WGPU by Examples

WGPU by Examples

From Basic 3D Shapes to Procedural Terrains
– Mastering Next-Generation Rust
Graphics and GPU Computing

Jack Xu, PhD

UniCAD Publishing

WGPU by Examples
Copyright © 2023 by Jack Xu, PhD
Printed and bound in the United States of America 9 8 7 6 5 4 3 2 1UC

Editor: Betty Hsu

Published by UniCAD Publishing.
New York, USA
ISBN: 979-8864220252

Publisher's Cataloging-in-Publication Data

Xu, Jack
WGPU by Examples: From Basic 3D Shapes to Procedural Terrains – Mastering Next-Generation Rust Graphics and GPU Computing / Jack Xu
– 1st ed.
p.cm.
ISBN 979-8864220252

1. wgpu. 2. 3D Graphics API. 3. WGSL Shaders. 4. Next-Generation Graphics API. 5. Games on GPU. 6. WebGL. 7. Graphics Rendering. 8. GPU Computing.
I. Title. II. Title. III Title: WGPU by Examples

Contents

Introduction

Overview

Welcome to *WGPU by Examples*! This book offers an immersive and practical approach to learning the next-generation graphics API, *wgpu*. The *wgpu* API is a cross-platform, safe, pure-Rust graphics API. Although it is based on the WebGPU standard, it can run not only on the web via WebAssembly but also on native devices with various backends such as Vulkan, Metal, DirectX12, DirectX11, and OpenGLES. With our step-by-step real-world examples, you will be able to create high-quality, real-time 3D graphics and GPU computing using this new *wgpu* graphics API. Whether you are a graphics creator, computer graphics programmer, game developer, or a student interested in the latest graphics development in Rust, this book is designed to help you acquire the skills and knowledge you need to succeed.

To understand the *wgpu* technology, it is essential to consider the evolution of graphics APIs. OpenGL has been one of the most popular graphics APIs for decades, but it was not designed for modern hardware and software architectures. As a result, optimizing graphics performance on newer hardware architectures became increasingly difficult. This led to the development of newer graphics APIs, including Vulkan, Metal, and DirectX 12, which were designed to take full advantage of modern hardware and software architectures.

Despite the availability of these newer graphics APIs, there is still a need for a unified graphics API that is designed for both the native devices and the Web. Unfortunately, Vulkan has run into trouble achieving true cross-platform reach due to its lack of support on Apple's MacOS and iOS, which only support Metal. Additionally, Vulkan's low-level nature, dealing with details such as GPU memory allocators, makes it less suitable for the web platform, where security is a significant concern. This is where WebGPU comes in. WebGPU is designed specifically for the Web, with a high-level approach that makes it usable and secure in a browser, and the ability to be implemented on top of Vulkan, Metal, and DirectX 12. WebGPU is the only truly cross-platform, and modern graphics API for web applications.

On the other hand, *wgpu* is a Rust implementation of the WebGPU API specifications. It allows developers to use the WebGPU API outside of web browsers, running natively on various platforms, including Vulkan, Metal, DirectX12, DirectX11, and OpenGLES. Rust's *wgpu* enables developers to create cross-platform applications that can take full advantage of modern graphics APIs on native devices, not just limited to the web environment. This means that Rust's *wgpu* extends the reach of the WebGPU API to native platforms, providing the benefits of low-level GPU access and performance on a broader range of devices.

Additionally, WebGPU and *wgpu* introduce a new shading language called WGSL (WebGPU Shading Language). This is because existing shading languages like GLSL and HLSL were not designed with WebGPU and *wgpu* in mind and lack some features that are important for efficient and safe execution. WGSL is designed specifically for WebGPU and *wgpu* and take into account the unique security and performance considerations of running graphics code in both native device and browser environments. Furthermore, WGSL provides a more concise and simplified syntax compared to older shading languages. This makes it easier for developers to write and maintain shaders, especially as graphics programming becomes more complex and powerful. Finally, WGSL is a cross-platform shading language that is designed to work across different devices and platforms, including desktop, mobile, and the Web. Having a unified shading language across all platforms makes it easier for developers to write code that can be run across different devices without worrying about compatibility issues.

WGPU by Examples is a comprehensive guide that equips you with all the tools you need to create stunning 3D graphics in your applications with the help of GPU acceleration. With this book, you will discover how to design an array of 3D graphics, from basic shapes like cubes, spheres, and cylinders to intricate 3D surface graphics like wireframes, surfaces, procedural terrains, volcanoes, Minecraft, voxel terrains, text rendering, and complex function visualization, and particle systems made using compute shaders. I have simplified the learning process by breaking down the concepts of *wgpu*, the cutting-edge graphics API in Rust, so even graphics developers with minimal experience can grasp the fundamentals of advanced graphics development. This book is an ideal resource to help you design a wide range of 3D graphics applications using the *wgpu* API and shader programs.

What this Book Includes

This book and its sample code listings, which are available for download at my website at https://drxudotnet.com, provide you with

- A complete and in-depth guide to practical 3D graphics programming with *wgpu* and Rust. After reading this book and running the example programs, you will be able to create various sophisticated 3D graphics with GPU acceleration in your graphics applications.

- Over 65 ready-to-run example projects that allow you to explore the 3D graphics techniques described in this book. You can use these examples to get better understanding of how the 3D graphics are created using the *wgpu* API and shader programs. You can also modify the code or add new features to them to form the basis of your own projects. Some of the example code listings provided with this book are already sophisticated graphics projects, and can be directly used in your own real-world web applications.

- Many functions and components in the sample code listings that you will find useful in your 3D graphics development. These functions and components include 3D transformation, projection, colormaps, lighting models, computer shader code, *wgpu* pipeline settings, as well as the other useful utility functions. You can extract these functions and components and plug them into your own web applications.

Is this Book for You?

The primary focus of this book is advanced GPU graphics programming with *wgpu* and WGSL. Therefore, I do not spend any time discussing the basics of programming with *wgpu* and Rust. To get the most out of this book, you should have some experience with graphics programming in OpenGL or

WebGPU and understand 3D rendering concepts such as model coordinates, view coordinates, perspective transformations, and other associated mathematical background. Some experience in *wgpu* and WGSL programming will also help, as I do not cover the absolute basics of dealing with code. For those new to *wgpu*, it is best to first read my introductory book *"Practical GPU Graphics with wgpu and Rust"*, where I provided step-by-step tutorials for creating simple graphics using *wgpu* and Rust.

It is worth noting that a significant portion of the information in this book about *wgpu* programming is not available in other tutorial and reference books. In addition, you can use most of the example programs contained in this book directly in your own real-world application development. This book will provide you with a level of detail, explanation, instruction, and sample program code that will enable you to do just about anything related to modern 3D graphics development using the next-generation *wgpu* graphics API.

Graphics programmers can use many of the example programs in this book routinely. Throughout the book, I emphasize the usefulness of *wgpu* graphics programming to real-world applications. If you follow the instructions presented in this book closely, you will easily be able to develop a variety of graphics applications with GPU acceleration, from simple 3D shapes to 3D surfaces with powerful colormap, wireframe, and texture mapping. You can build standard procedural terrains as well as voxel-based terrains and volcanoes using marching cubes and compute shaders. You can also create complex particle systems, text rendering, and domain coloring for complex functions using compute shaders. However, I will not spend too much time discussing program style and code optimization, as there are already plenty of books dealing with those topics. Most of the example programs you will find in this book omit error handling, which makes the code easier to understand by focusing only on the key concepts and practical applications.

What Do You Need to Use this Book?

You do not need any special equipment to make the most of this book and understand the algorithms presented. This book will take full advantage of open-source frameworks and libraries. The sample programs included with this book can run on various operating systems, including Windows, Linux, iOS, or MacOS. For development, this book uses Visual Studio Code (VS Code), Rust, and Cargo as the development environment and tools. VS Code is a lightweight IDE and powerful source code editor that runs on various operating systems, such as Windows, Linux, or MacOS.

Since the *wgpu* standard is still in development and has not been finalized, its API may change frequently. This book uses version 0.17.1 of *wgpu* for implementing *wgpu* applications. If you install other versions of the *wgpu* API, you may be able to run most of the sample code with few modifications. Please remember, however, that this book is intended for that specific version of the *wgpu* API on which all of the example programs were created and tested, so it is best to run the sample code on the same development environment and same version of the *wgpu* API.

Additionally, your operating system needs to have a modern GPU, as well as the DirectX 12, Metal, or Vulkan backend support on your graphics card.

How this Book Is Organized

This book is structured into twelve chapters, with each chapter exploring a distinct topic related to modern *wgpu* graphics programming. Below is a summary of each chapter to provide an overview of the book's contents:

Chapter 1, *Get Started*

This chapter covers the basics of *wgpu* graphics programming, including the structure of a wgpu application and how to initialize *wgpu*. It also includes step-by-step instructions for creating basic triangle examples using shaders and GPU buffers.

Chapter 2, *3D Shapes and Wireframes*

This chapter explains the creation of 3D shapes and wireframes using *wgpu*. It provides vertex data, shader code, and Rust code for creating a 3D cube, sphere, cylinder, and torus with wireframe, as well as adding multi-sample anti-aliasing (MSAA) to 3D shapes.

Chapter 3, *Lighting and Shading*

This chapter discusses how to simulate light and shading in computer graphics. It begins by introducing the different components of light, such as ambient, diffuse, and specular light. It then covers how to calculate normal vectors for surfaces, and how to use the Blinn-Phong light model to render 3D shapes. Finally, the chapter explains how to implement directional, point, and spot lights, as well as soft edge spot lights and fog effects.

Chapter 4, *Advanced Lighting*

This chapter covers advanced lighting techniques, including shadow mapping and physically-based rendering (PBR). It explains the microfacet model, bidirectional reflectance distribution function, and other components that make up PBR. The chapter also provides shader and Rust code for implementing both shadow mapping and PBR.

Chapter 5, *Colormap and 3D Surfaces*

This chapter focuses on creating colormap and 3D surfaces. It begins by discussing color models and colormaps, and then moves on to demonstrate how to create shaders with lighting and vertex colors. The chapter also includes examples of creating simple and parametric 3D surfaces, as well as rendering multiple surfaces.

Chapter 6, *Textures*

This chapter covers texture mapping in *wgpu*. It starts with an explanation of texture coordinates and mapping. Then, the chapter explains how to use textures in shaders, and provides examples of using textures with simple 3D shapes and surfaces. It also discusses advanced topics such as cube with multiple textures, normal mapping, and parallax mapping.

Chapter 7, *Compute Shaders for Surface Generation*

This chapter focuses on using compute shaders for surface generation. The chapter covers the basics of compute shaders, including compute space, workgroups, and buffer read/write operations. It then demonstrates the creation of simple and parametric 3D surfaces using compute shaders and provides shader and Rust code for generating vertices and indices. Finally, the chapter introduces the concept of super shapes and provides compute shader and Rust code for generating their vertex data.

Chapter 8, *Procedural Terrains*

This chapter covers the creation of procedural terrains using noise models. It explains the implementation of terrain chunks, instances, animation, and generation on both the CPU and GPU. Topics covered include Perlin noise, terrain chunks, level of detail algorithms, and the creation of Minecraft-style worlds using shaders. The reader will find WGSL code for the noise model, compute shaders, Rust code, and a detailed explanation of the implementation steps.

Chapter 9, *Marching Cubes*

This chapter focuses on the marching cubes algorithm, which is used to generate 3D surfaces from a volumetric dataset. The chapter covers implicit 3D surfaces, metaballs, voxel terrains, voxel volcanoes, and voxel Minecraft. It includes shader code, compute shader code, and Rust code to implement these techniques.

Chapter 10, *Visualizing Complex Functions*

This chapter discusses visualizing complex functions using surface plots and domain coloring. The chapter first explains complex functions and how to generate surface data on the CPU. Next, the chapter moves on to implementing complex functions in shaders and using compute shaders to generate surface data on the GPU. Finally, domain coloring is introduced as a way to visualize complex functions.

Chapter 11, *Particle System*

This chapter covers the topic of particle systems and simulations. It begins with a discussion of how to implement the compute boids algorithm using compute shaders. Next, the chapter moves on to particle simulations under gravity. It then covers firework simulations, fire simulations, gravity on a 2D grid, electric field distribution, and universe and star simulations. All of these simulations are performed on the GPU.

Chapter 12, *Text Rendering*

This chapter covers text rendering techniques in *wgpu*. It begins with an explanation of how to use bitmap fonts, where the chapter provides shader code for text rendering and Rust code for loading bitmap fonts. Next, the glyph geometry is introduced, which involves creating geometry for each character in a font and rendering the text as a regular 2D or 3D object.

Use Code Examples

You may use the code in this book in your own applications and documentation without needing to contact the author for permission, unless you are reproducing a significant portion of the code. For instance, writing a program that utilizes several code segments from this book does not necessitate permission. However, selling or distributing the example code listings requires permission. If you plan to integrate a substantial amount of example code from this book into your applications and documentation, you will also need permission. Integrating the example code from this book into commercial products is prohibited without written permission from the author.

Customer Support

I am always interested in hearing from readers and enjoy learning of your thoughts on this book. You can send me comments by e-mail to jxu@drxudotnet.com. I also provide updates, bug fixes, and ongoing support via my website: https://drxudotnet.com.

You can obtain the complete source code for all of examples in this book from the website.

1 Get Started

This chapter describes the necessary steps for setting up the required crates and tools for developing *wgpu* applications. The development environment will use Visual Studio Code (VS Code), Rust and Cargo. Through the use of simple triangle examples, I will illustrate the fundamental concepts of *wgpu*, including the *wgpu* instance, adapter, device, GPU buffers, rendering pipeline, WGSL shader program, and rendering graphics on a window surface.

1.1 Creating a Rust Application

I suppose you already installed Rust and Visual Studio Code on your local machine and also added the *rust-analyzer* extension to VS Code. The *rust-analyzer* provides support for the Rust programming language and features like intelligent code analysis, code completion, code navigation, and error highlighting.

Now, let's start a new rust library project with the following command in a command prompt window:

```
cargo new wgpu_book_examples --lib
```

The "*--lib*" flag tells Cargo that we want to create a library project rather than a binary-executable project. Here, the project name is *wgpu_book_examples*. Rust recommends that we should name our project using snake case, which means words in the name are in lowercase, with each space replaced by an underscore.

The *wgpu_book_examples* project contains a Rust file called *lib.rs* in the *src/* folder. This file serves as the entry point for our library code, where we will put commonly used Rust code. Additionally, we will add two new folders, *assets* and *examples* to the project's root directory. The *assets* folder will be used to store asset files such as image and font files, while the *examples* folder will contain the example projects. Thus, our project will have the following structure:

```
.
├── assets
├── examples
├── src/
│   └── lib.rs
├── Cargo.toml
```

For every Rust application, there is a *Cargo.toml* file in the root folder. This file is called manifest and is written in the TOML format, which aims to be a minimal configuration file format. The manifest file can consist of different sections such as cargo-features, package, target tables, dependency tables, etc.

Note that in Rust, crates are similar to the packages in some other languages. Crates compile individually. If a crate has child file modules, those files will get the merged with the crate file and compile as a single unit. In the *dependencies* section of the *Cargo.toml* file, the dependencies usually contain different crates.

Our *wgpu_book_examples* project will use the following manifest file:

```
[package]
name = "wgpu_book_examples"
version = "0.1.0"
edition = "2021"

[dependencies]
wgpu = "0.17.1"
cgmath = "0.18"
env_logger = "0.10"
futures = "0.3"
gfx-hal = "0.9"
image = "0.23"
log = "0.4"
pollster = "0.2"
winit = "0.28"
anyhow = "1.0"
```

Here, all the crates included in the [*dependencies*] section can be found at the https://crates.io/ website:

- *wgpu*: Rusty WebGPU API Wrapper that allows you to access the wgpu API.

- *cgmath*: A linear algebra and mathematics library for computer graphics.

- *env_logger*: A logging implementation for "log" that is configured via an environment variable.

- *futures*: An implementation of futures and streams featuring zero allocations, composability, and iterator-like interfaces.

- *gfx-hal*: *gfx-rs* hardware abstraction layer.

- *image*: An imaging library written in Rust, which provides basic filters and decoders for the most common image formats.

- *log*: A lightweight logging façade for Rust.

- *pollster*: A minimal async executor that lets you block on a future.

- *winit*: A cross-platform window creation library.

- *Anyhow*: Provides *anyhow::Error*, a trait object-based error type for easy idiomatic error handling in Rust applications.

Depending on the requirement of your applications, you may need to add more crates to the [dependencies] section later.

Since the WGSL shadering language will be used in our *wgpu* applications, we will also need to add the WGSL extension to VS Code. This extension will provide syntax highlight for your WGSL shaders.

1.2 wgpu initialization

To avoid code duplication, we will store commonly used files in the *src/* folder. First, add a new Rust file called *wgpu_simplified* to the *src/* folder and enter the following code into it:

```
use winit::window::Window;
```

```rust
use std::path::PathBuf;

pub struct IWgpuInit {
    pub instance: wgpu::Instance,
    pub surface: wgpu::Surface,
    pub adapter: wgpu::Adapter,
    pub device: wgpu::Device,
    pub queue: wgpu::Queue,
    pub config: wgpu::SurfaceConfiguration,
    pub size: winit::dpi::PhysicalSize<u32>,
    pub sample_count: u32,
}

impl IWgpuInit {
    pub async fn new(window: &Window, sample_count: u32, limits:Option<wgpu::Limits>) -> Self {
        let limits_device = limits.unwrap_or(wgpu::Limits::default());

        let size = window.inner_size();
        //let instance = wgpu::Instance::default();
        let instance = wgpu::Instance::new(wgpu::InstanceDescriptor {
            backends: wgpu::Backends::DX12,
            //dx12_shader_compiler: Default::default(),
            dx12_shader_compiler: {
                wgpu::Dx12Compiler::Dxc {
                    dxil_path: Some(PathBuf::from(r"assets/dxil.dll")),
                    dxc_path: Some(PathBuf::from(r"assets/dxcompiler.dll")),
                }
            }
        });
        let surface = unsafe { instance.create_surface(&window) }.unwrap();

        let adapter = instance
            .request_adapter(&wgpu::RequestAdapterOptions {
                power_preference: wgpu::PowerPreference::default(),
                compatible_surface: Some(&surface),
                force_fallback_adapter: false,
            })
            .await
            .expect("Failed to find an appropriate adapter");

        let (device, queue) = adapter
            .request_device(
                &wgpu::DeviceDescriptor {
                    label: None,
                    //features: wgpu::Features::empty(),
                    features:wgpu::Features::default() |
                        wgpu::Features::TEXTURE_ADAPTER_SPECIFIC_FORMAT_FEATURES,
                    limits: limits_device
                },
                None,
            )
            .await
            .expect("Failed to create device");

        let surface_caps = surface.get_capabilities(&adapter);
        let format = surface_caps.formats[0];

        let config = wgpu::SurfaceConfiguration {
            usage: wgpu::TextureUsages::RENDER_ATTACHMENT,
            format,
```

```
            width: size.width,
            height: size.height,
            present_mode: wgpu::PresentMode::Fifo,
            alpha_mode:surface_caps.alpha_modes[0],
            view_formats: vec![],
        };
        surface.configure(&device, &config);

        Self {
            instance,
            surface,
            adapter,
            device,
            queue,
            config,
            size,
            sample_count,
        }
    }
}
```

Here, we first create a struct named *IWgpuInit* that contains fields like *instance*, *surface*, *adapter*, *device*, etc. These fields will be initialized because they are common to most *wgpu* applications. Next, we add an implementation for this struct, in which the asynchronous *new* function is created. A detailed explanation of this *new* function will be provided in the following subsections.

1.2.1 wgpu Backends

It is clear that the *IWgpuInit*::*new* function has an *Option<wgpu::Limits>* input argument, which allows us to specify a custom *wgpu*::*Limits* parameter or use the default value by passing *None*. The code snippet:

```
    let limits_device = limits.unwrap_or(wgpu::Limits::default());
```

uses *unwrap_or* method to handle the *Option* and retrieve the value or use the default limits if *None* is provided.

Next, we set the physical size of the window and create an instance of the *wgpu* backend that depends on the graphics card installed on your local machine. In my case, the machine has an Nvidia GeForce RTX 3060 graphics card with both Vulkan and DX12 backends. The default backend is Vulkan, which can be specified using the following code:

```
    let instance = wgpu::Instance::default();
```

We can easily switch to the DX12 backend using the following code snippet:

```
    let instance = wgpu::Instance::new(wgpu::InstanceDescriptor {
        backends: wgpu::Backends::DX12,
        dx12_shader_compiler: {
            wgpu::Dx12Compiler::Dxc {
                dxil_path: Some(PathBuf::from(r"assets/dxil.dll")),
                dxc_path: Some(PathBuf::from(r"assets/dxcompiler.dll")),
            }
        }
    });
```

This code snippet specifies not only the *DX12* backend but also *dx12_shader_compiler*. You can also set *dx12_shader_compiler* to the default *Fxc* compiler using the following code:

```
    dx12_shader_compiler: Default::default(),
```

The *Fxc* compiler is an old, slow, and unmaintained compiler, but it does not require any additional *.dlls* to be shipped with the application. On the other hand, in the above code, we select the *Dxc* option, which is a new, fast, and maintained compiler. However, the *Dxc* compiler requires both dxcompiler.dll and dxil.dll to be shipped with the application. I have already included these two files in the *assets* folder. Alternatively, you can also download them from

https://github.com/microsoft/DirectXShaderCompiler/releases.

In addition to Vulkan and DX12, you can also set the other specific backends according to your machine. Here are some valid options:

- VULKAN: Supported on Windows, Linux/Android, and macOS/iOS via Vulkan Portability.

- GL: OpenGL, Supported on Linux/Android, the web through WebAssembly via WebGL, and Windows and macOS/iOS via ANGLE.

- METAL: Supported on macOS/iOS.

- DX12: Supported on Windows 10+.

- DX11: Supported on Windows 7+.

- BROWSER_WEBGPU: Supported when targeting the web through WebAssembly.

- PRIMARY: All the APIs that *wgpu* offers first tier of support for (Vulkan + Metal + DX12 + Browser WebGPU).

- SECONDARY: All the APIs that *wgpu* offers second tier of support for (OpenGL + DX11).

- all(): returns the set containing all backends supported by the *wgpu* API.

The example projects contained in this book will use the default Vulkan backend.

Next, we use the unsafe code to create a rendered surface for *winit* window:

```
let surface = unsafe { instance.create_surface(&window) }.unwrap();
```

This surface provides drawing functionality for the platform supported by *winit*.

Since the *wgpu* API is async when interacting with GPU, we need to place our rendering code inside the async function called *new* that is executed when the code is loaded. Within this async *new* function, we can access GPU in *wgpu* by calling the *request_adaptor* function.

```
let adapter = instance
    .request_adapter(&wgpu::RequestAdapterOptions {
        power_preference: wgpu::PowerPreference::default(),
        compatible_surface: Some(&surface),
        force_fallback_adapter: false,
    })
    .await
    .expect("Failed to find an appropriate adapter");
```

In the above code, the *compatible_surface* field is required to be representable with the requested adapter. This does not create the surface; it only guarantees that the adapter can present to said surface. The *force_fallback_adapter* field indicates that if it is *true*, only a fallback adapter can be returned. This is generally a "software" implementation on the system.

Once having the GPU adapter, we can call the *adapter.request_device* function to create a GPU device:

```
let (device, queue) = adapter
    .request_device(
        &wgpu::DeviceDescriptor {
```

```
            label: None,
            //features: wgpu::Features::empty(),
            features:wgpu::Features::default() |
                wgpu::Features::TEXTURE_ADAPTER_SPECIFIC_FORMAT_FEATURES,
            limits: limits_device
        },
        None,
    )
    .await
    .expect("Failed to create device");
```

Here, the *features* attribute on *DeviceDescriptor* allows you to specify the extra features you want. It is worth noting that the device configuration on your machine may limit the features you can use. If you want to use certain features, you may need to limit what devices you support, or provide work arounds. In the code above, we enable device specific texture format features needed for some example projects in later chapters of this book. By default, only texture format properties as defined by the *wgpu* specification are allowed. Enabling this feature flag extends the features of each format to the ones supported by the current device. Without this flag, read/write storage access is not allowed. Note that this is a native-only feature.

The *limits* attribute describes the constrains on certain types of resources that we can create. We can specify this field through the input argument. If we specify *None* as input for this field, we will use the default limits that are suitable for most devices.

1.2.2 Surface

As mentioned in the preceding section, we use the unsafe code to create a rendered surface, which is the part of the window that we draw to. We need it to write the results from the fragment shader directly to the screen.

Next, we use the *wgpu* adapter to configure the surface with the following code snippet:

```
let surface_caps = surface.get_capabilities(&adapter);
let format = surface_caps.formats[0];

let config = wgpu::SurfaceConfiguration {
    usage: wgpu::TextureUsages::RENDER_ATTACHMENT,
    format,
    width: size.width,
    height: size.height,
    present_mode: wgpu::PresentMode::Fifo,
    alpha_mode:surface_caps.alpha_modes[0],
    view_formats: vec![],
};
surface.configure(&device, &config);
```

This code first calls the *surface.get_capabilities* function, which returns the capabilities of the surface when used with the given adapter. This function will return specified values if the surface is incompatible with the adapter. The returned *SurfaceCapabilities* struct contains several fields, including *formats*, *present_mode*, *alpha_modes*, and *usages*.

The *format* field defines how the surface texture will be stored on the GPU. Different displays prefer different formats. Here, we using the *surface_caps.formats*[0] to figure out the best format to use based on the display we are using.

Inside the *SurfaceConfiguration*, the *usage* attribute describes how the surface textures will be used. The *RENDER _ATTACHMENT* field specifies that the textures will be used to write to the surface defined on the window. Currently, in *wgpu*, the only supported usage is *RENDER _ATTACHMENT*.

The *width* and *height* attributes define the size of the surface texture, which should usually be the width and height of the *winit* window. Make sure that the *width* and *height* of the surface texture are not zero; otherwise, it may cause your application to crash.

The *present_mode* attribute defines the behavior of the presentation engine based on the frame rate. Here, we set it to *Fifo*, which is the only mode guaranteed to be supported. The other possible modes like *FifoRelaxed*, *Immediate*, and *Mailbox* will crash if unsupported, while *AutoVsync* and *AutoNoVsync* will gracefully perform designed sets of fallbacks if their primary modes are unsupported.

The *alpha_mode* field specifies how the alpha channel of the textures should be handled during compositing.

In order to use the structs and functions defined in the *wgpu_simplified.rs* file, we need to declare it in the *lib.rs* file in the *src/* folder. Replace the content of the *lib.rs* file with the following code:

```
pub mod wgpu_simplified;
```

This declaration makes the public structs and functions accessible and usable from other parts of our project.

1.3 wgpu Information

In this section, we will create an example project that displays information about the *wgpu* API, such as adapter properties and GPU supported limits. To begin, add a new Rust file called *wgpu_info.rs* to the *examples/ch01/* folder with the following code:

```
use winit::{
    event::{Event, WindowEvent},
    event_loop::{ControlFlow, EventLoop},
    window::Window,
};
use wgpu_book_examples::wgpu_simplified as ws;

async fn get_wgpu_info(window: &Window) {

    let init = ws::IWgpuInit::new(&window, 1, None).await;

    println!("{:#?}", init.adapter.get_info());
    println!("Adapter{:#?}", init.adapter.limits());
    println!("Device{:#?}", init.device.limits());
}

fn main() {
    let event_loop = EventLoop::new();
    let window = Window::new(&event_loop).unwrap();
    window.set_title("wgpu_info");
    env_logger::init();

    event_loop.run(move |event, _, control_flow| {
        *control_flow = ControlFlow::Wait;
        match event {
            Event::RedrawRequested(_) => {
                pollster::block_on(get_wgpu_info(&window));
```

```
            }

            Event::WindowEvent {
                event: WindowEvent::CloseRequested,
                ..
            } => *control_flow = ControlFlow::Exit,
            _ => {}
        }
    });
}
```

This code first introduces the *winit* window and the *wgpu_simplified* module. Next, we implement the *get_wgpu_info* function. Inside this function, we call the *ws::IWgpuInit::new* method implemented in the *wgpu_simplified.rs* file, which returns the *IWgpuInit* struct. Next, we use *adapter.get_info*() method to get information about the adapter. Both the *adapter.limits*() and *device.limits*() methods provide the sets of limits the adapter and device support, respectively.

In the *main* function, we use the *block_on* function from the *pollster* crate to call our asynchronous *get_wgpu_info* function. The *pollster* is a minimal async executor that lets you block on a future.

Now, add the following code snippet to the *Cargo.toml* file:

```
[[example]]
name = "ch01_wgpu_info"
path = "examples/ch01/wgpu_info.rs"
```

Next, we can run the application by issuing the following *cargo run* command in a terminal window:

```
cargo run --example ch01_wgpu_info
```

This will bring up a new empty window, while the information about the adapter and limits will be displayed in the terminal window, as listed below:

```
AdapterInfo {
    name: "NVIDIA GeForce RTX 3060",
    vendor: 4318,
    device: 9476,
    device_type: DiscreteGpu,
    driver: "NVIDIA",
    driver_info: "531.30",
    backend: Vulkan,
}

AdapterLimits {
    max_texture_dimension_1d: 32768,
    max_texture_dimension_2d: 32768,
    max_texture_dimension_3d: 16384,
    max_texture_array_layers: 2048,
    max_bind_groups: 8,
    max_bindings_per_bind_group: 640,
    max_dynamic_uniform_buffers_per_pipeline_layout: 15,
    max_dynamic_storage_buffers_per_pipeline_layout: 16,
    max_sampled_textures_per_shader_stage: 1048576,
    max_samplers_per_shader_stage: 1048576,
    max_storage_buffers_per_shader_stage: 1048576,
    max_storage_textures_per_shader_stage: 1048576,
    max_uniform_buffers_per_shader_stage: 1048576,
    max_uniform_buffer_binding_size: 65536,
    max_storage_buffer_binding_size: 2147483648,
    max_vertex_buffers: 16,
    max_buffer_size: 18446744073709551615,
```

```
    max_vertex_attributes: 32,
    max_vertex_buffer_array_stride: 2048,
    min_uniform_buffer_offset_alignment: 64,
    min_storage_buffer_offset_alignment: 32,
    max_inter_stage_shader_components: 128,
    max_compute_workgroup_storage_size: 49152,
    max_compute_invocations_per_workgroup: 1024,
    max_compute_workgroup_size_x: 1024,
    max_compute_workgroup_size_y: 1024,
    max_compute_workgroup_size_z: 64,
    max_compute_workgroups_per_dimension: 65535,
    max_push_constant_size: 256,
}

DeviceLimits {
    max_texture_dimension_1d: 8192,
    max_texture_dimension_2d: 8192,
    max_texture_dimension_3d: 2048,
    max_texture_array_layers: 256,
    max_bind_groups: 4,
    max_bindings_per_bind_group: 640,
    max_dynamic_uniform_buffers_per_pipeline_layout: 8,
    max_dynamic_storage_buffers_per_pipeline_layout: 4,
    max_sampled_textures_per_shader_stage: 16,
    max_samplers_per_shader_stage: 16,
    max_storage_buffers_per_shader_stage: 8,
    max_storage_textures_per_shader_stage: 4,
    max_uniform_buffers_per_shader_stage: 12,
    max_uniform_buffer_binding_size: 65536,
    max_storage_buffer_binding_size: 134217728,
    max_vertex_buffers: 8,
    max_buffer_size: 268435456,
    max_vertex_attributes: 16,
    max_vertex_buffer_array_stride: 2048,
    min_uniform_buffer_offset_alignment: 256,
    min_storage_buffer_offset_alignment: 256,
    max_inter_stage_shader_components: 60,
    max_compute_workgroup_storage_size: 16384,
    max_compute_invocations_per_workgroup: 256,
    max_compute_workgroup_size_x: 256,
    max_compute_workgroup_size_y: 256,
    max_compute_workgroup_size_z: 64,
    max_compute_workgroups_per_dimension: 65535,
    max_push_constant_size: 0,
}
```

You can see from the above results that some limits from the adapter and device have different values, and usually the values from the device are smaller than those from the adapter. This is because the *adapter.limits*() function returns the limits of the physical device, while the *device.limits*() function returns the limits of the logical device. The physical device is the underlying hardware that the GPU is built on, while the logical device is a software abstraction that provides access to the physical device.

The limits of the physical device are the maximum values that can be used for certain resources, such as the number of buffers, the size of each buffer, and the number of threads that can be launched in parallel. These limits are generally determined by the hardware itself and are independent of any specific device or context.

On the other hand, the limits of the logical device are the limits that are actually enforced by the specific GPU driver that is currently in use by your application. The device-specific limits may be a subset of the adapter limits, as they can be further constrained by the device's capabilities or driver settings. For instance, the device might have less available memory than the adapter due to system resources being shared among multiple applications.

It is worth noting that the limits from the device displayed in the terminal are default values. You can change these limits using the *Option<wgpu::Limits>* argument when calling the *ws::IWgpuInit::new* function, as illustrated in the following code snippet:

```
let limits_input = wgpu::Limits {
    max_storage_buffer_binding_size: 1024*1024*1024,
    max_buffer_size: 1024*1024*1024,
    max_compute_invocations_per_workgroup: 512,
    ..Default::default()
};
let init = ws::IWgpuInit::new(&window, Some(limits_input)).await;
```

This code will change the default values for three device limits:

- *max_storage_buffer_binding_size*: change default 128 MiB to 1024 MiB.

- *max_buffer_size*: change default 256 MiB to 1024 MiB.

- *max_compute_invocation_per_workgroup*: change default 256 to 512.

Please keep in mind that these device limits have a hard constraint: they must be less than or equal to the corresponding adapter limits.

The information displayed in the terminal provides details about the adapter, device, and supported GPU limits. It is crucial to be aware of this information before starting to implement *wgpu* applications. It is worth noting that this information may change since *wgpu* is still in development.

1.4 wgpu Basics

We are now prepared to begin developing our *wgpu* applications. It is important to note the distinction between *wgpu* and OpenGL. *wgpu* separates resource management, work preparation, and command submission to the GPU, whereas in OpenGL, a single context object is responsible for all of these tasks and includes many associated states. In the following sections, I will walk you through three triangle examples to help you grasp the *wgpu* program structure and rendering pipeline.

1.4.1 Render Pipelines

In the previous sections, we have completed the basic initialization steps for *wgpu*, which include *adapter*, *device*, *instance*, and *surface*, among other objects. These objects are universal to all *wgpu* applications and they usually do not require resetting or modification. However, once this initialization process is complete, the rendering pipeline and the shading program will vary across different applications. In this section, we will discuss the code related to creating render pipelines.

Please add the following code to the *wgpu-simplified.rs* file in the *src/* folder:

```
pub struct IRenderPipeline<'a> {
    pub shader: Option<&'a wgpu::ShaderModule>,
    pub vs_shader: Option<&'a wgpu::ShaderModule>,
    pub fs_shader: Option<&'a wgpu::ShaderModule>,
    pub vertex_buffer_layout: &'a [wgpu::VertexBufferLayout<'a>],
    pub pipeline_layout: Option<&'a wgpu::PipelineLayout>,
```

```rust
    pub topology: wgpu::PrimitiveTopology,
    pub strip_index_format: Option<wgpu::IndexFormat>,
    pub cull_mode: Option<wgpu::Face>,
    pub is_depth_stencil: bool,
    pub vs_entry: String,
    pub fs_entry: String,
}

impl Default for IRenderPipeline<'_> {
    fn default() -> Self {
        Self {
            shader: None,
            vs_shader: None,
            fs_shader: None,
            vertex_buffer_layout: &[],
            pipeline_layout: None,
            topology: wgpu::PrimitiveTopology::TriangleList,
            strip_index_format: None,
            cull_mode: None,
            is_depth_stencil: true,
            vs_entry: String::from("vs_main"),
            fs_entry: String::from("fs_main"),
        }
    }
}

impl IRenderPipeline<'_> {
    pub fn new(&mut self, init: &IWgpuInit) -> wgpu::RenderPipeline {
        if self.shader.is_some() {
            self.vs_shader = self.shader;
            self.fs_shader = self.shader;
        }

        let mut depth_stencil:Option<wgpu::DepthStencilState> = None;
        if self.is_depth_stencil {
            depth_stencil = Some(wgpu::DepthStencilState {
                format: wgpu::TextureFormat::Depth24Plus,
                depth_write_enabled: true,
                depth_compare: wgpu::CompareFunction::LessEqual,
                stencil: wgpu::StencilState::default(),
                bias: wgpu::DepthBiasState::default(),
            });
        }

        init.device.create_render_pipeline(&wgpu::RenderPipelineDescriptor {
            label: Some("Render Pipeline"),
            layout: Some(&self.pipeline_layout.unwrap()),
            vertex: wgpu::VertexState {
                module: &&self.vs_shader.as_ref().unwrap(),
                entry_point: &self.vs_entry,
                buffers: &self.vertex_buffer_layout,
            },
            fragment: Some(wgpu::FragmentState {
                module: &&self.fs_shader.as_ref().unwrap(),
                entry_point: &self.fs_entry,
                targets: &[Some(init.config.format.into())],
            }),
            primitive: wgpu::PrimitiveState {
                topology: self.topology,
                strip_index_format: self.strip_index_format,
```

```
                ..Default::default()
        },
        depth_stencil,
        multisample: wgpu::MultisampleState{
            count: init.sample_count,
            ..Default::default()
        },
        multiview: None,
    })
  }
}
```

The *IRenderPipeline* struct contains the fields used as input arguments for creating a render pipeline. We use the *Default* trait to define the default values for the *IRenderPipeline* struct's fields when the struct is created without explicitly specifying values for those fields. Specifically, we explicitly set default values for these fields:

```
topology: wgpu::PrimitiveTopology::TriangleList,
vs_entry: String::from("vs_main"),
fs_entry: String::from("fs_main"),
sample_count: 1,
```

Inside the *new* method, we create the render pipeline using the *RederPipelineDescriptor*, which describes a render pipeline by configuring each of the render stages. The render pipeline descriptor includes the following members:

- *vertex*, of type *VertexState*: describes the vertex shader entry point of the pipeline and its input buffer layouts, which is a required field.

- *fragment*, of type *FragmentState*: describes the fragment shader entry point of the pipeline and its output colors. If undefined, no color output mode is enabled. However, in certain scenario, such as shadow rendering, the fragment state may be unnecessary.

- *primitive*, of type *PrimitiveState:* describes the primitive-related properties of the pipeline.

- *depthStencil,* of type *DepthStencilState:* describes the optional depth-stencil properties, including the testing, operations, and bias.

- *multisample,* of type *MultisampleState:* describes the multi-sampling anti-aliasing (MSAA) properties of the pipeline. It has a member called *count* (default to 1) that defines the number of samples per pixel. Currently, the *count* attribute in WebGPU can only have two possible numbers: 1 or 4, while *wgpu* extends this attribute to take more values like 1, 2, 4, 8, and 16. We use the *sample_count* member of the *IWgpuInit* struct to specify the MSAA property.

It is worth noting that while we can set the *sample_count* field up to 16 in *wgpu*, whether this extension is actually supported or not still depends on the GPU graphics card installed on your machine. For example, the Nvidia GeForce RTX 3060 graphics card on my machine only supports *sample_count* up to 8. Most new graphics cards on the market support MSAA *sample_count* up to 16, but there are currently no graphics cards that support MSAA with sample counts greater than 16.

Here is a list of Nvidia and AMD graphics cards that support MSAA *sample_count* up to 16:

Nvidia Graphics Card	AMD Graphics Card
GeForce GTX 480	Radeon HD 7970
GeForce GTX 470	Radeon R9 290X
GeForce GTX 580	Radeon R9 Fury X

GeForce GTX 680	Radeon RX Vega 64
GeForce GTX 780 Ti	Radeon RX Vega 56
GeForce GTX 980 Ti	Radeon RX 5700 XT
GeForce GTX 1080 Ti	Radeon RX 6800 XT
GeForce GTX 2080 Ti	Radeon RX 6900 XT
GeForce GTX 3080 Ti	

Please note that this list is not exhaustive, and there may be other graphics cards that support MSAA sample count up to 16. The performance of MSAA will vary depending on the graphics card and the graphics being processed. In general, higher sample counts will provide better image quality, but they will also come at a performance cost.

1.4.2 Render Passes

In *wgpu*, a render pass refers to execution of a single render pipeline, which produces an output image that is written to a set of framebuffer attachments in memory. Some of these attachments may be temporary or transient. For example, if a *wgpu* application uses both color and depth-stencil attachments during rendering but only requires the color attachments for subsequent rendering operations, then the depth-stencil attachment can be considered transient and can be safely discarded at the end of the render pass.

To simplify the process of creating render pass, we will place the commonly used code for defining the color attachment and depth-stencil attachment to the *wgpu_simplified.rs* file in the *src/* folder. Now, add the following code to the file:

```
pub fn create_color_attachment<'a>(texture_view: &'a wgpu::TextureView) ->
wgpu::RenderPassColorAttachment<'a> {
    wgpu::RenderPassColorAttachment {
        view: texture_view,
        resolve_target: None,
        ops: wgpu::Operations {
            load: wgpu::LoadOp::Clear(wgpu::Color::BLACK),
            store: true,
        },
    }
}

pub fn create_msaa_texture_view(init: &IWgpuInit) -> wgpu::TextureView{
    let msaa_texture = init.device.create_texture(&wgpu::TextureDescriptor {
        size: wgpu::Extent3d {
            width: init.config.width,
            height: init.config.height,
            depth_or_array_layers: 1,
        },
        mip_level_count: 1,
        sample_count: init.sample_count,
        dimension: wgpu::TextureDimension::D2,
        format: init.config.format,
        usage: wgpu::TextureUsages::RENDER_ATTACHMENT,
        label: None,
        view_formats: &[],
    });
```

```
        msaa_texture.create_view(&wgpu::TextureViewDescriptor::default())
}

pub fn create_msaa_color_attachment<'a>(texture_view: &'a wgpu::TextureView, msaa_view: &'a
wgpu::TextureView)
-> wgpu::RenderPassColorAttachment<'a> {
    wgpu::RenderPassColorAttachment {
        view: msaa_view,
        resolve_target: Some(texture_view),
        ops: wgpu::Operations {
            load: wgpu::LoadOp::Clear(wgpu::Color::BLACK),
            store: true,
        },
    }
}

pub fn create_depth_view(init: &IWgpuInit) -> wgpu::TextureView {
    let depth_texture = init.device.create_texture(&wgpu::TextureDescriptor {
        size: wgpu::Extent3d {
            width: init.config.width,
            height: init.config.height,
            depth_or_array_layers: 1,
        },
        mip_level_count: 1,
        sample_count: init.sample_count,
        dimension: wgpu::TextureDimension::D2,
        format:wgpu::TextureFormat::Depth24Plus,
        usage: wgpu::TextureUsages::RENDER_ATTACHMENT,
        label: None,
        view_formats: &[],
    });

    depth_texture.create_view(&wgpu::TextureViewDescriptor::default())
}

pub fn create_depth_stencil_attachment<'a>(depth_view: &'a wgpu::TextureView) ->
wgpu::RenderPassDepthStencilAttachment<'a> {
    wgpu::RenderPassDepthStencilAttachment {
        view: depth_view,
        depth_ops: Some(wgpu::Operations {
            load: wgpu::LoadOp::Clear(1.0),
            store: false,
        }),
        stencil_ops: None,
    }
}
```

The *create_color_attachment* function is a utility function used to configure a color attachment in a *wgpu* render pass. In the provided code, the color attachment is set to store the background color as follows:

```
    ops: wgpu::Operations {
        load: wgpu::LoadOp::Clear(wgpu::Color::BLACK),
        store: true,
    },
```

Here, the color *BLACK* is used to represent [R, G, B, alpha] in the *load* attribute, while the *view* attribute stores the rendering result on the current image of the surface texture. It is worth noting that the *SurfaceTexture* type is unique to the Rust API of *wgpu*. In the WebGPU specifications, the *GPUCanvasContext* provides a texture without any additional information.

The optional *resolve_target* field in the *RenderPassColorAttachment* struct defines a texture view that will receive the resolved output if multisampling is used.

When multisampling (*sample_count* greater than 1) is enabled, the definition of the *color attachment* attribute changes. In such cases, we need to create a texture view specifically for MSAA using the *create_msaa_texture_view* function, which is implemented in the above code. Once the MSAA texture view is available, we can then create a color attachment specifically for multisampling using the *create_msaa_color_attachment* function. This function takes two texture views as input arguments: one is the original surface texture view, and the other is the MSAA texture view returned from the *create_msaa_texture_view* function.

The render pass may also need a depth and stencil attachment to enable depth testing and stencil testing during rendering operations. Depth testing and stencil testing are fundamental techniques in computer graphics used to enhance the realism and visual quality of rendered scenes.

Depth testing involves comparing the depth value of a fragment (a pixel) being rendered with the depth value already stored in the depth buffer. The depth buffer keeps track of the depth information of each pixel on the screen. If the depth test passes, the new fragment replaces the old one in the depth buffer, ensuring proper rendering of closer objects. This process prevents objects that are farther away from being drawn on top of closer objects, ensuring that the scene is rendered correctly with respect to its spatial arrangement.

Stencil testing, on the other hand, involves comparing a fragment's stencil value with the value stored in the stencil buffer. The stencil buffer is a separate buffer used for storing arbitrary integer values for each pixel. Stencil testing is a versatile technique used for various purposes, such as creating special effects, shadows, or masking regions of the screen.

Using depth and stencil attachments in a render pass grants us control and customization over how fragments are processed based on their depth and stencil values. The attachments are usually provided as part of the render pass configuration, and they are used in the fragment shader to perform the necessary tests and operations.

The *create_depth_view* function create a depth texture and returns a depth texture view that can be used as a depth attachment in a render pass. This function is similar to the *create_msaa_texture_view* function, and the only difference is in the texture format. The MSAA texture uses the format from the surface capabilities to determine the best format to use based on the display, whereas the depth texture uses *Depth24Plus*, a special depth format with at least 24-bit integer depth.

Once the depth texture view is created, we can create depth stencil attachment using the *create_depth_stencil_attachment* function. The *RenderPassDepthStencilAttachment* descriptor contains three attributes: *view*, *depth_ops*, and *stencil_ops*. Here, we set *view* to the depth view, meaning that the depth information will be read and written to the specified depth view during the render pass. The *depth_ops* attribute represents what operations will be performed on the depth part of the attachment. The code snippet:

```
depth_ops: Some(wgpu::Operations {
    load: wgpu::LoadOp::Clear(1.0),
    store: false,
}),
```

specifies the load operation for the depth attachment. It means that before rendering, the depth attachment will be cleared to a depth value of 1.0 (fully far). Setting the depth clear value to 1.0 ensures that all fragments rendered in the current pass are considered closer than existing depth values, replacing the existing values in the depth buffer. This step initializes the depth buffer to its maximum value, effectively resetting the depth information for the new render pass. The *store* field is set to *false*, indicating that the depth information will not be preserved after the render pass is completed, thus, the depth information will not be usable in subsequent render passes. This might be the case if the depth buffer is not required in subsequent rendering stages.

The *stencil_ops* attribute is set to *None*, meaning that stencil testing will not be performed during the render pass. Stencil testing is a separate technique used for various purposes in computer graphics, but we will not use it in the example projects of this book.

1.5 Triangle with Distinct Vertex Colors

We are now prepared to embark on our first *wgpu* triangle example. The objective of this example is to create a straightforward triangle with distinct vertex colors using *wgpu*.

1.5.1 Shader Code

Create a new shader file called *triangle-vertex-color.wgsl* in the *examples/ch01/* folder and include the following code:

```
// vertex shader
struct Output {
    @builtin(position) Position : vec4f,
    @location(0) vColor : vec4f,
};

@vertex
fn vs_main(@builtin(vertex_index) VertexIndex: u32) -> Output {
    var pos = array<vec2f, 3>(
        vec2(0.0, 0.5),
        vec2(-0.5, -0.5),
        vec2(0.5, -0.5)
    );

    var color = array<vec3f, 3>(
        vec3(1.0, 0.0, 0.0),
        vec3(0.0, 1.0, 0.0),
        vec3(0.0, 0.0, 1.0)
    );

    var output: Output;
    output.Position = vec4(pos[VertexIndex], 0.0, 1.0);
    output.vColor = vec4(color[VertexIndex], 1.0);
    return output;
}

// fragment shader
@fragment
fn fs_main(@location(0) vColor: vec4f) -> @location(0) vec4f {
    return vColor;
}
```

The above WGSL shader code comprises both the vertex and fragment shaders. The vertex shader begins by defining a *vec2f* array that contains three vertex points that form our triangle. Next, we create a *vecf3* array that specifies the colors for each vertex. It is worth noting that we employ WGSL's predeclared alias, such as *vec2f = vec2<f32>* and *vec3f = vec3<f32>*, to define the triangle's vertices and colors.

Subsequently, we convert the *vec2f* vertices and *vec3f* colors into *vec4f* points and *vec4f* colors, respectively. This conversion is necessary for *wgpu* to render the triangle.

The fragment shader is relatively straightforward and merely returns the color processed in the vertex shader.

1.5.2 Common Code

As previously mentioned, our *wgpu-simplified* module in the *src/* folder comprises frequently used functions that streamline the process of developing *wgpu* applications. We will now leverage these common functions in the module to create *wgpu* applications.

In this section, we will discuss the control code of our *wgpu* application. The control code will be written in Rust. We will add commonly used Rust code called *common.rs* to the *examples/ch01/* folder, which will be shared across different example projects in this chapter. Type the following code in this *common.rs* file:

```rust
#![allow(dead_code)]
use wgpu::{IndexFormat, PrimitiveTopology, ShaderSource};
use winit::{
    event::{Event, WindowEvent},
    event_loop::{ControlFlow, EventLoop},
    window::Window,
};
use wgpu_book_examples::wgpu_simplified as ws;

pub struct Inputs<'a> {
    pub source: ShaderSource<'a>,
    pub topology: PrimitiveTopology,
    pub strip_index_format: Option<IndexFormat>,
}

impl Inputs<'_> {
    pub async fn new(&mut self, event_loop: EventLoop<()>, window: Window, num_vertices: u32) {
        let mut init = ws::IWgpuInit::new(&window, 1, None).await;

        let shader = init.device.create_shader_module(wgpu::ShaderModuleDescriptor {
            label: None,
            source: self.source.clone(),
        });

        let pipeline_layout = init.device.create_pipeline_layout(&wgpu::PipelineLayoutDescriptor {
            label: None,
            bind_group_layouts: &[],
            push_constant_ranges: &[],
        });

        let mut ppl = ws::IRenderPipeline{
            shader: Some(&shader),
            pipeline_layout: Some(&pipeline_layout),
            is_depth_stencil: false,
            topology: self.topology,
            strip_index_format:self.strip_index_format,
            ..Default::default()
        };
        let render_pipeline = ppl.new(&init);
```

```
event_loop.run(move |event, _, control_flow| {
    *control_flow = ControlFlow::Wait;
    match event {
        Event::WindowEvent {
            event: WindowEvent::Resized(size),
            ..
        } => {
            // Recreate the surface with the new size
            init.config.width = size.width;
            init.config.height = size.height;
            init.surface.configure(&init.device, &init.config);
        }
        Event::RedrawRequested(_) => {
            let frame = init.surface.get_current_texture().unwrap();

            let view = frame.texture.create_view(&wgpu::TextureViewDescriptor::default());
            let mut encoder =
                init.device.create_command_encoder(&wgpu::CommandEncoderDescriptor
                    { label: None });
            {
                let color_attachment = ws::create_color_attachment(&view);
                let mut rpass = encoder.begin_render_pass(&wgpu::RenderPassDescriptor {
                    label: None,
                    color_attachments: &[Some(color_attachment)],
                    depth_stencil_attachment: None,
                    occlusion_query_set: None,
                    timestamp_writes: None,
                });
                rpass.set_pipeline(&render_pipeline);
                rpass.draw(0..num_vertices, 0..1);
            }

            init.queue.submit(Some(encoder.finish()));
            frame.present();
        }
        Event::WindowEvent {
            event: WindowEvent::CloseRequested,
            ..
        } => *control_flow = ControlFlow::Exit,
        _ => {}
    }
});
}
}
```

This code begins by introducing a *winit* window, which is used to display the rendered image, and the *wgpu_simplified* module, which provided access the commonly used structs and functions. The code defines an *Inputs* struct with three fields: shader source, primitive topology, and index format for strip primitives. These fields will vary for different example projects.

Next, an implementation is added to the *Inputs* struct, containing an async function named *new*. This function first initializes the *wgpu* API by calling the async *IWgpuInit::new* function from the *wgpu_simplified* module. It then loads the shader module using the *create_shader_module* function, which can create a shader module from either SPIR-V or WGSL source code. In this book, we will use the official WGSL shader.

The code then proceeds to define the render pipeline layout, which is necessary when using GPU buffers. For our simple triangle examples, it is currently a placeholder without any meaningful content.

Subsequently, using the shader module, pipeline layout, and the members of the *Inputs* struct, a *IRenderPipeline* object is created, and its *new* method is called to create the render pipeline.

The next step involves recording and submitting GPU commands using a GPU command encoder. This process takes place within the *event_loop.run* function. The GPU Command Encoder, derived from Metal's MTLCommandEncoder, which is referred as GraphicsCommandList in DirectX 12 and CommandBuffer in Vulkan. Since the GPU is an independent coprocessor, all GPU commands are executed asynchronously. Consequently, a list of GPU commands is built up and sent in batches when needed. In *wgpu*, the GPU command encoder returned by the *device.create_command_encoder* function is a Rust object that assembles a batch of buffered commands to be sent to the GPU at an appropriate time.

Below is the code snippet demonstrating these steps:

```
let frame = init.surface.get_current_texture().unwrap();
let view = frame.texture.create_view(&wgpu::TextureViewDescriptor::default());
let color_attachment = ws::create_color_attachment(&view);

let mut encoder = init.device.create_command_encoder(&wgpu::CommandEncoderDescriptor { label: None });
{
    let mut rpass = encoder.begin_render_pass(&wgpu::RenderPassDescriptor {
        label: None,
        color_attachments: &[Some(color_attachment)],
        depth_stencil_attachment: None,
        occlusion_query_set: None,
        timestamp_writes: None,
    });
    rpass.set_pipeline(&render_pipeline);
    rpass.draw(0..num_vertices, 0..1);
}

init.queue.submit(Some(encoder.finish()));
frame.present();
```

In the above code snippet, we first create a texture view from the surface texture and then create a color attachment using the *create_color_attachment* function from the *wgpu_simplified* module.

Inside the *device.create_command_encoder* function, we open a render pass by calling the *encoder.begin_render_pass* function and name it *rpass* while making it mutable. This render pass accepts a parameter of type *RenderPassDescriptor* as a render pass option with several attributes. One required field is *color_attachments*, which is an array attached to the current render channel to store image information.

Another attribute in the *RenderPassDescriptor* is *depth_stencil_attachment*, which stores depth information for the rendering pass and its template information. Since our triangle examples do not require depth information (they draw 2D flat triangles), we set it to *None*.

Next, we assign the pipeline to the render pass and draw the triangle by calling *rpass.draw* with the specified number of vertices and instances.

To present the *SurfaceTexture* named *frame* returned by the *get_current_texture* method, we first need to submit all instructions to the GPU device's queue for execution with some work rendering to this texture. Then, we call the *frame.present()* method to schedule this texture for presentation on the surface.

1.5.3 Rust Code

The Rust code in this example is very simple because we can reuse the modules defined in the *common.rs* file. Add a new Rust file called *triangle_vertex_color.rs* to the *examples/ ch01/* folder with the following code:

```
mod common;
use winit::event_loop::EventLoop;
use std::borrow::Cow;

fn main() {
    let event_loop = EventLoop::new();
    let window = winit::window::Window::new(&event_loop).unwrap();
    window.set_title("ch01_triangle_vertex_color");
    env_logger::init();

    let mut inputs = common::Inputs{
        source: wgpu::ShaderSource::Wgsl(Cow::Borrowed(include_str!("triangle_vertex_color.wgsl"))),
        topology: wgpu::PrimitiveTopology::TriangleList,
        strip_index_format: None
    };

    pollster::block_on( inputs.new(event_loop, window, 3));
}
```

This code first loads the modules from the *common.rs* file, as well as *EventLoop* from the *winit* library and *Cow* from the standard library. *Cow* stands for "clone-on-write" and is used to handle the shader data efficiently by avoiding unnecessary cloning.

Inside the *main* function, we create an *EventLoop*, which manages events like code execution, user input, window resizing, etc. Next, we create a new window with the title *ch01_triangle_vertex_color*. Then, we instantiate an instance of the *Inputs* struct, which contains information related to shader, primitive topology, and strip index format. Finally, we use the *pollster::block_on* function to run the asynchronous *inputs.new* function, which handles the main logic of our application.

1.5.4 Run Application

To run this application, add the following code snippet to the *Cargo.toml* file:

```
[[example]]
name = "ch01_triangle_vertex_color"
path = "examples/ch01/triangle_vertex_color.rs"
```

Afterward, execute the following *cargo run* command in the terminal window:

```
cargo run --example ch01_triangle_vertex_color
```

This will produce a triangle with different vertex colors, shown in Fig.1-1.

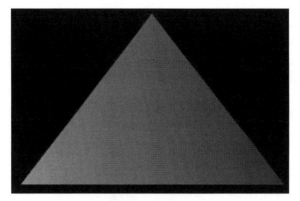

Fig.1-1. Triangle with different vertex colors.

1.6 Triangle Primitives

In this section, I will demonstrate how to use the *triangle-list* and *triangle-strip* primitives in *wgpu* to construct multiple triangles. If we employ the nine vertices and two distinct triangle primitives, the outcome would be as depicted in Fig.1-2.

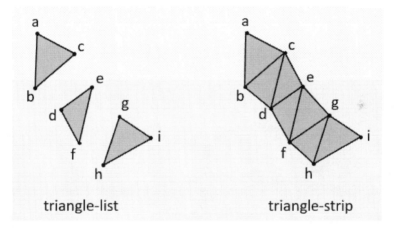

Fig.1-2. Triangles to be constructed using the triangle-list and triangle-strip primitives.

1.6.1 Shader Code

Add a new shader file called *triangle-primitive.wgsl* to the *examples/ch01/* folder with the following code:

```
struct Output {
    @builtin(position) Position : vec4f,
    @location(0) vColor : vec4f,
};

@vertex
fn vs_main(@builtin(vertex_index) VertexIndex: u32) -> Output {
```

```
    var pos : array<vec2f, 9> = array<vec2f, 9>(
        vec2(-0.63,  0.80),
        vec2(-0.65,  0.20),
        vec2(-0.20,  0.60),
        vec2(-0.37, -0.07),
        vec2( 0.05,  0.18),
        vec2(-0.13, -0.40),
        vec2( 0.30, -0.13),
        vec2( 0.13, -0.64),
        vec2( 0.70, -0.30)
    );

    var color : array<vec3f, 9> = array<vec3f, 9>(
        vec3(1.0, 0.0, 0.0),
        vec3(0.0, 1.0, 0.0),
        vec3(0.0, 0.0, 1.0),
        vec3(1.0, 0.0, 0.0),
        vec3(0.0, 1.0, 0.0),
        vec3(0.0, 0.0, 1.0),
        vec3(1.0, 0.0, 0.0),
        vec3(0.0, 1.0, 0.0),
        vec3(0.0, 0.0, 1.0),
    );
    var output: Output;
    output.Position = vec4(pos[VertexIndex], 0.0, 1.0);
    output.vColor = vec4(color[VertexIndex], 1.0);
    return output;
}

@fragment
fn fs_main(@location(0) vColor: vec4f) -> @location(0) vec4f {
    return vColor;
}
```

The current shader is very similar to the one used in the previous example, with the except of having nine vertices and colors.

1.6.2 Rust Code

Include a new Rust file called *triangle-primitive.rs* in the *examples/ch01/* folder and enter the following content into it:

```
mod common;
use winit::event_loop::EventLoop;
use std::borrow::Cow;

fn main() {
    let mut primitive_type = "triangle-list";
    let args: Vec<String> = std::env::args().collect();
    if args.len() > 1 {
        primitive_type = &args[1];
    }

    let mut topology = wgpu::PrimitiveTopology::TriangleList;
    let mut index_format = None;
    if  primitive_type == "triangle-list" {
        topology = wgpu::PrimitiveTopology::TriangleList;
        index_format = None;
    } else if  primitive_type == "triangle-strip" {
```

```
        topology = wgpu::PrimitiveTopology::TriangleStrip;
        index_format = Some(wgpu::IndexFormat::Uint32);
    }

    let mut inputs = common::Inputs{
        source: wgpu::ShaderSource::Wgsl(Cow::Borrowed(include_str!("triangle_primitive.wgsl"))),
        topology,
        strip_index_format: index_format
    };

    let event_loop = EventLoop::new();
    let window = winit::window::Window::new(&event_loop).unwrap();

    window.set_title(&*format!("{}{}", "ch01_primitive_", primitive_type));
    env_logger::init();
    pollster::block_on(inputs.new(event_loop, window, 9));
}
```

The code presented is comparable to the one used in the previous example. The difference is that in this instance, we provide a command line input named *primitive_type* as the *topology* field of the *Inputs* struct. This command line input can be either *triangle-list* or *triangle-strip*.

If we examine the *new* function of the *Inputs* struct defined in the *wgpu-simplified.rs* file in the *src/* folder, we can observe that for the *triangle-strip* primitive, we must assign the *index_format* attribute to *uint32*.

1.6.3 Run Application

To run this application, add the following code snippet to the *Cargo.toml* file:

```
[[example]]
name = "ch01_triangle_primitive"
path = "examples/ch01/triangle_primitive.rs"
```

Afterward, execute the following *cargo run* command in the terminal window:

```
cargo run --example ch01_triangle_primitive triangle-list
```

Here, triangle-list is the input argument for the *primitive_type* variable.

This will produce results shown in Fig.1-3.

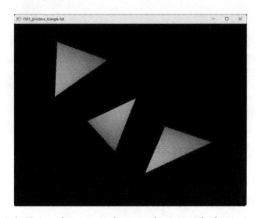

Fig.1-3. Triangles created using the triangle-list primitive.

Now, execute the following cargo run command in the terminal window:

```
cargo run --example ch01_triangle_primitive triangle-strip
```

Here, *triangle-strip* is the input argument for the *primitive_type* variable. This produces results shown in Fig.1-4.

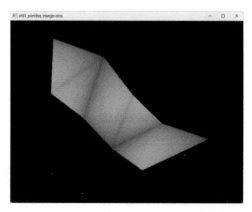

Fig.1-4. Triangles created using the triangle-strip primitive.

1.7 Create Triangle Using GPU Buffers

In the previous triangle examples, we directly entered the vertex data in the WGSL shader, which is solely viable for creating basic primitive shapes. Nonetheless, for complex 3D graphics objects, we usually void this direct approach. Therefore, in this section, we shall employ GPU buffers to store the vertex data and recreate the triangle with distinct vertex color, as shown in Fig.1-1.

A GPU buffer in *wgpu* represents a memory block used in GPU operations. Data is kept in a linear layout, implying that every byte of the allocation can be addressed by its offset from the start of the GPU buffer, with alignment constraints based on the operation.

Within *wgpu*, we can generate GPU buffers using the *device.create_buffer* function, which creates a new buffer in either mapped or unmapped state. Once the GPU buffer is created, we can write the data into it using the *queue.write_buffer* function. Alternatively, we can also create a GPU buffer with data to initialize it directly using the *device.create_buffer_init* function.

1.7.1 Shader Code

Add a new shader file called *triangle_gpu_buffer.wgsl* to the *examples/ch01/* folder with the following code:

```
struct VertexInput {
    @location(0) pos: vec2<f32>,
    @location(1) color: vec3<f32>,
};

struct VertexOutput {
    @builtin(position) position: vec4f,
    @location(0) color: vec4f,
};
```

```
@vertex
fn vs_main(in: VertexInput) -> VertexOutput {
    var out: VertexOutput;
    out.color = vec4(in.color, 1.0);
    out.position = vec4(in.pos, 0.0, 1.0);
    return out;
}

@fragment
fn fs_main(in: VertexOutput) -> @location(0) vec4f {
    return in.color;
}
```

This shader takes vertex position and color as inputs and produces an output struct containing the position and color of the vertex. The fragment shader then takes this output structure as input and outputs the color for each fragment to be displayed on the screen.

1.7.2 Rust Code

Add a new Rust file called *triangle-gpu_buffer.rs* to the *examples/ch01/* folder and enter the following content into it:

```
use bytemuck::{cast_slice, Pod, Zeroable};
use std::{iter, mem};
use wgpu::{util::DeviceExt, VertexBufferLayout};
use winit::{
    event::*,
    event_loop::{ControlFlow, EventLoop},
    window::{Window, WindowBuilder},
};
use wgpu_book_examples::wgpu_simplified as ws;

#[repr(C)]
#[derive(Copy, Clone, Debug, Pod, Zeroable)]
struct Vertex {
    position: [f32; 2],
    color: [f32; 3],
}

const VERTICES: &[Vertex] = &[
    Vertex {
        // vertex a
        position: [0.0, 0.5],
        color: [1.0, 0.0, 0.0],
    },
    Vertex {
        // vertex b
        position: [-0.5, -0.5],
        color: [0.0, 1.0, 0.0],
    },
    Vertex {
        // vertex c
        position: [0.5, -0.5],
        color: [0.0, 0.0, 1.0],
    },
];
```

```rust
struct State {
    init: ws::IWgpuInit,
    pipeline: wgpu::RenderPipeline,
    vertex_buffer: wgpu::Buffer,
}

impl State {
    async fn new(window: &Window) -> Self {
        let init = ws::IWgpuInit::new(&window, 1, None).await;

        let shader = init.device.create_shader_module(wgpu::include_wgsl!("triangle_gpu_buffer.wgsl"));

        let pipeline_layout = init.device.create_pipeline_layout(&wgpu::PipelineLayoutDescriptor {
            label: Some("Render Pipeline Layout"),
            bind_group_layouts: &[],
            push_constant_ranges: &[],
        });

        let vertex_buffer_layout = VertexBufferLayout {
            array_stride: mem::size_of::<Vertex>() as wgpu::BufferAddress,
            step_mode: wgpu::VertexStepMode::Vertex,
            attributes: &wgpu::vertex_attr_array![0 => Float32x2, 1 => Float32x3],
        };

        let mut ppl = ws::IRenderPipeline {
            shader: Some(&shader),
            pipeline_layout: Some(&pipeline_layout),
            is_depth_stencil: false,
            vertex_buffer_layout: &[vertex_buffer_layout],
            ..Default::default()
        };
        let pipeline = ppl.new(&init);

        let vertex_buffer = init.device.create_buffer_init(&wgpu::util::BufferInitDescriptor {
            label: Some("Vertex Buffer"),
            contents: cast_slice(VERTICES),
            usage: wgpu::BufferUsages::VERTEX,
        });

        Self {
            init,
            pipeline,
            vertex_buffer,
        }
    }

    pub fn resize(&mut self, new_size: winit::dpi::PhysicalSize<u32>) {
        if new_size.width > 0 && new_size.height > 0 {
            self.init.size = new_size;
            self.init.config.width = new_size.width;
            self.init.config.height = new_size.height;
            self.init.surface.configure(&self.init.device, &self.init.config);
        }
    }

    #[allow(unused_variables)]
    fn input(&mut self, event: &WindowEvent) -> bool {
        false
    }
```

```rust
    fn update(&mut self) {}

    fn render(&mut self) -> Result<(), wgpu::SurfaceError> {
        let output = self.init.surface.get_current_texture()?;
        let view = output
            .texture
            .create_view(&wgpu::TextureViewDescriptor::default());

        let mut encoder = self
            .init.device
            .create_command_encoder(&wgpu::CommandEncoderDescriptor {
                label: Some("Render Encoder"),
            });

        {
            let color_attachment = ws::create_color_attachment(&view);

            let mut render_pass = encoder.begin_render_pass(&wgpu::RenderPassDescriptor {
                label: Some("Render Pass"),
                color_attachments: &[Some(color_attachment)],
                depth_stencil_attachment: None,
                occlusion_query_set: None,
                timestamp_writes: None,
            });

            render_pass.set_pipeline(&self.pipeline);
            render_pass.set_vertex_buffer(0, self.vertex_buffer.slice(..));
            render_pass.draw(0..3, 0..1);
        }

        self.init.queue.submit(iter::once(encoder.finish()));
        output.present();

        Ok(())
    }
}

fn main() {
    env_logger::init();
    let event_loop = EventLoop::new();
    let window = WindowBuilder::new().build(&event_loop).unwrap();
    window.set_title(&*format!("{}", "ch01_triangle_gpu_buffer"));
    let mut state = pollster::block_on(State::new(&window));

    event_loop.run(move |event, _, control_flow| match event {
        Event::WindowEvent {
            ref event,
            window_id,
        } if window_id == window.id() => {
            if !state.input(event) {
                match event {
                    WindowEvent::CloseRequested
                    | WindowEvent::KeyboardInput {
                        input:
                            KeyboardInput {
                                state: ElementState::Pressed,
                                virtual_keycode: Some(VirtualKeyCode::Escape),
                                ..
                            },
                        ..
```

```
                    } => *control_flow = ControlFlow::Exit,
                    WindowEvent::Resized(physical_size) => {
                        state.resize(*physical_size);
                    }
                    WindowEvent::ScaleFactorChanged { new_inner_size, .. } => {
                        state.resize(**new_inner_size);
                    }
                    _ => {}
                }
            }
        }
        Event::RedrawRequested(_) => {
            state.update();
            match state.render() {
                Ok(_) => {}
                Err(wgpu::SurfaceError::Lost) => state.resize(state.init.size),
                Err(wgpu::SurfaceError::OutOfMemory) => *control_flow = ControlFlow::Exit,
                Err(e) => eprintln!("{:?}", e),
            }
        }
        Event::MainEventsCleared => {
            window.request_redraw();
        }
        _ => {}
    });
}
```

This code first define the *Vertex* struct that contains position and color for each vertex. The position is of type [f32; 2], representing the *x* and *y* coordinates in 2D space. The color is of type [f32; 3], representing the red, green, and blue components for the vertex color. We need the *Vertex* struct to be copyable so we can create the GPU buffer with it.

Next, we generate the actual data that will make up the triangle.

Subsequently, we pack all the fields required for the graphics output into the *State* struct and implement various functions on it. The asynchronous *State::new()* method consists of code for *wgpu* initialization, shader module, pipeline layout, and vertex buffer layout, which are required to build a render pipeline.

Additionally, the *State::new()* function creates a *vertex_buffer* with the vertex data to initialize it using the *device.create_buffer_init* function.

To support resizing in the application, we need to configure the surface every time the window's size changes. Inside the *resize* function, we store the physical *size* and the *config* used to configure the surface. If the window's size changes, we use the new *size* to reconfigure the surface.

Next, the *input()* function returns a Boolean result to indicate whether an event has been fully processed. If it returns *true*, the main loop will not process the event any further. Here, it just returns *false* because for our current example, there is no input events to capture.

The *update()* function is empty in this example because there is nothing to update yet. We will add some code here later on when we want to move some objects around.

The *render()* function defines the render pass, sets the pipeline and vertex buffer to the render pass, and calls the *draw* function to create our triangle.

Inside the *main* function, we need to update the event loop to call the *render()* function to create and render our graphics output.

1.7.3 Run Application

To run this application, add the following code snippet to the *Cargo.toml* file:

```
[[example]]
name = "ch01_triangle_gpu_buffer"
path = "examples/ch01/triangle_gpu_buffer.rs"
```

Afterward, execute the following *cargo run* command in the terminal window:

```
cargo run --example ch01_triangle_gpu_buffer
```

This will produce the same triangle with different vertex colors, as shown in Fig.1-1.

1.8 Create Lines with MSAA

The triangles in the previous examples display some jaggedness on the lines and edges. This aliasing effect occurs mathematically when a continuous signal is transformed into a discrete set of values by sampling. Rasterizing a line or object can also introduce spatial aliasing, meaning that using a fixed number of pixels to represent a line or object will always produce aliasing artifacts.

To mitigate this jagged effect, a technique known as super-sampling anti-aliasing (SSAA) can be employed. This method involves rendering a scene at a higher resolution and then down-sampling to a lower-resolution output. Higher resolutions make the jagged effect less noticeable. However, this approach requires more advanced hardware and greater processing power.

Multi-sampling anti-aliasing (MSAA) is a cost-effective method for enhancing the rendering quality by reducing the jaggedness along the lines and edges. MSAA operates by utilizing multiple samples per pixel for both color and depth during rendering process. It subsequently consolidates these samples to a single value per pixel once the rendering is complete. Most GPUs are optimized for storing 4 samples per pixel, but certain newer products can support MSAA *sample_count* up to 16. At present, WebGPU permits only 1 or 4 samples per pixel, which are determined by the MSAA count parameter. On the other hand, *wgpu* extends this attribute to take more values like 1, 2, 4, 8, and 16. We use the *sample_count* member of the *IWgpuInit* struct to specify the MSAA property.

In this example, we will use MSAA to create multiple line segments with line-list primitive to reduce jaggedness along the lines. This example allows you to compare the results with and without MSAA.

1.8.1 Rust Code

This example can reuse the shader file, *triangle_gpu_buffer.wgsl*, created in the previous example. Here, we only need the Rust control code. Add a new Rust file called *line_msaa.rs* to the *examples/ch01/* folder with the following code:

```
use bytemuck::{Pod, Zeroable};
use std::iter;
use wgpu::{util::DeviceExt, TextureView};
use winit::{
    event::*,
    event_loop::{ControlFlow, EventLoop},
    window::{Window, WindowBuilder},
};
use wgpu_book_examples::wgpu_simplified as ws;
```

```rust
#[repr(C)]
#[derive(Copy, Clone, Debug, Pod, Zeroable)]
struct Vertex {
    position: [f32; 2],
    color: [f32; 4],
}
struct State {
    init: ws::IWgpuInit,
    pipeline: wgpu::RenderPipeline,
    vertex_buffer: wgpu::Buffer,
    vertex_count: u32,
    msaa_texture_view: TextureView,
}

impl State {
    async fn new(window: &Window, sample_count: u32) -> Self {
        let init = ws::IWgpuInit::new(&window, sample_count, None).await;

        let shader = init.device.create_shader_module(wgpu::include_wgsl!("line_msaa.wgsl"));

        let pipeline_layout = init.device.create_pipeline_layout(&wgpu::PipelineLayoutDescriptor {
            label: Some("Render Pipeline Layout"),
            bind_group_layouts: &[],
            push_constant_ranges: &[],
        });

        let vertex_buffer_layout = wgpu::VertexBufferLayout {
            array_stride: std::mem::size_of::<Vertex>() as wgpu::BufferAddress,
            step_mode: wgpu::VertexStepMode::Vertex,
            attributes: &wgpu::vertex_attr_array![0 => Float32x2, 1 => Float32x4],
        };

        let mut ppl = ws::IRenderPipeline {
            shader: Some(&shader),
            topology: wgpu::PrimitiveTopology::LineList,
            pipeline_layout: Some(&pipeline_layout),
            is_depth_stencil: false,
            vertex_buffer_layout: &[vertex_buffer_layout],
            ..Default::default()
        };
        let pipeline = ppl.new(&init);

        let msaa_texture_view = ws::create_msaa_texture_view(&init);

        let mut vertex_data = vec![];

        let max = 50;
        for i in 0..max {
            let percent = i as f32 / max as f32;
            let (sin, cos) = (percent * 2.0 * std::f32::consts::PI).sin_cos();
            vertex_data.push(Vertex {
                position: [0.0, 0.0],
                color: [1.0, -sin, cos, 1.0],
            });
            vertex_data.push(Vertex {
                position: [1.0 * cos, 1.0 * sin],
                color: [sin, -cos, 1.0, 1.0],
            });
        }
```

```rust
    let vertex_buffer = init.device.create_buffer_init(&wgpu::util::BufferInitDescriptor {
        label: Some("Vertex Buffer"),
        contents: bytemuck::cast_slice(&vertex_data),
        usage: wgpu::BufferUsages::VERTEX,
    });
    let vertex_count = vertex_data.len() as u32;

    Self {
        init,
        pipeline,
        vertex_buffer,
        vertex_count,
        msaa_texture_view,
    }
}

pub fn resize(&mut self, new_size: winit::dpi::PhysicalSize<u32>) {
    if new_size.width > 0 && new_size.height > 0 {
        self.init.size = new_size;
        self.init.config.width = new_size.width;
        self.init.config.height = new_size.height;
        self.init.surface.configure(&self.init.device, &self.init.config);
        if self.init.sample_count > 1 {
            self.msaa_texture_view = ws::create_msaa_texture_view(&self.init);
        }
    }
}

#[allow(unused_variables)]
fn input(&mut self, event: &WindowEvent) -> bool {
    false
}

fn update(&mut self) {}

fn render(&mut self) -> Result<(), wgpu::SurfaceError> {
    let output = self.init.surface.get_current_texture()?;
    let view = output
        .texture
        .create_view(&wgpu::TextureViewDescriptor::default());

    let mut encoder = self
        .init.device
        .create_command_encoder(&wgpu::CommandEncoderDescriptor {
            label: Some("Render Encoder"),
        });

    {
        let color_attach = ws::create_color_attachment(&view);
        let msaa_attach = ws::create_msaa_color_attachment(&view, &self.msaa_texture_view);
        let color_attachment = if self.init.sample_count == 1 { color_attach } else { msaa_attach };

        let mut render_pass = encoder.begin_render_pass(&wgpu::RenderPassDescriptor {
            label: Some("Render Pass"),
            color_attachments: &[Some(color_attachment)],
            depth_stencil_attachment: None,
            occlusion_query_set: None,
            timestamp_writes: None,
        });
```

```rust
            render_pass.set_pipeline(&self.pipeline);
            render_pass.set_vertex_buffer(0, self.vertex_buffer.slice(..));
            render_pass.draw(0..self.vertex_count, 0..1);
        }

        self.init.queue.submit(iter::once(encoder.finish()));
        output.present();

        Ok(())
    }
}

fn main() {
    let mut sample_count = 1 as u32;
    let args: Vec<String> = std::env::args().collect();
    if args.len() > 1 {
        sample_count = args[1].parse::<u32>().unwrap();
    }

    env_logger::init();
    let event_loop = EventLoop::new();
    let window = WindowBuilder::new().build(&event_loop).unwrap();
    window.set_title(&*format!("{}_{}", "ch01_line_msaa", sample_count));
    let mut state = pollster::block_on(State::new(&window, sample_count));

    event_loop.run(move |event, _, control_flow| match event {
        Event::WindowEvent {
            ref event,
            window_id,
        } if window_id == window.id() => {
            if !state.input(event) {
                match event {
                    WindowEvent::CloseRequested
                    | WindowEvent::KeyboardInput {
                        input:
                            KeyboardInput {
                                state: ElementState::Pressed,
                                virtual_keycode: Some(VirtualKeyCode::Escape),
                                ..
                            },
                        ..
                    } => *control_flow = ControlFlow::Exit,
                    WindowEvent::Resized(physical_size) => {
                        state.resize(*physical_size);

                    }
                    WindowEvent::ScaleFactorChanged { new_inner_size, .. } => {
                        state.resize(**new_inner_size);
                    }
                    _ => {}
                }
            }
        }
        Event::RedrawRequested(_) => {
            state.update();
            match state.render() {
                Ok(_) => {}
                Err(wgpu::SurfaceError::Lost) => state.resize(state.init.size),
                Err(wgpu::SurfaceError::OutOfMemory) => *control_flow = ControlFlow::Exit,
                Err(e) => eprintln!("{:?}", e),
```

```
            }
        }
        Event::MainEventsCleared => {
            window.request_redraw();
        }
        _ => {}
    });
}
```

The code structure of this example is similar to the previous one. The main difference is that this example allows the user to set the MSAA *sample_count* parameter through the *State::new* function:

```
async fn new(window: &Window, sample_count: u32) -> Self {
    let init = ws::IWgpuInit::new(&window, sample_count, None).await;

    ...

}
```

Inside the *State::new* function, we use the *sample_count* parameter to initialize the *wgpu* API when calling the *ws::IWgpuInit::new* function. Additionally, we create a texture view specifically for MSAA multisampling:

```
let msaa_texture_view = ws::create_msaa_texture_view(&init);
```

In the *render* function, we define the color attachment depending on whether the *sample_count* is 1 or greater than 1:

```
let color_attach = ws::create_color_attachment(&view);
let msaa_attach = ws::create_msaa_color_attachment(&view, &self.msaa_texture_view);
let color_attachment = if self.init.sample_count == 1 { color_attach } else { msaa_attach };
```

In the *main* function, we specify the *sample_count* using a command line argument:

```
let mut sample_count = 1 as u32;
let args: Vec<String> = std::env::args().collect();
if args.len() > 1 {
    sample_count = args[1].parse::<u32>().unwrap();
}
```

The maximum value of the sample_count parameter depends on the graphics card installed on your machine. For example, the Nvidia GeForce RTX 3060 graphics card on my machine supports sample counts up to 8.

1.8.2 Run Application

To run this application, add the following code snippet to the *Cargo.toml* file:

```
[[example]]
name = "ch01_line_msaa"
path = "examples/ch01/line_msaa.rs"
```

Afterward, execute the following *cargo run* commands in the terminal window:

```
cargo run --example ch01_line msaa 1
cargo run --example ch01_line msaa 8
```

This will produce the line segments with different *sample_count*, as shown in Fig.1-5. These results provide a direct comparison of the line segments with and without MSAA. It can be observed that the line segments with MSAA appears smoother, indicating that MSAA can indeed enhance the quality of graphics objects in *wgpu*.

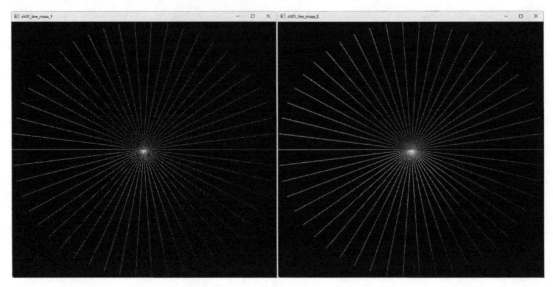

Fig.1-5. Line segments produced without (left) and with MSAA (right, sample_count = 8).

2 3D Shapes and Wireframes

In the previous chapter, we covered setting up the development environment and tools for building *wgpu* applications. We also discussed the basics of *wgpu* and demonstrated how to create triangles using WGSL shader and GPU buffers. While those examples were primarily two-dimensional, this chapter will cover creating real 3D shapes and wireframes, such as cube, sphere, cylinder, and tori.

Creating 3D objects in *wgpu* requires using various 3D coordinate systems, projection, and transformation. This book assumes that you have a mathematical background in 3D matrices and transformations. However, if you are new to 3D graphics, you can learn the basics from my previously published book "*Practical GPU Graphics with wgpu and Rust*", which provides the detailed explanation of 3D projections and transformations.

Similar to WebGPU, the *wgpu* API does not provide any functions for working with projection and transformations. In this book, we will use *cgmath* crate, a popular linear algebra and mathematics library for computer graphics, for performing 3D matrix operations and transformations in *wgpu*.

2.1 Transformations

Rendering 3D objects on a 2D screen requires a series of transformations to properly project the 3D world onto the 2D screen. These transformations are essential to create the illusion of depth and perspective in the final rendered image. The series of transformations typically include model transformation, view transformation, and projection transformation.

The model transformation involves transforming the 3D model's vertices from their local object space to a world coordinate system. This step allows positioning the model within the 3D world and enables it to be translated, rotated, and scaled.

The view transformation, also known as the camera transformation, places the virtual camera within the 3D world and adjusts its position and orientation. This transformation moves the entire scene relative to the camera, simulating the viewpoint from which the scene will be rendered.

The projection transformation is responsible for mapping the 3D scene onto a 2D screen. It converts the 3D coordinates into a 2D space that corresponds to the screen's viewport. This step simulates the perspective and foreshortening that occurs when looking at a 3D scene from a specific viewpoint.

We will implement helper functions for 3D transformations used to render 3D objects in *wgpu* in a Rust module. Add a new Rust file called *transforms.rs* in the *src/* folder and enter the following code into it:

```rust
#![allow(dead_code)]
use std::f32::consts::PI;
use cgmath::*;

#[rustfmt::skip]
#[allow(unused)]
pub const OPENGL_TO_WGPU_MATRIX: Matrix4<f32> = Matrix4::new(
    1.0, 0.0, 0.0, 0.0,
    0.0, 1.0, 0.0, 0.0,
    0.0, 0.0, 0.5, 0.0,
    0.0, 0.0, 0.5, 1.0,
);

pub fn create_model_mat(translation:[f32; 3], rotation:[f32; 3], scaling:[f32; 3]) -> Matrix4<f32> {
    // create transformation matrices
    let trans_mat = Matrix4::from_translation(Vector3::new(translation[0], translation[1],
        translation[2]));
    let rotate_mat_x = Matrix4::from_angle_x(Rad(rotation[0]));
    let rotate_mat_y = Matrix4::from_angle_y(Rad(rotation[1]));
    let rotate_mat_z = Matrix4::from_angle_z(Rad(rotation[2]));
    let scale_mat = Matrix4::from_nonuniform_scale(scaling[0], scaling[1], scaling[2]);

    // combine all transformation matrices together to form a final transform matrix: model matrix
    let model_mat = trans_mat * rotate_mat_z * rotate_mat_y * rotate_mat_x * scale_mat;

    // return final model matrix
    model_mat
}

pub fn create_view_mat(camera_position: Point3<f32>, look_direction: Point3<f32>, up_direction:
Vector3<f32>) -> Matrix4<f32> {
    Matrix4::look_at_rh(camera_position, look_direction, up_direction)
}

pub fn create_projection_mat(aspect:f32, is_perspective:bool) -> Matrix4<f32> {
    let project_mat:Matrix4<f32>;
    if is_perspective {
        project_mat = OPENGL_TO_WGPU_MATRIX * perspective(Rad(2.0*PI/5.0), aspect, 0.1, 1000.0);
    } else {
        project_mat = OPENGL_TO_WGPU_MATRIX * ortho(-4.0, 4.0, -3.0, 3.0, -1.0, 6.0);
    }
    project_mat
}

pub fn create_perspective_mat(fovy:Rad<f32>, aspect:f32, near: f32, far:f32) -> Matrix4<f32> {
    OPENGL_TO_WGPU_MATRIX * perspective(fovy, aspect, near, far)
}

pub fn create_ortho_mat(left: f32, right: f32, bottom: f32, top: f32, near: f32, far: f32) -> Matrix4<f32>
{
    OPENGL_TO_WGPU_MATRIX * ortho(left, right, bottom, top, near, far)
}

pub fn create_vp_ortho_mat(left: f32, right: f32, bottom: f32, top: f32, near: f32, far: f32,
camera_position: Point3<f32>,
    look_direction: Point3<f32>, up_direction: Vector3<f32>) -> (Matrix4<f32>, Matrix4<f32>, Matrix4<f32>)
{

    // construct view matrix
    let view_mat = Matrix4::look_at_rh(camera_position, look_direction, up_direction);
```

```
    // construct projection matrix
    let project_mat = OPENGL_TO_WGPU_MATRIX * ortho(left, right, bottom, top, near, far);

    // contruct view-projection matrix
    let vp_mat = project_mat * view_mat;

    // return various matrices
    (view_mat, project_mat, vp_mat)
}

pub fn create_vp_mat(camera_position: Point3<f32>, look_direction: Point3<f32>, up_direction:
Vector3<f32>,
    aspect:f32) -> (Matrix4<f32>, Matrix4<f32>, Matrix4<f32>) {

    // construct view matrix
    let view_mat = Matrix4::look_at_rh(camera_position, look_direction, up_direction);

    // construct projection matrix
    let project_mat = OPENGL_TO_WGPU_MATRIX * perspective(Rad(2.0*PI/5.0), aspect, 0.1, 1000.0);

    // contruct view-projection matrix
    let vp_mat = project_mat * view_mat;

    // return various matrices
    (view_mat, project_mat, vp_mat)
}

pub fn create_projection_ortho(left: f32, right: f32, bottom: f32, top: f32, near: f32, far: f32) ->
Matrix4<f32> {
    OPENGL_TO_WGPU_MATRIX * ortho(left, right, bottom, top, near, far)
}
```

Here, we first introduce a constant matrix called *OPENGL_TO_WGPU_MATRIX*, which is used to convert OpenGL's coordinate system into *wgpu*'s coordinate system. The coordinate system in *wgpu* is based on DirectX and Metal's coordinate system, meaning that in normalized device coordinates (NDC), the *x* axis and *y* axis are in the range of $[-1.0, 1.0]$, while the *z* axis is in the range of $[0.0, 1.0]$. While the *cgmath* library is built for OpenGL's coordinate system where the *x*, *y*, and *z*-axes are all in the range of $[-1.0, 1.0]$. We need this constant matrix to scale and translate our scene from OpenGL's coordinate system into *wgpu*'s coordinate system. Of course, we do not explicitly need this matrix, but models centered at (0, 0, 0) will be halfway inside the clipping area.

The *create_model_mat* function is responsible for combining the individual transformation matrices from translation, rotation, and scaling into a single *Matrix4* matrix using various matrix operation functions implemented in the *cgmath* library. It is important to note that when combining transformation matrices, you must multiply them in the reverse order of the desired transformation sequence. This is because matrix multiplication is not commutative, meaning that the order in which you multiply matrices affects the final results. For example, if we want to translate a 3D object, then rotate it, and then scale it, we must multiply the translation matrix by the rotation matrix by the scaling matrix, in that order. If we do it in the wrong order, we will get completely wrong transformations and the object will not appear correctly in the scene.

The *create_view_mat* function is responsible for creating a view matrix based on the camera position, look at direction, and up direction provided as input arguments. This function returns a view matrix of the *Matrix4* type.

The *create_projection_mat* function takes the aspect ratio as its input argument and returns a perspective or orthographic projection matrix depending on the *is_perspective* input argument.

The *create_vp_mat* function is used to create a view-projection matrix by combining the view and projection matrices together.

The above code also includes other helper functions such as *create_perspective_mat*, *create_ortho_mat*, and *create_vp_ortho_mat*. These functions may be useful for some 3D graphics applications.

2.2 Create 3D Cube

In this section, we will create a 3D cube with distinct vertex colors in *wgpu*. The vertices of a cube can be represented as eight points in 3D space, as shown in Fig.2-1.

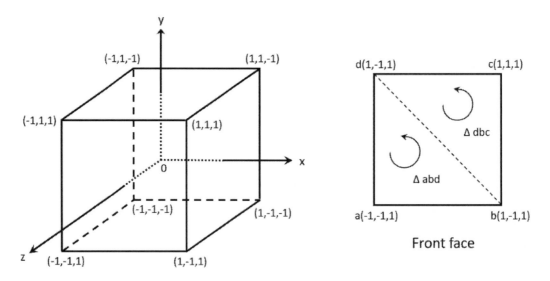

Fig.2-1. Coordinates of a cube. On the right shows triangular meshes for the front face.

2.2.1 Vertex Data

Let us consider the front face of the cube, which has four vertices and needs two triangle primitives to render it. There are two approaches to render this face: using six vertices or using four vertices with indices. In this example, we will use the index approach, which is more efficient and saves memory.

To define the vertex data for the cube, we will create a new Rust file called *vertex_data.rs* and save it in the *src/* folder. Here is code of this file:

```
pub fn create_cube_data(side:f32) -> (Vec<[f32; 3]>, Vec<[f32; 3]>,Vec<[f32; 3]>,
Vec<[f32; 2]>,Vec<u16>,Vec<u16>) {
    let s2 = side / 2.0;
    let positions = [
        [s2,  s2,  s2],     // index 0
        [s2,  s2, -s2],     // index 1
        [s2, -s2,  s2],     // index 2
        [s2, -s2, -s2],     // index 3
```

```
    [-s2,  s2, -s2],      // index 4
    [-s2,  s2,  s2],      // index 5
    [-s2, -s2, -s2],      // index 6
    [-s2, -s2,  s2],      // index 7
    [-s2,  s2, -s2],      // index 8
    [s2,   s2, -s2],      // index 9
    [-s2,  s2,  s2],      // index 10
    [s2,   s2,  s2],      // index 11
    [-s2, -s2,  s2],      // index 12
    [s2,  -s2,  s2],      // index 13
    [-s2, -s2, -s2],      // index 14
    [s2,  -s2, -s2],      // index 15
    [-s2,  s2,  s2],      // index 16
    [s2,   s2,  s2],      // index 17
    [-s2, -s2,  s2],      // index 18
    [s2,  -s2,  s2],      // index 19
    [s2,   s2, -s2],      // index 20
    [-s2,  s2, -s2],      // index 21
    [s2,  -s2, -s2],      // index 22
    [-s2, -s2, -s2],      // index 23
];

let colors = [
    [1., 1., 1.], [1., 1., 0.], [1., 0., 1.], [1., 0., 0.],
    [0., 1., 0.], [0., 1., 1.], [0., 0., 0.], [0., 0., 1.],
    [0., 1., 0.], [1., 1., 0.], [0., 1., 1.], [1., 1., 1.],
    [0., 0., 1.], [1., 0., 1.], [0., 0., 0.], [1., 0., 0.],
    [0., 1., 1.], [1., 1., 1.], [0., 0., 1.], [1., 0., 1.],
    [1., 1., 0.], [0., 1., 0.], [1., 0., 0.], [0., 0., 0.],
];

let normals = [
    [1.,  0.,  0.], [1.,  0.,  0.], [1.,  0.,  0.], [1.,  0.,  0.],
    [-1.,  0.,  0.], [-1.,  0.,  0.], [-1.,  0.,  0.], [-1.,  0.,  0.],
    [0.,  1.,  0.], [0.,  1.,  0.], [0.,  1.,  0.], [0.,  1.,  0.],
    [0., -1.,  0.], [0., -1.,  0.], [0., -1.,  0.], [0., -1.,  0.],
    [0.,  0.,  1.], [0.,  0.,  1.], [0.,  0.,  1.], [0.,  0.,  1.],
    [0.,  0., -1.], [0.,  0., -1.], [0.,  0., -1.], [0.,  0., -1.],
];

let uvs = [
    [0., 1.], [1., 1.], [0., 0.], [1., 0.], [0., 1.], [1., 1.], [0., 0.], [1., 0.],
    [0., 1.], [1., 1.], [0., 0.], [1., 0.], [0., 1.], [1., 1.], [0., 0.], [1., 0.],
    [0., 1.], [1., 1.], [0., 0.], [1., 0.], [0., 1.], [1., 1.], [0., 0.], [1., 0.],
];

let indices = [
    0,  2,  1, 2,  3,  1,
    4,  6,  5, 6,  7,  5,
    8, 10,  9, 10, 11,  9,
    12, 14, 13, 14, 15, 13,
    16, 18, 17, 18, 19, 17,
    20, 22, 21, 22, 23, 21,
];

let indices2 = [
    8, 9, 9, 11, 11, 10, 10, 8,     // top
    14, 15, 15, 13, 13, 12, 12, 14, // bottom
    11, 13, 9, 15, 8, 14, 10, 12,   // side
];
```

```
    (positions.to_vec(), colors.to_vec(), normals.to_vec(), uvs.to_vec(),
     indices.to_vec(), indices2.to_vec())
}
```

We can use the *create_cube_data* function to generate the positions, colors, normals, and UVs, as well as indices for rendering the cube. The normal data represents the normal vector for each vertex, while the UV data represents texture coordinates. The *indices2* data will be used to create a wireframe for the cube.

The index data is useful to avoid using duplicated vertex data. In the *triangle_gpu_buffer* example from the previous chapter, we created a triangle with just three vertices, without any duplicated vertices. However, for more complex objects, such as a square that requires 6 vertices (two triangles) but has 4 vertices, duplicating vertices would significantly increase CPU/GPU memory consumption. To address this issue, *wgpu* provides a function called *render_pass.draw_indexed*, which allows us to draw indexed shapes.

In the following chapters, we will use the normal data to compute lighting and the UV data to map a texture onto surfaces instead of the solid color.

2.2.2 Shader Code

Create a new shader file named *unlit-vertex-color.wgsl* in the *examples/ch02/* folder and insert the provided code into it:

```
@binding(0) @group(0) var<uniform> mvpMatrix : mat4x4f;

struct Output {
    @builtin(position) Position : vec4f,
    @location(0) vColor : vec4f,
};

@vertex
fn vs_main(@location(0) pos: vec3f, @location(1) color: vec3f) -> Output {
    var output: Output;
    output.Position = mvpMatrix * vec4(pos, 1.0);
    output.vColor = vec4(color, 1.0);
    return output;
}

@fragment
fn fs_main(@location(0) vColor: vec4f) -> @location(0) vec4f {
    return vColor;
}
```

This shader code is straightforward. We pass the model-view-projection matrix using the uniform buffer. The vertex data inputs include position and color, both of which are of type *vec3f*. In the vertex *vs_main* function, we convert them into the built-in position and color of type *vec4f*.

The fragment shader simply returns the color processed in the vertex shader.

2.2.3 Rust Code

Add a new Rust file called *cube_rotation.rs* file to the *examples/ch02/* folder and enter the following code into it:

```
use std:: {iter, mem};
```

```rust
use cgmath::Matrix4;
use wgpu:: {util::DeviceExt, VertexBufferLayout};
use winit::{
    event::*,
    event_loop::{ControlFlow, EventLoop},
    window::{Window, WindowBuilder},
};
use bytemuck:: {Pod, Zeroable, cast_slice};
use wgpu_book_examples:: { wgpu_simplified as ws, transforms as wt, vertex_data as vd };

#[repr(C)]
#[derive(Copy, Clone, Debug, Pod, Zeroable)]
struct Vertex {
    position: [f32; 3],
    color: [f32; 3],
}

fn create_vertices() -> (Vec<Vertex>, Vec<u16>) {
    let (pos, col, _, _, ind, _) = vd::create_cube_data(2.0);
    let mut data:Vec<Vertex> = vec![];
    for i in 0..pos.len() {
        data.push(Vertex { position:pos[i], color:col[i]});
    }
    (data.to_vec(), ind)
}

struct State {
    init: ws::IWgpuInit,
    pipeline: wgpu::RenderPipeline,
    vertex_buffer: wgpu::Buffer,
    index_buffer: wgpu::Buffer,
    uniform_bind_group:wgpu::BindGroup,
    uniform_buffer: wgpu::Buffer,
    view_mat: Matrix4<f32>,
    project_mat: Matrix4<f32>,
    msaa_texture_view: wgpu::TextureView,
    indices_len: u32,
    depth_texture_view: wgpu::TextureView,
    rotation_speed: f32,
}

impl State {
    async fn new(window: &Window, sample_count: u32) -> Self {
        let init = ws::IWgpuInit::new(&window, sample_count, None).await;

        let shader = init.device.create_shader_module(wgpu::include_wgsl!("unlit_vertex_color.wgsl"));

        // uniform data
        let camera_position = (3.0, 1.5, 3.0).into();
        let look_direction = (0.0,0.0,0.0).into();
        let up_direction = cgmath::Vector3::unit_y();

        let model_mat = wt::create_model_mat([0.0,0.0,0.0], [0.0,0.0,0.0], [1.0,1.0,1.0]);
        let (view_mat, project_mat, vp_mat) =
            wt::create_vp_mat(camera_position, look_direction, up_direction,
            init.config.width as f32 / init.config.height as f32);
        let mvp_mat = vp_mat * model_mat;

        let mvp_ref:&[f32; 16] = mvp_mat.as_ref();
        let uniform_buffer = init.device.create_buffer_init(
```

```rust
        &wgpu::util::BufferInitDescriptor {
            label: Some("Uniform Buffer"),
            contents: bytemuck::cast_slice(mvp_ref),
            usage: wgpu::BufferUsages::UNIFORM | wgpu::BufferUsages::COPY_DST,
        }
    );

    let (layout, uniform_bind_group) = ws::create_bind_group(
        &init.device,
        vec![wgpu::ShaderStages::VERTEX],
        &[uniform_buffer.as_entire_binding()]
    );

    let pipeline_layout = init.device.create_pipeline_layout(
        &wgpu::PipelineLayoutDescriptor {
            label: Some("Render Pipeline Layout"),
            bind_group_layouts: &[&layout],
            push_constant_ranges: &[],
        }
    );

    let vertex_buffer_layout = VertexBufferLayout {
        array_stride: mem::size_of::<Vertex>() as wgpu::BufferAddress,
        step_mode: wgpu::VertexStepMode::Vertex,
        attributes: &wgpu::vertex_attr_array![0 => Float32x3, 1 => Float32x3],
    };

    let mut ppl = ws::IRenderPipeline{
        shader: Some(&shader),
        pipeline_layout: Some(&pipeline_layout),
        vertex_buffer_layout: &[vertex_buffer_layout],
        ..Default::default()
    };
    let pipeline = ppl.new(&init);

    let msaa_texture_view = ws::create_msaa_texture_view(&init);
    let depth_texture_view = ws::create_depth_view(&init);

    let (vertex_data, index_data) = create_vertices();
    let vertex_buffer = init.device.create_buffer_init(
        &wgpu::util::BufferInitDescriptor {
            label: Some("Vertex Buffer"),
            contents: cast_slice(&vertex_data),
            usage: wgpu::BufferUsages::VERTEX,
        }
    );

    let index_buffer = init.device.create_buffer_init(
        &wgpu::util::BufferInitDescriptor{
            label: Some("Index Buffer"),
            contents: bytemuck::cast_slice(&index_data),
            usage: wgpu::BufferUsages::INDEX,
        }
    );

    Self {
        init,
        pipeline,
        vertex_buffer,
        index_buffer,
```

```rust
            uniform_bind_group,
            uniform_buffer,
            view_mat,
            project_mat,
            msaa_texture_view,
            indices_len: index_data.len() as u32,
            depth_texture_view,
            rotation_speed: 1.0,
        }
}

pub fn resize(&mut self, new_size: winit::dpi::PhysicalSize<u32>) {
    if new_size.width > 0 && new_size.height > 0 {
        self.init.size = new_size;
        self.init.config.width = new_size.width;
        self.init.config.height = new_size.height;
        self.init.surface.configure(&self.init.device, &self.init.config);

        self.project_mat = wt::create_projection_mat(new_size.width as f32 / new_size.height as f32,
            true);
        self.depth_texture_view = ws::create_depth_view(&self.init);
        if self.init.sample_count > 1 {
            self.msaa_texture_view = ws::create_msaa_texture_view(&self.init);
        }
    }
}

#[allow(unused_variables)]
fn input(&mut self, event: &WindowEvent) -> bool {
    match event {
        WindowEvent::KeyboardInput {
            input:
                KeyboardInput {
                    virtual_keycode: Some(keycode),
                    state: ElementState::Pressed,
                    ..
                },
            ..
        } => {
            match keycode {
                VirtualKeyCode::Q => {
                    self.rotation_speed += 0.1;
                    true
                },
                VirtualKeyCode::A => {
                    self.rotation_speed -= 0.1;
                    if self.rotation_speed < 0.0 {
                        self.rotation_speed = 0.0;
                    }
                    true
                },
                _ => false
            }
        }
        _ => false,
    }
}

fn update(&mut self, dt: std::time::Duration) {
    // update uniform buffer
```

```rust
        let dt = self.rotation_speed * dt.as_secs_f32();
        let model_mat = wt::create_model_mat([0.0,0.0,0.0], [dt.sin(), dt.cos(), 0.0], [1.0, 1.0, 1.0]);
        let mvp_mat = self.project_mat * self.view_mat * model_mat;
        let mvp_ref:&[f32; 16] = mvp_mat.as_ref();
        self.init.queue.write_buffer(&self.uniform_buffer, 0, bytemuck::cast_slice(mvp_ref));
    }

    fn render(&mut self) -> Result<(), wgpu::SurfaceError> {
        let output = self.init.surface.get_current_texture()?;
        let view = output
            .texture
            .create_view(&wgpu::TextureViewDescriptor::default());

        let mut encoder = self
            .init.device
            .create_command_encoder(&wgpu::CommandEncoderDescriptor {
                label: Some("Render Encoder"),
            });

        {
            let color_attach = ws::create_color_attachment(&view);
            let msaa_attach = ws::create_msaa_color_attachment(&view, &self.msaa_texture_view);
            let color_attachment = if self.init.sample_count == 1 { color_attach } else { msaa_attach };
            let depth_attachment = ws::create_depth_stencil_attachment(&self.depth_texture_view);

            let mut render_pass = encoder.begin_render_pass(&wgpu::RenderPassDescriptor {
                label: Some("Render Pass"),
                color_attachments: &[Some(color_attachment)],
                depth_stencil_attachment: Some(depth_attachment),
                occlusion_query_set: None,
                timestamp_writes: None,
            });

            render_pass.set_pipeline(&self.pipeline);
            render_pass.set_vertex_buffer(0, self.vertex_buffer.slice(..));
            render_pass.set_index_buffer(self.index_buffer.slice(..), wgpu::IndexFormat::Uint16);
            render_pass.set_bind_group(0, &self.uniform_bind_group, &[]);
            render_pass.draw_indexed(0..self.indices_len, 0, 0..1);
        }

        self.init.queue.submit(iter::once(encoder.finish()));
        output.present();

        Ok(())
    }
}

fn main() {
    let mut sample_count = 1 as u32;
    let args: Vec<String> = std::env::args().collect();
    if args.len() > 1 {
        sample_count = args[1].parse::<u32>().unwrap();
    }

    env_logger::init();
    let event_loop = EventLoop::new();
    let window = WindowBuilder::new().build(&event_loop).unwrap();
    window.set_title(&*format!("ch02_{}_{}", "cube_rotation", sample_count));
    let mut state = pollster::block_on(State::new(&window, sample_count));
```

```rust
    let render_start_time = std::time::Instant::now();

    event_loop.run(move |event, _, control flow| {
        match event {
            Event::WindowEvent {
                ref event,
                window_id,
            } if window_id == window.id() => {
                if !state.input(event) {
                    match event {
                        WindowEvent::CloseRequested
                        | WindowEvent::KeyboardInput {
                            input:
                                KeyboardInput {
                                    state: ElementState::Pressed,
                                    virtual_keycode: Some(VirtualKeyCode::Escape),
                                    ..
                                },
                            ..
                        } => *control flow = ControlFlow::Exit,
                        WindowEvent::Resized(physical_size) => {
                            state.resize(*physical_size);
                        }
                        WindowEvent::ScaleFactorChanged { new_inner_size, .. } => {
                            state.resize(**new_inner_size);
                        }
                        _ => {}
                    }
                }
            }
            Event::RedrawRequested(_) => {
                let now = std::time::Instant::now();
                let dt = now - render_start_time;
                state.update(dt);

                match state.render() {
                    Ok(_) => {}
                    Err(wgpu::SurfaceError::Lost) => state.resize(state.init.size),
                    Err(wgpu::SurfaceError::OutOfMemory) => *control flow = ControlFlow::Exit,
                    Err(e) => eprintln!("{:?}", e),
                }
            }
            Event::MainEventsCleared => {
                window.request_redraw();
            }
            _ => {}
        }
    });
}
```

Here, we first define a *Vertex* struct with two [f32; 3] fields that represents position and color for each vertex. We then implement a helper method called *create_vertices* that the *position*, *color*, and *indices* data from the *create_cube_data* function implemented in the *vertex_data.rs* file in the *src/* folder into a *Vertex* array and a *u16* array, which will be used to create our 3D cube.

Next, we pack all the fields required for drawing our graphics shape into another struct called *State*, and create some methods on it:

```rust
struct State {
    init: ws::IWgpuInit,
```

```
    pipeline: wgpu::RenderPipeline,
    vertex_buffer: wgpu::Buffer,
    index_buffer: wgpu::Buffer,
    uniform_bind_group:wgpu::BindGroup,
    uniform_buffer: wgpu::Buffer,
    view_mat: Matrix4<f32>,
    project_mat: Matrix4<f32>,
    msaa_texture_view: wgpu::TextureView,
    indices_len: u32,
    depth_texture_view: wgpu::TextureView,
    rotation_speed: f32,
}
```

Here, the *State* struct consists of a field called *init* that has the type of ws::*IWgpuInit*. That field contains various attributes associated with the *wgpu* initialization, such as device, surface, config, etc.

Inside the *State::new* function, we create a uniform buffer to store the model-view-projection matrix called *mvp_mat*. Note that we cannot use the *mvp_mat* matrix directly when creating the uniform buffer because *mvp_mat* is a *Matrix4<f32>* type and the "Pod" is not implemented for this type. As a workaround, we convert *mvp_mat* into *mvp_ref* with a &[f32; 16] type that can be used in creating our uniform buffer:

```
    let mvp_ref:&[f32; 16] = mvp_mat.as_ref();
    let uniform_buffer = init.device.create_buffer_init(
        &wgpu::util::BufferInitDescriptor {
            label: Some("Uniform Buffer"),
            contents: bytemuck::cast_slice(mvp_ref),
            usage: wgpu::BufferUsages::UNIFORM | wgpu::BufferUsages::COPY_DST,
        }
    );
```

With this uniform buffer, we create a uniform bind group layout and uniform bind group for it by calling the *create_bind_group* method implemented in the *wgpu_simplified* module. Here, we only need the uniform information in the vertex shader to manipulate our vertices, so we set its visibility attribute to *wgpu::ShaderStages::VERTEX*. Next, we register the uniform bind group layout with the render pipeline layout.

Subsequently, we use the *wgpu* macro, *vertex_attr_array*!, to create a vertex buffer layout. Here, we set the *attributes* of the layout using the following code snippet:

```
    attributes: &wgpu::vertex_attr_array![0 => Float32x3, 1 => Float32x3],
```

The first element corresponds to the positions, while the second element corresponds to the colors. Both have the same *VertexFormat*: '*Float32x3*', which corresponds to *vec3f* in the WGSL shader.

After creating the render pipeline, we proceed to create *position*, *color*, and *index* buffers for the vertex; Additionally, we create the depth texture using the *ws::create_depth_view* function, which will serve as the depth-stencil attachment in the render pass.

In the *render* function, we not only set the vertex buffer to the render pass but also set the bind group and index buffer to the render pass. It is worth noting that we need to call the *render_pass.draw_indexed* function in this example to draw the cube because the vertex data provided is indexed.

To rotate the cube automatically when the application starts, in the *update* function, we define a time-dependent rotation to create the model matrix. We then reconstruct the model-view-projection matrix by multiplying the model, view, and projection matrix together and update the uniform buffer with the updated data using the *write_buffer* function:

```
let dt = self.rotation_speed * dt.as_secs_f32();
let model_mat = wt::create_model_mat([0.0,0.0,0.0], [dt.sin(), dt.cos(), 0.0], [1.0, 1.0, 1.0]);
let mvp_mat = self.project_mat * self.view_mat * model_mat;
let mvp_ref:&[f32; 16] = mvp_mat.as_ref();
self.init.queue.write_buffer(&self.uniform_buffer, 0, cast_slice(mvp_ref));
```

Inside the *input* function, we add keyboard input to control the rotation speed: the *Q* key is used to increase the rotation speed, while the *A* key is used to decrease the rotation speed.

2.2.4 Run Application

To run this application, add the following code snippet to the *Cargo.toml* file:

```
[[example]]
name = "ch02_cube_rotation"
path = "examples/ch02/cube_rotation.rs"
```

Afterward, execute the following *cargo run* commands in the terminal window:

```
cargo run --example ch02_cube_rotation 8
```

This will produce the cube with different vertex colors, as shown in Fig.2-2.

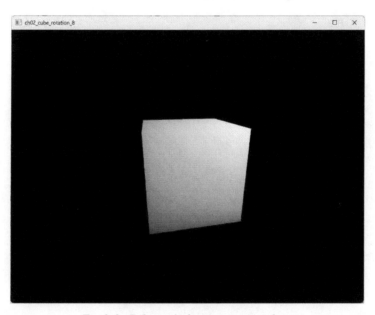

Fig.2-2. Cube with distinct vertex colors.

You can use *Q* and *A* keys to adjust the rotation speed of the cube.

2.3 Cube with Wireframe

In the previous example, we generated a cube with distinct vertex colors. However, in this section, we aim to produce the same cube but with a wireframe. Furthermore, we would like the user to be able to change the color of both the shape and wireframe independently.

2.3.1 Shader code

Create a new shader file called *unlit.wgsl* within the *examples/ch02/* folder and add the following code
to it:

```
@binding(0) @group(0) var<uniform> mvpMatrix: mat4x4f;

@vertex
fn vs_main(@location(0) pos: vec4f) -> @builtin(position) vec4f {
    return mvpMatrix * pos;
}

@binding(1) @group(0) var<uniform> color: vec4f;

@fragment
fn fs_main() -> @location(0) vec4f {
    return color;
}
```

The shader includes two uniform buffers – one for passing the model-view-projection matrix and the
other for passing the color. This shader will be used to generate both the cube shape and wireframe.

2.3.2 Rust Code

Now, add a new Rust file called *cube_wireframe.rs* to the *examples/ch02/* folder and type in the
following code into it:

```
use std:: {iter, mem};
use cgmath::Matrix4;
use wgpu:: {util::DeviceExt, VertexBufferLayout};
use winit::{
    event::*,
    event_loop::{ControlFlow, EventLoop},
    window::{Window, WindowBuilder},
};
use bytemuck:: {Pod, Zeroable, cast_slice};
use wgpu_book_examples:: { wgpu_simplified as ws, transforms as wt, vertex_data as vd };
use rand;

#[repr(C)]
#[derive(Copy, Clone, Debug, Pod, Zeroable)]
struct Vertex {
    position: [f32; 3],
}

fn create_vertices() -> (Vec<Vertex>, Vec<u16>, Vec<u16>) {
    let (pos, _, _, _, ind, ind2) = vd::create_cube_data(2.0);
    let mut data:Vec<Vertex> = vec![];
    for i in 0..pos.len() {
        data.push(Vertex { position:pos[i]});
    }
    (data.to_vec(), ind, ind2)
}

struct State {
    init: ws::IWgpuInit,
    pipelines: [wgpu::RenderPipeline; 2],
    vertex_buffer: wgpu::Buffer,
```

```
        index_buffers: [wgpu::Buffer; 2],
        uniform_bind_groups:[wgpu::BindGroup; 2],
        uniform_buffers: [wgpu::Buffer; 3],
        view_mat: Matrix4<f32>,
        project_mat: Matrix4<f32>,
        msaa_texture_view: wgpu::TextureView,
        depth_texture_view: wgpu::TextureView,
        indices_lens: [u32; 2],
        plot_type: u32,
        rotation_speed: f32,
}

impl State {
    async fn new(window: &Window, sample_count: u32) -> Self {
        let init = ws::IWgpuInit::new(&window, sample_count, None).await;

        let shader = init.device.create_shader_module(wgpu::include_wgsl!("unlit.wgsl"));

        // uniform data
        let camera_position = (3.0, 1.5, 3.0).into();
        let look_direction = (0.0,0.0,0.0).into();
        let up_direction = cgmath::Vector3::unit_y();

        let model_mat = wt::create_model_mat([0.0,0.0,0.0], [0.0,0.0,0.0], [1.0,1.0,1.0]);
        let (view_mat, project_mat, vp_mat) =
            wt::create_vp_mat(camera_position, look_direction, up_direction,
            init.config.width as f32 / init.config.height as f32);
        let mvp_mat = vp_mat * model_mat;

        let mvp_ref:&[f32; 16] = mvp_mat.as_ref();
        let uniform_buffer = init.device.create_buffer_init(&wgpu::util::BufferInitDescriptor {
            label: Some("Uniform Buffer"),
            contents: bytemuck::cast_slice(mvp_ref),
            usage: wgpu::BufferUsages::UNIFORM | wgpu::BufferUsages::COPY_DST,
        });

        // color uniform buffer for object and wireframe
        let color_buffer = init.device.create_buffer_init(&wgpu::util::BufferInitDescriptor {
            label: Some("Uniform Buffer"),
            contents: bytemuck::cast_slice([1.0 as f32, 0.0, 0.0].as_ref()),
            usage: wgpu::BufferUsages::UNIFORM | wgpu::BufferUsages::COPY_DST,
        });
        let color_buffer2 = init.device.create_buffer_init(&wgpu::util::BufferInitDescriptor {
            label: Some("Uniform Buffer"),
            contents: bytemuck::cast_slice([1.0 as f32, 1.0, 0.0].as_ref()),
            usage: wgpu::BufferUsages::UNIFORM | wgpu::BufferUsages::COPY_DST,
        });

        let (layout, uniform_bind_group) = ws::create_bind_group(
            &init.device,
            vec![wgpu::ShaderStages::VERTEX, wgpu::ShaderStages::FRAGMENT],
            &[uniform_buffer.as_entire_binding(), color_buffer.as_entire_binding()],
        );

        let(layout2, uniform_bind_group2) = ws::create_bind_group(
            &init.device,
            vec![wgpu::ShaderStages::VERTEX, wgpu::ShaderStages::FRAGMENT],
            &[uniform_buffer.as_entire_binding(), color_buffer2.as_entire_binding()],
        );
```

```rust
let pipeline_layout = init.device.create_pipeline_layout(&wgpu::PipelineLayoutDescriptor {
    label: Some("Render Pipeline Layout"),
    bind_group_layouts: &[&layout],
    push_constant_ranges: &[],
});

let vertex_buffer_layout = VertexBufferLayout {
    array_stride: mem::size_of::<Vertex>() as wgpu::BufferAddress,
    step_mode: wgpu::VertexStepMode::Vertex,
    attributes: &wgpu::vertex_attr_array![0 => Float32x3],
};

let mut ppl = ws::IRenderPipeline {
    shader: Some(&shader),
    pipeline_layout: Some(&pipeline_layout),
    vertex_buffer_layout: &[vertex_buffer_layout],
    ..Default::default()
};
let pipeline = ppl.new(&init);

let pipeline_layout2 = init.device.create_pipeline_layout(&wgpu::PipelineLayoutDescriptor {
    label: Some("Render Pipeline Layout 2"),
    bind_group_layouts: &[&layout2],
    push_constant_ranges: &[],
});

let vertex_buffer_layout2 = VertexBufferLayout {
    array_stride: mem::size_of::<Vertex>() as wgpu::BufferAddress,
    step_mode: wgpu::VertexStepMode::Vertex,
    attributes: &wgpu::vertex_attr_array![0 => Float32x3],
};

let mut ppl2 = ws::IRenderPipeline {
    topology: wgpu::PrimitiveTopology::LineList,
    shader: Some(&shader),
    pipeline_layout: Some(&pipeline_layout2),
    vertex_buffer_layout: &[vertex_buffer_layout2],
    ..Default::default()
};
let pipeline2 = ppl2.new(&init);

let msaa_texture_view = ws::create_msaa_texture_view(&init);
let depth_texture_view = ws::create_depth_view(&init);

let (vertex_data, index_data, index_data2) = create_vertices();
let vertex_buffer = init.device.create_buffer_init(&wgpu::util::BufferInitDescriptor {
    label: Some("Vertex Buffer"),
    contents: cast_slice(&vertex_data),
    usage: wgpu::BufferUsages::VERTEX,
});

let index_buffer = init.device.create_buffer_init(&wgpu::util::BufferInitDescriptor{
    label: Some("Index Buffer"),
    contents: bytemuck::cast_slice(&index_data),
    usage: wgpu::BufferUsages::INDEX,
});

let index_buffer2 = init.device.create_buffer_init(&wgpu::util::BufferInitDescriptor{
    label: Some("Index Buffer"),
    contents: bytemuck::cast_slice(&index_data2),
```

```
            usage: wgpu::BufferUsages::INDEX,
        });

        Self {
            init,
            pipelines: [pipeline, pipeline2],
            vertex_buffer,
            index_buffers: [index_buffer, index_buffer2],
            uniform_bind_groups: [uniform_bind_group, uniform_bind_group2],
            uniform_buffers: [uniform_buffer, color_buffer, color_buffer2],
            view_mat,
            project_mat,
            msaa_texture_view,
            depth_texture_view,
            indices_lens: [index_data.len() as u32, index_data2.len() as u32],
            plot_type: 0,
            rotation_speed: 1.0,
        }
    }

    pub fn resize(&mut self, new_size: winit::dpi::PhysicalSize<u32>) {
        if new_size.width > 0 && new_size.height > 0 {
            self.init.size = new_size;
            self.init.config.width = new_size.width;
            self.init.config.height = new_size.height;
            self.init.surface.configure(&self.init.device, &self.init.config);

            self.project_mat = wt::create_projection_mat(new_size.width as f32 / new_size.height as f32,
                true);
            self.depth_texture_view = ws::create_depth_view(&self.init);
            if self.init.sample_count > 1 {
                self.msaa_texture_view = ws::create_msaa_texture_view(&self.init);
            }
        }
    }
}

#[allow(unused_variables)]
fn input(&mut self, event: &WindowEvent) -> bool {
    match event {
        WindowEvent::KeyboardInput {
            input:
                KeyboardInput {
                    virtual_keycode: Some(keycode),
                    state: ElementState::Pressed,
                    ..
                },
            ..
        } => {
            match keycode {
                VirtualKeyCode::LControl => {
                    let scolor:[f32;3] = [rand::random(), rand::random(), rand::random()];
                    self.init.queue.write_buffer(&self.uniform_buffers[1], 0,
                        cast_slice(scolor.as_ref()));
                    true
                },
                VirtualKeyCode::LAlt => {
                    let wcolor:[f32;3] = [rand::random(), rand::random(), rand::random()];
                    self.init.queue.write_buffer(&self.uniform_buffers[2], 0,
                        cast_slice(wcolor.as_ref()));
                    true
```

```
                },
                VirtualKeyCode::Space => {
                    self.plot_type = (self.plot_type + 1) % 3;
                    true
                },
                VirtualKeyCode::Q => {
                    self.rotation_speed += 0.1;
                    true
                },
                VirtualKeyCode::A => {
                    self.rotation_speed -= 0.1;
                    if self.rotation_speed < 0.0 {
                        self.rotation_speed = 0.0;
                    }
                    true
                },
                _ => false
            }
        }
        _ => false,
    }
}

fn update(&mut self, dt: std::time::Duration) {
    // update uniform buffer
    let dt = self.rotation_speed * dt.as_secs_f32();
    let model_mat = wt::create_model_mat([0.0,0.0,0.0], [dt.sin(), dt.cos(), 0.0], [1.0, 1.0, 1.0]);
    let mvp_mat = self.project_mat * self.view_mat * model_mat;
    let mvp_ref:&[f32; 16] = mvp_mat.as_ref();
    self.init.queue.write_buffer(&self.uniform_buffers[0], 0, bytemuck::cast_slice(mvp_ref));
}

fn render(&mut self) -> Result<(), wgpu::SurfaceError> {
    let output = self.init.surface.get_current_texture()?;
    let view = output
        .texture
        .create_view(&wgpu::TextureViewDescriptor::default());

    let mut encoder = self
        .init.device
        .create_command_encoder(&wgpu::CommandEncoderDescriptor {
            label: Some("Render Encoder"),
        });

    {
        let color_attach = ws::create_color_attachment(&view);
        let msaa_attach = ws::create_msaa_color_attachment(&view, &self.msaa_texture_view);
        let color_attachment = if self.init.sample_count == 1 { color_attach } else { msaa_attach };
        let depth_attachment = ws::create_depth_stencil_attachment(&self.depth_texture_view);

        let mut render_pass = encoder.begin_render_pass(&wgpu::RenderPassDescriptor {
            label: Some("Render Pass"),
            color_attachments: &[Some(color_attachment)],
            depth_stencil_attachment: Some(depth_attachment),
            occlusion_query_set: None,
            timestamp_writes: None,
        });

        let plot_type = if self.plot_type == 1 { "shape_only" } else if self.plot_type == 2
            {"wireframe_only"} else {"both"};
```

```rust
        if plot_type == "shape_only" || plot_type == "both" {
            render_pass.set_pipeline(&self.pipelines[0]);
            render_pass.set_vertex_buffer(0, self.vertex_buffer.slice(..));
            render_pass.set_index_buffer(self.index_buffers[0].slice(..),
                wgpu::IndexFormat::Uint16);
            render_pass.set_bind_group(0, &self.uniform_bind_groups[0], &[]);
            render_pass.draw_indexed(0..self.indices_lens[0], 0, 0..1);
        }

        if plot_type == "wireframe_only" || plot_type == "both" {
            render_pass.set_pipeline(&self.pipelines[1]);
            render_pass.set_vertex_buffer(0, self.vertex_buffer.slice(..));
            render_pass.set_index_buffer(self.index_buffers[1].slice(..),
                wgpu::IndexFormat::Uint16);
            render_pass.set_bind_group(0, &self.uniform_bind_groups[1], &[]);
            render_pass.draw_indexed(0..self.indices_lens[1], 0, 0..1);
        }
    }

    self.init.queue.submit(iter::once(encoder.finish()));
    output.present();

    Ok(())
    }
}

fn main() {
    let mut sample_count = 1 as u32;
    let args: Vec<String> = std::env::args().collect();
    if args.len() > 1 {
        sample_count = args[1].parse::<u32>().unwrap();
    }

    env_logger::init();
    let event_loop = EventLoop::new();
    let window = WindowBuilder::new().build(&event_loop).unwrap();
    window.set_title(&*format!("ch02_{}_{}", "cube_wireframe", sample_count));
    let mut state = pollster::block_on(State::new(&window, sample_count));

    let render_start_time = std::time::Instant::now();

    event_loop.run(move |event, _, control_flow| {
        match event {
            Event::WindowEvent {
                ref event,
                window_id,
            } if window_id == window.id() => {
                if !state.input(event) {
                    match event {
                        WindowEvent::CloseRequested
                        | WindowEvent::KeyboardInput {
                            input:
                                KeyboardInput {
                                    state: ElementState::Pressed,
                                    virtual_keycode: Some(VirtualKeyCode::Escape),
                                    ..
                                },
                            ..
                        } => *control_flow = ControlFlow::Exit,
```

```
                    WindowEvent::Resized(physical_size) => {
                        state.resize(*physical_size);
                    }
                    WindowEvent::ScaleFactorChanged { new_inner_size, .. } => {
                        state.resize(**new_inner_size);
                    }
                    _ => {}
                }
            }
        }
        Event::RedrawRequested(_) => {
            let now = std::time::Instant::now();
            let dt = now - render_start_time;
            state.update(dt);

            match state.render() {
                Ok(_) => {}
                Err(wgpu::SurfaceError::Lost) => state.resize(state.init.size),
                Err(wgpu::SurfaceError::OutOfMemory) => *control_flow = ControlFlow::Exit,
                Err(e) => eprintln!("{:?}", e),
            }
        }
        Event::MainEventsCleared => {
            window.request_redraw();
        }
        _ => {}
    }
});
}
```

The above code closely resembles that of the previous example, with the exception that it requires the use of two render pipelines. One pipeline is responsible for generating the 3D shape using the "*triangle-list*" primitive, while the other creates the wireframe using the "*line-list*" primitive. The requirement for two pipelines arises due to their distinct primitive topologies.

As the color is determined by the user via the color uniform buffer, the attributes of the vertex buffer layout consist of only one element for the position:

```
attributes: &wgpu::vertex_attr_array![0 => Float32x3],
```

It is worth noting that in the *State::new* function, the uniform bind group incorporates two uniform buffers. One is used for the model-view-projection matrix, while the other is used for the color:

```
let (layout, uniform_bind_group) = ws::create_bind_group(
    &init.device,
    vec![wgpu::ShaderStages::VERTEX, wgpu::ShaderStages::FRAGMENT],
    &[uniform_buffer.as_entire_binding(), color_buffer.as_entire_binding()],
);
```

The *render* function now uses the *plot_type* parameter to determine whether we want to draw just the 3D shape, only the wireframe, or both. This choice can be made by pressing the *Space* key.

In addition, this example permits the user to modify the rotation speed, as well as the colors of both the shape and the wireframe using keyboard inputs.

Here is a list of controls using keyboard:

- *Space*: Changes the plot type.
- *LControl*: Changes color of the shape.

- *LAlt*: Changes color of the wireframe.
- *Q/A*: Increases/decreases the rotation speed.

2.3.3 Run Application

To run this application, add the following code snippet to the *Cargo.toml* file:

```
[[example]]
name = "ch02_cube_wireframe"
path = "examples/ch02/cube_wireframe.rs"
```

Afterward, execute the following *cargo run* commands in the terminal window:

```
cargo run --example ch02_cube_wireframe 8
```

This will produce the cube with wireframe, as shown in Fig.2-3.

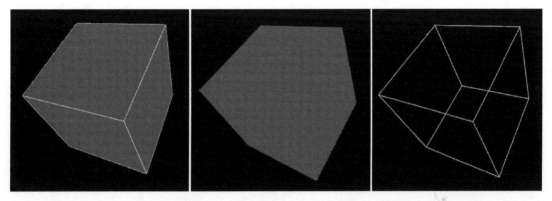

Fig.2-3. Cube with wireframe (left), shape only (middle), wireframe only (right).

2.4 Sphere with Wireframe

In this section, we will use *wgpu* to create a sphere shape with wireframe. To accomplish this, we need to have a good understanding of the spherical coordinate system. In this system, a point is defined by its distance from the origin, denoted as *r*, as well as two angles, θ, and φ. The angle θ represents the polar angle, which is the angle between the point and the positive *y*-axis. The angle φ represents the azimuthal angle, which is the angle between the projection of the point onto the *x-z* plane and the positive *x*-axis. In this notation, we will orient the conventional coordinate system so that the *y*- and *z*-axes are swapped, making it consistent with the coordinate system used in *wgpu*. Fig.2-4 provides a visualization of a point in this coordinate system.

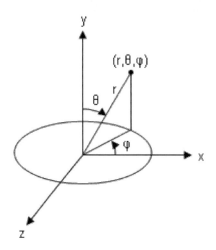

Fig.2-4. Spherical coordinate system.

From this figure, we can easily obtain the following relationships:

$$x = r \sin \theta \cos \phi$$
$$y = r \cos \theta$$
$$z = -r \sin \theta \sin \phi$$

To create a sphere with wireframe in *wgpu* using these relations, we can begin with the commonly used longitude and latitude approach (also known as the UV-sphere method). The method involves dividing the sphere into *u* segments and *v* rings, as illustrated in Fig.2-5. The *u* and *v* lines form grids on the sphere's surface. To create a 3D surface of the sphere, we can focus on just one unit grid, as shown on the right side of Fig.2-5.

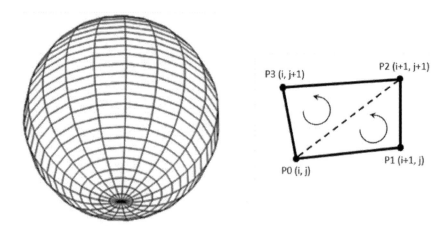

Fig.2-5. UV-sphere model and a unit grid used to create the sphere surface.

2.4.1 Vertex Data

After reviewing the previous section's discourse, generating vertex data for a sphere with wireframe is a simple process. To begin, include the following code to introduce two new functions: *sphere_position* and *create_sphere_data*, in the *vertex_data.rs* file in the *src/* folder:

```
fn sphere_position(r:f32, theta:Deg<f32>, phi:Deg<f32>) -> [f32; 3] {
    let x = r * theta.sin() * phi.cos();
    let y = r * theta.cos();
    let z =  -r * theta.sin() * phi.sin();
    [x, y, z]
}

pub fn create_sphere_data(r:f32, u:u16, v:u16) ->
(Vec<[f32; 3]>, Vec<[f32; 3]>, Vec<[f32; 2]>, Vec<u16>, Vec<u16>) {
    let mut positions: Vec<[f32; 3]> = vec![];
    let mut normals: Vec<[f32; 3]> = vec![];
    let mut uvs: Vec<[f32; 2]> = vec![];

    for i in 0..=u {
        for j in 0..=v {
            let theta = i as f32 *180.0/u as f32;
            let phi = j as f32 * 360.0/v as f32;
            let pos = sphere_position(r, Deg(theta), Deg(phi));
            positions.push(pos);
            normals.push([pos[0]/r, pos[1]/r, pos[2]/r]);
            uvs.push([i as f32/u as f32, j as f32/v as f32]);
        }
    }

    let mut indices: Vec<u16> = vec![];
    let mut indices2: Vec<u16> = vec![];

    for i in 0..u {
        for j in 0..v {
            let idx0 = j + i * (v as u16 + 1);
            let idx1 = j + 1 + i * (v as u16 + 1);
            let idx2 = j + 1 + (i + 1) * (v as u16 + 1);
            let idx3 = j + (i + 1) * (v as u16 + 1);

            let values: Vec<u16> = vec![idx0, idx1, idx2, idx2, idx3, idx0];
            indices.extend(values);

            let values2: Vec<u16> = vec![idx0, idx1, idx0, idx3];
            indices2.extend(values2);
        }
    }

    (positions, normals, uvs, indices, indices2)
}
```

In the *sphere_position* function, we compute a point on the sphere based on given (r, θ, φ) coordinates. Inside the *create_sphere_data* method, we begin by using the *sphere_position* function to calculate the positions, normals, and UVs for all grid points on the sphere's surface. We also define two arrays, *indices* and *indices2*, which will be employed to generate the sphere surface and wireframe respectively.

Within the *for* loop for calculating indices, we only need to account for a single unit grid with four grid points, namely *idx0*, *idx1*, *idx2*, and *idx3*. For each unit grid, we add six index numbers for two triangles to the *indices* array and four index numbers for two-line segments to the *indices2* array. This implies that we only need to draw two-line segments for each unit grid since the remaining two-line segments will be drawn by the other unit grids. This strategy avoids drawing the same line segment multiple times. By iterating through all grids, we can construct the wireframe for the entire sphere surface.

2.4.2 Rust Code

Add a new Rust file named *sphere_wireframe.rs* to the *examples/ch02/* folder. Since the structure of the Rust control code for this example is very similar to the previous example, I will only list the difference and omit the identical parts.

First, in the *create_vertices* function, we need to replace the vertex data for the cube with that for the sphere:

```rust
fn create_vertices(r:f32, u:u16, v:u16) -> (Vec<Vertex>, Vec<u16>, Vec<u16>) {
    let (pos, _, _, ind, ind2) = vd::create_sphere_data(r, u, v);
    let mut data:Vec<Vertex> = vec![];
    for i in 0..pos.len() {
        data.push(Vertex{position: pos[i]});
    }
    (data.to_vec(), ind, ind2)
}
```

Then, we need to add more fields to the *State* struct so that we can change the parameters, such as radius and *u*, *v* segments, to regenerate the vertex data for the sphere:

```rust
struct State {
    ... // code ommitted for brevity

    radius: f32,
    u_segments: u16,
    v_segments: u16,
    update_buffers: bool,
    recreate_buffers: bool,
}
```

Since the *State::new* function is identical to the previous example, we will omit its code here.

We add more keyboard controls in the *State::inputs* function so we can change the sphere's parameters using input keys:

```rust
    fn input(&mut self, event: &WindowEvent) -> bool {
        match event {
            WindowEvent::KeyboardInput {
                input:
                    KeyboardInput {
                        virtual_keycode: Some(keycode),
                        state: ElementState::Pressed,
                        ..
                    },
                ..
            } => {
                match keycode {

                    ... // identical code to the previous example is omitted for brevity

                    VirtualKeyCode::Q => {
                        self.radius += 0.1;
                        self.update_buffers = true;
```

```
                        true
                    },
                    VirtualKeyCode::A => {
                        self.radius -= 0.1;
                        self.update_buffers = true;
                        true
                    },
                    VirtualKeyCode::W => {
                        self.u_segments += 1;
                        self.recreate_buffers = true;
                        true
                    },
                    VirtualKeyCode::S => {
                        self.u_segments -= 1;
                        self.recreate_buffers = true;
                        true
                    },
                    VirtualKeyCode::E => {
                        self.v_segments += 1;
                        self.recreate_buffers = true;
                        true
                    },
                    VirtualKeyCode::D => {
                        self.v_segments -= 1;
                        self.recreate_buffers = true;
                        true
                    }
                    _ => false
                }
            }
            _ => false,
        }
    }
}
```

It is clear from the above code that varying the radius parameter only changes values of the vertex data, but not the size of the vertex and index buffers. In this case, we set the *update_buffers* parameter to *true*, meaning that we only need to update the original buffers with the new data. In contrast, altering the parameters, *u_segments* and *v_segments*, does affect the buffer size of the vertex buffer and index buffer, so we set the *recreate_buffers* parameter to *true*, indicating we need to destroy the original buffers and recreate them with the new data.

Subsequently, we add more code to update or recreate the vertex and index buffers when input parameters are being changed in the *State::update* method:

```
fn update(&mut self, dt: std::time::Duration) {

    ... // identical code omitted for brevity

    // update vertex buffer
    if self.update_buffers {
        let (pos, _ind, _ind2) = create_vertices(self.radius, self.u_segments, self.v_segments);
        self.init.queue.write_buffer(&self.vertex_buffer, 0, cast_slice(&pos));
        self.update_buffers = false;
    }

    // recreate vertex and index buffers
    if self.recreate_buffers {
        let (pos, ind, ind2) = create_vertices(self.radius, self.u_segments, self.v_segments);
        self.indices_lens = [ind.len() as u32, ind2.len() as u32];
```

```
    self.vertex_buffer.destroy();
    self.vertex_buffer = self.init.device.create_buffer_init(&wgpu::util::BufferInitDescriptor {
        label: Some("Vertex Buffer"),
        contents: cast_slice(&pos),
        usage: wgpu::BufferUsages::VERTEX | wgpu::BufferUsages::COPY_DST,
    });

    let indices_data = [ind, ind2];
    for i in 0..2 {
        self.index_buffers[i].destroy();
        self.index_buffers[i] = self.init.device.create_buffer_init(
        &wgpu::util::BufferInitDescriptor {
            label: Some("Index Buffer"),
            contents: cast_slice(&indices_data[i]),
            usage: wgpu::BufferUsages::INDEX | wgpu::BufferUsages::COPY_DST,
        });
    }
    self.recreate_buffers = false;
  }
}
```

Inside the *State::update* function, we just update the vertex buffer with the new vertex data when the *update_buffers* parameter is true. In this case, we can reuse the original index buffer because its buffer size is not changed. One the other hand, when the *recreate_buffers* parameter is true, we first need to destroy the original vertex buffer and index buffer, and then we recreate them with the new data using the *device.create_buffer_init* function.

The *render* and *main* functions are nearly identical to the previous example so we will omit their code here.

Additionally, this example permits the user to modify the rotation speed, the colors of both the shape and the wireframe, and parameters to generate vertex data using keyboard inputs.

Here is a list of controls using keyboard:

- *Space*: Changes the plot type.
- *LControl*: Changes color of the shape.
- *LAlt*: Changes color of the wireframe.
- *Q/A*: Increases/decreases the radius of the sphere.
- *W/S:* Increases/decreases the *u_segments* parameter.
- *E/D:* Increases/decreases the *u_segments* parameter.
- *R/F:* Increases/decreases the rotation speed.

2.4.3 Run Application

To run this application, add the following code snippet to the *Cargo.toml* file:

```
[[example]]
name = "ch02_sphere_wireframe"
path = "examples/ch02/sphere_wireframe.rs"
```

Afterward, execute the following *cargo run* commands in the terminal window:

```
cargo run --example ch02_sphere_wireframe 8
```

This will produce the cube with wireframe, as shown in Fig.2-6.

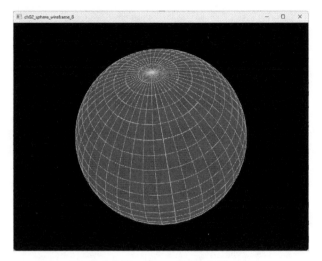

Fig.2-6. UV-sphere with wireframe.

This demonstration allows the manipulation of several input parameters, such as the plot type, rotation speed, *u_segments*, *v_segments*, and *radius* using keyboard inputs.

2.5 Cylinder with Wireframe

This section will demonstrate how to generate a cylinder with wireframe in *wgpu*. We will create a general cylinder shape that allows specification of its inner and outer radii. By setting a non-zero inner radius, a cylindrical tube shape can be produced.

In a cylindrical coordinate system, a point is defined by three parameters, r, θ, and y, which differ slightly from the conventional r, θ, and z notation. This notation is used for convenience since the computer screen can be described using the x-y plane. In this context, r refers to the distance of a projected point on the x-z plane from the origin, and θ represents the azimuthal angle. Fig.2-7 depicts a point within the cylindrical coordinate system.

From this figure, we have:

$$x = r\cos\theta$$
$$z = -r\sin\theta$$
$$y = y$$

Creating cylindrical objects in *wgpu* is made easy by using the cylindrical coordinate system. The initial step involves dividing the surface of the cylinder into slices. Fig.2-8 illustrates this process by partitioning the cylinder surface into n slices and creating a unit cell with the i-th and i+1-th slice lines. Each unit cell comprises eight vertices and four faces. Consequently, eight triangles and eight line segments must be drawn for every unit cell.

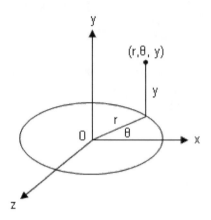

Fig.2-7. Cylindrical coordinate system.

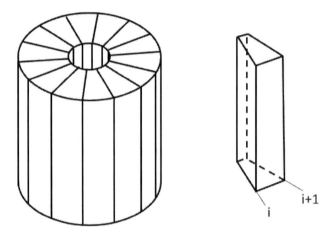

Fig.2-8. A cylinder and a unit cell.

2.5.1 Vertex Data

Given the background information discussed in the previous section, generating the vertex data for the cylinder with wireframe is straightforward. Add two new functions, *cylinder_position* and *create_cylinder_data*, to the *vertex_data.rs* file in the *src/* folder with the following code:

```
fn cylinder_position(r:f32, theta:Deg<f32>, y:f32) -> [f32; 3] {
    let x = r * theta.cos();
    let z = - r * theta.sin();
    [x, y, z]
}

pub fn create_cylinder_data(mut rin:f32, rout:f32, h:f32, n:u16) -> (Vec<[f32; 3]>, Vec<u16>, Vec<u16>) {
    if rin >= 0.999 * rout {
        rin = 0.999 * rout;
    }
```

```
let mut positions: Vec<[f32; 3]> = vec![];
for i in 0..=n {
    let theta = i as f32 * 360.0/n as f32;
    let p0 = cylinder_position(rout, Deg(theta), h/2.0);
    let p1 = cylinder_position(rout, Deg(theta), -h/2.0);
    let p2 = cylinder_position(rin, Deg(theta), -h/2.0);
    let p3 = cylinder_position(rin, Deg(theta), h/2.0);
    let values:Vec<[f32; 3]> = vec![p0, p1, p2, p3];
    positions.extend(values);
}

let mut indices: Vec<u16> = vec![];
let mut indices2: Vec<u16> = vec![];

for i in 0..n {
    let idx0 = i*4;
    let idx1 = i*4 + 1;
    let idx2 = i*4 + 2;
    let idx3 = i*4 + 3;
    let idx4 = i*4 + 4;
    let idx5 = i*4 + 5;
    let idx6 = i*4 + 6;
    let idx7 = i*4 + 7;

    // triangle indices
    let values: Vec<u16> = vec![
        idx0, idx4, idx7, idx7, idx3, idx0, // top
        idx1, idx2, idx6, idx6, idx5, idx1, // bottom
        idx0, idx1, idx5, idx5, idx4, idx0, // outer
        idx2, idx3, idx7, idx7, idx6, idx2  // inner
    ];
    indices.extend(values);

    // wireframe indices
    let values2: Vec<u16> = vec![
        idx0, idx3, idx3, idx7, idx4, idx0, // top
        idx1, idx2, idx2, idx6, idx5, idx1, // bottom
        idx0, idx1, idx3, idx2              // side
    ];
    indices2.extend(values2);
}

(positions, indices, indices2)
}
```

This *cylinder_position* function returns the position on the surface of the cylinder specified by given parameters r, θ, and y using the cylindrical coordinates.

The *create_cylinder_data* function is used to generate the vertex data for the cylinder with wireframe. This is achieved by specifying the inner and outer radii, and the height. In this function, eight vertices are constructed for each unit cell. For every unit cell, 24 index number (or vertices) are added to the *indices* array to form 8 triangles, consisting of two on each face of the top, bottom, outer, and inner surfaces. Additionally, 16 index numbers are added to the *indices2* array for 8 line-segments.

2.5.2 Rust Code

Add a new Rust file named *cylinder_wireframe.rs* to the *examples/ch02/* folder. Since the structure of the Rust control code for this example is very similar to the previous *cube_wireframe* example, I will only list the difference and omit the identical parts.

First, in the *create_vertices* function, we need to replace the vertex data for the cube with that for the cylinder:

```rust
fn create_vertices(rin:f32, rout:f32, h:f32, n:u16) -> (Vec<Vertex>, Vec<u16>, Vec<u16>) {
    let (pos, ind, ind2) = vd::create_cylinder_data(rin, rout, h, n);
    let mut data:Vec<Vertex> = vec![];
    for i in 0..pos.len() {
        data.push(Vertex{position:pos[i]});
    }
    (data.to_vec(), ind, ind2)
}
```

Then, we need to add more fields to the *State* struct so that we can change the parameters, such as inner and outer radii, height, *n* segments, to regenerate the vertex data for the cyliner:

```rust
struct State {
    ... // identical code is omitted for brevity

    rin: f32,
    rout: f32,
    h: f32,
    n_segments: u16,
    update_buffers: bool,
    recreate_buffers: bool,
}
```

Since the *State::new* function is identical to the previous example, we will omit its code here.

We add more keyboard controls in the *State::inputs* function so we can change the cylinder's parameters using input keys:

```rust
fn input(&mut self, event: &WindowEvent) -> bool {
    match event {
        WindowEvent::KeyboardInput {
            input:
                KeyboardInput {
                    virtual_keycode: Some(keycode),
                    state: ElementState::Pressed,
                    ..
                },
            ..
        } => {
            match keycode {

                ... // identical code is omitted for brevity

                VirtualKeyCode::Q => {
                    self.rin += 0.1;
                    self.update_buffers = true;
                    true
                },
                VirtualKeyCode::A => {
                    self.rin -= 0.1;
                    self.update_buffers = true;
```

```
                    true
                },
                VirtualKeyCode::W => {
                    self.rout += 0.1;
                    self.update_buffers = true;
                    true
                },
                VirtualKeyCode::S => {
                    self.rout -= 0.1;
                    self.update_buffers = true;
                    true
                },
                VirtualKeyCode::E => {
                    self.h += 0.1;
                    self.update_buffers = true;
                    true
                },
                VirtualKeyCode::D => {
                    self.h -= 0.1;
                    self.update_buffers = true;
                    true
                },
                VirtualKeyCode::R => {
                    self.n_segments += 1;
                    self.recreate_buffers = true;
                    true
                },
                VirtualKeyCode::F => {
                    self.n_segments -= 1;
                    self.recreate_buffers = true;
                    true
                },
                _ => false
            }
        }
        _ => false,
    }
}
```

It is clear from the above code that varying the radius and height parameters only changes values of the vertex data, but not the size of the vertex and index buffers. In this case, we set the *update_buffers* parameter to *true*, meaning that we only need to update the original buffers with the new data. In contrast, altering the parameter, *n_segments*, does affect the buffer size of the vertex buffer and index buffer, so we set the *recreate_buffers* parameter to *true*, indicating we need to destroy the original buffers and recreate them with the new data.

Subsequently, we add more code to update or recreate the vertex and index buffers when input parameters are being changed in the *State::update* method:

```
fn update(&mut self, dt: std::time::Duration) {

    ... // identical code omitted for brevity

    // update vertex buffer
    if self.update_buffers {
        let (pos, _ind, _ind2) = create_vertices(self.rin, self.rout, self.h, self.n_segments);
        self.init.queue.write_buffer(&self.vertex_buffer, 0, cast_slice(&pos));
        self.update_buffers = false;
    }
```

```
    // recreate vertex and index buffers
    if self.recreate_buffers {
        let (pos, ind, ind2) = create_vertices(self.rin, self.rout, self.h, self.n_segments);
        self.indices_lens = [ind.len() as u32, ind2.len() as u32];

        self.vertex_buffer.destroy();
        self.vertex_buffer = self.init.device.create_buffer_init(&wgpu::util::BufferInitDescriptor {
            label: Some("Vertex Buffer"),
            contents: cast_slice(&pos),
            usage: wgpu::BufferUsages::VERTEX | wgpu::BufferUsages::COPY_DST,
        });

        let indices_data = [ind, ind2];
        for i in 0..2 {
            self.index_buffers[i].destroy();
            self.index_buffers[i] = self.init.device.create_buffer_init(
            &wgpu::util::BufferInitDescriptor {
                label: Some("Index Buffer"),
                contents: cast_slice(&indices_data[i]),
                usage: wgpu::BufferUsages::INDEX | wgpu::BufferUsages::COPY_DST,
            });
        }
        self.recreate_buffers = false;
    }
}
```

Inside the *State::update* function, we just update the vertex buffer with the new vertex data when the *update_buffers* parameter is true. In this case, we can reuse the original index buffer because its buffer size is not changed. One the other hand, when the *recreate_buffers* parameter is true, we first need to destroy the original vertex buffer and index buffer, and then we recreate them with the new data using the *device.create_buffer_init* function.

The *render* and *main* functions are nearly identical to the previous example so we will omit their code here.

Additionally, this example permits the user to modify the rotation speed, the colors of both the shape and the wireframe, and parameters to generate vertex data using keyboard inputs.

Here is a list of controls using keyboard:

- *Space*: Changes the plot type.
- *LControl*: Changes color of the shape.
- *LAlt*: Changes color of the wireframe.
- *Q/A*: Increases/decreases the inner radius of the cylinder.
- *W/S:* Increases/decreases the outer radius of the cylinder.
- *E/D:* Increases/decreases the height of the cylinder.
- *R/F:* Increases/decreases the *n_segments* parameter.
- *T/G:* Increases/decreases the rotation speed.

2.5.3 Run Application

To run this application, add the following code snippet to the *Cargo.toml* file:

```
[[example]]
name = "ch02_cylinder_wireframe"
path = "examples/ch02/cylinder_wireframe.rs"
```

Afterward, execute the following *cargo run* commands in the terminal window:

```
cargo run --example ch02_cylinder_wireframe 8
```

This will produce the cube with wireframe, as shown in Fig.2-9.

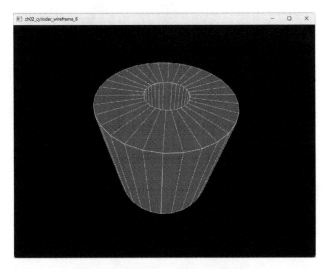

Fig.2-9. Cylinder with wireframe.

This demonstration allows the manipulation of several input parameters, such as the plot type, rotation speed, *n_segments*, *radius*, and height using keyboard inputs.

2.6 Torus with Wireframe

The torus is another popular 3D shape, which can be generated by revolving a circle around a specified axis in 3D space. It can be defined using the following set of parametric equations:

$$x = (R + r\cos v)\cos u$$
$$y = r\sin v$$
$$z = -(R + r\cos v)\sin u$$

where u and v are angles defined in the range of $[0, 2\pi]$, R is the distance from the center of the tube to the center of the torus, and r is the radius of the torus.

To create a torus shape with wireframe, we need to divide its surface using tube rings and torus rings, as illustrated in Fig.2-10.

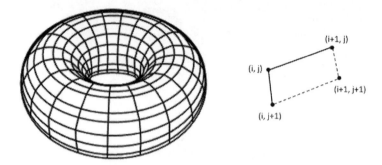

Fig.2-10. A torus and a unit cell.

The unit cell of the torus can be divided into a quad shape that consists of two triangles and four-line segments. To avoid drawing the same line segment multiple times, we only need to draw two solid-line segments for each unit cell. The dashed lines will be drawn by the other unit cells. By iterating over all the unit cells, we can construct the torus shape with wireframe.

2.6.1 Vertex Data

Using the information from the previous section, creating vertex data for the torus with wireframe is straightforward. Add two new functions, *torus_position* and *create_torus_data* to the *vertex_data.rs* file in the *src/* folder with the following code:

```
pub fn torus_position(r_torus:f32, r_tube:f32, u:Deg<f32>, v: Deg<f32>) -> [f32; 3] {
    let x = (r_torus + r_tube * v.cos()) * u.cos();
    let y = r_tube * v.sin();
    let z = -(r_torus + r_tube * v.cos()) * u.sin();
    [x, y, z]
}

pub fn create_torus_data(r_torus:f32, r_tube:f32, n_torus:u16, n_tube:u16)
-> (Vec<[f32; 3]>, Vec<[f32; 3]>, Vec<u16>, Vec<u16>) {
    let mut positions: Vec<[f32; 3]> = vec![];
    let mut normals: Vec<[f32; 3]> = vec![];
    let eps = 0.01 * 360.0/n_tube as f32;

    for i in 0..=n_torus {
        let du = i as f32 * 360.0/n_torus as f32;
        for j in 0..=n_tube {
            let dv = j as f32 * 360.0/n_tube as f32;
            let pos = torus_position(r_torus, r_tube, Deg(du), Deg(dv));
            positions.push(pos);

            // calculate normals
            let nu = Vector3::from(torus_position(r_torus, r_tube, Deg(du+eps), Deg(dv))) -
                    Vector3::from(torus_position(r_torus, r_tube, Deg(du-eps), Deg(dv)));
            let nv = Vector3::from(torus_position(r_torus, r_tube, Deg(du), Deg(dv+eps))) -
                    Vector3::from(torus_position(r_torus, r_tube, Deg(du), Deg(dv-eps)));
            let normal = nu.cross(nv).normalize();
            normals.push(normal.into());
        }
    }
```

```
let mut indices: Vec<u16> = vec![];
let mut indices2: Vec<u16> = vec![];
let vertices_per_row = n_tube + 1;

for i in 0..n_torus {
    for j in 0..n_tube {
        let idx0 = j + i * vertices_per_row;
        let idx1 = j + 1 + i * vertices_per_row;
        let idx2 = j + 1 + (i + 1) * vertices_per_row;
        let idx3 = j + (i + 1) * vertices_per_row;
        let values:Vec<u16> = vec![idx0, idx1, idx2, idx2, idx3, idx0];
        indices.extend(values);
        let values2:Vec<u16> = vec![idx0, idx1, idx0, idx3];
        indices2.extend(values2);
    }
}

(positions, normals, indices, indices2)
}
```

The *torus_position* function calculates the position on the torus surface using given parameters R, r, u, and v, and cylindrical coordinates.

The *create_torus_data* function generates the vertex data of the torus with wireframe similar to that of the UV sphere example, but with a difference in how normal vectors are calculated. To obtain the normal vector for each vertex, we first make small displacements along the u and v directions and then calculate the cross product of these displacements. This approach ensures that the normal vector is always perpendicular to the torus surface.

2.6.2 Rust Code

Add a new Rust file named *torus_wireframe.rs* to the *examples/ch02/* folder. Since the structure of the Rust control code for this example is very similar to the previous *cube_wireframe* example, I will only list the difference and omit the identical parts.

First, in the *create_vertices* function, we need to replace the vertex data for the cube with that for the torus:

```
fn create_vertices(r_torus:f32, r_tube:f32, u:u16, v:u16) -> (Vec<Vertex>, Vec<u16>, Vec<u16>) {
    let (pos, _, ind, ind2) = vd::create_torus_data(r_torus, r_tube, u, v);
    let mut data:Vec<Vertex> = vec![];
    for i in 0..pos.len() {
        data.push(Vertex {position: pos[i]});
    }
    (data.to_vec(), ind, ind2)
}
```

Then, we need to add more fields to the *State* struct so that we can change the parameters, such as torus and tube radii, and u, v segments, to regenerate the vertex data for the torus:

```
struct State {
    ... // identical code is omitted for brevity

    r_torus: f32,
    r_tube: f32,
    u_segments: u16,
    v_segments: u16,
    update_buffers: bool,
```

```
    recreate_buffers: bool,
}
```

Since the *State::new* function is identical to the previous example, we will omit its code here.

We add more keyboard controls in the *State::inputs* function so we can change the torus's parameters using input keys:

```
fn input(&mut self, event: &WindowEvent) -> bool {
    match event {
        WindowEvent::KeyboardInput {
            input:
                KeyboardInput {
                    virtual_keycode: Some(keycode),
                    state: ElementState::Pressed,
                    ..
                },
            ..
        } => {
            match keycode {

                ... // identical code is omitted for brevity

                VirtualKeyCode::Q => {
                    self.r_torus += 0.05;
                    self.update_buffers = true;
                    true
                },
                VirtualKeyCode::A => {
                    self.r_torus -= 0.05;
                    self.update_buffers = true;
                    true
                },
                VirtualKeyCode::W => {
                    self.r_tube += 0.02;
                    self.update_buffers = true;
                    true
                },
                VirtualKeyCode::S => {
                    self.r_tube -= 0.02;
                    self.update_buffers = true;
                    true
                },
                VirtualKeyCode::E => {
                    self.u_segments += 1;
                    self.recreate_buffers = true;
                    true
                },
                VirtualKeyCode::D => {
                    self.u_segments -= 1;
                    self.recreate_buffers = true;
                    true
                },
                VirtualKeyCode::R => {
                    self.v_segments += 1;
                    self.recreate_buffers = true;
                    true
                },
                VirtualKeyCode::F => {
                    self.v_segments -= 1;
                    self.recreate_buffers = true;
```

```
                    true
                },

                _ => false
            }
        }
        _ => false,
    }
}
```

It is clear from the above code that varying the tours and tube radius only changes values of the vertex data, but not the size of the vertex and index buffers. In this case, we set the *update_buffers* parameter to *true*, meaning that we only need to update the original buffers with the new data. In contrast, altering the parameters, *u_segments* and *v_segments*, does affect the buffer size of the vertex buffer and index buffer, so we set the *recreate_buffers* parameter to *true*, indicating we need to destroy the original buffers and recreate them with the new data.

Subsequently, we add more code to update or recreate the vertex and index buffers when input parameters are being changed in the *State::update* method:

```
fn update(&mut self, dt: std::time::Duration) {

    ... // identical code omitted for breviry

    // update vertex buffer
    if self.update_buffers {
        let (pos, _ind, _ind2) = create_vertices(self.r_torus, self.r_tube,
            self.u_segments, self.v_segments);
        self.init.queue.write_buffer(&self.vertex_buffer, 0, cast_slice(&pos));
        self.update_buffers = false;
    }

    // recreate vertex and index buffers
    if self.recreate_buffers {
        let (pos, ind, ind2) = create_vertices(self.r_torus, self.r_tube,
            self.u_segments, self.v_segments);
        self.indices_lens = [ind.len() as u32, ind2.len() as u32];

        self.vertex_buffer.destroy();
        self.vertex_buffer = self.init.device.create_buffer_init(&wgpu::util::BufferInitDescriptor {
            label: Some("Vertex Buffer"),
            contents: cast_slice(&pos),
            usage: wgpu::BufferUsages::VERTEX | wgpu::BufferUsages::COPY_DST,
        });

        let indices_data = [ind, ind2];
        for i in 0..2 {
            self.index_buffers[i].destroy();
            self.index_buffers[i] = self.init.device.create_buffer_init(
            &wgpu::util::BufferInitDescriptor {
                label: Some("Index Buffer"),
                contents: cast_slice(&indices_data[i]),
                usage: wgpu::BufferUsages::INDEX | wgpu::BufferUsages::COPY_DST,
            });
        }
        self.recreate_buffers = false;
    }
}
```

Inside the *State::update* function, we just update the vertex buffer with the new vertex data when the *update_buffers* parameter is true. In this case, we can reuse the original index buffer because its buffer size is not changed. One the other hand, when the *recreate_buffers* parameter is true, we first need to destroy the original vertex buffer and index buffer, and then we recreate them with the new data using the *device.create_buffer_init* function.

The *render* and *main* functions are nearly identical to the previous example so we will omit their code here.

Additionally, this example permits the user to modify the rotation speed, the colors of both the shape and the wireframe, and parameters to generate vertex data using keyboard inputs.

Here is a list of controls using keyboard:

- *Space*: Changes the plot type.
- *LControl*: Changes color of the shape.
- *LAlt*: Changes color of the wireframe.
- *Q/A*: Increases/decreases the torus radius.
- *W/S:* Increases/decreases the tube radius.
- *E/D:* Increases/decreases the *u_segments* parameter.
- *R/F:* Increases/decreases the *v_segments* parameter.
- *T/G:* Increases/decreases the rotation speed.

2.6.3 Run Application

To run this application, add the following code snippet to the *Cargo.toml* file:

```
[[example]]
name = "ch02_torus_wireframe"
path = "examples/ch02/torus_wireframe.rs"
```

Afterward, execute the following *cargo run* commands in the terminal window:

```
cargo run --example ch02_torus_wireframe 8
```

This will produce the cube with wireframe, as shown in Fig.2-11.

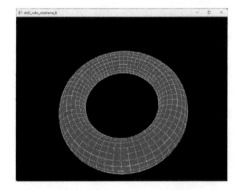

Fig.2-11. Torus with wireframe.

3 Lighting and Shading

In the previous chapters, we focused on creating simple primitives and various 3D shapes with wireframe. However, when it comes to rendering objects with solid colors, the resulting image may appear flat and fail to convey the object's 3D nature. This is due to the absence of interaction between light and surfaces of the objects. Lighting plays a critical role in creating visually recognizable 3D graphics that look realistic.

While lighting is an essential factor, *wgpu* does not offer built-in features for lighting. It only runs two functions – a vertex shader and a fragment shader – and expects you to write your lighting functions to achieve the desired results. This means that if you want lighting effects in your 3D scene, you need to create a lighting model yourself.

In this chapter, we will explore several lighting models in *wgpu* and demonstrate how to use them to simulate light sources and their interaction with objects in the scene. We will discuss three types of light sources: ambient light, diffuse light, and specular light, and explain how to implement directional, point, and spot lights, as well as soft edge spot lights and fog effects.

3.1 Light Components

Ambient, diffuse, and specular lights are distinct aspects of lighting. Ambient light uniformly illuminates all objects in an environment, regardless of their position or orientation. It serves as global illumination in a scene.

On the other hand, both diffuse and specular lighting depend on the angle of incidence of light on a surface. While diffuse reflection occurs in all directions after light hits a surface, specular reflection occurs only in a specific direction, as depicted in Fig.3-1.

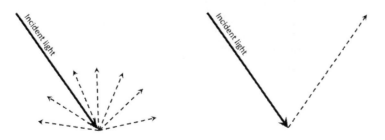

Fig.3-1. Diffuse reflection (left) and specular reflection (right).

Diffuse lighting is the major reflective component in reflection. Surfaces with matte or flat paint, as well as natural materials such as terrain seen from above, are examples of diffuse reflectors. Perfect diffuse surfaces scatter light evenly in all directions. On the other hand, specular reflection, also known as specular highlight produces a shiny glossiness as most of the reflected or scattered light is in a narrow range of angles close to the angle of reflection. The light reflected from a specific angle emerges at a single angle, following the rule that the angle of reflection equals the angle of incidence.

Fig.3-2 illustrates the impact of different lighting sources on the lighting effect of a torus surface.

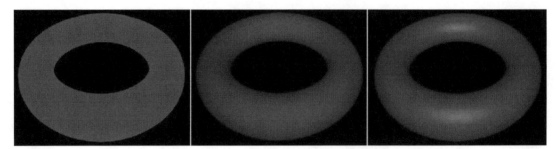

Fig.3-2. Light reflection on a torus surface from different light sources: ambient (left), diffuse (center), and specular (right).

The angle at which light hits a surface is a crucial factor in determining the reflection of light, as seen in Fig.3-2. This reflection is not only determined by the surface and light properties but also by the angle of incidence. This angle is closely related to the surface normal, which is perpendicular to the face at the vertex. Both specular and diffuse reflections are affected by this angle.

3.2 Normal Vectors

Building a lighting model requires calculating the surface normal, which indicates direction that the surface is facing. It is essential to normalize the normal to a unit vector, and it must be specified for each vertex.

Since a curved 3D object can face different directions at different vertices., each vertex needs its own normal vector. In *wgpu*, we can assign normal vectors to the vertices of a surface and use them to perform lighting calculations for the entire surface.

In the following subsections, I will explain how to calculate the surface normal for several simple 3D shapes, such as a cube, sphere, cylinder, and a general polyhedral surface.

3.2.1 Surface Normal of a Cube

If you have a unit cube, calculating the surface normal for each face is straightforward. Each normal simply points outwards from the respective face of the cube. For example, the front face, which is oriented toward to positive z direction, has four vertices: (-1, 1, 1), (-1, -1, 1), (1, -1, 1), and (1, 1, 1). They all have the same surface normal, which is equal to the unit vector along the position z-direction: (0, 0, 1). You can use this same approach to calculate the surface normal for the other five faces of the cube.

3.2.2 Surface Normal of a Sphere

Computing the surface normal of a sphere is straightforward. If shape is a unit sphere, then the surface normal of any point (x, y, z) on the unit sphere is simply (x, y, z). In other words, the normal data for a unit sphere is identical to its vertex data. The normal vector at point (x, y, z) can be expressed in spherical coordinate system the form:

$$x = \sin \theta \cos \varphi$$
$$y = \cos \theta$$
$$z = -\sin \theta \sin \varphi$$

3.2.3 Surface Normal of a Cylinder

The surface normal for a cylinder surface can be calculated by dividing it into three parts: the top face, the bottom face, and the round tube. The surface normal for the round tube point outward around the x-z plane. If we slice the tube into n equal parts, there will be n vertices with $y = 1$ and $y = -1$, and for any one of these vertices at point $P(x, y, z)$, its normal is $(x, 0, z)$. In the cylindrical coordinate system, it can be expressed as $(\cos \theta,\ 0, -\sin \theta)$.

The surface normals for the vertices on the top face and the bottom face are $(0, 1, 0)$ and $(0, -1, 0)$ respectively.

3.2.4 Surface Normal of a Polyhedral Surface

To determine the surface normals of a general polyhedral surface that includes faces and vertices, a two-step process can be used. First, we compute the weighted face normals, and then we use these to calculate the surface normals.

To calculate the weighted face normals, we first determine a normal vector for each face. We achieve this by multiplying the area of the face with the normal vector, which results in a weighted normal. We assign a higher weight to faces with larger areas. To calculate the normal vector for each face, we iterate through every three vertices in sequence around the face, and we use the following pseudo code to perform the cross product:

```
Vec3 ComputeTriangleNormal(vec3 a, vec3 b, vec3 c) {
    return normalize(CrossProduct(b-c, c-a);
}
```

It is important to note that the length of the cross product between two vectors is proportional to the area inside of the triangle abc. Therefore, to determine the surface normal at a vertex that is shared by several triangles, we need to sum up all of these cross products and normalize the result. The following pseudo code demonstrate how to calculate the surface normal for a general polyhedral surface:

```
vec3 ComputeSurfaceNormal(vextex v) {
    vec3 sum = vec3(0,0,0);
    list<vertex> adjacentVertices = getAdjacentVertice(a);
    for(var i = 1; i < adjacentVertices.length; ++i){
        vec3 b = adjacentVertices[i-1];
        vec3 c = adjacentVertices[i];
        sum += CrossProduct(b-a, c-a);
    }

    if(normalize(sum == 0)) return sum;
```

```
    return normalize(sum);
}
```

If the polyhedral surface is a quadrilateral (or quad), the surface normal calculation becomes much simpler. For a quad with vertices, *abcd*, arranged in counterclockwise order, we can use the following simple formula to calculate its surface normal:

```
normalize(CrossProduct(c-a, d-b));
```

This formula directly calculates the cross product of two diagonal vectors, which provides the normal vector of the quad. We normalize the result to obtain the final surface normal.

3.3 Blinn-Phong Light Model

Once we have computed the normal vector at a vertex, we can use it along with the direction of the light source to determine the lighting intensity. The resulting intensity value can then be used to contribute to the final color of the pixel by using the following formula in the fragment shader:

```
vec4 final_color = vec4(0.0, 0.0, 0.0, 1.0);
vec3 color = vec3(r, g, b);
final_color = vec4(color*intensity, 1.0);
```

It is worth noting that the output color value written to the image in *wgpu* are clamped to the range of [0, 1]. Therefore, any light intensity that exceeds 1, either individually or in combination with other lights, can result in unpleasant visual artifacts.

3.3.1 Diffuse Light

The intensity of diffuse light can be calculated by taking the dot product of the normalized light direction (L) and the surface normal (N), which gives us the cosine of the angle (α) between them:

$$\cos(\alpha) = \text{normalize}\,(L \cdot N)$$

The diffuse intensity Id is then calculated by multiplying the diffuse component of the object's material Kd with the maximum of the computed cosine value and 0 to avoid negative values:

$$Id = Kd * \max[\cos(\alpha), 0]$$

To account for ambient light, which is a uniform light source that does not depend on the direction, we can add the ambient light intensity Ia to the above result:

$$Id = \max\{Kd * \max[\cos(\alpha), 0], Ia\}$$

3.3.2 Specular Light

The Phong model is the simplest representation of specular light. It describes how the light reflected towards the viewer changes depending on the angle between the view direction and the direction of perfect reflection. Mathematically, the Phong model can be expressed as follows:

$$\text{Phong term} \sim (V \cdot R)^s$$

That is, the Phong term is proportional to the dot product of the view direction (V) and the reflect direction (R), raised to the power of the specular exponent (s). The specular exponent, s, represents the material property of shininess or roughness of a surface. A small value of s results in a rougher appearance, while a large s value indicates a shinier surface.

It is important to note that the Phong model is not based on real-world physics and simply generates a bright, circular region on the surface. The brightness of the region decreases as the viewer moves away from the direction of perfect reflection. It is essential to keep in mind that the formula only holds if the dot product is greater than zero; otherwise, the specular contribution is zero.

However, one of the primary drawbacks of the Phong model is that the angle between the view direction and the reflection direction must be less than 90 degrees for the specular Phong term to have any impact. To address this issue, the Blinn-Phong model can be used to compute the specular light. Unlike the Phong model, the Blinn-Phong model uses a different set of vectors that are based on the half-angle vector. The half-angle vector denotes the direction halfway between the view and light direction, as shown in Fig.3-3.

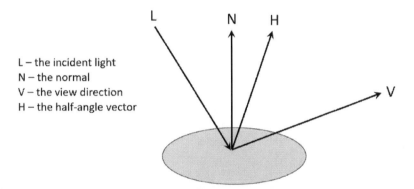

L – the incident light
N – the normal
V – the view direction
H – the half-angle vector

Fig.3-3. Blinn-Phong model based on half-angle vector.

The half-angle vector, denoted as H, can be obtained using the formula:

$$H = \frac{L - V}{|L - V|}$$

When the view direction aligns perfectly with the reflected direction, the half-angle vector will also be aligned with the surface normal. Hence, instead of comparing the reflection vector to the view direction, the Blinn-Phong model compares the half-angle vector to the surface normal. This value is then raised to a power that represents the shininess of the surface:

$$\text{Blinn-Phong term} \sim (N \cdot H)^s$$

Since the angle between the half-angle vector and the normal is always less than 90 degrees, the Blinn-Phong model produces comparable outcomes to the Phong model, but without the problems associated with the Phong model.

3.3.3 Normal Vector Transformation

As mentioned previously, normal vectors play a crucial role in lighting calculations. When a transformation is applied to a surface, it becomes necessary to derive normal vectors for the resulting surface from the original normal vectors. While translations do not alter the direction of the normals, non-uniform scaling requires special consideration. In this case, we must use the transpose of the inverse of the transform matrix used for the object's transformation to compute the transformed normal vectors. In OpenGL or WebGL, this operation is typically performed in the vertex shader using GLSL code:

```
vNormal = mat3(transpose(inverse(modelMat))) * normal;
```

However, WGSL does not currently support the matrix *inverse* function in its shader, making this calculation challenging. Instead, we can calculate the transpose and inverse transform matrix for the normal vectors in our application using CPU and then pass the resulting matrix to the WGSL shader for lighting calculation in GPU.

Fortunately, the *cgmath* library provides helpful functions such as *Invert* and *transpose*, which we can use to compute the transformed normal matrix from the model matrix used to transform the object:

```
let normal_mat = (model_mat.invert().unwrap()).transpose();
```

This Rust code calculates the inverse-transpose of *model_mat* and stores the result in *normal_mat*. After applying this transformation, we can pass the *normal_mat* to the shader program, where we will use it to compute the lighting.

3.3.4 Shader with Blinn-Phong Model

This section will demonstrate how to incorporate a basic lighting model into your shader program. This model accounts for the ambient, diffuse, and specular lighting, and is based on the Blinn-Phong model. To increase the code's reusability, we will separate the vertex and fragment shaders.

To begin, create a vertex shader file called *shader-vert.wgsl* in the *examples/ch03/* folder. Add the following code to the file:

```
// vertex shader
struct Uniforms {
    viewProjectMat : mat4x4f,
    modelMat : mat4x4f,
    normalMat : mat4x4f,
};
@binding(0) @group(0) var<uniform> uniforms : Uniforms;

struct Output {
    @builtin(position) position : vec4f,
    @location(0) vPosition : vec4f,
    @location(1) vNormal : vec4f,
};

@vertex
fn vs_main(@location(0) pos: vec3f, @location(1) normal: vec3f) -> Output {
    var output: Output;
    let mPosition = uniforms.modelMat * vec4(pos, 1.0);
    output.vPosition = mPosition;
    output.vNormal =  uniforms.normalMat * vec4(normal, 1.0);
    output.position = uniforms.viewProjectMat * mPosition;
    return output;
}
```

Here, we first pass three uniform matrices to the vertex shader: *ViewProjectMat*, *modelMat*, and *normalMat*. The input variables *pos* and *normal* represent the original vertex data and normal data, respectively. The output variables *vPosition* and *vNormal*, defined within the *Output* structure, hold the transformed vertex data and normal data, which we will pass to the fragment shader for lighting calculation.

Next, create a new fragment shader file called *blinn-phong-frag.wgsl* in the *examples/ch03/* folder, and insert the following code:

```
// fragment shader
struct LightUniforms {
    lightPosition: vec4f,
    eyePosition: vec4f,
    color: vec4f,
    specularColor: vec4f,
};
@group(1) @binding(0) var<uniform> light : LightUniforms;

struct MaterialUniforms {
    ambient: f32,
    diffuse: f32,
    specular: f32,
    shininess: f32,
};
@group(1) @binding(1) var<uniform> material : MaterialUniforms;

fn blinnPhong(N:vec3f, L:vec3f, V:vec3f) -> vec2f{
    let H = normalize(L + V);
    var diffuse = material.diffuse * max(dot(N, L), 0.0);
    diffuse += material.diffuse * max(dot(-N, L), 0.0);
    var specular = material.specular * pow(max(dot(N, H), 0.0), material.shininess);
    specular += material.specular * pow(max(dot(-N, H),0.0), material.shininess);
    return vec2(diffuse, specular);
}

@fragment
fn fs_main(@location(0) vPosition:vec4f, @location(1) vNormal:vec4f) ->  @location(0) vec4f {
    var N = normalize(vNormal.xyz);
    let L = normalize(light.lightPosition.xyz - vPosition.xyz);
    let V = normalize(light.eyePosition.xyz - vPosition.xyz);

    let bp = blinnPhong(N, L, V);

    let finalColor = light.color*(material.ambient + bp[0]) + light.specularColor * bp[1];
    return vec4(finalColor.rgb, 1.0);
}
```

Within the fragment shader, we define two uniform structures: *LightUniforms* and *MaterialUniforms*. *LightUniforms* is used to pass the *vec4f* type fields, such as the light and eye positions as well as the object and specular-light color. *MaterialUniforms* passes the material parameters of *f32* type, which are used for lighting computation. Of course, you can combine these two structures into one to achieve the same lighting effect.

The light calculation inside the *fs_main* function is straightforward. We first define various vectors N, L, and V, as explained earlier. We then invoke the *blinnPhong* function to compute the light contribution from the diffuse and specular sources. The *blinnPhong* function implements the Blinn-Phong lighting model. Additionally, it is worth noting that the ambient light is accounted for by simply adding the *material.ambient* constant to the diffuse light.

3.4 3D Shapes with Blinn-Phong Lighting

This section demonstrates the application of the Blinn-Phong model to multiple 3D shapes, including cube, sphere, and torus.

3.4.1 Common Code

To avoid code duplication, we will create a shared file called *common_blinn_phong.rs* in the *examples/ch03/* folder. This file can be reused to generate different 3D objects with lighting.

Add a new Rust file called *common_blinn_phong.rs* in the *examples/ch03/* folder and enter the following code into it:

```rust
use std:: {iter, mem};
use cgmath::{ Matrix, Matrix4, SquareMatrix };
use wgpu:: {util::DeviceExt, VertexBufferLayout};
use winit::{
    event::*,
    event_loop::{ControlFlow, EventLoop},
    window::Window,
};
use bytemuck:: {Pod, Zeroable, cast_slice};
use wgpu_book_examples:: { wgpu_simplified as ws, transforms as wt };
use rand;

#[repr(C)]
#[derive(Copy, Clone, Debug, Pod, Zeroable)]
struct IMaterial {
    ambient_intensity: f32,
    diffuse_intensity: f32,
    specular_intensity: f32,
    specular_shininess: f32,
}

impl Default for IMaterial {
    fn default() -> IMaterial {
        IMaterial {
            ambient_intensity: 0.2,
            diffuse_intensity: 0.8,
            specular_intensity: 0.4,
            specular_shininess: 30.0,
        }
    }
}

#[repr(C)]
#[derive(Copy, Clone, Debug, Pod, Zeroable)]
pub struct Vertex {
    pub position: [f32; 3],
    pub normal: [f32; 3],
}

struct State {
    init:  ws::IWgpuInit,
    pipelines: Vec<wgpu::RenderPipeline>,
    vertex_buffer: wgpu::Buffer,
    index_buffers: Vec<wgpu::Buffer>,
```

```
        uniform_bind_groups: Vec<wgpu::BindGroup>,
        uniform_buffers: Vec<wgpu::Buffer>,
        view_mat: Matrix4<f32>,
        project_mat: Matrix4<f32>,
        msaa_texture_view: wgpu::TextureView,
        depth_texture_view: wgpu::TextureView,
        indices_lens: Vec<u32>,
        plot_type: u32,
        rotation_speed: f32,

        ambient: f32,
        diffuse: f32,
        specular: f32,
        shininess: f32,
}

impl State {
    async fn new(window: &Window, vertex_data: &Vec<Vertex>, index_data: &Vec<u16>,
    index_data2: &Vec<u16>, sample_count:u32) -> Self {
        let init = ws::IWgpuInit::new(&window, sample_count, None).await;

        let vs_shader = init.device.create_shader_module(wgpu::include_wgsl!("shader_vert.wgsl"));
        let fs_shader = init.device.create_shader_module(wgpu::include_wgsl!("blinn_phong_frag.wgsl"));

        // uniform data
        let camera_position = (3.0, 1.5, 3.0).into();
        let look_direction = (0.0,0.0,0.0).into();
        let up_direction = cgmath::Vector3::unit_y();

        let (view_mat, project_mat, _) =
            wt::create_vp_mat(camera_position, look_direction, up_direction,
            init.config.width as f32 / init.config.height as f32);

        // create vertex uniform buffers

        // model_mat and vp_mat will be stored in vertex_uniform_buffer inside the update function
        let vert_uniform_buffer = init.device.create_buffer(&wgpu::BufferDescriptor{
            label: Some("Vertex Uniform Buffer"),
            size: 192,
            usage: wgpu::BufferUsages::UNIFORM | wgpu::BufferUsages::COPY_DST,
            mapped_at_creation: false,
        });

        // create light uniform buffer. here we set eye_position = camera_position and
        // light_position = eye_position
        let light_uniform_buffer = init.device.create_buffer(&wgpu::BufferDescriptor{
            label: Some("Light Uniform Buffer"),
            size: 64,
            usage: wgpu::BufferUsages::UNIFORM | wgpu::BufferUsages::COPY_DST,
            mapped_at_creation: false,
        });
        let light_uniform_buffer2 = init.device.create_buffer(&wgpu::BufferDescriptor{
            label: Some("Light Uniform Buffer 2"),
            size: 64,
            usage: wgpu::BufferUsages::UNIFORM | wgpu::BufferUsages::COPY_DST,
            mapped_at_creation: false,
        });

        let light_position:&[f32; 3] = camera_position.as_ref();
        let eye_position:&[f32; 3] = camera_position.as_ref();
```

```
init.queue.write_buffer(&light_uniform_buffer, 0, cast_slice(light_position));
init.queue.write_buffer(&light_uniform_buffer, 16, cast_slice(eye_position));
init.queue.write_buffer(&light_uniform_buffer2, 0, cast_slice(light_position));
init.queue.write_buffer(&light_uniform_buffer2, 16, cast_slice(eye_position));

// set specular light color to white
let specular_color:[f32; 3] = [1.0, 1.0, 1.0];
init.queue.write_buffer(&light_uniform_buffer, 48, cast_slice(specular_color.as_ref()));
init.queue.write_buffer(&light_uniform_buffer2, 48, cast_slice(specular_color.as_ref()));

// set default object color to red:
let object_color:[f32; 3] = [1.0, 0.0, 0.0];
init.queue.write_buffer(&light_uniform_buffer, 32, cast_slice(object_color.as_ref()));

// set default wireframe color to yellow:
let wireframe_color:[f32; 3] = [1.0, 1.0, 0.0];
init.queue.write_buffer(&light_uniform_buffer2, 32, cast_slice(wireframe_color.as_ref()));

// material uniform buffer
let material_uniform_buffer = init.device.create_buffer(&wgpu::BufferDescriptor{
    label: Some("Material Uniform Buffer"),
    size: 16,
    usage: wgpu::BufferUsages::UNIFORM | wgpu::BufferUsages::COPY_DST,
    mapped_at_creation: false,
});

// set default material parameters
let material = [0.2 as f32, 0.8, 0.4, 30.0];
init.queue.write_buffer(&material_uniform_buffer, 0, cast_slice(material.as_ref()));

// uniform bind group for vertex shader
let (vert_bind_group_layout, vert_bind_group) = ws::create_bind_group(
    &init.device,
    vec![wgpu::ShaderStages::VERTEX],
    &[vert_uniform_buffer.as_entire_binding()],
);
let (vert_bind_group_layout2, vert_bind_group2) = ws::create_bind_group(
    &init.device,
    vec![wgpu::ShaderStages::VERTEX],
    &[vert_uniform_buffer.as_entire_binding()],
);

// uniform bind group for fragment shader
let (frag_bind_group_layout, frag_bind_group) = ws::create_bind_group(
    &init.device,
    vec![wgpu::ShaderStages::FRAGMENT, wgpu::ShaderStages::FRAGMENT],
    &[light_uniform_buffer.as_entire_binding(), material_uniform_buffer.as_entire_binding()],
);
let (frag_bind_group_layout2, frag_bind_group2) = ws::create_bind_group(
    &init.device,
    vec![wgpu::ShaderStages::FRAGMENT, wgpu::ShaderStages::FRAGMENT],
    &[light_uniform_buffer2.as_entire_binding(), material_uniform_buffer.as_entire_binding()],
);

let vertex_buffer_layout = VertexBufferLayout {
    array_stride: mem::size_of::<Vertex>() as wgpu::BufferAddress,
    step_mode: wgpu::VertexStepMode::Vertex,
    attributes: &wgpu::vertex_attr_array![0 => Float32x3, 1 => Float32x3],
};
```

```rust
let pipeline_layout = init.device.create_pipeline_layout(&wgpu::PipelineLayoutDescriptor {
    label: Some("Render Pipeline Layout"),
    bind_group_layouts: &[&vert_bind_group_layout, &frag_bind_group_layout],
    push_constant_ranges: &[],
});

let mut ppl = ws::IRenderPipeline {
    vs_shader: Some(&vs_shader),
    fs_shader: Some(&fs_shader),
    pipeline_layout: Some(&pipeline_layout),
    vertex_buffer_layout: &[vertex_buffer_layout],
    ..Default::default()
};
let pipeline = ppl.new(&init);

let vertex_buffer_layout2 = VertexBufferLayout {
    array_stride: mem::size_of::<Vertex>() as wgpu::BufferAddress,
    step_mode: wgpu::VertexStepMode::Vertex,
    attributes: &wgpu::vertex_attr_array![0 => Float32x3, 1 => Float32x3],
};

let pipeline_layout2 = init.device.create_pipeline_layout(&wgpu::PipelineLayoutDescriptor {
    label: Some("Render Pipeline Layout 2"),
    bind_group_layouts: &[&vert_bind_group_layout2, &frag_bind_group_layout2],
    push_constant_ranges: &[],
});

let mut ppl2 = ws::IRenderPipeline {
    topology: wgpu::PrimitiveTopology::LineList,
    vs_shader: Some(&vs_shader),
    fs_shader: Some(&fs_shader),
    pipeline_layout: Some(&pipeline_layout2),
    vertex_buffer_layout: &[vertex_buffer_layout2],
    ..Default::default()
};
let pipeline2 = ppl2.new(&init);

let msaa_texture_view = ws::create_msaa_texture_view(&init);
let depth_texture_view = ws::create_depth_view(&init);

let vertex_buffer = init.device.create_buffer_init(&wgpu::util::BufferInitDescriptor {
    label: Some("Vertex Buffer"),
    contents: cast_slice(vertex_data),
    usage: wgpu::BufferUsages::VERTEX,
});

let index_buffer = init.device.create_buffer_init(&wgpu::util::BufferInitDescriptor{
    label: Some("Index Buffer"),
    contents: bytemuck::cast_slice(index_data),
    usage: wgpu::BufferUsages::INDEX,
});

let index_buffer2 = init.device.create_buffer_init(&wgpu::util::BufferInitDescriptor{
    label: Some("Index Buffer 2"),
    contents: bytemuck::cast_slice(index_data2),
    usage: wgpu::BufferUsages::INDEX,
});

Self {
    init,
```

```
            pipelines: vec![pipeline, pipeline2],
            vertex_buffer,
            index_buffers: vec![index_buffer, index_buffer2],
            uniform_bind_groups: vec![vert_bind_group, frag_bind_group, vert_bind_group2,
                frag_bind_group2],
            uniform_buffers: vec![vert_uniform_buffer, light_uniform_buffer, material_uniform_buffer,
                light_uniform_buffer2],
            view_mat,
            project_mat,
            msaa_texture_view,
            depth_texture_view,
            indices_lens: vec![index_data.len() as u32, index_data2.len() as u32],
            plot_type: 0,
            rotation_speed: 1.0,

            ambient: material[0],
            diffuse: material[1],
            specular: material[2],
            shininess: material[3],
        }
    }

    fn resize(&mut self, new_size: winit::dpi::PhysicalSize<u32>) {
        if new_size.width > 0 && new_size.height > 0 {
            self.init.size = new_size;
            self.init.config.width = new_size.width;
            self.init.config.height = new_size.height;
            self.init.surface.configure(&self.init.device, &self.init.config);

            self.project_mat = wt::create_projection_mat(new_size.width as f32 / new_size.height as f32,
                true);
            self.depth_texture_view = ws::create_depth_view(&self.init);
            if self.init.sample_count > 1 {
                self.msaa_texture_view = ws::create_msaa_texture_view(&self.init);
            }
        }
    }

    #[allow(unused_variables)]
    fn input(&mut self, event: &WindowEvent) -> bool {
        match event {
            WindowEvent::KeyboardInput {
                input:
                    KeyboardInput {
                        virtual_keycode: Some(keycode),
                        state: ElementState::Pressed,
                        ..
                    },
                ..
            } => {
                match keycode {
                    VirtualKeyCode::Key1 => {
                        let scolor:[f32;3] = [rand::random(), rand::random(), rand::random()];
                        self.init.queue.write_buffer(&self.uniform_buffers[1], 32,
                            cast_slice(scolor.as_ref()));
                        true
                    },
                    VirtualKeyCode::Key2 => {
                        let wcolor:[f32;3] = [rand::random(), rand::random(), rand::random()];
                        self.init.queue.write_buffer(&self.uniform_buffers[3], 32,
```

```
                    cast_slice(wcolor.as_ref())));
                true
            },
            VirtualKeyCode::Space => {
                self.plot_type = (self.plot_type + 1) % 3;
                true
            }
            VirtualKeyCode::Q => {
                self.ambient += 0.01;
                println!("ambient intensity = {}", self.ambient);
                true
            },
            VirtualKeyCode::A => {
                self.ambient -= 0.05;
                if self.ambient < 0.0 { self.ambient = 0.0; }
                println!("ambient intensity = {}", self.ambient);
                true
            },
            VirtualKeyCode::W => {
                self.diffuse += 0.05;
                println!("diffuse intensity = {}", self.diffuse);
                true
            },
            VirtualKeyCode::S => {
                self.diffuse -= 0.05;
                if self.diffuse < 0.0 { self.diffuse = 0.0; }
                println!("diffuse intensity = {}", self.diffuse);
                true
            }, VirtualKeyCode::E => {
                self.specular += 0.05;
                println!("specular intensity = {}", self.specular);
                true
            },
            VirtualKeyCode::D => {
                self.specular -= 0.05;
                if self.specular < 0.0 { self.specular = 0.0; }
                println!("specular intensity = {}", self.specular);
                true
            },
            VirtualKeyCode::R => {
                self.shininess += 5.0;
                println!("specular shininess = {}", self.shininess);
                true
            },
            VirtualKeyCode::F => {
                self.shininess -= 5.0;
                if self.shininess < 0.0 { self.shininess = 0.0; }
                println!("specular shininess = {}", self.shininess);
                true
            },
            _ => false
        }
    }
    _ => false,
    }
}

fn update(&mut self, dt: std::time::Duration) {
    // update uniform buffer
    let dt = self.rotation_speed * dt.as_secs_f32();
```

```rust
        let model_mat = wt::create_model_mat([0.0,0.0,0.0], [dt.sin(), dt.cos(), 0.0], [1.0, 1.0, 1.0]);
        let view_project_mat = self.project_mat * self.view_mat;

        let normal_mat = (model_mat.invert().unwrap()).transpose();

        let model_ref:&[f32; 16] = model_mat.as_ref();
        let view_projection_ref:&[f32; 16] = view_project_mat.as_ref();
        let normal_ref:&[f32; 16] = normal_mat.as_ref();

        self.init.queue.write_buffer(&self.uniform_buffers[0], 0,
            cast_slice(view_projection_ref));
        self.init.queue.write_buffer(&self.uniform_buffers[0], 64,
            cast_slice(model_ref));
        self.init.queue.write_buffer(&self.uniform_buffers[0], 128, bytemuck::cast_slice(normal_ref));

        // update material
        let material = [self.ambient, self.diffuse, self.specular, self.shininess];
        self.init.queue.write_buffer(&self.uniform_buffers[2], 0, cast_slice(material.as_ref()));
    }

    fn render(&mut self) -> Result<(), wgpu::SurfaceError> {
        //let output = self.init.surface.get_current_frame()?.output;
        let output = self.init.surface.get_current_texture()?;
        let view = output
            .texture
            .create_view(&wgpu::TextureViewDescriptor::default());

        let mut encoder = self
            .init.device
            .create_command_encoder(&wgpu::CommandEncoderDescriptor {
                label: Some("Render Encoder"),
            });

        {
            let color_attach = ws::create_color_attachment(&view);
            let msaa_attach = ws::create_msaa_color_attachment(&view, &self.msaa_texture_view);
            let color_attachment = if self.init.sample_count == 1 { color_attach } else { msaa_attach };
            let depth_attachment = ws::create_depth_stencil_attachment(&self.depth_texture_view);

            let mut render_pass = encoder.begin_render_pass(&wgpu::RenderPassDescriptor {
                label: Some("Render Pass"),
                color_attachments: &[Some(color_attachment)],
                depth_stencil_attachment: Some(depth_attachment),
                occlusion_query_set: None,
                timestamp_writes: None,
            });

            let plot_type = if self.plot_type == 1 { "shape_only" }
                else if self.plot_type == 2 {"wireframe_only"} else {"both"};

            if plot_type == "shape_only" || plot_type == "both" {
                render_pass.set_pipeline(&self.pipelines[0]);
                render_pass.set_vertex_buffer(0, self.vertex_buffer.slice(..));
                render_pass.set_index_buffer(self.index_buffers[0].slice(..),
                    wgpu::IndexFormat::Uint16);
                render_pass.set_bind_group(0, &self.uniform_bind_groups[0], &[]);
                render_pass.set_bind_group(1, &self.uniform_bind_groups[1], &[]);
                render_pass.draw_indexed(0..self.indices_lens[0], 0, 0..1);
            }
```

```
            if plot_type == "wireframe_only" || plot_type == "both" {
                render_pass.set_pipeline(&self.pipelines[1]);
                render_pass.set_vertex_buffer(0, self.vertex_buffer.slice(..));
                render_pass.set_index_buffer(self.index_buffers[1].slice(..),
                    wgpu::IndexFormat::Uint16);
                render_pass.set_bind_group(0, &self.uniform_bind_groups[2], &[]);
                render_pass.set_bind_group(1, &self.uniform_bind_groups[3], &[]);
                render_pass.draw_indexed(0..self.indices_lens[1], 0, 0..1);
            }
        }

        self.init.queue.submit(iter::once(encoder.finish()));
        output.present();

        Ok(())
    }
}

pub fn run(vertex_data: &Vec<Vertex>, index_data: &Vec<u16>, index_data2: &Vec<u16>, sample_count:u32,
title: &str) {
    env_logger::init();
    let event_loop = EventLoop::new();
    let window = winit::window::WindowBuilder::new().build(&event_loop).unwrap();
    window.set_title(&*format!("ch03_{}", title));

    let mut state = pollster::block_on(State::new(&window, &vertex_data, index_data,
        index_data2, sample_count));
    let render_start_time = std::time::Instant::now();

    event_loop.run(move |event, _, control_flow| {
        match event {
            Event::WindowEvent {
                ref event,
                window_id,
            } if window_id == window.id() => {
                if !state.input(event) {
                    match event {
                        WindowEvent::CloseRequested
                        | WindowEvent::KeyboardInput {
                            input:
                                KeyboardInput {
                                    state: ElementState::Pressed,
                                    virtual_keycode: Some(VirtualKeyCode::Escape),
                                    ..
                                },
                            ..
                        } => *control_flow = ControlFlow::Exit,
                        WindowEvent::Resized(physical_size) => {
                            state.resize(*physical_size);
                        }
                        WindowEvent::ScaleFactorChanged { new_inner_size, .. } => {
                            state.resize(**new_inner_size);
                        }
                        _ => {}
                    }
                }
            }
            Event::RedrawRequested(_) => {
                let now = std::time::Instant::now();
                let dt = now - render_start_time;
```

```
            state.update(dt);

        match state.render() {
            Ok(_) => {}
            Err(wgpu::SurfaceError::Lost) => state.resize(state.init.size),
            Err(wgpu::SurfaceError::OutOfMemory) => *control_flow = ControlFlow::Exit,
            Err(e) => eprintln!("{:?}", e),
        }
    }
    Event::MainEventsCleared => {
        window.request_redraw();
    }
    _ => {}
    }
});
}
```

Within the *State::new* function, we define three uniform buffers for transform matrices, light, and material parameters, as well as two bind groups, each with a different layout. One bind group is used for vertex shader, while the other is used for fragment shader. The vertex bind group is created using the following code:

```
// uniform bind group for vertex shader
let (vert_bind_group_layout, vert_bind_group) = ws::create_bind_group(
    &init.device,
    vec![wgpu::ShaderStages::VERTEX],
    &[vert_uniform_buffer.as_entire_binding()],
);
```

Similarly, we create the fragment bind group using the following code:

```
// uniform bind group for fragment shader
let (frag_bind_group_layout, frag_bind_group) = ws::create_bind_group(
    &init.device,
    vec![wgpu::ShaderStages::FRAGMENT, wgpu::ShaderStages::FRAGMENT],
    &[light_uniform_buffer.as_entire_binding(), material_uniform_buffer.as_entire_binding()],
);
```

To pass the uniform buffers properly, we use the *@group*(0) annotation in the vertex shader and the *@group*(1) annotation in the fragment shader.

We then proceed to generate two render pipelines: one for creating the 3D shape and another for creating the wireframe. For each pipeline, we use two elements to configure the *attributes* of the vertex buffer layout, with the first element containing the vertex position and second element containing the normal-vector data:

```
attributes: &wgpu::vertex_attr_array![0 => Float32x3, 1 => Float32x3],
```

Both elements have the same data type of *Float32x3*, which corresponds to *vec3f* in the WGSL shader. We then construct the corresponding buffers using the position, normal, and index data.

In the *State::render* function, to render 3D shape with lighting, we need to set the position, normal, and index buffers, along with two bind groups to the render pass in the *draw* function:

```
render_pass.set_pipeline(&self.pipelines[0]);
render_pass.set_vertex_buffer(0, self.vertex_buffer.slice(..));
render_pass.set_index_buffer(self.index_buffers[0].slice(..), wgpu::IndexFormat::Uint16);
render_pass.set_bind_group(0, &self.uniform_bind_groups[0], &[]);
render_pass.set_bind_group(1, &self.uniform_bind_groups[1], &[]);
render_pass.draw_indexed(0..self.indices_lens[0], 0, 0..1);
```

Within the *State::update* function, we update the uniform and material buffers whenever the model matrix, light, or material parameters change. The normal matrix is also recalculated by performing the inversion and transpose on the updated model matrix:

```
let normal_mat = (model_mat.invert().unwrap()).transpose();
```

It is worth noting that to update the uniform buffers correctly, we must ensure that the offsets are set correctly. For instance, to update the uniform buffer for the transform matrices, we use the following code snippet:

```
self.init.queue.write_buffer(&self.uniform_buffers[0], 0, cast_slice(view_projection_ref));
self.init.queue.write_buffer(&self.uniform_buffers[0], 64, cast_slice(model_ref));
self.init.queue.write_buffer(&self.uniform_buffers[0], 128, cast_slice(normal_ref));
```

In this code snippet, *uniform_buffers*[0] corresponds to the uniform buffer used to pass the three transform matrices: view-projection matrix, model matrix, and normal matrix. These matrices have the corresponding offsets of 0, 64, and 128, respectively.

Additionally, the code permits the user to modify the plot type, the colors of both the shape and the wireframe, and material parameters for lighting computation using keyboard inputs.

Here is a list of controls using keyboard:

- *Space*: Changes the plot type.
- *LControl*: Changes color of the shape.
- *LAlt*: Changes color of the wireframe.
- *Q/A*: Increases/decreases the ambient light intensity.
- *W/S:* Increases/decreases the diffuse light intensity.
- *E/D:* Increases/decreases the specular light intensity.
- *R/F:* Increases/decreases the shininess of the specular light.

3.4.2 Cube with Lighting

This section will demonstrate how to apply the Blinn-Phong lighting model to a simple 3D cube. To do this, we will use the normal data created for the cube in the *create_cube_data* function from the *vertex_data.rs* file located in the *src/* folder. We will also use the Blinn-Phong shader and the common functions presented in the preceding section to compute lighting for the cube.

To get started, create a new Rust file called *cube_blinn_phong.rs* file in the *examples/ch03/* folder and enter the following code into it:

```
use common_blinn_phong::Vertex;
use wgpu_book_examples:: vertex_data as vd;
mod common_blinn_phong;

fn create_vertices() -> (Vec<common_blinn_phong::Vertex>, Vec<u16>, Vec<u16>) {
    let(pos, _, normal, _, ind, ind2) = vd::create_cube_data(2.0);
    let mut data:Vec<common_blinn_phong::Vertex> = Vec::with_capacity(pos.len());
    for i in 0..pos.len() {
        data.push(Vertex{position:pos[i], normal: normal[i]});
    }
    (data.to_vec(), ind, ind2)
}
```

```
fn main(){
    let mut sample_count = 1 as u32;
    let args: Vec<String> = std::env::args().collect();
    if args.len() > 1 {
        sample_count = args[1].parse::<u32>().unwrap();
    }

    let (vertex_data, index_data, index_data2) = create_vertices();
    common_blinn_phong::run(&vertex_data, &index_data, &index_data2, sample_count, "cube_blinn_phong");
}
```

In the above code, we first introduce the *common_blinn_phong* module and then implement the *create_vertices* function using the vertex data for the cube.

Inside the main function, we invoke the *run* function defined in the *common_blinn_phong* module, using the vertex and index data returned by the *create_vertices* function as its input arguments. This will render the cube with lighting on the screen.

By changing the light and material parameters using the keyboard inputs, we can obtain different types of lighting, such as ambient, diffuse, and specular lighting. For instance, if we set the *ambient* parameter to 1, and both the *diffuse* and *specular* parameters to 0, we will get only ambient lighting. Similarly, we can obtain pure diffuse or specular lighting by setting the other two components to zero. To achieve mixed lighting, we can set a small value such as 0.1 for ambient and set values for diffuse and specular in the middle of the [0, 1] range. For the specular lighting, we can also set the light color and shininess. A small shininess such 5 represents a rough surface, while a large value such as 300 represents a metallic surface.

To run this application, add the following code snippet to the *Cargo.toml* file:

```
[[example]]
name = "ch03_cube_blinn_phong"
path = "examples/ch03/cube_blinn_phong.rs"
```

Afterward, execute the following *cargo run* commands in the terminal window:

```
cargo run --example ch03_cube_blinn_phong 8
```

This will produce the cube with lighting, as shown in Fig.3-4.

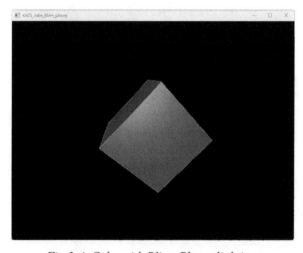

Fig.3-4. Cube with Blinn-Phong lighting.

3.4.3 Sphere with Lighting

We will use the vertex and normal data generated for a UV sphere in the previous chapter to add the lighting effect to the sphere using the Blinn-Phong shader. The Rust file for this example is similar to the one used in the previous example, but instead of the cube vertex and normal data, we will use the sphere's data.

Create a new Rust file called *sphere_blinn_phong.rs* in the *examples/ch03/* folder and add the following code to it:

```
use wgpu_book_examples:: vertex_data as vd;
mod common_blinn_phong;
use common_blinn_phong::Vertex;

fn create_vertices() -> (Vec<Vertex>, Vec<u16>, Vec<u16>) {
    let (pos, norm, _, ind, ind2) = vd::create_sphere_data(2.2, 20, 30);
    let mut data:Vec<Vertex> = Vec::with_capacity(pos.len());
    for i in 0..pos.len() {
        data.push(Vertex{position: pos[i], normal: norm[i]});
    }
    (data.to_vec(), ind, ind2)
}

fn main(){
    let mut sample_count = 1 as u32;
    let args: Vec<String> = std::env::args().collect();
    if args.len() > 1 {
        sample_count = args[1].parse::<u32>().unwrap();
    }

    let (vertex_data, index_data, index_data2) = create_vertices();
    common_blinn_phong::run(&vertex_data, &index_data, &index_data2, sample_count, "sphere_blinn_phong");
}
```

The code used in this example is similar to the previous one, with the exception that it uses the sphere data to create the vertex and index data using the *create_vertices* method.

To run this application, add the following code snippet to the *Cargo.toml* file:

```
[[example]]
name = "ch03_sphere_blinn_phong"
path = "examples/ch03/sphere_blinn_phong.rs"
```

Afterward, execute the following *cargo run* commands in the terminal window:

```
cargo run --example ch03_sphere_blinn_phong 8
```

This will produce the sphere with lighting, as shown in Fig.3-5.

3.4.4 Torus with Lighting

We have generated vertex data and normal-vector data for a torus shape in the previous chapter. In this section, we will use this data along with the Blinn-Phong shader to apply lighting effects to the torus shape.

Add a new Rust file called *torus_blinn_phong.rs* to the *examples/ch03/* folder and include the following code:

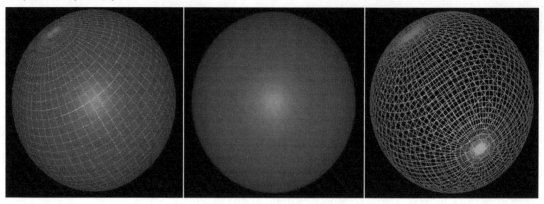

Fig.3-5. Sphere with lighting: shape with wireframe (left), shape only (middle), wireframe only (right).

```
use wgpu_book_examples:: vertex_data as vd;
mod common_blinn_phong;
use common_blinn_phong::Vertex;

fn create_vertices() -> (Vec<Vertex>, Vec<u16>, Vec<u16>) {
    let (pos, norm, ind, ind2) = vd::create_torus_data(1.8, 0.4, 60, 20);
    let mut data:Vec<Vertex> = Vec::with_capacity(pos.len());
    for i in 0..pos.len() {
        data.push(Vertex{position:pos[i], normal:norm[i]});
    }
    (data.to_vec(), ind, ind2)
}

fn main(){
    let mut sample_count = 1 as u32;
    let args: Vec<String> = std::env::args().collect();
    if args.len() > 1 {
        sample_count = args[1].parse::<u32>().unwrap();
    }

    let (vertex_data, index_data, index_data2) = create_vertices();
    common_blinn_phong::run(&vertex_data, &index_data, &index_data2, sample_count, "torus_blinn_phong");
}
```

The code used in this example is similar to the one used in the previous example, but it generates a torus shape with lighting effect instead.

To run this application, add the following code snippet to the *Cargo.toml* file:

```
[[example]]
name = "ch03_torus_blinn_phong"
path = "examples/ch03/torus_blinn_phong.rs"
```

Afterward, execute the following *cargo run* commands in the terminal window:

```
cargo run --example ch03_torus_blinn_phong 8
```

This will produce the torus with lighting, as shown in Fig.3-6.

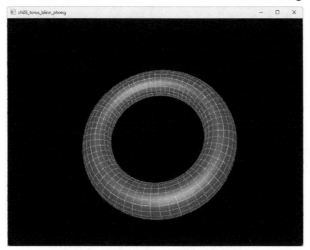

Fig.3-6. Torus with Blinn-Phong lighting.

3.5 Directional Light

A directional light emits light in a specific direction and behaves as though it is infinitely far away, with all rays produced being parallel. This type of light is commonly used to simulate daylight, where the sun or moon is far enough away that its position can be considered infinite and all rays from it are parallel.

Since the direction of the light remains the same for each object in the scene, and all light rays are parallel, the relationship between each object and the light source's position does not matter, resulting in similar lighting calculations for each object in the scene.

3.5.1 Instanced Drawing

In this section, we will explore how to effectively add directional lighting to multiple 3D objects using *wgpu*'s instanced drawing feature. Instanced drawing allows us to draw multiple instances of the same object with a single call to the *draw_indexed* function, resulting in faster rendering time:

```
drawIndexed(indices, baseVertex, instances)
```

You can see that the *draw_indexed* function accepts several input arguments. The *indices* parameter specifies the range of indices to draw. The *base_vertex* is added to each index value before indexing into the vertex buffers. Finally, the *instances* argument indicates the range of instances to draw.

In previous examples, we have drawn a single object because we specify the *instances* argument using 0..1. However, by setting *instances* to a range like 0..*instance_count* with the *instance_count* parameter value greater than 1, we can draw multiple instances of an object. Additionally, we can also draw instances in a specific range. For example, setting *instances* 10..40 would draw 30 instances from 10 to 40.

In this example, we will create multiple instances of three types of shapes: cubes, spheres, and tori, using instanced drawing to effectively render them with directional lighting.

3.5.2 Shader Code

To improve code reusability, we will separate the vertex shader and fragment shader code. Create a new vertex shader file called *shader-instance-vert.wgsl* in the *examples/ch03/* folder, and then copy and paste the following code into the file:

```
// vertex shader
@group(0) @binding(0) var<uniform> viewProjectMat: mat4x4f;
@group(0) @binding(1) var<storage> modelMat: array<mat4x4f>;
@group(0) @binding(2) var<storage> normalMat: array<mat4x4f>;
@group(0) @binding(3) var<storage> colorVec: array<vec4f>;

struct Input {
    @builtin(instance_index) idx: u32,
    @location(0) position: vec3f,
    @location(1) normal: vec3f
}

struct Output {
    @builtin(position) position: vec4f,
    @location(0) vPosition: vec4f,
    @location(1) vNormal: vec4f,
    @location(2) vColor: vec4f,
};

@vertex
fn vs_main(in:Input) -> Output {
    var output: Output;
    let modelMat = modelMat[in.idx];
    let normalMat = normalMat[in.idx];
    let mPosition:vec4<f32> = modelMat * vec4(in.position, 1.0);
    output.vPosition = mPosition;
    output.vNormal =  normalMat * vec4(in.normal, 1.0);
    output.position = viewProjectMat * mPosition;
    output.vColor = colorVec[in.idx];
    return output;
}
```

The reason for using arrays of *mat4x4f* matrices for model matrix and normal matrix, and an array of *vec4f* vectors for color vector, is to enable the creation of multiple instances for each shape, with different locations and colors. To pass these arrays, storage buffers are used because their sizes are unspecified. Runtime sized arrays in *wgpu* can only be used in the *<storage>* address space. However, the view-projection matrix remains in the uniform buffer because all instances will have the same view-projection matrix.

Within the *vs_main* function, the built-in *instance_index* parameter is used to represent the transformation and color for each instance, and the position, normal, and color for each instance are processed as output. The fragment shader then uses this output to calculate the lighting effect and color. This vertex shader will be reused in the examples presented in the following sections.

Create a new fragment shader file called *directional-frag.wgsl* in the *examples/ch03/* folder and include the following code:

```
struct LightUniforms {
    lightDirection : vec4f,
    eyePosition : vec4f,
    specularColor : vec4f,
}
```

```
@group(1) @binding(0) var<uniform> light : LightUniforms;

struct MaterialUniforms {
    ambient: f32,
    diffuse: f32,
    specular: f32,
    shininess: f32,
}
@group(1) @binding(1) var<uniform> material : MaterialUniforms;

struct Input {
    @location(0) vPosition:vec4f,
    @location(1) vNormal:vec4f,
    @location(2) vColor: vec4f,
}

fn blinnPhong(N:vec3f, L:vec3f, V:vec3f) -> vec2f{
    let H = normalize(L + V);
    var diffuse = material.diffuse * max(dot(N, L), 0.0);
    diffuse += material.diffuse * max(dot(-N, L), 0.0);
    var specular = material.specular * pow(max(dot(N, H), 0.0), material.shininess);
    specular += material.specular * pow(max(dot(-N, H),0.0), material.shininess);
    return vec2(diffuse, specular);
}

@fragment
fn fs_main(in:Input) -> @location(0) vec4f {
    var N = normalize(in.vNormal.xyz);
    let L = normalize(-light.lightDirection.xyz);
    let V = normalize(light.eyePosition.xyz - in.vPosition.xyz);

    let bp = blinnPhong(N, L, V);

    let finalColor = in.vColor * (material.ambient + bp[0]) + light.specularColor * bp[1];
    return vec4<f32>(finalColor.rgb, 1.0);
}
```

This fragment shader code shares similarities with the one in the *blinn-phong-frag.wgsl* file, but instead of specifying the position of the light source, we set the direction of the light rays.

3.5.3 Common Code

Similar to what we have done before, we will consolidate commonly used code for instanced drawing into a common file within this chapter. Create a new Rust file called *common_instance.rs* in the *examples/ch03/* folder and insert the code below:

```
use wgpu_book_examples:: { vertex_data as vd, transforms as wt };
use wgpu::util::DeviceExt;
use bytemuck:: {Pod, Zeroable, cast_slice};
use cgmath::{ Matrix, SquareMatrix };
use rand::Rng;

#[repr(C)]
#[derive(Copy, Clone, Debug, Pod, Zeroable)]
pub struct Vertex {
    pub position: [f32; 3],
    pub normal: [f32; 3],
}
```

```rust
pub fn cube_vertices() -> (Vec<Vertex>, Vec<u16>) {
    let(pos, _, norm, _, ind, _) = vd::create_cube_data(2.0);
    let mut data:Vec<Vertex> = Vec::with_capacity(pos.len());
    for i in 0..pos.len() {
        data.push(Vertex{position: pos[i], normal: norm[i]});
    }
    (data.to_vec(), ind)
}

pub fn sphere_vertices() -> (Vec<Vertex>, Vec<u16>) {
    let (pos, norm, _, ind, _) = vd::create_sphere_data(2.2, 20, 30);
    let mut data:Vec<Vertex> = Vec::with_capacity(pos.len());
    for i in 0..pos.len() {
        data.push(Vertex{position: pos[i], normal: norm[i]});
    }
    (data.to_vec(), ind)
}

pub fn torus_vertices() -> (Vec<Vertex>, Vec<u16>) {
    let (pos, norm, ind, _) = vd::create_torus_data(1.8, 0.4, 60, 20);
    let mut data:Vec<Vertex> = Vec::with_capacity(pos.len());
    for i in 0..pos.len() {
        data.push(Vertex{position: pos[i], normal: norm[i]});
    }
    (data.to_vec(), ind)
}

pub fn create_object_buffers(device: &wgpu::Device) -> (Vec<wgpu::Buffer>, Vec<wgpu::Buffer>, Vec<u32>) {
    let (cube_vertex_data, cube_index_data) = cube_vertices();
    let (sphere_vertex_data, sphere_index_data) = sphere_vertices();
    let (torus_vertex_data, torus_index_data) = torus_vertices();

    let cube_vertex_buffer = device.create_buffer_init(&wgpu::util::BufferInitDescriptor {
        label: Some("Cube Vertex Buffer"),
        contents: cast_slice(&cube_vertex_data),
        usage: wgpu::BufferUsages::VERTEX,
    });

    let cube_index_buffer = device.create_buffer_init(&wgpu::util::BufferInitDescriptor{
        label: Some("Cube Index Buffer"),
        contents: cast_slice(&cube_index_data),
        usage: wgpu::BufferUsages::INDEX,
    });

    let sphere_vertex_buffer = device.create_buffer_init(&wgpu::util::BufferInitDescriptor {
        label: Some("sphere Vertex Buffer"),
        contents: cast_slice(&sphere_vertex_data),
        usage: wgpu::BufferUsages::VERTEX,
    });

    let sphere_index_buffer = device.create_buffer_init(&wgpu::util::BufferInitDescriptor{
        label: Some("Sphere Index Buffer"),
        contents: cast_slice(&sphere_index_data),
        usage: wgpu::BufferUsages::INDEX,
    });

    let torus_vertex_buffer = device.create_buffer_init(&wgpu::util::BufferInitDescriptor {
        label: Some("Torus Vertex Buffer"),
        contents: cast_slice(&torus_vertex_data),
```

```
        usage: wgpu::BufferUsages::VERTEX,
    });

    let torus_index_buffer = device.create_buffer_init(&wgpu::util::BufferInitDescriptor{
        label: Some("Torus Index Buffer"),
        contents: cast_slice(&torus_index_data),
        usage: wgpu::BufferUsages::INDEX,
    });

    (
        vec![cube_vertex_buffer, sphere_vertex_buffer, torus_vertex_buffer],
        vec![cube_index_buffer, sphere_index_buffer, torus_index_buffer],
        vec![cube_index_data.len() as u32, sphere_index_data.len() as u32, torus_index_data.len() as u32]
    )
}

#[allow(dead_code)]
pub fn create_transform_mat_color(objects_count:u32, translate_default:bool) -> (Vec<[f32; 16]>, Vec<[f32;
16]>, Vec<[f32; 4]>){
    let mut model_mat:Vec<[f32; 16]> = vec![];
    let mut normal_mat:Vec<[f32; 16]> = vec![];
    let mut color_vec:Vec<[f32; 4]> = vec![];

    for _i in 0..objects_count {
        let mut rng = rand::thread_rng();
        let mut translation = [rng.gen::<f32>() * 60.0 - 53.0,
            rng.gen::<f32>() * 50.0 - 45.0, -15.0 - rng.gen::<f32>() * 50.0];
        if !translate_default {
            translation = [rng.gen::<f32>() * 50.0 - 25.0,
                rng.gen::<f32>() * 40.0 - 18.0, -30.0 - rng.gen::<f32>() * 50.0];
        }
        let rotation = [rng.gen::<f32>(), rng.gen::<f32>(), rng.gen::<f32>()];
        let scale = [1.0, 1.0, 1.0];
        let m = wt::create_model_mat(translation, rotation, scale);
        let n = (m.invert().unwrap()).transpose();
        let color = [rng.gen::<f32>(), rng.gen::<f32>(), rng.gen::<f32>(), 1.0];
        model_mat.push(*(m.as_ref()));
        normal_mat.push(*(n.as_ref()));
        color_vec.push(color);
    }

    (model_mat, normal_mat, color_vec)
}
```

The above code first implements three public functions, *cube_vertices*, *sphere_vertices*, and *torus_vertices*. These functions return the vertex data and index data for the cube, sphere, and torus using their respective position, normal, and index data.

The *create_object_buffers* method uses this vertex and index data to create the vertex buffers and index buffers for the cube, sphere, and torus.

Finally, the *create_transform_mat_color* function defines the model and normal matrices, along with color, for each instance using the random function. This will create a distinct location, orientation, and color for each instance.

Previously, we implemented two functions, *create_bind_group_layout* and *create_bind_group*, in the *wgpu_simplified.rs* in the *src/* folder. These functions require that all buffers have a *Uniform* binding type. However, in instanced drawing, the vertex shader uses storage buffers to pass the model and normal matrices because their sizes are unspecified. Runtime-sized arrays in *wgpu* can only be used in the

<storage> address space. In order to use buffers with a *Storage* binding type in a bind group, we need to create two new functions: one is the *create_bind_group_layout_storage* and the other is *create_bind_group_storage*, in the *wgpu_simplefied.rs* file with the following code:

```rust
pub fn create_bind_group_layout_storage(
    device: &wgpu::Device,
    shader_stages: Vec<wgpu::ShaderStages>,
    binding_types: Vec<wgpu::BufferBindingType>
) -> wgpu::BindGroupLayout {
    let mut entries = vec![];

    for i in 0..shader_stages.len() {
        entries.push(wgpu::BindGroupLayoutEntry {
            binding: i as u32,
            visibility: shader_stages[i],
            ty: wgpu::BindingType::Buffer {
                ty: binding_types[i],
                has_dynamic_offset: false,
                min_binding_size: None,
            },
            count: None,
        });
    }

    device.create_bind_group_layout(&wgpu::BindGroupLayoutDescriptor{
        entries: &entries,
        label: Some("Uniform Bind Group Layout"),
    })
}

pub fn create_bind_group_storage(
    device: &wgpu::Device,
    shader_stages: Vec<wgpu::ShaderStages>,
    binding_types: Vec<wgpu::BufferBindingType>,
    resources: &[wgpu::BindingResource<'_>]
) -> ( wgpu::BindGroupLayout, wgpu::BindGroup) {
    let entries: Vec<_> = resources.iter().enumerate().map(|(i, resource)| {
        wgpu::BindGroupEntry {
            binding: i as u32,
            resource: resource.clone(),
        }
    }).collect();

    let layout = create_bind_group_layout_storage(device, shader_stages, binding_types);
    let bind_group = device.create_bind_group(&wgpu::BindGroupDescriptor {
        layout: &layout,
        entries: &entries,
        label: Some("Uniform Bind Group"),
    });

    (layout, bind_group)
}
```

These two functions in the code above takes an extra input argument named *bind_types* with a type of *Vec<wgpu::BufferBindingType>*, which allows you to specify the binding type for each buffer when creating a bind group.

3.5.4 Rust Code

Create a new Rust file called *directional_light.rs* in the *examples/ch03/* folder and include the following code:

```rust
use std:: {iter, mem};
use cgmath::{ Matrix4, Point3 };
use wgpu::VertexBufferLayout;
use winit::{
    event::*,
    event_loop::{ControlFlow, EventLoop},
    window::Window,
};
use bytemuck::cast_slice;
use wgpu_book_examples:: { wgpu_simplified as ws, transforms as wt };
mod common_instance;

const NUM_CUBES:u32 = 50;
const NUM_SPHERES:u32 = 50;
const NUM_TORI:u32 = 50;

struct State {
    init:  ws::IWgpuInit,
    pipeline: wgpu::RenderPipeline,
    vertex_buffers: Vec<wgpu::Buffer>,
    index_buffers: Vec<wgpu::Buffer>,
    uniform_bind_groups: Vec<wgpu::BindGroup>,
    uniform_buffers: Vec<wgpu::Buffer>,
    view_mat: Matrix4<f32>,
    project_mat: Matrix4<f32>,
    msaa_texture_view: wgpu::TextureView,
    depth_texture_view: wgpu::TextureView,
    indices_lens: Vec<u32>,
    animation_speed: f32,

    ambient: f32,
    diffuse: f32,
    specular: f32,
    shininess: f32,
}

impl State {
    async fn new(window: &Window, sample_count:u32) -> Self {
        let init = ws::IWgpuInit::new(&window, sample_count, None).await;

        let vs_shader = init.device.create_shader_module(
            wgpu::include_wgsl!("shader_instance_vert.wgsl"));
        let fs_shader = init.device.create_shader_module(wgpu::include_wgsl!("directional_frag.wgsl"));

        let objects_count = NUM_CUBES + NUM_SPHERES + NUM_TORI;

        // uniform data
        let camera_position = (8.0, 8.0, 16.0).into();
        let look_direction = (0.0, 0.0, 0.0).into();
        let up_direction = cgmath::Vector3::unit_y();
        let light_direction: Point3<f32> = (0.2, 1.0, 0.3).into();

        let (model_mat, normal_mat, color_vec) =
            common_instance::create_transform_mat_color(objects_count, true);
```

```
let (view_mat, project_mat, vp_mat) =
    wt::create_vp_mat(camera_position, look_direction, up_direction,
    init.config.width as f32 / init.config.height as f32);

// create uniform view-projection buffers
let vp_uniform_buffer = init.device.create_buffer(&wgpu::BufferDescriptor{
    label: Some("View-Projection Buffer"),
    size: 64,
    usage: wgpu::BufferUsages::UNIFORM | wgpu::BufferUsages::COPY_DST,
    mapped_at_creation: false,
});
init.queue.write_buffer(&vp_uniform_buffer, 0, cast_slice(vp_mat.as_ref() as &[f32; 16]));

// model storage buffer
let model_uniform_buffer = init.device.create_buffer(&wgpu::BufferDescriptor{
    label: Some("Model Uniform Buffer"),
    size: 64 * objects_count as u64,
    usage: wgpu::BufferUsages::STORAGE | wgpu::BufferUsages::COPY_DST,
    mapped_at_creation: false,
});
init.queue.write_buffer(&model_uniform_buffer, 0, cast_slice(&model_mat));

// normal storage buffer
let normal_uniform_buffer = init.device.create_buffer(&wgpu::BufferDescriptor{
    label: Some("Normal Uniform Buffer"),
    size: 64 * objects_count as u64,
    usage: wgpu::BufferUsages::STORAGE | wgpu::BufferUsages::COPY_DST,
    mapped_at_creation: false,
});
init.queue.write_buffer(&normal_uniform_buffer, 0, cast_slice(&normal_mat));

// color storage buffer
let color_uniform_buffer = init.device.create_buffer(&wgpu::BufferDescriptor{
    label: Some("color Uniform Buffer"),
    size: 16 * objects_count as u64,
    usage: wgpu::BufferUsages::STORAGE | wgpu::BufferUsages::COPY_DST,
    mapped_at_creation: false,
});
init.queue.write_buffer(&color_uniform_buffer, 0, cast_slice(&color_vec));

// light uniform buffer.
let light_uniform_buffer = init.device.create_buffer(&wgpu::BufferDescriptor{
    label: Some("Light Uniform Buffer"),
    size: 48,
    usage: wgpu::BufferUsages::UNIFORM | wgpu::BufferUsages::COPY_DST,
    mapped_at_creation: false,
});
init.queue.write_buffer(&light_uniform_buffer, 0,
    cast_slice(light_direction.as_ref() as &[f32; 3]));
init.queue.write_buffer(&light_uniform_buffer, 16,
    cast_slice(camera_position.as_ref() as &[f32; 3]));

// set specular light color to white
let specular_color:[f32; 3] = [1.0, 1.0, 1.0];
init.queue.write_buffer(&light_uniform_buffer, 32, cast_slice(specular_color.as_ref()));

// material uniform buffer
let material_uniform_buffer = init.device.create_buffer(&wgpu::BufferDescriptor{
    label: Some("Material Uniform Buffer"),
    size: 16,
```

```
        usage: wgpu::BufferUsages::UNIFORM | wgpu::BufferUsages::COPY_DST,
        mapped_at_creation: false,
});

// set default material parameters
let material = [0.1 as f32, 0.6, 0.4, 30.0];
init.queue.write_buffer(&material_uniform_buffer, 0, cast_slice(material.as_ref()));

// uniform bind group for vertex shader
let (vert_bind_group_layout, vert_bind_group) = ws::create_bind_group_storage(
    &init.device,
    vec![
        wgpu::ShaderStages::VERTEX, wgpu::ShaderStages::VERTEX,
        wgpu::ShaderStages::VERTEX, wgpu::ShaderStages::VERTEX
    ],
    vec![
        wgpu::BufferBindingType::Uniform,
        wgpu::BufferBindingType::Storage { read_only: true },
        wgpu::BufferBindingType::Storage { read_only: true },
        wgpu::BufferBindingType::Storage { read_only: true },
    ],
    &[
        vp_uniform_buffer.as_entire_binding(),
        model_uniform_buffer.as_entire_binding(),
        normal_uniform_buffer.as_entire_binding(),
        color_uniform_buffer.as_entire_binding()
    ],
);

// uniform bind group for fragment shader
let (frag_bind_group_layout, frag_bind_group) = ws::create_bind_group(
    &init.device,
    vec![wgpu::ShaderStages::FRAGMENT, wgpu::ShaderStages::FRAGMENT],
    &[light_uniform_buffer.as_entire_binding(), material_uniform_buffer.as_entire_binding()],
);

let vertex_buffer_layout = VertexBufferLayout {
    array_stride: mem::size_of::<common_instance::Vertex>() as wgpu::BufferAddress,
    step_mode: wgpu::VertexStepMode::Vertex,
    attributes: &wgpu::vertex_attr_array![0 => Float32x3, 1 => Float32x3],
};

let pipeline_layout = init.device.create_pipeline_layout(&wgpu::PipelineLayoutDescriptor {
    label: Some("Render Pipeline Layout"),
    bind_group_layouts: &[&vert_bind_group_layout, &frag_bind_group_layout],
    push_constant_ranges: &[],
});

let mut ppl = ws::IRenderPipeline {
    vs_shader: Some(&vs_shader),
    fs_shader: Some(&fs_shader),
    pipeline_layout: Some(&pipeline_layout),
    vertex_buffer_layout: &[vertex_buffer_layout],
    ..Default::default()
};
let pipeline = ppl.new(&init);

let msaa_texture_view = ws::create_msaa_texture_view(&init);
let depth_texture_view = ws::create_depth_view(&init);
```

```
    // vertex and index buffers for objects:
    let (vertex_buffers, index_buffers, index_lens) =
        common_instance::create_object_buffers(&init.device);

    Self {
        init,
        pipeline,
        vertex_buffers,
        index_buffers,
        uniform_bind_groups: vec![vert_bind_group, frag_bind_group],
        uniform_buffers: vec![
            vp_uniform_buffer,
            model_uniform_buffer,
            normal_uniform_buffer,
            color_uniform_buffer,
            light_uniform_buffer,
            material_uniform_buffer
        ],
        view_mat,
        project_mat,
        msaa_texture_view,
        depth_texture_view,
        indices_lens: index_lens.to_vec(),
        animation_speed: 1.0,

        ambient: material[0],
        diffuse: material[1],
        specular: material[2],
        shininess: material[3],
    }
}

fn resize(&mut self, new_size: winit::dpi::PhysicalSize<u32>) {
    if new_size.width > 0 && new_size.height > 0 {
        self.init.size = new_size;
        self.init.config.width = new_size.width;
        self.init.config.height = new_size.height;
        self.init.surface.configure(&self.init.device, &self.init.config);

        self.project_mat = wt::create_projection_mat(new_size.width as f32 / new_size.height as f32,
            true);
        self.depth_texture_view = ws::create_depth_view(&self.init);
        if self.init.sample_count > 1 {
            self.msaa_texture_view = ws::create_msaa_texture_view(&self.init);
        }
    }
}

#[allow(unused_variables)]
fn input(&mut self, event: &WindowEvent) -> bool {
    match event {
        WindowEvent::KeyboardInput {
            input:
                KeyboardInput {
                    virtual_keycode: Some(keycode),
                    state: ElementState::Pressed,
                    ..
                },
            ..
        } => {
```

```
            match keycode {
                VirtualKeyCode::Q => {
                    self.ambient += 0.01;
                    true
                },
                VirtualKeyCode::A => {
                    self.ambient -= 0.05;
                    if self.ambient < 0.0 { self.ambient = 0.0; }
                    true
                },
                VirtualKeyCode::W => {
                    self.diffuse += 0.05;
                    true
                },
                VirtualKeyCode::S => {
                    self.diffuse -= 0.05;
                    if self.diffuse < 0.0 { self.diffuse = 0.0; }
                    true
                }, VirtualKeyCode::E => {
                    self.specular += 0.05;
                    true
                },
                VirtualKeyCode::D => {
                    self.specular -= 0.05;
                    if self.specular < 0.0 { self.specular = 0.0; }
                    true
                },
                VirtualKeyCode::R => {
                    self.shininess += 5.0;
                    true
                },
                VirtualKeyCode::F => {
                    self.shininess -= 5.0;
                    if self.shininess < 0.0 { self.shininess = 0.0; }
                    true
                },
                _ => false
            }
        }
        _ => false,
    }
}

fn update(&mut self, dt: std::time::Duration) {
    // update uniform buffer
    let dt = self.animation_speed * dt.as_secs_f32();
    let sn = 10.0 * (0.5 + dt.sin());
    let cn = 10.0 * (0.5 + dt.cos());
    self.init.queue.write_buffer(&self.uniform_buffers[4], 0,
        cast_slice([-0.2*sn, -0.3*cn, -1.0].as_ref()));

    let view_project_mat = self.project_mat * self.view_mat;
    let view_projection_ref:&[f32; 16] = view_project_mat.as_ref();
    self.init.queue.write_buffer(&self.uniform_buffers[0], 0, cast_slice(view_projection_ref));

    // update material
    let material = [self.ambient, self.diffuse, self.specular, self.shininess];
    self.init.queue.write_buffer(&self.uniform_buffers[5], 0, cast_slice(material.as_ref()));
}
```

```rust
    fn render(&mut self) -> Result<(), wgpu::SurfaceError> {
        let output = self.init.surface.get_current_texture()?;
        let view = output
            .texture
            .create_view(&wgpu::TextureViewDescriptor::default());

        let mut encoder = self
            .init.device
            .create_command_encoder(&wgpu::CommandEncoderDescriptor {
                label: Some("Render Encoder"),
            });

        {
            let color_attach = ws::create_color_attachment(&view);
            let msaa_attach = ws::create_msaa_color_attachment(&view, &self.msaa_texture_view);
            let color_attachment = if self.init.sample_count == 1 { color_attach } else { msaa_attach };
            let depth_attachment = ws::create_depth_stencil_attachment(&self.depth_texture_view);

            let mut render_pass = encoder.begin_render_pass(&wgpu::RenderPassDescriptor {
                label: Some("Render Pass"),
                color_attachments: &[Some(color_attachment)],
                depth_stencil_attachment: Some(depth_attachment),
                occlusion_query_set: None,
                timestamp_writes: None,
            });

            render_pass.set_pipeline(&self.pipeline);
            render_pass.set_bind_group(0, &self.uniform_bind_groups[0], &[]);
            render_pass.set_bind_group(1, &self.uniform_bind_groups[1], &[]);

            // draw cubes
            render_pass.set_vertex_buffer(0, self.vertex_buffers[0].slice(..));
            render_pass.set_index_buffer(self.index_buffers[0].slice(..), wgpu::IndexFormat::Uint16);
            render_pass.draw_indexed(0..self.indices_lens[0], 0, 0..NUM_CUBES);

            // draw spheres
            render_pass.set_vertex_buffer(0, self.vertex_buffers[1].slice(..));
            render_pass.set_index_buffer(self.index_buffers[1].slice(..), wgpu::IndexFormat::Uint16);
            render_pass.draw_indexed(0..self.indices_lens[1], 0, NUM_CUBES..NUM_CUBES+NUM_SPHERES);

            // draw tori
            render_pass.set_vertex_buffer(0, self.vertex_buffers[2].slice(..));
            render_pass.set_index_buffer(self.index_buffers[2].slice(..), wgpu::IndexFormat::Uint16);
            render_pass.draw_indexed(0..self.indices_lens[2], 0,
                NUM_CUBES+NUM_SPHERES..NUM_CUBES+NUM_SPHERES+NUM_TORI);
        }
        self.init.queue.submit(iter::once(encoder.finish()));
        output.present();

        Ok(())
    }
}

fn main() {
    let mut sample_count = 1 as u32;
    let args: Vec<String> = std::env::args().collect();
    if args.len() > 1 {
        sample_count = args[1].parse::<u32>().unwrap();
    }
```

```
env_logger::init();
let event_loop = EventLoop::new();
let window = winit::window::WindowBuilder::new().build(&event_loop).unwrap();
window.set_title(&*format!("ch03_{}", "directional_light"));

let mut state = pollster::block_on(State::new(&window, sample_count));
let render_start_time = std::time::Instant::now();

event_loop.run(move |event, _, control_flow| {
    match event {
        Event::WindowEvent {
            ref event,
            window_id,
        } if window_id == window.id() => {
            if !state.input(event) {
                match event {
                    WindowEvent::CloseRequested
                    | WindowEvent::KeyboardInput {
                        input:
                            KeyboardInput {
                                state: ElementState::Pressed,
                                virtual_keycode: Some(VirtualKeyCode::Escape),
                                ..
                            },
                        ..
                    } => *control_flow = ControlFlow::Exit,
                    WindowEvent::Resized(physical_size) => {
                        state.resize(*physical_size);
                    }
                    WindowEvent::ScaleFactorChanged { new_inner_size, .. } => {
                        state.resize(**new_inner_size);
                    }
                    _ => {}
                }
            }
        }
        Event::RedrawRequested(_) => {
            let now = std::time::Instant::now();
            let dt = now - render_start_time;
            state.update(dt);

            match state.render() {
                Ok(_) => {}
                Err(wgpu::SurfaceError::Lost) => state.resize(state.init.size),
                Err(wgpu::SurfaceError::OutOfMemory) => *control_flow = ControlFlow::Exit,
                Err(e) => eprintln!("{:?}", e),
            }
        }
        Event::MainEventsCleared => {
            window.request_redraw();
        }
        _ => {}
    }
});
}
```

The code structure is similar to previous examples. Here, I will only discuss the different parts. The first difference is that we define three constants: NUM_CUBES, NUM_SPHERES, and NUM_TOTI, all with a value of 50, meaning that we want to draw 50 instances of each shape.

The other difference is that we set the buffer usage to *STORAGE* when creating the model, normal, and color buffers:

```
usage: wgpu::BufferUsages::STORAGE | wgpu::BufferUsages::COPY_DST,
```

Correspondingly, we create the bind group using the new *ws::create_bind_group_storage* function with specified bind types, as shown in the following code snippet:

```
let (vert_bind_group_layout, vert_bind_group) = ws::create_bind_group_storage(
    &init.device,
    vec![
        wgpu::ShaderStages::VERTEX, wgpu::ShaderStages::VERTEX,
        wgpu::ShaderStages::VERTEX, wgpu::ShaderStages::VERTEX
    ],
    vec![
        wgpu::BufferBindingType::Uniform,
        wgpu::BufferBindingType::Storage { read_only: true },
        wgpu::BufferBindingType::Storage { read_only: true },
        wgpu::BufferBindingType::Storage { read_only: true },
    ],
    &[
        vp_uniform_buffer.as_entire_binding(),
        model_uniform_buffer.as_entire_binding(),
        normal_uniform_buffer.as_entire_binding(),
        color_uniform_buffer.as_entire_binding()
    ],
);
```

It is clear that the first buffer for the view-projection matrix has a *Uniform* binding type, while the remaining three buffers for model, normal, and color have a *Storage* binding type.

In the *State::render* function, we need to set the render pass properly to draw multiple instances, as shown in the following code snippet:

```
render_pass.set_pipeline(&self.pipeline);
render_pass.set_bind_group(0, &self.uniform_bind_groups[0], &[]);
render_pass.set_bind_group(1, &self.uniform_bind_groups[1], &[]);

// draw cubes
render_pass.set_vertex_buffer(0, self.vertex_buffers[0].slice(..));
render_pass.set_index_buffer(self.index_buffers[0].slice(..), wgpu::IndexFormat::Uint16);
render_pass.draw_indexed(0..self.indices_lens[0], 0, 0..NUM_CUBES);

// draw spheres
render_pass.set_vertex_buffer(0, self.vertex_buffers[1].slice(..));
render_pass.set_index_buffer(self.index_buffers[1].slice(..), wgpu::IndexFormat::Uint16);
render_pass.draw_indexed(0..self.indices_lens[1], 0, NUM_CUBES..NUM_CUBES+NUM_SPHERES);

// draw tori
render_pass.set_vertex_buffer(0, self.vertex_buffers[2].slice(..));
render_pass.set_index_buffer(self.index_buffers[2].slice(..), wgpu::IndexFormat::Uint16);
render_pass.draw_indexed(0..self.indices_lens[2], 0,
    NUM_CUBES+NUM_SPHERES..NUM_CUBES+NUM_SPHERES+NUM_TORI);
```

Here, it is essential to set the *instances* parameter accurately; otherwise, some instances may overlap others.

Notably, the light direction is animated within the *State::update* function using the following code snippet:

```
let dt = self.animation_speed * dt.as_secs_f32();
```

```
let sn = 10.0 * (0.5 + dt.sin());
let cn = 10.0 * (0.5 + dt.cos());
self.init.queue.write_buffer(&self.uniform_buffers[4],0,cast_slice([-0.2*sn,-0.3*cn,-1.0].as_ref()));
```

In the code snippet above, *uniform_buffers*[4] refers to the light uniform buffer.

Additionally, the code permits the user to modify material parameters for lighting computation using keyboard inputs.

Here is a list of controls using keyboard:

- *Q/A*: Increases/decreases the ambient light intensity.

- *W/S:* Increases/decreases the diffuse light intensity.

- *E/D:* Increases/decreases the specular light intensity.

- *R/F:* Increases/decreases the shininess of the specular light.

3.5.5 Run Application

To run this application, add the following code snippet to the *Cargo.toml* file:

```
[[example]]
name = "ch03_directional_light"
path = "examples/ch03/directional_light.rs"
```

Afterward, execute the following *cargo run* commands in the terminal window:

```
cargo run --example ch03_directional_light 8
```

This will produce the objects under directional light, as shown in Fig.3-7.

Fig.3-7. 3D objects under directional light.

3.6 Point Light

A point light is a type of light source that has a specified position within the scene and illuminates in all directions. The light rays from a point light source gradually fade out over distance. We can think of the Blinn-Phong light model as a special type of point light where we neglect attenuation. Typically, light bulbs are a common example of a point light source.

One way to calculate the attenuation over distance of a point light is to use the following formula:

$$F_{att} = \frac{1.0}{K_c + K_l * d + k_q * d^2}$$

In this formula, d represents the distance from the fragment to the light source. The constants K_c, K_l, and K_q represent the constant, linear, and quadratic coefficients, respectively. In practice, the constant term is usually set to 1.0. The linear term reduces the intensity in a linear manner, while the quadratic term sets a quadratic decrease of intensity for the light source. It is worth noting that the quadratic term is less significant in comparison to the linear term when the distance is small. However, it gets significantly larger as the distance increases.

3.6.1 Shader Code

For this example, we will use the same vertex shader code as used in the preceding example. However, we will use a different fragment shader. To achieve this, add a new fragment shader file called *point_frag.wgsl* to the *examples/ch03/* folder with the following code:

```
struct LightUniforms {
    lightPosition : vec4f,
    eyePosition : vec4f,
    specularColor : vec4f,
};
@group(1) @binding(0) var<uniform> light : LightUniforms;

struct MaterialUniforms {
    // blinn-phong
    ambient: f32,
    diffuse: f32,
    specular: f32,
    shininess: f32,

    // attenuation for point light
    attConstant: f32,
    attLinear: f32,
    attQuadratic: f32,
}
@group(1) @binding(1) var<uniform> material : MaterialUniforms;

struct Input {
    @location(0) vPosition:vec4f,
    @location(1) vNormal:vec4f,
    @location(2) vColor:vec4f,
}

fn blinnPhong(N:vec3f, L:vec3f, V:vec3f) -> vec2f{
    let H = normalize(L + V);
    var diffuse = material.diffuse * max(dot(N, L), 0.0);
    diffuse += material.diffuse * max(dot(-N, L), 0.0);
```

```
    var specular = material.specular * pow(max(dot(N, H), 0.0), material.shininess);
    specular += material.specular * pow(max(dot(-N, H),0.0), material.shininess);
    return vec2(diffuse, specular);
}

@fragment
fn fs_main(in:Input) -> @location(0) vec4f {
    var N = normalize(in.vNormal.xyz);
    let L = normalize(light.lightPosition.xyz - in.vPosition.xyz);
    let V = normalize(light.eyePosition.xyz - in.vPosition.xyz);

    let distance = length(L);
    let att = 1.0 / (material.attConstant + material.attLinear * distance +
        material.attQuadratic * distance * distance);

    let bp = blinnPhong(N, L, V);

    let finalColor = (in.vColor*(material.ambient + bp[0]) + light.specularColor * bp[1]) * att;
    return vec4<f32>(finalColor.rgb, 1.0);
}
```

This code is similar to that in the *blinn_phong_frag.wgsl* file, with exception that we incorporate the attenuation to the Blinn-Phong light and include it in the lighting calculations. To achieve this, we multiply the attenuation value with the final color:

```
    let distance = length(L);
    let att = 1.0 / (material.attConstant + material.attLinear * distance +
        material.attQuadratic * distance * distance);

    let bp = blinnPhong(N, L, V);

    let finalColor = (in.vColor*(material.ambient + bp[0]) + light.specularColor * bp[1]) * att;
    return vec4<f32>(finalColor.rgb, 1.0);
```

3.6.2 Rust Code

Create a new Rust file called *point_light.rs* in the *examples/ch03/* folder. This code is very similar to the previous example. Here, I only list the different parts.

First, we add two extra fields: *linear_attenuation* and *quadratic_attenuation*, to the *State* struct, which represent the linear and quadratic attenuation parameters for the point light. These two parameters allow you to examine their effect on the light by changing them with the keyboard inputs.

We have also animated the position of the point-light within the *State::update* function, so you can see real-time changes in the lighting effect in the scene, as shown in the following code snippet:

```
    let dt = self.animation_speed * dt.as_secs_f32();
    let sn = 10.0 * (0.5 + dt.sin());
    let cn = 10.0 * (0.5 + dt.cos());
    let cn1 = 10.0 * (1.0 + (2.0 * dt).cos());
    self.init.queue.write_buffer(&self.uniform_buffers[4], 0,
        cast_slice([2.0*sn, 4.0*cn, 8.0*cn1].as_ref()));
```

In the code snippet above, *uniform_buffers*[4] refers to the light uniform buffer.

Additionally, the code permits the user to modify material parameters for lighting computation using keyboard inputs.

Here is a list of controls using keyboard:

- *Q/A*: Increases/decreases the ambient light intensity.
- *W/S:* Increases/decreases the diffuse light intensity.
- *E/D:* Increases/decreases the specular light intensity.
- *R/F:* Increases/decreases the shininess of the specular light.
- *T/G:* Increases/decreases the linear attenuation.
- *Y/H:* Increases/decreases the quadratic attenuation.

3.6.3 Run Application

To run this application, add the following code snippet to the *Cargo.toml* file:

```
[[example]]
name = "ch03_point_light"
path = "examples/ch03/point_light.rs"
```

Afterward, execute the following *cargo run* commands in the terminal window:

```
cargo run --example ch03_point_light 8
```

This will produce objects under point light, as shown in Fig.3-8.

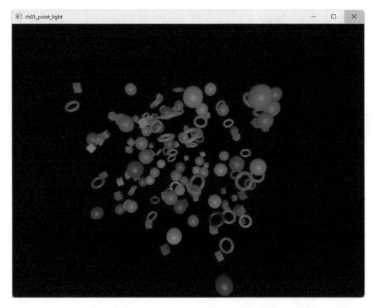

Fig.3-8. 3D objects under point light.

You can see that only the objects in the front are lit, with the closest objects being the brightest. The objects in the back are not lit since they are too far away from the light source. You can change the linear or quadratic terms to examine the attenuation effect on the light brightness.

3.7 Spotlight

A spotlight emits light rays in a cone shape from the apex located at the light source, illuminating only the objects within the cone while leaving everything else in the dark. Examples of spotlights include street lamps and flashlights. Like point lights, spotlights also have attenuation, where the light intensity is highest along the axis of the cone and decreases toward the outside edges, resulting in a realistic spotlight effect.

To represent a spotlight, you need to define its light position, light direction, and a cutoff angle that determines the radius of the spotlight cone. For each fragment, you calculate whether it is inside the cone (using the cutoff angle), and lit it accordingly.

3.7.1 Shader Code

Create a new fragment shader file called *spot_frag.wgsl* in the *examples/ch03/* folder and enter the following code into it:

```
const pi = 3.14159265358979323846;

struct LightUniforms {
    lightPosition : vec4f,
    lightDirection: vec4f,
    eyePosition : vec4f,
    specularColor : vec4f,
}
@group(1) @binding(0) var<uniform> light : LightUniforms;

struct MaterialUniforms {
    // blinn-phong
    ambient: f32,
    diffuse: f32,
    specular: f32,
    shininess: f32,
    // spot light
    attConstant: f32,
    attLinear: f32,
    attQuadratic: f32,
    cutoff: f32,
}
@group(1) @binding(1) var<uniform> material : MaterialUniforms;

struct Input {
    @location(0) vPosition:vec4f,
    @location(1) vNormal:vec4f,
    @location(2) vColor:vec4f,
}

fn blinnPhong(N:vec3f, L:vec3f, V:vec3f) -> vec2f{
    let H = normalize(L + V);
    var diffuse = material.diffuse * max(dot(N, L), 0.0);
    diffuse += material.diffuse * max(dot(-N, L), 0.0);
    var specular = material.specular * pow(max(dot(N, H), 0.0), material.shininess);
    specular += material.specular * pow(max(dot(-N, H),0.0), material.shininess);
    return vec2(diffuse, specular);
}
```

```
@fragment
fn fs_main(in:Input) -> @location(0) vec4f {
    let L = normalize(light.lightPosition.xyz - in.vPosition.xyz);
    let theta = dot(L, normalize(-light.lightDirection.xyz));

    if(theta > cos(material.cutoff *pi/180)){
        var N = normalize(in.vNormal.xyz);
        let V = normalize(light.eyePosition.xyz - in.vPosition.xyz);
        let bp = blinnPhong(N, L, V);

        let distance = length(L);
        let att = 1.0 / (material.attConstant + material.attLinear * distance +
            material.attQuadratic * distance * distance);

        let finalColor = (in.vColor*(material.ambient + bp[0]) + light.specularColor * bp[1]) * att;
        return vec4(finalColor.rgb, 1.0);
    } else {
        let finalColor = in.vColor*(material.ambient);
        return vec4<f32>(finalColor.rgb, 1.0);
    }
}
```

Here, we calculate the angle between the light direction and the direction from the spotlight to the fragment. We then compare the angle value with the cutoff angle of the spotlight. If the angle is less than the cutoff, the fragment is considered inside the spotlight cone and is lit accordingly. Otherwise, the fragment is outside of the cone and only receives the ambient light. The code for calculating the attenuation for the spotlight is similar to that used for the point-light in the preceding example.

3.7.2 Rust Code

Add a new Rust file called *spot_light.rs* to the *examples/ch03/* folder. This code is very similar to the previous example. Here, I only list the different parts.

First, this example renders a total of 300 objects, including 100 instances of cubes, spheres, and tori. In addition to the linear and quadratic attenuation parameters, we have added the *cutoff* angle to the *State* struct, allowing you to explore their effect on the light by changing the parameters with the keyboard inputs. We also animate the position of the spotlight source in the *State::update* function, allowing you to see real-time changes in the lighting effect within the scene.

Additionally, the code permits the user to modify material parameters for lighting computation using keyboard inputs.

Here is a list of controls using keyboard:

- *Q/A:* Increases/decreases the ambient light intensity.
- *W/S:* Increases/decreases the diffuse light intensity.
- *E/D:* Increases/decreases the specular light intensity.
- *R/F:* Increases/decreases the shininess of the specular light.
- *T/G:* Increases/decreases the linear attenuation.
- *Y/H:* Increases/decreases the quadratic attenuation.
- *U/J:* Increases/decreases the cutoff angle.

3.7.3 Run Application

To run this application, add the following code snippet to the *Cargo.toml* file:

```
[[example]]
name = "ch03_spot_light"
path = "examples/ch03/spot_light.rs"
```

Afterward, execute the following *cargo run* commands in the terminal window:

```
cargo run --example ch03_spot_light 8
```

This will produce objects under spotlight, as shown in Fig.3-9.

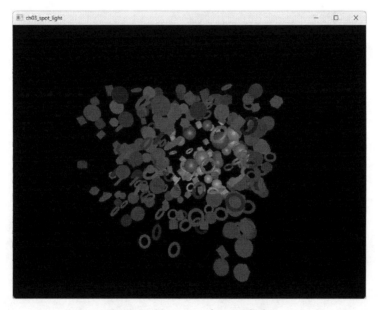

Fig.3-9. Objects under spotlight.

As you can see, only the objects within the cone of the spotlight are illuminated, while the objects outside the cone receive only weak ambient light.

3.8 Soft Edge Spotlight

In the previous section, we discussed a spotlight that illuminates objects inside a cone shape. However, this spotlight has a hard edge that abruptly cuts off the light beyond the cone. To create a more realistic spotlight with a smooth attenuation around the edge, we can use a two-cone approach.

The inner cone is the same as the one used in the previous example. For the outer cone, we gradually dim the light from the inner cone to the edge of the outer cone. This way, the light attenuates smoothly instead of shutting down completely at the cone edge.

3.8.1 Shader Code

create a new fragment shader file called *soft_spot_frag.wgsl* in the *examples/ch03/* folder and enter the following code into it:

```
const pi = 3.14159265358979323846;

struct LightUniforms {
    lightPosition : vec4f,
    lightDirection: vec4f,
    eyePosition : vec4f,
    specularColor : vec4f,
}
@group(1) @binding(0) var<uniform> light : LightUniforms;

struct MaterialUniforms {
    // blinn-phong
    ambient: f32,
    diffuse: f32,
    specular: f32,
    shininess: f32,
    // spot light
    attConstant: f32,
    attLinear: f32,
    attQuadratic: f32,
    cutoff: f32,
    outerCutoff: f32,
};
@group(1) @binding(1) var<uniform> material : MaterialUniforms;

struct Input {
    @location(0) vPosition:vec4f,
    @location(1) vNormal:vec4f,
    @location(2) vColor:vec4f,
}

fn blinnPhong(N:vec3f, L:vec3f, V:vec3f) -> vec2f{
    let H = normalize(L + V);
    var diffuse = material.diffuse * max(dot(N, L), 0.0);
    diffuse += material.diffuse * max(dot(-N, L), 0.0);
    var specular = material.specular * pow(max(dot(N, H), 0.0), material.shininess);
    specular += material.specular * pow(max(dot(-N, H),0.0), material.shininess);
    return vec2(diffuse, specular);
}

@fragment
fn fs_main(in:Input) -> @location(0) vec4f {
    let L = normalize(light.lightPosition.xyz - in.vPosition.xyz);
    var N = normalize(in.vNormal.xyz);
    let V = normalize(light.eyePosition.xyz - in.vPosition.xyz);
    var bp = blinnPhong(N, L, V);

    // soft-edge spot light
    var cutoff = material.cutoff * pi/180;
    let outerCutoff = material.outerCutoff*pi/180;
    let theta = dot(L, normalize(-light.lightDirection.xyz));
    if(cutoff > outerCutoff){
        cutoff = outerCutoff;
    }
    let epsilon = cos(cutoff) - cos(outerCutoff);
```

```
let spotIntensity = clamp((theta - cos(outerCutoff)) / epsilon, 0.0, 1.0);
bp[0] *= spotIntensity;
bp[1] *= spotIntensity;

let distance = length(L);
let att = 1.0 / (material.attConstant + material.attLinear * distance +
    material.attQuadratic * distance * distance);

let finalColor = (in.vColor*(material.ambient + bp[0]) + light.specularColor * bp[1]) * att;
return vec4(finalColor.rgb, 1.0);
}
```

Here, we calculate the spotlight intensity use the formula:

```
let epsilon = cos(cutoff) - cos(outerCutoff);
let spotIntensity = clamp((theta - cos(outerCutoff)) / epsilon, 0.0, 1.0);
```

This indicates that if a fragment is between the inner and the outer cones, we calculate the intensity value between 0 and 1 using the formula (theta - cos(outerCutoff)) / epsilon, where epsilon is the cosine difference between the inner and outer cones. The resulting value represents the intensity of the spotlight at the current fragment. The *clamp* function is used here to ensure that the intensity value is always in the range of [0, 1].

3.8.2 Rust Code

Add a new Rust file called *soft_spot_light.rs* to the *examples/ch03/* folder. This code is very similar to the previous example. Here, I only list the different parts.

First, in addition to the inner *cutoff* angle, we add an extra field named *outer_cutoff* to the *State* struct, which allows the user to change the inner and outer cutoff angles of the spotlight cone using the keyboard inputs. This provides flexibility to customize the spotlight to meet specific requirements. The position of the spotlight source is also animated in real-time within the *State::update* function, enabling the user to observe changes in the lighting effect.

Additionally, the code permits the user to modify material parameters for lighting computation using keyboard inputs.

Here is a list of controls using keyboard:

- *Q/A:* Increases/decreases the ambient light intensity.
- *W/S:* Increases/decreases the diffuse light intensity.
- *E/D:* Increases/decreases the specular light intensity.
- *R/F:* Increases/decreases the shininess of the specular light.
- *T/G:* Increases/decreases the linear attenuation.
- *Y/H:* Increases/decreases the quadratic attenuation.
- *U/J:* Increases/decreases the inner cutoff angle.
- *I/K:* Increases/decreases the outer cutoff angle.

3.8.3 Run Application

To run this application, add the following code snippet to the *Cargo.toml* file:

```
[[example]]
name = "ch03_soft_spot_light"
path = "examples/ch03/soft_spot_light.rs"
```

Afterward, execute the following *cargo run* commands in the terminal window:

```
cargo run --example ch03_soft_spot_light 8
```

Fig.3-10 illustrates the output of this example project, demonstrating that the spotlight with a soft edge appears more natural and realistic.

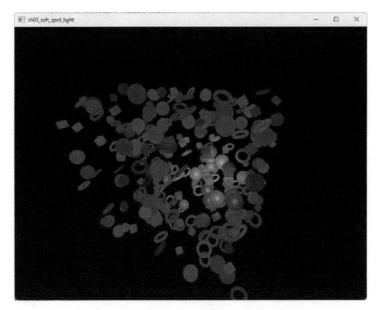

Fig.3-10. Objects under spotlight with soft edge.

3.9 Fog Effect

We can simulate a fog effect by blending the color of each fragment with a constant fog color, which can be specified by the user. The intensity of the fog is based on distance between the camera and the fragment, and can be controlled using a function that describes the relationship between the distance and the amount of fog color. Typically, functions like linear or exponential can be used to achieve this effect. In this example, we use a simple linear function, which can be expressed as follows:

$$\alpha = 1 - \frac{F_{max} - d}{F_{max} - F_{min}}$$

Where F_{min} and F_{max} are the minimum and maximum distances, respectively, within which the fog effect is applied. Beyond the minimum distance, the fragment will be completely visible, while beyond the maximum distance, the fragment will not be visible at all. The value of α represents the fog coefficient, with a value of 1 indicating 100% fog, and a value of 0 indicating no fog.

3.9.1 Shader Code

Add a new fragment shader file called *fog_frag.wgsl* to the *examples/ch03/* folder with the following code:

```
struct LightUniforms {
    lightPosition: vec4f,
    eyePosition: vec4f,
    specularColor: vec4f,
    fogColor: vec4f,
}
@group(1) @binding(0) var<uniform> light : LightUniforms;

struct MaterialUniforms {
    // blinn-phong
    ambient: f32,
    diffuse: f32,
    specular: f32,
    shininess: f32,
    // fog
    minDist: f32,
    maxDist: f32,
}
@group(1) @binding(1) var<uniform> material : MaterialUniforms;

struct Input {
    @location(0) vPosition:vec4f,
    @location(1) vNormal:vec4f,
    @location(2) vColor: vec4f,
}

fn blinnPhong(N:vec3f, L:vec3f, V:vec3f) -> vec2f {
    let H = normalize(L + V);
    var diffuse = material.diffuse * max(dot(N, L), 0.0);
    diffuse += material.diffuse * max(dot(-N, L), 0.0);
    var specular = material.specular * pow(max(dot(N, H), 0.0), material.shininess);
    specular += material.specular * pow(max(dot(-N, H),0.0), material.shininess);
    return vec2(diffuse, specular);
}

@fragment
fn fs_main(in:Input) -> @location(0) vec4f {
    var N = normalize(in.vNormal.xyz);
    let L = normalize(light.lightPosition.xyz - in.vPosition.xyz);
    let V = normalize(light.eyePosition.xyz - in.vPosition.xyz);
    let z = abs(in.vPosition.z);
    var alpha = 1 - (material.maxDist - z)/(material.maxDist - material.minDist);
    alpha = clamp(alpha, 0.0, 1.0);

    let bp = blinnPhong(N, L, V);

    let shaderColor = in.vColor*(material.ambient + bp[0]) + light.specularColor * bp[1];
    let finalColor = mix(shaderColor.rgb, light.fogColor.rgb, alpha);
    return vec4(finalColor, 1.0);
}
```

In this shader, we use the *z* coordinate to represent the distance between the eye position and the fragment point. Then, we calculate the fog coefficient with the linear equation. Since the *z* distance may not fall between `material.minDist` and `material.maxDist`, we clamp the coefficient to be in the range of 0 and 1.

Afterward, we call the *blinnPhong* function to evaluate the reflection model and use the result to obtain the shader color. Finally, we blend the shader color and the frag color together based on the fog coefficient, and the result is returned as the fragment color.

3.9.2 Rust Code

Create a new Rust file called *fog_effect.rs* in the *examples/ch03/* folder. This code is very similar to the previous examples. Here, I only list the different parts.

First, we add the fog parameters *min_dist* and *max_dist* to the *State* struct, allowing you to adjust them using the keyboard inputs. You can experiment with these parameters to observe the fog effect. Additionally, the position of the light source is animated within the *State::update* function to provide real-time changes in the lighting effect.

Additionally, the code permits the user to modify material parameters for lighting computation using keyboard inputs.

Here is a list of controls using keyboard:

- *Q/A*: Increases/decreases the ambient light intensity.
- *W/S:* Increases/decreases the diffuse light intensity.
- *E/D:* Increases/decreases the specular light intensity.
- *R/F:* Increases/decreases the shininess of the specular light.
- *T/G:* Increases/decreases the *min_dist* parameter.
- *Y/H:* Increases/decreases the *max_dist* parameter.

3.9.3 Run Application

To run this application, add the following code snippet to the *Cargo.toml* file:

```
[[example]]
name = "ch03_fog_effect"
path = "examples/ch03/fog_effect.rs"
```

Afterward, execute the following *cargo run* commands in the terminal window:

```
cargo run --example ch03_fog_effect 8
```

Fig.3-11 shows the output of this example project. You can change the *min_dist* and *max_dist* parameters using keyboard inputs to examine their effect on the fog.

Fig.3-11. Simulate the fog effect.

4 Advanced Lighting

The preceding chapter introduced Blinn-Phong based lighting models for basic 3D graphics object lighting. The Blinn-Phong model is widely used in real-time rendering applications, but it has limitations in accurately rendering complex materials as it does not consider physical properties like energy conservation, reflectivity, and roughness.

This chapter aims to improve the Blinn-Phong lighting effect by adding shadows and using physically based rendering (PBR). Shadows create depth and realism in a scene, while PBR provides more accurate and consistent results when rendering complex materials by considering physical properties like energy conservation. PBR is preferred for high-end applications like video games, film, and product visualization that require realistic rendering.

4.1 Shadow Mapping

Shadows occur when objects block the path of light rays from a light source, resulting in areas of reduced or absent light. This phenomenon, known as occlusion, creates the impression of depth and enhances the realism of a lit scene. Shadows provide a way for viewers to perceive the spatial relationships between objects and enhance the overall sense of depth in the scene.

Shadows are not straightforward to implement in real-time graphics due to the absence of a perfect shadow algorithm. While there are several good shadow approximation techniques available, they have their unique quirks and limitations that need to be considered.

This section discusses using the shadow mapping technique to add shadows to a scene. This approach is commonly used in video games, as it provides satisfactory results and is relatively easy to implement. Moreover, it does not impose a significant performance cost and can be extended to more advanced algorithms without much difficulty.

The basic shadow mapping algorithm consists of two passes. First, the scene is rendered from the point of view of the light, with only the depth of each fragment computed. Next, the scene is rendered as usual, but with an extra test to determine whether the current fragment is in shadow. The test for being in shadow is actually quite simple. If the current sample is further from the light than the corresponding point in the shadow map, it means that the scene contains an object that is closer to the light, and the current fragment is therefore in shadow.

In this example, we only consider a Blinn-Phong lighting model and use an orthographic projection to render the shadow map.

4.1.1 Shader Code

The first pass requires us to generate a depth map for the shadow. The shader used during this pass is very simple – it only includes a vertex shader that transforms the vertices to light space, and does not require a fragment shader since there is no color needed for the shadow. Create a new vertex shader file named *shadow_depth.wgsl* in the *examples/ch04/* folder and include the following code:

```
@group(0) @binding(0) var<storage> modelMat: array<mat4x4f>;
@group(0) @binding(1) var<uniform> lightProjectMat: mat4x4f;

struct Input {
    @builtin(instance_index) idx : u32,
    @location(0) position : vec4f,
    @location(1) normal: vec4f,
};

@vertex
fn vs_main(in:Input) -> @builtin(position) vec4f {
    let mPosition = modelMat[in.idx] * in.position;
    return lightProjectMat * mPosition;
}
```

The main task of this vertex shader is to calculate the positions of vertices and then convert them into light space using a light projection matrix. It should be noted that the *modelMat* is a 4x4 matrix array that is used for generating multiple instances.

We now need to implement the Blinn-Phong model with a shadow test in the usual shader. We need to test whether each computed fragment is behind the shadow map or not. As before, we will separate this shader into two parts, the vertex shader and fragment shader.

Create a new vertex shader file named *shadow_vert.wgsl* in the *examples/ch04/* folder and enter the following code into it:

```
// vertex shader
@group(0) @binding(0) var<uniform> viewProjectMat: mat4x4f;
@group(0) @binding(1) var<storage> modelMat: array<mat4x4f>;
@group(0) @binding(2) var<storage> normalMat: array<mat4x4f>;
@group(0) @binding(3) var<uniform> lightProjectMat: mat4x4f;
@group(0) @binding(4) var<storage> colorVec: array<vec4f>;

struct Input {
    @builtin(instance_index) idx : u32,
    @location(0) position : vec4f,
    @location(1) normal : vec4f,
};

struct Output {
    @builtin(position) position: vec4f,
    @location(0) vPosition: vec4f,
    @location(1) vNormal: vec4f,
    @location(2) vShadowPos: vec4f,
    @location(3) vColor: vec4f,
};

@vertex
fn vs_main(in:Input) -> Output {
    var output: Output;
    let modelMat = modelMat[in.idx];
    let normalMat = normalMat[in.idx];
```

```
    let mPosition = modelMat * in.position;
    output.vPosition = mPosition;
    output.vNormal = normalMat * in.normal;
    output.position = viewProjectMat * mPosition;
    output.vColor = colorVec[in.idx];

    let lightPosition = lightProjectMat * mPosition;
    output.vShadowPos = vec4(lightPosition.xy*vec2(0.5, -0.5) + vec2(0.5, 0.5), lightPosition.z, 1.0);

    return output;
}
```

The shader code here is very similar to the code in the *shader-instance-vert.wgsl* file in the *examples/ch03/* folder, which was used to create multiple instances with lighting effects in the previous chapter. The difference is that we now pass an extra uniform buffer, *lightProjectMat*, to this shader. Furthermore, the *vs_main* function returns an additional shadow position named *vShadowPos*. Here, we use the same light projection matrix as in the previous depth map shader to transform the positions of vertices in world space to light space, which will be used in the fragment shader.

It is worth noting that in the *vs_main* function, we cannot use *lightPosition* directly as the shadow position because its *x* and *y* components are defined in the range of [-1, 1] and *z*-component is in the range of [0, 1], while shadow texture sampling must be done in the range of [0, 1]. To address this issue, we perform a coordinate transformation on *lightPosition* to obtain the shadow position using the following code snippet:

```
    output.vShadowPos = vec4(lightPosition.xy*vec2(0.5, -0.5) + vec2(0.5, 0.5), lightPosition.z, 1.0);
```

During the transformation, it can be observed that the *z*-component remains unchanged, while the *y*-component is inverted, in accordance with the y-down convention for texture coordinates.

Next, add a new fragment shader file named *shadow-frag.wgsl* to the *examples/ch04/* folder and include the following code:

```
struct LightUniforms {
    lightPosition: vec4f,
    eyePosition: vec4f,
    specularColor: vec4f,
};
@group(1) @binding(0) var<uniform> light : LightUniforms;

struct MaterialUniforms {
    ambient: f32,
    diffuse: f32,
    specular: f32,
    shininess: f32,
};
@group(1) @binding(1) var<uniform> material : MaterialUniforms;
@group(1) @binding(2) var shadowTexture: texture_depth_2d;
@group(1) @binding(3) var shadowSampler: sampler_comparison;

struct Input {
    @location(0) vPosition: vec4f,
    @location(1) vNormal: vec4f,
    @location(2) vShadowPos: vec4f,
    @location(3) vColor: vec4f,
};

fn blinnPhong(N:vec3f, L:vec3f, V:vec3f) -> vec2f {
```

```
    let H = normalize(L + V);
    var diffuse = material.diffuse * max(dot(N, L), 0.0);
    diffuse += material.diffuse * max(dot(-N, L), 0.0);
    var specular = material.specular * pow(max(dot(N, H), 0.0), material.shininess);
    specular += material.specular * pow(max(dot(-N, H),0.0), material.shininess);
    return vec2(diffuse, specular);
}

@fragment
fn fs_main(in:Input) ->  @location(0) vec4f {
    var N = normalize(in.vNormal.xyz);
    let L = normalize(light.lightPosition.xyz - in.vPosition.xyz);
    let V = normalize(light.eyePosition.xyz - in.vPosition.xyz);

    let bp = blinnPhong(N, L, V);

    var visibility = 0.0;
    let size = f32(textureDimensions(shadowTexture).x);
    let oneOverSize = 1.0/size;
    for (var y: i32 = -1 ; y <= 1 ; y = y + 1) {
        for (var x: i32 = -1 ; x <= 1 ; x = x + 1) {
            let offset = vec2(f32(x)*oneOverSize, f32(y)*oneOverSize);
            visibility += textureSampleCompare(
                shadowTexture,
                shadowSampler,
                in.vShadowPos.xy + offset,
                in.vShadowPos.z - 0.007
            );
        }
    }
    visibility /= 0.9;
    let finalColor = in.vColor * (material.ambient + visibility * bp[0]) + light.specularColor * bp[1];
    return vec4(finalColor.rgb, 1.0);
}
```

The fragment shader code here is very similar to that in the *blinn-phong-frag.wgsl* file located in the *examples/ch03/* folder, which implements a standard Blinn-Phong lighting model. However, in this example, we add shadow calculation. To do this, we pass the shadow depth texture and its sampler to the shader. It is worth noting that the shadows obtained from shadow mapping can have a lot of aliasing. To reduce aliasing, we use the percentage closer filtering (PCF) technique in the *fs_main* function. The concept of PCF is to sample from the shadow map around the current pixel and compare its depth to all the samples. By averaging out the results, we obtain a smoother transition between light and shadow. From the PCF calculation, we obtain an average *visibility* value, which we use to multiply the resulting diffuse and specular components from the Blinn-Phong model. Since shadows are rarely completely dark due to light scattering, we leave the ambient component out of the *visibility* multiplications.

4.1.2 Rust Code

Include a new function named *create_shadow_texture_view* in the *wgpu_simplified.rs* file in the *src/* folder with the following code:

```
pub fn create_shadow_texture_view(init: &IWgpuInit, width:u32, height:u32) -> wgpu::TextureView {
    let shadow_depth_texture = init.device.create_texture(&wgpu::TextureDescriptor {
        size: wgpu::Extent3d {
            width,
            height,
            depth_or_array_layers: 1,
```

```
        },
        mip_level_count: 1,
        sample_count: init.sample_count,
        dimension: wgpu::TextureDimension::D2,
        format:wgpu::TextureFormat::Depth24Plus,
        usage: wgpu::TextureUsages::RENDER_ATTACHMENT | wgpu::TextureUsages::TEXTURE_BINDING,
        label: None,
        view_formats: &[],
    });

    shadow_depth_texture.create_view(&wgpu::TextureViewDescriptor::default())
}
```

Typically, the size of the depth texture used for conventional object rendering should match the size of the *winit* window. However, this method allows you to set the size of the shadow depth texture independently using the width and height input arguments, since the depth texture is used only for generating shadows.

Now, create a new Rust file named *shadow.rs* in the *examples/ch04/* folder and enter the following code into it:

```
use std:: {iter, mem};
use cgmath::{ Matrix4, SquareMatrix, Matrix };
use wgpu::VertexBufferLayout;
use winit::{
    event::*,
    event_loop::{ControlFlow, EventLoop},
    window::Window,
};
use bytemuck::cast_slice;
use wgpu_book_examples::{ wgpu_simplified as ws, transforms as wt };
use rand::Rng;
#[path="../ch03/common_instance.rs"]
mod common_instance;

const ANIMATION_SPEED:f32 = 1.0;

#[derive(Debug)]
struct Scene {
    translation: [f32;3],
    rotation: [f32;3],
    scale: [f32;3],
    v: f32
}

fn create_transform_mat() -> (Vec<Scene>, Vec<[f32; 16]>, Vec<[f32; 16]>, Vec<[f32; 4]>) {
    let mut scenes:Vec<Scene> = vec![];
    let mut model_mat:Vec<[f32; 16]> = vec![];
    let mut normal_mat:Vec<[f32; 16]> = vec![];
    let mut color_vec:Vec<[f32; 4]> = vec![];

    let mut rng = rand::thread_rng();

    // add a cube as  floor
    let translation_cube = [0.0f32, -13.0, -20.0];
    let rotation_cube = [0.0f32, 0.0, 0.0];
    let scale_cube = [30.0f32, 0.1, 20.0];
    let m_cube = wt::create_model_mat(translation_cube, rotation_cube, scale_cube);
    let n_cube = (m_cube.invert().unwrap()).transpose();
    let c_cube = [0.5f32, 0.5, 0.7, 1.0];
```

```rust
        model_mat.push(*(m_cube.as_ref()));
        normal_mat.push(*(n_cube.as_ref()));
        color_vec.push(c_cube);
        scenes.push(Scene{
            translation: translation_cube,
            rotation: rotation_cube,
            scale: scale_cube,
            v: 0.0,
        });

        // add a torus
        let translation_torus = [0.0f32, -4.7, -20.0];
        let rotation_torus = [1.57f32, 0.0, 0.0];
        let scale_torus = [4.0f32, 4.0, 4.0];
        let m_torus = wt::create_model_mat(translation_torus, rotation_torus, scale_torus);
        let n_torus = (m_torus.invert().unwrap()).transpose();
        let c_torus = [rng.gen::<f32>(), rng.gen::<f32>(), rng.gen::<f32>(), 1.0];
        model_mat.push(*(m_torus.as_ref()));
        normal_mat.push(*(n_torus.as_ref()));
        color_vec.push(c_torus);
        scenes.push(Scene{
            translation: translation_torus,
            rotation: rotation_torus,
            scale: scale_torus,
            v: 0.0,
        });

        // add spheres
        for _i in 2..20 {
            let mut v1 = -1.0f32;
            if rng.gen::<f32>() > 0.5 {
                v1 = 1.0;
            }
            let tx = v1 * (4.0 + rng.gen::<f32>() * 12.0);
            let translation_sphere = [tx, -11.0 + rng.gen::<f32>() * 15.0, -20.0 + tx];
            let rotation_sphere = [rng.gen::<f32>(), rng.gen::<f32>(), rng.gen::<f32>()];
            let s = [0.5f32, rng.gen::<f32>()].iter().fold(f32::NEG_INFINITY, |a, &b| a.max(b));
            let scale_sphere = [s, s, s];
            let m_sphere = wt::create_model_mat(translation_sphere, rotation_sphere, scale_sphere);
            let n_sphere = (m_torus.invert().unwrap()).transpose();
            let c_sphere = [rng.gen::<f32>(), rng.gen::<f32>(), rng.gen::<f32>(), 1.0];
            model_mat.push(*(m_sphere.as_ref()));
            normal_mat.push(*(n_sphere.as_ref()));
            color_vec.push(c_sphere);
            let v = v1 * [0.09, rng.gen::<f32>()/10.0].iter().fold(f32::NEG_INFINITY, |a, &b| a.max(b));
            scenes.push(Scene{
                translation: translation_sphere,
                rotation: rotation_sphere,
                scale: scale_sphere,
                v,
            });
        }

        (scenes, model_mat, normal_mat, color_vec)
}


struct State {
    init:  ws::IWgpuInit,
    pipelines: Vec<wgpu::RenderPipeline>,
```

```rust
    vertex_buffers: Vec<wgpu::Buffer>,
    index_buffers: Vec<wgpu::Buffer>,
    uniform_bind_groups: Vec<wgpu::BindGroup>,
    uniform_buffers: Vec<wgpu::Buffer>,
    view_mat: Matrix4<f32>,
    project_mat: Matrix4<f32>,
    depth_texture_views: Vec<wgpu::TextureView>,
    indices_lens: Vec<u32>,

    light_position: [f32; 3],
    scenes: (Vec<Scene>, Vec<[f32; 16]>, Vec<[f32; 16]>, Vec<[f32; 4]>),

    ambient: f32,
    diffuse: f32,
    specular: f32,
    shininess: f32,
}

impl State {
    async fn new(window: &Window) -> Self {
        let init = ws::IWgpuInit::new(&window, 1, None).await;

        let vs_shader = init.device.create_shader_module(wgpu::include_wgsl!("shadow_vert.wgsl"));
        let fs_shader = init.device.create_shader_module(wgpu::include_wgsl!("shadow_frag.wgsl"));
        let depth_shader = init.device.create_shader_module(wgpu::include_wgsl!("shadow_depth.wgsl"));

        // uniform data
        let camera_position = (0.0, 10.0, 20.0).into();
        let look_direction = (0.0, 0.0, 0.0).into();
        let up_direction = cgmath::Vector3::unit_y();
        let (view_mat, project_mat, vp_mat) =
            wt::create_vp_mat(camera_position, look_direction, up_direction,
            init.config.width as f32 / init.config.height as f32);

        // create uniform view-projection buffers
        let vp_uniform_buffer = init.device.create_buffer(&wgpu::BufferDescriptor{
            label: Some("View-Projection Buffer"),
            size: 64,
            usage: wgpu::BufferUsages::UNIFORM | wgpu::BufferUsages::COPY_DST,
            mapped_at_creation: false,
        });
        init.queue.write_buffer(&vp_uniform_buffer, 0, cast_slice(vp_mat.as_ref() as &[f32; 16]));

        // model storage buffer
        let objects_count = 20;
        let model_uniform_buffer = init.device.create_buffer(&wgpu::BufferDescriptor{
            label: Some("Model Uniform Buffer"),
            size: 64 * objects_count as u64,
            usage: wgpu::BufferUsages::STORAGE | wgpu::BufferUsages::COPY_DST,
            mapped_at_creation: false,
        });

        // normal storage buffer
        let normal_uniform_buffer = init.device.create_buffer(&wgpu::BufferDescriptor{
            label: Some("Normal Uniform Buffer"),
            size: 64 * objects_count as u64,
            usage: wgpu::BufferUsages::STORAGE | wgpu::BufferUsages::COPY_DST,
            mapped_at_creation: false,
        });
```

```rust
// color storage buffer
let color_uniform_buffer = init.device.create_buffer(&wgpu::BufferDescriptor{
    label: Some("color Uniform Buffer"),
    size: 16 * objects_count as u64,
    usage: wgpu::BufferUsages::STORAGE | wgpu::BufferUsages::COPY_DST,
    mapped_at_creation: false,
});

// uniform buffer for  light projection
let light_projection_uniform_buffer = init.device.create_buffer(&wgpu::BufferDescriptor{
    label: Some("Light Projection Uniform Buffer"),
    size: 64,
    usage: wgpu::BufferUsages::UNIFORM | wgpu::BufferUsages::COPY_DST,
    mapped_at_creation: false,
});

// light uniform buffer.
let light_uniform_buffer = init.device.create_buffer(&wgpu::BufferDescriptor{
    label: Some("Light Uniform Buffer"),
    size: 48,
    usage: wgpu::BufferUsages::UNIFORM | wgpu::BufferUsages::COPY_DST,
    mapped_at_creation: false,
});
init.queue.write_buffer(&light_uniform_buffer, 16,
    cast_slice(camera_position.as_ref() as &[f32; 3]));
// set specular light color to white
let specular_color:[f32; 3] = [1.0, 1.0, 1.0];
init.queue.write_buffer(&light_uniform_buffer, 32, cast_slice(specular_color.as_ref()));

// material uniform buffer
let material_uniform_buffer = init.device.create_buffer(&wgpu::BufferDescriptor{
    label: Some("Material Uniform Buffer"),
    size: 16,
    usage: wgpu::BufferUsages::UNIFORM | wgpu::BufferUsages::COPY_DST,
    mapped_at_creation: false,
});

// set default material parameters
let material = [0.4 as f32, 0.04, 0.4, 30.0];
init.queue.write_buffer(&material_uniform_buffer, 0, cast_slice(material.as_ref()));

// uniform bind group for vertex shader
let (vert_bind_group_layout, vert_bind_group) = ws::create_bind_group_storage(
    &init.device,
    vec![
        wgpu::ShaderStages::VERTEX, wgpu::ShaderStages::VERTEX,
        wgpu::ShaderStages::VERTEX, wgpu::ShaderStages::VERTEX,
        wgpu::ShaderStages::VERTEX
    ],
    vec![
        wgpu::BufferBindingType::Uniform,
        wgpu::BufferBindingType::Storage { read_only: true },
        wgpu::BufferBindingType::Storage { read_only: true },
        wgpu::BufferBindingType::Uniform,
        wgpu::BufferBindingType::Storage { read_only: true },
    ],
    &[
        vp_uniform_buffer.as_entire_binding(),
        model_uniform_buffer.as_entire_binding(),
        normal_uniform_buffer.as_entire_binding(),
```

```
            light_projection_uniform_buffer.as_entire_binding(),
            color_uniform_buffer.as_entire_binding()
        ],
    );

    // uniform bind group for shadow
    let (shadow_bind_group_layout, shadow_bind_group) = ws::create_bind_group_storage(
        &init.device,
        vec![
            wgpu::ShaderStages::VERTEX, wgpu::ShaderStages::VERTEX,
        ],
        vec![
            wgpu::BufferBindingType::Storage { read_only: true },
            wgpu::BufferBindingType::Uniform,
        ],
        &[
            model_uniform_buffer.as_entire_binding(),
            light_projection_uniform_buffer.as_entire_binding(),
        ],
    );

    // uniform bind group for fragment shader
    let (frag_bind_group_layout, frag_bind_group) = ws::create_bind_group(
        &init.device,
        vec![wgpu::ShaderStages::FRAGMENT, wgpu::ShaderStages::FRAGMENT],
        &[light_uniform_buffer.as_entire_binding(), material_uniform_buffer.as_entire_binding()],
    );
    // shadow texturebind group for fragment shader
    let shadow_depth_texture_view = ws::create_shadow_texture_view(&init, 2048, 2048);
    let shadow_depth_sampler = init.device.create_sampler(&wgpu::SamplerDescriptor {
        label: Some("Shadow Sampler"),
        compare: Some(wgpu::CompareFunction::Less),
        ..Default::default()
    });
    let frag_bind_group_layout2 = init.device.create_bind_group_layout(
    &wgpu::BindGroupLayoutDescriptor{
        entries: &[
            wgpu::BindGroupLayoutEntry {
                binding: 0,
                visibility: wgpu::ShaderStages::FRAGMENT,
                ty: wgpu::BindingType::Texture {
                    multisampled: false,
                    view_dimension: wgpu::TextureViewDimension::D2,
                    sample_type: wgpu::TextureSampleType::Depth,
                },
                count: None,
            },
            wgpu::BindGroupLayoutEntry {
                binding: 1,
                visibility: wgpu::ShaderStages::FRAGMENT,
                ty: wgpu::BindingType::Sampler(wgpu::SamplerBindingType::Comparison),
                count: None,
            },
        ],
        label: Some("Fragment Bind Group Layout 2"),
    });

    let frag_bind_group2 = init.device.create_bind_group(
        &wgpu::BindGroupDescriptor {
            layout: &frag_bind_group_layout2,
```

```
            entries: &[
                wgpu::BindGroupEntry {
                    binding: 0,
                    resource: wgpu::BindingResource::TextureView(&shadow_depth_texture_view),
                },
                wgpu::BindGroupEntry {
                    binding: 1,
                    resource: wgpu::BindingResource::Sampler(&shadow_depth_sampler),
                }
            ],
            label: Some("Fragment Bind  Group 2"),
        }
    );

    let vertex_buffer_layout = VertexBufferLayout {
        array_stride: mem::size_of::<common_instance::Vertex>() as wgpu::BufferAddress,
        step_mode: wgpu::VertexStepMode::Vertex,
        attributes: &wgpu::vertex_attr_array![0 => Float32x3, 1 => Float32x3],
    };

    let pipeline_layout = init.device.create_pipeline_layout(&wgpu::PipelineLayoutDescriptor {
        label: Some("Render Pipeline Layout"),
        bind_group_layouts: &[&vert_bind_group_layout, &frag_bind_group_layout,
            &frag_bind_group_layout2],
        push_constant_ranges: &[],
    });

    let mut ppl = ws::IRenderPipeline {
        vs_shader: Some(&vs_shader),
        fs_shader: Some(&fs_shader),
        pipeline_layout: Some(&pipeline_layout),
        vertex_buffer_layout: &[vertex_buffer_layout],
        ..Default::default()
    };
    let pipeline = ppl.new(&init);

    // pipeline for shadow
    let vertex_buffer_layout2 = VertexBufferLayout {
        array_stride: mem::size_of::<common_instance::Vertex>() as wgpu::BufferAddress,
        step_mode: wgpu::VertexStepMode::Vertex,
        attributes: &wgpu::vertex_attr_array![0 => Float32x3, 1 => Float32x3],
    };

    let pipeline_layout2 = init.device.create_pipeline_layout(&wgpu::PipelineLayoutDescriptor {
        label: Some("Render Pipeline Layout 2"),
        bind_group_layouts: &[&shadow_bind_group_layout],
        push_constant_ranges: &[],
    });

    let pipeline2 = init.device.create_render_pipeline(&wgpu::RenderPipelineDescriptor {
        label: Some("Render Pipeline 2"),
        layout: Some(&pipeline_layout2),
        vertex: wgpu::VertexState {
            module: &depth_shader,
            entry_point: "vs_main",
            buffers: &[vertex_buffer_layout2],
        },
        fragment: None,
        primitive: wgpu::PrimitiveState {
            topology: wgpu::PrimitiveTopology::TriangleList,
```

```
                ..Default::default()
            },
            depth_stencil: Some(wgpu::DepthStencilState {
                format: wgpu::TextureFormat::Depth24Plus,
                depth_write_enabled: true,
                depth_compare: wgpu::CompareFunction::LessEqual,
                stencil: wgpu::StencilState::default(),
                bias: wgpu::DepthBiasState::default(),
            }),
            multisample: wgpu::MultisampleState::default(),
            multiview: None,
        });

        let depth_texture_view = ws::create_depth_view(&init);

        // vertex and index buffers for objects:
        let (vertex_buffers, index_buffers, index_lens) =
            common_instance::create_object_buffers(&init.device);
        let (scenes, model_mat, normal_mat, color_vec) = create_transform_mat();
        init.queue.write_buffer(&color_uniform_buffer, 0, cast_slice(color_vec.as_ref()));

        Self {
            init,
            pipelines: vec![pipeline, pipeline2],
            vertex_buffers,
            index_buffers,
            uniform_bind_groups: vec![vert_bind_group, frag_bind_group, frag_bind_group2,
                shadow_bind_group],
            uniform_buffers: vec![
                vp_uniform_buffer,
                model_uniform_buffer,
                normal_uniform_buffer,
                light_projection_uniform_buffer,
                color_uniform_buffer,
                light_uniform_buffer,
                material_uniform_buffer
            ],
            view_mat,
            project_mat,
            depth_texture_views: vec![depth_texture_view, shadow_depth_texture_view],
            indices_lens: index_lens,

            light_position: [0.0, 100.0, 0.0],
            scenes: (scenes, model_mat, normal_mat, color_vec),

            ambient: material[0],
            diffuse: material[1],
            specular: material[2],
            shininess: material[3],
        }
    }

    fn resize(&mut self, new_size: winit::dpi::PhysicalSize<u32>) {
        if new_size.width > 0 && new_size.height > 0 {
            self.init.size = new_size;
            self.init.config.width = new_size.width;
            self.init.config.height = new_size.height;
            self.init.surface.configure(&self.init.device, &self.init.config);

            self.project_mat = wt::create_projection_mat(new_size.width as f32 / new_size.height as f32,
```

```
                true);
            self.depth_texture_views[0] = ws::create_depth_view(&self.init);
        }
    }

    #[allow(unused_variables)]
    fn input(&mut self, event: &WindowEvent) -> bool {
        match event {
            WindowEvent::KeyboardInput {
                input:
                    KeyboardInput {
                        virtual_keycode: Some(keycode),
                        state: ElementState::Pressed,
                        ..
                    },
                ..
            } => {
                match keycode {
                    VirtualKeyCode::Q => {
                        self.ambient += 0.01;
                        true
                    },
                    VirtualKeyCode::A => {
                        self.ambient -= 0.05;
                        if self.ambient < 0.0 { self.ambient = 0.0; }
                        true
                    },
                    VirtualKeyCode::W => {
                        self.diffuse += 0.005;
                        true
                    },
                    VirtualKeyCode::S => {
                        self.diffuse -= 0.005;
                        if self.diffuse < 0.0 { self.diffuse = 0.0; }
                        true
                    }, VirtualKeyCode::E => {
                        self.specular += 0.05;
                        true
                    },
                    VirtualKeyCode::D => {
                        self.specular -= 0.05;
                        if self.specular < 0.001 { self.specular = 0.001; }
                        true
                    },
                    VirtualKeyCode::R => {
                        self.shininess += 5.0;
                        true
                    },
                    VirtualKeyCode::F => {
                        self.shininess -= 5.0;
                        if self.shininess < 0.01 { self.shininess = 0.01; }
                        true
                    },
                    _ => false
                }
            }
            _ => false,
        }
    }
}
```

```rust
fn update(&mut self, dt: std::time::Duration) {
    // update uniform buffer
    let dt = ANIMATION_SPEED * dt.as_secs_f32();
    self.light_position[0]= 50.0 * dt.sin();
    self.light_position[2]= 50.0 * dt.cos();
    self.init.queue.write_buffer(&self.uniform_buffers[5], 0,
        cast_slice(self.light_position.as_ref()));

    let light_mat = wt::create_view_mat(self.light_position.into(), [0.0, 0.0, 0.0].into(),
        cgmath::Vector3::unit_y());
    let mut light_projection_mat = wt::create_ortho_mat(-40.0, 40.0, -40.0, 40.0, -50.0, 200.0);
    light_projection_mat = light_projection_mat * light_mat;
    self.init.queue.write_buffer(&self.uniform_buffers[3], 0,
        cast_slice(light_projection_mat.as_ref() as &[f32; 16]));

    // update positions
    let torus  = &mut self.scenes.0[1];
    torus.rotation[1] = 2.0 * dt;
    let m_torus = wt::create_model_mat(torus.translation, torus.rotation, torus.scale);
    let n_torus = (m_torus.invert().unwrap()).transpose();
    self.scenes.1[1] = *m_torus.as_ref();
    self.scenes.2[1] = *n_torus.as_ref();

    for i in 2..20 {
        let sphere = &mut self.scenes.0[i];
        sphere.translation[1] += sphere.v;
        if sphere.translation[1] < -11.0 || sphere.translation[1] > 11.0 {
            sphere.v *= -1.0;
        }
        let m_sphere = wt::create_model_mat(sphere.translation, sphere.rotation, sphere.scale);
        let n_sphere = (m_sphere.invert().unwrap()).transpose();
        self.scenes.1[i] = *m_sphere.as_ref();
        self.scenes.2[i] = *n_sphere.as_ref();
    }
    self.init.queue.write_buffer(&self.uniform_buffers[1], 0, cast_slice(self.scenes.1.as_ref()));
    self.init.queue.write_buffer(&self.uniform_buffers[2], 0, cast_slice(self.scenes.2.as_ref()));

    let view_project_mat = self.project_mat * self.view_mat;
    let view_projection_ref:&[f32; 16] = view_project_mat.as_ref();
    self.init.queue.write_buffer(&self.uniform_buffers[0], 0, cast_slice(view_projection_ref));

    // update material
    let material = [self.ambient, self.diffuse, self.specular, self.shininess];
    self.init.queue.write_buffer(&self.uniform_buffers[6], 0, cast_slice(material.as_ref()));
}

fn render(&mut self) -> Result<(), wgpu::SurfaceError> {
    let output = self.init.surface.get_current_texture()?;
    let view = output
        .texture
        .create_view(&wgpu::TextureViewDescriptor::default());

    let mut encoder = self
        .init.device
        .create_command_encoder(&wgpu::CommandEncoderDescriptor {
            label: Some("Render Encoder"),
        });

    // draw shadow
    {
```

```
let mut shadow_pass = encoder.begin_render_pass(&wgpu::RenderPassDescriptor {
    label: Some("Shadow Pass"),
    color_attachments: &[],
    depth_stencil_attachment: Some(wgpu::RenderPassDepthStencilAttachment{
        view: &self.depth_texture_views[1],
        depth_ops: Some(wgpu::Operations {
            load: wgpu::LoadOp::Clear(1.0),
            store: true,
        }),
        stencil_ops: None,
        occlusion_query_set: None,
        timestamp_writes: None,
    }),
});

shadow_pass.set_pipeline(&self.pipelines[1]);
shadow_pass.set_bind_group(0, &self.uniform_bind_groups[3], &[]);

// draw shadow for cube
shadow_pass.set_vertex_buffer(0, self.vertex_buffers[0].slice(..));
shadow_pass.set_index_buffer(self.index_buffers[0].slice(..), wgpu::IndexFormat::Uint16);
shadow_pass.draw_indexed(0..self.indices_lens[0], 0, 0..1);

// draw shadow for torus
shadow_pass.set_vertex_buffer(0, self.vertex_buffers[2].slice(..));
shadow_pass.set_index_buffer(self.index_buffers[2].slice(..), wgpu::IndexFormat::Uint16);
shadow_pass.draw_indexed(0..self.indices_lens[2], 0, 1..2);

// draw shadow for spheres
shadow_pass.set_vertex_buffer(0, self.vertex_buffers[1].slice(..));
shadow_pass.set_index_buffer(self.index_buffers[1].slice(..), wgpu::IndexFormat::Uint16);
shadow_pass.draw_indexed(0..self.indices_lens[1], 0, 2..20);
}

// draw objects
{
    let color_attach = ws::create_color_attachment(&view);
    let depth_attachment = ws::create_depth_stencil_attachment(&self.depth_texture_views[0]);

    let mut render_pass = encoder.begin_render_pass(&wgpu::RenderPassDescriptor {
        label: Some("Render Pass"),
        color_attachments: &[Some(color_attach)],
        depth_stencil_attachment: Some(depth_attachment),
        occlusion_query_set: None,
        timestamp_writes: None,
    });

    render_pass.set_pipeline(&self.pipelines[0]);
    render_pass.set_bind_group(0, &self.uniform_bind_groups[0], &[]);
    render_pass.set_bind_group(1, &self.uniform_bind_groups[1], &[]);
    render_pass.set_bind_group(2, &self.uniform_bind_groups[2], &[]);

    // draw cube
    render_pass.set_vertex_buffer(0, self.vertex_buffers[0].slice(..));
    render_pass.set_index_buffer(self.index_buffers[0].slice(..), wgpu::IndexFormat::Uint16);
    render_pass.draw_indexed(0..self.indices_lens[0], 0, 0..1);

    // draw torus
    render_pass.set_vertex_buffer(0, self.vertex_buffers[2].slice(..));
    render_pass.set_index_buffer(self.index_buffers[2].slice(..), wgpu::IndexFormat::Uint16);
```

```
                render_pass.draw_indexed(0..self.indices_lens[2], 0, 1..2);

                // draw spheres
                render_pass.set_vertex_buffer(0, self.vertex_buffers[1].slice(..));
                render_pass.set_index_buffer(self.index_buffers[1].slice(..), wgpu::IndexFormat::Uint16);
                render_pass.draw_indexed(0..self.indices_lens[1], 0, 2..20);

            }
        self.init.queue.submit(iter::once(encoder.finish()));
        output.present();

        Ok(())
    }
}

fn main() {
    env_logger::init();
    let event_loop = EventLoop::new();
    let window = winit::window::WindowBuilder::new().build(&event_loop).unwrap();
    window.set_title(&*format!("ch04_{}", "shadow_mapping"));

    let mut state = pollster::block_on(State::new(&window));
    let render_start_time = std::time::Instant::now();

    event_loop.run(move |event, _, control_flow| {
        match event {
            Event::WindowEvent {
                ref event,
                window_id,
            } if window_id == window.id() => {
                if !state.input(event) {
                    match event {
                        WindowEvent::CloseRequested
                        | WindowEvent::KeyboardInput {
                            input:
                                KeyboardInput {
                                    state: ElementState::Pressed,
                                    virtual_keycode: Some(VirtualKeyCode::Escape),
                                    ..
                                },
                            ..
                        } => *control_flow = ControlFlow::Exit,
                        WindowEvent::Resized(physical_size) => {
                            state.resize(*physical_size);
                        }
                        WindowEvent::ScaleFactorChanged { new_inner_size, .. } => {
                            state.resize(**new_inner_size);
                        }
                        _ => {}
                    }
                }
            }
            Event::RedrawRequested(_) => {
                let now = std::time::Instant::now();
                let dt = now - render_start_time;
                state.update(dt);

                match state.render() {
                    Ok(_) => {}
                    Err(wgpu::SurfaceError::Lost) => state.resize(state.init.size),
```

```
                Err(wgpu::SurfaceError::OutOfMemory) => *control_flow = ControlFlow::Exit,
                Err(e) => eprintln!("{:?}", e),
            }
        }
        Event::MainEventsCleared => {
            window.request_redraw();
        }
        _ => {}
    }
});
}
```

The above code defines a *Scene* struct that contains four fields allowing you to position a 3D object in the scene. These fields include *translation*, *rotation*, *scale*, and *v*, where the *v* field is used to specify the vertical or *y* movement of an object. Then, the code implements a *create_transform_mat* method, which generates the model and normal matrices as well as colors for a cube, a torus, and 18 spheres. The method also uses a vector of the *Scene* struct to position these instances in a 3D scene by specifying their translation, rotation, scale, and vertical movement. Particularly, we set the cube as a floor object by scaling it with a very small value in the *y* direction:

```
let scale_cube = [30.0f32, 0.1, 20.0];
```

Additionally, the initial vertical location is set to zero for both the cube and torus, meaning that both objects are located on the floor. On the other hand, for the 18 spheres, we set their initial vertical locations randomly using random numbers:

```
let v = v1 * [0.09, rng.gen::<f32>()/10.0].iter().fold(f32::NEG_INFINITY, |a, &b| a.max(b));
```

Within the *State::new* function, we create two render pipelines: one is for rendering 3D objects and the other is for generating shadows. It is worth noting that we set the *fragment* state to *None* when creating the render pipeline for the shadow. This indicates that the shadow pipeline does not need a fragment state since we are not interested in rendering color output for the shadows.

Furthermore, we create vertex buffers for several 3D objects, including a cube for the ground floor, a torus that rotates at the center of the floor, and 18 instances of spheres as bouncing balls from the floor.

Additionally, we create the shadow depth texture using the code snippet shown below:

```
let shadow_depth_texture_view = ws::create_shadow_texture_view(&init, 2048, 2048);
```

In this example, we have set the size to 2048 by 2048, which is the texture resolution. Increasing the texture resolution will result in higher-definition shadows, but it is also possible to use lower resolutions such as 1024x1024 or 512x512.

Moreover, we include the shadow depth texture view and simpler to a separate bind group, which will be passed to the fragment shader using the following code snippet:

```
let frag_bind_group2 = init.device.create_bind_group(
    &wgpu::BindGroupDescriptor {
        layout: &frag_bind_group_layout2,
        entries: &[
            wgpu::BindGroupEntry {
                binding: 0,
                resource: wgpu::BindingResource::TextureView(&shadow_depth_texture_view),
            },
            wgpu::BindGroupEntry {
                binding: 1,
                resource: wgpu::BindingResource::Sampler(&shadow_depth_sampler),
            }
```

```
        ],
        label: Some("Fragment Bind  Group 2"),
    }
);
```

Within the *State::render* function, we first draw shadows and then the 3D objects by setting appropriate vertex buffers, index buffers, and bind group for each render pass. It is worth noting that when creating the render pass descriptor for the shadow pass, we set the *color_attachments* to &[], i.e., an empty array, indicating that we do not need to render any color output for the shadows and thus do not require a color attachment for the shadow pass.

To see the shadows clearly, we position the light source above the floor by specifying the light position, which is a field of the *State* struct, with the following code:

```
light_position: [0.0, 100.0, 0.0],
```

This means that the light source is located far away above (100 units) the ground floor, making it a directional light source with almost all of its light rays parallel. Therefore, we can use an orthographic projection to create the light projection matrix as there is minimal perspective distortion for this type of light source, as demonstrated in the following code snippet inside the *State::update* function:

```
let light_mat = wt::create_view_mat(self.light_position.into(), [0.0, 0.0, 0.0].into(),
    cgmath::Vector3::unit_y());
let mut light_projection_mat = wt::create_ortho_mat(-40.0, 40.0, -40.0, 40.0, -50.0, 200.0);
light_projection_mat = light_projection_mat * light_mat;
self.init.queue.write_buffer(&self.uniform_buffers[3], 0,
    cast_slice(light_projection_mat.as_ref() as &[f32; 16]));
```

Within the *State::update* function, we also perform various animations, including rotating the light source around the *y*-axis, automatically rotating the torus object by updating its rotation vector's the *z*-component with a time-dependent parameter, and making 18 spheres bounce as bouncing balls by updating their *y*-position within the range of [-11, 11].

Additionally, the code permits the user to modify material parameters for lighting computation using keyboard inputs.

Here is a list of controls using keyboard:

- *Q/A:* Increases/decreases the ambient light intensity.

- *W/S:* Increases/decreases the diffuse light intensity.

- *E/D:* Increases/decreases the specular light intensity.

- *R/F:* Increases/decreases the shininess of the specular light.

4.1.3 Run Application

To run this application, add the following code snippet to the *Cargo.toml* file:

```
[[example]]
name = "ch04_shadow"
path = "examples/ch04/shadow.rs"
```

Afterward, execute the following *cargo run* commands in the terminal window:

```
cargo run --example ch04_shadow
```

Fig.4-1 displays the output from this example.

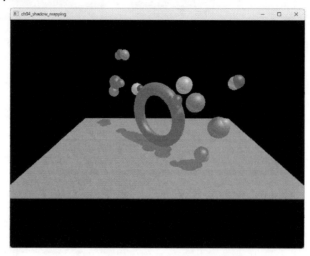

Fig.4-1. Creating shadows in wgpu.

4.2 Introduction to PBR

The Blinn-Phong based lighting model is an empirical model based on observations, and its parameters are not physically based. For example, the separation of the light intensity into ambient, diffuse, and specular components is not physically accurate. However, the model provides several parameters that can be tuned to achieve the desired results.

To improve the lighting effects of the Blinn-Phong model, the PBR technique can be used. PBR is becoming increasingly importance in high-end applications such as film and video games. By using physically based, energy-conserving rendering models, we can easily create high quality and realistic lighting effects under a variety of lighting environments.

4.2.1 Microfacet Model

Almost all PBR approaches are based on the theory of microfacets. The microfacet model is used to simulate the way that light interacts with surfaces at a microscopic level. Most surfaces of 3D objects are not perfectly smooth but have small bumps and imperfections, which can be modeled as a collection of small microfacets. These microfacets have different orientations and surface roughness, which determine how much light is reflected in each direction. The microfacet model takes into account the statistical distribution of these facets, which affects the overall appearance of the surface.

The amount of light that gets into a specific direction from a given point on an object can be described by the reflectance equation:

$$L_0(p, v) = \int_{\Omega} f_r(p, l, v) L_i(p, l)(n \cdot l) \, dl$$

Where $L_0(p, v)$ is the outgoing radiance at point p in the view direction with direction vector v, $f_r(p, l, v)$ is the bidirectional reflectance distribution function (BRDF) at point p for incoming light with direction vector l and outgoing view direction vector v, $L_i(p, l)$ is the incoming radiance at point p from direction vector l, $(n \cdot l)$ is the cosine of the angle between the surface normal at point p and the incoming light direction l, and dl is the infinitesimal solid angle around l.

The integral is over the hemisphere above the surface for all incoming radiance within that hemisphere weighted by the cosine factor. If the incoming light sources are restricted to a certain number of point light sources, the above integral can be replaced with a sum over these individual point light sources.

4.2.2 Bidirectional Reflectance Distribution Function

The only unknown in the integral above is the $f_r(p, l, v)$, or BRDF, which determines the amount of reflected light based on material properties. Several approximations for this function have been proposed to simulate real-life material behavior while obeying the energy conservation law. However, most real-time PBR techniques use the Cook-Torrance BRDF model, which contains two parts: the diffuse BRDF and the specular BRDF:

$$f_r = k_d f_l + k_s f_{ct}$$

Where k_d is the amount of refracted light that gets re-emitted, and k_s is the amount of reflected light with $k_d = 1 - k_s$. The f_l term represents he Lambertian diffuse distribution (corresponding to the diffuse part of the Blinn-Phong model) and can be approximated as evenly spread on all direction:

$$f_l = \frac{C_{diff}}{\pi}$$

Here, C_{diff} represents the albedo of the object surface at point p, which is the fraction of light radiated diffusely. The normalization factor π accounts for the fact that incoming light is integrated over the hemisphere at point p.

The Cook-Torrance specular term f_{ct} represents surface reflectance based on microfacet theory. This term is composed of three functions with a normalization factor in the denominator, as shown in the following formula:

$$f_{ct} = \frac{D(h)F(l, h)G(l, v, h)}{4(n \cdot v)(n \cdot l)}$$

The D, F, and G in the above formula represent functions that approximate specific parts of the surface's reflective properties. D is the normal distribution function (NDF), which represents the alignment of the surface's microfacets to the halfway vector h, influenced by the roughness of the surface. G represents the geometry function that describes the self-shadowing property of the microfacets. F is the Fresnel equation that represents the ratio of surface reflection at different surface angles. In the above expression, l, v, n, and h represent the light direction, view direction, surface normal, and halfway vector respectively.

4.2.3 Normal Distribution Function

The normal distribution function D in the specular BRDF describes the statistical distribution of microfacets on a surface. The function takes as input the halfway vector h, and describes the probability density of microfacets oriented in a particular direction. The roughness of the surface determines the width of the NDF, with rougher surfaces having wider NDFs and smoother surfaces having narrower NDFs.

There are several different functions that can be used as the NDF, each with its own strengths and weaknesses. These distribution functions have different shapes and properties, and the choice of which one to use can depend on factors such as the desired level of realism and the computational efficiency of the function.

In this book, we will use the popular Trowbridge-Reitz GGX function for D, which can be expressed in the form:

$$D(h) = \frac{\alpha^2}{\pi[(n \cdot h)^2(\alpha^2 - 1) + 1]^2}$$

In this equation, the value of α depends on the surface roughness. Assuming that r is a roughness parameter, we can set α to r^2.

4.2.4 Geometry Function

The geometry function G in the specular BRDF accounts for the self-shadowing and occlusion effects of microfacets on a surface. It represents the proportion of microfacets that are visible from both the view direction and the light direction while also considering occlusion by neighboring microfacets. The Schlick-GGX approximation is used in this book for the geometry function:

$$G(l, v, h) = G_s(l)G_s(v)$$

Where $G_s(v)$ represents the obstruction from the view direction and $G_s(l)$ represents the shadowing from the light direction. $G_s(l)$ and $G_s(v)$ can be expressed as:

$$G_s(l) = \frac{n \cdot l}{(n \cdot l)(1 - k) + k}$$

$$G_s(v) = \frac{n \cdot v}{(n \cdot v)(1 - k) + k}$$

The constant k is a remapping of the roughness parameter r, and can be calculated as follows:

$$k = \frac{(r + 1)^2}{8}$$

4.2.5 Fresnel Equation

The Fresnel equation in the specular BRDF describes the ratio of reflected light to incident light at different angles of incidence and reflection on a surface. One popular approximation of the Fresnel equation used in real-time rendering is the Fresnel-Schlick approximation. It assumes that the amount of reflected light is proportional to the amount of incident light and is given by the following formula:

$$F(l, h) = F_0 + (1 - F_0)[1 - (l \cdot h)]^5$$

In this formula, F_0 represents the reflectance of the surface at normal incidence, and $(l \cdot h)$ represents the cosine of the angle between the light direction l and the halfway vector h. The power of 5 is used to increase the reflectivity for grazing angles of incidence.

It is worth noting that in the Fresnel-Schlick approximation formula, the term $(l \cdot h)$ can be replaced by $(v \cdot h)$. This is because the angle between the view direction and the halfway vector is equal to the angle between the light direction and the halfway vector in a perfect specular surface.

The Fresnel-Schlick approximation provides a good estimate for many materials, but it is not universally accurate. Typically, dielectric materials exhibit very low values of F_0, usually in the range of 0.05 (for all RGB components). Whereas metals lack diffuse reflection and have a higher F_0 value, ranging between 0.5 and 1.0. To accommodate these differences, a common practice is to set F_0 to a small value such as (0.04, 0.04, 0.04) for dielectric materials and use color as the value for C_{diff}. Conversely, for metallic surfaces, C_{diff} can be set to (0, 0, 0) (no diffuse) and use color as the value for F_0. Thus, two slightly different models can be employed for metals and dielectrics as necessary.

We now have a complete representation of the PBR theory based on the microfacet model. Before diving into the code, let's revisit the reflectance equation that involves an integral over all directions in the hemisphere above the surface. We can simplify this equation by assuming that all incoming light comes directly from point light sources. With this assumption, we can convert the integral into the following summation:

$$L_0(p, v) = \pi \sum_{i=1}^{N} f_r(p, l_i, v) \, L_i(p, l_i)(n \cdot l_i)$$

Here, N is the number of point light sources, L_i is the illumination received at the surface due to ith light source, and l_i is the light position of the ith light source. Since the intensity of light decreases with distance, we will use an inverse-square relationship to calculate point light attenuation:

$$L_i = \frac{I_i}{d_i^2}$$

Here, I_i is the intensity of the light source, and d_i is the distance from the surface point to the light source.

We have now a complete microfacet-based model that can be applied to both metallic and dielectric surfaces. As mentioned earlier, slight adjustments for the standard BRDF are required depending on whether we are working with a metal or a dielectric material. The number of parameters required for the BRDF is relatively small, and here we consider only the following two parameters:

- *Roughness*, which represents the surface roughness with a value in the range of [0, 1].

- *Metallic*, which represents the material property with a value in the range of [0, 1]. Generally, dielectric materials have a smaller metallic value (i.e., < 0.05), while metallic materials have a larger metallic value (0.5 ~ 1).

4.3 PBR Implementation

In the previous section, we laid the foundation for getting a physically based rendering off the ground. This section focuses on translating the PBR theory into an actual renderer. In this implementation, we assume that there are total of four-point light sources. To satisfy the reflectance equation, we will loop over each light source, calculate its radiance, and sum its contribution scaled by the BRDF and the light's incident angle.

4.3.1 Shader Code

For this example, we will use the vertex shader that was implemented in the previous chapter. The vertex shader code is present in the *shader_instance_vert.wgsl* file located in the *examples/ch03/* folder. This shader serves the purpose of producing multiple instances with lighting effect. Our focus now is to develop the fragment shader. To achieve this, we need to create a new fragment shader file named *pbr_frag.wgsl* in the *examples/ch04/* folder and add the code given below:

```
const pi = 3.14159265358979323846;

struct LightUniforms {
    lightPosition : vec4f,
    lightIntensity : vec4f,
};
@group(1) @binding(0) var<uniform> light:array<LightUniforms, 4>;

struct MaterialUniforms {
    eyePosition : vec4f,
    roughness: f32,
    metallic: f32,
};
@group(1) @binding(1) var<uniform> material : MaterialUniforms;

fn ggxDistrbution(dotNh: f32) -> f32 {
    let a = material.roughness * material.roughness * material.roughness * material.roughness;
    let b = (dotNh * dotNh) * (a - 1.0) + 1.0;
    return r / (pi * b * b);
}

fn geomSmith(dotProd: f32) -> f32 {
    let a = (material.roughness + 1.0) * (material.roughness + 1.0) /8.0;
    return 1.0 / (dotProd * (1.0 - a) + a);
}

fn schlickFresnel(dotHv:f32, vColor:vec4f) -> vec3f {
    var f0 = vec3(0.04);
    f0 = mix(f0, vColor.rgb, material.metallic);
    return f0 + (1.0 - f0) * pow(clamp(1.0 - dotHv, 0.0, 1.0), 5.0);
}

fn microfacetModel(idx: u32, position: vec3f, n: vec3f, vColor:vec4f) -> vec3f {
    var l = normalize(light[idx].lightPosition.xyz - position);
    let v = normalize(material.eyePosition.xyz - position);
    let h = normalize( v + l);
    let dist = length(light[idx].lightPosition.xyz - position);
    var intensity = light[idx].lightIntensity.xyz;
    intensity /= (dist * dist);
    let dotNh = dot(n, h);
    let dotLh = dot(l, h);
    let dotNl = max(dot(n, l), 0.0);
    let dotNv = max(dot(n, v), 0.0);
    let dotHv = dot(h, v);

    let ndf = ggxDistrbution(dotNh);
    let g = geomSmith(dotNv) * geomSmith(dotNl);
    let f = schlickFresnel(dotHv, vColor);

    let specularBrdf = 0.25 * ndf * g * f / (0.0001 + dotNv * dotNl);

    let ks = f;
    var kd = vec3(1.0) - ks;
    kd *= 1.0 - material.metallic;

    return (kd *vColor.rgb / pi + specularBrdf) * intensity * dotNl;
}

struct Input {
    @location(0) vPosition:vec4f,
```

```
    @location(1) vNormal:vec4f,
    @location(2) vColor:vec4f,
}

@fragment
fn fs_main(in:Input) -> @location(0) vec4f {
    var color = vec3(0.0);
    var n = normalize(in.vNormal.xyz);
    for(var i: u32 = 0; i < 4u; i = i + 1u){
        color += microfacetModel(i, in.vPosition.xyz, n, in.vColor);
        color += microfacetModel(i, in.vPosition.xyz, -n, in.vColor);
    }

    // Reinhard operator
    color = color / (color + vec3(1.0));
    // gamma correction
    color = pow(color, vec3(1.0/2.2));

    return vec4(color, 1.0);
}
```

The above code starts by defining two uniform structures that contain the necessary PBR input parameters required for the shader, such as light position, intensity for point light sources, surface roughness, and metallic property.

Then, three functions are defined to compute the complete Cook-Torrance specular PBR terms. These functions include *ggxDistribution* for the normal distribution function D based on Trowbridge-Reitz approximation, *geoSmith* for the geometry term G, and *schlickFresnel* for the Fresnel term using the Schlick approximation.

The *microfacetModel* function is introduced to calculate the entire BRDF model for a single light source. Firstly, the function computes the attenuation for point light sources by scaling the light intensity with the inverse-square law. Then, using the functions defined earlier, the specular BRDF (*specularBrdf*) is calculated, as shown in the following code snippet:

```
let specularBrdf = 0.25 * ndf * g * f / (0.0001 + dotNv * dotNl);
```

Note that 0.0001 is added to the denominator to prevent a divide-by-zero error in case any dot product equals zero. Since the Fresnel term directly corresponds to k_s in the BRDF equation, we can use F term to denote the specular contribution of any light that hits the surface. From k_s, we can then calculate the ratio of diffuse k_d, using the following code snippet:

```
let ks = f;
var kd = vec3(1.0) - ks;
kd *= 1.0 - material.metallic;
```

Here, k_s represents the energy of light that gets reflected, and k_d represents the remaining ratio of light energy that gets diffused. Note that k_d is nullified if the surface is metallic because metallic surfaces do not refract light and, therefore, have no diffuse reflections. This provides the final result necessary to calculate each light's outgoing reflectance.

In the *fs_main* function, we assume that the scene's irradiance is represented by four-point light sources. To satisfy the reflectance equation, we iterate over each light source using a for-loop, calculate its individual radiance, and sum its contribution scaled by the BRDF and the incident angle of the light.

Our light calculation, as presented above, is performed in a linear color space, which is important because PBR requires all input parameters to be linear. However, we also want the light inputs to be close to their physical equivalents so that their radiance or color can vary significantly. As a result, the light radiance calculated from linear inputs can increase quickly to a large value that gets clamped between 0 and 1 due to the default low dynamic range (LDR) output. We can use the Reinhard operator to tone map the linear result with the high dynamic range (HDR) to LDR before gamma correction, as shown in the following code snippet:

```
// Reinhard operator
color = color / (color + vec3(1.0));
// gamma correction
color = pow(color, vec3(1.0/2.2));
```

4.3.2 Rust Code

This example can reuse the common code implemented in the *common_instance.rs* file located in the *examples/ch03/* folder. To begin, create a new Rust file named *pbr.rs* in the *examples/ch04/* folder and enter the following code into it:

```
use std:: {iter, mem};
use cgmath::Matrix4;
use wgpu::VertexBufferLayout;
use winit::{
    event::*,
    event_loop::{ControlFlow, EventLoop},
    window::Window,
};
use bytemuck::cast_slice;
use wgpu_book_examples:: { wgpu_simplified as ws, transforms as wt };
#[path="../ch03/common_instance.rs"]
mod common_instance;

const ANIMATION_SPEED:f32 = 1.0;
const NUM_CUBES:u32 = 50;
const NUM_SPHERES:u32 = 50;
const NUM_TORI:u32 = 50;

struct State {
    init:  ws::IWgpuInit,
    pipeline: wgpu::RenderPipeline,
    vertex_buffers: Vec<wgpu::Buffer>,
    index_buffers: Vec<wgpu::Buffer>,
    uniform_bind_groups: Vec<wgpu::BindGroup>,
    uniform_buffers: Vec<wgpu::Buffer>,
    view_mat: Matrix4<f32>,
    project_mat: Matrix4<f32>,
    msaa_texture_view: wgpu::TextureView,
    depth_texture_view: wgpu::TextureView,
    indices_lens: Vec<u32>,

    intensity: f32,
    metallic: f32,
    roughness: f32,
}

impl State {
    async fn new(window: &Window, sample_count:u32) -> Self {
        let init = ws::IWgpuInit::new(&window, sample_count, None).await;

        let vs_shader = init.device.create_shader_module(
            wgpu::include_wgsl!("../ch03/shader_instance_vert.wgsl"));
```

```
let fs_shader = init.device.create_shader_module(wgpu::include_wgsl!("pbr_frag.wgsl"));

let objects_count = NUM_CUBES + NUM_SPHERES + NUM_TORI;

// uniform data
let camera_position = (0.0, 0.0, 1.0).into();
let look_direction = (0.0, 0.0, 0.0).into();
let up_direction = cgmath::Vector3::unit_y();
let eye_position = camera_position;
let light_position = camera_position;

let (model_mat, normal_mat, color_vec) =
    common_instance::create_transform_mat_color(objects_count, false);

let (view_mat, project_mat, vp_mat) =
    wt::create_vp_mat(camera_position, look_direction, up_direction,
    init.config.width as f32 / init.config.height as f32);

// create uniform view-projection buffers
let vp_uniform_buffer = init.device.create_buffer(&wgpu::BufferDescriptor{
    label: Some("View-Projection Buffer"),
    size: 64,
    usage: wgpu::BufferUsages::UNIFORM | wgpu::BufferUsages::COPY_DST,
    mapped_at_creation: false,
});
init.queue.write_buffer(&vp_uniform_buffer, 0, cast_slice(vp_mat.as_ref() as &[f32; 16]));

// model uniform buffer
let model_uniform_buffer = init.device.create_buffer(&wgpu::BufferDescriptor{
    label: Some("Model Uniform Buffer"),
    size: 64 * objects_count as u64,
    usage: wgpu::BufferUsages::STORAGE | wgpu::BufferUsages::COPY_DST,
    mapped_at_creation: false,
});
init.queue.write_buffer(&model_uniform_buffer, 0, cast_slice(&model_mat));

// normal storage buffer
let normal_uniform_buffer = init.device.create_buffer(&wgpu::BufferDescriptor{
    label: Some("Normal Uniform Buffer"),
    size: 64 * objects_count as u64,
    usage: wgpu::BufferUsages::STORAGE | wgpu::BufferUsages::COPY_DST,
    mapped_at_creation: false,
});
init.queue.write_buffer(&normal_uniform_buffer, 0, cast_slice(&normal_mat));

// color storage buffer
let color_uniform_buffer = init.device.create_buffer(&wgpu::BufferDescriptor{
    label: Some("color Uniform Buffer"),
    size: 16 * objects_count as u64,
    usage: wgpu::BufferUsages::STORAGE | wgpu::BufferUsages::COPY_DST,
    mapped_at_creation: false,
});
init.queue.write_buffer(&color_uniform_buffer, 0, cast_slice(&color_vec));

// light uniform buffer.
let light_uniform_buffer = init.device.create_buffer(&wgpu::BufferDescriptor{
    label: Some("Light Uniform Buffer"),
    size: 128,
    usage: wgpu::BufferUsages::UNIFORM | wgpu::BufferUsages::COPY_DST,
    mapped_at_creation: false,
```

```
    });
    init.queue.write_buffer(&light_uniform_buffer, 0,
        cast_slice(light_position.as_ref() as &[f32; 3]));

    // material uniform buffer
    let material_uniform_buffer = init.device.create_buffer(&wgpu::BufferDescriptor{
        label: Some("Material Uniform Buffer"),
        size: 32,
        usage: wgpu::BufferUsages::UNIFORM | wgpu::BufferUsages::COPY_DST,
        mapped_at_creation: false,
    });

    // set default material parameters
    init.queue.write_buffer(&material_uniform_buffer, 0,
        cast_slice(eye_position.as_ref() as &[f32; 3]));
    let material = [0.2 as f32, 0.8];
    init.queue.write_buffer(&material_uniform_buffer, 16, cast_slice(material.as_ref()));

    // uniform bind group for vertex shader
    let (vert_bind_group_layout, vert_bind_group) = ws::create_bind_group_storage(
        &init.device,
        vec![
            wgpu::ShaderStages::VERTEX, wgpu::ShaderStages::VERTEX,
            wgpu::ShaderStages::VERTEX, wgpu::ShaderStages::VERTEX
        ],
        vec![
            wgpu::BufferBindingType::Uniform,
            wgpu::BufferBindingType::Storage { read_only: true },
            wgpu::BufferBindingType::Storage { read_only: true },
            wgpu::BufferBindingType::Storage { read_only: true },
        ],
        &[
            vp_uniform_buffer.as_entire_binding(),
            model_uniform_buffer.as_entire_binding(),
            normal_uniform_buffer.as_entire_binding(),
            color_uniform_buffer.as_entire_binding()
        ],
    );

    // uniform bind group for fragment shader
    let (frag_bind_group_layout, frag_bind_group) = ws::create_bind_group(
        &init.device,
        vec![wgpu::ShaderStages::FRAGMENT, wgpu::ShaderStages::FRAGMENT],
        &[light_uniform_buffer.as_entire_binding(), material_uniform_buffer.as_entire_binding()],
    );

    let vertex_buffer_layout = VertexBufferLayout {
        array_stride: mem::size_of::<common_instance::Vertex>() as wgpu::BufferAddress,
        step_mode: wgpu::VertexStepMode::Vertex,
        attributes: &wgpu::vertex_attr_array![0 => Float32x3, 1 => Float32x3],
    };

    let pipeline_layout = init.device.create_pipeline_layout(&wgpu::PipelineLayoutDescriptor {
        label: Some("Render Pipeline Layout"),
        bind_group_layouts: &[&vert_bind_group_layout, &frag_bind_group_layout],
        push_constant_ranges: &[],
    });

    let mut ppl = ws::IRenderPipeline {
        vs_shader: Some(&vs_shader),
```

```
            fs_shader: Some(&fs_shader),
            pipeline_layout: Some(&pipeline_layout),
            vertex_buffer_layout: &[vertex_buffer_layout],
            ..Default::default()
        };
        let pipeline = ppl.new(&init);

        let msaa_texture_view = ws::create_msaa_texture_view(&init);
        let depth_texture_view = ws::create_depth_view(&init);

        // vertex and index buffers for objects:
        let (vertex_buffers, index_buffers, index_lens) =
            common_instance::create_object_buffers(&init.device);

        Self {
            init,
            pipeline,
            vertex_buffers,
            index_buffers,
            uniform_bind_groups: vec![vert_bind_group, frag_bind_group],
            uniform_buffers: vec![
                vp_uniform_buffer,
                model_uniform_buffer,
                normal_uniform_buffer,
                color_uniform_buffer,
                light_uniform_buffer,
                material_uniform_buffer
            ],
            view_mat,
            project_mat,
            msaa_texture_view,
            depth_texture_view,
            indices_lens: index_lens,

            intensity: 300.0,
            roughness: material[0],
            metallic: material[1],
        }
    }

    fn resize(&mut self, new_size: winit::dpi::PhysicalSize<u32>) {
        if new_size.width > 0 && new_size.height > 0 {
            self.init.size = new_size;
            self.init.config.width = new_size.width;
            self.init.config.height = new_size.height;
            self.init.surface.configure(&self.init.device, &self.init.config);

            self.project_mat = wt::create_projection_mat(new_size.width as f32 / new_size.height as f32,
                true);
            self.depth_texture_view = ws::create_depth_view(&self.init);
            if self.init.sample_count > 1 {
                self.msaa_texture_view = ws::create_msaa_texture_view(&self.init);
            }
        }
    }

    #[allow(unused_variables)]
    fn input(&mut self, event: &WindowEvent) -> bool {
        match event {
            WindowEvent::KeyboardInput {
```

```rust
                input:
                    KeyboardInput {
                        virtual_keycode: Some(keycode),
                        state: ElementState::Pressed,
                        ..
                    },
                    ..
            } => {
                match keycode {
                    VirtualKeyCode::Q => {
                        self.intensity += 10.0;
                        true
                    },
                    VirtualKeyCode::A => {
                        self.intensity -= 10.0;
                        if self.intensity < 10.0 { self.intensity = 10.0; }
                        true
                    },
                    VirtualKeyCode::W => {
                        self.roughness += 0.01;
                        true
                    },
                    VirtualKeyCode::S => {
                        self.roughness -= 0.01;
                        if self.roughness < 0.05 { self.roughness = 0.05; }
                        true
                    }, VirtualKeyCode::E => {
                        self.metallic += 0.01;
                        true
                    },
                    VirtualKeyCode::D => {
                        self.metallic -= 0.01;
                        if self.metallic < 0.001 { self.metallic = 0.001; }
                        true
                    },
                    _ => false
                }
            }
        }
        _ => false,
    }
}

fn update(&mut self, dt: std::time::Duration) {
    // update uniform buffer
    let dt = ANIMATION_SPEED * dt.as_secs_f32();
    let sn = (2.0 + (ANIMATION_SPEED * dt).sin()) / 3.0;
    let cn = (2.0 + (ANIMATION_SPEED * dt).cos()) / 3.0;
    let dz = 5.0;
    let factor = 15.0;
    let light_pos0 = [-factor*sn, factor*cn,  factor*cn - dz, 1.0];
    let light_pos1 = [ factor*sn, factor*cn,  factor*cn - dz, 1.0];
    let light_pos2 = [-factor*sn, -factor*cn, factor*cn - dz, 1.0];
    let light_pos3 = [ factor*sn, -factor*cn, factor*cn - dz, 1.0];
    let intensity = [self.intensity, self.intensity, self.intensity, 1.0];

    let data  = [
        light_pos0, intensity, light_pos1, intensity,
        light_pos2, intensity, light_pos3, intensity,
    ].concat();
```

```
        self.init.queue.write_buffer(&self.uniform_buffers[4], 0, cast_slice(data.as_ref()));

        let view_project_mat = self.project_mat * self.view_mat;
        let view_projection_ref:&[f32; 16] = view_project_mat.as_ref();
        self.init.queue.write_buffer(&self.uniform_buffers[0], 0, cast_slice(view_projection_ref));

        // update material
        let material = [[self.roughness, self.metallic]];
        self.init.queue.write_buffer(&self.uniform_buffers[5], 16, cast_slice(material.as_ref()));
    }

    fn render(&mut self) -> Result<(), wgpu::SurfaceError> {
        let output = self.init.surface.get_current_texture()?;
        let view = output
            .texture
            .create_view(&wgpu::TextureViewDescriptor::default());

        let mut encoder = self
            .init.device
            .create_command_encoder(&wgpu::CommandEncoderDescriptor {
                label: Some("Render Encoder"),
            });

        {
            let color_attach = ws::create_color_attachment(&view);
            let msaa_attach = ws::create_msaa_color_attachment(&view, &self.msaa_texture_view);
            let color_attachment = if self.init.sample_count == 1 { color_attach } else { msaa_attach };
            let depth_attachment = ws::create_depth_stencil_attachment(&self.depth_texture_view);

            let mut render_pass = encoder.begin_render_pass(&wgpu::RenderPassDescriptor {
                label: Some("Render Pass"),
                color_attachments: &[Some(color_attachment)],
                depth_stencil_attachment: Some(depth_attachment),
                occlusion_query_set: None,
                timestamp_writes: None,
            });

            render_pass.set_pipeline(&self.pipeline);
            render_pass.set_bind_group(0, &self.uniform_bind_groups[0], &[]);
            render_pass.set_bind_group(1, &self.uniform_bind_groups[1], &[]);

            // draw cubes
            render_pass.set_vertex_buffer(0, self.vertex_buffers[0].slice(..));
            render_pass.set_index_buffer(self.index_buffers[0].slice(..), wgpu::IndexFormat::Uint16);
            render_pass.draw_indexed(0..self.indices_lens[0], 0, 0..NUM_CUBES);

            // draw spheres
            render_pass.set_vertex_buffer(0, self.vertex_buffers[1].slice(..));
            render_pass.set_index_buffer(self.index_buffers[1].slice(..), wgpu::IndexFormat::Uint16);
            render_pass.draw_indexed(0..self.indices_lens[1], 0, NUM_CUBES..NUM_CUBES+NUM_SPHERES);

            // draw tori
            render_pass.set_vertex_buffer(0, self.vertex_buffers[2].slice(..));
            render_pass.set_index_buffer(self.index_buffers[2].slice(..), wgpu::IndexFormat::Uint16);
            render_pass.draw_indexed(0..self.indices_lens[2], 0,
                NUM_CUBES+NUM_SPHERES..NUM_CUBES+NUM_SPHERES+NUM_TORI);

        }
        self.init.queue.submit(iter::once(encoder.finish()));
        output.present();
```

```rust
        Ok(())
    }
}
fn main() {
    let mut sample_count = 1 as u32;
    let args: Vec<String> = std::env::args().collect();
    if args.len() > 1 {
        sample_count = args[1].parse::<u32>().unwrap();
    }

    env_logger::init();
    let event_loop = EventLoop::new();
    let window = winit::window::WindowBuilder::new().build(&event_loop).unwrap();
    window.set_title(&*format!("ch04_{}", "pbr_light"));

    let mut state = pollster::block_on(State::new(&window, sample_count));
    let render_start_time = std::time::Instant::now();

    event_loop.run(move |event, _, control_flow| {
        match event {
            Event::WindowEvent {
                ref event,
                window_id,
            } if window_id == window.id() => {
                if !state.input(event) {
                    match event {
                        WindowEvent::CloseRequested
                        | WindowEvent::KeyboardInput {
                            input:
                                KeyboardInput {
                                    state: ElementState::Pressed,
                                    virtual_keycode: Some(VirtualKeyCode::Escape),
                                    ..
                                },
                            ..
                        } => *control_flow = ControlFlow::Exit,
                        WindowEvent::Resized(physical_size) => {
                            state.resize(*physical_size);
                        }
                        WindowEvent::ScaleFactorChanged { new_inner_size, .. } => {
                            state.resize(**new_inner_size);
                        }
                        _ => {}
                    }
                }
            }
            Event::RedrawRequested(_) => {
                let now = std::time::Instant::now();
                let dt = now - render_start_time;
                state.update(dt);

                match state.render() {
                    Ok(_) => {}
                    Err(wgpu::SurfaceError::Lost) => state.resize(state.init.size),
                    Err(wgpu::SurfaceError::OutOfMemory) => *control_flow = ControlFlow::Exit,
                    Err(e) => eprintln!("{:?}", e),
                }
            }
            Event::MainEventsCleared => {
                window.request_redraw();
```

```
        }
        _ => {}
    }
});
}
```

In the code above, we add three parameters, namely *intensity*, *roughness*, and *metallic*, to the *State* struct. These parameters will be used for the light calculation in the fragment shader based on the PBR model. Within the *State::update* function, we define four-point light sources using their positions and light intensity with the following code snippet:

```
let dt = ANIMATION_SPEED * dt.as_secs_f32();
let sn = (2.0 + dt.sin()) / 3.0;
let cn = (2.0 + dt.cos()) / 3.0;
let dz = 5.0;
let factor = 15.0;
let light_pos0 = [-factor*sn,  factor*cn,  factor*cn - dz, 1.0];
let light_pos1 = [ factor*sn,  factor*cn,  factor*cn - dz, 1.0];
let light_pos2 = [-factor*sn, -factor*cn,  factor*cn - dz, 1.0];
let light_pos3 = [ factor*sn, -factor*cn,  factor*cn - dz, 1.0];
let intensity = [self.intensity, self.intensity, self.intensity, 1.0];

let data  = [
    light_pos0, intensity, light_pos1, intensity,
    light_pos2, intensity, light_pos3, intensity,
].concat();

self.init.queue.write_buffer(&self.uniform_buffers[4], 0, cast_slice(data.as_ref()));
```

Here, we are also animating the light sources by varying their positions.

Additionally, the code permits the user to modify input parameters through keyboard inputs.

Here is a list of controls using keyboard:

- *Q/A*: Increases/decreases the *intensity* parameter.

- *W/S:* Increases/decreases the *roughness* parameter.

- *E/D:* Increases/decreases the *metallic* parameter.

4.3.3 Run Application

To run this application, add the following code snippet to the *Cargo.toml* file:

```
[[example]]
name = "ch04_pbr"
path = "examples/ch04/pbr.rs"
```

Afterward, execute the following *cargo run* commands in the terminal window:

```
cargo run --example ch04_pbr 8
```

Fig.4-2 displays the results of this example. As you can see, by only changing the *metallic* and *roughness* parameters, we are able to display a wide range of different materials.

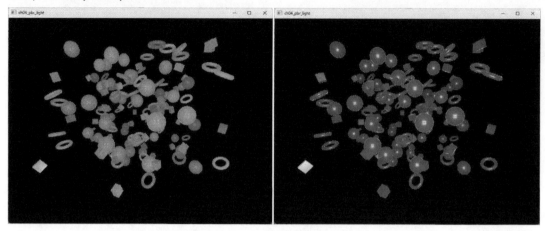

Fig.4-2. PRB lighting model: dielectric material (left) and metal (right).

It is clear that the PBR model provides a more accurate and consistent way of simulating lighting and materials, resulting in more realistic and visually pleasing graphics.

5 Colormap and 3D Surfaces

So far, most examples in this book have used a solid color to render an entire 3D object or a specific part of it. Solid color rendering is commonly used in simple graphics applications where a uniform appearance is desired. It does not incorporate any gradient color data, and the color applied to the object is typically specified manually by passing a uniform color variable to the shader.

In fact, *wgpu* builds objects using sets of vertices, each of which has a position and a color. By default, colors and other attributes of all other pixels are computed using interpolation, resulting in smooth gradients. In Chapter 2, we demonstrated this by applying distinct colors for different vertices in a rotating cube, which produced a smooth colormap effect.

Colormap rendering involves assigning a color value to each vertex of an object based on its color data. This is commonly used in scientific and engineering applications where data sets need to be visualized. The color values are typically mapped to a predefined gradient color list or table, where each color represents a specific value or range of values.

In this chapter, we will explore how to create a color model and colormap and how to use them to render 3D simple and parametric surfaces using various mathematical functions. Surfaces play an important role in various applications, including computer graphics, virtual reality, computer games, and 3D data visualization.

5.1 Color Models

The color used in *wgpu* is created by combining red, green, and blue light, with different colors generated by varying the intensity of each type of light. The RGB color model specifies a color using three numbers that represent the intensity of each color component, with each component specified as a number in the range of [0, 1]. For example, the number (1, 1, 0) represents a yellow color obtained by setting red and green to full intensity, while blue is set to minimum intensity.

In computer graphics, RGB colors are often represented using 8 bits per color component, or a total of 24 bits for a color. Each component can be set to a value in the range of [0, 255]. However, to avoid visual artifact caused by rounding errors in color calculations, it is common to use additional bits per color component. For example, 16-bit integers or 32-bit floating-point values can be used to represent each color component.

The RGBA color model adds a fourth component to the RGB model called alpha, which represents transparency. A color with maximum alpha value is fully opaque, while a color with zero alpha is completely transparent and therefore invisible. Intermediate alpha values give translucent or partly transparent colors. In this book, we will use a *float32* value to represent each color component.

5.2 Colormap

In certain graphics and chart applications, the custom colormaps may be necessary to achieve specific visual effects. These colormaps are simply tables or lists of colors organized in a desired fashion. The surface, patch, and image objects can be associated with a custom colormap by creating an $m \times 3$ color map matrix. Each row of this matrix represents RGB values, with the row index representing the y data of a 2D chart or the height (the y data) of a 3D surface plot. For a given colormap matrix with m rows, the color data values can be linearly scaled to the color map.

For example, if you want to use a colormap to represent the y coordinates of a 2D graphics object, you can use the *Ymin* and *Ymax* to linearly transform the y data values to indices where each index identifies an RGB row (i.e., a color) in the color map matrix. The mathematical transformation of the color index values is described by the formula:

$$Color\ Index = \begin{cases} 1 & y < Y\min \\ (\text{int})\left(\dfrac{(y - Y\min)m}{Y\max - Y\min}\right) & Y\min \le y < Y\max \\ m & y \ge Y\max \end{cases}$$

Here y is the individual value of y data and m is the length of the colormap matrix. This allows you to use the entire range of colors in the colormap over the plotted data. For 3D graphics objects and 3D surface charts, the y data should be replaced with the height (z or y depending on your coordinate system) data.

5.2.1 Colormap Data

It is easy to create your own custom colormap using simple mathematical formula. Here, we provide 23 commonly used colormaps created using various $m \times 3$ colormap array. Create a new Rust file called *colormap.rs* in the *src/* folder and enter the following code into it:

```rust
#![allow(dead_code)]
pub fn colormap_data(colormap_name: &str) -> [[f32; 3]; 11] {
    let colors = match colormap_name {
        "hsv" => [[1.0,0.0,0.0],[1.0,0.5,0.0],[0.97,1.0,0.01],[0.0,0.99,0.04],[0.0,0.98,0.52],
            [0.0,0.98,1.0],[0.01,0.49,1.0],[0.03,0.0,0.99],[1.0,0.0,0.96],[1.0,0.0,0.49],[1.0,0.0,0.02]],

        "hot" => [[0.0,0.0,0.0],[0.3,0.0,0.0],[0.6,0.0,0.0],[0.9,0.0,0.0],[0.93,0.27,0.0],
            [0.97,0.55,0.0],[1.0,0.82,0.0],[1.0,0.87,0.25],[1.0,0.91,0.5],[1.0,0.96,0.75],[1.0,1.0,1.0]],

        "cool" => [[0.49,0.0,0.7],[0.45,0.0,0.85],[0.42,0.15,0.89],[0.38,0.29,0.93],[0.27,0.57,0.91],
            [0.0,0.8,0.77],[0.0,0.97,0.57],[0.0,0.98,0.46],[0.0,1.0,0.35],[0.16,1.0,0.03],[0.58,1.0,0.0]],

        "spring" => [[1.0,0.0,1.0],[1.0,0.1,0.9],[1.0,0.2,0.8],[1.0,0.3,0.7],[1.0,0.4,0.6],
            [1.0,0.5,0.5],[1.0,0.6,0.4],[1.0,0.7,0.3],[1.0,0.8,0.2],[1.0,0.9,0.1],[1.0,1.0,0.0]],

        "summer" => [[0.0,0.5,0.4],[0.1,0.55,0.4],[0.2,0.6,0.4],[0.3,0.65,0.4],[0.4,0.7,0.4],
            [0.5,0.75,0.4],[0.6,0.8,0.4],[0.7,0.85,0.4],[0.8,0.9,0.4],[0.9,0.95,0.4],[1.0,1.0,0.4]],

        "autumn" => [[1.0,0.0,0.0],[1.0,0.1,0.0],[1.0,0.2,0.0],[1.0,0.3,0.0],[1.0,0.4,0.0],[1.0,0.5,0.0],
```

```
    [1.0,0.6,0.0],[1.0,0.7,0.0],[1.0,0.8,0.0],[1.0,0.9,0.0],[1.0,1.0,0.0]],

"winter" => [[0.0,0.0,1.0],[0.0,0.1,0.95],[0.0,0.2,0.9],[0.0,0.3,0.85],[0.0,0.4,0.8],
    [0.0,0.5,0.75],[0.0,0.6,0.7],[0.0,0.7,0.65],[0.0,0.8,0.6],[0.0,0.9,0.55],[0.0,1.0,0.5]],

"bone" => [[0.0,0.0,0.0],[0.08,0.08,0.11],[0.16,0.16,0.23],[0.25,0.25,0.34],[0.33,0.33,0.45],
    [0.41,0.44,0.54],[0.5,0.56,0.62],[0.58,0.67,0.7],[0.66,0.78,0.78],[0.83,0.89,0.89],
    [1.0,1.0,1.0]],

"cooper" => [[0.0,0.0,0.0],[0.13,0.08,0.05],[0.25,0.16,0.1],[0.38,0.24,0.15],[0.5,0.31,0.2],
    [0.62,0.39,0.25],[0.75,0.47,0.3],[0.87,0.55,0.35],[1.0,0.63,0.4],[1.0,0.71,0.45],
    [1.0,0.78,0.5]],

"greys" => [[0.0,0.0,0.0],[0.1,0.1,0.1],[0.2,0.2,0.2],[0.3,0.3,0.3],[0.4,0.4,0.4],[0.5,0.5,0.5],
    [0.6,0.6,0.6],[0.7,0.7,0.7],[0.8,0.8,0.8],[0.9,0.9,0.9],[1.0,1.0,1.0]],

"rainbow" => [[0.588, 0.000, 0.353],[0.118, 0.000, 0.698],[0.000, 0.059, 0.914],
    [0.000, 0.297, 1.000],[0.035, 0.677, 0.918],[0.173, 1.000, 0.588],
    [0.508, 1.000, 0.118],[0.837, 0.951, 0.000],[1.000, 0.725, 0.000],
    [1.000, 0.348, 0.000],[1.000, 0.000, 0.000]],

"rainbow_soft" => [[0.490, 0.000, 0.702],[0.780, 0.000, 0.706],[1.000, 0.000, 0.475],
    [1.000, 0.424, 0.000],[0.871, 0.761, 0.000],[0.588, 1.000, 0.000],
    [0.000, 1.000, 0.216],[0.000, 0.965, 0.588],[0.196, 0.655, 0.871],
    [0.404, 0.200, 0.922],[0.486, 0.000, 0.729]],

"white" => convert_f32([[1,1,1],[1,1,1],[1,1,1],[1,1,1],[1,1,1],[1,1,1],[1,1,1],[1,1,1],
    [1,1,1],[1,1,1],[1,1,1]]),

"black" => convert_f32([[0,0,0],[0,0,0],[0,0,0],[0,0,0],[0,0,0],[0,0,0],[0,0,0],[0,0,0],
    [0,0,0],[0,0,0],[0,0,0]]),

"red" => convert_f32([[1,0,0],[1,0,0],[1,0,0],[1,0,0],[1,0,0],[1,0,0],[1,0,0],[1,0,0],
    [1,0,0],[1,0,0],[1,0,0]]),

"green" => convert_f32([[0,1,0],[0,1,0],[0,1,0],[0,1,0],[0,1,0],[0,1,0],[0,1,0],[0,1,0],
    [0,1,0],[0,1,0],[0,1,0]]),

"blue" => convert_f32([[0,0,1],[0,0,1],[0,0,1],[0,0,1],[0,0,1],[0,0,1],[0,0,1],[0,0,1],
    [0,0,1],[0,0,1],[0,0,1]]),

"yellow" => convert_f32([[1,1,0],[1,1,0],[1,1,0],[1,1,0],[1,1,0],[1,1,0],[1,1,0],[1,1,0],
    [1,1,0],[1,1,0],[1,1,0]]),

"cyan" => convert_f32([[0,1,1],[0,1,1],[0,1,1],[0,1,1],[0,1,1],[0,1,1],[0,1,1],[0,1,1],
    [0,1,1],[0,1,1],[0,1,1]]),

"fuchsia" => convert_f32([[1,0,1],[1,0,1],[1,0,1],[1,0,1],[1,0,1],[1,0,1],[1,0,1],[1,0,1],
    [1,0,1],[1,0,1],[1,0,1]]),

"terrain" => [[0.1765,0.2471,0.6471],[0.0392,0.5176,0.9176],[0.0000,0.7451,0.5725],
    [0.3098,0.8627,0.4588],[0.7098,0.9451,0.5451],[0.9686,0.9608,0.5843],[0.7686,0.7059,0.4784],
    [0.5451,0.4196,0.3529],[0.6196,0.5098,0.4863],[0.7765,0.7137,0.7020],[0.9490,0.9333,0.9333]],

"ocean" => [[0.0000,0.4627,0.0275],[0.0000,0.3216,0.1176],[0.0000,0.1686,0.2196],
    [0.0000,0.0392,0.3098],[0.0000,0.0902,0.3961],[0.0000,0.2275,0.4863],[0.0000,0.3804,0.5843],
    [0.0510,0.5255,0.6863],[0.3137,0.6549,0.7686],[0.5922,0.7961,0.8627],[0.9020,0.9490,0.9647]],

// "jet" as default
_ => [[0.0,0.0,0.51],[0.0,0.24,0.67],[0.01,0.49,0.78],[0.01,0.75,0.89],[0.02,1.0,1.0],
```

```
                [0.51,1.0,0.5],[1.0,1.0,0.0],[0.99,0.67,0.0],[0.99,0.33,0.0],[0.98,0.0,0.0],[0.5,0.0,0.0]],
    };

    colors
}

fn convert_f32(a: [[i32; 3]; 11]) -> [[f32; 3]; 11] {
    let b: Vec<[f32;3]> = a.iter().map(|&c| [c[0] as f32, c[1] as f32, c[2] as f32]).collect();
    let mut arr:[[f32; 3]; 11] = [[0.0; 3]; 11];
    for i in 0..11 {
        arr[i] = b[i].clone();
    }
    arr
}
```

The above code defines a function called *colormap_data* that takes in a string parameter representing the name of the colormap. Inside the function, a *match* statement is used to select the appropriate colormap array based on the input string. Each selected colormap contains eleven RGB color arrays and has a corresponding colormap name. The purpose of this function is to provide users with pre-defined colormaps containing color gradients that they can use in their graphics and chart applications.

The *convert_f32* function is a helper function, which can be used to convert the *i32* array into *f32* array. This means that using this function, we can simply enter integers as color components without needing to type floating points for the data.

5.2.2 Color Interpolation

The *colormap_data* function presented in the previous section assumes that the 11-color arrays for each colormap are uniformly distributed within the range of [0, 1]. For instance, *colors[0]* represents a color at 0, and *colors[5]* represents a color at 0.5. However, if we want to obtain a color at an arbitrary location, such as 0.55, we need to use an interpolation method.

Add a new function called *color_lerp* to the *colormap.rs* file with the following code:

```
pub fn color_lerp(colors:[[f32;3];11], min:f32, max:f32, mut t:f32) -> [f32; 3]{
    if t < min {
        t = min;
    }
    if t > max {
        t = max;
    }
    let tn = (t-min)/(max - min);
    let indx = (10.0 * tn).floor() as usize;

    if indx as f32 == 10.0 * tn {
        colors[indx]
    } else {
        let tn1 = (tn - 0.1 * indx as f32)*10.0; // rescale
        let a = colors[indx];
        let b = colors[indx+1];
        let color_r = a[0] + (b[0] - a[0]) * tn1;
        let color_g = a[1] + (b[1] - a[1]) * tn1;
        let color_b = a[2] + (b[2] - a[2]) * tn1;
        [color_r, color_g, color_b]
    }
}
```

This function accepts colormap data array and an argument *t* whose value is in the range of [*min*, *max*]. It allows you to interpolate a color for an arbitrary *t* value. Within the function, we first ensure the input *t* parameter is within the [*min*, *max*] range. Next, we normalize the *t* variable to the range of [0, 1], and finally, interpolate the color for the *t* variable. The function returns an array [*r*, *g*, *b*] with each color component being in the range of [0, 1].

5.3 Framerate and FPS

In the previous chapters, we created simple 3D shapes in *wgpu*, which did not have performance issues. However, rendering complex graphics may lead to a drop in framerate (also known as frames per second or FPS), which can negatively impact the immersion, responsiveness, and overall quality of the user experience.

Measuring framerate is crucial to assess rendering performance of *wgpu* applications. FPS represents the number of executions over a given time period and is directly linked to the time it takes for the code to execute.

Usually, the rendering code is executed at the beginning of each frame at the same refresh rate as the display. For most displays, this refresh rate is 60 Hz, or 60 FPS. Thus, the rendering code will be called a maximum of 60 times per second. The shortest possible time to execute the rendering code is approximately 16.67 ms. If the execution time exceeds this threshold, the next frame's time will be impacted, resulting in dropped frames and reduced framerate.

Here, we will create a simple struct with its implementations to calculate the framerate. Add the following code to the *wgpu_simplified.rs* file in the *src/* folder:

```rust
#[derive(Debug)]
pub struct FpsCounter {
    last_second_frames: VecDeque<Instant>,
    last_print_time: Instant,
}

impl Default for FpsCounter {
    fn default() -> Self {
        Self::new()
    }
}

impl FpsCounter {
    // Creates a new FpsCounter.
    pub fn new() -> Self {
        Self {
            last_second_frames: VecDeque::with_capacity(128),
            last_print_time: Instant::now(),
        }
    }

    // updates the fps counter and print fps.
    pub fn print_fps(&mut self, interval:u64) {
        let now = Instant::now();
        let a_second_ago = now - Duration::from_secs(1);

        while self.last_second_frames.front().map_or(false, |t| *t < a_second_ago) {
            self.last_second_frames.pop_front();
        }
```

```
        self.last_second_frames.push_back(now);

        // Check if the interval seconds have passed since the last print time
        if now - self.last_print_time >= Duration::from_secs(interval) {
            let fps = self.last_second_frames.len();
            println!("FPS: {}", fps);
            self.last_print_time = now;
        }
    }
}
```

This code first defines a simple *FpsCounter* struct that contains two fields: *last_second_frames*, which is a *VecDeque* of *Instant* timestamps used to store the times of the most recent frames, and *last_print_time*, which is an *Instant* timestamp used to keep track of the last time the FPS was printed.

The code then implements the *Default* trait for the struct, which provides a default value for a type. The *default()* function creates a new *FpsCounter* with default values. In this case, it calls the *new()* method to create a new *FpsCounter* with the default settings.

Next, the code defines the implementation block for the struct. The *new* function in this block is a constructor method for creating a new instance of *FpsCounter*. It initializes the *last_second_frames* with a capacity of 128 and sets the *last_print_time* to the current time using *Instant::now()*.

The *print_fps* function in the block updates the FPS counter and prints the FPS value at a specified interval (in seconds).

The *FpsCounter* struct and its implementations allow you to keep track of the frames per second and print the FPS value at desired intervals, which can be useful for performance monitoring and debugging in *wgpu* applications like games or real-time graphics.

5.4 Shaders with Lighting and Vertex Color

For the sake of simplicity, we will reuse the fragment shader for a directional light source implemented in the *directional_frag.wgsl* file located in the *examples/ch03/* folder. However, we need to create a new vertex shader file named *shader-vert.wgsl* in the *examples/ch05/* folder that incorporates both the lighting and vertex color. The following code can be used for the new vertex shader:

```
// vertex shader
struct Uniforms {
    vpMat : mat4x4f,
    modelMat : mat4x4f,
    normalMat : mat4x4f,
};
@binding(0) @group(0) var<uniform> uniforms : Uniforms;

struct Input {
    @location(0) position: vec4f,
    @location(1) normal: vec4f,
    @location(2) color: vec4f,
}

struct Output {
    @builtin(position) position : vec4f,
    @location(0) vPosition : vec4f,
    @location(1) vNormal : vec4f,
    @location(2) vColor: vec4f,
```

```
};

@vertex
fn vs_main(in:Input) -> Output {
    var output: Output;
    let mPosition = uniforms.modelMat * in.position;
    output.vPosition = mPosition;
    output.vNormal =  uniforms.normalMat * in.normal;
    output.position = uniforms.vpMat * mPosition;
    output.vColor = in.color;
    return output;
}
```

This vertex shader is very similar to the one used in Chapter 3, with the exception that in addition to the *position* and *normal* data, we also pass the *color* data to it. Within the *vs_main* function, we process the color data and assign it to the *vColor* variable defined in the *Output* struct, which is used in the fragment shader to generate the color for rendering the object.

5.5 Simple 3D Surfaces

In the *wgpu*'s coordinate system, a simple 3D surface represents a y function on a surface for each x and z coordinate within a defined region. Each x and z value pair on a simple surface can have at most one y value. We can define a simple surface by specifying the y-coordinates of points above a rectangular grid in the x-z plane, which are then connected with line segments. Simple surfaces are particularly useful for visualizing large 2D data arrays (matrices) that cannot be displayed numerically or for graphing functions of two variables.

Traditionally, surfaces are formed using quadrilateral meshes, but *wgpu* only provides triangles as the basic units to represent any 3D surface. To represent a surface using quadrilaterals in *wgpu*, custom functions must be written.

5.5.1 Vertex Data

In this section, we will generate vertex data for a 3D simple surface described by a math function $y = f(x, z)$ using a rectangular mesh or quad mesh to approximate it. To accomplish this, create a new Rust file called *surface_date.rs* in the *src/* folder and include the following code:

```
#![allow(dead_code)]
use cgmath::*;
use std::f32::consts::PI;
use std::collections::HashMap;
use super::colormap;
use super::math_func as mf;

#[derive(Default)]
pub struct ISurfaceOutput {
    pub positions: Vec<[f32; 3]>,
    pub normals: Vec<[f32; 3]>,
    pub colors: Vec<[f32; 3]>,
    pub colors2: Vec<[f32; 3]>,
    pub uvs: Vec<[f32; 2]>,
    pub indices: Vec<u16>,
    pub indices2: Vec<u16>,
}
```

```rust
pub struct ISimpleSurface {
    pub surface_type: u32,
    pub xmin: f32,
    pub xmax: f32,
    pub zmin: f32,
    pub zmax: f32,
    pub x_resolution: u16,
    pub z_resolution: u16,
    pub scale: f32,
    pub aspect_ratio: f32,
    pub colormap_name: String,
    pub wireframe_color: String,
    pub colormap_direction: u32, // 0: x-direction, 1: y-direction, 2: z-direction
    pub t: f32,   // animation time parameter
    pub uv_lens: [f32; 2],
}

impl Default for ISimpleSurface {
    fn default() -> Self {
        Self {
            surface_type: 0,
            xmin: -1.0,
            xmax: 1.0,
            zmin: -1.0,
            zmax: 1.0,
            x_resolution: 30,
            z_resolution: 30,
            scale: 1.0,
            aspect_ratio: 1.0,
            colormap_name: "jet".to_string(),
            wireframe_color: "white".to_string(),
            colormap_direction: 1,
            t: 0.0,
            uv_lens: [1.0, 1.0],
        }
    }
}

impl ISimpleSurface {
    pub fn new(&mut self) -> ISurfaceOutput {
        if self.surface_type == 0 {
            (self.xmin, self.xmax, self.zmin, self.zmax) = (-8.0, 8.0, -8.0, 8.0);
            self.aspect_ratio = 0.5;
            self.simple_surface_data(&mf::sinc)
        } else if self.surface_type == 1 {
            (self.xmin, self.xmax, self.zmin, self.zmax) = (-8.0, 8.0, -8.0, 8.0);
            self.aspect_ratio = 0.6;
            self.simple_surface_data(&mf::poles)
        } else {
            (self.xmin, self.xmax, self.zmin, self.zmax) = (-3.0, 3.0, -3.0, 3.0);
            self.aspect_ratio = 0.9;
            self.simple_surface_data(&mf::peaks)
        }
    }

    fn simple_surface_data(&mut self, f:&dyn Fn(f32, f32, f32) -> [f32; 3]) -> ISurfaceOutput {
        let mut positions: Vec<[f32; 3]> = vec![];
        let mut normals: Vec<[f32; 3]> = vec![];
        let mut colors: Vec<[f32; 3]> = vec![];
```

```rust
let mut colors2: Vec<[f32; 3]> = vec![];
let mut uvs: Vec<[f32; 2]> = vec![];

let dx = (self.xmax- self.xmin) / self.x_resolution as f32;
let dz = (self.zmax - self.zmin) / self.z_resolution as f32;
let (epsx, epsz) = (0.01 * dx, 0.01 * dz);

let (ymin, ymax) = self.yrange(f);
let cdata = colormap::colormap_data(&self.colormap_name);
let cdata2 = colormap::colormap_data(&self.wireframe_color);

for i in 0..=self.x_resolution {
    let x = self.xmin + dx * i as f32;
    for j in 0..=self.z_resolution {
        let z = self.zmin + dz * j as f32;
        let pos = self.normalize_data(f(x,z,self.t), ymin, ymax);
        positions.push(pos);

        // calculate normals
        let nx = Vector3::from(self.normalize_data(f(x+epsx, z, self.t), ymin, ymax)) -
                Vector3::from(self.normalize_data(f(x-epsx, z, self.t), ymin, ymax));
        let nz = Vector3::from(self.normalize_data(f(x, z+epsz, self.t), ymin, ymax)) -
                Vector3::from(self.normalize_data(f(x, z-epsz, self.t), ymin, ymax));
        let normal = nx.cross(nz).normalize();
        normals.push(normal.into());

        // colormap
        let range = if self.colormap_direction == 1 { self.scale * self.aspect_ratio}
            else {self.scale};
        let color = colormap::color_lerp(cdata, -range, range,
            pos[self.colormap_direction as usize]);
        let color2 = colormap::color_lerp(cdata2, -range, range,
            pos[self.colormap_direction as usize]);
        colors.push(color);
        colors2.push(color2);

        // uvs
        uvs.push([self.uv_lens[0]*(x-self.xmin)/(self.xmax-self.xmin),
            self.uv_lens[1]*(z-self.zmin)/(self.zmax-self.zmin)
        ]);
    }
}

// calculate indices
let mut indices: Vec<u16> = vec![];
let mut indices2: Vec<u16> = vec![];
let vertices_per_row = self.z_resolution + 1;

for i in 0..self.x_resolution {
    for j in 0..self.z_resolution {
        let idx0 = j + i * vertices_per_row;
        let idx1 = j + 1 + i * vertices_per_row;
        let idx2 = j + 1 + (i + 1) * vertices_per_row;
        let idx3 = j + (i + 1) * vertices_per_row;

        let values:Vec<u16> = vec![idx0, idx1, idx2, idx2, idx3, idx0];
        indices.extend(values);

        let values2:Vec<u16> = vec![idx0, idx1, idx0, idx3];
        indices2.extend(values2);
```

```
                if i == self.x_resolution - 1 || j == self.z_resolution - 1 {
                    let edge_values:Vec<u16> = vec![idx1, idx2, idx2, idx3];
                    indices2.extend(edge_values);
                }
            }
        }

        ISurfaceOutput { positions, normals, colors, colors2, uvs, indices, indices2 }
    }

    fn normalize_data(&mut self, point:[f32; 3], ymin:f32, ymax:f32) -> [f32; 3] {
        let mut pt = point.clone();
        pt[0] = (-1.0 + 2.0 * (pt[0] - self.xmin) / (self.xmax - self.xmin)) * self.scale;
        pt[1] = (-1.0 + 2.0 * (pt[1] - ymin) / (ymax - ymin)) * self.scale * self.aspect_ratio;
        pt[2] = (-1.0 + 2.0 * (pt[2] - self.zmin) / (self.zmax - self.zmin)) * self.scale;
        pt
    }

    fn yrange(&mut self, f:&dyn Fn(f32, f32, f32) -> [f32; 3]) -> (f32, f32) {
        let dx = (self.xmax- self.xmin) / self.x_resolution as f32;
        let dz = (self.zmax - self.zmin) / self.z_resolution as f32;
        let mut ymin = f32::MAX;
        let mut ymax = f32::MIN;

        for i in 0..=self.x_resolution {
            let x = self.xmin + dx * i as f32;
            for j in 0..=self.z_resolution {
                let z = self.zmin + dz * j as f32;
                let pt = f(x, z, self.t);
                ymin = if pt[1] < ymin { pt[1] } else { ymin };
                ymax = if pt[1] > ymax { pt[1] } else { ymax };
            }
        }
        (ymin, ymax)
    }
}
```

The code above defines two structs, *ISurfaceOutput* and *ISimpleSurface*, used as output and input when generating 3D surfaces. Two implementations are added to the *ISimpleSurface* struct: one for setting the default values and the other for implementing various functions, including two utility functions: *normalize_data* and *y_range*.

The *normalize_data* function maps the region of a surface onto a region of [-1, 1], providing a consistent size for different 3D surfaces in the scene when using the same camera and transformations. The *scale* and *aspect* parameters defined in the *ISimpleSurface* struct allow the user to control the size and aspect ratio of the surface. The *y_range* function calculates the range of *y*-values for a simple 3D surface. This range is used to normalize the surface data.

The main function in the code above is *simple_surface_data*, which takes the math function *f* as input. The *f* function is separately defined as a mathematical expression, and the *ISimpleSurface* struct allows the user to specify the data region and 2D grid points in the *x-z* plane. This function contains data arrays for storing the *position*, *normal*, *color*, *uv*, and *index* data.

In the *for*-loop, the *positions* array is populated with the normalized data of the function $f(x, z)$ on the 2D grid. The normal vector for each vertex is then calculated by making small displacements along the *x* and *z* directions and computing the cross product of these displacements, ensuring perpendicularity to the surface.

Next, two colormaps are calculated for the surface and wireframe by invoking the *color_lerp* function defined earlier in the *colormap.rs* file. The UV data for the surface and two index data (one for the surface and the other for the wireframe) are also calculated. Finally, the *simple_surface_data* function returns an object of the *ISurfaceOutput* type.

The public *new* function returns different surface data specified by the *surface_type* field defined in the *ISimpleSurface* struct by calling the *simple_surface_data* function. Specifically, *surface_type* with value of 0, 1, or any other value corresponds to the *sinc*, *poles*, or *peaks* surface, respectively.

5.5.2 Math Functions for Simple surfaces

This subsection implements three mathematical functions, *sinc*, *peaks*, and *poles*, which will be used to create different simple 3D surfaces.

The *sinc* function is defined by the following math formula:

$$f(x,z) = \frac{\sin r}{r}, \quad \text{with } r = \sqrt{x^2 + z^2}$$

Add a new function called *sinc* to the *math_func.rs* file in the *src/* folder with the following code:

```
pub fn sinc(x:f32, z:f32, t:f32) -> [f32; 3] {
    let a = 1.01 + t.sin();
    let r = a * (x*x + z*z).sqrt();
    let y = if r == 0.0 { 1.0 } else { r.sin()/r };
    [x, y, z]
}
```

The *t* input argument is an animation parameter. This function computes the *sinc* function with respect to *x*, *z*, and *t*, and returns a [*f32; 3*] point.

The *peaks* function can be described using the following math expression:

$$f(x,z) = 3(1-z)^2 e^{-[z^2+(1+x)^2]} - 10\left(\frac{z}{5} - z^3 - x^5\right)e^{-(x^2+z^2)} - \frac{1}{3}e^{-[(1+z)^2+x^2]}$$

Create a new function called *peaks* in the *math-func.rs* file located in the *src/* folder and include the following code:

```
pub fn peaks(x:f32, z:f32, t:f32) -> [f32; 3] {
    let a = 1.00001 + t.sin();
    let b = 1.00001 + (1.5*t).sin();
    let c = 1.00001 + (2.0*t).sin();
    let y = 3.0*(1.0-x)*(1.0-x)*(-a*(x*x)-a*(z+1.0)*(z+1.0)).exp()-
    10.0*(x/5.0-x*x*x-z*z*z*z*z)*(-b*x*x-b*z*z).exp() - 1.0/3.0*(-c*(x+1.0)*(x+1.0)-c*z*z).exp();
    [z, y, x]
}
```

Here, we also add an animation parameter *t* to this function.

Finally, the *poles* function is defined by the following math formula:

$$f(x,z) = \frac{xz}{|(x-3)^3| + (z-6)^2 + 2}$$

Add a new function called *poles* to the *math-func.rs* file in the *src/* folder with the following code:

```
pub fn poles(x:f32, z:f32, t:f32) -> [f32; 3] {
    let a = 1.5 * t.sin();
```

```
    let y =  x*z/(((x-a)*(x-a)*(x-a)).abs() + (z- 2.0*a)*(z- 2.0*a) + 2.0);
    [x, y, z]
}
```

Here, an animation parameter *t* is also included in this function.

5.5.3 Rust Code

With the background presented in the previous sections, we are ready to render simple 3D surfaces in
wgpu. To do this, create a new Rust file named *simple_surface.rs* in the *examples/ch05/* folder and enter
the following code into it:

```
use std:: {iter, mem};
use cgmath::{ Matrix, Matrix4, SquareMatrix };
use wgpu:: {util::DeviceExt, VertexBufferLayout};
use winit::{
    event::*,
    event_loop::{ControlFlow, EventLoop},
    window::Window,
};
use bytemuck:: {Pod, Zeroable, cast_slice};
use wgpu_book_examples:: { wgpu_simplified as ws, transforms as wt, surface_data as sd };

#[repr(C)]
#[derive(Copy, Clone, Debug, Pod, Zeroable)]
pub struct Vertex {
    pub position: [f32; 3],
    pub normal: [f32; 3],
    pub color: [f32; 3],
}

fn create_vertices(ss_data: sd::ISurfaceOutput) -> (Vec<Vertex>, Vec<Vertex>, Vec<u16>, Vec<u16>) {
    let mut data:Vec<Vertex> = vec![];
    let mut data2:Vec<Vertex> = vec![];
    for i in 0..ss_data.positions.len() {
        data.push(Vertex{position:ss_data.positions[i], normal:ss_data.normals[i],
            color:ss_data.colors[i]});
        data2.push(Vertex{position:ss_data.positions[i], normal:ss_data.normals[i],
            color:ss_data.colors2[i]});
    }
    (data.to_vec(), data2.to_vec(), ss_data.indices, ss_data.indices2)
}

struct State {
    init:  ws::IWgpuInit,
    pipelines: Vec<wgpu::RenderPipeline>,
    vertex_buffers: Vec<wgpu::Buffer>,
    index_buffers: Vec<wgpu::Buffer>,
    uniform_bind_groups: Vec<wgpu::BindGroup>,
    uniform_buffers: Vec<wgpu::Buffer>,
    view_mat: Matrix4<f32>,
    project_mat: Matrix4<f32>,
    msaa_texture_view: wgpu::TextureView,
    depth_texture_view: wgpu::TextureView,
    indices_lens: Vec<u32>,
    plot_type: u32,
    recreate_buffers: bool,
    animation_speed: f32,
    rotation_speed: f32,
```

```
        simple_surface: sd::ISimpleSurface,
        fps_counter: ws::FpsCounter,
}

impl State {
    async fn new(
        window:&Window,
        sample_count:u32,
        colormap_name:&str,
        wireframe_color:&str
    ) -> Self {
        let init = ws::IWgpuInit::new(&window, sample_count, None).await;

        let vs_shader = init.device.create_shader_module(wgpu::include_wgsl!("shader_vert.wgsl"));
        let fs_shader = init.device.create_shader_module(
            wgpu::include_wgsl!("../ch03/directional_frag.wgsl"));

        // uniform data
        let camera_position = (4.0, 4.0, 4.0).into();
        let look_direction = (0.0,0.0,0.0).into();
        let up_direction = cgmath::Vector3::unit_y();
        let light_direction = [-0.5f32, -0.5, -0.5];

        let (view_mat, project_mat, _) =
            wt::create_vp_mat(camera_position, look_direction, up_direction,
            init.config.width as f32 / init.config.height as f32);

        // create vertex uniform buffers
        // model_mat and vp_mat will be stored in vertex_uniform_buffer inside the update function
        let vert_uniform_buffer = init.device.create_buffer(&wgpu::BufferDescriptor{
            label: Some("Vertex Uniform Buffer"),
            size: 192,
            usage: wgpu::BufferUsages::UNIFORM | wgpu::BufferUsages::COPY_DST,
            mapped_at_creation: false,
        });

        // create light uniform buffer. here we set eye_position = camera_position
        let light_uniform_buffer = init.device.create_buffer(&wgpu::BufferDescriptor{
            label: Some("Light Uniform Buffer"),
            size: 48,
            usage: wgpu::BufferUsages::UNIFORM | wgpu::BufferUsages::COPY_DST,
            mapped_at_creation: false,
        });

        let eye_position:&[f32; 3] = camera_position.as_ref();
        init.queue.write_buffer(&light_uniform_buffer, 0, cast_slice(light_direction.as_ref()));
        init.queue.write_buffer(&light_uniform_buffer, 16, cast_slice(eye_position));

        // set specular light color to white
        let specular_color:[f32; 3] = [1.0, 1.0, 1.0];
        init.queue.write_buffer(&light_uniform_buffer, 32, cast_slice(specular_color.as_ref()));

        // material uniform buffer
        let material_uniform_buffer = init.device.create_buffer(&wgpu::BufferDescriptor{
            label: Some("Material Uniform Buffer"),
            size: 16,
            usage: wgpu::BufferUsages::UNIFORM | wgpu::BufferUsages::COPY_DST,
            mapped_at_creation: false,
        });
```

```
// set default material parameters
let material = [0.1f32, 0.7, 0.4, 30.0];
init.queue.write_buffer(&material_uniform_buffer, 0, cast_slice(material.as_ref()));

// uniform bind group for vertex shader
let (vert_bind_group_layout, vert_bind_group) = ws::create_bind_group(
    &init.device,
    vec![wgpu::ShaderStages::VERTEX],
    &[vert_uniform_buffer.as_entire_binding()],
);
let (vert_bind_group_layout2, vert_bind_group2) = ws::create_bind_group(
    &init.device,
    vec![wgpu::ShaderStages::VERTEX],
    &[vert_uniform_buffer.as_entire_binding()],
);

// uniform bind group for fragment shader
let (frag_bind_group_layout, frag_bind_group) = ws::create_bind_group(
    &init.device,
    vec![wgpu::ShaderStages::FRAGMENT, wgpu::ShaderStages::FRAGMENT],
    &[light_uniform_buffer.as_entire_binding(), material_uniform_buffer.as_entire_binding()],
);
let (frag_bind_group_layout2, frag_bind_group2) = ws::create_bind_group(
    &init.device,
    vec![wgpu::ShaderStages::FRAGMENT, wgpu::ShaderStages::FRAGMENT],
    &[light_uniform_buffer.as_entire_binding(), material_uniform_buffer.as_entire_binding()],
);

let vertex_buffer_layout = VertexBufferLayout {
    array_stride: mem::size_of::<Vertex>() as wgpu::BufferAddress,
    step_mode: wgpu::VertexStepMode::Vertex,
    attributes: &wgpu::vertex_attr_array![0 => Float32x3, 1 => Float32x3, 2 => Float32x3],
    // pos, norm, col
};

let pipeline_layout = init.device.create_pipeline_layout(&wgpu::PipelineLayoutDescriptor {
    label: Some("Render Pipeline Layout"),
    bind_group_layouts: &[&vert_bind_group_layout, &frag_bind_group_layout],
    push_constant_ranges: &[],
});

let mut ppl = ws::IRenderPipeline {
    vs_shader: Some(&vs_shader),
    fs_shader: Some(&fs_shader),
    pipeline_layout: Some(&pipeline_layout),
    vertex_buffer_layout: &[vertex_buffer_layout],
    ..Default::default()
};
let pipeline = ppl.new(&init);

let vertex_buffer_layout2 = VertexBufferLayout {
    array_stride: mem::size_of::<Vertex>() as wgpu::BufferAddress,
    step_mode: wgpu::VertexStepMode::Vertex,
    attributes: &wgpu::vertex_attr_array![0 => Float32x3, 1 => Float32x3, 2 => Float32x3],
    // pos, norm, col
};

let pipeline_layout2 = init.device.create_pipeline_layout(&wgpu::PipelineLayoutDescriptor {
    label: Some("Render Pipeline Layout 2"),
```

```
        bind_group_layouts: &[&vert_bind_group_layout2, &frag_bind_group_layout2],
        push_constant_ranges: &[],
    });

    let mut ppl2 = ws::IRenderPipeline {
        topology: wgpu::PrimitiveTopology::LineList,
        vs_shader: Some(&vs_shader),
        fs_shader: Some(&fs_shader),
        pipeline_layout: Some(&pipeline_layout2),
        vertex_buffer_layout: &[vertex_buffer_layout2],
        ..Default::default()
    };
    let pipeline2 = ppl2.new(&init);

    let msaa_texture_view = ws::create_msaa_texture_view(&init);
    let depth_texture_view = ws::create_depth_view(&init);

    let mut ss = sd::ISimpleSurface {
        scale: 3.0,
        colormap_name: colormap_name.to_string(),
        wireframe_color: wireframe_color.to_string(),
        ..Default::default()
    };
    let data = create_vertices(ss.new());

    let vertex_buffer = init.device.create_buffer_init(&wgpu::util::BufferInitDescriptor {
        label: Some("Vertex Buffer"),
        contents: cast_slice(&data.0),
        usage: wgpu::BufferUsages::VERTEX | wgpu::BufferUsages::COPY_DST,
    });

    let vertex_buffer2 = init.device.create_buffer_init(&wgpu::util::BufferInitDescriptor {
        label: Some("Vertex Buffer 2"),
        contents: cast_slice(&data.1),
        usage: wgpu::BufferUsages::VERTEX | wgpu::BufferUsages::COPY_DST,
    });

    let index_buffer = init.device.create_buffer_init(&wgpu::util::BufferInitDescriptor{
        label: Some("Index Buffer"),
        contents: bytemuck::cast_slice(&data.2),
        usage: wgpu::BufferUsages::INDEX | wgpu::BufferUsages::COPY_DST,
    });

    let index_buffer2 = init.device.create_buffer_init(&wgpu::util::BufferInitDescriptor{
        label: Some("Index Buffer 2"),
        contents: bytemuck::cast_slice(&data.3),
        usage: wgpu::BufferUsages::INDEX | wgpu::BufferUsages::COPY_DST,
    });

    Self {
        init,
        pipelines: vec![pipeline, pipeline2],
        vertex_buffers: vec![vertex_buffer, vertex_buffer2],
        index_buffers: vec![index_buffer, index_buffer2],
        uniform_bind_groups: vec![vert_bind_group, frag_bind_group, vert_bind_group2,
            frag_bind_group2],
        uniform_buffers: vec![vert_uniform_buffer, light_uniform_buffer, material_uniform_buffer],
        view_mat,
        project_mat,
        msaa_texture_view,
```

```rust
                depth_texture_view,
                indices_lens: vec![data.2.len() as u32, data.3.len() as u32],
                plot_type: 0,
                recreate_buffers: false,
                animation_speed: 1.0,
                rotation_speed: 1.0,

                simple_surface: ss,
                fps_counter: ws::FpsCounter::default(),
        }
    }

    fn resize(&mut self, new_size: winit::dpi::PhysicalSize<u32>) {
        if new_size.width > 0 && new_size.height > 0 {
            self.init.size = new_size;
            self.init.config.width = new_size.width;
            self.init.config.height = new_size.height;
            self.init.surface.configure(&self.init.device, &self.init.config);

            self.project_mat = wt::create_projection_mat(new_size.width as f32 / new_size.height as f32,
                true);
            self.depth_texture_view = ws::create_depth_view(&self.init);
            if self.init.sample_count > 1 {
                self.msaa_texture_view = ws::create_msaa_texture_view(&self.init);
            }
        }
    }

    #[allow(unused_variables)]
    fn input(&mut self, event: &WindowEvent) -> bool {
        match event {
            WindowEvent::KeyboardInput {
                input:
                    KeyboardInput {
                        virtual_keycode: Some(keycode),
                        state: ElementState::Pressed,
                        ..
                    },
                ..
            } => {
                match keycode {
                    VirtualKeyCode::Space => {
                        self.plot_type = (self.plot_type + 1) % 3;
                        true
                    }
                    VirtualKeyCode::LControl => {
                        self.simple_surface.surface_type =
                            (self.simple_surface.surface_type + 1) % 3;
                        true
                    },
                    VirtualKeyCode::LAlt => {
                        self.simple_surface.colormap_direction =
                            (self.simple_surface.colormap_direction + 1) % 3;
                        true
                    },
                    VirtualKeyCode::Q => {
                        self.simple_surface.x_resolution += 1;
                        if self.simple_surface.x_resolution > 250 {
                            self.simple_surface.x_resolution = 250;
                        }
```

```rust
                    println!("x_resolution: {}", self.simple_surface.x_resolution);
                    self.recreate_buffers = true;
                    true
                },
                VirtualKeyCode::A => {
                    self.simple_surface.x_resolution -= 1;
                    if self.simple_surface.x_resolution < 8 {
                        self.simple_surface.x_resolution = 8;
                    }
                    println!("x_resolution: {}", self.simple_surface.x_resolution);
                    self.recreate_buffers = true;
                    true
                },
                VirtualKeyCode::W => {
                    self.simple_surface.z_resolution += 1;
                    if self.simple_surface.z_resolution > 250 {
                        self.simple_surface.z_resolution = 250;
                    }
                    println!("z_resolution: {}", self.simple_surface.z_resolution);
                    self.recreate_buffers = true;
                    true
                },
                VirtualKeyCode::S => {
                    self.simple_surface.z_resolution -= 1;
                    if self.simple_surface.z_resolution < 8 {
                        self.simple_surface.z_resolution = 8;
                    }
                    println!("z_resolution: {}", self.simple_surface.z_resolution);
                    self.recreate_buffers = true;
                    true
                } ,
                VirtualKeyCode::E => {
                    self.animation_speed += 0.1;
                    true
                },
                VirtualKeyCode::D => {
                    self.animation_speed -= 0.1;
                    if self.animation_speed < 0.0 {
                        self.animation_speed = 0.0;
                    }
                    true
                } ,
                VirtualKeyCode::R => {
                    self.rotation_speed += 0.1;
                    true
                },
                VirtualKeyCode::F => {
                    self.rotation_speed -= 0.1;
                    if self.rotation_speed < 0.0 {
                        self.rotation_speed = 0.0;
                    }
                    true
                } ,
                _ => false
            }
        }
        _ => false,
    }
}
```

```rust
fn update(&mut self, dt: std::time::Duration) {
    // update uniform buffer
    let dt1 = self.rotation_speed * dt.as_secs_f32();

    let model_mat = wt::create_model_mat([0.0,1.0,0.0], [dt1.sin(), dt1.cos(), 0.0], [1.0, 1.0, 1.0]);
    let view_project_mat = self.project_mat * self.view_mat;

    let normal_mat = (model_mat.invert().unwrap()).transpose();

    let model_ref:&[f32; 16] = model_mat.as_ref();
    let view_projection_ref:&[f32; 16] = view_project_mat.as_ref();
    let normal_ref:&[f32; 16] = normal_mat.as_ref();

    self.init.queue.write_buffer(&self.uniform_buffers[0], 0, cast_slice(view_projection_ref));
    self.init.queue.write_buffer(&self.uniform_buffers[0], 64, cast_slice(model_ref));
    self.init.queue.write_buffer(&self.uniform_buffers[0], 128, cast_slice(normal_ref));

    // recreate vertex and index buffers
    if self.recreate_buffers {
        let data = create_vertices(self.simple_surface.new());
        self.indices_lens = vec![data.2.len() as u32, data.3.len() as u32];
        let vertex_data = [data.0, data.1];
        let index_data = [data.2, data.3];

        for i in 0..2 {
            self.vertex_buffers[i].destroy();
            self.vertex_buffers[i] = self.init.device.create_buffer_init(
            &wgpu::util::BufferInitDescriptor {
                label: Some("Vertex Buffer"),
                contents: cast_slice(&vertex_data[i]),
                usage: wgpu::BufferUsages::VERTEX | wgpu::BufferUsages::COPY_DST,
            });
            self.index_buffers[i].destroy();
            self.index_buffers[i] = self.init.device.create_buffer_init(
            &wgpu::util::BufferInitDescriptor {
                label: Some("Index Buffer"),
                contents: cast_slice(&index_data[i]),
                usage: wgpu::BufferUsages::INDEX | wgpu::BufferUsages::COPY_DST,
            });
        }
        self.recreate_buffers = false;
    }

    // update vertex buffer for every frame
    self.simple_surface.t = self.animation_speed * dt.as_secs_f32();
    let data = create_vertices(self.simple_surface.new());
    self.init.queue.write_buffer(&self.vertex_buffers[0], 0, cast_slice(&data.0));
    self.init.queue.write_buffer(&self.vertex_buffers[1], 0, cast_slice(&data.1));
}

fn render(&mut self) -> Result<(), wgpu::SurfaceError> {
    let output = self.init.surface.get_current_texture()?;
    let view = output
        .texture
        .create_view(&wgpu::TextureViewDescriptor::default());

    let mut encoder = self
        .init.device
        .create_command_encoder(&wgpu::CommandEncoderDescriptor {
            label: Some("Render Encoder"),
```

```
        });

    {
        let color_attach = ws::create_color_attachment(&view);
        let msaa_attach = ws::create_msaa_color_attachment(&view, &self.msaa_texture_view);
        let color_attachment = if self.init.sample_count == 1 { color_attach } else { msaa_attach };
        let depth_attachment = ws::create_depth_stencil_attachment(&self.depth_texture_view);

        let mut render_pass = encoder.begin_render_pass(&wgpu::RenderPassDescriptor {
            label: Some("Render Pass"),
            color_attachments: &[Some(color_attachment)],
            depth_stencil_attachment: Some(depth_attachment),
            occlusion_query_set: None,
            timestamp_writes: None,
        });

        let plot_type = if self.plot_type == 1 { "shape_only" }
            else if self.plot_type == 2 {"wireframe_only"} else {"both"};

        if plot_type == "shape_only" || plot_type == "both" {
            render_pass.set_pipeline(&self.pipelines[0]);
            render_pass.set_vertex_buffer(0, self.vertex_buffers[0].slice(..));
            render_pass.set_index_buffer(self.index_buffers[0].slice(..),
                wgpu::IndexFormat::Uint16);
            render_pass.set_bind_group(0, &self.uniform_bind_groups[0], &[]);
            render_pass.set_bind_group(1, &self.uniform_bind_groups[1], &[]);
            render_pass.draw_indexed(0..self.indices_lens[0], 0, 0..1);
        }

        if plot_type == "wireframe_only" || plot_type == "both" {
            render_pass.set_pipeline(&self.pipelines[1]);
            render_pass.set_vertex_buffer(0, self.vertex_buffers[1].slice(..));
            render_pass.set_index_buffer(self.index_buffers[1].slice(..),
                wgpu::IndexFormat::Uint16);
            render_pass.set_bind_group(0, &self.uniform_bind_groups[2], &[]);
            render_pass.set_bind_group(1, &self.uniform_bind_groups[3], &[]);
            render_pass.draw_indexed(0..self.indices_lens[1], 0, 0..1);
        }

        self.fps_counter.print_fps(5);
    }

    self.init.queue.submit(iter::once(encoder.finish()));
    output.present();

    Ok(())
    }
}

fn main() {
    let mut sample_count = 1 as u32;
    let mut colormap_name = "jet";
    let mut wireframe_color = "white";
    let args: Vec<String> = std::env::args().collect();
    if args.len() > 1 {
        sample_count = args[1].parse::<u32>().unwrap();
    }
    if args.len() > 2 {
        colormap_name = &args[2];
    }
```

```rust
    if args.len() > 3 {
        wireframe_color = &args[3];
    }

    env_logger::init();
    let event_loop = EventLoop::new();
    let window = winit::window::WindowBuilder::new().build(&event_loop).unwrap();
    window.set_title(&*format!("ch05_{}", "simple_surface"));

    let mut state = pollster::block_on(State::new(&window, sample_count, colormap_name,
        wireframe_color));
    let render_start_time = std::time::Instant::now();

    event_loop.run(move |event, _, control_flow| {
        match event {
            Event::WindowEvent {
                ref event,
                window_id,
            } if window_id == window.id() => {
                if !state.input(event) {
                    match event {
                        WindowEvent::CloseRequested
                        | WindowEvent::KeyboardInput {
                            input:
                                KeyboardInput {
                                    state: ElementState::Pressed,
                                    virtual_keycode: Some(VirtualKeyCode::Escape),
                                    ..
                                },
                            ..
                        } => *control_flow = ControlFlow::Exit,
                        WindowEvent::Resized(physical_size) => {
                            state.resize(*physical_size);
                        }
                        WindowEvent::ScaleFactorChanged { new_inner_size, .. } => {
                            state.resize(**new_inner_size);
                        }
                        _ => {}
                    }
                }
            }
            Event::RedrawRequested(_) => {
                let now = std::time::Instant::now();
                let dt = now - render_start_time;
                state.update(dt);

                match state.render() {
                    Ok(_) => {}
                    Err(wgpu::SurfaceError::Lost) => state.resize(state.init.size),
                    Err(wgpu::SurfaceError::OutOfMemory) => *control_flow = ControlFlow::Exit,
                    Err(e) => eprintln!("{:?}", e),
                }
            }
            Event::MainEventsCleared => {
                window.request_redraw();
            }
            _ => {}
        }
    });
}
```

The *State::new* and *State::render* functions in the above code are similar to those used in the *ch03-common_blinn_phong.rs* file located in the *examples/ch03/* folder, with the exception that this example uses different shader code and adds an extra color field to the *Vertex* struct that is used to store the colormap data when creating the render pipelines for both the surface and the wireframe.

This code also checks the *recreate_buffers* variable to determine whether the vertex and index buffers need to be regenerated. The variable will be set to *true* if either the *x_resolution* or *z_resolution* is changed. In this case, we will regenerate the buffers using the following code snippet:

```
if self.recreate_buffers {
    let data = create_vertices(self.simple_surface.new());
    self.indices_lens = vec![data.2.len() as u32, data.3.len() as u32];
    let vertex_data = [data.0, data.1];
    let index_data = [data.2, data.3];

    for i in 0..2 {
        self.vertex_buffers[i].destroy();
        self.vertex_buffers[i] = self.init.device.create_buffer_init(
        &wgpu::util::BufferInitDescriptor {
            label: Some("Vertex Buffer"),
            contents: cast_slice(&vertex_data[i]),
            usage: wgpu::BufferUsages::VERTEX | wgpu::BufferUsages::COPY_DST,
        });
        self.index_buffers[i].destroy();
        self.index_buffers[i] = self.init.device.create_buffer_init(
        &wgpu::util::BufferInitDescriptor {
            label: Some("Index Buffer"),
            contents: cast_slice(&index_data[i]),
            usage: wgpu::BufferUsages::INDEX | wgpu::BufferUsages::COPY_DST,
        });
    }
    self.recreate_buffers = false;
}
```

Unlike the previous examples, where the change in vertex data comes from varying user input parameters, this example also animates the vertex data directly by updating it with a time dependent parameter within the *State::update* function. The following code snippet illustrates this process:

```
self.simple_surface.t = self.animation_speed * dt.as_secs_f32();
let data = create_vertices(self.simple_surface.new());
self.init.queue.write_buffer(&self.vertex_buffers[0], 0, cast_slice(&data.0));
self.init.queue.write_buffer(&self.vertex_buffers[1], 0, cast_slice(&data.1));
```

The above code snippet is executed continuously inside the *State::update* function for every frame. However, this is a computation-intensive process, particularly when the grid points have a high resolution, controlled by the *x_resolution* and *z_resolution* parameters.

To examine the rendering performance of this application, we print the FPS value in every 5 seconds inside the *State::render* function by calling the *print_fps* method implemented in the *wgpu_simplified* module:

```
self.fps_counter.print_fps(5);
```

This code allows you to monitor the performance during the rendering process.

In the *State::inputs* function, the user can manipulate various input parameters via the keyboard inputs, such as the surface type, plot type, colormap of the surface, color of the wireframe, number of grid points along the *x*- and *z*-axis.

Here is a list of controls using keyboard:

- *Space*: Changes the plot type: surface, wireframe, or both.
- *LControl*: Changes the surface type: *sinc*, *peaks*, or *poles*.
- *LAlt*: Changes colormap direction: *x*, *y*, or *z*.
- *Q/A*: Increases/decreases *x_resolution*.
- *W/S:* Increases/decreases *z_resolution*.
- *E/D:* Increases/decreases the animation speed.
- *R/F:* Increases/decreases the rotation speed.

5.5.4 Run Application

To run this application, add the following code snippet to the *Cargo.toml* file:

```
[[example]]
name = "ch05_simple_surface"
path = "examples/ch05/simple_surface.rs"
```

Afterward, execute the following *cargo run* commands in the terminal window:

```
cargo run --example ch05_simple_surface 8
```

Fig.5-1 shows the results of this example by varying the input parameters via the keyboard inputs.

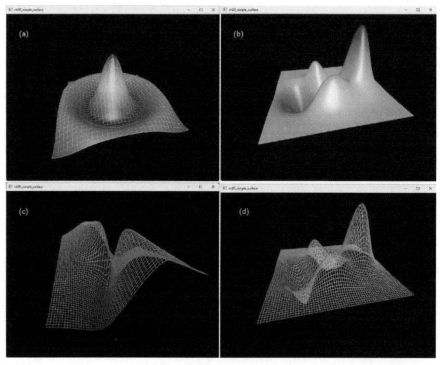

Fig.5-1. Simple 3D surfaces generated by varying input parameters.

It is evident from the results displayed in Fig.5-1 that by manipulating the input parameters from the keyboard inputs, various simple 3D surfaces can be created. The figure showcases the following: (a) the *sinc* surface with wireframe, (b) the *peaks* surface without wireframe, (c) the *poles* wireframe with the *cool* colormap, and (d) the peaks wireframe with a yellow color. Furthermore, both the surface and the wireframe feature a lighting effect.

The default values for both *x_resolution* and *z_resolution* are set to 30. On my machine with an Nvidia GeForce RTX 3060 GPU, the FPS value displayed in the terminal is 60 FPS, in sync with my 60 Hz display's refresh rate, indicating that the rendering time for creating a simple 3D surface is less or equal to 16.67 ms. However, if the resolution is increased to 250 by setting both *x_resolution* and *z_resolution* to 250, the framerate drops to 16 FPS.

For rendering a single 3D surface, using the default resolution of 30 is good enough. However, rendering more complex objects with detailed structures in a scene, such as those found in video games, requires higher resolution (>1000). Unfortunately, it is currently impossible to achieve such resolutions with our current implementation. The reason for this limitation is that the code used to create the vertex data in the current example is written in Rust and runs on the CPU. The CPU typically has a limited number of cores and, therefore, limited parallel processing power. Updating the vertex data for every frame with high resolution using the CPU can lead to frame drops, causing the application to become unresponsive and appear to lag or freeze.

In order to overcome this problem, we will explore how to use a compute shader to generate the vertex data directly on the GPU in future chapters. By leveraging the GPU's parallel processing capabilities, we can update the vertex data for every frame with high resolution (> 1000) while maintaining a frame rate of 60 FPS.

5.6 Parametric 3D Surfaces

In the preceding sections, you learned how to create simple 3D surfaces. A key characteristic of this type of surface is that there is at most one *y* value for each pair of *x* and *z* values. However, sometimes you may want to create a complex surface of a certain shape that cannot be represented by a simple mathematical formula. For certain values of *x* and *z*, this type of surface has more than one *y* value, making the approach discussed in the preceding sections unsuitable for storing and displaying the data.

One way to represent such a surface is to use a set of parametric equations that define the *x*, *y*, and *z* coordinates of points on the surface in terms of the parametric variables *u* and *v*. Many complex surfaces can be represented using parametric equations. For example, the sphere, torus, Klein bottle, and quadric surfaces are all parametric surfaces.

5.6.1 Vertex Data

In this section, we will generate vertex data for a 3D parametric surface described by a set of parametric equations:

$$x = x(u, v)$$
$$y = y(u, v)$$
$$z = z(u, v)$$

We will approximate the parametric surface using a rectangular mesh or quad mesh in the parametric *u*-*v* space. To achieve this, add the following code to the *surface_data.rs* file in the *src/* folder:

```rust
pub struct IParametricSurface {
    pub surface_type: u32,
    pub surface_type_map: HashMap<u32, String>,
    pub umin: f32,
    pub umax: f32,
    pub vmin: f32,
    pub vmax: f32,
    pub u_resolution: u16,
    pub v_resolution: u16,
    pub scale: f32,
    pub aspect_ratio: f32,
    pub colormap_name: String,
    pub wireframe_color: String,
    pub colormap_direction: u32, // 0: x-direction, 1: y-direction, 2: z-direction
    pub uv_lens: [f32; 2],
}

fn surface_type_map() -> HashMap<u32,String> {
    let mut surface_type = HashMap::new();
    surface_type.insert(0, String::from("klein_bottle"));
    surface_type.insert(1, String::from("astroid"));
    surface_type.insert(2, String::from("astroid2"));
    surface_type.insert(3, String::from("astrodal_torus"));
    surface_type.insert(4, String::from("bohemian_dome"));
    surface_type.insert(5, String::from("boy_shape"));
    surface_type.insert(6, String::from("breather"));
    surface_type.insert(7, String::from("enneper"));
    surface_type.insert(8, String::from("figure8"));
    surface_type.insert(9, String::from("henneberg"));
    surface_type.insert(10, String::from("kiss"),);
    surface_type.insert(11, String::from("klein_bottle2"));
    surface_type.insert(12, String::from("klein_bottle3"));
    surface_type.insert(13, String::from("kuen"));
    surface_type.insert(14, String::from("minimal"));
    surface_type.insert(15, String::from("parabolic_cyclide"));
    surface_type.insert(16, String::from("pear"));
    surface_type.insert(17, String::from("plucker_conoid"));
    surface_type.insert(18, String::from("seashell"));
    surface_type.insert(19, String::from("sievert_enneper"));
    surface_type.insert(20, String::from("steiner"));
    surface_type.insert(21, String::from("torus"));
    surface_type.insert(22, String::from("wellenkugel"));
    surface_type
}

impl Default for IParametricSurface {
    fn default() -> Self {
        Self {
            surface_type: 0,
            surface_type_map: surface_type_map(),
            umin: -1.0,
            umax: 1.0,
            vmin: -1.0,
            vmax: 1.0,
            u_resolution: 80,
            v_resolution: 80,
            scale: 1.0,
            aspect_ratio: 1.0,
            colormap_name: "jet".to_string(),
            wireframe_color: "white".to_string(),
```

```rust
            colormap_direction: 1,
            uv_lens: [1.0, 1.0],
        }
    }
}


impl IParametricSurface {
    pub fn new(&mut self) -> ISurfaceOutput {
        if self.surface_type == 1 {
            (self.umin, self.umax, self.vmin, self.vmax) = (0.0, 2.0*PI, 0.0, 2.0*PI);
            self.parametric_surface_data(&mf::astroid)
        } else if self.surface_type == 2 {
            (self.umin, self.umax, self.vmin, self.vmax) = (0.0, 2.0*PI, 0.0, 2.0*PI);
            self.parametric_surface_data(&mf::astroid2)
        } else if self.surface_type == 3 {
            (self.umin, self.umax, self.vmin, self.vmax) = (-PI, PI, 0.0, 5.0);
            self.parametric_surface_data(&mf::astroidal_torus)
        } else if self.surface_type == 4 {
            (self.umin, self.umax, self.vmin, self.vmax) = (0.0, 2.0*PI, 0.0, 2.0*PI);
            self.parametric_surface_data(&mf::bohemian_dome)
        } else if self.surface_type == 5 {
            (self.umin, self.umax, self.vmin, self.vmax) = (0.0, PI, 0.0, PI);
            self.parametric_surface_data(&mf::boy_shape)
        } else if self.surface_type == 6 {
            (self.umin, self.umax, self.vmin, self.vmax) = (-14.0, 14.0, -12.0*PI, 12.0*PI);
            self.parametric_surface_data(&mf::breather)
        } else if self.surface_type == 7 {
            (self.umin, self.umax, self.vmin, self.vmax) = (-3.3, 3.3, -3.3, 3.3);
            self.parametric_surface_data(&mf::enneper)
        } else if self.surface_type == 8 {
            (self.umin, self.umax, self.vmin, self.vmax) = (0.0, 4.0*PI, 0.0, 2.0*PI);
            self.parametric_surface_data(&mf::figure8)
        } else if self.surface_type == 9 {
            (self.umin, self.umax, self.vmin, self.vmax) = (0.0, 1.0, 0.0, 2.0*PI);
            self.parametric_surface_data(&mf::henneberg)
        } else if self.surface_type == 10 {
            (self.umin, self.umax, self.vmin, self.vmax) = (-0.99999, 0.99999, 0.0, 2.0*PI);
            self.parametric_surface_data(&mf::kiss)
        } else if self.surface_type == 11 {
            (self.umin, self.umax, self.vmin, self.vmax) = (0.0, 2.0*PI, 0.0, 2.0*PI);
            self.parametric_surface_data(&mf::klein_bottle2)
        } else if self.surface_type == 12 {
            (self.umin, self.umax, self.vmin, self.vmax) = (0.0, 4.0*PI, 0.0, 2.0*PI);
            self.parametric_surface_data(&mf::klein_bottle3)
        } else if self.surface_type == 13 {
            (self.umin, self.umax, self.vmin, self.vmax) = (-4.5, 4.5, -5.0, 5.0);
            self.parametric_surface_data(&mf::kuen)
        } else if self.surface_type == 14 {
            (self.umin, self.umax, self.vmin, self.vmax) = (-3.0, 1.0, -3.0*PI, 3.0*PI);
            self.parametric_surface_data(&mf::minimal)
        } else if self.surface_type == 15 {
            (self.umin, self.umax, self.vmin, self.vmax) = (-5.0, 5.0, -5.0, 5.0);
            self.parametric_surface_data(&mf::parabolic_cyclide)
        } else if self.surface_type == 16 {
            (self.umin, self.umax, self.vmin, self.vmax) = (0.0, 1.0, 0.0, 2.0*PI);
            self.parametric_surface_data(&mf::pear)
        } else if self.surface_type == 17 {
            (self.umin, self.umax, self.vmin, self.vmax) = (-2.0, 2.0, 0.0, 2.0*PI);
            self.parametric_surface_data(&mf::plucker_conoid)
        } else if self.surface_type == 18 {
```

```rust
            (self.umin, self.umax, self.vmin, self.vmax) = (0.0, 6.0*PI, 0.0, 2.0*PI);
            self.parametric_surface_data(&mf::seashell)
        } else if self.surface_type == 19 {
            (self.umin, self.umax, self.vmin, self.vmax) = (-PI/2.1, PI/2.1, 0.001, PI/1.001);
            self.parametric_surface_data(&mf::sievert_enneper)
        } else if self.surface_type == 20 {
            (self.umin, self.umax, self.vmin, self.vmax) = (0.0, 1.999999*PI, 0.0, 0.999999*PI);
            self.parametric_surface_data(&mf::steiner)
        } else if self.surface_type == 21 {
            (self.umin, self.umax, self.vmin, self.vmax) = (0.0, 2.0*PI, 0.0, 2.0*PI);
            self.parametric_surface_data(&mf::torus)
        } else if self.surface_type == 22 {
            (self.umin, self.umax, self.vmin, self.vmax) = (0.0, 14.5, 0.0, 5.2);
            self.parametric_surface_data(&mf::wellenkugel)
        } else {
            (self.umin, self.umax, self.vmin, self.vmax) = (0.0, PI, 0.0, 2.0*PI);
            self.parametric_surface_data(&mf::klein_bottle)
        }
    }

    fn parametric_surface_data(&mut self, f:&dyn Fn(f32, f32) -> [f32; 3]) -> ISurfaceOutput {
        let mut positions: Vec<[f32; 3]> = vec![];
        let mut normals: Vec<[f32; 3]> = vec![];
        let mut colors: Vec<[f32; 3]> = vec![];
        let mut colors2: Vec<[f32; 3]> = vec![];
        let mut uvs: Vec<[f32; 2]> = vec![];

        let du = (self.umax - self.umin)/self.u_resolution as f32;
        let dv = (self.vmax - self.vmin)/self.v_resolution as f32;
        let (epsu, epsv) = (0.01 * du, 0.01 * dv);

        let (min_val, max_val, pts) = self.parametric_surface_range(f);
        let cdata = colormap::colormap_data(&self.colormap_name);
        let cdata2 = colormap::colormap_data(&self.wireframe_color);

        for i in 0..=self.u_resolution {
            let u = self.umin + du * i as f32;
            for j in 0..=self.v_resolution {
                let v = self.vmin + dv * j as f32;
                positions.push(pts[i as usize][j as usize]);

                // calculate normals
                let nu = Vector3::from(f(u+epsu, v)) - Vector3::from(f(u-epsu, v));
                let nv = Vector3::from(f(u, v+epsv)) - Vector3::from(f(u, v-epsv));
                let normal = nu.cross(nv).normalize();
                normals.push(normal.into());

                // colormap
                let color = colormap::color_lerp(cdata, min_val, max_val,
                    pts[i as usize][j as usize][self.colormap_direction as usize]);
                let color2 = colormap::color_lerp(cdata2, min_val, max_val,
                    pts[i as usize][j as usize][self.colormap_direction as usize]);
                colors.push(color);
                colors2.push(color2);

                // uvs
                uvs.push([self.uv_lens[0]*(u-self.umin)/(self.umax-self.umin),
                    self.uv_lens[1]*(v-self.vmin)/(self.vmax-self.vmin)
                ]);
            }
```

```rust
    }

    // calculate indices
    let mut indices: Vec<u16> = vec![];
    let mut indices2: Vec<u16> = vec![];
    let vertices_per_row = self.v_resolution + 1;

    for i in 0..self.u_resolution {
        for j in 0..self.v_resolution {
            let idx0 = j + i * vertices_per_row;
            let idx1 = j + 1 + i * vertices_per_row;
            let idx2 = j + 1 + (i + 1) * vertices_per_row;
            let idx3 = j + (i + 1) * vertices_per_row;

            let values:Vec<u16> = vec![idx0, idx1, idx2, idx2, idx3, idx0];
            indices.extend(values);

            let values2:Vec<u16> = vec![idx0, idx1, idx0, idx3];
            indices2.extend(values2);
            if i == self.u_resolution - 1 || j == self.v_resolution - 1 {
                let edge_values:Vec<u16> = vec![idx1, idx2, idx2, idx3];
                indices2.extend(edge_values);
            }
        }
    }

    ISurfaceOutput { positions, normals, colors, colors2, uvs, indices, indices2 }
}

fn parametric_surface_range(&mut self, f:&dyn Fn(f32, f32) -> [f32; 3])
-> (f32, f32, Vec<Vec<[f32;3]>>) {
    let du = (self.umax - self.umin)/self.u_resolution as f32;
    let dv = (self.vmax - self.vmin)/self.v_resolution as f32;
    let (mut xmin, mut ymin, mut zmin) = (f32::MAX, f32::MAX, f32::MAX);
    let (mut xmax, mut ymax, mut zmax) = (f32::MIN, f32::MIN, f32::MIN);

    let mut pts: Vec<Vec<[f32; 3]>> = vec![];
    for i in 0..=self.u_resolution {
        let u = self.umin + du * i as f32;
        let mut pt1: Vec<[f32; 3]> = vec![];
        for j in 0..=self.v_resolution {
            let v = self.vmin + dv * j as f32;
            let pt = f(u, v);
            xmin = if pt[0] < xmin { pt[0] } else { xmin };
            xmax = if pt[0] > xmax { pt[0] } else { xmax };
            ymin = if pt[1] < ymin { pt[1] } else { ymin };
            ymax = if pt[1] > ymax { pt[1] } else { ymax };
            zmin = if pt[2] < zmin { pt[2] } else { zmin };
            zmax = if pt[2] > zmax { pt[2] } else { zmax };
            pt1.push(pt);
        }
        pts.push(pt1);
    }

    let (mut min_val, mut max_val) = (f32::MAX, f32::MIN);
    let dist = (xmax - xmin).max(ymax - ymin).max(zmax - zmin);

    for i in 0..=self.u_resolution {
        for j in 0..=self.v_resolution {
            let mut pt = pts[i as usize][j as usize];
```

```
            pt[0] = self.scale * (pt[0] - 0.5 * (xmin + xmax)) / dist;
            pt[1] = self.scale * (pt[1] - 0.5 * (ymin + ymax)) / dist;
            pt[2] = self.scale * (pt[2] - 0.5 * (zmin + zmax)) / dist;
            let pt1 = pt[self.colormap_direction as usize];
            min_val = if pt1 < min_val { pt1 } else { min_val };
            max_val = if pt1 > max_val { pt1 } else { max_val };
            pts[i as usize][j as usize] = pt;
        }
    }
    (min_val, max_val, pts)
    }
}
```

The above code first creates a struct names *IParametricSurface*, which contains various fields used as input parameters for generating vertex data of a parametric 3D surface. It then implements a private *surface_type_map* function that returns a *HashMap*, a dictionary-like key-value pair collection. This *HashMap* uses a *u32* integer key to map the name of a parametric 3D surface, making it easier to manipulate the integer key than the string name directly.

The code then implements the *Default* trait for the *IParametricSurface* struct, which provides a default value for a type. The *default()* function creates a new *IParametricSurface* with default values.

Next, the code defines the implementation block for the struct. The *parametric_surface_range* and *parametric_surface_data* functions in the block are similar to those used in creating simple 3D surfaces. The difference is that here, the input function is defined using the parametric variables *u* and *v* instead of *x* and *z*. The data region parameters, *umin*, *umax*, *vmin*, and *vmax*, defined in the *IParametricSurface* struct, set the parametric region in the parametric space. This means that in the parametric space, we create a constant *u-v* grid with equal spacing in the respective *u* and *v* directions, and the input function $f(u, v)$ has at most one value for each pair of *u* and *v* values. Therefore, we create a simple surface in the *u-v* space using an approach similar to the one for creating actual simple surfaces. The trick for creating a parametric surface is to map the simple surface in the *u-v* space back to the *x-y-z* coordinate system using the parametric equations. The resulting surface in the real-world space can be very different from the one in the parametric space.

The *parametric_surface_range* function in the above code begins by computing the data region in the *x-y-z* coordinate system using the parametric equations. It then uses this data range to normalize the data, providing a consistent size for different parametric 3D surfaces in the scene when using the same camera and transformations. Additionally, the function calculates the color region specified by *min_value* and *max_value*, which will be used for colormap.

The *parametric_surface_data* function is our main function, which will used to generate the vertex data for a parametric 3D surface. Within the function, we first introduce several arrays for holding the position, normal, colormap, and UV data. In the *for*-loop, the *positions* array is populated with the normalized data calculated from the *parametric_surface_range* function. Subsequently, the normal vector for each vertex is calculated by making small displacements along the *u* and *v* directions in the parametric space and calculating the cross product of these displacements. This approach ensures that the normal vector is always perpendicular to the surface.

Next, two colormaps are calculated: one for the surface and the other for the wireframe, by calling the *color_learp* function defined earlier in the *colormap.rs* file. The UV data for the surface and two index data, one for the surface and the other for the wireframe, are also calculated. The private function *parametric_surface_data* returns an object of the *ISurfaceOutput* type.

The public *new* function is specifically designed to generate surface data for 23 different parametric surfaces. Within this function, different data ranges in the parametric space are set depending on the surface type selected. The function then calls the *parametric_surface_data* function to generate the surface data.

5.6.2 Math Functions for Parametric Surfaces

This subsection implements 23 mathematical functions used to create different parametric 3D surfaces, including popular shapes such as the Klein bottle, figure-8, seashell, and Wellenkugel surface. Please add 23 new functions to the *math_func.rs* file located in the *src/* folder and include the following code:

```rust
pub fn torus(u:f32, v:f32) -> [f32; 3] {
    let x = (1.0 + 0.3 * v.cos()) * u.cos();
    let y = 0.3 * v.sin();
    let z = (1.0 + 0.3 * v.cos()) * u.sin();
    [x, y, z]
}

pub fn sphere(u:f32, v:f32) -> [f32; 3] {
    let x = v.sin() * u.cos();
    let y = v.cos();
    let z = -v.sin() * u.sin();
    [x, y, z]
}

pub fn breather(u:f32, v:f32) -> [f32; 3] {
    const A:f32 = 0.4; // where 0 < A < 1

    let de = A*((1.0-A*A)* ((A*u).cosh()).powf(2.0)+A*A*((((1.0-A*A).sqrt()*v).sin()).powf(2.0)));

    let x = -u+(2.0*(1.0-A*A)*(A*u).cosh()*(A*u).sinh())/de;

    let y = (2.0*(1.0-A*A).sqrt()*(A*u).cosh()*(-((1.0-A*A).sqrt()*v.cos()*((1.0-A*A).sqrt()*v).cos()) -
        v.sin()*((1.0-A*A).sqrt()*v).sin()))/de;

    let z = (2.0*(1.0-A*A).sqrt()*(A*u).cosh()*(-((1.0-A*A).sqrt()*v.sin()*((1.0-A*A).sqrt()*v).cos()) +
        v.cos()*((1.0-A*A).sqrt()*v).sin()))/de;

    [x, y, z]
}

pub fn sievert_enneper(u:f32, v:f32) -> [f32; 3] {
    const A:f32 = 1.0;

    let pu = -u/(1.0+A).sqrt() + (u.tan()*(1.0+A).sqrt()).atan();
    let auv = 2.0/(1.0+A-A*v.sin()*v.sin()*u.cos()*u.cos());
    let ruv = auv*v.sin()*((1.0+1.0/A)*(1.0+A*u.sin()*u.sin())).sqrt();

    let x = (((v/2.0).tan()).ln() + (1.0+A)*auv*v.cos()) /A.sqrt();
    let y = ruv*pu.cos();
    let z = ruv*pu.sin();

    [x, y, z]
}

pub fn seashell(u:f32, v:f32) -> [f32; 3] {
    let x = 2.0*(-1.0+(u/(6.0*PI)).exp())*u.sin()*(((v/2.0).cos()).powf(2.0));
```

```
    let y = 1.0 - (u/(3.0*PI)).exp()-v.sin() + (u/(6.0*PI)).exp()*v.sin();

    let z = 2.0*(1.0-(u/(6.0*PI)).exp())*u.cos()*((v/2.0).cos()).powf(2.0);

    [x, y, z]
}

pub fn wellenkugel(u:f32, v:f32) -> [f32; 3] {
    let x = u*(u.cos()).cos()*v.sin();
    let y = u*(u.cos()).sin();
    let z = u*(u.cos()).cos()*v.cos();
    [x, y, z]
}

pub fn figure8(u:f32, v:f32) -> [f32; 3] {
    let a = 2.5f32;
    let x = (a + (0.5 * u).cos() * v.sin() - (0.5 * u).sin() * (2.0 * v).sin()) * u.cos();
    let y = (a + (0.5 * u).cos() * v.sin() - (0.5 * u).sin() * (2.0 * v).sin()) * u.sin();
    let z = (0.5 * u).sin() * v.sin() + (0.5 * u).cos() * (2.0 * v).sin();
    [x, y, z]
}

pub fn klein_bottle3(u:f32, v:f32) -> [f32; 3] {
    let a = 8f32;
    let n = 3f32;
    let m = 1f32;

    let x = (a + (0.5 * u * n).cos() * v.sin() - (0.5 * u * n).sin() * (2.0 * v).sin()) *
        (0.5 * u * m).cos();
    let y = (0.5 * u * n).sin() * v.sin() + (0.5 * u * n).cos() * (2.0 * v).sin();
    let z = (a + (0.5 * u * n).cos() * v.sin() - (0.5 * u * n).sin() * (2.0 * v).sin()) *
        (0.5 * u * m).sin();
    [x, y, z]
}

pub fn klein_bottle2(u:f32, v:f32) -> [f32; 3] {
    let (mut x, mut z) = (0f32, 0f32);
    let r = 4.0 * (1.0 - 0.5 * u.cos());
    if u >= 0.0 && u <= PI {
        x = 6.0 * u.cos() * (1.0 + u.sin()) + r * u.cos() * v.cos();
        z = 16.0 * u.sin() + r * u.sin() * v.cos();
    } else if u > PI && u <= 2.0 * PI {
        x = 6.0 * u.cos() * (1.0 + u.sin()) + r *(v + PI).cos();
        z = 16.0 * u.sin();
    }
    let y = r * v.sin();
    [x, y, z]
}

pub fn klein_bottle(u:f32, v:f32) -> [f32; 3] {
    let x = 2.0/15.0*(3.0+5.0*u.cos()*u.sin())*v.sin();

    let y = -1.0/15.0*u.sin()*(3.0*v.cos()-3.0*(u.cos()).powf(2.0)*v.cos()-
    48.0*(u.cos()).powf(4.0)*v.cos()+48.0*(u.cos()).powf(6.0)*v.cos()-
    60.0*u.sin()+5.0*u.cos()*v.cos()*u.sin()-5.0*(u.cos()).powf(3.0)*v.cos()*u.sin()-
    80.0*(u.cos()).powf(5.0)*v.cos()*u.sin()+80.0*(u.cos()).powf(7.0)*v.cos()*u.sin());

    let z = -2.0/15.0*u.cos()*(3.0*v.cos()-30.0*u.sin() +
    90.0*(u.cos()).powf(4.0)*u.sin()-60.0*(u.cos()).powf(6.0)*u.sin() + 5.0*u.cos()*v.cos()*u.sin());
```

```
        [x, y, z]
}

pub fn astroid(u:f32, v:f32) -> [f32; 3] {
    let a = 1.5f32;
    let x = a * (u.cos()).powf(3.0) * (v.cos()).powf(3.0);
    let y = a * (u.sin()).powf(3.0);
    let z = a * (u.sin()).powf(3.0) * (v.cos()).powf(3.0);
    [x, y, z]
}

pub fn astroid2(u:f32, v:f32) -> [f32; 3] {
    let x = (u.sin()).powf(3.0) * v.cos();
    let y = (u.cos()).powf(3.0);
    let z = (u.sin()).powf(3.0) * v.sin();
    [x, y, z]
}

pub fn astroidal_torus(u:f32, v:f32) -> [f32; 3] {
    let a = 2.0;
    let b = 1.0;
    let c = 7854.0f32;
    let x = (a + b * (u.cos()).powf(3.0) * c.cos() - b * (u.sin()).powf(3.0) * c.sin()) * v.cos();
    let y = b * (u.cos()).powf(3.0) * c.sin() + b * (u.sin()).powf(3.0) * c.cos();
    let z = (a + b * (u.cos()).powf(3.0) * c.cos() - b * (u.sin()).powf(3.0) * c.sin()) * v.sin();
    [x, y, z]
}

pub fn bohemian_dome(u:f32, v:f32) -> [f32; 3] {
    let a = 0.7;
    let x = a * u.cos();
    let y = v.cos();
    let z = a * u.sin() + v.sin();
    [x, y, z]
}

pub fn boy_shape(u:f32, v:f32) -> [f32; 3] {
    let x = u.cos() * (1.0 / 3.0 * 2.0f32.sqrt() * u.cos() * (2.0 * v).cos() +
        2.0 / 3.0 * u.sin() * v.cos()) / (1.0 - 2.0f32.sqrt() * u.sin() * u.cos() * (3.0 * v).sin());
    let y = u.cos() * u.cos() / (1.0 - 2.0f32.sqrt() * u.sin() * u.cos() * (3.0 * v).sin()) - 1.0;
    let z = u.cos() * (1.0 / 3.0 * 2.0f32.sqrt() * u.cos() * (2.0 * v).sin() -
        2.0 / 3.0 * u.sin() * v.sin()) / (1.0 - 2.0f32.sqrt() * u.sin() * u.cos() * (3.0 * v).sin());
    [x, y, z]
}

pub fn enneper(u:f32, v:f32) -> [f32; 3] {
    let a = 1.0/3.0;
    let x = a * u * (1.0 - u * u / 3.0 + v * v);
    let y = a * (u * u - v * v);
    let z = a * v * (1.0 - v * v / 3.0 + u * u);
    [x, y, z]
}

pub fn henneberg(u:f32, v:f32) -> [f32; 3] {
    let x = u.sinh() * v.cos() - (3.0*u).sinh() * (3.0*v).cos()/3.0;
    let y = (2.0*u).cosh() * (2.0*v).cos();
    let z = u.sinh() * v.sin() - (3.0*u).sinh() * (3.0*v).sin()/3.0;
    [x, y, z]
}
```

```rust
pub fn kiss(u:f32, v:f32) -> [f32; 3] {
    let x = u * u * (1.0-u).sqrt() * v.cos();
    let y = u;
    let z = u * u * (1.0-u).sqrt() * v.sin();
    [x, y, z]
}

pub fn kuen(u:f32, v:f32) -> [f32; 3] {
    let x = 2.0 * u * v.cos();
    let y = 2.0 * (3.0 * v).cos();
    let z = 2.0 * u * v.sin();
    [x, y, z]
}

pub fn minimal(u:f32, v:f32) -> [f32; 3] {
    let x = u - (2.0*u).exp() * (2.0 *v).cos() /2.0 ;
    let y = 2.0 * u.exp() * v.cos();
    let z = -(v + (2.0*u).exp() * (2.0 * v).sin()/2.0);
    [x, y, z]
}

pub fn parabolic_cyclide(u:f32, v:f32) -> [f32; 3] {
    let x = u * (0.5 + v*v)/(1.0 + u*u + v*v);
    let y = 0.5 * (2.0*v*v + 0.5*(1.0 - u*u - v*v))/(1.0 + u*u + v*v);
    let z = v * (1.0 + u*u -0.5)/(1.0 + u*u + v*v);
    [x, y, z]
}

pub fn pear(u:f32, v:f32) -> [f32; 3] {
    let x = u * (u * (1.0 - u)).sqrt() * v.cos();
    let y = -u;
    let z = u * (u * (1.0 - u)).sqrt() * v.sin();
    [x, y, z]
}

pub fn plucker_conoid(u:f32, v:f32) -> [f32; 3] {
    let x = 2.0 * u * v.cos();
    let y = 2.0 * (3.0 * v).cos();
    let z = 2.0 * u * v.sin();
    [x, y, z]
}

pub fn steiner(u:f32, v:f32) -> [f32; 3] {
    let x = u.cos() * v.cos() * v.sin();
    let y = u.cos() * u.sin() * (v.cos()).powf(2.0);
    let z = u.sin() * v.cos() * v.sin();
    [x, y, z]
}
```

These functions accept the parametric variables *u* and *v* as input arguments and calculate the *x*, *y*, and *z* values using different parametric equations. The functions return a *vec3* point in real-world space.

5.6.3 Rust Code

With the background presented in the previous sections, we are now ready to render parametric 3D surfaces in *wgpu*. To do this, create a new Rust file named *parametric_surface.rs* in the *examples/ch05/* folder. The code for both the *State::new* and *State::render* functions is similar to that used in the previous simple 3D surface example, except that we use the vertex and index data for the parametric surface to create the vertex and index buffers.

The other difference from the previous example occurs inside the *State::update* function, where, when the condition *self.random_shape_change* = 1 is met, we use the following code to update the vertex buffers every 5 seconds:

```
// update vertex buffer for every 5 seconds
let elapsed = self.t0.elapsed();
if elapsed >= std::time::Duration::from_secs(5) && self.random_shape_change == 1 {
    self.parametric_surface.surface_type = self.rng.gen_range(0..=23) as u32;
    let data = create_vertices(self.parametric_surface.new());
    self.init.queue.write_buffer(&self.vertex_buffers[0], 0, cast_slice(&data.0));
    self.init.queue.write_buffer(&self.vertex_buffers[1], 0, cast_slice(&data.1));
    self.t0 = std::time::Instant::now();

    println!("key = {:?}, value = {:?}", self.parametric_surface.surface_type,
        self.parametric_surface.surface_type_map[&self.parametric_surface.surface_type]);
}
```

This code snippet randomly selects a new surface type, generates new vertex data for that surface, writes the data to the vertex buffers, and prints the selected surface type and corresponding surface name in the terminal. On the other hand, when *self.random_shape_change* != 1, which can be changed using the *LAlt* key, you can then use the *LControl* key to change the surface type manually.

Unlike the previous simple-surface example, where the vertex data is updated for every frame within the *State::update* function, this example does not animate the vertex data using a time-dependent variable; thus, it is not necessary to update the vertex data for every frame. Instead, this code checks the *updata_buffers* and *recreate_buffers* variables to determine if the vertex data and corresponding buffers need to be updated or regenerated.

Additionally, the code permits the user to modify input parameters using keyboard inputs.

Here is a list of controls using keyboard:

- *Space*: Changes the plot type: surface, wireframe, or both.
- *LControl*: Changes the surface type when *random_shape_change* != 1.
- *LShift*: Changes colormap direction: *x, y,* or *z*.
- *LAlt*: Changes the *random_shape_change* value between 0 and 1.
- *Q/A*: Increases/decreases *u_resolution*.
- *W/S:* Increases/decreases *v_resolution*.
- *E/D:* Increases/decreases the rotation speed.

5.6.4 Run Application

To run this application, add the following code snippet to the *Cargo.toml* file:

```
[[example]]
name = "ch05_parametric_surface"
path = "examples/ch05/parametric_surface.rs"
```

Afterward, execute the following *cargo run* commands in the terminal window:

```
cargo run --example ch05_parametric_surface 8
```

Fig.5-2 shows the outputs of this example by manipulating the input parameters.

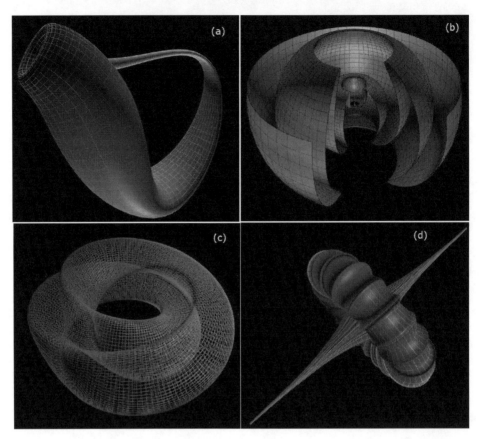

Fig.5-2. Parametric 3D surfaces: (a) Klein bottle, (b) Wellenkugel surface, (c) Figure-8 shape, and (d) Breather surface.

5.7 Multiple Surfaces

In this section, we will use *wgpu*'s instanced drawing feature to efficiently render multiple 3D surfaces in a single scene, as we did in Chapter 3 for different lighting models. Instanced drawing lets us draw more than one of the same objects faster than drawing them one by one. It reduces the number of draw calls and state changes that the GPU has to perform, which improves performance and efficiency. We will use this feature to render 10,000 simple or parametric surfaces in the following examples.

5.7.1 Rendering Multiple Simple Surfaces

To render multiple surfaces in a single scene using instanced drawing, we need a new vertex shader program. Create a new file named *shader_instance_vert.wgsl* in the *examples/ch05/* folder and add the following code:

```
// vertex shader
@group(0) @binding(0)  var<uniform> vpMat: mat4x4f;
```

```
@group(0) @binding(1)  var<storage> modelMat: array<mat4x4f>;
@group(0) @binding(2)  var<storage> normalMat: array<mat4x4f>;

struct Input {
    @builtin(instance_index) idx: u32,
    @location(0) position: vec4f,
    @location(1) normal: vec4f,
    @location(2) color: vec4f,
};

struct Output {
    @builtin(position) position: vec4f,
    @location(0) vPosition: vec4f,
    @location(1) vNormal: vec4f,
    @location(2) vColor: vec4f,
};

@vertex
fn vs_main(in: Input) -> Output {
    var output: Output;
    let modelMat = modelMat[in.idx];
    let normalMat = normalMat[in.idx];
    let mPosition = modelMat * in.position;
    output.vPosition = mPosition;
    output.vNormal =  normalMat * in.normal;
    output.position = vpMat * mPosition;
    output.vColor = in.color;
    return output;
}
```

This vertex shader is very similar to the one used in Chapter 3 with the same name, except that in addition to the *position* and *normal* data, we also pass the *color* data to it. In the *vs_main* function, we process the color data and assign it to the *vColor* variable defined in the *Output* structure. The fragment shader will use this variable to generate the color for rendering the object.

Next, create a new Rust file named *multiple_simple_surfaces.rs* in the *examples/ch05/* folder. The code for the *State::new* function is similar to that used in the previous simple-surface example, except that we add three new fields, *x_num*, *z_num*, and *objects_count*, to the *State* struct. Inside the *State::new* function, we define these three fields as:

```
let x_num = 100u32;
let z_num = 100u32;
let objects_count = x_num * z_num;
```

It is evident that the grid is a 100x100 square in the *x-z* plane, which can position a total of 10,000 surfaces, with one on each grid point.

The *State::render* function is implemented using the following code:

```
fn render(&mut self) -> Result<(), wgpu::SurfaceError> {
    let output = self.init.surface.get_current_texture()?;
    let view = output
        .texture
        .create_view(&wgpu::TextureViewDescriptor::default());

    let mut encoder = self
        .init.device
        .create_command_encoder(&wgpu::CommandEncoderDescriptor {
            label: Some("Render Encoder"),
        });
```

```
        {
            let color_attach = ws::create_color_attachment(&view);
            let msaa_attach = ws::create_msaa_color_attachment(&view, &self.msaa_texture_view);
            let color_attachment = if self.init.sample_count == 1 { color_attach } else { msaa_attach };
            let depth_attachment = ws::create_depth_stencil_attachment(&self.depth_texture_view);
            let mut render_pass = encoder.begin_render_pass(&wgpu::RenderPassDescriptor {
                label: Some("Render Pass"),
                color_attachments: &[Some(color_attachment)],
                depth_stencil_attachment: Some(depth_attachment),
                occlusion_query_set: None,
                timestamp_writes: None,
            });

            let plot_type = if self.plot_type == 1 { "shape_only" }
                else if self.plot_type == 2 {"wireframe_only"} else {"both"};

            if plot_type == "shape_only" || plot_type == "both" {
                render_pass.set_pipeline(&self.pipelines[0]);
                render_pass.set_vertex_buffer(0, self.vertex_buffers[0].slice(..));
                render_pass.set_index_buffer(self.index_buffers[0].slice(..),
                    wgpu::IndexFormat::Uint16);
                render_pass.set_bind_group(0, &self.uniform_bind_groups[0], &[]);
                render_pass.set_bind_group(1, &self.uniform_bind_groups[1], &[]);
                render_pass.draw_indexed(0..self.indices_lens[0], 0, 0..self.objects_count);
            }

            if plot_type == "wireframe_only" || plot_type == "both" {
                render_pass.set_pipeline(&self.pipelines[1]);
                render_pass.set_vertex_buffer(0, self.vertex_buffers[1].slice(..));
                render_pass.set_index_buffer(self.index_buffers[1].slice(..),
                    wgpu::IndexFormat::Uint16);
                render_pass.set_bind_group(0, &self.uniform_bind_groups[2], &[]);
                render_pass.set_bind_group(1, &self.uniform_bind_groups[3], &[]);
                render_pass.draw_indexed(0..self.indices_lens[1], 0, 0..self.objects_count);
            }
        }

        self.init.queue.submit(iter::once(encoder.finish()));
        output.present();

        Ok(())
    }
```

The *State::render* function in the above code is very similar to that used in the previous simple-surface example, except that we use *objects_count* to set the *instances* input argument when invoking the *draw_indexed* function, as demonstrated in the following code snippet:

```
...
// for rendering surface
render_pass.draw_indexed(0..self.indices_lens[0], 0, 0..self.objects_count);
...
// for rendering wireframe
render_pass.draw_indexed(0..self.indices_lens[1], 0, 0..self.objects_count);
...
```

Here, the *instances* argument tells the GPU how many copies, or instances, of the object we want to draw.

Inside the *State::update* function, we position these surfaces using translation transformations along the *x* and *z* directions. Additionally, we allow each surface to have a time-dependent rotation. This process is illustrated with the following code snippet:

```
let mut model_mat:Vec<[f32; 16]> = vec![];
let mut normal_mat:Vec<[f32; 16]> = vec![];
let dt1 = self.rotation_speed * dt.as_secs_f32();
for i in 0..self.x_num {
    for j in 0..self.z_num {
        let translation = [-150.0 + 2.0 * i as f32, 2.0, -180.0 + 2.0 * j as f32];
        let rotation = [
            (dt1* i as f32 /self.x_num as f32).sin(),
            (dt1* j as f32 /self.z_num as f32).sin(),
            ((i*j) as f32 * dt1/self.objects_count as f32).cos()
        ];
        let scale = [1.0f32, 1.0, 1.0];
        let m = wt::create_model_mat(translation, rotation, scale);
        let n = (m.invert().unwrap()).transpose();
        model_mat.push(*(m.as_ref()));
        normal_mat.push(*(n.as_ref()));
    }
}
self.init.queue.write_buffer(&self.uniform_buffers[1], 0, cast_slice(&model_mat));
self.init.queue.write_buffer(&self.uniform_buffers[2], 0, cast_slice(&normal_mat));
```

Additionally, the code permits the user to modify input parameters using keyboard inputs.

Here is a list of controls using keyboard:

- *Space*: Changes the plot type: surface, wireframe, or both.
- *LControl*: Changes the surface type among *sinc*, *peaks*, and *poles*.
- *LShift*: Changes colormap direction: *x*, *y*, or *z*.
- *Q/A*: Increases/decreases the animation speed.
- *W/S:* Increases/decreases the rotation speed.

To run this application, add the following code snippet to the *Cargo.toml* file:

```
[[example]]
name = "ch05_multiple_simple_surfaces"
path = "examples/ch05/ multiple_simple_surfaces.rs"
```

Afterward, execute the following *cargo run* commands in the terminal window:

```
cargo run --example ch05_ multiple_simple_surfaces 8
```

Fig.5-3 shows the outputs of this example.

As in the previous simple-surface example, this example also regenerates vertex data and vertex buffers for every frame. The previous example demonstrated that the framerate for a single surface with a default resolution of 30 is 60 FPS. In the current example, the framerate for 10,000 surfaces with the same resolution is about 13 FPS.

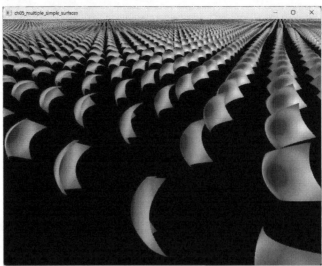

Fig.5-3. Multiple simple 3D surfaces.

5.7.2 Rendering Multiple Parametric Surfaces

As we did for simple surfaces in the previous section, we will use *wgpu*'s instanced drawing feature here to render multiple parametric surfaces. To do this, create a new Rust file named *multiple_parametric_surfaces.rs* in the *examples/ch06/* folder. The code for both the *State::new* and *State::render* functions is similar to that used in the previous example. Here, I only need to list the code of the *State::update* function, as shown in the following code:

```rust
fn update(&mut self, dt: std::time::Duration) {
    // update uniform buffer
    let mut model_mat:Vec<[f32; 16]> = vec![];
    let mut normal_mat:Vec<[f32; 16]> = vec![];
    let dt1 = self.rotation_speed * dt.as_secs_f32();

    for i in 0..self.x_num {
        for j in 0..self.z_num {
            let translation = [-150.0 + 2.0 * i as f32, 2.0, -180.0 + 2.0 * j as f32];
            let rotation = [
                (dt1* i as f32 /self.x_num as f32).sin(),
                (dt1* j as f32 /self.z_num as f32).sin(),
                ((i*j) as f32 * dt1/self.objects_count as f32).cos()
            ];
            let scale = [1.0f32, 1.0, 1.0];
            let m = wt::create_model_mat(translation, rotation, scale);
            let n = (m.invert().unwrap()).transpose();
            model_mat.push(*(m.as_ref()));
            normal_mat.push(*(n.as_ref()));
        }
    }
    self.init.queue.write_buffer(&self.uniform_buffers[1], 0, cast_slice(&model_mat));
    self.init.queue.write_buffer(&self.uniform_buffers[2], 0, cast_slice(&normal_mat));

    let view_project_mat = self.project_mat * self.view_mat;
    let view_projection_ref:&[f32; 16] = view_project_mat.as_ref();
```

```
self.init.queue.write_buffer(&self.uniform_buffers[0], 0, cast_slice(view_projection_ref));

// recreate vertex and index buffers
if self.recreate_buffers {
    let data = create_vertices(self.parametric_surface.new());
    self.indices_lens = vec![data.2.len() as u32, data.3.len() as u32];
    let vertex_data = [data.0, data.1];
    let index_data = [data.2, data.3];

    for i in 0..2 {
        self.vertex_buffers[i].destroy();
        self.vertex_buffers[i] = self.init.device.create_buffer_init(
        &wgpu::util::BufferInitDescriptor {
            label: Some("Vertex Buffer"),
            contents: cast_slice(&vertex_data[i]),
            usage: wgpu::BufferUsages::VERTEX | wgpu::BufferUsages::COPY_DST,
        });
        self.index_buffers[i].destroy();
        self.index_buffers[i] = self.init.device.create_buffer_init(
        &wgpu::util::BufferInitDescriptor {
            label: Some("Index Buffer"),
            contents: cast_slice(&index_data[i]),
            usage: wgpu::BufferUsages::INDEX | wgpu::BufferUsages::COPY_DST,
        });
    }
    self.recreate_buffers = false;
}

// update vertex buffer for every 5 seconds
let elapsed = self.t0.elapsed();
if elapsed >= std::time::Duration::from_secs(5) && self.random_shape_change == 0 {
    self.parametric_surface.surface_type = self.rng.gen_range(0..=23) as u32;
    let data = create_vertices(self.parametric_surface.new());
    self.init.queue.write_buffer(&self.vertex_buffers[0], 0, cast_slice(&data.0));
    self.init.queue.write_buffer(&self.vertex_buffers[1], 0, cast_slice(&data.1));
    self.t0 = std::time::Instant::now();

    println!("key = {:?}, value = {:?}", self.parametric_surface.surface_type,
        self.parametric_surface.surface_type_map[&self.parametric_surface.surface_type]);
}

// update vertex buffer when data changed
if self.update_buffers {
    let data = create_vertices(self.parametric_surface.new());
    self.init.queue.write_buffer(&self.vertex_buffers[0], 0, cast_slice(&data.0));
    self.init.queue.write_buffer(&self.vertex_buffers[1], 0, cast_slice(&data.1));
    self.update_buffers = false;
}
}
}
```

As we did in the previous example for simple surfaces, in this example, we also define a 100×100 square grid in the *x-z* plane, which can accommodate a total of 10,000 parametric surfaces, with one on each grid point. Within the *State::update* function, we position these surfaces using translations along the *x* and *z* directions.

To run this application, add the following code snippet to the *Cargo.toml* file:

```
[[example]]
name = "ch05_multiple_parametric_surfaces"
```

```
path = "examples/ch05/ multiple_parametric_surfaces.rs"
```

Afterward, execute the following *cargo run* commands in the terminal window:

```
cargo run --example ch05_ multiple_parametric_surfaces 8
```

Fig.5-4 shows the outputs of this example.

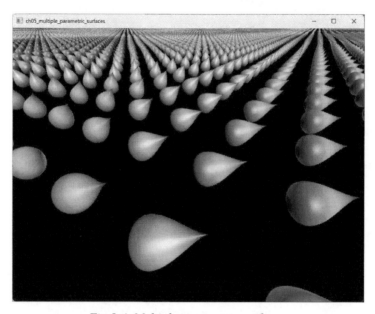

Fig.5-4. Multiple parametric surfaces.

6 Textures

In the previous chapters, we used solid color, such as vertex color and colormap, to render various 3D shapes and surfaces. This approach is often used for simple graphics objects because it is fast, efficient, and straightforward to implement. The solid color rendering can be useful when the focus is on the shape and structure of an object rather than its surface details. Objects with solid color rendering, particularly using colormap, look nice enough, but they lack depth and realism.

On the other hand, texture mapping involves the application of a texture or image onto the surface of a 3D object. The texture can be a picture, a painting, or a procedural pattern generated by a computer program. Texture mapping follows the curvatures of an object and covers its surface like a skin. This technique can add visual detail, depth, and realism to 3D objects.

Currently, support for texture mapping has been built into GPUs at the hardware level. Modern GPUs have dedicated hardware units called texture mapping units (TMUs) that are specifically designed to handle texture mapping operations. TMUs are responsible for accessing and retrieving the textures stored in GPU buffers and mapping them onto the surface of the 3D object. Furthermore, modern GPUs often include support for advanced texture mapping techniques, such as parallax mapping, bump mapping, and displacement mapping. These techniques enable the creation of highly detailed and realistic surfaces by simulating the effects of lighting and shading on the texture.

In this chapter, we will consider 2D image textures that can be mapped onto a surface to make the color of the surface vary from point to point, similar to painting a copy of the image onto the surface. It is worth noting that the width and height of a texture image are usually powers of 2, such as 64, 128, 256, 512, etc. This requirement might be relaxed in modern GPU hardware, but it is still a good idea to use power of two textures. In the following sections, I will show you how to map 2D image textures onto surfaces of various 3D objects in *wgpu*.

6.1 Texture Coordinates

Although there are multiple ways to perform texture mapping, all requiring a sequence of steps that involve mappings among several coordinate systems. At various stages in the process, we will be working with screen coordinates, where the final images is produced; object coordinates, where we describe the objects upon which the textures will be mapped; texture coordinates, which we use to locate positions in the texture; and parametric coordinates, which we use to specify parametric surfaces.

When a texture is applied to a surface, each point on the surface corresponds to a point in the texture. A texture image comes with its own 2D coordinate system $T(u, v)$, where u is used for the horizontal coordinate on the image and v is used for the vertical coordinate. Note that in OpenGL and WebGL, s

and t are usually used for texture coordinates, while *wgpu* uses u and v for texture coordinates. Please do not confuse u and v with the u and v used in parametric equations. Without loss of generality, we usually scale our texture coordinates to vary over the range of [0, 1]. Fig.6-1 shows the coordinates of an image and its equivalent texture coordinates.

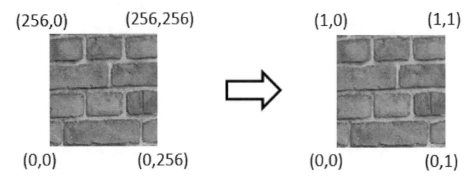

Fig.6-1. Image coordinates (left) and corresponding texture coordinates (right).

You can see from the figure that for an image size of 256×256 pixels, all points will be divided by 256 to lie within this range. The texture coordinate (0.5, 0.25) for a 256×256 image refers to the texture coordinate (128, 64).

Note that values of u or v outside of the range of 0 and 1 are not inside the image, but such values are still valid as texture coordinates. Values over the range of [0, 1] can be used for repeating the texture image.

To map a texture onto a surface, we need a pair of texture coordinates (u, v) for each vertex. These texture coordinates indicate which point in the image is mapped to the vertex. The texture coordinates of a vertex are an attribute of the vertex, just like color and normal vectors. They are typically provided to the shader program as an attribute variable.

The texture coordinates should usually be computed from the object coordinates of the object being rendered. Namely, they are calculated from the original vertex coordinates before any transformation has been applied. Then, when the object is transformed, the texture will be transformed along with the object so that it will look like the texture is attached to the object.

With an image texture, a color is computed by sampling the image based on a pair of texture coordinates. The image essentially defines a function that takes texture coordinates as input and returns a color as output. However, we can also use procedural approach to determine texture mapping. A procedural texture is defined by a function whose value is computed rather than looked up. Namely, the texture coordinates are used as input to a code snippet whose output is a color value.

In *wgpu*, procedural textures can be defined in the fragment shader: take a *vec2* representing a set of texture coordinates and then, instead of using a *sampler* to look up a color in the texture image, use the *vec2* as input to some mathematical computation that computes a *vec4* vector representing a color. In theory any computation could be used as long as the components of the *vec4* are in the range of [0,1].

6.2 Texture Mapping in wgpu

In *wgpu*, a texture is stored within a *wgpu::Texture* object. The most common approach to populate texture data is by using an image file. Here, we will use the *image* crate, which is included in the *Cargo.toml* file, to process the image file. The *image* crate offers fundamental image processing functions and methods for seamless conversion between various image formats.

Create a new Rust file named *texture_data.rs* in the *src/* folder and enter the following code into it:

```rust
use image::GenericImageView;
use image::io::Reader as ImageReader;
use anyhow::*;

pub struct ITexture {
    pub texture: wgpu::Texture,
    pub view: wgpu::TextureView,
    pub sampler: wgpu::Sampler,
}

impl ITexture {
    pub fn create_texture_data(
        device:&wgpu::Device,
        queue: &wgpu::Queue,
        img_file: &str,
        u_mode:wgpu::AddressMode,
        v_mode:wgpu::AddressMode
    ) -> Result<Self> {

        let img = ImageReader::open(img_file)?.decode()?;
        let rgba = img.as_rgba8().unwrap();
        let dimensions = img.dimensions();

        let size = wgpu::Extent3d {
            width: dimensions.0,
            height: dimensions.1,
            depth_or_array_layers: 1,
        };
        let texture = device.create_texture(
            &wgpu::TextureDescriptor {
                label: Some("Image Texture"),
                size,
                mip_level_count: 1,
                sample_count: 1,
                dimension: wgpu::TextureDimension::D2,
                format: wgpu::TextureFormat::Rgba8UnormSrgb,
                usage: wgpu::TextureUsages::TEXTURE_BINDING | wgpu::TextureUsages::COPY_DST,
                view_formats: &[],
            }
        );

        queue.write_texture(
            wgpu::ImageCopyTexture {
                aspect: wgpu::TextureAspect::All,
                texture: &texture,
                mip_level: 0,
                origin: wgpu::Origin3d::ZERO,
            },
            rgba,
            wgpu::ImageDataLayout {
```

```
                offset: 0,
                bytes_per_row: Some(4*dimensions.0),
                rows_per_image:Some(dimensions.1),
            },
            size,
        );

        let view = texture.create_view(&wgpu::TextureViewDescriptor::default());

        let sampler = device.create_sampler(
            &wgpu::SamplerDescriptor {
                address_mode_u: u_mode,
                address_mode_v: v_mode,
                address_mode_w: wgpu::AddressMode::ClampToEdge,
                mag_filter: wgpu::FilterMode::Linear,
                min_filter: wgpu::FilterMode::Nearest,
                mipmap_filter: wgpu::FilterMode::Nearest,
                ..Default::default()
            }
        );

        Ok(Self { texture, view, sampler })
    }

    pub fn create_texture_store_data(
        device:&wgpu::Device,
        width: u32,
        height:u32
    ) -> Result<Self> {
        let texture = device.create_texture(&wgpu::TextureDescriptor {
            label: Some("Texture Image"),
            size: wgpu::Extent3d{ width, height, depth_or_array_layers: 1 },
            mip_level_count: 1,
            sample_count: 1,
            dimension: wgpu::TextureDimension::D2,
            format: wgpu::TextureFormat::Rgba8Unorm,
            usage: wgpu::TextureUsages::STORAGE_BINDING | wgpu::TextureUsages::TEXTURE_BINDING
                    | wgpu::TextureUsages::COPY_DST,
            view_formats: &[],
        });

        let view = texture.create_view(&wgpu::TextureViewDescriptor::default());

        let sampler = device.create_sampler(
            &wgpu::SamplerDescriptor {
                address_mode_u: wgpu::AddressMode::ClampToEdge,
                address_mode_v: wgpu::AddressMode::ClampToEdge,
                address_mode_w: wgpu::AddressMode::ClampToEdge,
                mag_filter: wgpu::FilterMode::Linear,
                min_filter: wgpu::FilterMode::Nearest,
                mipmap_filter: wgpu::FilterMode::Nearest,
                ..Default::default()
            }
        );
        Ok(Self { texture, view, sampler })
    }
}
```

The above code begins by defining an *ITexture* struct and subsequently implementing a *create_texture_data* method. This method facilitates the creation of texture data from an image file. Within the *create_texture_data* method, the process unfolds as follows:

- The image is loaded into memory using *ImageReader*, and then decoded into an RGBA format.

- The image's dimensions are extracted to determine the texture size.

- A new texture is created using the provided dimensions and format via the *device.create_texture* function call.

- The image data is written to the texture utilizing the *queue.write_texture* method.

- A sampler is created to enable texture sampling by invoking the *device.create_sampler* function.

In the context of *wgpu*, a *wgpu::Sampler* object is employed to encode transformation and filtering information used in shaders for interpreting texture resource data. Notably, when applying a texture to a surface, the pixel mapping between the texture and the surface is often not one-to-one. Thus, filtering becomes necessary to account for this discrepancy. When scaling down a texture, a minification filter is used, while magnification filtering is necessary when one pixel from the texture covers multiple pixels on the surface.

The *wgpu* API offers properties like *min_filter* and *mag_filter* to specify the sampling behavior. *wgpu::FilterMode* is used to determine sampler behavior when the sample footprint does not precisely match a single texel. The two available options are *nearest* and *linear*, with *nearest* selecting the nearest texel's value and *linear* performing linear interpolation between two neighboring texels.

To mitigate the inefficiency of linear filtering for large textures applied to smaller surfaces, mipmaps are utilized. Mipmaps are scaled-down versions of the original texture, and a complete set consists of progressively smaller versions. These mipmaps allow for efficient filtering during texture scaling.

For addressing texture coordinates outside the [0, 1] range, the *address_mode* property comes into play. It has four options: *ClampToEdge*, *Repeat*, *MirrorRepeat*, and *ClampToBorder*. These options dictate how the sampler behaves when texture coordinates fall beyond the normal range.

It's important to note that mipmaps are primarily used for minification filtering. *wgpu* also provides a *mipmap_filter* property for sampling between different mipmap levels.

The *ITexture* struct's implementation block further includes a public *create_texture_store_data* function. This function is designed for textures storing pixel values computed via a compute shader. It takes the desired texture size as input and creates the corresponding texture and sampler. This function will be useful when creating textures for the results obtained from compute shaders.

6.3 Shaders with Texture

Our shader program is expected to become more complicated because we want to incorporate texture and lighting into the shaders.

6.3.1 Vertex Shader

Create a new vertex shader file named *shader_vert.wgsl* in the *examples/ch06/* folder and add the following code to it:

```
// vertex shader
```

```
struct Uniforms {
    vpMat : mat4x4f,
    modelMat : mat4x4f,
    normalMat : mat4x4f,
};
@binding(0) @group(0) var<uniform> uniforms : Uniforms;

struct Input {
    @location(0) pos: vec4f,
    @location(1) normal: vec4f,
    @location(2) uv: vec2f,
};

struct Output {
    @builtin(position) position : vec4f,
    @location(0) vPosition : vec4f,
    @location(1) vNormal : vec4f,
    @location(2) vUv: vec2f,
};

@vertex
fn vs_main(in: Input) -> Output {
    var output: Output;
    let mPosition = uniforms.modelMat * in.pos;
    output.vPosition = mPosition;
    output.vNormal =  uniforms.normalMat * in.normal;
    output.position = uniforms.vpMat * mPosition;
    output.vUv = in.uv;
    return output;
}
```

This vertex shader is very similar to the one used in Chapter 3, with the exception that in addition to the *position* and *normal* data, we also pass the UV data to it. Within the *vs_main* function, we process the UV data and assign it to the *vUv* variable defined in the *Output* structure, which is used in the fragment shader to generate the color for rendering the object.

6.3.2 Fragment Shader

Add a new fragment shader file called *shader-frag.wgsl* to the *examples/ch06/* folder and include the following code:

```
struct LightUniforms {
    lightDirection : vec4f,
    eyePosition : vec4f,
    specularColor : vec4f,
};
@group(1) @binding(0) var<uniform> light: LightUniforms;
struct MaterialUniforms {
    ambient: f32,
    diffuse: f32,
    specular: f32,
    shininess: f32,
};
@group(1) @binding(1) var<uniform> material : MaterialUniforms;
@group(2) @binding(0) var textureSampler: sampler;
@group(2) @binding(1) var textureData : texture_2d<f32>;

struct Input {
```

```
    @location(0) vPosition: vec4f,
    @location(1) vNormal: vec4f,
    @location(2) vUv: vec2f,
};
fn blinnPhong(N:vec3f, L:vec3f, V:vec3f) -> vec2f {
    let H = normalize(L + V);
    var diffuse:f32 = material.diffuse * max(dot(N, L), 0.0);
    diffuse += material.diffuse * max(dot(-N, L), 0.0);
    var specular: f32 = material.specular * pow(max(dot(N, H), 0.0), material.shininess);
    specular += material.specular * pow(max(dot(-N, H),0.0), material.shininess);
    return vec2(diffuse, specular);
}


@fragment
fn fs_main(in: Input) ->  @location(0) vec4f {
    var N = normalize(in.vNormal.xyz);
    let L = normalize(-light.lightDirection.xyz);
    let V = normalize(light.eyePosition.xyz - in.vPosition.xyz);
    let bp = blinnPhong(N, L, V);

    let texColor = (textureSample(textureData, textureSampler, in.vUv)).rgb;

    var finalColor = texColor * (material.ambient + bp[0]) + light.specularColor.rgb * bp[1];
    finalColor = pow(finalColor, vec3<f32>(1.0/2.2));
    return vec4(finalColor.rgb, 1.0);
}
```

The above code is similar to the one used in the *directional-frag.wgsl* file located in the *examples/ch03/* folder, which is based on the Blinn-Phong model for directional light sources. The main difference is that this example uses the texture data, sampler, and the processed UV data from the vertex shader as inputs to obtain color, as described in the following code snippet:

```
    let texColor = (textureSample(textureData, textureSampler, in.vUv)).rgb;
```

The final color is obtained by

```
    let finalColor = texColor * (material.ambient + bp[0]) + light.specularColor.rgb * bp[1];
```

Here, the ambient and diffuse light components are multiplied by the color from the texture.

6.4 Common Code

As we did earlier, to avoid code duplication, we will place commonly used code in the *wgpu_simplified.rs* file in the *src/* folder. Add the following two functions, *create_texture_bind_groups* and *create_texture_bind_group_layouts*, to the file with the following code:

```
use super::texture_data as tex;

fn create_texture_bind_group_layout(
    device: &wgpu::Device,
    img_files:Vec<&str>
) -> wgpu::BindGroupLayout {
    let mut entries:Vec<wgpu::BindGroupLayoutEntry> = vec![];
    for i in 0..img_files.len() {
        entries.push( wgpu::BindGroupLayoutEntry {
            binding: (2*i) as u32,
            visibility: wgpu::ShaderStages::FRAGMENT,
            ty: wgpu::BindingType::Texture {
```

```
                multisampled: false,
                view_dimension: wgpu::TextureViewDimension::D2,
                sample_type: wgpu::TextureSampleType::Float { filterable: true },
            },
            count: None,
        });
        entries.push(wgpu::BindGroupLayoutEntry {
            binding: (2*i+1) as u32,
            visibility: wgpu::ShaderStages::FRAGMENT,
            ty: wgpu::BindingType::Sampler(wgpu::SamplerBindingType::Filtering),
            count: None,
        })
    }

    device.create_bind_group_layout(&wgpu::BindGroupLayoutDescriptor {
        entries: &entries,
        label: Some("texture_bind_group_layout"),
    })
}

pub fn create_texture_bind_group(
    device: &wgpu::Device,
    queue: &wgpu::Queue,
    img_files:Vec<&str>,
    u_mode:wgpu::AddressMode,
    v_mode:wgpu::AddressMode,
) -> (wgpu::BindGroupLayout, wgpu::BindGroup) {
    let mut img_textures:Vec<tex::ITexture> = vec![];
    let mut entries:Vec<wgpu::BindGroupEntry<'_>> = vec![];
    for i in 0..img_files.len() {
        img_textures.push(tex::ITexture::create_texture_data(device, queue, img_files[i],
            u_mode, v_mode).unwrap());
    }
    for i in 0..img_files.len() {
        entries.push( wgpu::BindGroupEntry {
            binding: (2*i) as u32,
            resource: wgpu::BindingResource::TextureView(&img_textures[i].view),
        });
        entries.push( wgpu::BindGroupEntry {
            binding: (2*i + 1) as u32,
            resource: wgpu::BindingResource::Sampler(&img_textures[i].sampler),
        })
    }

    let layout = create_texture_bind_group_layout(device, img_files);

    let bind_group = device.create_bind_group(&wgpu::BindGroupDescriptor{
        layout: &layout,
        label: Some("texture_bind_group"),
        entries: &entries
    });
    (layout, bind_group)
}
```

The two functions in the above code are designed to facilitate the creation of bind group layout and bind group for textures generated from image files. The code begins by importing the *texture_data* module, which was previously implemented, and then assigns it an alias, *tex*.

The *create_texture_bind_group_layout* function is tasked with generating a bind group layout, wherein each image file corresponds to two bindings: one for the texture view and another for the sampler. These bindings are marked with a visibility of *wgpu::ShaderStages::FRAGMENT*, ensuring their accessibility solely within the fragment shader.

Moving on, the *create_texture_bind_group* function constructs a bind group utilizing the provided texture bind group layout and a collection of image files. This function proceeds by creating a collection of *ITexture* objects, each representing a texture to be bound within the bind group. Subsequently, it generates a list of *wgpu::BindGroupEntry* instances, with each entry corresponding to a texture. The *resource* field of each *BindGroupEntry* is set to either the view or sampler attribute of the relevant *ITexture* object.

In essence, these functions offer a structured and efficient approach to handling textures, while also enabling the seamless creation of texture bind group layout and bind group for use within the context of *wgpu* shaders.

6.5 Simple 3D Shapes

With the background presented in previous sections, this section will demonstrate how to map 2D texture images onto two 3D shapes, cube and sphere. In order to create textures, I have added several 512×512 images with PNG format to the *assets/* folder.

6.5.1 Cube with Texture

Texture mapping requires the texture coordinates or UV data. For a cube object, we have generated the UV data using the *create_cube_data* function in the *vertex-data.rs* file located in the *src/* folder. This section will use this UV data to create a texture map for a cube.

Create a new Rust file called *cube_texture.rs* in the *examples/ch06/* folder and enter the following code into it:

```rust
use std:: {iter, mem, collections::HashMap};
use cgmath::{ Matrix, Matrix4, SquareMatrix };
use wgpu::{util::DeviceExt, VertexBufferLayout};
use winit::{
    event::*,
    event_loop::{ControlFlow, EventLoop},
    window::Window,
};
use bytemuck:: {Pod, Zeroable, cast_slice};
use wgpu_book_examples::{ wgpu_simplified as ws, transforms as wt, vertex_data as vd };

#[repr(C)]
#[derive(Copy, Clone, Debug, Pod, Zeroable)]
struct Vertex {
    position: [f32; 3],
    normal: [f32; 3],
    uv: [f32; 2],
}

fn create_vertices(ul:f32, vl:f32) -> (Vec<Vertex>, Vec<u16>) {
    let(pos, _, norm, uv, ind, _) = vd::create_cube_data(2.0);
    let mut data:Vec<Vertex> = vec![];
    for i in 0..pos.len() {
        data.push(Vertex{position: pos[i], normal: norm[i], uv: [uv[i][0]*ul, uv[i][1]*vl]});
    }
```

```
        (data.to_vec(), ind)
}

fn image_file_map(n:u32) -> Option<&'static str> {
    let mut d: HashMap<u32, &'static str> = HashMap::new();
    d.insert(0, "assets/brick.png");
    d.insert(1, "assets/grass.png");
    d.insert(2, "assets/wood.png");
    d.insert(3, "assets/marble.png");

    d.get(&n).cloned()
}

const ADDRESS_MODE:wgpu::AddressMode = wgpu::AddressMode::MirrorRepeat;

struct State {
    init:  ws::IWgpuInit,
    pipeline: wgpu::RenderPipeline,
    vertex_buffer: wgpu::Buffer,
    index_buffer: wgpu::Buffer,
    uniform_bind_groups: Vec<wgpu::BindGroup>,
    uniform_buffers: Vec<wgpu::Buffer>,
    view_mat: Matrix4<f32>,
    project_mat: Matrix4<f32>,
    msaa_texture_view: wgpu::TextureView,
    depth_texture_view: wgpu::TextureView,
    animation_speed: f32,
    indices_len: u32,
    image_selection: u32,
    u_len: f32,
    v_len: f32,
    update_buffers: bool,
}

impl State {
    async fn new(window: &Window, sample_count:u32) -> Self {
        let init = ws::IWgpuInit::new(&window, sample_count, None).await;

        let vs_shader = init.device.create_shader_module(wgpu::include_wgsl!("shader_vert.wgsl"));
        let fs_shader = init.device.create_shader_module(wgpu::include_wgsl!("shader_frag.wgsl"));

        // uniform data
        let camera_position = (2.5, 1.5, 3.0).into();
        let look_direction = (0.0,0.0,0.0).into();
        let up_direction = cgmath::Vector3::unit_y();

        let (view_mat, project_mat, _) =
            wt::create_vp_mat(camera_position, look_direction, up_direction,
            init.config.width as f32 / init.config.height as f32);

        // create vertex uniform buffers

        // model_mat and vp_mat will be stored in vertex_uniform_buffer inside the update function
        let vert_uniform_buffer = init.device.create_buffer(&wgpu::BufferDescriptor{
            label: Some("Vertex Uniform Buffer"),
            size: 192,
            usage: wgpu::BufferUsages::UNIFORM | wgpu::BufferUsages::COPY_DST,
            mapped_at_creation: false,
        });
```

```
// create light uniform buffer. here we set eye_position = camera_position and
// light_position = eye_position
let light_uniform_buffer = init.device.create_buffer(&wgpu::BufferDescriptor{
    label: Some("Light Uniform Buffer"),
    size: 48,
    usage: wgpu::BufferUsages::UNIFORM | wgpu::BufferUsages::COPY_DST,
    mapped_at_creation: false,
});

let light_direction = [-0.5f32, -0.5, -0.5];
let eye_position:&[f32; 3] = camera_position.as_ref();
init.queue.write_buffer(&light_uniform_buffer, 0, cast_slice(&light_direction));
init.queue.write_buffer(&light_uniform_buffer, 16, cast_slice(eye_position));

// set specular light color to white
let specular_color:[f32; 3] = [1.0, 1.0, 1.0];
init.queue.write_buffer(&light_uniform_buffer, 32, cast_slice(specular_color.as_ref()));

// material uniform buffer
let material_uniform_buffer = init.device.create_buffer(&wgpu::BufferDescriptor{
    label: Some("Material Uniform Buffer"),
    size: 16,
    usage: wgpu::BufferUsages::UNIFORM | wgpu::BufferUsages::COPY_DST,
    mapped_at_creation: false,
});

// set default material parameters
let material = [0.1 as f32, 0.7, 0.4, 30.0];
init.queue.write_buffer(&material_uniform_buffer, 0, cast_slice(&material));

// uniform bind group for vertex shader
let (vert_bind_group_layout, vert_bind_group) = ws::create_bind_group(
    &init.device,
    vec![wgpu::ShaderStages::VERTEX],
    &[vert_uniform_buffer.as_entire_binding()],
);

// uniform bind group for fragment shader
let (frag_bind_group_layout, frag_bind_group) = ws::create_bind_group(
    &init.device,
    vec![wgpu::ShaderStages::FRAGMENT, wgpu::ShaderStages::FRAGMENT],
    &[light_uniform_buffer.as_entire_binding(), material_uniform_buffer.as_entire_binding()],
);

// create image texture and image texture bind group
let img_file = image_file_map(0).unwrap();
let(texture_bind_group_layout, texture_bind_group) =
    ws::create_texture_bind_group(&init.device, &init.queue, vec![img_file],
        ADDRESS_MODE, ADDRESS_MODE);

let vertex_buffer_layout = VertexBufferLayout {
    array_stride: mem::size_of::<Vertex>() as wgpu::BufferAddress,
    step_mode: wgpu::VertexStepMode::Vertex,
    attributes: &wgpu::vertex_attr_array![0 => Float32x3, 1 => Float32x3, 2 => Float32x2],
    // pos, normal, uv
};

let pipeline_layout = init.device.create_pipeline_layout(&wgpu::PipelineLayoutDescriptor {
    label: Some("Render Pipeline Layout"),
    bind_group_layouts: &[&vert_bind_group_layout, &frag_bind_group_layout,
```

```rust
                    &texture_bind_group_layout],
            push_constant_ranges: &[],
        });

        let mut ppl = ws::IRenderPipeline {
            vs_shader: Some(&vs_shader),
            fs_shader: Some(&fs_shader),
            pipeline_layout: Some(&pipeline_layout),
            vertex_buffer_layout: &[vertex_buffer_layout],
            ..Default::default()
        };
        let pipeline = ppl.new(&init);

        let msaa_texture_view = ws::create_msaa_texture_view(&init);
        let depth_texture_view = ws::create_depth_view(&init);

        let (vertex_data, index_data) = create_vertices(1.0, 1.0);

        let vertex_buffer = init.device.create_buffer_init(&wgpu::util::BufferInitDescriptor {
            label: Some("Vertex Buffer"),
            contents: cast_slice(&vertex_data),
            usage: wgpu::BufferUsages::VERTEX | wgpu::BufferUsages::COPY_DST,
        });

        let index_buffer = init.device.create_buffer_init(&wgpu::util::BufferInitDescriptor{
            label: Some("Index Buffer"),
            contents: bytemuck::cast_slice(&index_data),
            usage: wgpu::BufferUsages::INDEX,
        });

        Self {
            init,
            pipeline,
            vertex_buffer,
            index_buffer,
            uniform_bind_groups: vec![vert_bind_group, frag_bind_group, texture_bind_group],
            uniform_buffers: vec![vert_uniform_buffer, light_uniform_buffer, material_uniform_buffer],
            view_mat,
            project_mat,
            msaa_texture_view,
            depth_texture_view,
            animation_speed: 1.0,
            indices_len: index_data.len() as u32,
            image_selection: 0,
            u_len: 1.0,
            v_len: 1.0,
            update_buffers: false,
        }
    }

    fn resize(&mut self, new_size: winit::dpi::PhysicalSize<u32>) {
        if new_size.width > 0 && new_size.height > 0 {
            self.init.size = new_size;
            self.init.config.width = new_size.width;
            self.init.config.height = new_size.height;
            self.init.surface.configure(&self.init.device, &self.init.config);

            self.project_mat = wt::create_projection_mat(new_size.width as f32 / new_size.height as f32,
                true);
            self.depth_texture_view = ws::create_depth_view(&self.init);
```

```rust
        if self.init.sample_count > 1 {
            self.msaa_texture_view = ws::create_msaa_texture_view(&self.init);
        }
    }
}

#[allow(unused_variables)]
fn input(&mut self, event: &WindowEvent) -> bool {
    match event {
        WindowEvent::KeyboardInput {
            input:
                KeyboardInput {
                    virtual_keycode: Some(keycode),
                    state: ElementState::Pressed,
                    ..
                },
            ..
        } => {
            match keycode {
                VirtualKeyCode::Space => {
                    self.image_selection = (self.image_selection + 1) % 4;
                    let img_file = image_file_map(self.image_selection).unwrap();
                    let(_, bind_group) =
                        ws::create_texture_bind_group(&self.init.device, &self.init.queue,
                            vec![img_file], ADDRESS_MODE, ADDRESS_MODE);
                    self.uniform_bind_groups[2] = bind_group;
                    true
                },
                VirtualKeyCode::Q => {
                    self.u_len += 0.1;
                    self.update_buffers = true;
                    true
                },
                VirtualKeyCode::A => {
                    self.u_len -= 0.1;
                    if self.u_len < 0.1 {
                        self.u_len = 0.1;
                    }
                    self.update_buffers = true;
                    true
                },
                VirtualKeyCode::W => {
                    self.v_len += 0.1;
                    self.update_buffers = true;
                    true
                },
                VirtualKeyCode::S => {
                    self.v_len -= 0.1;
                    if self.v_len < 0.1 {
                        self.v_len = 0.1;
                    }
                    self.update_buffers = true;
                    true
                },
                VirtualKeyCode::E => {
                    self.animation_speed += 0.1;
                    true
                },
                VirtualKeyCode::D => {
                    self.animation_speed -= 0.1;
```

```rust
                    if self.animation_speed < 0.0 {
                        self.animation_speed = 0.0;
                    }
                    true
                },
                _ => false
            }
        }
        _ => false,
    }
}

fn update(&mut self, dt: std::time::Duration) {
    // update uniform buffer
    let dt = self.animation_speed * dt.as_secs_f32();
    let model_mat = wt::create_model_mat([0.0,0.0,0.0], [dt.sin(), dt.cos(), 0.0], [1.0, 1.0, 1.0]);
    let view_project_mat = self.project_mat * self.view_mat;
    let normal_mat = (model_mat.invert().unwrap()).transpose();

    let model_ref:&[f32; 16] = model_mat.as_ref();
    let view_projection_ref:&[f32; 16] = view_project_mat.as_ref();
    let normal_ref:&[f32; 16] = normal_mat.as_ref();

    self.init.queue.write_buffer(&self.uniform_buffers[0], 0, cast_slice(view_projection_ref));
    self.init.queue.write_buffer(&self.uniform_buffers[0], 64, cast_slice(model_ref));
    self.init.queue.write_buffer(&self.uniform_buffers[0], 128, cast_slice(normal_ref));

    // update vertex buffer
    if self.update_buffers {
        let (vertex_data, _) = create_vertices(self.u_len, self.v_len);
        self.init.queue.write_buffer(&self.vertex_buffer, 0, cast_slice(&vertex_data));
        self.update_buffers = false;
    }
}

fn render(&mut self) -> Result<(), wgpu::SurfaceError> {
    let output = self.init.surface.get_current_texture()?;
    let view = output
        .texture
        .create_view(&wgpu::TextureViewDescriptor::default());

    let mut encoder = self
        .init.device
        .create_command_encoder(&wgpu::CommandEncoderDescriptor {
            label: Some("Render Encoder"),
        });

    {
        let color_attach = ws::create_color_attachment(&view);
        let msaa_attach = ws::create_msaa_color_attachment(&view, &self.msaa_texture_view);
        let color_attachment = if self.init.sample_count == 1 { color_attach } else { msaa_attach };
        let depth_attachment = ws::create_depth_stencil_attachment(&self.depth_texture_view);

        let mut render_pass = encoder.begin_render_pass(&wgpu::RenderPassDescriptor {
            label: Some("Render Pass"),
            color_attachments: &[Some(color_attachment)],
            depth_stencil_attachment: Some(depth_attachment),
            occlusion_query_set: None,
            timestamp_writes: None,
        });
```

```
        render_pass.set_pipeline(&self.pipeline);
        render_pass.set_vertex_buffer(0, self.vertex_buffer.slice(..));
        render_pass.set_index_buffer(self.index_buffer.slice(..), wgpu::IndexFormat::Uint16);
        render_pass.set_bind_group(0, &self.uniform_bind_groups[0], &[]);
        render_pass.set_bind_group(1, &self.uniform_bind_groups[1], &[]);
        render_pass.set_bind_group(2, &self.uniform_bind_groups[2], &[]);
        render_pass.draw_indexed(0..self.indices_len, 0, 0..1);
    }

    self.init.queue.submit(iter::once(encoder.finish()));
    output.present();

    Ok(())
    }
}

fn main() {
    env_logger::init();
    let event_loop = EventLoop::new();
    let window = winit::window::WindowBuilder::new().build(&event_loop).unwrap();
    window.set_title(&*format!("ch06_{}", "cube_texture"));

    let mut state = pollster::block_on(State::new(&window, 8));
    let render_start_time = std::time::Instant::now();

    event_loop.run(move |event, _, control_flow| {
        match event {
            Event::WindowEvent {
                ref event,
                window_id,
            } if window_id == window.id() => {
                if !state.input(event) {
                    match event {
                        WindowEvent::CloseRequested
                        | WindowEvent::KeyboardInput {
                            input:
                                KeyboardInput {
                                    state: ElementState::Pressed,
                                    virtual_keycode: Some(VirtualKeyCode::Escape),
                                    ..
                                },
                            ..
                        } => *control_flow = ControlFlow::Exit,
                        WindowEvent::Resized(physical_size) => {
                            state.resize(*physical_size);
                        }
                        WindowEvent::ScaleFactorChanged { new_inner_size, .. } => {
                            state.resize(**new_inner_size);
                        }
                        _ => {}
                    }
                }
            }
            Event::RedrawRequested(_) => {
                let now = std::time::Instant::now();
                let dt = now - render_start_time;
                state.update(dt);

                match state.render() {
                    Ok(_) => {}
```

```
                    Err(wgpu::SurfaceError::Lost) => state.resize(state.init.size),
                    Err(wgpu::SurfaceError::OutOfMemory) => *control_flow = ControlFlow::Exit,
                    Err(e) => eprintln!("{:?}", e),
                }
            }
            Event::MainEventsCleared => {
                window.request_redraw();
            }
            _ => {}
        }
    });
}
```

At the beginning of the above code, the *image_file_map* function is introduced, serving as a utility to establish mapping between specific numbers and corresponding image files through the use of a *HashMap*. This utility function streamlines the process of changing image files by specifying an integer key.

In contrast to the *State::new* function used in prior examples, the function featured in this example incorporates multiple new code blocks. First, we leverage helper functions from the *wgpu_simplified* module to create a texture bind group layout and a bind group from an image file. The following code snippet illustrates this procedure:

```
// create image texture and image texture bind group
let img_file = image_file_map(0).unwrap();
let(texture_bind_group_layout, texture_bind_group) = ws::create_texture_bind_group(
    &init.device, &init.queue, vec![img_file], ADDRESS_MODE, ADDRESS_MODE);
```

To facilitate the passage of UV data to the shader, the subsequent code snippet accomplishes this objective:

```
let vertex_buffer_layout = VertexBufferLayout {
    array_stride: mem::size_of::<Vertex>() as wgpu::BufferAddress,
    step_mode: wgpu::VertexStepMode::Vertex,
    attributes: &wgpu::vertex_attr_array![0 => Float32x3, 1 => Float32x3, 2 => Float32x2],
    // pos, normal, uv
};
```

In the *attributes* field, the entries correspond to *position*, *normal*, and *UV* data.

To enable the user to select different image files by pressing the *Space* key, a mechanism is implemented to regenerate the texture bind group within the *State::input* method. The following code block fulfills this requirement:

```
VirtualKeyCode::Space => {
    self.image_selection = (self.image_selection + 1) % 4;
    let img_file = image_file_map(self.image_selection).unwrap();
    let(_, bind_group) = ws::create_texture_bind_group(
        &self.init.device, &self.init.queue, vec![img_file], ADDRESS_MODE, ADDRESS_MODE);
    self.uniform_bind_groups[2] = bind_group;
    true
},
```

Additionally, the code permits the user to modify input parameters using keyboard inputs.

Here is a list of controls using keyboard:

- *Space*: Selects a different image file.

- *Q/A*: Increases/decreases the range of texture coordinates along the *u* direction.

- *W/S:* Increases/decreases the range of texture coordinates along the *v* direction.

- *E/D:* Increases/decreases the rotation speed.

To run this application, add the following code snippet to the *Cargo.toml* file:

```
[[example]]
name = "ch06_cube_texture"
path = "examples/ch06/cube_texture.rs"
```

Afterward, execute the following *cargo run* commands in the terminal window:

```
cargo run --example ch06_cube_texture
```

Fig.6-2 shows the textured cubes of this example using different image files.

Fig.6-2. Cube with different texture maps.

Fig.6-3 shows the results using a different range of texture coordinates by setting the *u_len* and *v_len* parameter to 0.5. This means that the cube is texture-mapped using only a quarter of the brick image.

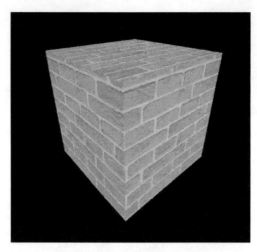

Fig.6-3. Cube with a brick image texture map in the range of [0, 0.5].

6.5.2 Sphere with Texture

We previously implemented the *create_sphere_data* function in the *vertex-data.rs* file within the *src/* folder. This function already includes computations for the UV texture coordinates on a sphere. In this example, we will use this UV data to map a 2D image onto the sphere's surface.

Create a new Rust file named *sphere_texture.rs* in the *examples/ch06/* folder. The code structure of this file closely resembles that of the previous cube texture example. The key difference lies in the utilization of the sphere's vertex data to instantiate instances of the *Vertex* struct, as demonstrated in the following code snippet:

```rust
pub struct Vertex {
    pub position: [f32; 3],
    pub normal: [f32; 3],
    pub uv: [f32; 2],
}

fn create_vertices() -> (Vec<Vertex>, Vec<u16>) {
    let(pos, norm, uv, ind, _) = vd::create_sphere_data(2.0, 20, 32);
    let mut data:Vec<Vertex> = vec![];
    for i in 0..pos.len() {
        data.push(Vertex{position:pos[i], normal:norm[i], uv:uv[i]});
    }
    (data.to_vec(), ind)
}
```

Moreover, we designate the *earth.png* file as the default image texture:

```rust
fn image_file_map(n:u32) -> Option<&'static str> {
    let mut d: HashMap<u32, &'static str> = HashMap::new();
    d.insert(0, "assets/earth.png");
    d.insert(1, "assets/brick.png");
    d.insert(2, "assets/grass.png");
    d.insert(3, "assets/wood.png");
    d.insert(4, "assets/marble.png");
    d.get(&n).cloned()
}
```

Additionally, the code enables users to adjust input parameters using keyboard inputs.

Here is a list of controls using keyboard:

- *Space*: Selects a different image file.
- *Q/A:* Increases/decreases the rotation speed.

To run this application, add the following code snippet to the *Cargo.toml* file:

```
[[example]]
name = "ch06_sphere_texture"
path = "examples/ch06/sphere_texture.rs"
```

Afterward, execute the following *cargo run* commands in the terminal window:

```
cargo run --example ch06_sphere_texture
```

Fig.6-4 displays the result of this example: a textured sphere mapped by an earth image.

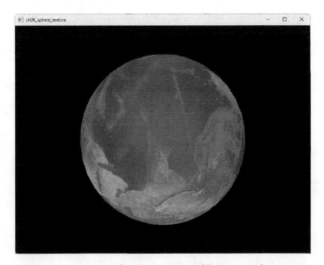

Fig.6-4. A textured sphere mapped by an earth image.

6.6 3D Surfaces

Earlier, we implemented a range of functions in the *surface-data.rs* file within the *src/ folder*. These functions serve to generate various vertex data, including the position, normal, colormap, and UV data. In this section, I will demonstrate the application of this data for mapping 2D texture images onto 3D surfaces, including simple and parametric surfaces.

6.6.1 Simple Surfaces with Texture

Create a new Rust file named *simple_surface_texture.rs* in the *examples/ch06/* folder. The code structure within this file closely resembles that of the preceding texture examples. The primary distinction lies in the utilization of the vertex data from simple surfaces to instantiate instances of the *Vertex* struct, as illustrated in the following code snippet:

```
pub struct Vertex {
```

```
    pub position: [f32; 3],
    pub normal: [f32; 3],
    pub uv: [f32; 2],
}

fn create_vertices(ss_data:sd::ISurfaceOutput) -> (Vec<Vertex>, Vec<u16>) {
    let mut data:Vec<Vertex> = vec![];
    for i in 0..ss_data.positions.len() {
        data.push(Vertex{position:ss_data.positions[i], normal:ss_data.normals[i], uv:ss_data.uvs[i]});
    }
    (data.to_vec(), ss_data.indices)
}
```

Within the *State*::*new* method, we invoke the *create_vertices* function to generate vertex and index data by instantiating the *ISimpleSurface* struct, as demonstrated by this code snippet:

```
    let mut ss = sd::ISimpleSurface {
        scale: 1.8,
        x_resolution: 64,
        z_resolution: 64,
        ..Default::default()
    };
    let (vertex_data, index_data) = create_vertices(ss.new());
```

Here, the resolution is increased to 64 to enhance texture map quality.

Similar to the previous chapter, for simple 3D surfaces with colormap, we implement vertex data animation. In the *State*::*update* function, vertex data and vertex buffers are updated per frame by introducing a time-dependent parameter to the *self.simple_surface.t* field, as depicted below:

```
    // update vertex buffer
    self.simple_surface.t = self.animation_speed * dt.as_secs_f32();
    let (vertex_data, _) = create_vertices(self.simple_surface.new());
    self.init.queue.write_buffer(&self.vertex_buffer, 0, cast_slice(&vertex_data));
```

The index buffer remains unchanged due to the fixed resolution of 64.

Moreover, the code in the *simple_surface_texture.rs* file facilitates parameter adjustment via keyboard inputs.

Here is a list of controls using keyboard:

- *Space*: Selects a different image file.
- *LControl*: Changes the surface type among *sinc*, *peaks*, and *poles*.
- *Q/A*: Increases/decreases the range of texture coordinates along the *u* direction.
- *W/S:* Increases/decreases the range of texture coordinates along the *v* direction.
- *E/D:* Increases/decreases the animation speed.
- *R/F:* Increases/decreases the rotation speed.

To run this application, add the following code snippet to the *Cargo.toml* file:

```
[[example]]
name = "ch06_simple_surface_texture"
path = "examples/ch06/simple_surface_texture.rs"
```

Afterward, execute the following *cargo run* commands in the terminal window:

```
cargo run --example ch06_simple_surface_texture
```

Fig.6-5 displays the results of this example.

Fig.6-5. Textured simple 3D surfaces with different images.

6.6.2 Parametric Surfaces with Texture

Introduce a new Rust file named *parametric_surface_texture.rs* into the *examples/ch06/* folder. The code structure within this file closely parallels that of the previous example. The key distinction lies in utilizing vertex data from parametric surfaces to instantiate instances of the *Vertex* struct, as illustrated in the subsequent code snippet:

```rust
pub struct Vertex {
    pub position: [f32; 3],
    pub normal: [f32; 3],
    pub uv: [f32; 2],
}

fn create_vertices(ss_data:sd::ISurfaceOutput) -> (Vec<Vertex>, Vec<u16>) {
    let mut data:Vec<Vertex> = vec![];
    for i in 0..ss_data.positions.len() {
        data.push(Vertex{position:ss_data.positions[i], normal:ss_data.normals[i], uv:ss_data.uvs[i]});
    }
    (data.to_vec(), ss_data.indices)
}
```

Inside the *State::new* method, we invoke the *create_vertices* function to generate vertex and index data by instantiating the *IParametricSurface* struct, as demonstrated here:

```rust
    let mut ps = sd::IParametricSurface {
        scale: 3.5,
        surface_type: 0,
        ..Default::default()
    };
    let (vertex_data, index_data) = create_vertices(ps.new());
```

In contrast to the previous example, vertex data and vertex buffers are not updated every frame. Instead, updates occurs solely when users modify the input parameters like *scale*, *u_len*, or *v_len*.

Similar to the prior chapter, for parametric 3D surfaces with colormap, within the *State::update* function, when the condition *self.random_shape_change* = 1 is met, we use the following code to update vertex buffers every 5 seconds:

```rust
    let elapsed = self.t0.elapsed();
    if elapsed >= std::time::Duration::from_secs(5) && self.random_shape_change == 1 {
        self.parametric_surface.surface_type = self.rng.gen_range(0..=23) as u32;
```

```
    let (vertex_data, _) = create_vertices(self.parametric_surface.new());
    self.init.queue.write_buffer(&self.vertex_buffer, 0, cast_slice(&vertex_data));
    self.t0 = std::time::Instant::now();

    println!("key = {:?}, value = {:?}", self.parametric_surface.surface_type,
        self.parametric_surface.surface_type_map[&self.parametric_surface.surface_type]);
}
```

This code snippet randomly selects a new surface type, generates new vertex data, writes it to the vertex buffers, and prints the selected surface type and corresponding surface name in the terminal. On the other hand, when *self.random_shape_change* != 1 (alterable via the *LAlt* key), you can manually modify the surface type using the *LControl* key.

Moreover, the code in the *parametric_surface_texture.rs* file facilitates parameter adjustment via keyboard inputs.

Here is a list of controls using keyboard:

- *Space*: Selects a different image file.
- *LControl*: Changes the surface type manually when *random_shape_change* != 1.
- *LAlt*: Alters the *random_shape_change* parameter value between 0 and 1.
- *Q/A*: Increases/decreases the range of texture coordinates along the *u* direction.
- *W/S:* Increases/decreases the range of texture coordinates along the *v* direction.
- *E/D:* Increases/decreases the rotation speed.

To run this application, add the following code snippet to the *Cargo.toml* file:

```
[[example]]
name = "ch06_parametric_surface_texture"
path = "examples/ch06/parametric_surface_texture.rs"
```

Afterward, execute the following *cargo run* commands in the terminal window:

```
cargo run --example ch06_parametric_surface_texture
```

Fig.6-6 shows the results of this example.

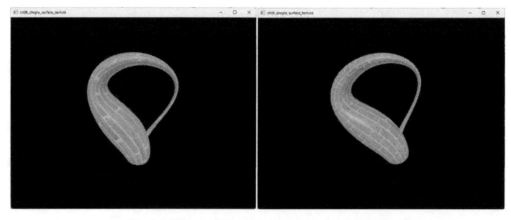

Fig.6-6. Textured Klein bottle using a brick image.

In the figure above, we observe a parametric 3D surface, the Klein bottle, that has been texture-mapped using a brick image. On the left side of the figure, the surface is mapped with the default parameters: *u_len* = 1 and *v_len* = 1. As a result, the texture map appears distorted – each brick seems overly elongated. In contrast, the right side of the figure portrays a more visually pleasing representation, achieved by adjusting the parameters to *u_len* = 4 and *v_len* = 1. This adjustment results in a more proportionate appearance for each brick on the surface. By fine-tuning these parameters, you can achieve suitable texture mapping for various parametric 3D surfaces.

6.7 Cube with Multiple Textures

In previous examples, we have consistently employed a single image to map onto the surface of a 3D object. However, it is possible to apply multiple textures to a surface, thereby creating a diverse range of visual effects. One effective approach to achieve this involves the creation of a texture atlas. This atlas is a single image file housing multiple sub-images, each representing distinct textures. By mapping the texture coordinates of the surface to the corresponding sub-image within the texture atlas, we enable the application of multiple textures to the surface. This technique is extensively detailed in my previously published book, titled "*Practical GPU Graphics with wgpu and Rust*."

Another approach involves layering multiple textures atop one another using the texture blending. The base layer texture might portray the surface's base color or base texture, while additional textures could convey intricate details such as cracks, bumps, blemishes, or damage. Through the blending of these textures, we can craft surfaces that appear more authentic and varied.

This upcoming example will showcase the texture blending technique by applying two layers of texture onto a cube's surface. The base layer will feature a fully opaque image, while the second layer will incorporate a partially transparent image. To facilitate the creation of multiple textures, I have introduced a selection of partial transparent images with PNG format to the *assets/* folder.

6.7.1 Shader Code

We can still use the same vertex shader as the one used in the previous example. But, to map two textures onto a surface we need a new fragment shader. Create a fragment shader file called *multiple-frag.wgsl* in the *examples/ch06/* folder and enter the following code into it:

```
struct LightUniforms {
    lightDirection : vec4f,
    eyePosition : vec4f,
    specularColor : vec4f,
};
@group(1) @binding(0) var<uniform> light : LightUniforms;

struct MaterialUniforms {
    ambient: f32,
    diffuse: f32,
    specular: f32,
    shininess: f32,
};
@group(1) @binding(1) var<uniform> material: MaterialUniforms;
@group(2) @binding(0) var textureSampler: sampler;
@group(2) @binding(1) var textureData: texture_2d<f32>;
@group(3) @binding(0) var textureSampler2: sampler;
@group(3) @binding(1) var textureData2: texture_2d<f32>;
```

```
struct Input {
    @location(0) vPosition: vec4f,
    @location(1) vNormal: vec4f,
    @location(2) vUv: vec2f,
};

fn blinnPhong(N:vec3f, L:vec3f, V:vec3f) -> vec2f{
    let H = normalize(L + V);
    var diffuse = material.diffuse * max(dot(N, L), 0.0);
    diffuse += material.diffuse * max(dot(-N, L), 0.0);
    var specular = material.specular * pow(max(dot(N, H), 0.0), material.shininess);
    specular += material.specular * pow(max(dot(-N, H),0.0), material.shininess);
    return vec2(diffuse, specular);
}

@fragment
fn fs_main(in: Input) ->  @location(0) vec4f {
    var N = normalize(in.vNormal.xyz);
    let L = normalize(-light.lightDirection.xyz);
    let V = normalize(light.eyePosition.xyz - in.vPosition.xyz);
    let bp = blinnPhong(N, L, V);

    let texColor = (textureSample(textureData, textureSampler, in.vUv));
    let texColor2 = (textureSample(textureData2, textureSampler2, in.vUv));
    let col = mix(texColor.rgb, texColor2.rgb, texColor2.a);

    let finalColor = col.rgb * (material.ambient + bp[0]) + light.specularColor.rgb * bp[1];
    return vec4(finalColor.rgb, 1.0);
}
```

This fragment shader code is based on the code in the *directional-frag.wgsl* file located in the *examples/ch03/* folder, with certain modifications. Firstly, we replace the vertex color data with the UV coordinate data. Then, we pass two textures and samplers to the shader, with each representing data from a different image file. Furthermore, within the *fs_main* function, we blend these two textures together to create the final color, as illustrated in the following code snippet:

```
let texColor = (textureSample(textureData, textureSampler, in.vUv));
let texColor2 = (textureSample(textureData2, textureSampler2, in.vUv));
let col = mix(texColor.rgb, texColor2.rgb, texColor2.a);
let finalColor = col.rgb * (material.ambient + bp[0]) + light.specularColor.rgb * bp[1];
```

Here, we blend two colors from textures together using the WGSL built-in function *mix*. The third argument in the *mix* function is the percentage used when mixing the two colors. We use the *alpha* value from the second texture for the argument. This causes the result to be a linear interpolation of the two colors based on the value of the *alpha* in the second texture. Finally, the ambient and diffuse components are multiplied by the result of the *mix* function to obtain the fragment color.

6.7.2 Rust Code

Create a new Rust file called *multiple_textures.rs* in the *examples/ch06/* folder and include the following code:

```
use std:: {iter, mem, collections::HashMap};
use cgmath::{ Matrix, Matrix4, SquareMatrix };
use wgpu::{util::DeviceExt, VertexBufferLayout};
use winit::{
    event::*,
```

```
        event_loop::{ControlFlow, EventLoop},
        window::Window,
};
use bytemuck:: {Pod, Zeroable, cast_slice};
use wgpu_book_examples::{ wgpu_simplified as ws, transforms as wt, vertex_data as vd };

#[repr(C)]
#[derive(Copy, Clone, Debug, Pod, Zeroable)]
struct Vertex {
    position: [f32; 3],
    normal: [f32; 3],
    uv: [f32; 2],
}

fn create_vertices(ul:f32, vl:f32) -> (Vec<Vertex>, Vec<u16>) {
    let(pos, _, norm, uv, ind, _) = vd::create_cube_data(2.0);
    let mut data:Vec<Vertex> = vec![];
    for i in 0..pos.len() {
        data.push(Vertex{position: pos[i], normal: norm[i], uv: [uv[i][0]*ul, uv[i][1]*vl]});
    }
    (data.to_vec(), ind)
}

fn image_file_map(n:u32) -> Option<&'static str> {
    let mut d: HashMap<u32, &'static str> = HashMap::new();
    d.insert(0, "assets/brick.png");
    d.insert(1, "assets/wood.png");
    d.insert(2, "assets/marble.png");

    d.get(&n).cloned()
}

const ADDRESS_MODE:wgpu::AddressMode = wgpu::AddressMode::MirrorRepeat;

struct State {
    init:  ws::IWgpuInit,
    pipeline: wgpu::RenderPipeline,
    vertex_buffer: wgpu::Buffer,
    index_buffer: wgpu::Buffer,
    uniform_bind_groups: Vec<wgpu::BindGroup>,
    uniform_buffers: Vec<wgpu::Buffer>,
    view_mat: Matrix4<f32>,
    project_mat: Matrix4<f32>,
    msaa_texture_view: wgpu::TextureView,
    depth_texture_view: wgpu::TextureView,
    animation_speed: f32,
    indices_len: u32,
    image_selection: u32,
    u_len: f32,
    v_len: f32,
    update_buffers: bool,
}

impl State {
    async fn new(window: &Window, sample_count:u32) -> Self {
        let init = ws::IWgpuInit::new(&window, sample_count, None).await;

        let vs_shader = init.device.create_shader_module(wgpu::include_wgsl!("shader_vert.wgsl"));
        let fs_shader = init.device.create_shader_module(wgpu::include_wgsl!("multiple_frag.wgsl"));
```

```
// uniform data
let camera_position = (2.5, 1.5, 3.0).into();
let look_direction = (0.0,0.0,0.0).into();
let up_direction = cgmath::Vector3::unit_y();


let (view_mat, project_mat, _) =
    wt::create_vp_mat(camera_position, look_direction, up_direction,
    init.config.width as f32 / init.config.height as f32);

// create vertex uniform buffers

// model_mat and vp_mat will be stored in vertex_uniform_buffer inside the update function
let vert_uniform_buffer = init.device.create_buffer(&wgpu::BufferDescriptor{
    label: Some("Vertex Uniform Buffer"),
    size: 192,
    usage: wgpu::BufferUsages::UNIFORM | wgpu::BufferUsages::COPY_DST,
    mapped_at_creation: false,
});

// create light uniform buffer. here we set eye_position = camera_position and
// light_position = eye_position
let light_uniform_buffer = init.device.create_buffer(&wgpu::BufferDescriptor{
    label: Some("Light Uniform Buffer"),
    size: 48,
    usage: wgpu::BufferUsages::UNIFORM | wgpu::BufferUsages::COPY_DST,
    mapped_at_creation: false,
});

let light_direction = [-0.5f32, -0.5, -0.5];
let eye_position:&[f32; 3] = camera_position.as_ref();
init.queue.write_buffer(&light_uniform_buffer, 0, cast_slice(&light_direction));
init.queue.write_buffer(&light_uniform_buffer, 16, cast_slice(eye_position));

// set specular light color to white
let specular_color:[f32; 3] = [1.0, 1.0, 1.0];
init.queue.write_buffer(&light_uniform_buffer, 32, cast_slice(specular_color.as_ref()));

// material uniform buffer
let material_uniform_buffer = init.device.create_buffer(&wgpu::BufferDescriptor{
    label: Some("Material Uniform Buffer"),
    size: 16,
    usage: wgpu::BufferUsages::UNIFORM | wgpu::BufferUsages::COPY_DST,
    mapped_at_creation: false,
});

// set default material parameters
let material = [0.1 as f32, 0.7, 0.4, 30.0];
init.queue.write_buffer(&material_uniform_buffer, 0, cast_slice(&material));

// uniform bind group for vertex shader
let (vert_bind_group_layout, vert_bind_group) = ws::create_bind_group(
    &init.device,
    vec![wgpu::ShaderStages::VERTEX],
    &[vert_uniform_buffer.as_entire_binding()],
);

// uniform bind group for fragment shader
let (frag_bind_group_layout, frag_bind_group) = ws::create_bind_group(
    &init.device,
    vec![wgpu::ShaderStages::FRAGMENT, wgpu::ShaderStages::FRAGMENT],
```

```
        &[light_uniform_buffer.as_entire_binding(), material_uniform_buffer.as_entire_binding()],
);

// create image texture and image texture bind group
let img_file = image_file_map(0).unwrap();
let(texture_bind_group_layout, texture_bind_group) =
    ws::create_texture_bind_group(&init.device, &init.queue, vec![img_file],
        ADDRESS_MODE, ADDRESS_MODE);

let img_file2 = "assets/trans-africa-moss.png";
let(texture_bind_group_layout2, texture_bind_group2) =
    ws::create_texture_bind_group(&init.device, &init.queue, vec![img_file2],
        ADDRESS_MODE, ADDRESS_MODE);

let vertex_buffer_layout = VertexBufferLayout {
    array_stride: mem::size_of::<Vertex>() as wgpu::BufferAddress,
    step_mode: wgpu::VertexStepMode::Vertex,
    attributes: &wgpu::vertex_attr_array![0 => Float32x3, 1 => Float32x3, 2 => Float32x2],
    // pos, normal, uv
};

let pipeline_layout = init.device.create_pipeline_layout(&wgpu::PipelineLayoutDescriptor {
    label: Some("Render Pipeline Layout"),
    bind_group_layouts: &[&vert_bind_group_layout, &frag_bind_group_layout,
        &texture_bind_group_layout, &texture_bind_group_layout2],
    push_constant_ranges: &[],
});

let mut ppl = ws::IRenderPipeline {
    vs_shader: Some(&vs_shader),
    fs_shader: Some(&fs_shader),
    pipeline_layout: Some(&pipeline_layout),
    vertex_buffer_layout: &[vertex_buffer_layout],
    ..Default::default()
};
let pipeline = ppl.new(&init);

let msaa_texture_view = ws::create_msaa_texture_view(&init);
let depth_texture_view = ws::create_depth_view(&init);

let (vertex_data, index_data) = create_vertices(1.0, 1.0);

let vertex_buffer = init.device.create_buffer_init(&wgpu::util::BufferInitDescriptor {
    label: Some("Vertex Buffer"),
    contents: cast_slice(&vertex_data),
    usage: wgpu::BufferUsages::VERTEX | wgpu::BufferUsages::COPY_DST,
});

let index_buffer = init.device.create_buffer_init(&wgpu::util::BufferInitDescriptor{
    label: Some("Index Buffer"),
    contents: bytemuck::cast_slice(&index_data),
    usage: wgpu::BufferUsages::INDEX,
});

Self {
    init,
    pipeline,
    vertex_buffer,
    index_buffer,
    uniform_bind_groups: vec![vert_bind_group, frag_bind_group, texture_bind_group,
```

```
                texture_bind_group2],
            uniform_buffers: vec![vert_uniform_buffer, light_uniform_buffer, material_uniform_buffer],
            view_mat,
            project_mat,
            msaa_texture_view,
            depth_texture_view,
            animation_speed: 1.0,
            indices_len: index_data.len() as u32,
            image_selection: 0,
            u_len: 1.0,
            v_len: 1.0,
            update_buffers: false,
        }
    }

    fn resize(&mut self, new_size: winit::dpi::PhysicalSize<u32>) {
        if new_size.width > 0 && new_size.height > 0 {
            self.init.size = new_size;
            self.init.config.width = new_size.width;
            self.init.config.height = new_size.height;
            self.init.surface.configure(&self.init.device, &self.init.config);

            self.project_mat = wt::create_projection_mat(new_size.width as f32 / new_size.height as f32,
                true);
            self.depth_texture_view = ws::create_depth_view(&self.init);
            if self.init.sample_count > 1 {
                self.msaa_texture_view = ws::create_msaa_texture_view(&self.init);
            }
        }
    }

    #[allow(unused_variables)]
    fn input(&mut self, event: &WindowEvent) -> bool {
        match event {
            WindowEvent::KeyboardInput {
                input:
                    KeyboardInput {
                        virtual_keycode: Some(keycode),
                        state: ElementState::Pressed,
                        ..
                    },
                ..
            } => {
                match keycode {
                    VirtualKeyCode::Space => {
                        self.image_selection = (self.image_selection + 1) % 3;
                        let img_file = image_file_map(self.image_selection).unwrap();
                        let(_, bind_group) = ws::create_texture_bind_group(
                            &self.init.device, &self.init.queue, vec![img_file],
                            ADDRESS_MODE, ADDRESS_MODE);
                        self.uniform_bind_groups[2] = bind_group;
                        true
                    },
                    VirtualKeyCode::Q => {
                        self.u_len += 0.1;
                        self.update_buffers = true;
                        true
                    },
                    VirtualKeyCode::A => {
                        self.u_len -= 0.1;
```

```
                if self.u_len < 0.1 {
                    self.u_len = 0.1;
                }
                self.update_buffers = true;
                true
            },
            VirtualKeyCode::W => {
                self.v_len += 0.1;
                self.update_buffers = true;
                true
            },
            VirtualKeyCode::S => {
                self.v_len -= 0.1;
                if self.v_len < 0.1 {
                    self.v_len = 0.1;
                }
                self.update_buffers = true;
                true
            },
            VirtualKeyCode::E => {
                self.animation_speed += 0.1;
                true
            },
            VirtualKeyCode::D => {
                self.animation_speed -= 0.1;
                if self.animation_speed < 0.0 {
                    self.animation_speed = 0.0;
                }
                true
            } ,
            _ => false
        }
    }
    _ => false,
    }
}

fn update(&mut self, dt: std::time::Duration) {
    // update uniform buffer
    let dt = self.animation_speed * dt.as_secs_f32();
    let model_mat = wt::create_model_mat([0.0,0.0,0.0], [dt.sin(), dt.cos(), 0.0], [1.0, 1.0, 1.0]);
    let view_project_mat = self.project_mat * self.view_mat;

    let normal_mat = (model_mat.invert().unwrap()).transpose();

    let model_ref:&[f32; 16] = model_mat.as_ref();
    let view_projection_ref:&[f32; 16] = view_project_mat.as_ref();
    let normal_ref:&[f32; 16] = normal_mat.as_ref();

    self.init.queue.write_buffer(&self.uniform_buffers[0], 0, cast_slice(view_projection_ref));
    self.init.queue.write_buffer(&self.uniform_buffers[0], 64, cast_slice(model_ref));
    self.init.queue.write_buffer(&self.uniform_buffers[0], 128, cast_slice(normal_ref));

    // update vertex buffer
    if self.update_buffers {
        let (vertex_data, _) = create_vertices(self.u_len, self.v_len);
        self.init.queue.write_buffer(&self.vertex_buffer, 0, cast_slice(&vertex_data));
        self.update_buffers = false;
    }
}
```

```rust
fn render(&mut self) -> Result<(), wgpu::SurfaceError> {
    //let output = self.init.surface.get_current_frame()?.output;
    let output = self.init.surface.get_current_texture()?;
    let view = output
        .texture
        .create_view(&wgpu::TextureViewDescriptor::default());

    let mut encoder = self
        .init.device
        .create_command_encoder(&wgpu::CommandEncoderDescriptor {
            label: Some("Render Encoder"),
        });

    {
        let color_attach = ws::create_color_attachment(&view);
        let msaa_attach = ws::create_msaa_color_attachment(&view, &self.msaa_texture_view);
        let color_attachment = if self.init.sample_count == 1 { color_attach } else { msaa_attach };
        let depth_attachment = ws::create_depth_stencil_attachment(&self.depth_texture_view);

        let mut render_pass = encoder.begin_render_pass(&wgpu::RenderPassDescriptor {
            label: Some("Render Pass"),
            color_attachments: &[Some(color_attachment)],
            depth_stencil_attachment: Some(depth_attachment),
            occlusion_query_set: None,
            timestamp_writes: None,
        });
        render_pass.set_pipeline(&self.pipeline);
        render_pass.set_vertex_buffer(0, self.vertex_buffer.slice(..));
        render_pass.set_index_buffer(self.index_buffer.slice(..), wgpu::IndexFormat::Uint16);
        render_pass.set_bind_group(0, &self.uniform_bind_groups[0], &[]);
        render_pass.set_bind_group(1, &self.uniform_bind_groups[1], &[]);
        render_pass.set_bind_group(2, &self.uniform_bind_groups[2], &[]);
        render_pass.set_bind_group(3, &self.uniform_bind_groups[3], &[]);
        render_pass.draw_indexed(0..self.indices_len, 0, 0..1);
    }

    self.init.queue.submit(iter::once(encoder.finish()));
    output.present();

    Ok(())
}
}

fn main() {
    env_logger::init();
    let event_loop = EventLoop::new();
    let window = winit::window::WindowBuilder::new().build(&event_loop).unwrap();
    window.set_title(&*format!("ch06_{}", "multiple_textures"));

    let mut state = pollster::block_on(State::new(&window, 8));
    let render_start_time = std::time::Instant::now();

    event_loop.run(move |event, _, control_flow| {
        match event {
            Event::WindowEvent {
                ref event,
                window_id,
            } if window_id == window.id() => {
                if !state.input(event) {
```

```
                match event {
                    WindowEvent::CloseRequested
                    | WindowEvent::KeyboardInput {
                        input:
                            KeyboardInput {
                                state: ElementState::Pressed,
                                virtual_keycode: Some(VirtualKeyCode::Escape),
                                ..
                            },
                        ..
                    } => *control_flow = ControlFlow::Exit,
                    WindowEvent::Resized(physical_size) => {
                        state.resize(*physical_size);
                    }
                    WindowEvent::ScaleFactorChanged { new_inner_size, .. } => {
                        state.resize(**new_inner_size);
                    }
                    _ => {}
                }
            }
        }
        Event::RedrawRequested(_) => {
            let now = std::time::Instant::now();
            let dt = now - render_start_time;
            state.update(dt);

            match state.render() {
                Ok(_) => {}
                Err(wgpu::SurfaceError::Lost) => state.resize(state.init.size),
                Err(wgpu::SurfaceError::OutOfMemory) => *control_flow = ControlFlow::Exit,
                Err(e) => eprintln!("{:?}", e),
            }
        }
        Event::MainEventsCleared => {
            window.request_redraw();
        }
        _ => {}
    }
    });
}
```

In the above code, we set the base image for the first texture using the image files: *brick.png*, *wood.png*, or *marble.png*, and then set the secondary image for the second texture using the image file: *trans-africa-moss.png*. The user can choose the base image from the keyboard inputs.

Subsequently, we use the selected base and secondary images, as well as the helper functions implemented in the *wgpu-simplified.rs* file, to create two separate textures/samplers and corresponding texture bind groups, as described in the following code snippet:

```
// create image texture and image texture bind group
let img_file = image_file_map(0).unwrap();
let(texture_bind_group_layout, texture_bind_group) =
    ws::create_texture_bind_group(&init.device, &init.queue, vec![img_file],
        ADDRESS_MODE, ADDRESS_MODE);

let img_file2 = "assets/trans-africa-moss.png";
let(texture_bind_group_layout2, texture_bind_group2) =
    ws::create_texture_bind_group(&init.device, &init.queue, vec![img_file2],
        ADDRESS_MODE, ADDRESS_MODE);
```

Moreover, the above code facilitates parameter adjustment via keyboard inputs. Here is a list of controls using keyboard:

- *Space*: Selects a different base image file.
- *Q/A*: Increases/decreases the range of texture coordinates along the *u* direction.
- *W/S:* Increases/decreases the range of texture coordinates along the *v* direction.
- *E/D:* Increases/decreases the rotation speed.

To run this application, add the following code snippet to the *Cargo.toml* file:

```
[[example]]
name = "ch06_multiple_textures"
path = "examples/ch06/multiple_textures.rs"
```

Afterward, execute the following *cargo run* commands in the terminal window:

```
cargo run --example ch06_multiple_textures
```

Fig.6-7 displays the results of this examples with different base images.

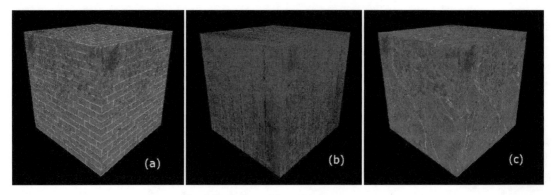

Fig.6-7. Cubes with multiple textures.

It is evident from Fig.6-7 that applying multiple textures on a surface is a powerful technique that can help create a wide variety of visual effects, from realistic natural surfaces to fantastical and surreal ones. In the figure, the base and second layers are shown for a textured cube using different base images: brick (a), wood (b), and marble (c). The transparent parts of the secondary texture reveal the base texture underneath.

6.8 Normal Mapping

Normal mapping is a texture mapping technique used to simulate surface variations without actually modeling every small detail. Normal maps are commonly used for creating realistic 3D surfaces that have bumps, dents, roughness, or wrinkles, which enhances the quality of details on those surfaces without increasing the polygon count or complexity. This technique uses a texture called a normal map, which stores per-pixel surface normal information that perturbs the surface normals of an object at runtime.

In normal mapping, the normal map is applied to the object's surface, in addition to its regular texture map. The normal map perturbs the surface normals of the object to make it appear as if there are bumps, scratches, or other small details on its surface, even though the underlying geometry is still smooth.

The process of applying a normal map to an object involves generating tangent and bitangent vectors for each vertex of the object, which define the orientation of the texture space (also known as the tangent space). This is followed by mapping the normal map onto this tangent space, and the resulting texture is then used to modify the surface normals of the object in the shading calculations.

When creating normal maps, the normal vectors are typically transformed into a color space that maps the x, y, and z components to the range of $[0, 1]$. As blue is often associated with a positive z direction, the blue channel of the texture is typically emphasized to make the surface orientation more visible. Hence, the normal map of a brick surface shown in Fig.6-8 has a blue tone as the normals are closely pointing outwards towards the positive z-axis $(0, 0, 1)$.

Fig.6-8. A brick normal map texture.

The deviations in color indicate normal vectors that are slightly offset from the general positive z direction, giving depth to the texture. It is noteworthy that the color tends to be more greenish at the top of each brick as the top side of the brick would have normals pointing more in the positive y direction $(0, 1, 0)$ which happens to be green color.

There are several ways to generate a normal map. Many 3D modeling programs include tools for generating normal maps, such as *ZBrush*, *Blender*, or *Maya*. These tools often use ray-tracing techniques to project the surface detail onto the low-poly model. There are also standalone applications that specialize in generating normal maps, such as *xNormal* or *CrazyBump*. These tools can take a high-poly model and a low-poly model as input and generate maps as output. Additionally, it is possible to use Photoshop to generate a basic normal map by converting a height map into a normal map using a filter.

Once the normal map is generated, it can be used in conjunction with a 3D model and *wgpu* to create the illusion of surface detail.

6.8.1 Calculating Tangents and Bitangents

To make the normal map work, we need to evaluate the reflection model in tangent space, which requires transforming the vectors used in the camera space into tangent space. Such a transformation matrix (known as TBN matrix) can be constructed using tangent vector, bitangent vector, and the vertex normal vector as the columns of a 3×3 matrix. This matrix can then be multiplied by any vector in camera space to get its corresponding vector in tangent space.

Transforming vectors from camera space to tangent space is useful for techniques such as normal mapping and parallax mapping, where you want to apply texture that are given in tangent space coordinates. By doing this transformation, you can avoid expensive computations in the fragment shader and achieve more realistic lighting effects.

The TBN matrix requires three vectors: normal, tangent, and bitangent vectors. We usually already know the normal vector as it is necessary for lighting calculation. Since the normal vector is perpendicular to the surface at each vertex, we can think of the direction of tangent and bitangent vectors as aligning with the direction of a surface's UV coordinates. We can use this fact to calculate tangent and bitangent vectors for various surfaces.

Add a new function named *create_tangent_data* to the *vertex_data.rs* file located in the *src/* folder and enter the following code into it:

```
#[derive(Default, Debug)]
pub struct Vertex {
    pub pos: [f32; 3],
    pub uv: [f32; 2],
    pub norm: [f32; 3],
    pub tang: [f32; 3],
    pub bitang: [f32; 3],
}

pub fn create_tangent_data(
    positions:&Vec<[f32;3]>,
    normals:&Vec<[f32;3]>,
    uvs:&Vec<[f32;2]>,
    indices:&Vec<u16>
) -> Vec<Vertex> {
    let mut vertices:Vec<Vertex> = vec![];
    for i in 0..positions.len() {
        vertices.push(Vertex {
            pos: positions[i],
            uv: uvs[i],
            norm: normals[i],
            tang: [0.0; 3],
            bitang: [0.0; 3],
        })
    }

    let mut triangles:Vec<u16> = vec![0; vertices.len()];
    for i in (0..indices.len()).step_by(3) {
        let c = [indices[i], indices[i+1], indices[i+2]];
        let v0 = &vertices[c[0] as usize];
        let v1 = &vertices[c[1] as usize];
        let v2 = &vertices[c[2] as usize];

        let pos0 = Vector3::from(v0.pos);
        let pos1 = Vector3::from(v1.pos);
        let pos2 = Vector3::from(v2.pos);
```

```
    let uv0 = Vector2::from(v0.uv);
    let uv1 = Vector2::from(v1.uv);
    let uv2 = Vector2::from(v2.uv);

    let dp1 = pos1 - pos0;
    let dp2 = pos2 - pos0;
    let duv1 = uv1 - uv0;
    let duv2 = uv2 - uv0;

    let d = 1.0/(duv1[0]*duv2[1] - duv1[1]*duv2[0]);
    let tangent = [
        (dp1[0]*duv2[1] - dp2[0]*duv1[1])*d,
        (dp1[1]*duv2[1] - dp2[1]*duv1[1])*d,
        (dp1[2]*duv2[1] - dp2[2]*duv1[1])*d,
    ];
    let bitangent = [
        (dp2[0]*duv1[0] - dp1[0]*duv2[0])*(-d),
        (dp2[1]*duv1[0] - dp1[1]*duv2[0])*(-d),
        (dp2[2]*duv1[0] - dp1[2]*duv2[0])*(-d),
    ];

    vertices[c[0] as usize].tang =(Vector3::from(tangent) + Vector3::from(vertices[c[0]
        as usize].tang)).into();
    vertices[c[1] as usize].tang =(Vector3::from(tangent) + Vector3::from(vertices[c[1]
        as usize].tang)).into();
    vertices[c[2] as usize].tang =(Vector3::from(tangent) + Vector3::from(vertices[c[2]
        as usize].tang)).into();
    vertices[c[0] as usize].bitang =(Vector3::from(bitangent) + Vector3::from(vertices[c[0]
        as usize].bitang)).into();
    vertices[c[1] as usize].bitang =(Vector3::from(bitangent) + Vector3::from(vertices[c[1]
        as usize].bitang)).into();
    vertices[c[2] as usize].bitang =(Vector3::from(bitangent) + Vector3::from(vertices[c[2]
        as usize].bitang)).into();

    triangles[c[0] as usize] += 1;
    triangles[c[1] as usize] += 1;
    triangles[c[2] as usize] += 1;
}

// average tangents and bitangents
for i in 0..triangles.len() {
    let n = triangles[i];
    vertices[i].tang = (Vector3::from(vertices[i].tang)/n as f32).into();
    vertices[i].bitang = (Vector3::from(vertices[i].bitang)/n as f32).into();
}

// Gram-Schmidt orthogonalization
for i in 0..vertices.len() {
    let v = &mut vertices[i];
    let n = Vector3::from(v.norm);
    let t = Vector3::from(v.tang);
    let b = Vector3::from(v.bitang);

    // calculate t1
    let dot_tn = t.dot(n);
    let mut t1 = n * dot_tn;
    t1 = (t - t1).normalize();

    // calculate b1
    let dot_bn = b.dot(n);
```

```
        let dot_bt = b.dot(t1);
        let b_bn = n * dot_bn;
        let b_bt = t1 * dot_bt;
        let mut b1 = b - b_bn;
        b1 = (b1 - b_bt).normalize();

        v.tang = t1.into();
        v.bitang = b1.into();
    }
    vertices
}
```

The *create_tangent_data* function accepts the position, normal, UV, and index data as its input arguments. Within this function, we first retrieve the position, UV, and normal vectors for each vertex from the respective data arrays. Additionally, we define the tangent and bitangent vectors for each vertex with an empty vector as placeholders. These five vectors will be treated as basis vectors. We then compute the edge (*dp1, dp2*) and delta UV (*duv1, duv2*) for each triangle. Subsequently, we use these deltas to compute the tangent and bitangent vectors, as described in the following code snippet:

```
let d = 1.0/(duv1[0]*duv2[1] - duv1[1]*duv2[0]);
let tangent = [
    (dp1[0]*duv2[1] - dp2[0]*duv1[1])*d,
    (dp1[1]*duv2[1] - dp2[1]*duv1[1])*d,
    (dp1[2]*duv2[1] - dp2[2]*duv1[1])*d,
];
let bitangent = [
    (dp2[0]*duv1[0] - dp1[0]*duv2[0])*(-d),
    (dp2[1]*duv1[0] - dp1[1]*duv2[0])*(-d),
    (dp2[2]*duv1[0] - dp1[2]*duv2[0])*(-d),
];
```

After obtaining the tangent and bitangent vectors for each triangle, we take the average of these vectors to smooth out the variations in the surface orientation and texture mapping. This can help to avoid artifacts and discontinuities when applying normal mapping or other shading techniques. However, averaging tangent and bitangent vectors may also introduce some problems such as losing orthogonality between them or between them and the normal vector. This can affect how accurately the normal map reflects light. Therefore, to overcome this problem, we need to perform the Gram-Schmidt orthogonalization for the normal, tangent, and bitangent vectors. Finally, the function returns an object containing the tangent and bitangent data arrays, which can be used for normal mapping.

6.8.2 Shader Code

Normal mapping requires new shader code for both vertex and fragment shaders. Create a new vertex shader file named *normal_vert.wgsl* in the *examples/ch06/* folder and include the following code:

```
// vertex shader
struct Uniforms {
    vpMat : mat4x4f,
    modelMat : mat4x4f,
    normalMat : mat4x4f,

};
@binding(0) @group(0) var<uniform> uniforms : Uniforms;

struct Light {
    lightPosition: vec4f,
    eyePosition: vec4f,
```

```
}
@binding(1) @group(0) var<uniform> light : Light;

struct Input {
    @location(0) pos: vec4f,
    @location(1) normal: vec4f,
    @location(2) uv: vec2f,
    @location(3) tangent: vec4f,
    @location(4) bitangent: vec4f,
};

struct Output {
    @builtin(position) position : vec4f,
    @location(0) vUv: vec2f,
    @location(1) tPosition: vec3f,
    @location(2) tLightPosition: vec3f,
    @location(3) tEyePosition: vec3f,
};

@vertex
fn vs_main(in:Input) -> Output {
    var output: Output;

    // create the tangent matrix
    let wNormal = normalize(uniforms.normalMat * in.normal);
    let wTangent = normalize(uniforms.normalMat * in.tangent);
    let wBitangent = normalize(uniforms.normalMat * in.bitangent);
    let tbnMat = transpose(mat3x3(wTangent.xyz, wBitangent.xyz, wNormal.xyz));

    let wPosition = uniforms.modelMat * in.pos;
    output.position = uniforms.vpMat * wPosition;
    output.vUv  = in.uv;
    output.tPosition = tbnMat * wPosition.xyz;
    output.tEyePosition = tbnMat * light.eyePosition.xyz;
    output.tLightPosition = tbnMat * light.lightPosition.xyz;

    return output;
}
```

In the above code, the *Input* structure contains not only the position, normal, and UV data, but also the tangent and bitangent data, which are necessary for normal mapping. Furthermore, the *Output* structure includes the position, light position, and eye position in the tangent space, which will be calculated within the *vs_main* function.

In the *vs_main* function, we first construct the TBN matrix using the following code snippet:

```
// create the tangent matrix
let wNormal = normalize(uniforms.normalMat * in.normal);
let wTangent = normalize(uniforms.normalMat * in.tangent);
let wBitangent = normalize(uniforms.normalMat * in.bitangent);
let tbnMat = transpose(mat3x3(wTangent.xyz, wBitangent.xyz, wNormal.xyz));
```

We then use this BTN matrix to transform the relevant vectors from the camera space to the tangent space, as shown in the following code snippet:

```
output.tPosition = tbnMat * wPosition.xyz;
output.tEyePosition = tbnMat * light.eyePosition.xyz;
output.tLightPosition = tbnMat * light.lightPosition.xyz;
```

Next, add a new fragment shader file called *normal-frag.wgsl* to the *examples/ch06/* folder and enter the following code into it:

```
struct LightUniforms {
    specularColor : vec4f,
};
@group(1) @binding(0) var<uniform> light : LightUniforms;

struct MaterialUniforms {
    ambient: f32,
    diffuse: f32,
    specular: f32,
    shininess: f32,
    withGammaCorrection: f32,
};
@group(1) @binding(1) var<uniform> material: MaterialUniforms;
@group(2) @binding(0) var textureSampler: sampler;        // base texture and sampler
@group(2) @binding(1) var textureData: texture_2d<f32>;
@group(2) @binding(2) var textureSampler2: sampler;       // normal texture and sampler
@group(2) @binding(3) var textureData2: texture_2d<f32>;

struct Input {
    @location(0) vUv: vec2f,
    @location(1) tPosition: vec3f,
    @location(2) tLightPosition: vec3f,
    @location(3) tEyePosition: vec3f,
};

fn blinnPhong(N:vec3f, L:vec3f, V:vec3f) -> vec2f{
    let H = normalize(L + V);
    var diffuse = material.diffuse * max(dot(N, L), 0.0);
    diffuse += material.diffuse * max(dot(-N, L), 0.0);
    var specular = material.specular * pow(max(dot(N, H), 0.0), material.shininess);
    specular += material.specular * pow(max(dot(-N, H),0.0), material.shininess);
    return vec2(diffuse, specular);
}

@fragment
fn fs_main(in: Input) -> @location(0) vec4f {
    let texColor = textureSample(textureData, textureSampler, in.vUv);
    let texNormal = textureSample(textureData2, textureSampler2, in.vUv);

    var N = texNormal.xyz * 2.0 - 1.0;
    let L = normalize(in.tLightPosition - in.tPosition);
    let V = normalize(in.tEyePosition - in.tPosition);
    let bp = blinnPhong(N, L, V);

    var finalColor = texColor.rgb * (material.ambient + bp[0]) + light.specularColor.rgb * bp[1];
    if(material.withGammaCorrection == 1.0){
        finalColor = pow(finalColor, vec3(1.0/2.2));
    }
    return vec4(finalColor, 1.0);
}
```

The code above includes two sets of textures and samplers: one for the regular texture and the other for the normal map texture. The position, light position, and eye position in the tangent space, which are processed in the vertex shader, are included in the *Input* structure.

Within the *fs_main* function, instead of using the standard normal vector as in previous examples, the normal vector in this example is retrieved from the normal map texture, as shown in the following code snippet:

```
let texNormal = textureSample(textureData2, textureSampler2, in.vUv);
var N = texNormal.xyz * 2.0 - 1.0;
```

Since textures store values in the range of [0, 1], while normal vectors have components in the range of [-1, 1], we need to rescale the value to that range. This is achieved by multiplying by 2 and then subtracting 1.

Finally, we calculate light reflection by invoking the *blinnPhong* function. It is worth noting that the *blinnPhong* function evaluates the reflection model using *N*, *L*, and *V* vectors, all of which are defined in tangent space.

6.8.3 Cube with Normal Map

With the background presented in the previous sections, we are ready to generate normal mapping for a 3D cube in this section. To do this, create a new Rust file named *cube_normal.rs* in the *examples/ch06/* folder and include the following code:

```
use std:: {iter, mem};
use cgmath::{ Matrix, Matrix4, SquareMatrix };
use wgpu::{util::DeviceExt, VertexBufferLayout};
use winit::{
    event::*,
    event_loop::{ControlFlow, EventLoop},
    window::Window,
};
use bytemuck:: {Pod, Zeroable, cast_slice};
use wgpu_book_examples::{ wgpu_simplified as ws, transforms as wt, vertex_data as vd };

#[repr(C)]
#[derive(Copy, Clone, Debug, Pod, Zeroable)]
struct Vertex {
    position: [f32; 3],
    normal: [f32; 3],
    uv: [f32; 2],
    tangent: [f32; 3],
    bitangent: [f32; 3],
}

fn create_vertices(ul:f32, vl:f32) -> (Vec<Vertex>, Vec<u16>) {
    let(pos, _, normal, uv, ind, _) = vd::create_cube_data(2.5);
    let tan = vd::create_tangent_data(&pos, &normal, &uv, &ind);

    let mut data:Vec<Vertex> = vec![];
    for i in 0..pos.len() {
        data.push(Vertex{
            position: pos[i],
            normal: normal[i],
            uv: [uv[i][0]*ul, uv[i][1]*vl],
            tangent: tan[i].tang,
            bitangent: tan[i].bitang,
        });
    }

    (data.to_vec(), ind)
```

```rust
}

const ADDRESS_MODE:wgpu::AddressMode = wgpu::AddressMode::MirrorRepeat;

struct State {
    init:  ws::IWgpuInit,
    pipeline: wgpu::RenderPipeline,
    vertex_buffer: wgpu::Buffer,
    index_buffer: wgpu::Buffer,
    uniform_bind_groups: Vec<wgpu::BindGroup>,
    uniform_buffers: Vec<wgpu::Buffer>,
    view_mat: Matrix4<f32>,
    project_mat: Matrix4<f32>,
    msaa_texture_view: wgpu::TextureView,
    depth_texture_view: wgpu::TextureView,
    animation_speed: f32,
    indices_len: u32,
    u_len: f32,
    v_len: f32,
    update_buffers: bool,
    gamma_correction: u32,
}

impl State {
    async fn new(window: &Window, sample_count:u32) -> Self {
        let init = ws::IWgpuInit::new(&window, sample_count, None).await;

        let vs_shader = init.device.create_shader_module(wgpu::include_wgsl!("normal_vert.wgsl"));
        let fs_shader = init.device.create_shader_module(wgpu::include_wgsl!("normal_frag.wgsl"));

        // uniform data
        let camera_position = (2.0, 3.0, 4.0).into();
        let look_direction = (0.0,0.0,0.0).into();
        let up_direction = cgmath::Vector3::unit_y();

        let (view_mat, project_mat, _) =
            wt::create_vp_mat(camera_position, look_direction, up_direction,
            init.config.width as f32 / init.config.height as f32);

        // create vertex uniform buffers

        // model_mat and vp_mat will be stored in vertex_uniform_buffer inside the update function
        let vert_uniform_buffer = init.device.create_buffer(&wgpu::BufferDescriptor{
            label: Some("Vertex Uniform Buffer"),
            size: 192,
            usage: wgpu::BufferUsages::UNIFORM | wgpu::BufferUsages::COPY_DST,
            mapped_at_creation: false,
        });

        // create light uniform buffer. here we set eye_position = camera_position
        // and light_position = eye_position
        let vert_light_uniform_buffer = init.device.create_buffer(&wgpu::BufferDescriptor{
            label: Some("Vertex Light Uniform Buffer"),
            size: 32,
            usage: wgpu::BufferUsages::UNIFORM | wgpu::BufferUsages::COPY_DST,
            mapped_at_creation: false,
        });

        let eye_position:&[f32; 3] = camera_position.as_ref();
        let light_position = eye_position;
```

```
init.queue.write_buffer(&vert_light_uniform_buffer, 0, cast_slice(light_position));
init.queue.write_buffer(&vert_light_uniform_buffer, 16, cast_slice(eye_position));

// fragment light unifrom buffer
let light_uniform_buffer = init.device.create_buffer(&wgpu::BufferDescriptor{
    label: Some("fragment Light Uniform Buffer"),
    size: 16,
    usage: wgpu::BufferUsages::UNIFORM | wgpu::BufferUsages::COPY_DST,
    mapped_at_creation: false,
});

// set specular light color to white
let specular_color:[f32; 3] = [1.0, 1.0, 1.0];
init.queue.write_buffer(&light_uniform_buffer, 0, cast_slice(specular_color.as_ref()));

// material uniform buffer
let material_uniform_buffer = init.device.create_buffer(&wgpu::BufferDescriptor{
    label: Some("Material Uniform Buffer"),
    size: 20,
    usage: wgpu::BufferUsages::UNIFORM | wgpu::BufferUsages::COPY_DST,
    mapped_at_creation: false,
});

// set default material parameters
let material = [0.1 as f32, 0.4, 0.1, 5.0, 0.0];
init.queue.write_buffer(&material_uniform_buffer, 0, cast_slice(&material));

// uniform bind group for vertex shader
let (vert_bind_group_layout, vert_bind_group) = ws::create_bind_group(
    &init.device,
    vec![wgpu::ShaderStages::VERTEX, wgpu::ShaderStages::VERTEX],
    &[vert_uniform_buffer.as_entire_binding(), vert_light_uniform_buffer.as_entire_binding()],
);

// uniform bind group for fragment shader
let (frag_bind_group_layout, frag_bind_group) = ws::create_bind_group(
    &init.device,
    vec![wgpu::ShaderStages::FRAGMENT, wgpu::ShaderStages::FRAGMENT],
    &[light_uniform_buffer.as_entire_binding(), material_uniform_buffer.as_entire_binding()],
);

// create image texture and image texture bind group
let img_files = vec!["assets/brick.png", "assets/brick-normal.png"];
let(texture_bind_group_layout, texture_bind_group) =
    ws::create_texture_bind_group(&init.device, &init.queue, img_files,
        ADDRESS_MODE, ADDRESS_MODE);

let vertex_buffer_layout = VertexBufferLayout {
    array_stride: mem::size_of::<Vertex>() as wgpu::BufferAddress,
    step_mode: wgpu::VertexStepMode::Vertex,
    attributes: &wgpu::vertex_attr_array![
        0 => Float32x3, // position
        1 => Float32x3, // normal
        2 => Float32x2, // uv
        3 => Float32x3, // tangent
        4 => Float32x3, // bitangent
    ],
};

let pipeline_layout = init.device.create_pipeline_layout(&wgpu::PipelineLayoutDescriptor {
```

```
            label: Some("Render Pipeline Layout"),
            bind_group_layouts: &[&vert_bind_group_layout, &frag_bind_group_layout,
                &texture_bind_group_layout],
            push_constant_ranges: &[],
        });

        let mut ppl = ws::IRenderPipeline {
            vs_shader: Some(&vs_shader),
            fs_shader: Some(&fs_shader),
            pipeline_layout: Some(&pipeline_layout),
            vertex_buffer_layout: &[vertex_buffer_layout],
            ..Default::default()
        };
        let pipeline = ppl.new(&init);

        let msaa_texture_view = ws::create_msaa_texture_view(&init);
        let depth_texture_view = ws::create_depth_view(&init);

        let (vertex_data, index_data) = create_vertices(1.0, 1.0);

        let vertex_buffer = init.device.create_buffer_init(&wgpu::util::BufferInitDescriptor {
            label: Some("Vertex Buffer"),
            contents: cast_slice(&vertex_data),
            usage: wgpu::BufferUsages::VERTEX | wgpu::BufferUsages::COPY_DST,
        });

        let index_buffer = init.device.create_buffer_init(&wgpu::util::BufferInitDescriptor{
            label: Some("Index Buffer"),
            contents: bytemuck::cast_slice(&index_data),
            usage: wgpu::BufferUsages::INDEX,
        });

        Self {
            init,
            pipeline,
            vertex_buffer,
            index_buffer,
            uniform_bind_groups: vec![vert_bind_group, frag_bind_group, texture_bind_group],
            uniform_buffers: vec![vert_uniform_buffer, light_uniform_buffer, material_uniform_buffer,
                vert_light_uniform_buffer],
            view_mat,
            project_mat,
            msaa_texture_view,
            depth_texture_view,
            animation_speed: 1.0,
            indices_len: index_data.len() as u32,
            u_len: 1.0,
            v_len: 1.0,
            update_buffers: false,
            gamma_correction: 0,
        }
    }

    fn resize(&mut self, new_size: winit::dpi::PhysicalSize<u32>) {
        if new_size.width > 0 && new_size.height > 0 {
            self.init.size = new_size;
            self.init.config.width = new_size.width;
            self.init.config.height = new_size.height;
            self.init.surface.configure(&self.init.device, &self.init.config);
```

```
        self.project_mat = wt::create_projection_mat(new_size.width as f32 / new_size.height as f32,
            true);
        self.depth_texture_view = ws::create_depth_view(&self.init);
        if self.init.sample_count > 1 {
            self.msaa_texture_view = ws::create_msaa_texture_view(&self.init);
        }
    }
}

#[allow(unused_variables)]
fn input(&mut self, event: &WindowEvent) -> bool {
    match event {
        WindowEvent::KeyboardInput {
            input:
                KeyboardInput {
                    virtual_keycode: Some(keycode),
                    state: ElementState::Pressed,
                    ..
                },
            ..
        } => {
            match keycode {
                VirtualKeyCode::Space => {
                    self.gamma_correction = (self.gamma_correction + 1) % 2;
                    let material = [0.1 as f32, 0.4, 0.1, 5.0, self.gamma_correction as f32];
                    self.init.queue.write_buffer(&self.uniform_buffers[2], 0, cast_slice(&material));
                    true
                },
                VirtualKeyCode::Q => {
                    self.u_len += 0.1;
                    self.update_buffers = true;
                    true
                },
                VirtualKeyCode::A => {
                    self.u_len -= 0.1;
                    if self.u_len < 0.1 {
                        self.u_len = 0.1;
                    }
                    self.update_buffers = true;
                    true
                },
                VirtualKeyCode::W => {
                    self.v_len += 0.1;
                    self.update_buffers = true;
                    true
                },
                VirtualKeyCode::S => {
                    self.v_len -= 0.1;
                    if self.v_len < 0.1 {
                        self.v_len = 0.1;
                    }
                    self.update_buffers = true;
                    true
                },
                VirtualKeyCode::E => {
                    self.animation_speed += 0.1;
                    true
                },
                VirtualKeyCode::D => {
                    self.animation_speed -= 0.1;
```

```
                    if self.animation_speed < 0.0 {
                        self.animation_speed = 0.0;
                    }
                    true
                },
                _ => false
            }
        }
        _ => false,
    }
}
fn update(&mut self, dt: std::time::Duration) {
    // update uniform buffer
    let dt = self.animation_speed * dt.as_secs_f32();
    let model_mat = wt::create_model_mat([0.0, 0.5, 0.0], [0.0, dt, 0.0], [1.0, 1.0, 1.0]);
    let view_project_mat = self.project_mat * self.view_mat;

    let normal_mat = (model_mat.invert().unwrap()).transpose();

    let model_ref:&[f32; 16] = model_mat.as_ref();
    let view_projection_ref:&[f32; 16] = view_project_mat.as_ref();
    let normal_ref:&[f32; 16] = normal_mat.as_ref();

    self.init.queue.write_buffer(&self.uniform_buffers[0], 0, cast_slice(view_projection_ref));
    self.init.queue.write_buffer(&self.uniform_buffers[0], 64, cast_slice(model_ref));
    self.init.queue.write_buffer(&self.uniform_buffers[0], 128, bytemuck::cast_slice(normal_ref));

    // update vertex buffer
    if self.update_buffers {
        let (vertex_data, _) = create_vertices(self.u_len, self.v_len);
        self.init.queue.write_buffer(&self.vertex_buffer, 0, cast_slice(&vertex_data));
        self.update_buffers = false;
    }
}

fn render(&mut self) -> Result<(), wgpu::SurfaceError> {
    //let output = self.init.surface.get_current_frame()?.output;
    let output = self.init.surface.get_current_texture()?;
    let view = output
        .texture
        .create_view(&wgpu::TextureViewDescriptor::default());

    let mut encoder = self
        .init.device
        .create_command_encoder(&wgpu::CommandEncoderDescriptor {
            label: Some("Render Encoder"),
        });

    {
        let color_attach = ws::create_color_attachment(&view);
        let msaa_attach = ws::create_msaa_color_attachment(&view, &self.msaa_texture_view);
        let color_attachment = if self.init.sample_count == 1 { color_attach } else { msaa_attach };
        let depth_attachment = ws::create_depth_stencil_attachment(&self.depth_texture_view);
        let mut render_pass = encoder.begin_render_pass(&wgpu::RenderPassDescriptor {
            label: Some("Render Pass"),
            color_attachments: &[Some(color_attachment)],
            depth_stencil_attachment: Some(depth_attachment),
            occlusion_query_set: None,
            timestamp_writes: None,
        });
```

```
            render_pass.set_pipeline(&self.pipeline);
            render_pass.set_vertex_buffer(0, self.vertex_buffer.slice(..));
            render_pass.set_index_buffer(self.index_buffer.slice(..), wgpu::IndexFormat::Uint16);
            render_pass.set_bind_group(0, &self.uniform_bind_groups[0], &[]);
            render_pass.set_bind_group(1, &self.uniform_bind_groups[1], &[]);
            render_pass.set_bind_group(2, &self.uniform_bind_groups[2], &[]);
            render_pass.draw_indexed(0..self.indices_len, 0, 0..1);
        }

        self.init.queue.submit(iter::once(encoder.finish()));
        output.present();

        Ok(())
    }
}

fn main() {
    env_logger::init();
    let event_loop = EventLoop::new();
    let window = winit::window::WindowBuilder::new().build(&event_loop).unwrap();
    window.set_title(&*format!("ch06_{}", "cube_normal"));

    let mut state = pollster::block_on(State::new(&window, 8));
    let render_start_time = std::time::Instant::now();

    event_loop.run(move |event, _, control_flow| {
        match event {
            Event::WindowEvent {
                ref event,
                window_id,
            } if window_id == window.id() => {
                if !state.input(event) {
                    match event {
                        WindowEvent::CloseRequested
                        | WindowEvent::KeyboardInput {
                            input:
                                KeyboardInput {
                                    state: ElementState::Pressed,
                                    virtual_keycode: Some(VirtualKeyCode::Escape),
                                    ..
                                },
                            ..
                        } => *control_flow = ControlFlow::Exit,
                        WindowEvent::Resized(physical_size) => {
                            state.resize(*physical_size);
                        }
                        WindowEvent::ScaleFactorChanged { new_inner_size, .. } => {
                            state.resize(**new_inner_size);
                        }
                        _ => {}
                    }
                }
            }
            Event::RedrawRequested(_) => {
                let now = std::time::Instant::now();
                let dt = now - render_start_time;
                state.update(dt);

                match state.render() {
                    Ok(_) => {}
```

```
                    Err(wgpu::SurfaceError::Lost) => state.resize(state.init.size),
                    Err(wgpu::SurfaceError::OutOfMemory) => *control_flow = ControlFlow::Exit,
                    Err(e) => eprintln!("{:?}", e),
                }
            }
            Event::MainEventsCleared => {
                window.request_redraw();
            }
            _ => {}
        }
    });
}
```

At the beginning of the above code, we introduce a *Vertex* struct with five fields: *position*, *normal*, *uv*, *tangent*, and *bitangent*. Subsequently, we implement the *create_vertices* function. Within this function, we first create vertex data for the cube using the *create_cube_data* function. We then proceed to generate the tangent and bitangent data by invoking the newly implemented *create_tangent_data* method found in the *vertex_data.rs* file. The data is utilized to populate instances of the *Vertex* struct, thus encompassing the complete range of attributes: *position*, *normal*, *uv*, *tangent*, and *bitangent* data.

Within the *State::new* function of the above code, the *attributes* field within the vertex buffer layout is enriched to encompass not only *position*, *normal*, and *uv* data, but also *tangent* and *bitangent* data. This is depicted in the following code snippet:

```
let vertex_buffer_layout = VertexBufferLayout {
    array_stride: mem::size_of::<Vertex>() as wgpu::BufferAddress,
    step_mode: wgpu::VertexStepMode::Vertex,
    attributes: &wgpu::vertex_attr_array![
        0 => Float32x3, // position
        1 => Float32x3, // normal
        2 => Float32x2, // uv
        3 => Float32x3, // tangent
        4 => Float32x3, // bitangent
    ],
};
```

Additionally, we create two separate textures and samplers using two different image files, as described in the following code snippet:

```
// create image texture and image texture bind group
let img_files = vec!["assets/brick.png", "assets/brick-normal.png"];
let(texture_bind_group_layout, texture_bind_group) =
    ws::create_texture_bind_group(&init.device, &init.queue, img_files, ADDRESS_MODE, ADDRESS_MODE);
```

The first image file, *brick.png*, serves for standard texture mapping, while the second, *brick-normal.png*, is dedicated to normal mapping.

In the *State::render* function, we also need to set the tangent and bitangent buffers for inclusion within the render pass.

Moreover, the above code facilitates parameter adjustment via keyboard inputs. Here is a list of controls using keyboard:

- *Space*: Determines whether the Gamma correction is used for the color or not.
- *Q/A*: Increases/decreases the range of texture coordinates along the *u* direction.
- *W/S:* Increases/decreases the range of texture coordinates along the *v* direction.
- *E/D:* Increases/decreases the rotation speed.

To run this application, add the following code snippet to the *Cargo.toml* file:

```
[[example]]
name = "ch06_cube_normal"
path = "examples/ch06/cube_normal.rs"
```

Afterward, execute the following *cargo run* commands in the terminal window:

```
cargo run --example ch06_cube_normal
```

Fig.6-9 displays the result of this example. It is evident that normal mapping makes the brick texture on the cube surface look more realistic and provides an enormous boost in detail.

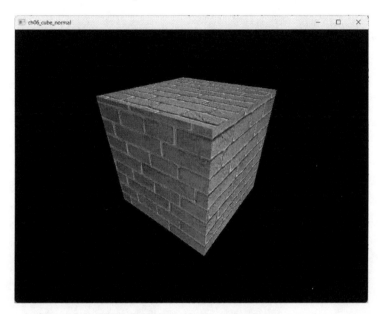

Fig.6-9. Cube with normal mapping.

6.8.4 Sphere with Normal Mapping

Create a new Rust file named *sphere_normal.rs* in the *examples/ch06/* folder. The code in this file is similar to the one used in the previous cube example, except that this example uses the vertex data for a sphere, as illustrated in the following code snippet:

```
struct Vertex {
    position: [f32; 3],
    normal: [f32; 3],
    uv: [f32; 2],
    tangent: [f32; 3],
    bitangent: [f32; 3],
}

fn create_vertices(ul:f32, vl:f32) -> (Vec<Vertex>, Vec<u16>) {
    let(pos, normal, uv, ind, _) = vd::create_sphere_data(2.5, 20, 32);
    let tan = vd::create_tangent_data(&pos, &normal, &uv, &ind);

    let mut data:Vec<Vertex> = vec![];
    for i in 0..pos.len() {
```

```
    data.push(Vertex{
        position: pos[i],
        normal: normal[i],
        uv: [uv[i][0]*ul, uv[i][1]*vl],
        tangent: tan[i].tang,
        bitangent: tan[i].bitang,
    });
}

(data.to_vec(), ind)
}
```

Additionally, we use the *earth.png* and *earth-normal.png* files to create the standard texture mapping and normal mapping by using the following code snippet:

```
// create image texture and image texture bind group
let img_files = vec!["assets/earth.png", "assets/earth-normal.png"];
let(texture_bind_group_layout, texture_bind_group) =
    ws::create_texture_bind_group(&init.device, &init.queue, img_files, ADDRESS_MODE, ADDRESS_MODE);
```

Moreover, the above code facilitates parameter adjustment via keyboard inputs. Here is a list of controls using keyboard:

- *Space*: Determines whether the Gamma correction is used for the color or not.

- *Q/A*: Increases/decreases the range of texture coordinates along the *u* direction.

- *W/S:* Increases/decreases the range of texture coordinates along the *v* direction.

- *E/D:* Increases/decreases the rotation speed.

To run this application, add the following code snippet to the *Cargo.toml* file:

```
[[example]]
name = "ch06_sphere_normal"
path = "examples/ch06/sphere_normal.rs"
```

Afterward, execute the following *cargo run* commands in the terminal window:

```
cargo run --example ch06_sphere_normal
```

Fig.6-10 shows a direct comparison of a sphere with and without normal mapping. It is evident that the sphere without normal mapping looks smooth and flat, as if it had no features or relief. Normal mapping makes the sphere look more like the real earth with more details and realism by faking the lighting of mountains, valleys, oceans, and continents on its surface.

6.9 Parallax Mapping

In the previous sections, we presented normal mapping for a cube and a sphere. Normal mapping uses a texture map called a normal map to encodes surface normals at each vertex. By altering the surface normals in the normal map, the lighting on the surface can be changed to create an illusion of depth.

Parallax mapping, on the other hand, uses a height map or displacement map to encode depth information in the form of grayscale values. The height map is applied to the surface, and as camera moves, the texture coordinates on the surface are shifted based on the depth information in the height map. This shift in texture coordinates creates an illusion of depth and adds a sense of relief to the surface, making it appear as if it has bumps, wrinkles, and other 3D features.

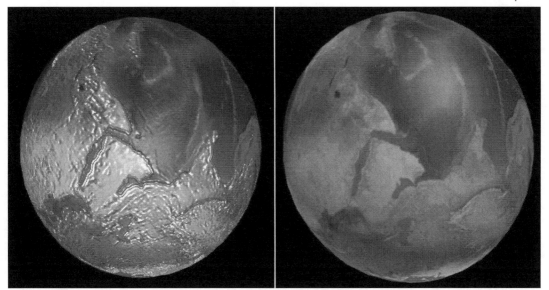

Fig.6-10. Sphere with (left) and without (right) normal mapping.

One of the key differences between normal mapping and parallax mapping is the level of depth that can be achieved. Normal mapping can create a surface that appears to have small bumps or ridges, but it cannot create a significant amount of depth. Parallax mapping, on the other hand, can create a much deeper sense of relief on a flat surface.

In this section, I will show you how to create parallax mapping for a 3D cube. Similar to the previous example, we will work with tangent space. For parallax mapping, we need three textures: a height map texture, a normal map texture, and a color texture. We could combine the height map and normal map into a single texture, storing the height values in the *alpha* channel and the normal in the R, G, and B channels. This can save memory space and make application run more efficiently. But in this example, we will treat them as separate textures.

6.9.1 Shader Code

We can use the same vertex shader as we did in the previous normal mapping example. The vertex shader transforms the view and light directions from camera space to tangent space, and passes the results to the fragment shader.

Create a new fragment shader file called *parallax_frag.wgsl* file in the *examples/ch06/* folder and add the following code to it:

```
struct LightUniforms {
    specularColor : vec4f,
};
@group(1) @binding(0) var<uniform> light : LightUniforms;

struct MaterialUniforms {
    ambient: f32,
    diffuse: f32,
    specular: f32,
    shininess: f32,
```

```
        withGammaCorrection: f32,
        heightScale: f32,
};
@group(1) @binding(1) var<uniform> material: MaterialUniforms;

@group(2) @binding(0) var textureSampler: sampler;          // base texture and sampler
@group(2) @binding(1) var textureData: texture_2d<f32>;
@group(2) @binding(2) var textureSampler2: sampler;         // normal texture and sampler
@group(2) @binding(3) var textureData2: texture_2d<f32>;
@group(2) @binding(4) var textureSampler3: sampler;         // depth texture and sampler
@group(2) @binding(5) var textureData3: texture_2d<f32>;

struct Input {
        @location(0) vUv: vec2f,
        @location(1) tPosition: vec3f,
        @location(2) tLightPosition: vec3f,
        @location(3) tEyePosition: vec3f,
};

fn blinnPhong(N:vec3f, L:vec3f, V:vec3f) -> vec2f{
        let H = normalize(L + V);
        var diffuse = material.diffuse * max(dot(N, L), 0.0);
        diffuse += material.diffuse * max(dot(-N, L), 0.0);
        var specular = material.specular * pow(max(dot(N, H), 0.0), material.shininess);
        specular += material.specular * pow(max(dot(-N, H),0.0), material.shininess);
        return vec2(diffuse, specular);
}

fn parallaxMap(uv:vec2f, eyeDirection:vec3f) -> vec2f {
        let height = 1 - textureSample(textureData3, textureSampler3, uv).r;
        let delta = eyeDirection.xy * height * material.heightScale / eyeDirection.z;
        return uv - delta;
}

@fragment
fn fs_main(in: Input) ->  @location(0) vec4f {
        let L = normalize(in.tLightPosition - in.tPosition);
        let V = normalize(in.tEyePosition - in.tPosition);

        var uv = parallaxMap(in.vUv, V);
        let tf = select(1.0, 0.0, (uv.x > 1.0 || uv.y > 1.0 || uv.x < 0.0 || uv.y < 0.0));
        if(tf == 0.0){
            discard;
        }
        let texColor = textureSample(textureData, textureSampler, uv);
        let texNormal = textureSample(textureData2, textureSampler2, uv);

        var N = normalize(texNormal.xyz * 2.0 - 1.0);
        let bp = blinnPhong(N, L, V);

        var finalColor = texColor.rgb * (material.ambient + bp[0] + light.specularColor.rgb * bp[1]);
        if(material.withGammaCorrection == 1.0){
            finalColor = pow(finalColor, vec3(1.0/2.2));
        }
        return vec4(finalColor, 1.0);
}
```

The code above includes three sets of textures and samplers: one for the color (or regular) texture, one for the height map texture, and the other for the normal map texture. The position, light position, and eye position in the tangent space, which are processed in the vertex shader, are included in the *Input* structure.

In the *parallaxMap* function, we use the tangent space view direction and height map value at the current texture coordinate to offset the texture coordinates. The *heightScale* factor, which is passed as a uniform variable defined in the *MaterialUniforms* structure, is usually in the range of [0, 0.05]. You can tune this value for your particular normal and height maps. Here, we offset the texture coordinate by the value of *delta*. We subtract rather than add here because *eyeDirection* is actually pointing toward the viewer, so we need to offset in the opposite direction.

Inside the *fs_main* function, using the offset texture coordinate returned from the *parallaxMap* function, we compute the light reflection using the Blinn-Phong model with data from the normal map and color texture.

6.9.2 Rust Code

In this section, we will generate parallax mapping for a 3D cube. Create a new Rust file named *cube_parallax.rs* in the *examples/ch06/* folder. The code struct is similar to the previous example. The difference is that we need to use the *parallax_frag.wgsl* file to generate the fragment shader module within the *State::new* function:

```
let vs_shader = init.device.create_shader_module(wgpu::include_wgsl!("normal_vert.wgsl"));
let fs_shader = init.device.create_shader_module(wgpu::include_wgsl!("parallax_frag.wgsl"));
```

Subsequently, this example uses three image files: *brick1.png*, *brick1-normal.png*, and *brick1-height.png*, to create three sets of textures and samplers for the color texture, normal map texture, and height map texture, respectively. We then use these textures and samplers to construct the texture bind group, as described in the following code snippet:

```
// create image texture and image texture bind group
let img_files = vec!["assets/brick1.png", "assets/brick1-normal.png", "assets/brick1-height.png"];
let(texture_bind_group_layout, texture_bind_group) = ws::create_texture_bind_group(
    &init.device, &init.queue, img_files, ADDRESS_MODE, ADDRESS_MODE);
```

This texture bind group will be passed to the fragment shader to calculate the light reflection using the Blinn-Phong model with offset texture coordinates from parallax mapping and data from the normal map and color texture.

Moreover, the code in the *cube_parallax.rs* file facilitates parameter adjustment via keyboard inputs. Here is a list of controls using keyboard:

- *Space*: Determines whether the Gamma correction is used for the color or not.
- *Q/A*: Increases/decreases the range of texture coordinates along the *u* direction.
- *W/S:* Increases/decreases the range of texture coordinates along the *v* direction.
- *E/D:* Increases/decreases the rotation speed.

To run this application, add the following code snippet to the *Cargo.toml* file:

```
[[example]]
name = "ch06_cube_parallax"
path = "examples/ch06/cube_parallax.rs"
```

Afterward, execute the following *cargo run* commands in the terminal window:

```
cargo run --example ch06_cube_parallax
```

Fig.6-11 displays the results of this example.

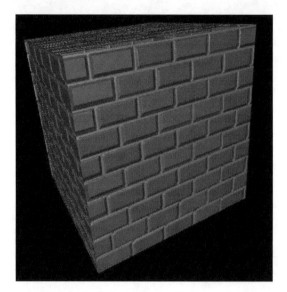

Fig.6-11. Cube with parallax mapping.

The parallax mapping is considered an improvement over normal mapping because it simulates depth in textures and creates an illusion of height displacement that normal mapping cannot achieve. It allows for more realistic and intricate textures that can create the appearance of depth, such as materials like brick or cobblestone.

7 Compute Shaders for Surface Generation

In the preceding chapters, we have explored diverse techniques for visually rendering 3D objects and surfaces within a scene, employing both vertex and fragment shaders. Notably, *wgpu* offers an expanded range of GPU capabilities, including features not found in OpenGL, such as compute shaders and storage buffers. These resources enable developers to craft potent GPU compute applications.

In *wgpu*, the compute shader operates within a distinct stage of the GPU pipeline, separating it from the rest of the graphics rendering process. It harnesses the GPU's capabilities for general-purpose tasks, whether or not they are graphically related. While the compute shader can access many of the same resources as graphics shaders, it offers a higher degree of control over its execution flow.

In our prior work, we generated 3D surface vertex data, encompassing attributes such as positions, normals, colors, and indices, through Rust code executed on the CPU. However, a potential concern with this approach arises when animating surfaces at higher resolutions. As depicted in Figure 5-1, elevating the resolution to 250 leads to a substantial framerate reduction to 16 FPS, causing the application to become unresponsive and appear to lag or freeze. This highlights the challenge posed by updating vertex data for each frame at higher resolutions using the CPU.

This decrease in framerate can be attributed to the fact that increased resolution necessitates greater computational work per frame to derive new vertex data on the CPU. Furthermore, a larger volume of data must be transmitted to the GPU with each rendering request. This transmission is required since the GPU relies on up-to-date vertex data to calculate the final image displayed on the screen.

The upcoming chapter delves into the realm of compute shaders and elucidates their application in generating vertex data for 3D surfaces directly within the GPU. This approach leverages compute shaders to exploit parallelism by simultaneously updating vertex data for a group of vertices, as opposed to a single vertex at a time. Consequently, the need to upload new vertex data for each frame is circumvented, as the requisite data is already resident within the GPU. With compute shaders at our disposal, executing a 3D surface animation on the GPU at significantly higher resolutions (exceeding 1,000) can be achieved without encountering framerate drops.

This chapter will comprehensively demonstrate the use of compute shaders in the creation of a diverse array of 3D surfaces. These include simple 3D surfaces, parametric 3D surfaces, and 3D super shapes.

7.1 Compute Shaders

The graphics processor is a powerful device, capable of performing trillions of calculations per second. Over the years, it has been developed to crunch the huge amount of math operations required to render real-time graphics such as video games. However, it is also possible to use the computational power of the GPU for general-purpose applications that may not be related to graphics. To enable this type of application, *wgpu* implements a special shader stage called the compute shader.

7.1.1 Compute Space and Workgroups

Like vertex and fragment shaders, which fit into the pipeline at specific points and operate on graphics-specific elements, compute shaders also fit into the compute pipeline and operate on compute-specific elements. The performance of the GPU is achieved through parallelism, which, in turn is obtained by launching work in groups known as workgroups. Workgroups have a local neighborhood known as a local workgroup, and these are again grouped to form a global workgroup, as shown in Fig.7-1.

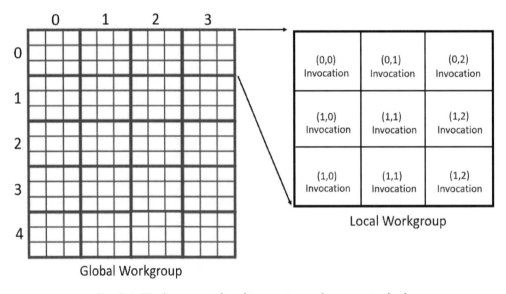

Fig.7-1. Workgroup grid and invocations of a compute shader.

You can see from the figure that the number of invocations of a compute shader is determined by the user-defined compute space. This space can be divided into a number of workgroups. A global workgroup can then be divided into a number of local workgroups, and each local workgroup contains a number of invocations. The compute space can be defined as a one-, two-, or three-dimensional space.

The invocations of the compute shader can communicate with each other via variables and memory and can perform operations to keep their work coherent. The order of execution of the workgroups and, thereby, the individual shader invocations is not specified, and the GPU can execute them in any order.

The *wgpu* API contains several built-in variables that can be used to access the workgroups and invocations of the compute shader:

- *local_invocation_id*: is a type of *vec3u* variable that represents the current invocation's local invocation ID, i.e., its position in the workgroup grid.

- *local_invocation_index*: is a type of *u32* variable that represents the current invocation's local invocation index, which is a linearized index of the invocation's position within the workgroup grid.

- *global_invocation_id:* is a type of *vec3u* variable that represents the current invocation's global invocation ID, i.e., its position in the compute shader grid.

- *workgroup_id:* is a type of *vec3u* type variable that represents the current invocation's workgroup ID, i.e., the position of the workgroup in the workgroup grid.

- *workgroup_size:* is a type of *vec3u* variable that represents the workgroup size of the current entry point.

With these built-in variables, you can easily access workgroups and invocations of a compute shader in *wgpu*. For example, you can use both *workgroup_id* and *local_invocation_id* to access the invocation location, as demonstrated in the following code snippet:

```
@compute @workgroup_size(8, 8, 1)
fn cs_main(@builtin(workgroup_id) workGroupId: vec3u, @builtin(local_invocation_id) localId: vec3u) {
    let x = localId.x + workGroupId.x * 8u;
    let y = localId.y + workGroupId.y * 8u;
    ...
}
```

Alternatively, you can use *global_invocation_id* to directly access the invocation location, as illustrated in the following code snippet:

```
@compute @workgroup_size(8, 8, 1)
fn cs_main(@builtin(global_invocation_id) id: vec3u) {
    let i = id.x;
    let j = id.y;
    ...
}
```

You can think of *global_invocation_id* as a shortcut of *workgroup_id*, *local_invocation_id* and *workgroup_size* size. It can be expressed as:

```
global_invocation_id = local_invocation_id + workgroup_id * workgroup_size;
```

7.1.2 Write and Read Buffer

The *wgpu* API allows you to write data to memory for the GPU, a process that is not straightforward due to the sandboxing model used in modern GPU hardware. Let us examine the following code snippet:

```
Let numbers = [0.1, 1.0, 2.0, 3.0];
Let write_buffer = device.create_buffer_init(&wgpu::util::BufferInitDescriptor {
    label: Some("Write Buffer"),
    contents: bytemuck::cast_slices(&numbers),
    usage: wgpu::BufferUsage::MAP_WRITE,
});
```

This is the standard method for creating a GPU buffer with data to initialize it. We have extensively used this approach in preceding chapters. The only distinction is the usage flag – here we employ *wgpu::BufferUsage::MAP_WRITE*.

The above code snippet illustrates writing 16 bytes to buffer memory. Upon close inspection of the source code of the *create_buffer_init* method, you will notice it must be unmapped by invoking the *buffer.unmap* function. We must specify whether a buffer is mapped or unmapped to avoid race conditions arising from simultaneous CPU and GPU memory access.

Having created a GPU buffer using the above code snippet, our next objective is to copy the buffer to a second GPU buffer. This can be achieved by simply replacing the original usage flag with the following code:

```
Usage: wgpu::BufferUsage::MAP_WRITE | wgpu::BufferUsage::COPY_SRC
```

In this manner, we can use the buffer as a destination of the first GPU buffer and read it in Rust code after the GPU copy command has been executed. Here is the code sequence for this purpose:

```
let read_buffer = device.create_buffer(&wgpu::BufferDescriptor {
    label: None,
    size: result_buffer_size,
    usage: wgpu::BufferUsage::MAP_READ | wgpu::BufferUsage::COPY_DST,
    mapped_at_creation: false,
});
```

Subsequently, we use *device.create_command_encoder* to obtain a GPU command encoder – a Rust object containing buffered commands that will be submitted to the GPU as a batch. The methods on the GPU buffer are unbuffered, thus executing sequentially when called.

Following that, we invoke *encoder.copy_buffer_to_buffer* on the GPU command encoder to add the buffered commands to the command queue for later execution. This is illustrated in the following code snippet:

```
let emcoder = device.create_command_encoder();
encoder.copy_buffer_to_buffer(&write_buffer, 0, &read_buffer, 0, 16);
queue.submit(Some(encoder.finish()));
```

Now, it is time to execute the GPU queue commands we have dispatched. To read from the second GPU buffer for execution, we must first specify which portion of the buffer we are using for a given operation. Here, we use the entire buffer with a total unbounded range. Subsequently, we acquire the future representing when the buffer can be read by invoking the *read_buffer_slice.map_async* method with *wgpu::MapMode::Read*:

```
let read_buffer_slice = read_buffer.slice();
let read_buffer_future = read_buffer_slice.map_async(wgpu::MapMode::Read);
```

This returns a promise that resolves when the GPU buffer is mapped. We can then access the mapped range using the *read_buffer_slice.get_mapped_range* method, which contains the same values as the first GPU buffer once all of the queued GPU commands have been executed. This is demonstrated in the following code snippet:

```
let data = read_buffer.slice.get_mapped_range();
let result = bytemuck::cast_slice(&data).to_vec();
drop(data);
read_buffer.unmap();
```

Note that we invoke the *drop(data)* method to ensure all mapped views are dropped before we unmap the buffer. It is evident that for using GPU buffers in device queue submission, the buffers must be unmapped, while for writing/reading GPU buffers in Rust, they must be mapped.

7.2 Simple 3D Surfaces

In this section, we will try to reproduce simple 3D surfaces presented in Chapter 5, but using the compute shader to generate the vertex data. Here, we can reuse the vertex and fragment shader files, *shader-vert.wgsl* and *shader-frag.wgsl*, located in the *examples/ch05/* folder.

7.2.1 Compute Shader for Generating Indices

To avoid duplicating code, we separate the indices data from the other vertex data. This is because the indices data is used not only for creating the simple 3D surfaces, but also for creating the other 3D surfaces, such as parametric surfaces.

Create a new WGSL shader file named *indices_comp.wgsl* in the *examples/ch07/* folder and enter the following code into it:

```
@group(0) @binding(0) var<storage, read_write> indices: array<u32>;
@group(0) @binding(1) var<storage, read_write> indices2: array<u32>;
@group(0) @binding(2) var<uniform> resolution: u32;

@compute @workgroup_size(8, 8, 1)
fn cs_main(@builtin(workgroup_id) wid : vec3u, @builtin(local_invocation_id) lid: vec3u) {
    let i = lid.x + wid.x * 8u;
    let j = lid.y + wid.y * 8u;

    if(i >= resolution - 1u || j >= resolution - 1u ) { return; }

    let idx = (i + j * (resolution - 1u)) * 6u;

    // first triangle
    indices[idx] = i + j * resolution;
    indices[idx + 1u] = i + (j + 1u) * resolution;
    indices[idx + 2u] = i + 1u + j * resolution;
    // second triangle
    indices[idx + 3u] = i + 1u + j * resolution;
    indices[idx + 4u] = i + (j + 1u) * resolution;
    indices[idx + 5u] = i + 1u + (j  + 1u) * resolution;

    // wireframe
    let tdx = (i + j * (resolution - 1u)) * 8u;
    indices2[tdx] = i + j * resolution;
    indices2[tdx + 1u] = i + 1u + j * resolution;
    indices2[tdx + 2u] = i + 1u + j * resolution;
    indices2[tdx + 3u] = i + 1u + (j + 1u) * resolution;
    indices2[tdx + 4u] = i + 1u + (j + 1u) * resolution;
    indices2[tdx + 5u] = i + (j + 1u) * resolution;
    indices2[tdx + 6u] = i + (j + 1u) * resolution;
    indices2[tdx + 7u] = i + j * resolution;
}
```

The code above uses the *@compute @workgroup_size* decorator to specify that it is a compute shader and to set the workgroup size to $8 \times 8 \times 1$. This shader takes three variables: *indices*, *indices2*, and *resolution*. *indices* and *indices2* are arrays of unsigned 32-bit integers that are used to store the generated indices. The *resolution* parameter is a uniform variable that specifies the resolution of the grid that the indices are generated for. For sake of simplicity, we use a square grid with a size of *resolution* by *resolution*.

The shader generates the indices by iterating over the grid and calculating the indices for each triangle. The indices are stored in the *indices* array as two triangles per unit quad. The shader also generates a wireframe by storing the indices for the four edges (or line segments) of each quad in the *indices2* array.

It is worth noting that this shader uses the *workgroup_id* and *local_invocation_id* to specify the invocation location. Alternatively, you can use the *global_invocation_id* instead.

7.2.2 Shader Code for Math Functions

We also need to convert the Rust code of the math functions used for creating simple 3D surfaces into WGSL shader code. Create a new WGSL shader file named *simple_surface_func.wgsl* in the *examples/ch07/* folder and include the following code:

```
struct DataRange {
    xRange: vec2f,
    yRange: vec2f,
    zRange: vec2f,
}

fn sinc(x:f32, z:f32, t:f32) -> vec3f{
    let a = 1.01 + sin(t);

    let r = a * sqrt(x*x + z*z);
    var y = 1.0;
    if(r != 0.0){
        y = sin(r)/r;
    }
    return vec3(x, y, z);
}

fn peaks(x:f32, z:f32, t:f32) -> vec3f{
    let a = 1.0 + 0.2*sin(t);
    let b = 1.0 + 0.2*sin(1.5*t);
    let c = 1.0 + 0.2*sin(2.0*t);

    let y = 3.0 * (1.0 - z) * (1.0 - z) * exp(-a* (z * z) - a * (x + 1.0) * (x + 1.0)) -
        10.0 * (z / 5.0 - z * z * z - x * x * x * x * x) * exp(-b * z * z - b * x * x)
        - 1.0 / 3.0 * exp(- c * (z + 1.0) * (z + 1.0) - c * x * x);

    return vec3(z, y, x);
}

fn poles(x:f32, z:f32, t:f32) -> vec3f{
    let a = 1.5*(sin(t));
    let y = x*z/(abs((x-a)*(x-a)*(x-a)) + (z- 2.0*a)*(z- 2.0*a) + 2.0);

    return vec3(x, y, z);
}

fn getDataRange(funcSelection:u32) -> DataRange{
    var dr:DataRange;

    if (funcSelection == 0u) { // sinc
        dr.xRange = vec2(-8.0, 8.0);
        dr.yRange = vec2(-0.3, 1.0);
        dr.zRange = vec2(-8.0, 8.0);
    } else if (funcSelection == 1u) { // peaks
        dr.xRange = vec2(-3.0, 3.0);
```

```
        dr.yRange = vec2(-6.5, 8.1);
        dr.zRange = vec2(-3.0, 3.0);
    } else if (funcSelection == 2u) { // poles
        dr.xRange = vec2(-8.0, 8.0);
        dr.yRange = vec2(-0.4, 3.3);
        dr.zRange = vec2(-8.0, 8.0);
    }
    return dr;
}

fn simpleSurfaceFunc(x:f32, z:f32, t:f32, funcSelection:u32) -> vec3f{
    var pos = vec3(0.0, 0.0, 0.0);

    if (funcSelection == 0u) { // sinc
        pos = sinc(x, z, t);
    }
    else if (funcSelection == 1u) { // peaks
        pos = peaks(x, z, t);
    }
    else if (funcSelection == 2u) { // poles
        pos = poles(x, z, t);
    }
    return pos;
}
```

The code above defines three functions: *sinc*, *peaks*, and *poles*, which will be used to create different simple 3D surfaces. The *setDataRange* function is used to set the data ranges of these three functions. Meanwhile, the *simpleSurfaceFunc* function is specifically designed to select one of these three mathematical functions. Note that, in addition to the *x* and *z* arguments, we also pass a time dependent parameter *t* to these functions, which will be used to perform animation for 3D surfaces.

7.2.3 Compute Shader for Vertex Data

Create a new compute shader file called *simple_surface_comp.wgsl* in the *examples/ch07/* folder and include the following code:

```
struct VertexData{
    position: vec4f,
    normal: vec4f,
    color: vec4f,
}
struct VertexDataArray{
    vertexDataArray: array<VertexData>,
}

struct SimpleSurfaceParams {
    resolution: f32,
    funcSelection: f32,
    colormapDirection: f32,
    colormapReverse: f32,
    animationTime: f32,
}

@group(0) @binding(0) var<storage, read_write> vda : VertexDataArray;
@group(0) @binding(1) var<storage, read_write> vda2 : VertexDataArray;
@group(0) @binding(2) var<storage> colormap: array<vec4f>;
@group(0) @binding(3) var<storage> colormap2: array<vec4f>;
@group(0) @binding(4) var<uniform> ssp: SimpleSurfaceParams;
```

```
var<private> xmin:f32;
var<private> xmax:f32;
var<private> ymin:f32;
var<private> ymax:f32;
var<private> zmin:f32;
var<private> zmax:f32;
var<private> dx:f32;
var<private> dz:f32;
var<private> aspect:f32;

fn getUv(i:u32, j:u32) -> vec2f {
    var dr = getDataRange(u32(ssp.funcSelection));
    xmin = dr.xRange[0];
    xmax = dr.xRange[1];
    ymin = dr.yRange[0];
    ymax = dr.yRange[1];
    zmin = dr.zRange[0];
    zmax = dr.zRange[1];
    aspect = dr.aspectRatio;

    dx = (xmax - xmin)/(ssp.resolution - 1.0);
    dz = (zmax - zmin)/(ssp.resolution - 1.0);
    var x = xmin + f32(i) * dx;
    var z = zmin + f32(j) * dz;
    return vec2(x, z);
}

fn normalizePoint(u:f32, v:f32) -> vec3f {
    var pos = simpleSurfaceFunc(u, v, ssp.animationTime, u32(ssp.funcSelection));
    pos.x = 2.0 * (pos.x - xmin)/(xmax - xmin) - 1.0;
    pos.y = 2.0 * (pos.y - ymin)/(ymax - ymin) - 1.0;
    pos.z = 2.0 * (pos.z - zmin)/(zmax - zmin) - 1.0;
    pos.y = pos.y * aspect;
    return pos;
}

fn colorLerp(is_surface:bool, tmin:f32, tmax:f32, t:f32, colormapReverse:u32) -> vec4f{
    var t1 = t;
    if (t1 < tmin) {t1 = tmin;}
    if (t1 > tmax) {t1 = tmax;}
    var tn = (t1-tmin)/(tmax-tmin);

    if(colormapReverse >= 1u) {tn = 1.0 - tn;}

    var idx = u32(floor(10.0*tn));
    var color = vec4(0.0,0.0,0.0, 1.0);

    if(is_surface){
        if(f32(idx) == 10.0*tn) {
            color = colormap[idx];
        } else {
            var tn1 = (tn - 0.1*f32(idx))*10.0;
            var a = colormap[idx];
            var b = colormap[idx+1u];
            color.x = a.x + (b.x - a.x)*tn1;
            color.y = a.y + (b.y - a.y)*tn1;
            color.z = a.z + (b.z - a.z)*tn1;
        }
    } else {
```

```
            if(f32(idx) == 10.0*tn) {
                color = colormap2[idx];
            } else {
                var tn1 = (tn - 0.1*f32(idx))*10.0;
                var a = colormap2[idx];
                var b = colormap2[idx+1u];
                color.x = a.x + (b.x - a.x)*tn1;
                color.y = a.y + (b.y - a.y)*tn1;
                color.z = a.z + (b.z - a.z)*tn1;
            }
        }
        return color;
}


@compute @workgroup_size(8, 8, 1)
fn cs_main(@builtin(global_invocation_id) id : vec3u) {
    let i = id.x;
    let j = id.y;
    var uv = getUv(i, j);
    var p0 = normalizePoint(uv.x, uv.y);

    // calculate normals
    let epsx = 0.01 * dx;
    let epsz = 0.01 * dz;

    let nx = normalizePoint(uv.x + epsx, uv.y) - normalizePoint(uv.x - epsx, uv.y);
    let nz = normalizePoint(uv.x, uv.y + epsz) - normalizePoint(uv.x, uv.y - epsz);
    let normal = normalize(cross(nx, nz));

    // colormap
    var range = 1.0;
    if(u32(ssp.colormapDirection) == 1u){
        range = aspect;
    }

    let color = colorLerp(true, -range, range, p0[u32(ssp.colormapDirection)], u32(ssp.colormapReverse));
    let color2 = colorLerp(false, -range, range, p0[u32(ssp.colormapDirection)],
        u32(ssp.colormapReverse));

    var idx = i + j * u32(ssp.resolution);

    // for surface
    vda.vertexDataArray[idx].position = vec4(p0, 1.0);
    vda.vertexDataArray[idx].normal = vec4(normal, 1.0);
    vda.vertexDataArray[idx].color = color;

    // for wireframe
    vda2.vertexDataArray[idx].position = vec4(p0, 1.0);
    vda2.vertexDataArray[idx].normal = vec4(normal, 1.0);
    vda2.vertexDataArray[idx].color = color2;
}
```

The above code introduces the *VertexData* struct, which specify the data to be generated for each vertex, encompassing attributes such as *position*, *normal*, and *color*. Building upon this, the *VertexDataArray* struct is designed to create a dynamic array utilizing the *VertexData* struct. This array serves as a repository for the vertex data essential for a basic 3D surface representation. Additionally, we employ the *SimpleSurfaceParams* struct to establish diverse parameters that drive the generation of vertex data.

Subsequently, we define a pair of storage buffers, namely, *vda* and *vda2*. Both buffers are configured with *read-write* access mode and act as containers for the vertex data arrays associated with the surface and wireframe, respectively. In addition, we define another pair of storage buffers, *colormap* and *colormap2*, configured with *read* access mode. These buffers are used to pass the colormap data, as previously defined in the *colormap.rs* file within the *src/* folder, to the shader components responsible for rendering the surface and wireframe.

The *getUv* function calculates the *x* and *z* coordinates in the square grid, crucial for generating the simple 3D surface. Meanwhile, the *normalizePoint* function performs a mapping of a region defined by different math functions onto a region of [-1, 1] range. This scaling accounts for the aspect ratio in the *y* direction, ensuring uniform sizing of different 3D surfaces in the scene when employing the same camera and transformations.

Subsequently, we introduce a utility function named *colorLerp*, which specializes in color interpolation based on a given *t* value within a predetermined range. This function computes the color corresponding to a specific position within a colormap or its reverse, contingent upon whether it pertains to a surface or wireframe representation. The *colorLerp* function serves to create seamlessly transitioning colormaps for rendering simple 3D surfaces.

The focal point of the above code is the *cs_main* function, which accepts the *global_invocation_id* as input. The global ID designates the invocation locations, feeding into the *getUv* function to determine the *x* and *z* coordinates. Subsequently, these coordinates drive the calculation of vertex positions corresponding to distinct mathematical functions through the *normalizePoint* function. Furthermore, the normal vector for each vertex is computed by making small displacements along the *x* and *z* directions, followed by cross product calculations. This approach guarantees that the normal vectors remain perpendicular to the respective surfaces.

Following this, two colormaps are generated – one for the surface and another for the wireframe, via the *colorLerp* function. Lastly, we populate the *vda* and *vda2* buffers with vertex data, encompassing attributes like *position*, *normal*, and *color*. These buffers will be used to generate simple 3D surfaces.

It is noteworthy that the *cs_main* function orchestrates simultaneous vertex data generation for all vertices, devoid of explicit for-loops. This parallelized approach, optimized for the GPU, contrasts with CPU-based computation, where nested for-loops are necessary to perform individual vertex computations.

7.2.4 Rust Code

With the background presented in the previous sections, we are ready to create simple 3D surfaces using compute shaders. To do so, add a new Rust file called *simple_surface.rs* to the *examples/ch07/* folder and include the following code:

```rust
use std::iter;
use cgmath::{ Matrix, Matrix4, SquareMatrix };
use wgpu:: { VertexBufferLayout, util::DeviceExt };
use winit::{
    event::*,
    event_loop::{ControlFlow, EventLoop},
    window::Window,
};
use bytemuck::cast_slice;
use wgpu_book_examples::{ wgpu_simplified as ws, transforms as wt, colormap };

fn create_color_data(colormap_name: &str) -> Vec<[f32; 4]> {
```

```rust
    let cdata = colormap::colormap_data(colormap_name);
    let mut data:Vec<[f32; 4]> = vec![[]];
    for i in 0..cdata.len() {
        data.push([cdata[i][0], cdata[i][1], cdata[i][2], 1.0 ]);
    }
    data
}

struct State {
    init:  ws::IWgpuInit,
    pipelines: Vec<wgpu::RenderPipeline>,
    uniform_bind_groups: Vec<wgpu::BindGroup>,
    uniform_buffers: Vec<wgpu::Buffer>,

    cs_pipelines: Vec<wgpu::ComputePipeline>,
    cs_vertex_buffers: Vec<wgpu::Buffer>,
    cs_index_buffers: Vec<wgpu::Buffer>,
    cs_uniform_buffers: Vec<wgpu::Buffer>,
    cs_bind_groups: Vec<wgpu::BindGroup>,

    view_mat: Matrix4<f32>,
    project_mat: Matrix4<f32>,
    msaa_texture_view: wgpu::TextureView,
    depth_texture_view: wgpu::TextureView,
    plot_type: u32,
    animation_speed: f32,
    rotation_speed: f32,

    resolution: u32,
    triangles_count: u32,
    lines_count: u32,

    surface_type: u32,
    colormap_direction: u32,
    colormap_reverse: u32,
    fps_counter: ws::FpsCounter,
}

impl State {
    async fn new(window:&Window, sample_count:u32, resolution:u32, colormap_name:&str,
wireframe_color:&str) -> Self {
        let init = ws::IWgpuInit::new(&window, sample_count, None).await;

        let vs_shader = init.device.create_shader_module(wgpu::include_wgsl!("../ch05/shader_vert.wgsl"));
        let fs_shader = init.device.create_shader_module(wgpu::include_wgsl!("../ch05/shader_frag.wgsl"));

        let cs_surface_func_file = include_str!("simple_surface_func.wgsl");
        let cs_surface_file = include_str!("simple_surface_comp.wgsl");
        let cs_comp_file = [cs_surface_func_file, cs_surface_file].join("\n");

        let cs_comp = init.device.create_shader_module(wgpu::ShaderModuleDescriptor {
            label: Some("Compute Shader"),
            source: wgpu::ShaderSource::Wgsl(cs_comp_file.into()),
        });

        let cs_indices = init.device.create_shader_module(wgpu::include_wgsl!("indices_comp.wgsl"));

        // uniform data
        let camera_position = (1.5, 1.5, 1.5).into();
        let look_direction = (0.0,0.0,0.0).into();
```

```
let up_direction = cgmath::Vector3::unit_y();
let light_direction = [-0.5f32, -0.5, -0.5];

let (view_mat, project_mat, _) =
    wt::create_vp_mat(camera_position, look_direction, up_direction,
    init.config.width as f32 / init.config.height as f32);

// create vertex uniform buffers

// model_mat and vp_mat will be stored in vertex_uniform_buffer inside the update function
let vert_uniform_buffer = init.device.create_buffer(&wgpu::BufferDescriptor{
    label: Some("Vertex Uniform Buffer"),
    size: 192,
    usage: wgpu::BufferUsages::UNIFORM | wgpu::BufferUsages::COPY_DST,
    mapped_at_creation: false,
});

// create light uniform buffer. here we set eye_position = camera_position
let light_uniform_buffer = init.device.create_buffer(&wgpu::BufferDescriptor{
    label: Some("Light Uniform Buffer"),
    size: 48,
    usage: wgpu::BufferUsages::UNIFORM | wgpu::BufferUsages::COPY_DST,
    mapped_at_creation: false,
});

let eye_position:&[f32; 3] = camera_position.as_ref();
init.queue.write_buffer(&light_uniform_buffer, 0, cast_slice(light_direction.as_ref()));
init.queue.write_buffer(&light_uniform_buffer, 16, cast_slice(eye_position));

// set specular light color to white
let specular_color:[f32; 3] = [1.0, 1.0, 1.0];
init.queue.write_buffer(&light_uniform_buffer, 32, cast_slice(specular_color.as_ref()));

// material uniform buffer
let material_uniform_buffer = init.device.create_buffer(&wgpu::BufferDescriptor{
    label: Some("Material Uniform Buffer"),
    size: 16,
    usage: wgpu::BufferUsages::UNIFORM | wgpu::BufferUsages::COPY_DST,
    mapped_at_creation: false,
});

// set default material parameters
let material = [0.1f32, 0.7, 0.4, 30.0];
init.queue.write_buffer(&material_uniform_buffer, 0, cast_slice(material.as_ref()));

// uniform bind group for vertex shader
let (vert_bind_group_layout, vert_bind_group) = ws::create_bind_group(
    &init.device,
    vec![wgpu::ShaderStages::VERTEX],
    &[vert_uniform_buffer.as_entire_binding()],
);
let (vert_bind_group_layout2, vert_bind_group2) = ws::create_bind_group(
    &init.device,
    vec![wgpu::ShaderStages::VERTEX],
    &[vert_uniform_buffer.as_entire_binding()],
);

// uniform bind group for fragment shader
let (frag_bind_group_layout, frag_bind_group) = ws::create_bind_group(
    &init.device,
```

```
        vec![wgpu::ShaderStages::FRAGMENT, wgpu::ShaderStages::FRAGMENT],
        &[light_uniform_buffer.as_entire_binding(), material_uniform_buffer.as_entire_binding()],
);
let (frag_bind_group_layout2, frag_bind_group2) = ws::create_bind_group(
    &init.device,
    vec![wgpu::ShaderStages::FRAGMENT, wgpu::ShaderStages::FRAGMENT],
    &[light_uniform_buffer.as_entire_binding(), material_uniform_buffer.as_entire_binding()],
);

let vertex_buffer_layout = VertexBufferLayout {
    array_stride: 48,
    step_mode: wgpu::VertexStepMode::Vertex,
    attributes: &wgpu::vertex_attr_array![0 => Float32x4, 1 => Float32x4, 2 => Float32x4],
};

let pipeline_layout = init.device.create_pipeline_layout(&wgpu::PipelineLayoutDescriptor {
    label: Some("Render Pipeline Layout"),
    bind_group_layouts: &[&vert_bind_group_layout, &frag_bind_group_layout],
    push_constant_ranges: &[],
});

let mut ppl = ws::IRenderPipeline {
    vs_shader: Some(&vs_shader),
    fs_shader: Some(&fs_shader),
    pipeline_layout: Some(&pipeline_layout),
    vertex_buffer_layout: &[vertex_buffer_layout],
    ..Default::default()
};
let pipeline = ppl.new(&init);

let vertex_buffer_layout2 = VertexBufferLayout {
    array_stride: 48,
    step_mode: wgpu::VertexStepMode::Vertex,
    attributes: &wgpu::vertex_attr_array![0 => Float32x4, 1 => Float32x4, 2 => Float32x4],
};

let pipeline_layout2 = init.device.create_pipeline_layout(&wgpu::PipelineLayoutDescriptor {
    label: Some("Render Pipeline Layout 2"),
    bind_group_layouts: &[&vert_bind_group_layout2, &frag_bind_group_layout2],
    push_constant_ranges: &[],
});
let mut ppl2 = ws::IRenderPipeline {
    topology: wgpu::PrimitiveTopology::LineList,
    vs_shader: Some(&vs_shader),
    fs_shader: Some(&fs_shader),
    pipeline_layout: Some(&pipeline_layout2),
    vertex_buffer_layout: &[vertex_buffer_layout2],
    ..Default::default()
};
let pipeline2 = ppl2.new(&init);

let msaa_texture_view = ws::create_msaa_texture_view(&init);
let depth_texture_view = ws::create_depth_view(&init);

let resol = ws::round_to_multiple(resolution, 8);
let vertices_count = resol * resol;
let triangles_count = 6 * (resol - 1) * (resol - 1);
let lines_count = 8 * (resol - 1) * (resol - 1);

println!("resolution = {}", resol);
```

```
// create compute pipeline for indices
let cs_index_buffer = init.device.create_buffer(&wgpu::BufferDescriptor{
    label: Some("Index Buffer"),
    size:  4 * triangles_count as u64,
    usage: wgpu::BufferUsages::INDEX | wgpu::BufferUsages::STORAGE | wgpu::BufferUsages::COPY_DST,
    mapped_at_creation: false,
});

let cs_index_buffer2 = init.device.create_buffer(&wgpu::BufferDescriptor{
    label: Some("Index 2 Buffer"),
    size:  4 * lines_count as u64,
    usage: wgpu::BufferUsages::INDEX | wgpu::BufferUsages::STORAGE | wgpu::BufferUsages::COPY_DST,
    mapped_at_creation: false,
});

let cs_index_uniform_buffer = init.device.create_buffer(&wgpu::BufferDescriptor{
    label: Some("Index Uniform Buffer"),
    size:  4,
    usage: wgpu::BufferUsages::UNIFORM | wgpu::BufferUsages::COPY_DST,
    mapped_at_creation: false,
});
init.queue.write_buffer(&cs_index_uniform_buffer, 0, cast_slice(&[resol]));

let (cs_index_bind_group_layout, cs_index_bind_group) = ws::create_bind_group_storage(
    &init.device,
    vec![
        wgpu::ShaderStages::COMPUTE, wgpu::ShaderStages::COMPUTE,
        wgpu::ShaderStages::COMPUTE,
    ],
    vec![
        wgpu::BufferBindingType::Storage { read_only: false },
        wgpu::BufferBindingType::Storage { read_only: false },
        wgpu::BufferBindingType::Uniform,
    ],
    &[
        cs_index_buffer.as_entire_binding(),
        cs_index_buffer2.as_entire_binding(),
        cs_index_uniform_buffer.as_entire_binding(),
    ],
);

let cs_index_pipeline_layout = init.device.create_pipeline_layout(&wgpu::PipelineLayoutDescriptor{
    label: Some("Compute Index Pipeline Layout"),
    bind_group_layouts: &[&cs_index_bind_group_layout],
    push_constant_ranges: &[],
});

let cs_index_pipeline = init.device.create_compute_pipeline(&wgpu::ComputePipelineDescriptor{
    label: Some("Compute Index Pipeline"),
    layout: Some(&cs_index_pipeline_layout),
    module: &cs_indices,
    entry_point: "cs_main",
});

// create compute pipeline for simple surface
let cs_vertex_buffer = init.device.create_buffer(&wgpu::BufferDescriptor{
    label: Some("Vertex Buffer"),
    size:  48 * vertices_count as u64,
    usage: wgpu::BufferUsages::VERTEX | wgpu::BufferUsages::STORAGE |
```

```
        wgpu::BufferUsages::COPY_DST,
    mapped_at_creation: false,
});

let cs_vertex_buffer2 = init.device.create_buffer(&wgpu::BufferDescriptor{
    label: Some("Vertex Buffer 2"),
    size:  48 * vertices_count as u64,
    usage: wgpu::BufferUsages::VERTEX | wgpu::BufferUsages::STORAGE |
        wgpu::BufferUsages::COPY_DST,
    mapped_at_creation: false,
});

let cdata = create_color_data(colormap_name);
let cs_colormap_uniform_buffer = init.device.create_buffer_init(
&wgpu::util::BufferInitDescriptor{
    label: Some("Colormap Uniform Buffer"),
    contents: bytemuck::cast_slice(&cdata),
    usage: wgpu::BufferUsages::STORAGE | wgpu::BufferUsages::COPY_DST,
});

let cdata2 = create_color_data(wireframe_color);
let cs_colormap_uniform_buffer2 = init.device.create_buffer_init(
&wgpu::util::BufferInitDescriptor{
    label: Some("Wireframe Colormap Uniform Buffer"),
    contents: bytemuck::cast_slice(&cdata2),
    usage: wgpu::BufferUsages::STORAGE | wgpu::BufferUsages::COPY_DST,
});

let params = [resol as f32, 0.0, 1.0, 0.0, 0.0];
let cs_vertex_uniform_buffer = init.device.create_buffer_init(
&wgpu::util::BufferInitDescriptor{
    label: Some("Vertex Uniform Buffer"),
    contents: bytemuck::cast_slice(&params),
    usage: wgpu::BufferUsages::UNIFORM | wgpu::BufferUsages::COPY_DST,
});

let (cs_vertex_bind_group_layout, cs_vertex_bind_group) = ws::create_bind_group_storage(
    &init.device,
    vec![
        wgpu::ShaderStages::COMPUTE, wgpu::ShaderStages::COMPUTE, wgpu::ShaderStages::COMPUTE,
        wgpu::ShaderStages::COMPUTE, wgpu::ShaderStages::COMPUTE,
    ],
    vec![
        wgpu::BufferBindingType::Storage { read_only: false },
        wgpu::BufferBindingType::Storage { read_only: false },
        wgpu::BufferBindingType::Storage { read_only: true },
        wgpu::BufferBindingType::Storage { read_only: true },
        wgpu::BufferBindingType::Uniform,
    ],
    &[
        cs_vertex_buffer.as_entire_binding(),
        cs_vertex_buffer2.as_entire_binding(),
        cs_colormap_uniform_buffer.as_entire_binding(),
        cs_colormap_uniform_buffer2.as_entire_binding(),
        cs_vertex_uniform_buffer.as_entire_binding(),
    ],
);

let cs_pipeline_layout = init.device.create_pipeline_layout(&wgpu::PipelineLayoutDescriptor{
    label: Some("Compute Pipeline Layout"),
```

```
            bind_group_layouts: &[&cs_vertex_bind_group_layout],
            push_constant_ranges: &[],
        });

        let cs_pipeline = init.device.create_compute_pipeline(&wgpu::ComputePipelineDescriptor{
            label: Some("Compute Pipeline"),
            layout: Some(&cs_pipeline_layout),
            module: &cs_comp,
            entry_point: "cs_main",
        });

        Self {
            init,
            pipelines: vec![pipeline, pipeline2],
            uniform_bind_groups: vec![vert_bind_group, frag_bind_group, vert_bind_group2,
                frag_bind_group2],
            uniform_buffers: vec![vert_uniform_buffer, light_uniform_buffer, material_uniform_buffer],

            cs_pipelines: vec![cs_index_pipeline, cs_pipeline],
            cs_vertex_buffers: vec![cs_vertex_buffer, cs_vertex_buffer2],
            cs_index_buffers: vec![cs_index_buffer, cs_index_buffer2],
            cs_uniform_buffers: vec![cs_index_uniform_buffer, cs_vertex_uniform_buffer],
            cs_bind_groups: vec![cs_index_bind_group, cs_vertex_bind_group],

            view_mat,
            project_mat,
            msaa_texture_view,
            depth_texture_view,

            plot_type: 1,
            animation_speed: 1.0,
            rotation_speed: 1.0,

            resolution: resol,
            triangles_count,
            lines_count,

            surface_type: 0,
            colormap_direction: 1,
            colormap_reverse: 0,
            fps_counter: ws::FpsCounter::default(),
        }
    }

    fn resize(&mut self, new_size: winit::dpi::PhysicalSize<u32>) {
        if new_size.width > 0 && new_size.height > 0 {
            self.init.size = new_size;
            self.init.config.width = new_size.width;
            self.init.config.height = new_size.height;
            self.init.surface.configure(&self.init.device, &self.init.config);

            self.project_mat = wt::create_projection_mat(new_size.width as f32 / new_size.height as f32,
                true);
            self.depth_texture_view = ws::create_depth_view(&self.init);
            if self.init.sample_count > 1 {
                self.msaa_texture_view = ws::create_msaa_texture_view(&self.init);
            }
        }
    }
```

```rust
#[allow(unused_variables)]
fn input(&mut self, event: &WindowEvent) -> bool {
    match event {
        WindowEvent::KeyboardInput {
            input:
                KeyboardInput {
                    virtual_keycode: Some(keycode),
                    state: ElementState::Pressed,
                    ..
                },
            ..
        } => {
            match keycode {
                VirtualKeyCode::Space => {
                    self.plot_type = (self.plot_type + 1) % 3;
                    true
                }
                VirtualKeyCode::LControl => {
                    self.surface_type = (self.surface_type + 1) % 3;
                    true
                },
                VirtualKeyCode::LShift => {
                    self.colormap_direction = (self.colormap_direction + 1) % 3;
                    true
                },
                VirtualKeyCode::LAlt => {
                    self.colormap_reverse = if self.colormap_reverse == 0 {1} else {0};
                    true
                },
                VirtualKeyCode::Q => {
                    self.animation_speed += 0.1;
                    true
                },
                VirtualKeyCode::A => {
                    self.animation_speed -= 0.1;
                    if self.animation_speed < 0.0 {
                        self.animation_speed = 0.0;
                    }
                    true
                } ,
                VirtualKeyCode::W => {
                    self.rotation_speed += 0.1;
                    true
                },
                VirtualKeyCode::S => {
                    self.rotation_speed -= 0.1;
                    if self.rotation_speed < 0.0 {
                        self.rotation_speed = 0.0;
                    }
                    true
                } ,
                _ => false
            }
        }
        _ => false,
    }
}

fn update(&mut self, dt: std::time::Duration) {
    // update uniform buffer
```

```rust
        let dt1 = self.rotation_speed * dt.as_secs_f32();

        let model_mat = wt::create_model_mat([0.0,0.0,0.0], [dt1.sin(), dt1.cos(), 0.0], [1.0, 1.0, 1.0]);
        let view_project_mat = self.project_mat * self.view_mat;

        let normal_mat = (model_mat.invert().unwrap()).transpose();

        let model_ref:&[f32; 16] = model_mat.as_ref();
        let view_projection_ref:&[f32; 16] = view_project_mat.as_ref();
        let normal_ref:&[f32; 16] = normal_mat.as_ref();

        self.init.queue.write_buffer(&self.uniform_buffers[0], 0, cast_slice(view_projection_ref));
        self.init.queue.write_buffer(&self.uniform_buffers[0], 64, cast_slice(model_ref));
        self.init.queue.write_buffer(&self.uniform_buffers[0], 128, cast_slice(normal_ref));

        // update buffers for compute pipeline
        let params = [
            self.resolution as f32,
            self.surface_type as f32,
            self.colormap_direction as f32,
            self.colormap_reverse as f32,
            self.animation_speed * dt.as_secs_f32()
        ];
        self.init.queue.write_buffer(&self.cs_uniform_buffers[1], 0, bytemuck::cast_slice(&params));
    }

    fn render(&mut self) -> Result<(), wgpu::SurfaceError> {
        let output = self.init.surface.get_current_texture()?;
        let view = output
            .texture
            .create_view(&wgpu::TextureViewDescriptor::default());

        let mut encoder = self
            .init.device
            .create_command_encoder(&wgpu::CommandEncoderDescriptor {
                label: Some("Render Encoder"),
            });

        // compute pass for indices
        {
            let mut cs_index_pass = encoder.begin_compute_pass(&wgpu::ComputePassDescriptor {
                label: Some("Compute Index Pass"),
                timestamp_writes: None,
            });
            cs_index_pass.set_pipeline(&self.cs_pipelines[0]);
            cs_index_pass.set_bind_group(0, &self.cs_bind_groups[0], &[]);
            cs_index_pass.dispatch_workgroups(self.resolution/8, self.resolution/8, 1);
        }

        // compute pass for vertices
        {
            let mut cs_pass = encoder.begin_compute_pass(&wgpu::ComputePassDescriptor {
                label: Some("Compute Pass"),
                timestamp_writes: None,
            });
            cs_pass.set_pipeline(&self.cs_pipelines[1]);
            cs_pass.set_bind_group(0, &self.cs_bind_groups[1], &[]);
            cs_pass.dispatch_workgroups(self.resolution/8, self.resolution/8, 1);
        }
```

```rust
    // render pass
    {
        let color_attach = ws::create_color_attachment(&view);
        let msaa_attach = ws::create_msaa_color_attachment(&view, &self.msaa_texture_view);
        let color_attachment = if self.init.sample_count == 1 { color_attach } else { msaa_attach };
        let depth_attachment = ws::create_depth_stencil_attachment(&self.depth_texture_view);

        let mut render_pass = encoder.begin_render_pass(&wgpu::RenderPassDescriptor {
            label: Some("Render Pass"),
            color_attachments: &[Some(color_attachment)],
            depth_stencil_attachment: Some(depth_attachment),
            occlusion_query_set: None,
            timestamp_writes: None,
        });

        let plot_type = if self.plot_type == 1 { "shape_only" }
            else if self.plot_type == 2 {"wireframe_only"} else {"both"};

        if plot_type == "shape_only" || plot_type == "both" {
            render_pass.set_pipeline(&self.pipelines[0]);
            render_pass.set_vertex_buffer(0, self.cs_vertex_buffers[0].slice(..));
            render_pass.set_index_buffer(self.cs_index_buffers[0].slice(..),
                wgpu::IndexFormat::Uint32);
            render_pass.set_bind_group(0, &self.uniform_bind_groups[0], &[]);
            render_pass.set_bind_group(1, &self.uniform_bind_groups[1], &[]);
            render_pass.draw_indexed(0..self.triangles_count, 0, 0..1);
        }

        if plot_type == "wireframe_only" || plot_type == "both" {
            render_pass.set_pipeline(&self.pipelines[1]);
            render_pass.set_vertex_buffer(0, self.cs_vertex_buffers[1].slice(..));
            render_pass.set_index_buffer(self.cs_index_buffers[1].slice(..),
                wgpu::IndexFormat::Uint32);
            render_pass.set_bind_group(0, &self.uniform_bind_groups[2], &[]);
            render_pass.set_bind_group(1, &self.uniform_bind_groups[3], &[]);
            render_pass.draw_indexed(0..self.lines_count, 0, 0..1);
        }
    }
    self.fps_counter.print_fps(5);
    self.init.queue.submit(iter::once(encoder.finish()));
    output.present();

    Ok(())
    }
}
fn main() {
    let mut sample_count = 1u32;
    let mut resolution = 64u32;
    let mut colormap_name = "jet";
    let mut wireframe_color = "white";
    let args: Vec<String> = std::env::args().collect();
    if args.len() > 1 {
        sample_count = args[1].parse::<u32>().unwrap();
    }
    if args.len() > 2 {
        resolution = args[2].parse::<u32>().unwrap();
    }
    if args.len() > 3 {
        colormap_name = &args[3];
    }
```

```
    if args.len() > 4 {
        wireframe_color = &args[4];
    }

    env_logger::init();
    let event_loop = EventLoop::new();
    let window = winit::window::WindowBuilder::new().build(&event_loop).unwrap();
    window.set_title(&*format!("ch07_{}", "simple_surface"));

    let mut state = pollster::block_on(State::new(&window, sample_count, resolution, colormap_name,
        wireframe_color));
    let render_start_time = std::time::Instant::now();

    event_loop.run(move |event, _, control_flow| {
        match event {
            Event::WindowEvent {
                ref event,
                window_id,
            } if window_id == window.id() => {
                if !state.input(event) {
                    match event {
                        WindowEvent::CloseRequested
                        | WindowEvent::KeyboardInput {
                            input:
                                KeyboardInput {
                                    state: ElementState::Pressed,
                                    virtual_keycode: Some(VirtualKeyCode::Escape),
                                    ..
                                },
                            ..
                        } => *control_flow = ControlFlow::Exit,
                        WindowEvent::Resized(physical_size) => {
                            state.resize(*physical_size);
                        }
                        WindowEvent::ScaleFactorChanged { new_inner_size, .. } => {
                            state.resize(**new_inner_size);
                        }
                        _ => {}
                    }
                }
            }
            Event::RedrawRequested(_) => {
                let now = std::time::Instant::now();
                let dt = now - render_start_time;
                state.update(dt);

                match state.render() {
                    Ok(_) => {}
                    Err(wgpu::SurfaceError::Lost) => state.resize(state.init.size),
                    Err(wgpu::SurfaceError::OutOfMemory) => *control_flow = ControlFlow::Exit,
                    Err(e) => eprintln!("{:?}", e),
                }
            }
            Event::MainEventsCleared => {
                window.request_redraw();
            }
            _ => {}
        }
    });
}
```

The above code begins by introducing the *create_color_data* function, which generates a color data vector based on a specified colormap name. Within the function, the colormap data is sourced from the *colormap.rs* file in the *src/* folder. A data conversion is carried out where the data type transition from [[*f32*; 3]; 11] to *Vec<[f32; 4]>*. This alteration involves the addition of an alpha value of 1.0. This conversion is necessary to ensure proper buffer alignment for compute shaders.

The *State* struct undergoes expansion to accommodate various fields associated with compute pipelines, including *cs_pipelines*, *cs_vertex_buffers*, and *cs_index_buffers*, among others. Furthermore, the *resolution*, *triangle_count*, and *lines_count* fields within the struct offer accessible values for different functions without necessitating their explicit input.

Within the *State::new* function, we reuse the vertex and fragment shader files created earlier in Chapter 5, located in the *examples/ch05/* folder. As both *simple_surface_comp.wgsl* and *simple_surface_func.wgsl* are required for generating vertex data, these files are amalgamated to form the compute shader module. The process is demonstrated in the following code:

```
let cs_surface_func_file = include_str!("simple_surface_func.wgsl");
let cs_surface_file = include_str!("simple_surface_comp.wgsl");
let cs_comp_file = [cs_surface_func_file, cs_surface_file].join("\n");

let cs_comp = init.device.create_shader_module(wgpu::ShaderModuleDescriptor {
    label: Some("Compute Shader"),
    source: wgpu::ShaderSource::Wgsl(cs_comp_file.into()),
});
```

For the compute shader tasked with calculating indices, a single file, *indices_comp.wgsl*, is employed, and the customary method is employed to generate its shader module:

```
let cs_indices = init.device.create_shader_module(wgpu::include_wgsl!("indices_comp.wgsl"));
```

Subsequently, akin to previous examples, similar uniform buffers and bind groups are used for transformations and the light model. However, a slight variation is introduced in the vertex buffer layout: the format *Float32×3* utilized for transmitting *position*, *normal*, and *color* data in prior examples is substituted with *Float32×4* in the current instance:

```
let vertex_buffer_layout = VertexBufferLayout {
    array_stride:  48,
    step_mode: wgpu::VertexStepMode::Vertex,
    attributes: &wgpu::vertex_attr_array![0 => Float32x4, 1 => Float32x4, 2 => Float32x4],
    // pos, norm, col
};
```

It is important to emphasize that in the current example, a compute shader is harnessed to directly generate vertex data on the GPU. Modern GPUs often feature memory architectures tailored for optimal access to data aligned on power-of-2 boundaries. Leveraging this characteristic can significantly enhance memory access performance and overall GPU efficiency. The subsequent table illustrates byte sizes and alignments for different data types:

Type	Size in Bytes	Alignment in Bytes
scalar (f32, u32, i32)	4	4
vec2<T>	8	8
vec3<T>	12	16
vec4<T>	16	16

Evidently, the byte size coincides with the byte alignment across all data types, barring *vec3*. In the case of *vec3*, alignment shifts to the next power of 2 from its size, i.e., 16 rather than the actual byte size of 12. Consequently, the *Float32×4* format is adopted for transmitting vertex data. Alternatively, if the *Float32×3* format were utilized, the need to ensure proper buffer alignment would demand the incorporation of a 4-byte padding for each *Float32×3* field.

Within the *State*::*new* function, a noteworthy departure from previous examples emerges: the current approach circumvents the creation of vertex buffers for position, normal, and colormap using Rust-generated data. Instead, we will harness compute shaders to generate these very vertex buffers.

The State::*new* function introduces a distinctive code segment dedicated to crafting a compute pipeline for indices. In this section, we commence by crafting two index buffers: *cs_index_buffer* and *cs_index_buffer2*, earmarked for the surface and wireframe, respectively. Concurrently, a uniform buffer is fashioned to relay the resolution parameter to the shader. This collection of buffers then aids in the creation of a bind group layout and subsequently, a bind group, pivotal for the compute pipeline.

The subsequent code segment forges a compute pipeline tailored for vertex data generation. Within this context, we introduce two distinct vertex buffers, namely *cs_vertex_buffer* and *cs_vertex_buffer2*. These buffers are allocated a size of 48 bytes, derived from three *Float32×4* fields – *position*, *normal*, and *color* – each spanning a size of 16 bytes.

Following this, we proceed to define an array of storage and uniform buffers. These buffers are pivotal for conveying colormap data and input parameters indispensable for vertex data calculation. By amalgamating these buffers, we pave the way for the formulation of both the bind group layout and the corresponding bind group for the compute pipeline. The code snippet below elucidates this process:

```
let (cs_vertex_bind_group_layout, cs_vertex_bind_group) = ws::create_bind_group_storage(
    &init.device,
    vec![
        wgpu::ShaderStages::COMPUTE, wgpu::ShaderStages::COMPUTE, wgpu::ShaderStages::COMPUTE,
        wgpu::ShaderStages::COMPUTE, wgpu::ShaderStages::COMPUTE,
    ],
    vec![
        wgpu::BufferBindingType::Storage { read_only: false },
        wgpu::BufferBindingType::Storage { read_only: false },
        wgpu::BufferBindingType::Storage { read_only: true },
        wgpu::BufferBindingType::Storage { read_only: true },
        wgpu::BufferBindingType::Uniform,
    ],
    &[
        cs_vertex_buffer.as_entire_binding(),
        cs_vertex_buffer2.as_entire_binding(),
        cs_colormap_uniform_buffer.as_entire_binding(),
        cs_colormap_uniform_buffer2.as_entire_binding(),
        cs_vertex_uniform_buffer.as_entire_binding(),
    ],
);
```

Here, the assortment of five buffers, encompassing four storage buffers and one uniform buffer, seamlessly aligns with the quintet of bindings within the compute shader. Notably, we designate all five buffers for access within the *COMPUTE* shader stage, thereby limiting their accessibility to the compute shader exclusively.

The *State*::*render* function encompasses three distinctive passes, comprising two compute passes followed by a render pass. In the first compute pass, index calculation takes the center stage. Here, the bind group is configured for the pass, and the *dispatch_workgroups* function is invoked. This function orchestrates the launch of a predefined number of workgroups, initiating the execution of the compute shader functions. The *dispatch_workgroups* function necessitates three inputs: the count of workgroups to dispatch along the *x*, *y*, and *z* dimensions.

A subsequent compute pass is dedicated to vertex data generation. In this case, the bind group configuration remains pertinent, as one of the resource attributes hinges on the vertex buffer. This setup serves as a precursor to the ensuing render pass.

In the realm of the render pass, we diverge from preceding examples. Here, the vertex buffer and index buffer sourced from the compute pipelines are instrumental in defining these buffers within the render pass. This is a departure from earlier instances, where the vertex buffer and index buffer were generated using data originating from Rust code executed on the CPU.

The *State::update* function largely resembles its counterparts in previous examples. However, in this instance, an innovative approach to animating the vertex data and vertex buffer is adopted. Unlike prior scenarios wherein vertex data and buffers required regeneration or updates on a per-frame basis, the focus shifts here. Instead, the emphasis lies in updating solely the uniform parameters essential for vertex data computation within the compute shader. This novel approach can be observed in the subsequent code excerpt:

```
// update buffers for compute pipeline
let params = [
    self.resolution as f32,
    self.surface_type as f32,
    self.colormap_direction as f32,
    self.colormap_reverse as f32,
    self.animation_speed * dt.as_secs_f32()
];
self.init.queue.write_buffer(&self.cs_uniform_buffers[1], 0, cast_slice(&params));
```

Additionally, the code permits the user to modify input parameters through keyboard inputs.

Here is a list of controls using keyboard:

- *Space*: Changes plot type among surface, wireframe, and both.
- *LControl*: Changes surface type among *sinc, peaks,* and *poles.*
- *LShift*: Changes colormap direction among *x, y* and *z.*
- *LAlt*: Reverses colormap or not.
- *Q/A*: Increases/decreases the animation speed.
- *W/S:* Increases/decreases the rotation speed.

7.2.5 Run Application

To run this application, add the following code snippet to the *Cargo.toml* file:

```
[[example]]
name = "ch07_simple_surface"
path = "examples/ch07/simple_surface.rs"
```

Afterward, execute the following *cargo run* commands in the terminal window:

```
cargo run --example ch07_simple_surface 8 1000
```

Fig.7-2 shows the results of this example.

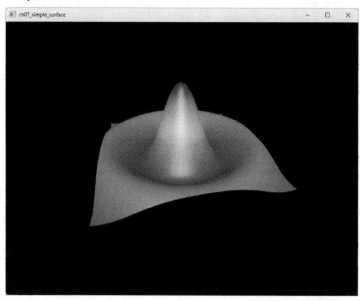

Fig.7-2. Simple 3D surface generated using compute shaders.

The figure effectively illustrates how employing compute shaders results in the creation of a smooth animated 3D surface, maintaining a steady 60 FPS frame rate, even for higher resolutions such as 1000. In contrast, when attempting to generate the same animated surface using CPU computations as demonstrated in Chapter 5, the frame rate drops notably to 16 FPS for a resolution of 250. This stark contrast underscores the remarkable computational prowess of compute shaders in generating vertex data.

It is worth noting that if the resolution is further increased beyond 1680, an error arises with the following cause:

```
Caused by:
    In Device::create_bind_group
      note: label = `Uniform Bind Group`
    Buffer binding 0 range 135475200 exceeds `max_*_buffer_binding_size` limit 134217728.
```

This error emanates from the use of the default setting (128 MiB) for the *max_storage_buffer_binding _size limit* during GPU device creation within the *IWgpuInit*::new function as defined in the *wgpu-simplified* module. To address this, the *IWgpuInit*::new function offers an optional argument named limits that empowers users to adjust this limit. For instance, the code snippet below raises the *max_storage_buffer_binding_size limit* to 1024 MiB (with the maximum possible value being 2048 MiB):

```
let limits = wgpu::Limits {
    max_storage_buffer_binding_size: 1024*1024*1024, //1024 MiB, defaulting to 128MiB
    max_buffer_size: 1024*1024*1024, // 1024 MiB, defaulting to 256 MiB
    max_compute_invocations_per_workgroup: 512, // dafaulting to 256
    ..Default::default()
};
let init = ws::IWgpuInit::new(&window, sample_count, Some(limits)).await;
```

By employing this snippet, the resolution for rendering 3D surfaces can be elevated. For example, even at a resolution as high as 3000, the application runs smoothly without errors. In such instances, a steady 60 FPS frame rate is sustained.

7.3 Parametric 3D Surfaces

In this section, we will attempt to reproduce the parametric 3D surfaces presented in Chapter 5 using a compute shader to create the vertex data, as we did for simple 3D surfaces in previous sections. We will reuse the vertex and fragment shaders from Chapter 5, as well as the compute shader for indices from the previous example.

7.3.1 Shader Code for Math Functions

We need to convert the Rust code of the math functions used for generating parametric 3D surfaces into WGSL shader code. Create a new WGSL shader file named *parametric_surface_func.wgsl* in the *examples/ch07/* folder and include the following code:

```
const pi:f32 = 3.14159265359;

struct DataRange {
    uRange: vec2f,
    vRange: vec2f,
    xRange: vec2f,
    yRange: vec2f,
    zRange: vec2f,
};

fn p2(x:f32) -> f32 {
    return pow(x, 2.0);
}

fn p3(x:f32) -> f32 {
    if(x >= 0.0){
        return pow(x,3.0);
    } else{
        return -pow(abs(x), 3.0);
    }
}

fn p4(x:f32) -> f32 {
    return pow(x, 4.0);
}

fn p5(x:f32) -> f32{
    if(x >= 0.0){
        return pow(x,5.0);
    } else{
        return -pow(abs(x), 5.0);
    }
}

fn p6(x:f32) -> f32 {
    return pow(x, 6.0);
}
```

```
fn p7(x:f32) -> f32 {
    if(x >= 0.0){
        return pow(x,7.0);
    } else{
        return -pow(abs(x), 7.0);
    }
}

fn p8(x:f32) -> f32 {
    return pow(x, 8.0);
}

fn astroid(u:f32, v:f32) -> vec3f {
    var x = p3(cos(u)) * p3(cos(v));
    var y = p3(sin(v));
    var z = p3(sin(u)) * p3(cos(v));
    return vec3(z, y, x);
}

fn astroid2(u:f32, v:f32) -> vec3f {
    var x = p3(sin(u)) * cos(v);
    var y = p3(cos(u));
    var z = p3(sin(u)) * sin(v);
    return vec3(x, y, z);
}

fn astroidal_torus(u:f32, v:f32) -> vec3f {
    let a = 2.0;
    let b = 1.0;
    let c = 0.7854;
    var x = (a + b * pow(cos(u), 3.0) * cos(c) - b * pow(sin(u), 3.0) * sin(c)) * cos(v);
    var y = b * pow(cos(u), 3.0) * sin(c) + b * pow(sin(u), 3.0) * cos(c);
    var z = (a + b * pow(cos(u), 3.0) * cos(c) - b * pow(sin(u), 3.0) * sin(c)) * sin(v);
    return vec3(z, y, x);
}

fn bohemian_dome(u:f32, v:f32) -> vec3f {
    let a = 0.7;
    let b = 1.0;
    var x = a * cos(u);
    var y = b * cos(v);
    var z = a * sin(u) + b * sin(v);
    return vec3(x, y, z);
}

fn boy_shape(u:f32, v:f32) -> vec3f {
    var x = cos(u) * (1.0 / 3.0 * sqrt(2.0) * cos(u) * cos(2.0 * v) + 2.0 / 3.0 * sin(u) * cos(v)) /
        (1.0 - sqrt(2.0) * sin(u) * cos(u) * sin(3.0 * v));
    var y = cos(u) * cos(u) / (1.0 - sqrt(2.0) * sin(u) * cos(u) * sin(3.0 * v)) - 1.0;
    var z = cos(u) * (1.0 / 3.0 * sqrt(2.0) * cos(u) * sin(2.0 * v) - 2.0 / 3.0 * sin(u) * sin(v)) /
        (1.0 - sqrt(2.0) * sin(u) * cos(u) * sin(3.0 * v));
    return vec3(z, y, x);
}

fn breather(u:f32, v:f32) -> vec3f {
    let a = 0.4;
    let ch = cosh(a * u);
    let sh = sinh(a * u);

    var x = -u + (2.0 * (1.0 - a * a) * ch * sh) / (a * ((1.0 - a * a) * p2(ch) +
```

```
            a * a * p2(sin(sqrt(1.0 - a * a) * v))));
    var y = (2.0 * sqrt(1.0 - a * a) * ch * (-(sqrt(1.0 - a * a) * cos(v) * cos(sqrt(1.0 - a * a) * v)) -
        sin(v) * sin(sqrt(1.0 - a * a) * v))) / (a * ((1.0 - a * a) * p2(ch) +
        a * a * p2(sin(sqrt(1.0 - a * a) * v))));
    var z = (2.0 * sqrt(1.0 - a * a) * ch * (-(sqrt(1.0 - a * a) * sin(v) * cos(sqrt(1.0 - a * a) * v)) +
        cos(v) * sin(sqrt(1.0 - a * a) * v))) / (a * ((1.0 - a * a) * p2(ch) +
        a * a * p2(sin(sqrt(1.0 - a * a) * v))));
    return vec3(x, y, z);
}

fn enneper(u:f32, v:f32) -> vec3f {
    var x = u * (1.0 - u * u / 3.0 + v * v);
    var y = u * u - v * v;
    var z = v * (1.0 - v * v / 3.0 + u * u);
    return vec3(x, y, z);
}

fn figure8(u:f32, v:f32) -> vec3f {
    let a = 2.5;
    var x = (a + cos(0.5 * u) * sin(v) - sin(0.5 * u) * sin(2.0 * v)) * cos(u);
    var y = (a + cos(0.5 * u) * sin(v) - sin(0.5 * u) * sin(2.0 * v)) * sin(u);
    var z = sin(0.5 * u) * sin(v) + cos(0.5 * u) * sin(2.0 * v);
    return vec3(x, z, y);
}

fn henneberg(u:f32, v:f32) -> vec3f {
    var x = (sinh(u) * cos(v) - sinh(3.0 * u) * cos(3.0 * v) / 3.0);
    var y = cosh(2.0 * u) * cos(2.0 * v);
    var z = (sinh(u) * sin(v) - sinh(3.0 * u) * sin(3.0 * v) / 3.0);
    return vec3(x, y, z);
}

fn kiss(u:f32, v:f32) -> vec3f {
    var x = u * u * sqrt(1.0 - u) * cos(v);
    var y = u;
    var z = u * u * sqrt(1.0 - u) * sin(v);
    return vec3(z, y, x);
}

fn klein_bottle(u:f32, v:f32) -> vec3f {
    var x = 2.0 / 15.0 * (3.0 + 5.0 * cos(u) * sin(u)) * sin(v);

    var y = -1.0 / 15.0 * sin(u) * (3.0 * cos(v) - 3.0 * p2(cos(u)) * cos(v) -
        48.0 * p4(cos(u)) * cos(v) + 48.0 * p6(cos(u)) * cos(v) -
        60.0 * sin(u) + 5.0 * cos(u) * cos(v) * sin(u) - 5.0 * p3(cos(u)) * cos(v) * sin(u) -
        80.0 * p5(cos(u)) * cos(v) * sin(u) + 80.0 * p7(cos(u)) * cos(v) * sin(u));

    var z = -2.0 / 15.0 * cos(u) * (3.0 * cos(v) - 30.0 * sin(u) +
        90.0 * p4(cos(u)) * sin(u) - 60.0 * p6(cos(u)) * sin(u) +
        5.0 * cos(u) * cos(v) * sin(u));

    return vec3(x, y, z);
}

fn klein_bottle2(u:f32, v:f32) -> vec3f {
    var x = 0.0;
    var z = 0.0;
    var r = 4.0 * (1.0 - 0.5 * cos(u));

    if (u >= 0.0 && u <= pi)
```

```
    {
        x = 6.0 * cos(u) * (1.0 + sin(u)) + r * cos(u) * cos(v);
        z = 16.0 * sin(u) + r * sin(u) * cos(v);
    }
    else if (u > pi && u <= 2.0 * pi)
    {
        x = 6.0 * cos(u) * (1.0 + sin(u)) + r * cos(v + pi);
        z = 16.0 * sin(u);
    }
    var y = r * sin(v);

    return vec3(x, z, y);
}

fn klein_bottle3(u:f32, v:f32) -> vec3f {
    let a = 8.0;
    let n = 3.0;
    let m = 1.0;
    var x = (a + cos(0.5 * u * n) * sin(v) - sin(0.5 * u * n) * sin(2.0 * v)) * cos(0.5 * u * m);
    var y = sin(0.5 * u * n) * sin(v) + cos(0.5 * u * n) * sin(2.0 * v);
    var z = (a + cos(0.5 * u * n) * sin(v) - sin(0.5 * u * n) * sin(2.0 * v)) * sin(0.5 * u * m);
    return vec3(x, y, z);
}

fn kuen(u:f32, v:f32) -> vec3f {
    var x = 2.0 * cosh(v) * (cos(u) + u * sin(u)) / (p2(cosh(v)) + u * u);
    var y = v - (2.0 * sinh(v) * cosh(v)) / (p2(cosh(v)) + u * u);
    var z = 2.0 * cosh(v) * (-u * cos(u) + sin(u)) / (p2(cosh(v)) + u * u);
    return vec3(x, y, z);
}

fn minimal(u:f32, v:f32) -> vec3f {
    let a = 1.0;
    let b = -4.0;
    let c = 1.0;
    var x = a * (u - sin(u) * cosh(v));
    var y = b * sin(u / 2.0) * sinh(v / 2.0);
    var z = c * (1.0 - cos(u) * cosh(v));
    return vec3(x, y, z);
}

fn parabolic_cyclide(u:f32, v:f32) -> vec3f {
    let a = 1.0;
    let b = 0.5;
    var x = a * u * (v * v + b) / (1.0 + u * u + v * v);
    var y = (a / 2.0) * (2.0 * v * v + b * (1.0 - u * u - v * v)) / (1.0 + u * u + v * v);
    var z = a * v * (1.0 + u * u - b) / (1.0 + u * u + v * v);
    return vec3(z, y, x);
}

fn pear(u:f32, v:f32) -> vec3f {
    var x = u * sqrt(u * (1.0 - u)) * cos(v);
    var y = -u;
    var z = u * sqrt(u * (1.0 - u)) * sin(v);
    return vec3(x, y, z);
}

fn plucker_conoid(u:f32, v:f32) -> vec3f {
    let a = 2.0;
    let b = 3.0;
```

```
    var x = a * u * cos(v);
    var y = a * cos(b * v);
    var z = a * u * sin(v);
    return vec3(x, y, z);
}

fn seashell(u:f32, v:f32) -> vec3f {
    var x = 2.0 * (-1.0 + exp(u / (6.0 * pi))) * sin(u) * p2(cos(v / 2.0));
    var y = 1.0 - exp(u / (3.0 * pi)) - sin(v) + exp(u / (6.0 * pi)) * sin(v);
    var z = 2.0 * (1.0 - exp(u / (6.0 * pi))) * cos(u) * p2(cos(v / 2.0));
    return vec3(x, y, z);
}

fn sievert_enneper(u:f32, v:f32) -> vec3f {
    let a = 1.0;
    var x = log(tan(v / 2.0)) / sqrt(a) + 2.0 * (1.0 + a) * cos(v) /
        (1.0 + a - a * sin(v) * sin(v) * cos(u) * cos(u)) / sqrt(a);

    var y = (2.0 * sin(v) * sqrt((1.0 + 1.0 / a) * (1.0 + a * sin(u) * sin(u)))) /
        (1.0 + a - a * sin(v) * sin(v) * cos(u) *
        cos(u)) * sin(atan(sqrt(1.0 + a) * tan(u)) - u / sqrt(1.0 + a));

    var z = (2.0 * sin(v) * sqrt((1.0 + 1.0 / a) * (1.0 + a * sin(u) * sin(u)))) /
        (1.0 + a - a * sin(v) * sin(v) * cos(u) *
        cos(u)) * cos(atan(sqrt(1.0 + a) * tan(u)) - u / sqrt(1.0 + a));

    return vec3(z, y, x);
}

fn steiner(u:f32, v:f32) -> vec3f {
    var x = cos(u) * cos(v) * sin(v);
    var y = cos(u) * sin(u) * p2(cos(v));
    var z = sin(u) * cos(v) * sin(v);
    return vec3(x, y, z);
}

fn torus(u:f32, v:f32) -> vec3f {
    let r1 = 1.0;
    let r2 = 0.3;
    var x = (r1 + r2 * cos(v)) * cos(u);
    var y = r2 * sin(v);
    var z = (r1 + r2 * cos(v)) * sin(u);
    return vec3(x, y, z);
}

fn wellenkugel(u:f32, v:f32) -> vec3f {
    var x = u * cos(cos(u)) * cos(v);
    var y = u * sin(cos(u));
    var z = u * cos(cos(u)) * sin(v);

    return vec3(x, y, z);
}

fn getDataRange(funcSelection:u32) -> DataRange {
    var dr:DataRange;
    if (funcSelection == 0u) { // klein-bottle
        dr.uRange = vec2<f32>(0.0, pi);
        dr.vRange = vec2<f32>(0.0, 2.0 * pi);
        dr.xRange = vec2<f32>(-0.734, 0.734);
        dr.yRange = vec2<f32>(0.0, 4.21);
```

```
            dr.zRange = vec2<f32>(-1.517, 1.824);
    } else if (funcSelection == 1u) { // astroid
            dr.uRange = vec2(0.0, 2.0 * pi);
            dr.vRange = vec2(0.0, 2.0 * pi);
            dr.xRange = vec2(-1.0, 1.0);
            dr.yRange = vec2(-1.0, 1.0);
            dr.zRange = vec2(-1.0, 1.0);
    } else if (funcSelection == 2u) { // astroid 2
            dr.uRange = vec2(0.0, 2.0 * pi);
            dr.vRange = vec2(0.0, 2.0 * pi);
            dr.xRange = vec2(-1.0, 1.0);
            dr.yRange = vec2(-1.0, 1.0);
            dr.zRange = vec2(-1.0, 1.0);
    } else if (funcSelection == 3u) { // astroidal torus
            dr.uRange = vec2<f32>(-pi, pi);
            dr.vRange = vec2<f32>(0.0, 5.0);
            dr.xRange = vec2<f32>(-2.71, 2.71);
            dr.yRange = vec2<f32>(-0.7071,0.7071);
            dr.zRange = vec2<f32>(-2.707, 2.707);
    } else if (funcSelection == 4u) { // bohemian dome
            dr.uRange = vec2<f32>(0.0, 2.0*pi);
            dr.vRange = vec2<f32>(0.0, 2.0*pi);
            dr.xRange = vec2<f32>(-0.7, 0.7);
            dr.yRange = vec2<f32>(-1.0, 1.0);
            dr.zRange = vec2<f32>(-1.7, 1.7);
    } else if (funcSelection == 5u) { // boy shape
            dr.uRange = vec2<f32>(0.0, pi);
            dr.vRange = vec2<f32>(0.0, pi);
            dr.xRange = vec2<f32>(-1.383, 1.187);
            dr.yRange = vec2<f32>(-1.0, 1.0);
            dr.zRange = vec2<f32>(-0.964, 1.469);
    } else if (funcSelection == 6u) { // breather
            dr.uRange = vec2<f32>(-14.0, 14.0);
            dr.vRange = vec2<f32>(-12.0*pi, 12.0*pi);
            dr.xRange = vec2<f32>(-9.0, 9.0);
            dr.yRange = vec2<f32>(-4.984, 4.998);
            dr.zRange = vec2<f32>(-4.946, 4.946);
    } else if (funcSelection == 7u) { // enneper
            dr.uRange = vec2<f32>(-3.3, 3.3);
            dr.vRange = vec2<f32>(-3.3, 3.3);
            dr.xRange = vec2<f32>(-27.258, 27.258);
            dr.yRange = vec2<f32>(-10.8898, 10.8898);
            dr.zRange = vec2<f32>(-27.258, 27.258);
    } else if (funcSelection == 8u) { // figure 8
            dr.uRange = vec2<f32>(0.0, 4.0*pi);
            dr.vRange = vec2<f32>(0.0, 2.0*pi);
            dr.xRange = vec2<f32>(-3.517, 3.5);
            dr.yRange = vec2<f32>(-1.25, 1.25);
            dr.zRange = vec2<f32>(-3.745, 3.745);
    } else if (funcSelection == 9u) { // Henneberg
            dr.uRange = vec2<f32>(0.0, 1.0);
            dr.vRange = vec2<f32>(0.0, 2.0*pi);
            dr.xRange = vec2<f32>(-3.942, 3.944);
            dr.yRange = vec2<f32>(-3.762, 3.763);
            dr.zRange = vec2<f32>(-4.514, 4.514);
    } else if (funcSelection == 10u) { // kiss
            dr.uRange = vec2<f32>(-0.9999, 0.9999);
            dr.vRange = vec2<f32>(0.0, 2.0 * pi);
            dr.xRange = vec2<f32>(-1.383, 1.383);
            dr.yRange = vec2<f32>(-1.0, 1.0);
```

```
        dr.zRange = vec2<f32>(-1.383, 1.383);
} else if (funcSelection == 11u) { // klein-bottle 2
        dr.uRange = vec2<f32>(0.0, 2.0 * pi);
        dr.vRange = vec2<f32>(0.0, 2.0 * pi);
        dr.xRange = vec2<f32>(-13.1, 9.761);
        dr.yRange = vec2<f32>(-16.0, 20.1);
        dr.zRange = vec2<f32>(-6.0, 6.0);
} else if (funcSelection == 12u) { // klein-bottle 3
        dr.uRange = vec2<f32>(0.0, 4.0 * pi);
        dr.vRange = vec2<f32>(0.0, 2.0 * pi);
        dr.xRange = vec2<f32>(-9.055, 9.055);
        dr.yRange = vec2<f32>(-1.25, 1.25);
        dr.zRange = vec2<f32>(-9.127, 9.127);
} else if (funcSelection == 13u) { // kuen
        dr.uRange = vec2<f32>(-4.5, 4.5);
        dr.vRange = vec2<f32>(-5.0, 5.0);
        dr.xRange = vec2<f32>(-1.025, 2.0);
        dr.yRange = vec2<f32>(-3.0, 3.0);
        dr.zRange = vec2<f32>(-1.063, 1.063);
} else if (funcSelection == 14u) { // minimal
        dr.uRange = vec2<f32>(-8.2, 8.2);
        dr.vRange = vec2<f32>(-2.2, 2.2);
        dr.xRange = vec2<f32>(-9.39, 9.39);
        dr.yRange = vec2<f32>(-5.342, 5.342);
        dr.zRange = vec2<f32>(-3.57, 5.566);
} else if (funcSelection == 15u) { // parabolic cyclide
        dr.uRange = vec2<f32>(-5.0, 5.0);
        dr.vRange = vec2<f32>(-5.5, 5.5);
        dr.xRange = vec2<f32>(-2.5, 2.5);
        dr.yRange = vec2<f32>(-0.231, 0.734);
        dr.zRange = vec2<f32>(-2.734, 2.734);
} else if (funcSelection == 16u) { // pear
        dr.uRange = vec2<f32>(0.0, 1.0);
        dr.vRange = vec2<f32>(0.0, 2.0 * pi);
        dr.xRange = vec2<f32>(-0.325, 0.325);
        dr.yRange = vec2<f32>(-1.0, 0.0);
        dr.zRange = vec2<f32>(-0.325, 0.325);
} else if (funcSelection == 17u) { // plucker conoid
        dr.uRange = vec2<f32>(-2.0, 2.0);
        dr.vRange = vec2<f32>(0.0, 2.0 * pi);
        dr.xRange = vec2<f32>(-4.0, 4.0);
        dr.yRange = vec2<f32>(-2.0, 2.0);
        dr.zRange = vec2<f32>(-4.0, 4.0);
} else if (funcSelection == 18u) { // seashell
        dr.uRange = vec2<f32>(0.0, 6.0 * pi);
        dr.vRange = vec2<f32>(0.0, 2.0 * pi);
        dr.xRange = vec2<f32>(-3.012, 2.245);
        dr.yRange = vec2<f32>(-8.108, 0.0);
        dr.zRange = vec2<f32>(-3.437, 2.613);
} else if (funcSelection == 19u) { // sievert-enneper
        dr.uRange = vec2<f32>(-pi / 2.1, pi / 2.1);
        dr.vRange = vec2<f32>(0.001, pi / 1.001);
        dr.xRange = vec2<f32>(-0.00142, 2.829);
        dr.yRange = vec2<f32>(-0.917, 0.917);
        dr.zRange = vec2<f32>(-5.6, 4.458);
} else if (funcSelection == 20u) { // steiner
        dr.uRange = vec2<f32>(0.0, 1.999999*pi);
        dr.vRange = vec2<f32>(0.0, 1.999999*pi);
        dr.xRange = vec2<f32>(-0.5, 0.5);
        dr.yRange = vec2<f32>(-0.5, 0.5);
```

```
            dr.zRange = vec2<f32>(-0.5, 0.5);
        } else if (funcSelection == 21u) { // torus
            dr.uRange = vec2<f32>(0.0, 2.0 * pi);
            dr.vRange = vec2<f32>(0.0, 2.5 * pi);
            dr.xRange = vec2<f32>(-1.3, 1.3);
            dr.yRange = vec2<f32>(-0.3, 0.3);
            dr.zRange = vec2<f32>(-1.3, 1.3);
        } else if (funcSelection == 22u) { // wellenkugel
            dr.uRange = vec2<f32>(0.0, 14.5);
            dr.vRange = vec2<f32>(0.0, 5.2);
            dr.xRange = vec2<f32>(-14.171, 14.173);
            dr.yRange = vec2<f32>(-8.0, 10.626);
            dr.zRange = vec2<f32>(-14.172, 14.172);
        }
        return dr;
}

fn parametricSurfaceFunc(u:f32, v:f32, funcSelection:u32) -> vec3f {
    var pos = vec3(0.0, 0.0, 0.0);

    if (funcSelection == 0u) { // klein bottle
        pos = klein_bottle(u, v);
    } else if (funcSelection == 1u) { // astroid
        pos = astroid(u, v);
    } else if (funcSelection == 2u) { // astroid2
        pos = astroid2(u, v);
    } else if (funcSelection == 3u) { // astroidal torus
        pos = astroidal_torus(u, v);
    } else if (funcSelection == 4u) { // bohemian dome
        pos = bohemian_dome(u, v);
    } else if (funcSelection == 5u) { // boy shape
        pos = boy_shape(u, v);
    } else if (funcSelection == 6u) { // breather
        pos = breather(u, v);
    } else if (funcSelection == 7u) { // enneper
        pos = enneper(u, v);
    } else if (funcSelection == 8u) { // figure 8
        pos = figure8(u, v);
    } else if (funcSelection == 9u) { // henneberg
        pos = henneberg(u, v);
    } else if (funcSelection == 10u) { // kiss
        pos = kiss(u, v);
    } else if (funcSelection == 11u) { // klein-bottle 2
        pos = klein_bottle2(u, v);
    }
    else if (funcSelection == 12u) { // klein-bottle 3
        pos = klein_bottle3(u, v);
    } else if (funcSelection == 13u) { // kuen
        pos = kuen(u, v);
    } else if (funcSelection == 14u) { // minimal
        pos = minimal(u, v);
    } else if (funcSelection == 15u) { // parabolic cyclide
        pos = parabolic_cyclide(u, v);
    } else if (funcSelection == 16u) { // pear
        pos = pear(u, v);
    } else if (funcSelection == 17u) { // plucker conoid
        pos = plucker_conoid(u, v);
    } else if (funcSelection == 18u) { // seashell
        pos = seashell(u, v);
    } else if (funcSelection == 19u) { // sievert-enneper
```

```
        pos = sievert_enneper(u, v);
    } else if (funcSelection == 20u) { // steiner
        pos = steiner(u, v);
    } else if (funcSelection == 21u) { // torus
        pos = torus(u, v);
    } else if (funcSelection == 22u) { // wellenkugel
        pos = wellenkugel(u, v);
    }
    return pos;
}
```

The code above defines twenty-three parametric functions, including certain well-known functions such as the Klein bottle, figure-8, breather, Sievert-Enneper, and Wellenkugel. These functions will be used to create various parametric 3D surfaces. The *setDataRange* function is used to set the data ranges of these functions in both the parametric space and real-world space. Meanwhile, the *parametricSurfaceFunc* function is specifically designed to select one of these twenty-three parametric functions.

7.3.2 Compute Shader for Vertex Data

Create a new compute shader file called *parametric_surface_comp.wgsl* in the *examples/ch07/* folder and add the following code to it:

```
struct VertexData{
    position: vec4f,
    normal: vec4f,
    color: vec4f,
}

struct VertexDataArray{
    vertexDataArray: array<VertexData>,
}

struct ParametricSurfaceParams{
    resolution: u32,
    funcSelection: u32,
    colormapDirection: u32,
    colormapReverse: u32,
}

@group(0) @binding(0) var<storage, read_write> vda : VertexDataArray;
@group(0) @binding(1) var<storage, read_write> vda2 : VertexDataArray;
@group(0) @binding(2) var<storage> colormap: array<vec4f>;
@group(0) @binding(3) var<storage> colormap2: array<vec4f>;
@group(0) @binding(4) var<uniform> psp: ParametricSurfaceParams;

var<private> umin:f32;
var<private> umax:f32;
var<private> vmin:f32;
var<private> vmax:f32;
var<private> xmin:f32;
var<private> xmax:f32;
var<private> ymin:f32;
var<private> ymax:f32;
var<private> zmin:f32;
var<private> zmax:f32;
var<private> range:f32 = 1.0;
var<private> du:f32;
```

```
var<private> dv:f32;

fn getUv(id: vec3u) -> vec2f {
    var dr = getDataRange(psp.funcSelection);
    umin = dr.uRange[0];
    umax = dr.uRange[1];
    vmin = dr.vRange[0];
    vmax = dr.vRange[1];
    xmin = dr.xRange[0];
    xmax = dr.xRange[1];
    ymin = dr.yRange[0];
    ymax = dr.yRange[1];
    zmin = dr.zRange[0];
    zmax = dr.zRange[1];

    du = (umax - umin)/(f32(psp.resolution) - 1.0);
    dv = (vmax - vmin)/(f32(psp.resolution) - 1.0);
    var u = umin + f32(id.x) * du;
    var v = vmin + f32(id.y) * dv;
    return vec2(u, v);
}

fn normalizePoint(u:f32, v:f32) -> vec3f {
    var pos = parametricSurfaceFunc(u, v, psp.funcSelection);
    var distance = max(max(xmax - xmin, ymax - ymin), zmax - zmin);

    if(psp.colormapDirection == 0u){
        range = (xmax - xmin)/distance;
    } else if(psp.colormapDirection == 2u){
        range = (zmax - zmin)/distance;
    } else {
        range = (ymax - ymin)/distance;
    }

    pos.x = 2.0 * (pos.x - xmin)/(xmax - xmin) - 1.0;
    pos.y = 2.0 * (pos.y - ymin)/(ymax - ymin) - 1.0;
    pos.z = 2.0 * (pos.z - zmin)/(zmax - zmin) - 1.0;

    pos.x = pos.x * (xmax - xmin)/distance;
    pos.y = pos.y * (ymax - ymin)/distance;
    pos.z = pos.z * (zmax - zmin)/distance;

    return pos;
}

fn colorLerp(is_surface:bool, tmin:f32, tmax:f32, t:f32, colormapReverse:u32) -> vec4f{
    var t1 = t;
    if (t1 < tmin) {t1 = tmin;}
    if (t1 > tmax) {t1 = tmax;}
    var tn = (t1-tmin)/(tmax-tmin);

    if(colormapReverse >= 1u) {tn = 1.0 - tn;}

    var idx = u32(floor(10.0*tn));
    var color = vec4(0.0,0.0,0.0, 1.0);

    if(is_surface){
        if(f32(idx) == 10.0*tn) {
            color = colormap[idx];
        } else {
```

```
            var tn1 = (tn - 0.1*f32(idx))*10.0;
            var a = colormap[idx];
            var b = colormap[idx+1u];
            color.x = a.x + (b.x - a.x)*tn1;
            color.y = a.y + (b.y - a.y)*tn1;
            color.z = a.z + (b.z - a.z)*tn1;
        }
    } else {
        if(f32(idx) == 10.0*tn) {
            color = colormap2[idx];
        } else {
            var tn1 = (tn - 0.1*f32(idx))*10.0;
            var a = colormap2[idx];
            var b = colormap2[idx+1u];
            color.x = a.x + (b.x - a.x)*tn1;
            color.y = a.y + (b.y - a.y)*tn1;
            color.z = a.z + (b.z - a.z)*tn1;
        }
    }
    return color;
}


@compute @workgroup_size(8, 8, 1)
fn cs_main(@builtin(global_invocation_id) id : vec3u) {
    var i = id.x;
    var j = id.y;
    var idx = i + j * psp.resolution;
    var uv = getUv(id);

    var p0 = normalizePoint(uv.x, uv.y);

    // calculate normals
    let epsu = 0.01 * du;
    let epsv = 0.01 * dv;

    let nu = normalizePoint(uv.x + epsu, uv.y) - normalizePoint(uv.x - epsu, uv.y);
    let nv = normalizePoint(uv.x, uv.y + epsv) - normalizePoint(uv.x, uv.y - epsv);
    let normal = normalize(cross(nu, nv));

    // colormap
    var color = colorLerp(true, -range, range, p0[psp.colormapDirection], psp.colormapReverse);
    var color2 = colorLerp(false, -range, range, p0[psp.colormapDirection], psp.colormapReverse);

    // for surface
    vda.vertexDataArray[idx].position = vec4(p0, 1.0);
    vda.vertexDataArray[idx].normal = vec4(normal, 1.0);
    vda.vertexDataArray[idx].color = color;

    // for wireframe
    vda2.vertexDataArray[idx].position = vec4(p0, 1.0);
    vda2.vertexDataArray[idx].normal = vec4(normal, 1.0);
    vda2.vertexDataArray[idx].color = color2;
}
```

The compute shader responsible for vertex data generation closely resembles the previous simple-surface example. However, a key distinction lies in the usage of parametric variables, namely u and v, instead of x and z. The introduction of private variables, *umin*, *umax*, *vmin*, and *vmax*, defines data region in the parametric space.

In the parametric realm, a consistent *u-v* grid is established, featuring uniform intervals in the corresponding *u* and *v* dimensions. The input function *f(u, v)* is designed to yield, at most, one value for every combination of *u* and *v*. Creating a parametric surface entails a clever maneuver: the simple surface within the *u-v* space is mapped back to the *x-y-z* coordinate system via parametric equations. This ingenious technique transforms the resultant surface in the physical world into a unique entity, quite distinct from its counterpart in the parametric space.

Just as in the previous example, the *vda* and *vda2* buffers are populated with essential vertex data. This data encompasses crucial attributes including *position*, *normal*, and *color*. These buffers are poised to play a pivotal role in the generation of parametric 3D surfaces.

7.3.3 Rust Code

With the background presented in the previous sections, we are ready to create parametric 3D surfaces using compute shaders. To do so, add a new Rust file called *parametric_surface.rs* to the *examples/ch07/* folder.

The code above for this example is structurally similar to that used in the previous example on simple 3D surfaces. Here, I only list the different parts of the code:

```rust
// ... code identical to the previous example omitted for brevity

use wgpu_book_examples::{ wgpu_simplified as ws, transforms as wt, colormap,
    surface_data::get_surface_type };


struct State {

    // ... code identical to the previous example omitted for brevity

    rng: ThreadRng,
    t0: std::time::Instant,
    random_shape_change: u32,
    data_changed: bool,
    fps_counter: ws::FpsCounter,
}

impl State {
    async fn new(window:&Window, sample_count:u32, resolution:u32, colormap_name:&str,
    wireframe_color:&str) -> Self {

        //let init = ws::IWgpuInit::new(&window, sample_count, None).await;

        let limits = wgpu::Limits {
            max_storage_buffer_binding_size: 1024*1024*1024, //1024 MB, defaulting to 128MB
            max_buffer_size: 1024*1024*1024, // 1024MB, defaulting to 256MB
            max_compute_invocations_per_workgroup: 512, // dafaulting to 256
            ..Default::default()
        };
        let init = ws::IWgpuInit::new(&window, sample_count, Some(limits)).await;

        let vs_shader = init.device.create_shader_module(wgpu::include_wgsl!("../ch05/shader_vert.wgsl"));
        let fs_shader = init.device.create_shader_module(wgpu::include_wgsl!("../ch05/shader_frag.wgsl"));

        let cs_surface_func_file = include_str!("parametric_surface_func.wgsl");
        let cs_surface_file = include_str!("parametric_surface_comp.wgsl");
        let cs_comp_file = [cs_surface_func_file, cs_surface_file].join("\n");
```

```rust
let cs_comp = init.device.create_shader_module(wgpu::ShaderModuleDescriptor {
    label: Some("Compute Shader"),
    source: wgpu::ShaderSource::Wgsl(cs_comp_file.into()),
});

let cs_indices = init.device.create_shader_module(wgpu::include_wgsl!("indices_comp.wgsl"));

// uniform data

// ... code identical to the previous example omitted for brevity

// create compute pipeline for indices

// ... code identical to the previous example omitted for brevity

// create compute pipeline for simple surface

// ... code identical to the previous example omitted for brevity

    Self {

        // ... code identical to the previous example omitted for brevity

        rng: rand::thread_rng(),
        t0:  std::time::Instant::now(),
        random_shape_change: 1,
        data_changed: false,
        fps_counter: ws::FpsCounter::default(),
    }
}

fn resize(&mut self, new_size: winit::dpi::PhysicalSize<u32>) {

    // ... code identical to the previous example omitted for brevity

}

#[allow(unused_variables)]
fn input(&mut self, event: &WindowEvent) -> bool {
    match event {
        WindowEvent::KeyboardInput {
            input:
                KeyboardInput {
                    virtual_keycode: Some(keycode),
                    state: ElementState::Pressed,
                    ..
                },
            ..
        } => {
            match keycode {
                VirtualKeyCode::Space => {
                    self.plot_type = (self.plot_type + 1) % 3;
                    true
                }
                VirtualKeyCode::LControl => {
                    self.surface_type = (self.surface_type + 1) % 23;
                    self.data_changed = true;
                    true
                },
```

```rust
                    VirtualKeyCode::LShift => {
                        self.colormap_direction = (self.colormap_direction + 1) % 3;
                        self.data_changed = true;
                        true
                    },
                    VirtualKeyCode::LAlt => {
                        self.random_shape_change = (self.random_shape_change + 1) % 2;
                        true
                    },
                    VirtualKeyCode::RControl => {
                        self.colormap_reverse = if self.colormap_reverse == 0 { 1 } else { 0 };
                        self.data_changed = true;
                        true
                    },
                    VirtualKeyCode::Q => {
                        self.rotation_speed += 0.1;
                        true
                    },
                    VirtualKeyCode::A => {
                        self.rotation_speed -= 0.1;
                        if self.rotation_speed < 0.0 {
                            self.rotation_speed = 0.0;
                        }
                        true
                    },
                    _ => false
                }
            }
            _ => false,
        }
    }

    fn update(&mut self, dt: std::time::Duration) {
        // update uniform buffer

        // ... code identical to the previous example omitted for brevity

        // change surface type for every 5 seconds
        let elapsed = self.t0.elapsed();
        if elapsed >= std::time::Duration::from_secs(5) && self.random_shape_change == 1 {
            self.surface_type = self.rng.gen_range(0..=22) as u32;
            let params = [self.resolution, self.surface_type, self.colormap_direction,
                self.colormap_reverse];
            self.init.queue.write_buffer(&self.cs_uniform_buffers[1], 0, cast_slice(&params));
            self.t0 = std::time::Instant::now();
            println!("key = {:?}, surface_type = {:?}", self.surface_type,
                get_surface_type(self.surface_type));
        }

        // update buffers for compute pipeline
        if self.data_changed {
            let params = [
                self.resolution,
                self.surface_type,
                self.colormap_direction,
                self.colormap_reverse
            ];
            self.init.queue.write_buffer(&self.cs_uniform_buffers[1], 0, bytemuck::cast_slice(&params));
            self.data_changed = false;
            println!("key = {:?}, surface_type = {:?}", self.surface_type,
```

```
                get_surface_type(self.surface_type));
        }
    }

    fn render(&mut self) -> Result<(), wgpu::SurfaceError> {

        // ... code identical to the previous example omitted for brevity

    }

fn main() {
    // ... code identical to the previous example omitted for brevity

    window.set_title(&*format!("ch07_{}", "parametric_surface"));

    // ... code identical to the previous example omitted for brevity
}
```

Diverging from the previous example, this code introduces the utilization of the *get_surface_type* method sourced from the *surface_data* module. This method will be used to extract a surface type name via an integer key. Moreover, the *State* struct is augmented with several new fields, tailored to the realm of parametric surfaces.

Within the *State::new* function, we amalgamate two distinct compute shader files, namely *parametric_ surface_func.wgsl* and *parametric_surface_comp.wgsl*, to construct the shader module for the compute pipeline primarily responsible for vertex data generation. It is worth noting that the code for generating uniform buffers, uniform bind groups, and compute pipelines mirrors that of the prior example. For the sake of brevity, we have omitted this code here.

Another distinction from the preceding example manifests within the *State::update* function. Here, a specific condition, denoted by *self.random_shape_change* = 1, triggers a notable behavior. When this condition is met, the subsequent code block engages to update the uniform buffers at 5-second intervals:

```
// change surface type for every 5 seconds
let elapsed = self.t0.elapsed();
if elapsed >= std::time::Duration::from_secs(5) && self.random_shape_change == 1 {
    self.surface_type = self.rng.gen_range(0..=22) as u32;
    let params = [self.resolution, self.surface_type, self.colormap_direction, self.colormap_reverse];
    self.init.queue.write_buffer(&self.cs_uniform_buffers[1], 0, bytemuck::cast_slice(&params));
    self.t0 = std::time::Instant::now();
    println!("key = {:?}, surface_type = {:?}", self.surface_type,
        get_surface_type(self.surface_type));
}
```

In this code snippet, a new surface type is selected at random, thereby instigating the generation of fresh parameter data tailored to the chosen surface. Subsequently, this data is inscribed into the uniform buffers. Additionally, this action prompts the display of the selected surface type and its corresponding name in the terminal.

Conversely, when *self.random_shape_change* does not equal 1, a scenario attainable through the *LAlt* key, you then possess the ability to manually alter the surface type using the *LControl* key.

Additionally, the code permits the user to modify input parameters using keyboard inputs.

Here is a list of controls using keyboard:

- *Space*: Changes the plot type: surface, wireframe, or both.

- *LControl*: Changes the surface type when *random_shape_change* != 1.

- *LShift*: Changes colormap direction: x, y, or z.
- *LAlt*: Changes the *random_shape_change* value between 0 and 1.
- *Q/A:* Increases/decreases the rotation speed.

7.3.4 Run Application

To run this application, add the following code snippet to the *Cargo.toml* file:

```
[[example]]
name = "ch07_parametric_surface"
path = "examples/ch07/parametric_surface.rs"
```

Afterward, execute the following *cargo run* commands in the terminal window:

```
cargo run --example ch07_parametric_surface 8 1000
```

Fig.7-3 shows the result of this example, where the Wellenkugel surface is selected.

You can play around with this example by choosing different parametric surfaces. You can also customize the surface by changing other parameters, such as colormap, plot type, and wireframe color.

Fig.7-3. Wellenkugel surface created using compute shaders.

7.4 Super Shapes

The super-shape or super-formula is a mathematical formula that can be used to generate a wide variety of complex shapes and patterns. In polar coordinates, the super-shape equation is defined as follows:

$$r(\phi) = \left(\left| \frac{\cos\left(\frac{m\phi}{4}\right)}{a} \right|^{n_2} + \left| \frac{\sin\left(\frac{m\phi}{4}\right)}{b} \right|^{n_3} \right)^{-\frac{1}{n_1}}$$

Where r is the radial distance from the origin, ϕ is the angle, and a, b, m, n_1, n_2, and n_3 are parameters that can be adjusted to create different shapes. The super-formula can be used to create shapes that resemble animals, shells, and other natural forms, as well as more abstract shapes.

It is possible to extend the super-shape equation to higher dimensions such as 3, 4, or n dimensions by using the spherical product of super-formulas. For example, the 3D parametric surface can be obtained by multiplying two super-formulas r_1 and r_2. The coordinates are defined by the relations:

$$x = r_1(\theta)\cos\theta \cdot r_2(\phi)\cos\phi$$
$$y = r_1(\theta)\sin\theta \cdot r_2(\phi)\cos\phi$$
$$z = r_2(\phi)\sin\phi$$

Where $-\frac{\pi}{2} \le \phi \le \frac{\pi}{2}$ and $-\pi \le \theta \le \pi$.

In this section, we will use compute shaders to implement super-shapes in 3D dimension.

7.4.1 Compute Shader for Vertex Data

This example can still reuse the vertex and fragment shaders implemented in Chapter 5, as well as the compute shader for indices from the previous example. The only shader we need to code is the compute shader for generating the vertex data of the super-shapes. To achieve this, create a new compute shader file named *super_shape_comp.wgsl* in the *examples/ch07/* folder and add the following code to it:

```
const pi:f32 = 3.14159265359;
struct VertexData{
    position: vec4f,
    normal: vec4f,
    color: vec4f,
}

struct VertexDataArray{
    vertexDataArray: array<VertexData>,
}

struct SuperShapeParams {
    n1:vec4f,
    n2:vec4f,
    a1:vec2f,
    a2:vec2f,
    resolution: f32,
    colormapDirection: f32,
    colormapReverse: f32,
    animationTime: f32,
    scaling:f32,
    aspectRatio: f32,
}

@group(0) @binding(0) var<storage, read_write> vda : VertexDataArray;
@group(0) @binding(1) var<storage, read_write> vda2 : VertexDataArray;
@group(0) @binding(2) var<storage> colormap: array<vec4f>;
```

```
@group(0) @binding(3) var<storage> colormap2: array<vec4f>;
@group(0) @binding(4) var<uniform> ssp: SuperShapeParams;

var<private> umin:f32;
var<private> umax:f32;
var<private> vmin:f32;
var<private> vmax:f32;
var<private> du:f32;
var<private> dv:f32;

fn superShape3D(u:f32, v:f32, t:f32, n1:vec4f, n2:vec4f, a1:vec2f, a2:vec2f) -> vec3f {
    var raux1 = pow(abs(1.0 / a1.x * cos(n1.x * u /4.0)), n1.z) +
        pow(abs(1.0 / a1.y * sin(n1.x * u /4.0)), n1.w);
    var r1 = pow(abs(raux1), -1.0 / n1.y);
    var raux2 = pow(abs(1.0 / a2.x * cos(n2.x * v /4.0)), n2.z) +
        pow(abs(1.0 / a2.y * sin(n2.x * v /4.0)), n2.w);
    var r2 = pow(abs(raux2), -1.0 / n2.y);

    var a = 0.334*(2.0 + sin(t));
    var v1 = v*a;
    var x = r1 * cos(u) * r2 * cos(v1);
    var y = r2 * sin(v1);
    var z = r1 * sin(u) * r2 * cos(v1);
    return vec3(x, y, z);
}
fn getUv(id: vec3u) -> vec2f {
    umin = -pi;
    umax = pi;
    vmin = -0.5*pi;
    vmax = 0.5*pi;

    du = (umax - umin)/(f32(ssp.resolution) - 1.0);
    dv = (vmax - vmin)/(f32(ssp.resolution) - 1.0);
    var u = umin + f32(id.x) * du;
    var v = vmin + f32(id.y) * dv;
    return vec2(u, v);
}

fn normalizePoint(u:f32, v:f32) -> vec3f {
    var t = ssp.animationTime;
    var pos = superShape3D(u, v, t, ssp.n1, ssp.n2, ssp.a1, ssp.a2);
    pos.y = pos.y*ssp.aspectRatio;
    return pos*ssp.scaling;
}

fn colorLerp(is_surface:bool, tmin:f32, tmax:f32, t:f32, colormapReverse:u32) -> vec4f{
    var t1 = t;
    if (t1 < tmin) {t1 = tmin;}
    if (t1 > tmax) {t1 = tmax;}
    var tn = (t1-tmin)/(tmax-tmin);

    if(colormapReverse >= 1u) {tn = 1.0 - tn;}

    var idx = u32(floor(10.0*tn));
    var color = vec4(0.0,0.0,0.0, 1.0);

    if(is_surface){
        if(f32(idx) == 10.0*tn) {
            color = colormap[idx];
        } else {
```

```
                var tn1 = (tn - 0.1*f32(idx))*10.0;
                var a = colormap[idx];
                var b = colormap[idx+1u];
                color.x = a.x + (b.x - a.x)*tn1;
                color.y = a.y + (b.y - a.y)*tn1;
                color.z = a.z + (b.z - a.z)*tn1;
            }
        } else {
            if(f32(idx) == 10.0*tn) {
                color = colormap2[idx];
            } else {
                var tn1 = (tn - 0.1*f32(idx))*10.0;
                var a = colormap2[idx];
                var b = colormap2[idx+1u];
                color.x = a.x + (b.x - a.x)*tn1;
                color.y = a.y + (b.y - a.y)*tn1;
                color.z = a.z + (b.z - a.z)*tn1;
            }
        }
    }
    return color;
}


@compute @workgroup_size(8, 8, 1)
fn cs_main(@builtin(global_invocation_id) id : vec3u) {
    var i = id.x;
    var j = id.y;
    var idx = i + j * u32(ssp.resolution);
    var uv = getUv(id);

    var p0 = normalizePoint(uv.x, uv.y);

    // calculate normals
    let epsu = 0.01 * du;
    let epsv = 0.01 * dv;

    let nx = normalizePoint(uv.x + epsu, uv.y) - normalizePoint(uv.x - epsu, uv.y);
    let nz = normalizePoint(uv.x, uv.y + epsv) - normalizePoint(uv.x, uv.y - epsv);
    let normal = normalize(cross(nx, nz));

    // colormap
    var range = 1.0;
    if(ssp.colormapDirection == 1.0){
        range = ssp.aspectRatio;
    }
    let color = colorLerp(true, -range, range, p0[u32(ssp.colormapDirection)], u32(ssp.colormapReverse));
    let color2 = colorLerp(false, -range, range, p0[u32(ssp.colormapDirection)],
        u32(ssp.colormapReverse));

    // for surface
    vda.vertexDataArray[idx].position = vec4(p0, 1.0);
    vda.vertexDataArray[idx].normal = vec4(normal, 1.0);
    vda.vertexDataArray[idx].color = color;

    // for wireframe
    vda2.vertexDataArray[idx].position = vec4(p0, 1.0);
    vda2.vertexDataArray[idx].normal = vec4(normal, 1.0);
    vda2.vertexDataArray[idx].color = color2;
}
```

The *VertexData* struct within the provided code delineates the vertex data that is generated for each vertex, encompassing attributes such as *position*, *normal*, and *color*. Meanwhile, the *VertexDataArray* struct constructs a dynamic array employing the *VertexData* struct. This array serves as a repository for the vertex data pertinent to 3D super-shapes. Moreover, the *SuperShapeParams* struct furnishes a collection of parameters pivotal in generating the said vertex data.

The *superShape3D* function implements a super-shape using the super-formula. Within this function, *n1* of *vec4f* type and *a1* of *vec2f* type are employed to symbolize the parameters for r_1, specifically $\vec{n1} = (m, n1, n2, n3)$ and $\vec{a1} = (a, b)$. A parallel approach is taken for r_2, utilizing *n2* of *vec4f* type and *a2* of *vec2f* type. The *superShape3D* function also incorporates the *t* argument, instrumental in animating the super-shape.

The *getUv* function's role is in calculating the *u* and *v* coordinates within the square grid in the parametric space. These coordinates subsequently contribute to the creation of 3D super-shapes. In contrast, the *normalizePoint* function facilitates a simple *y*-component scaling operation via the aspect ratio. It is important to note that within the *normalizePoint* function, data normalization is not performed, as the data values intrinsic to super-shapes are inherently confined within the $[-1, 1]$ range.

Unfolding akin to the prior example, the *cs_main* function remains unchanged. Here, the *vda* and *vda2* buffers are furnished with pivotal vertex data. This dataset encompasses critical attributes such as *position*, *normal*, and *color*. These buffers stand poised to undertake a crucial role in the intricate process of 3D super shape generation.

7.4.2 Rust Code

With the background presented in the previous section, we are ready to create 3D super-shapes using compute shaders. To do so, add a new Rust file called *super_shape.rs* to the *examples/ch07/* folder and add the following code to it:

```
// ... code identical to the previous example omitted for brevity

struct State {

    // ... code identical to the previous example omitted for brevity

    n1: Vec<f32>,
    n2: Vec<f32>,
    a1: Vec<f32>,
    a2: Vec<f32>,
    scale: f32,
    aspect_ratio: f32,
}

impl State {
    async fn new(window:&Window, sample_count:u32, resolution:u32, colormap_name:&str,
    wireframe_color:&str) -> Self {
        let init = ws::IWgpuInit::new(&window, sample_count, None).await;

        let vs_shader = init.device.create_shader_module(wgpu::include_wgsl!("../ch05/shader_vert.wgsl"));
        let fs_shader = init.device.create_shader_module(wgpu::include_wgsl!("../ch05/shader_frag.wgsl"));
        let cs_comp = init.device.create_shader_module(wgpu::include_wgsl!("super_shape_comp.wgsl"));
        let cs_indices = init.device.create_shader_module(wgpu::include_wgsl!("indices_comp.wgsl"));

        // uniform data
```

```rust
// ... code identical to the previous example omitted for brevity

// create compute pipeline for indices

// ... code identical to the previous example omitted for brevity

// create compute pipeline for surface

// ... code identical to the previous example omitted for brevity
let params = [
    7.0f32, 0.2, 1.7, 1.7,   // n1
    7.0, 0.2, 1.7, 1.7,      // n2
    1.0, 1.0, 1.0, 1.0,      // a1, a2
    resol as f32, 1.0, 0.0, 0.0, 1.2, 1.0,
    0.0, 0.0    // padding
];

let cs_vertex_uniform_buffer = init.device.create_buffer_init(&wgpu::util::BufferInitDescriptor{
    label: Some("Vertex Uniform Buffer"),
    contents: bytemuck::cast_slice(&params),
    usage: wgpu::BufferUsages::UNIFORM | wgpu::BufferUsages::COPY_DST,
});

// ... code identical to the previous example omitted for brevity

Self {

    // ... code identical to the previous example omitted for brevity

    n1: params[0..4].to_vec(),
    n2: params[4..8].to_vec(),
    a1: params[8..10].to_vec(),
    a2: params[10..12].to_vec(),
    scale: params[16],
    aspect_ratio: params[17],
    }
}

fn resize(&mut self, new_size: winit::dpi::PhysicalSize<u32>) {

    // ... code identical to the previous example omitted for brevity

}

#[allow(unused_variables)]
fn input(&mut self, event: &WindowEvent) -> bool {
    match event {
        WindowEvent::KeyboardInput {
            input:
                KeyboardInput {
                    virtual_keycode: Some(keycode),
                    state: ElementState::Pressed,
                    ..
                },
            ..
        } => {
            match keycode {
                VirtualKeyCode::Space => {
                    self.plot_type = (self.plot_type + 1) % 3;
                    true
```

```
        }
        VirtualKeyCode::LControl => {
            self.surface_type = (self.surface_type + 1) % 9;
            self.scale = 1.0;
            if self.surface_type == 0 {
                self.n1 = [7.0, 0.2, 1.7, 1.7].to_vec();
                self.n2 = [7.0, 0.2, 1.7, 1.7].to_vec();
            } else if self.surface_type == 1 {
                self.n1 = [0.0, 1.0, 1.0, 1.0].to_vec();
                self.n2 = [0.0, 1.0, 1.0, 1.0].to_vec();
            } else if self.surface_type == 2 {
                self.n1 = [4.0, 1.0, 1.0, 1.0].to_vec();
                self.n2 = [4.0, 1.0, 1.0, 1.0].to_vec();
            } else if self.surface_type == 3 {
                self.n1 = [6.0, 1.0, 1.0, 1.0].to_vec();
                self.n2 = [3.0, 1.0, 1.0, 1.0].to_vec();
            } else if self.surface_type == 4 {
                self.n1 = [5.0, 0.1, 1.7, 1.7].to_vec();
                self.n2 = [1.0, 0.3, 0.5, 0.5].to_vec();
            } else if self.surface_type == 5 {
                self.n1 = [6.0, 0.25, 47.6, -0.66].to_vec();
                self.n2 = [7.0, -77.0, 0.52, -56.7].to_vec();
                self.scale = 0.5;
            } else if self.surface_type == 6 {
                self.n1 = [0.0, 0.48, 30.25, 0.35].to_vec();
                self.n2 = [5.0, 15.4, -0.45, 97.0].to_vec();
            } else if self.surface_type == 7 {
                self.n1 = [2.0, 1.0, 97.7, -0.44].to_vec();
                self.n2 = [7.0, -8.1, -0.09, 93.0].to_vec();
            } else if self.surface_type == 8 {
                self.n1 = [6.0, 0.77, 52.3, -0.2].to_vec();
                self.n2 = [5.0, 37.7, 0.53, -19.0].to_vec();
            }
            println!("i = {}, n1 = {:?}, n2 = {:?}", self.surface_type, self.n1, self.n2);
            true
        },
        VirtualKeyCode::LShift => {
            self.colormap_direction = (self.colormap_direction + 1) % 3;
            true
        },
        VirtualKeyCode::LAlt => {
            self.colormap_reverse = if self.colormap_reverse == 0 { 1 } else { 0 };
            true
        },
        VirtualKeyCode::Q => {
            self.animation_speed += 0.1;
            true
        },
        VirtualKeyCode::A => {
            self.animation_speed -= 0.1;
            if self.animation_speed < 0.0 {
                self.animation_speed = 0.0;
            }
            true
        } ,
        VirtualKeyCode::W => {
            self.rotation_speed += 0.1;
            true
        },
        VirtualKeyCode::S => {
```

```
                    self.rotation_speed -= 0.1;
                    if self.rotation_speed < 0.0 {
                        self.rotation_speed = 0.0;
                    }
                    true
                } ,
                _ => false
            }
        }
        _ => false,
    }
}

fn update(&mut self, dt: std::time::Duration) {
    // update uniform buffer

    // ... code identical to the previous example omitted for brevity

    // update buffers for compute pipeline
    let params = [
        self.n1[0], self.n1[1], self.n1[2], self.n1[3],
        self.n2[0], self.n2[1], self.n2[2], self.n2[3],
        self.a1[0], self.a1[1], self.a2[0], self.a2[1],
        self.resolution as f32,
        self.colormap_direction as f32,
        self.colormap_reverse as f32,
        self.animation_speed * dt.as_secs_f32(),
        self.scale,
        self.aspect_ratio,
    ];
    self.init.queue.write_buffer(&self.cs_uniform_buffers[1], 0, bytemuck::cast_slice(&params));
}

fn render(&mut self) -> Result<(), wgpu::SurfaceError> {

 // ... code identical to the previous example omitted for brevity

}
}

fn main() {

    // ... code identical to the previous example omitted for brevity

    window.set_title(&*format!("ch07_{}", "super_shape"));

    // ... code identical to the previous example omitted for brevity
}
```

The code above for this example is structurally similar to that used in previous examples on 3D surfaces. Hence, we do not list the identical code segments for brevity. The code for the creation of compute pipeline for vertex data generation is also similar to that used in previous examples, except that the parameter buffer is created using the parameters for the super-shapes.

Within the *State::input* function, users can define two parameter sets by triggering the *LControl* key. Each set comprises four parameters (m, $n1$, $n2$, $n3$), with the remaining parameters, a and b, being set to 1. These parameters are integral in crafting the distinct super shapes. The default values for these two parameter sets align, both featuring the values (7, 0.2, 1.7, 1.7). By manipulating these parameter sets, a diverse array of super shapes can be crafted. To facilitate this, nine predefined surface types are provided, each equipped with two parameter sets catering to the creation of specific super shape. Through continuous *LControl* key presses, users can seamlessly navigate across these various super shapes.

Additionally, the code permits the user to modify the other input parameters using keyboard inputs.

Here is a list of controls using keyboard:

- *Space*: Changes the plot type: surface, wireframe, or both.
- *LControl*: Changes the surface type.
- *LShift*: Changes colormap direction: *x*, *y*, or *z*.
- *LAlt*: Triggers whether colormap reverses or not.
- *Q/A:* Increases/decreases the animation speed.
- *W/S:* Increases/decreases the rotation speed.

7.4.3 Run Application

To run this application, add the following code snippet to the *Cargo.toml* file:

```
[[example]]
name = "ch07_super_shape"
path = "examples/ch07/super_shape.rs"
```

Afterward, execute the following *cargo run* commands in the terminal window:

```
cargo run --example ch07_super_shape 8
```

Fig.7-4 shows the results of this example, where various super-shapes are displayed by changing surface types using the *LControl* key.

It is evident from the figure that we can use the 3D super-shape equation to create various 3D graphics objects, including basic shapes such as spheres, diamonds, and cones, as shown in Fig.7-4 (a)-(c), and other complex 3D surfaces, as displayed in Fig.7-4 (d)-(i).

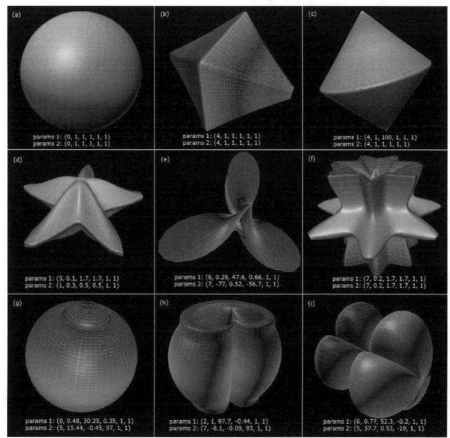

Fig.7-4. Super-shapes generated using compute shaders.

8 Procedural Terrains

Terrain refers to the generation and rendering of 3D landscapes or environments, which can range from realistic representations of real-world locations to completely fictional worlds. It is widely used in a variety of applications, including video games, virtual reality, movies, and simulation software. In particular, terrain in video games is often a crucial component of the game world, providing players with a sense of exploration and immersion.

Game engines like Unity and Unreal Engine provide tools that let you create and edit terrain objects. The process typically involves sculpting the terrain and populating it with objects such as textures, trees, rocks, water, and grass. The advantage of this manual approach is the ability to create highly detailed and precise terrain that can be customized to meet specific design goals. However, manually creating terrain can also be time-consuming and resource-intensive, requiring a significant amount of effort.

On the other hand, procedural terrain refers to the generation of terrain using mathematical algorithms. Procedural terrain algorithms can generate vast and diverse landscapes without the need for manually creating each individual part of the terrain. This is much more efficient than manually creating and editing the terrain as the algorithms can generate the terrain automatically, reducing the time and resources required for development. Furthermore, procedural terrain can be modified and adjusted easily by tuning a few parameters, allowing developers to quickly iterate on their designs and make changes without having to manually edit the terrain. Another advantage of procedural terrain is that it can ensure a consistent level of detail and quality across the entire terrain. Additionally, procedural terrain can be designed to mimic real-world environments, with realistic features such as mountains, valleys, and rivers. This can enhance the realism and immersion of the game or simulation.

In this chapter, I will explain the process of creating procedural terrains in *wgpu* using a noise model, which is a popular technique used in game development and other applications, and how to use terrain chunks and level of detail techniques to improve performance and manage memory. Furthermore, I will illustrate how compute shaders on the GPU can improve the process of terrain generation.

8.1 Noise Model

So far in this book, I have demonstrated how to create various 3D objects that have a smooth-looking surface. However, in some cases, such as the terrain in video games, we want to create objects that look more realistic by simulating the imperfections of real surfaces. Most effects and patterns in nature exhibit a certain degree of randomness and non-linearity. One way to simulate this randomness is by using random data generated from a pseudo-random number generator. However, this approach can result in a surface that appears too uniform or has abrupt changes, which is not suitable for creating natural-looking terrain.

To create a natural-looking terrain, we actually need a surface that is continuous but still gives the appearance of randomness. Purely random data does not have this continuity property. Therefore, we need a more sophisticated technique to generate terrain that mimic the natural environment.

8.1.1 Perlin Noise

Perlin noise is a type of procedural noise commonly used to generate natural-looking patterns. It works by generating a grid of random gradient vectors and then interpolating between those vectors to create a smooth, continuous noise function.

In Rust, the *noise* crate provides implementation of the Perlin noise function in multiple dimensions (1D, 2D, 3D, and 4D), which can be used to generate coherent and natural-looking procedural noise. Here, we will use this crate to create our procedural terrains. You can install the crate by adding it to the *dependencies* in the *Cargo.toml* file:

```
[dependencies]
noise = "0.8"
```

In the *noise* crate, you can easily use the *noise::Perlin* struct to create a Perlin noise generator. This struct provides methods to generate Perlin noise values. Here is an example of how you might use it to generate 2D noise:

```
use noise::{ NoiseFn, Perlin };

fn main() {
    let perlin = Perlin::new(1232);
    let noise_value = perlin.get([x, y]); // Replace x, y with your coordinates
    println!("Perlin Noise Value: {}", noise_value);
}
```

Note that you can create Perlin noise in different dimensions based on the input coordinates you provided. For instance, if you provide a 1D input vector [x], you will get a noise value in 1D. If you provide a 2D input vector [x, y], you will get a noise value in 2D. Similarly, if you provide a 3D input vector [x, y, z], you will get a noise value in 3D.

We will use Perlin function in the *noise* crate for procedural terrain generation in the following sections.

8.1.2 Noise Map

In this section, we will use the Perlin function in the *noise* crate to generate a 2D noise map. To achieve this, create a new Rust file called *terrain_data.rs* file in the *src/* folder and add the following code to it:

```
use noise::{NoiseFn, Perlin};
use super::wgpu_simplified as ws;
use super::colormap;

pub struct ITerrain {
    pub width: u32,
    pub height: u32,
    pub seed: u32,
    pub octaves: u32,
    pub persistence: f32,
```

```
        pub lacunarity: f32,
        pub offsets: [f32; 2],
        pub water_level: f32,
        pub scale: f32,
        pub colormap_name: String,
        pub wireframe_color: String,
        pub chunk_size: u32,
        pub level_of_detail: u32,
        pub normalize_mode: String,
    }

    impl Default for ITerrain {
        fn default() -> Self {
            Self {
                width: 200,
                height: 200,
                seed: 1232,
                octaves: 5,
                persistence: 0.5,
                lacunarity: 2.0,
                offsets: [0.0, 0.0],
                water_level: 0.0,
                scale: 10.0,
                colormap_name: "terrain".to_string(),
                wireframe_color: "white".to_string(),
                chunk_size: 241,
                level_of_detail: 0,
                normalize_mode: "local".to_string(),
            }
        }
    }

    impl ITerrain {
        pub fn new() -> Self {
            Default::default()
        }

        fn create_noise_map(&mut self, width: u32, height: u32) -> Vec<Vec<f32>>{
            let rng = ws::seed_random_number(self.seed as u64);
            let perlin = Perlin::new(self.seed);

            let mut offsets:Vec<[f32;2]> = vec![];
            for _i in 0..self.octaves {
                let offsetx = 100000f32 * (2.0 * rng - 1.0) + self.offsets[0];
                let offsetz = 100000f32 * (2.0 * rng - 1.0) + self.offsets[1];
                offsets.push([offsetx, offsetz]);
            }

            let mut noise_map:Vec<Vec<f32>> = vec![];
            let mut height_min = f32::MAX;
            let mut height_max = f32::MIN;
            let halfw = 0.5 * width as f32;
            let halfh = 0.5 * height as f32;

            for x in 0..width {
                let mut p1:Vec<f32> = vec![];
                for z in 0..height {
                    let mut amplitude = 1f32;
                    let mut frequency = 1f32;
                    let mut noise_height = 0f32;
```

```
            for i in 0..self.octaves {
                let sample_x = (x as f32 - halfw + offsets[i as usize][0]) * frequency / self.scale;
                let sample_y = (z as f32 - halfh + offsets[i as usize][1]) * frequency / self.scale;
                let y = perlin.get([sample_x as f64, sample_y as f64]) as f32;
                noise_height += y * amplitude;
                amplitude *= self.persistence;
                frequency *= self.lacunarity;
            }
            height_min = if noise_height < height_min { noise_height } else { height_min };
            height_max = if noise_height > height_max { noise_height } else { height_max };
            p1.push(noise_height);
        }
        noise_map.push(p1);
    }

    if self.normalize_mode == "global" {
        height_min = -1.0;
        height_max = 1.0;
    }

    for x in 0..width as usize {
        for z in 0..height as usize {
            noise_map[x][z] = (noise_map[x][z] - height_min)/(height_max - height_min);
        }
    }

    noise_map
    }
}
```

The provided code begins by defining a struct called *ITerrain* that encompasses the input parameters required for generating procedural terrains. It then implements the *Default* trait for this struct, enabling the default initialization of its members. Following this, the code introduces the *create_noise_map* function for the *ITerrain* struct, which employs the Perlin noise algorithm to create a 2D noise map. This function accepts two arguments: the *width* and *height* of the noise map.

To initiate, the function defines offsets utilized to shift the noise function in different directions. By introducing random offsets to the *x* and *z* coordinates of the sample point within each octave, the noise function gains increased variation. In this context, the offsets are randomly generated through a seeded random number generator function, *ws::seed_random_number*, which is defined in the *wgpu_simplified* module.

The *create_noise_map* function leverages the octaves parameter within the *ITerrain* struct to determine the number of noise layers produced. Each octave engenders a distinct noise function, with varying frequency and amplitude, duly scaled by the lacunarity and persistence parameters. Additionally, the function's scale parameter dictates the dimensions of the noise function – smaller scales yield more intricate noise patterns, while larger scales yield smoother ones. This scale parameter modifies the frequency of the noise function within each octave.

The Perlin noise value for the sample point is calculated using the Perlin function from the *noise* crate, and is scaled to a range of $[-1, 1]$. Noise height for a given point is computed by adding the product of the Perlin noise value and the present amplitude value to the running total of *noise_height*. Subsequently, the *noise_map* data undergoes normalization to transition from its original value range (between *height_min* and *height_max*) to the range of $[0, 1]$. Ultimately, the *create_noise_map* function yields the normalized *noise_map*, an essential component in generating the final terrain data

8.2 Creating Terrains on CPU

With the noise model and noise map presented in the previous section, we are ready to use them to generate a simple procedural terrain on the CPU.

8.2.1 Terrain Data

Open the *terrain_data.rs* file located in the *src/* folder and insert the following code snippet at the top of the file, right after the *use* statements:

```rust
use bytemuck:: {Pod, Zeroable};

#[repr(C)]
#[derive(Copy, Clone, Debug, Pod, Zeroable)]
pub struct Vertex {
    pub position: [f32; 3],
    pub color: [f32; 3],
}
```

The *Vertex* struct serves the purpose of generating vertex data for our procedural terrains. It is important to note that this struct comprises only two members: *position* and *color*, omitting the *normal* field. Consequently, for simplicity, we will create procedural terrains without implementing the lighting effect in this chapter. However, should you wish to incorporate lighting effects into your terrains, you can refer to the procedure for creating 3D surfaces with lighting effects in Chapter 5.

Afterwards, incorporate two new functions, *create_indices* and *create_terrain_data*, into the implementation of the *ITerrain* struct. Insert the following code snippet immediately following the *create_noise_map* method:

```rust
pub fn create_indices(&mut self, width: u32, height: u32) -> (Vec<u32>, Vec<u32>) {
    let n_vertices_per_row = height;
    let mut indices:Vec<u32> = vec![];
    let mut indices2:Vec<u32> = vec![];

    for i in 0..width - 1 {
        for j in 0..height - 1 {
            let idx0 = j + i * n_vertices_per_row;
            let idx1 = j + 1 + i * n_vertices_per_row;
            let idx2 = j + 1 + (i + 1) * n_vertices_per_row;
            let idx3 = j + (i + 1) * n_vertices_per_row;
            indices.extend([idx0, idx1, idx2, idx2, idx3, idx0]);
            indices2.extend([idx0, idx1, idx0, idx3]);
            if i == width - 2 || j == height - 1 {
                indices2.extend([idx1, idx2, idx2, idx3]);
            }
        }
    }
    (indices, indices2)
}

pub fn create_terrain_data(&mut self) -> (Vec<Vertex>, Vec<Vertex>) {
    let cdata = colormap::colormap_data(&self.colormap_name);
    let cdata2 = colormap::colormap_data(&self.wireframe_color);
    let noise_map = self.create_noise_map(self.width, self.height);
```

```
        let mut data:Vec<Vertex> = vec![];
        let mut data2:Vec<Vertex> = vec![];

        for x in 0..self.width as usize {
            for z in 0..self.height as usize {
                let y = if noise_map[x][z].is_finite() { noise_map[x][z] } else { 0.0 };

                let position = [x as f32, y, z as f32];
                let color = colormap::color_lerp(cdata, 0.0, 1.0, y);
                let color2 = colormap::color_lerp(cdata2, 0.0, 1.0, y);

                data.push(Vertex { position, color });
                data2.push(Vertex { position, color: color2 });
            }
        }
        (data, data2)
    }
```

These two functions, *create_indices* and *create_terrain_data*, closely resemble the *simple_surface_data* function previously implemented in the *surface_data.rs* file within the *src/* folder. However, in this instance, they are used to generate indices and terrain data separately. This separation is intended to enable the reuse of the *create_indices* function for the generation of diverse terrains.

The *create_indices* function returns two arrays of indices – one for the creation of the terrain surface, and the other for the terrain wireframe. Meanwhile, the *create_terrain_data* function employs the noise map data from the *create_noise_map* function to generate terrain data, encompassing position and colormap data. Notably, the *create_terrain_data* function omits the computation of normal data, as this chapter focuses on generating procedural terrains using an unlit shader that does not necessitate normal data. The primary aim here is to emphasize terrain generation over lighting effects.

8.2.2 Shader Code

In this chapter, we will use an unlit shader for procedural terrain generation. Add a new WGSL shader file named *shader_unlit.wgsl* to the *examples/ch08/* folder and include the following code:

```
// vertex shader
@binding(0) @group(0) var<uniform> mvp_mat : mat4x4f;

struct Output {
    @builtin(position) position : vec4f,
    @location(0) vColor: vec4f,
};

@vertex
fn vs_main(@location(0) pos: vec4f, @location(1) color: vec4f) -> Output {
    var output: Output;
    output.position = mvp_mat * pos;
    output.vColor = color;
    return output;
}

@fragment
fn fs_main(@location(0) vColor: vec4f) ->  @location(0) vec4f {
    return vec4(vColor.rgb, 1.0);
}
```

This shader is very simple: we just pass the position and colormap data to the vertex shader, and the fragment shader uses the processed colormap data to generate the final fragment color.

8.2.3 Rust Code

Create a new Rust file named *terrain_cpu.rs* in the *examples/ch08/* folder and add the following code to it:

```rust
use std:: {iter, mem, f32::consts::PI};
use rand::Rng;
use cgmath::Matrix4;
use wgpu:: {util::DeviceExt, VertexBufferLayout};
use winit::{
    event::*,
    event_loop::{ControlFlow, EventLoop},
    window::Window,
};
use bytemuck::cast_slice;
use wgpu_book_examples::{ wgpu_simplified as ws, transforms as wt, terrain_data };

struct State {
    init:  ws::IWgpuInit,
    pipelines: Vec<wgpu::RenderPipeline>,
    vertex_buffers: Vec<wgpu::Buffer>,
    index_buffers: Vec<wgpu::Buffer>,
    uniform_bind_groups: Vec<wgpu::BindGroup>,
    uniform_buffers: Vec<wgpu::Buffer>,
    model_mat: Matrix4<f32>,
    view_mat: Matrix4<f32>,
    project_mat: Matrix4<f32>,
    msaa_texture_view: wgpu::TextureView,
    depth_texture_view: wgpu::TextureView,
    indices_lens: Vec<u32>,
    plot_type: u32,

    terrain: terrain_data::ITerrain,
    update_buffers: bool,
    aspect_ratio: f32,
    fps_counter: ws::FpsCounter,
}

impl State {
    async fn new(
        window:&Window,
        sample_count:u32,
        width:u32,
        height:u32,
        colormap_name:&str,
        wireframe_color:&str
    ) -> Self {
        let init = ws::IWgpuInit::new(&window, sample_count, None).await;

        let shader = init.device.create_shader_module(wgpu::include_wgsl!("shader_unlit.wgsl"));

        // uniform data
        let model_mat = wt::create_model_mat([-0.65*width as f32, 5.0, -0.5*height as f32],
            [0.0, PI/15.0, 0.0], [1.0, 10.0, 1.0]);
        let camera_position = (40.0, 50.0, 60.0).into();
```

```
let look_direction = (0.0,0.0,0.0).into();
let up_direction = cgmath::Vector3::unit_y();

let (view_mat, project_mat, vp_mat) =
    wt::create_vp_mat(camera_position, look_direction, up_direction,
    init.config.width as f32 / init.config.height as f32);

let mvp_mat = vp_mat * model_mat;

// create vertex uniform buffers
let vert_uniform_buffer = init.device.create_buffer_init(&wgpu::util::BufferInitDescriptor{
    label: Some("Vertex Uniform Buffer"),
    contents: cast_slice(mvp_mat.as_ref() as &[f32; 16]),
    usage: wgpu::BufferUsages::UNIFORM | wgpu::BufferUsages::COPY_DST,
});

// uniform bind group for vertex shader
let (vert_bind_group_layout, vert_bind_group) = ws::create_bind_group(
    &init.device,
    vec![wgpu::ShaderStages::VERTEX],
    &[vert_uniform_buffer.as_entire_binding()],
);
let (vert_bind_group_layout2, vert_bind_group2) = ws::create_bind_group(
    &init.device,
    vec![wgpu::ShaderStages::VERTEX],
    &[vert_uniform_buffer.as_entire_binding()],
);

let vertex_buffer_layout = VertexBufferLayout {
    array_stride: mem::size_of::<terrain_data::Vertex>() as wgpu::BufferAddress,
    step_mode: wgpu::VertexStepMode::Vertex,
    attributes: &wgpu::vertex_attr_array![0 => Float32x3, 1 => Float32x3], // pos, col
};

let pipeline_layout = init.device.create_pipeline_layout(&wgpu::PipelineLayoutDescriptor {
    label: Some("Render Pipeline Layout"),
    bind_group_layouts: &[&vert_bind_group_layout],
    push_constant_ranges: &[],
});

let mut ppl = ws::IRenderPipeline {
    shader: Some(&shader),
    pipeline_layout: Some(&pipeline_layout),
    vertex_buffer_layout: &[vertex_buffer_layout],
    ..Default::default()
};
let pipeline = ppl.new(&init);

let vertex_buffer_layout2 = VertexBufferLayout {
    array_stride: mem::size_of::<terrain_data::Vertex>() as wgpu::BufferAddress,
    step_mode: wgpu::VertexStepMode::Vertex,
    attributes: &wgpu::vertex_attr_array![0 => Float32x3, 1 => Float32x3], // pos, col
};

let pipeline_layout2 = init.device.create_pipeline_layout(&wgpu::PipelineLayoutDescriptor {
    label: Some("Render Pipeline Layout 2"),
    bind_group_layouts: &[&vert_bind_group_layout2],
    push_constant_ranges: &[],
});
```

```
let mut ppl2 = ws::IRenderPipeline {
    topology: wgpu::PrimitiveTopology::LineList,
    shader: Some(&shader),
    pipeline_layout: Some(&pipeline_layout2),
    vertex_buffer_layout: &[vertex_buffer_layout2],
    ..Default::default()
};
let pipeline2 = ppl2.new(&init);

let msaa_texture_view = ws::create_msaa_texture_view(&init);
let depth_texture_view = ws::create_depth_view(&init);

let mut terrain = terrain_data::ITerrain{
    scale: 50.0,
    colormap_name: colormap_name.to_string(),
    wireframe_color: wireframe_color.to_string(),
    width,
    height,
    ..Default::default()
};
let vertex_data = terrain.create_terrain_data();
let index_data = terrain.create_indices(width, height);

let vertex_buffer = init.device.create_buffer_init(&wgpu::util::BufferInitDescriptor {
    label: Some("Vertex Buffer"),
    contents: cast_slice(&vertex_data.0),
    usage: wgpu::BufferUsages::VERTEX | wgpu::BufferUsages::COPY_DST,
});

let vertex_buffer2 = init.device.create_buffer_init(&wgpu::util::BufferInitDescriptor {
    label: Some("Vertex Buffer 2"),
    contents: cast_slice(&vertex_data.1),
    usage: wgpu::BufferUsages::VERTEX | wgpu::BufferUsages::COPY_DST,
});

let index_buffer = init.device.create_buffer_init(&wgpu::util::BufferInitDescriptor{
    label: Some("Index Buffer"),
    contents: bytemuck::cast_slice(&index_data.0),
    usage: wgpu::BufferUsages::INDEX | wgpu::BufferUsages::COPY_DST,
});

let index_buffer2 = init.device.create_buffer_init(&wgpu::util::BufferInitDescriptor{
    label: Some("Index Buffer 2"),
    contents: bytemuck::cast_slice(&index_data.1),
    usage: wgpu::BufferUsages::INDEX | wgpu::BufferUsages::COPY_DST,
});

Self {
    init,
    pipelines: vec![pipeline, pipeline2],
    vertex_buffers: vec![vertex_buffer, vertex_buffer2],
    index_buffers: vec![index_buffer, index_buffer2],
    uniform_bind_groups: vec![vert_bind_group, vert_bind_group2],
    uniform_buffers: vec![vert_uniform_buffer],
    model_mat,
    view_mat,
    project_mat,
    msaa_texture_view,
    depth_texture_view,
    indices_lens: vec![index_data.0.len() as u32, index_data.1.len() as u32],
```

```
            plot_type: 1,

            terrain,
            update_buffers: false,
            aspect_ratio: 10.0,
            fps_counter: ws::FpsCounter::default(),
        }
    }

    fn resize(&mut self, new_size: winit::dpi::PhysicalSize<u32>) {
        if new_size.width > 0 && new_size.height > 0 {
            self.init.size = new_size;
            self.init.config.width = new_size.width;
            self.init.config.height = new_size.height;
            self.init.surface.configure(&self.init.device, &self.init.config);

            self.project_mat = wt::create_projection_mat(new_size.width as f32 / new_size.height as f32,
                true);
            let mvp_mat = self.project_mat * self.view_mat * self.model_mat;
            self.init.queue.write_buffer(&self.uniform_buffers[0], 0,
                cast_slice(mvp_mat.as_ref() as &[f32;16]));

            self.depth_texture_view = ws::create_depth_view(&self.init);
            if self.init.sample_count > 1 {
                self.msaa_texture_view = ws::create_msaa_texture_view(&self.init);
            }
        }
    }

    #[allow(unused_variables)]
    fn input(&mut self, event: &WindowEvent) -> bool {
        match event {
            WindowEvent::KeyboardInput {
                input:
                    KeyboardInput {
                        virtual_keycode: Some(keycode),
                        state: ElementState::Pressed,
                        ..
                    },
                ..
            } => {
                match keycode {
                    VirtualKeyCode::Space => {
                        self.plot_type = (self.plot_type + 1) % 3;
                        true
                    },
                    VirtualKeyCode::LControl => {
                        let mut rng = rand::thread_rng();
                        self.terrain.seed = rng.gen_range(1..65536);
                        self.update_buffers = true;
                        println!("seed = {}", self.terrain.seed);
                        true
                    },
                    VirtualKeyCode::Q => {
                        self.terrain.scale += 1.0;
                        self.update_buffers = true;
                        println!("scale = {}", self.terrain.scale);
                        true
                    },
                    VirtualKeyCode::A => {
```

```rust
                self.terrain.scale -= 1.0;
                if self.terrain.scale < 1.0 {
                    self.terrain.scale = 1.0;
                }
                self.update_buffers = true;
                println!("scale = {}", self.terrain.scale);
                true
            },
            VirtualKeyCode::W => {
                self.terrain.octaves += 1;
                self.update_buffers = true;
                println!("octaves = {}", self.terrain.octaves);
                true
            },
            VirtualKeyCode::S => {
                self.terrain.octaves -= 1;
                if self.terrain.octaves < 1 {
                    self.terrain.octaves = 1;
                }
                self.update_buffers = true;
                println!("octaves = {}", self.terrain.octaves);
                true
            },
            VirtualKeyCode::E => {
                self.terrain.offsets[0] += 1.0;
                self.update_buffers = true;
                println!("offset_x = {}", self.terrain.offsets[0]);
                true
            },
            VirtualKeyCode::D => {
                self.terrain.offsets[0] -= 1.0;
                self.update_buffers = true;
                println!("offset_x = {}", self.terrain.offsets[0]);
                true
            },
            VirtualKeyCode::R => {
                self.terrain.offsets[1] += 1.0;
                self.update_buffers = true;
                println!("offset_z = {}", self.terrain.offsets[1]);
                true
            },
            VirtualKeyCode::F => {
                self.terrain.offsets[1] -= 1.0;
                self.update_buffers = true;
                println!("offset_z = {}", self.terrain.offsets[1]);
                true
            },
            VirtualKeyCode::T => {
                self.aspect_ratio += 1.0;
                self.update_buffers = true;
                println!("aspect_ratio = {}", self.aspect_ratio);
                true
            },
            VirtualKeyCode::G => {
                self.aspect_ratio -= 1.0;
                self.update_buffers = true;
                println!("aspect_ratio = {}", self.aspect_ratio);
                true
            },
            _ => false
```

```
                }
            }
            _ => false,
        }
    }

    fn update(&mut self) {
        // update buffers:
        if self.update_buffers {
            self.model_mat = wt::create_model_mat([-0.65*self.terrain.width as f32,
                5.0, -0.5*self.terrain.height as f32],
                [0.0, PI/15.0, 0.0], [1.0, self.aspect_ratio, 1.0]);
            let mvp_mat = self.project_mat * self.view_mat * self.model_mat;
            self.init.queue.write_buffer(&self.uniform_buffers[0], 0,
                cast_slice(mvp_mat.as_ref() as &[f32;16]));

            let vertex_data = self.terrain.create_terrain_data();
            self.init.queue.write_buffer(&self.vertex_buffers[0], 0, cast_slice(&vertex_data.0));
            self.init.queue.write_buffer(&self.vertex_buffers[1], 0, cast_slice(&vertex_data.1));
            self.update_buffers = false;
        }
    }

    fn render(&mut self) -> Result<(), wgpu::SurfaceError> {
        //let output = self.init.surface.get_current_frame()?.output;
        let output = self.init.surface.get_current_texture()?;
        let view = output
            .texture
            .create_view(&wgpu::TextureViewDescriptor::default());

        let mut encoder = self
            .init.device
            .create_command_encoder(&wgpu::CommandEncoderDescriptor {
                label: Some("Render Encoder"),
            });

        {
            let color_attach = ws::create_color_attachment(&view);
            let msaa_attach = ws::create_msaa_color_attachment(&view, &self.msaa_texture_view);
            let color_attachment = if self.init.sample_count == 1 { color_attach } else { msaa_attach };
            let depth_attachment = ws::create_depth_stencil_attachment(&self.depth_texture_view);

            let mut render_pass = encoder.begin_render_pass(&wgpu::RenderPassDescriptor {
                label: Some("Render Pass"),
                color_attachments: &[Some(color_attachment)],
                depth_stencil_attachment: Some(depth_attachment),
                occlusion_query_set: None,
                timestamp_writes: None,
            });

            let plot_type = if self.plot_type == 1 { "shape_only" }
                else if self.plot_type == 2 {"wireframe_only"} else {"both"};

            if plot_type == "shape_only" || plot_type == "both" {
                render_pass.set_pipeline(&self.pipelines[0]);
                render_pass.set_vertex_buffer(0, self.vertex_buffers[0].slice(..));
                render_pass.set_index_buffer(self.index_buffers[0].slice(..),
                    wgpu::IndexFormat::Uint32);
                render_pass.set_bind_group(0, &self.uniform_bind_groups[0], &[]);
                render_pass.draw_indexed(0..self.indices_lens[0], 0, 0..1);
```

```
                }

                if plot_type == "wireframe_only" || plot_type == "both" {
                    render_pass.set_pipeline(&self.pipelines[1]);
                    render_pass.set_vertex_buffer(0, self.vertex_buffers[1].slice(..));
                    render_pass.set_index_buffer(self.index_buffers[1].slice(..),
                        wgpu::IndexFormat::Uint32);
                    render_pass.set_bind_group(0, &self.uniform_bind_groups[1], &[]);
                    render_pass.draw_indexed(0..self.indices_lens[1], 0, 0..1);
                }
            }

            self.fps_counter.print_fps(5);
            self.init.queue.submit(iter::once(encoder.finish()));
            output.present();

            Ok(())
        }
    }

fn main() {
    let mut sample_count = 1 as u32;
    let mut width = 200u32;
    let mut height = 200u32;
    let mut colormap_name = "terrain";
    let mut wireframe_color = "white";
    let args: Vec<String> = std::env::args().collect();
    if args.len() > 1 {
        sample_count = args[1].parse::<u32>().unwrap();
    }
    if args.len() > 2 {
        width = args[2].parse::<u32>().unwrap();
    }
    if args.len() > 3 {
        height = args[3].parse::<u32>().unwrap();
    }
    if args.len() > 4 {
        colormap_name = &args[4];
    }
    if args.len() > 5 {
        wireframe_color = &args[5];
    }

    env_logger::init();
    let event_loop = EventLoop::new();
    let window = winit::window::WindowBuilder::new().build(&event_loop).unwrap();
    window.set_title(&*format!("ch08_{}", "terrain_cpu"));

    let mut state = pollster::block_on(State::new(&window, sample_count, width, height,
        colormap_name, wireframe_color));

    event_loop.run(move |event, _, control_flow| {
        match event {
            Event::WindowEvent {
                ref event,
                window_id,
            } if window_id == window.id() => {
                if !state.input(event) {
                    match event {
                        WindowEvent::CloseRequested
```

```
                            | WindowEvent::KeyboardInput {
                                input:
                                    KeyboardInput {
                                        state: ElementState::Pressed,
                                        virtual_keycode: Some(VirtualKeyCode::Escape),
                                        ..
                                    },
                                ..
                            } => *control_flow = ControlFlow::Exit,
                            WindowEvent::Resized(physical_size) => {
                                state.resize(*physical_size);
                            }
                            WindowEvent::ScaleFactorChanged { new_inner_size, .. } => {
                                state.resize(**new_inner_size);
                            }
                            _ => {}
                        }
                    }
                }
                Event::RedrawRequested(_) => {
                    state.update();

                    match state.render() {
                        Ok(_) => {}
                        Err(wgpu::SurfaceError::Lost) => state.resize(state.init.size),
                        Err(wgpu::SurfaceError::OutOfMemory) => *control_flow = ControlFlow::Exit,
                        Err(e) => eprintln!("{:?}", e),
                    }
                }
                Event::MainEventsCleared => {
                    window.request_redraw();
                }
                _ => {}
            }
        });
}
```

The *State::new* and *State::render* functions in the above code is similar to those used in the creation of simple 3D surfaces detailed in Chapter 5. However, the distinction arises from the use of an unlit shader and terrain data without normal data.

Within the *State::new* function, we employ the following code snippet to generate the terrain data:

```
let mut terrain = terrain_data::ITerrain {
    scale: 50.0,
    colormap_name: colormap_name.to_string(),
    wireframe_color: wireframe_color.to_string(),
    width,
    height,
    ..Default::default()
};
let vertex_data = terrain.create_terrain_data();
let index_data = terrain.create_indices(width, height);
```

This code snippet initializes a *terrain* object of the *ITerrain* struct, configures its fields, and generates both vertex and index data for a procedural terrain.

Subsequently, the terrain data and vertex buffers are updated within the *State::update* function when the user modifies the input parameters. This is demonstrated in the following code snippet:

```
// update buffers:
if self.update_buffers {
    // ......

    let vertex_data = self.terrain.create_terrain_data();
    self.init.queue.write_buffer(&self.vertex_buffers[0], 0, cast_slice(&vertex_data.0));
    self.init.queue.write_buffer(&self.vertex_buffers[1], 0, cast_slice(&vertex_data.1));
    self.update_buffers = false;
}
```

This code shows that when the *update_buffers* flag is set, the terrain data is recalculated, and the changes are reflected in the updated vertex buffers.

Additionally, the code permits the user to modify input parameters through keyboard inputs.

Here is a list of controls using keyboard:

- *Space*: Changes plot type among surface, wireframe, and both.

- *LControl*: Changes the *seed* value for the terrain.

- *Q/A*: Increases/decreases the *scale* parameter.

- *W/S:* Increases/decreases the *octaves* parameter.

- *E/D:* Increases/decreases the *offect_x* parameter.

- *R/F:* Increases/decreases the *offect_z* parameter.

- *T/G:* Increases/decreases the *aspect_ratio* parameter.

8.2.4 Run Application

To run this application, add the following code snippet to the *Cargo.toml* file:

```
[[example]]
name = "ch08_terrain_cpu"
path = "examples/ch08/ terrain_cpu.rs"
```

Afterward, execute the following *cargo run* commands in the terminal window:

```
cargo run --example ch08_ terrain_cpu 8
```

Fig.8-1 shows the results of this example by manipulating the plot type with the *Space* key.

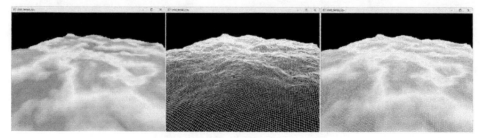

Fig.8-1. Procedural terrains generated on the CPU: terrain only (left), wireframe only (middle), and both the terrain and wireframe (right).

In Fig.8-1, you can play around with the procedural terrain by varying the input parameters. In particular, you can modify the *seed, persistence, lacunarity, offset_x, offset_z,* or *scale* parameters using the keyboard inputs to examine their effect on the terrain.

8.3 Water Level

While the terrain created in the previous section appears to be functioning adequately, an issue arises with the water's appearance (displayed in a bluish color), where it appears to be influenced, leading to a hilly visual effect. This becomes particularly evident when the *scale* and *aspect_ratio* parameters are increased, as depicted in Fig.8-2.

Fig.8-2. Water with a hilly appearance.

To address this issue, we can incorporate a curve, akin to an animation curve in Unity, that defines the degree to which various height values are influenced by the aspect ratio (or height multiplier). A typical curve we want to use is shown in Fig.8-3.

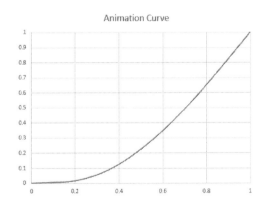

Fig.8-3. Animation curve can be used to adjust the water level in a terrain.

The figure reveals that the curve remains nearly level below 0.2 on the horizontal axis – precisely the behavior we desire for the water level. However, for the sake of simplicity, we will adopt a manual approach. Instead of employing an animation curve, we will directly set the water level through hard coding.

8.3.1 Colormap for Terrain

To conveniently introduce a water level to a terrain, we can create a simple colormap tailored for terrains. To accomplish this, navigate to the *terrain_data.rs* file within the *src/* folder and integrate the following code into the implementation of the *ITerain* struct. Place it immediately after the *create_terrain_data* method:

```
fn terrian_colormap_data(&mut self) -> (Vec<[f32; 3]>, Vec<[f32; 3]>, Vec<f32>) {
    let cdata = vec![
        [0.055f32, 0.529, 0.8],
        [0.761, 0.698, 0.502],
        [0.204, 0.549, 0.192],
        [0.353, 0.302, 0.255],
        [1.0, 0.98, 0.98]
    ];
    let cdata2 = vec![[1f32, 1.0, 1.0]; 5];
    let ta = vec![0.0f32, 0.3, 0.35, 0.6, 0.9, 1.0];
    (cdata, cdata2, ta)
}


fn shift_water_level(&mut self, ta:&Vec<f32>) -> Vec<f32> {
    let mut t1 = vec![0f32; 6];
    let r = (1.0 - self.water_level)/(1.0 - ta[1]);
    t1[1] = self.water_level;
    for i in 1..5usize {
        let del = ta[i+1] - ta[i];
        t1[i+1] = t1[i] + r * del;
    }
    t1
}


fn color_lerp(&mut self, color:&Vec<[f32;3]>, ta:&Vec<f32>, t:f32) -> [f32;3] {
    let len = 6usize;
    let mut res = [0f32;3];
    for i in 0..len - 1 {
        if t >= ta[i] && t < ta[i + 1] {
            res = color[i];
        }
    }
    if t == ta[len-1] {
        res = color[len-2];
    }
    res
}


fn add_terrain_colors(&mut self, color:&Vec<[f32;3]>, ta:&Vec<f32>, tmin:f32, tmax:f32, t:f32)
-> [f32;3] {
    let mut tt = if t < tmin { tmin } else if t > tmax { tmax } else { t };
    tt = (tt - tmin)/(tmax - tmin);
    let t1 = self.shift_water_level(ta);
    self.color_lerp(color, &t1, tt)
}
```

The *terrain_colormap_data* function in the above code houses two colormaps: *cdata* and *cdata2*. The former is intended for rendering the terrain, while the latter is for rendering the wireframe. Each colormap comprises a 5-element vector. Additionally, the *ta* vector is employed to store the location at which the colormap is defined.

The *shift_water_level* function uses the water level parameter to shift the locations of the colormap data stored in the original location *ta* vector to new locations, which are stored in a new vector named *t1*. Simultaneously, leveraging the utility function *color_lerp*, the *add_terrain_colors* function interpolates colormap data at an arbitrary location, taking the water level shift into account.

8.3.2 Terrain Data with Water Level

Open the *terrain_data.rs* file within the *src/* folder, and augment the implementation of the *ITerrain* struct by introducing a new function called *create_terrain_data_with_water_level*. Include the following code:

```
pub fn create_terrain_data_with_water_level(&mut self) -> (Vec<Vertex>, Vec<Vertex>) {
    let (cdata, cdata2, ta) = self.terrian_colormap_data();

    let noise_map = self.create_noise_map(self.width, self.height);

    let mut data:Vec<Vertex> = vec![];
    let mut data2:Vec<Vertex> = vec![];

    for x in 0..self.width as usize {
        for z in 0..self.height as usize {
            let mut y = if noise_map[x][z].is_finite() { noise_map[x][z] } else { 0.0 };
            if y < self.water_level {
                y = self.water_level - 0.01;
            }

            let position = [x as f32, y, z as f32];
            let color = self.add_terrain_colors(&cdata, &ta, 0.0, 1.0, y);
            let color2 = self.add_terrain_colors(&cdata2, &ta, 0.0, 1.0, y);

            data.push(Vertex { position, color });
            data2.push(Vertex { position, color: color2 });
        }
    }
    (data, data2)
}
```

The *create_terrain_data_with_water_level* function in the above code is similar in structure to the previously demonstrated *create_terrain_data* function. However, in this version, the function introduces a water level adjustment using hard coded logic:

```
let mut y = if noise_map[x][z].is_finite() { noise_map[x][z] } else { 0.0 };
if y < self.water_level {
    y = self.water_level - 0.01;
}
```

In this code segment, the *y* value is manually set to a constant slightly below the specified water level. This adjustment serves to ensure a clear visual distinction between the water level and the land surface. While this approach directly embeds the water level offset, game developers often use animation curves, as demonstrated in Unity, for a similar purpose.

When generating a procedural terrain, it is important to ensure that the water surface is clearly distinguishable from the land surface. If vertices representing the water's surface are exactly at the water level, it might be challenging to visually perceive where the water surface begins due to anti-aliasing and graphical effects. By positioning these vertices slightly below the water level, even if only by a very small amount, it ensures that the water surface has a distinct visual appearance.

Notably, the *y* values or noise map values correlate with the *water_level* parameter, providing users with the flexibility to customize the water level as needed by altering this parameter.

Consequently, the *create_terrain_data_with_water_level* function appropriately returns terrain data while accommodating the adjusted water level.

8.3.3 Rust Code

Create a new Rust file named *terrain_water_level.rs* within the *examples/ch08/* folder. The code structure of this example closely resembles the previous one. The key difference lies in the method used to generate the vertex data: we utilize the *create_terrian_data_with_water_level* method implemented in the preceding section of the *terrain-data.rs* file. This can be observed in the following code snippet:

```
let mut terrain = terrain_data::ITerrain {
    scale: 50.0,
    water_level: 0.3,
    width,
    height,
    ..Default::default()
};
let vertex_data = terrain.create_terrain_data_with_water_level();
let index_data = terrain.create_indices(width, height);
```

Additionally, the code permits the user to modify input parameters through keyboard inputs.

Here is a list of controls using keyboard:

- *Space*: Changes plot type among surface, wireframe, and both.
- *LControl*: Changes the *seed* value for the terrain.
- *Q/A*: Increases/decreases the *scale* parameter.
- *W/S:* Increases/decreases the *octaves* parameter.
- *E/D:* Increases/decreases the *offect_x* parameter.
- *R/F:* Increases/decreases the *offect_z* parameter.
- *T/G:* Increases/decreases the *aspect_ratio* parameter.
- *Y/H:* Increases/decreases the *water_level* parameter.

8.3.4 Run Application

To run this application, add the following code snippet to the *Cargo.toml* file:

```
[[example]]
name = "ch08_terrain_water_level"
path = "examples/ch08/ terrain_ water_level.rs"
```

Afterward, execute the following *cargo run* commands in the terminal window:

```
cargo run --example ch08_ terrain_ water_level 8
```

Fig.8-4 displays the results of this example. The terrain in this figure clearly demonstrates that the water level looks flat and does not have a hilly appearance anymore.

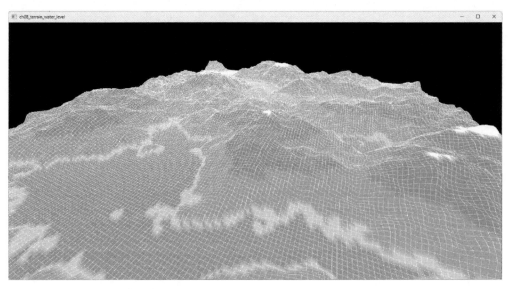

Fig.8-4. Terrain with water_level = 0.3.

In Fig.8-4, the *water_level* parameter is set to 0.3. If this parameter is changed to 0.6 using the *Y* key and all the other parameters are kept unchanged, we will obtain a new terrain with more water, as shown in Fig.8-5.

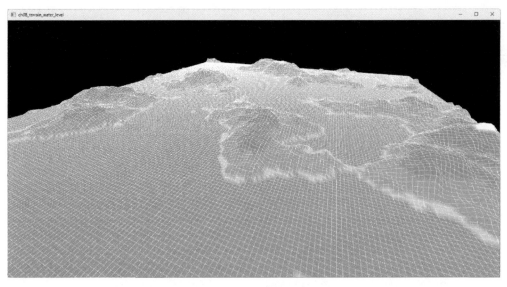

Fig.8-5. Terrain with water_level = 0.6.

8.4 Terrain Chunks

Terrain chunks and level of detail (LOD) are important concepts in procedural terrain generation and they are used to optimize the rendering of large terrains and to balance the trade-off between visual quality and performance.

Chunks are smaller pieces of the terrain that are generated separately and then combined to create the overall terrain. By dividing the terrain into smaller chunks, the system can generate and render only the visible parts of the terrain, reducing the amount of memory and processing power required. As the player moves through the terrain, new chunks are generated and old ones are discarded, providing a seamless and continuous experience.

Level of detail is a technique used to adjust the visual complexity of the terrain based on the distance from the viewer. As the viewer moves further away from the terrain, details become less noticeable, and thus, lower levels of detail can be used to save on computational resources. This technique allows for the generation of highly detailed terrains that can be rendered at high framerates.

Together, chunks and LOD work in tandem to provide an efficient way to generate and render large, detailed terrains. As the player moves through the terrain, new chunks are loaded and older ones are unloaded. Additionally, the system adjusts the level of detail of the terrain based on the viewer's distance, providing a visually pleasing experience while maintaining performance.

In this section, we will create a terrain chunk that is a conventional terrain with a fix size. For convenience, we will consider a square terrain with a size of 241 × 241.

8.4.1 Level of Detail Algorithm

To improve the performance of terrain generation, we want to add support for multiple resolutions for a terrain with a fix size. By implementing this LOD feature, we can render terrain chunks in the distance with fewer vertices, ensuring smooth gameplay even in a large terrain composed of multiple chunks.

As demonstrated in previous examples, when generating the terrain data, we loop through each vertex in the terrain, incrementing by 1. To simplify this process, we can set the increment to a number that is larger than 1. Actually, the possible increment numbers can be easily calculated: they must be a factor of (size − 1). For the terrain chunk with a size of 241 × 241, the possible increment numbers will be 1, 2, 3, 4, 5, 6, 8, 10, and 12. Thus, we can use the following formula to calculate the number of vertices in one direction:

$$numVertices = \frac{size - 1}{increment} + 1$$

The following table list the LOD levels, increment number, and corresponding number of vertices for a terrain chunk with a size of 241 × 241:

LOD Levels	Increments	Number of Vertices
0	1	241 × 241 = 58,081
1	2	121 × 121 = 14,641
2	3	81 × 81 = 6,561
3	4	61 × 61 = 3,721

4	5	$49 \times 49 = 2,401$
5	6	$41 \times 41 = 1,681$
6	8	$31 \times 31 = 961$
7	10	$25 \times 25 = 625$
8	12	$21 \times 21 = 441$

It is evident from the above table that we can define a parameter named *level_of_detail* that can be used for vertex simplification. Specifically, we can set it to 0, if there is no simplification, or 1, 2, …, or 8 for increasing levels of simplification. The highest LOD is obtained by setting the *level_of_detail* parameter to 0.

8.4.2 Terrain Chunk Data

Navigate to the *terrain_data.rs* file within the *src/* folder and introduce a new Rust function within the implementation of the ITerrain struct. This function is named *create_terrain_data_chunk*, and here is the corresponding code:

```
pub fn create_terrain_data_chunk(&mut self) -> (Vec<Vertex>, Vec<Vertex>, u32) {
    let increment_count = if self.level_of_detail <= 5 { self.level_of_detail + 1} else
        { 2*(self.level_of_detail - 2) };

    let vertices_per_row = (self.chunk_size - 1)/increment_count + 1;

    let (cdata, cdata2, ta) = self.terrian_colormap_data();

    let noise_map = self.create_noise_map(self.chunk_size, self.chunk_size);

    let mut data:Vec<Vertex> = vec![];
    let mut data2:Vec<Vertex> = vec![];

    for x in (0..self.chunk_size as usize).step_by(increment_count as usize) {
        for z in (0..self.chunk_size as usize).step_by(increment_count as usize) {
            let mut y = if noise_map[x][z].is_finite() { noise_map[x][z] } else { 0.0 };
            if y < self.water_level {
                y = self.water_level - 0.01;
            }

            let position = [x as f32, y, z as f32];
            let color = self.add_terrain_colors(&cdata, &ta, 0.0, 1.0, y);
            let color2 = self.add_terrain_colors(&cdata2, &ta, 0.0, 1.0, y);

            data.push(Vertex { position, color });
            data2.push(Vertex { position, color: color2 });
        }
    }
    (data, data2, vertices_per_row)
}
```

In the above code, the *create_terrain_data_chunk* function begins by calculating the increment number and the count of vertices per row based on the *level_of_detail* parameter, as demonstrated below:

```
let increment_count = if self.level_of_detail <= 5 { self.level_of_detail + 1} else
    { 2*(self.level_of_detail - 2) };

let vertices_per_row = (self.chunk_size - 1)/increment_count + 1;
```

The function then proceeds to generate terrain data with an associated water level, akin to the approach taken in the previous example. Notably, the *for* loops are modified to use *increment_count* as the increment step, resulting in the following code snippet:

```
for x in (0..self.chunk_size as usize).step_by(increment_count as usize) {
    for z in (0..self.chunk_size as usize).step_by(increment_count as usize) {
        ...
    }
}
```

Another key difference from the previous example is the inclusion of an additional *u32* value named *vertices_per_row* within the returned tuple. This value plays a role in calculating the index data, particularly by invoking the *create_indices* method in the following manner:

```
let index_data = self.create_indices(vertices_per_row, vertices_per_row);
```

This modification is necessary since *vertices_per_row* represents the actual count of vertices required for constructing triangles or the terrain surface. Consequently, this adjustment ensures that the generated indices accurately reflect the specified level of detail for the terrain.

8.4.3 Rust Code

Create a new Rust file named *terrain_chunk.rs* within the *examples/ch08/* folder. The code structure of this example closely resembles that of the previous *terrain_cpu* example. However, the key difference lies in the method used to generate the vertex data. Here, we make use of the *create_terrian_data_chunk* method of the *terrain-data.rs* file implemented in the preceding section. This is illustrated in the following code snippet:

```
let mut terrain = terrain_data::ITerrain {
    scale: 50.0,
    water_level: 0.3,
    width,
    height,
    ..Default::default()
};
let vertex_data = terrain.create_terrain_data_chunk();
let index_data = terrain.create_indices(vertex_data.2, vertex_data.2);
```

In this snippet, we initialize a terrain object of the *ITerrain* struct. The scale parameter is set to 50.0, the *water_level* is set to 0.3, and the width and height parameters are specified accordingly. Notably, we use the default *chunk_size* = 241 and *level_of_detail* = 0 values to generate the terrain chunk. However, these input parameters are adjustable by the user via keyboard inputs. The *level_of_detail* parameter, for instance, can be changed using the *LAlt* key to modify the level of detail within the terrain chunk.

Within the *State::update* function, there is a distinction from the previous example. While previously only the vertex buffer required updating for a given resolution during the application's startup, here, both the vertex and index buffers need updating. This is due to the fact that the index data varies depending on the level of detail, even for a fixed terrain chunk size (or resolution). This distinction is apparent in the following code snippet:

```
if self.update_buffers {

    // ...

    let vertex_data = self.terrain.create_terrain_data_chunk();
    self.init.queue.write_buffer(&self.vertex_buffers[0], 0, cast_slice(&vertex_data.0));
```

```
        self.init.queue.write_buffer(&self.vertex_buffers[1], 0, cast_slice(&vertex_data.1));
        let index_data = self.terrain.create_indices(vertex_data.2, vertex_data.2);
        self.init.queue.write_buffer(&self.index_buffers[0], 0, cast_slice(&index_data.0));
        self.init.queue.write_buffer(&self.index_buffers[1], 0, cast_slice(&index_data.1));
        self.indices_lens = vec![index_data.0.len() as u32, index_data.1.len() as u32];
        self.update_buffers = false;
    }
```

In this code excerpt, when the *update_buffers* flag is *true*, we update both the vertex and index buffers. The *create_terrain_data_chunk* method generates new vertex data, which is then written to the appropriate vertex buffers. Similarly, the *create_indices* method is employed to generate index data specific to the level of detail, and this data is written to the index buffers. Furthermore, the lengths of the index data arrays are stored to the *self.indices_lens* vector, which will be used when drawing the terrain and its wireframe within the *State::render* method.

Here is a list of controls using keyboard:

- *Space*: Changes plot type among surface, wireframe, and both.

- *LControl*: Changes the *seed* value for the terrain.

- *LAlt*: Changes the *level_of_detail* parameter.

- *Q/A*: Increases/decreases the *scale* parameter.

- *W/S:* Increases/decreases the *octaves* parameter.

- *E/D:* Increases/decreases the *offect_x* parameter.

- *R/F:* Increases/decreases the *offect_z* parameter.

- *T/G:* Increases/decreases the *aspect_ratio* parameter.

- *Y/H:* Increases/decreases the *water_level* parameter.

8.4.4 Run Application

To run this application, add the following code snippet to the *Cargo.toml* file:

```
[[example]]
name = "ch08_terrain_chunk"
path = "examples/ch08/ terrain_ chunk.rs"
```

Afterward, execute the following *cargo run* commands in the terminal window:

```
cargo run --example ch08_ terrain_ chunk 8
```

Fig.8-6 displays the results of this example with the highest level of detail, where the *level_of_detail* parameter is set to 0.

To examine how LOD works, you can change the *level_of_detail* parameter to 5 by pressing the LAlt key and keep all other parameters unchanged. You can clearly see that the mesh of the terrain chunk gets simplified, as shown in Fig.8-7.

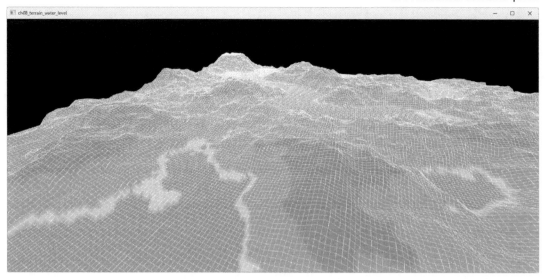

Fig.8-6. Terrain chunk with level_of_detail = 0.

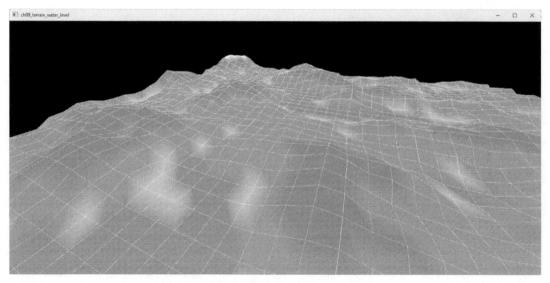

Fig.8-7. Terrain chunk with level_of_detail = 5.

8.5 Terrain Instances

With the terrain chunk presented in the previous example, we can create multiple instances of a terrain chunk to form a large terrain, as we did earlier for 3D surfaces in chapter 5. Creating multiple instances of a terrain chunk is more efficient than creating multiple chunks one-by-one because it reduces the overhead of creating new terrain chunks. Additionally, when creating multiple instances of a terrain chunk, the data for that chunk only needs to be created once. This can save a lot of memory, especially if the chunk is large and complex.

8.5.1 Shader Code

To create multiple instances of a terrain chunk, we need to implement a new unlit shader that supports multiple instances. Please create a new WGSL shader file called *shader_unlit_instance.wgsl* in the *examples/ch08/* folder and add the following code to it:

```wgsl
// vertex shader
@binding(0) @group(0) var<uniform> vpMat: mat4x4f;
@group(0) @binding(1)  var<storage> modelMat: array<mat4x4f>;

struct Input {
    @builtin(instance_index) idx: u32,
    @location(0) position: vec4f,
    @location(1) color: vec4f
};

struct Output {
    @builtin(position) position : vec4f,
    @location(0) vColor: vec4f,
};

@vertex
fn vs_main(in:Input) -> Output {
    var output: Output;
    output.position = vpMat * modelMat[in.idx] * in.position;
    output.vColor = in.color;
    return output;
}

// fragment shader
@fragment
fn fs_main(@location(0) vColor: vec4f) ->  @location(0) vec4f {
    return vec4(vColor.rgb, 1.0);
}
```

The only difference between this shader and the one used to create a single terrain is that the model-view-projection matrix is separated into two matrices: model and view-projection matrices. Additionally, the model matrix in this case is an array of 4×4 matrices accounting for multiple instances.

8.5.2 Rust Code

Create a new Rust file named *terrain_instance.rs* in *examples/ch08/* folder and include the following code:

```rust
use std:: {iter, mem};
use rand::Rng;
use cgmath::Matrix4;
use wgpu:: {util::DeviceExt, VertexBufferLayout};
use winit::{
    event::*,
    event_loop::{ControlFlow, EventLoop},
    window::Window,
};
use bytemuck::cast_slice;
use wgpu_book_examples:: { wgpu_simplified as ws, transforms as wt, terrain_data };

const X_CHUNKS_COUNT:u32 = 4;
const Z_CHUNKS_COUNT:u32 = 4;
```

```rust
const CHUNKS_COUNT:u32 = 16;

struct State {
    init:  ws::IWgpuInit,
    pipelines: Vec<wgpu::RenderPipeline>,
    vertex_buffers: Vec<wgpu::Buffer>,
    index_buffers: Vec<wgpu::Buffer>,
    uniform_bind_groups: Vec<wgpu::BindGroup>,
    uniform_buffers: Vec<wgpu::Buffer>,
    view_mat: Matrix4<f32>,
    project_mat: Matrix4<f32>,
    msaa_texture_view: wgpu::TextureView,
    depth_texture_view: wgpu::TextureView,
    indices_lens: Vec<u32>,
    plot_type: u32,

    terrain: terrain_data::ITerrain,
    update_buffers: bool,
    fps_counter: ws::FpsCounter,
}

impl State {
    async fn new(window:&Window, sample_count:u32, width:u32, height:u32) -> Self {
        let init = ws::IWgpuInit::new(&window, sample_count, None).await;

        let shader = init.device.create_shader_module(wgpu::include_wgsl!("shader_unlit_instance.wgsl"));

        let mut terrain = terrain_data::ITerrain {
            scale: 40.0,
            water_level: 0.3,
            width,
            height,
            ..Default::default()
        };

        // uniform data
        let mut model_mat:Vec<[f32; 16]> = vec![];
        let chunk_size1 = (terrain.chunk_size - 1) as f32;
        for i in 0..X_CHUNKS_COUNT {
            for j in 0..Z_CHUNKS_COUNT {
                let xt = -0.5 * X_CHUNKS_COUNT as f32 * chunk_size1 + i as f32 * chunk_size1;
                let zt = -0.5 * Z_CHUNKS_COUNT as f32 * chunk_size1 + j as f32 * chunk_size1;
                let translation = [xt, 100.0, zt];
                let m = wt::create_model_mat(translation, [0.0, 0.0, 0.0], [1.0, 25.0, 1.0]);
                model_mat.push(*(m.as_ref()));
            }
        }
        let model_storage_buffer = init.device.create_buffer_init(&wgpu::util::BufferInitDescriptor{
            label: Some("Model Matrix Storage Buffer"),
            contents: cast_slice(&model_mat),
            usage: wgpu::BufferUsages::STORAGE | wgpu::BufferUsages::COPY_DST,
        });

        let camera_position = (250.0, 300.0, 300.0).into();
        let look_direction = (0.0,0.0,0.0).into();
        let up_direction = cgmath::Vector3::unit_y();

        let (view_mat, project_mat, vp_mat) =
            wt::create_vp_mat(camera_position, look_direction, up_direction,
            init.config.width as f32 / init.config.height as f32);
```

```
// create vertex uniform buffers
let vp_uniform_buffer = init.device.create_buffer_init(&wgpu::util::BufferInitDescriptor{
    label: Some("View-Projection Matrix Uniform Buffer"),
    contents: cast_slice(vp_mat.as_ref() as &[f32; 16]),
    usage: wgpu::BufferUsages::UNIFORM | wgpu::BufferUsages::COPY_DST,
});

// uniform bind group for vertex shader
let (vert_bind_group_layout, vert_bind_group) = ws::create_bind_group_storage(
    &init.device,
    vec![wgpu::ShaderStages::VERTEX, wgpu::ShaderStages::VERTEX],
    vec![
        wgpu::BufferBindingType::Uniform,
        wgpu::BufferBindingType::Storage { read_only: true },
    ],
    &[vp_uniform_buffer.as_entire_binding(), model_storage_buffer.as_entire_binding()],
);

let (vert_bind_group_layout2, vert_bind_group2) = ws::create_bind_group_storage(
    &init.device,
    vec![wgpu::ShaderStages::VERTEX, wgpu::ShaderStages::VERTEX],
    vec![
        wgpu::BufferBindingType::Uniform,
        wgpu::BufferBindingType::Storage { read_only: true },
    ],
    &[vp_uniform_buffer.as_entire_binding(), model_storage_buffer.as_entire_binding()],
);

let vertex_buffer_layout = VertexBufferLayout {
    array_stride: mem::size_of::<terrain_data::Vertex>() as wgpu::BufferAddress,
    step_mode: wgpu::VertexStepMode::Vertex,
    attributes: &wgpu::vertex_attr_array![0 => Float32x3, 1 => Float32x3], // pos, col
};

let pipeline_layout = init.device.create_pipeline_layout(&wgpu::PipelineLayoutDescriptor {
    label: Some("Render Pipeline Layout"),
    bind_group_layouts: &[&vert_bind_group_layout],
    push_constant_ranges: &[],
});

let mut ppl = ws::IRenderPipeline {
    shader: Some(&shader),
    pipeline_layout: Some(&pipeline_layout),
    vertex_buffer_layout: &[vertex_buffer_layout],
    ..Default::default()
};
let pipeline = ppl.new(&init);

let vertex_buffer_layout2 = VertexBufferLayout {
    array_stride: mem::size_of::<terrain_data::Vertex>() as wgpu::BufferAddress,
    step_mode: wgpu::VertexStepMode::Vertex,
    attributes: &wgpu::vertex_attr_array![0 => Float32x3, 1 => Float32x3], // pos, col
};

let pipeline_layout2 = init.device.create_pipeline_layout(&wgpu::PipelineLayoutDescriptor {
    label: Some("Render Pipeline Layout 2"),
    bind_group_layouts: &[&vert_bind_group_layout2],
    push_constant_ranges: &[],
});
```

```
let mut ppl2 = ws::IRenderPipeline {
    topology: wgpu::PrimitiveTopology::LineList,
    shader: Some(&shader),
    pipeline_layout: Some(&pipeline_layout2),
    vertex_buffer_layout: &[vertex_buffer_layout2],
    ..Default::default()
};
let pipeline2 = ppl2.new(&init);

let msaa_texture_view = ws::create_msaa_texture_view(&init);
let depth_texture_view = ws::create_depth_view(&init);

let vertex_data = terrain.create_terrain_data_chunk();
let index_data = terrain.create_indices(vertex_data.2, vertex_data.2);

let vertex_buffer = init.device.create_buffer_init(&wgpu::util::BufferInitDescriptor {
    label: Some("Vertex Buffer"),
    contents: cast_slice(&vertex_data.0),
    usage: wgpu::BufferUsages::VERTEX | wgpu::BufferUsages::COPY_DST,
});

let vertex_buffer2 = init.device.create_buffer_init(&wgpu::util::BufferInitDescriptor {
    label: Some("Vertex Buffer 2"),
    contents: cast_slice(&vertex_data.1),
    usage: wgpu::BufferUsages::VERTEX | wgpu::BufferUsages::COPY_DST,
});

let index_buffer = init.device.create_buffer_init(&wgpu::util::BufferInitDescriptor{
    label: Some("Index Buffer"),
    contents: bytemuck::cast_slice(&index_data.0),
    usage: wgpu::BufferUsages::INDEX | wgpu::BufferUsages::COPY_DST,
});

let index_buffer2 = init.device.create_buffer_init(&wgpu::util::BufferInitDescriptor{
    label: Some("Index Buffer 2"),
    contents: bytemuck::cast_slice(&index_data.1),
    usage: wgpu::BufferUsages::INDEX | wgpu::BufferUsages::COPY_DST,
});

Self {
    init,
    pipelines: vec![pipeline, pipeline2],
    vertex_buffers: vec![vertex_buffer, vertex_buffer2],
    index_buffers: vec![index_buffer, index_buffer2],
    uniform_bind_groups: vec![vert_bind_group, vert_bind_group2],
    uniform_buffers: vec![vp_uniform_buffer, model_storage_buffer],
    view_mat,
    project_mat,
    msaa_texture_view,
    depth_texture_view,
    indices_lens: vec![index_data.0.len() as u32, index_data.1.len() as u32],
    plot_type: 0,

    terrain,
    update_buffers: false,
    fps_counter: ws::FpsCounter::default(),
}
}
```

```rust
fn resize(&mut self, new_size: winit::dpi::PhysicalSize<u32>) {
    if new_size.width > 0 && new_size.height > 0 {
        self.init.size = new_size;
        self.init.config.width = new_size.width;
        self.init.config.height = new_size.height;
        self.init.surface.configure(&self.init.device, &self.init.config);

        self.project_mat = wt::create_projection_mat(new_size.width as f32 / new_size.height as f32,
            true);
        let vp_mat = self.project_mat * self.view_mat;
        self.init.queue.write_buffer(&self.uniform_buffers[0], 0,
            cast_slice(vp_mat.as_ref() as &[f32;16]));

        self.depth_texture_view = ws::create_depth_view(&self.init);
        if self.init.sample_count > 1 {
            self.msaa_texture_view = ws::create_msaa_texture_view(&self.init);
        }
    }
}

#[allow(unused_variables)]
fn input(&mut self, event: &WindowEvent) -> bool {
    match event {
        WindowEvent::KeyboardInput {
            input:
                KeyboardInput {
                    virtual_keycode: Some(keycode),
                    state: ElementState::Pressed,
                    ..
                },
            ..
        } => {
            match keycode {
                VirtualKeyCode::Space => {
                    self.plot_type = (self.plot_type + 1) % 3;
                    true
                },
                VirtualKeyCode::LControl => {
                    let mut rng = rand::thread_rng();
                    self.terrain.seed = rng.gen_range(1..65536);
                    self.update_buffers = true;
                    println!("seed = {}", self.terrain.seed);
                    true
                },
                VirtualKeyCode::LAlt => {
                    self.terrain.level_of_detail = (self.terrain.level_of_detail + 1) % 7;
                    self.update_buffers = true;
                    println!("LOD = {}", self.terrain.level_of_detail);
                    true
                },
                VirtualKeyCode::Q => {
                    self.terrain.scale += 1.0;
                    self.update_buffers = true;
                    println!("scale = {}", self.terrain.scale);
                    true
                },
                VirtualKeyCode::A => {
                    self.terrain.scale -= 1.0;
                    if self.terrain.scale < 1.0 {
                        self.terrain.scale = 1.0;
```

```
                }
                self.update_buffers = true;
                println!("scale = {}", self.terrain.scale);
                true
            },
            VirtualKeyCode::W => {
                self.terrain.octaves += 1;
                self.update_buffers = true;
                println!("octaves = {}", self.terrain.octaves);
                true
            },
            VirtualKeyCode::S => {
                self.terrain.octaves -= 1;
                if self.terrain.octaves < 1 {
                    self.terrain.octaves = 1;
                }
                self.update_buffers = true;
                println!("octaves = {}", self.terrain.octaves);
                true
            },
            VirtualKeyCode::E => {
                self.terrain.offsets[0] += 1.0;
                self.update_buffers = true;
                println!("offset_x = {}", self.terrain.offsets[0]);
                true
            },
            VirtualKeyCode::D => {
                self.terrain.offsets[0] -= 1.0;
                self.update_buffers = true;
                println!("offset_x = {}", self.terrain.offsets[0]);
                true
            },
            VirtualKeyCode::R => {
                self.terrain.offsets[1] += 1.0;
                self.update_buffers = true;
                println!("offset_z = {}", self.terrain.offsets[1]);
                true
            },
            VirtualKeyCode::F => {
                self.terrain.offsets[1] -= 1.0;
                self.update_buffers = true;
                println!("offset_z = {}", self.terrain.offsets[1]);
                true
            },
            VirtualKeyCode::T => {
                self.terrain.water_level += 0.01;
                self.update_buffers = true;
                println!("water_level = {}", self.terrain.water_level);
                true
            },
            VirtualKeyCode::G => {
                self.terrain.water_level -= 0.01;
                self.update_buffers = true;
                println!("water_level = {}", self.terrain.water_level);
                true
            },
            _ => false
        }
    }
    _ => false,
```

```
        }
    }

    fn update(&mut self) {
        // update buffers:
        if self.update_buffers {
            let vertex_data = self.terrain.create_terrain_data_chunk();
            self.init.queue.write_buffer(&self.vertex_buffers[0], 0, cast_slice(&vertex_data.0));
            self.init.queue.write_buffer(&self.vertex_buffers[1], 0, cast_slice(&vertex_data.1));
            let index_data = self.terrain.create_indices(vertex_data.2, vertex_data.2);
            self.init.queue.write_buffer(&self.index_buffers[0], 0, cast_slice(&index_data.0));
            self.init.queue.write_buffer(&self.index_buffers[1], 0, cast_slice(&index_data.1));
            self.indices_lens = vec![index_data.0.len() as u32, index_data.1.len() as u32];
            self.update_buffers = false;
        }
    }

    fn render(&mut self) -> Result<(), wgpu::SurfaceError> {
        //let output = self.init.surface.get_current_frame()?.output;
        let output = self.init.surface.get_current_texture()?;
        let view = output
            .texture
            .create_view(&wgpu::TextureViewDescriptor::default());

        let mut encoder = self
            .init.device
            .create_command_encoder(&wgpu::CommandEncoderDescriptor {
                label: Some("Render Encoder"),
            });

        {
            let color_attach = ws::create_color_attachment(&view);
            let msaa_attach = ws::create_msaa_color_attachment(&view, &self.msaa_texture_view);
            let color_attachment = if self.init.sample_count == 1 { color_attach } else { msaa_attach };
            let depth_attachment = ws::create_depth_stencil_attachment(&self.depth_texture_view);

            let mut render_pass = encoder.begin_render_pass(&wgpu::RenderPassDescriptor {
                label: Some("Render Pass"),
                color_attachments: &[Some(color_attachment)],
                depth_stencil_attachment: Some(depth_attachment),
                occlusion_query_set: None,
                timestamp_writes: None,
            });

            let plot_type = if self.plot_type == 1 { "shape_only" }
                else if self.plot_type == 2 {"wireframe_only"} else {"both"};

            if plot_type == "shape_only" || plot_type == "both" {
                render_pass.set_pipeline(&self.pipelines[0]);
                render_pass.set_vertex_buffer(0, self.vertex_buffers[0].slice(..));
                render_pass.set_index_buffer(self.index_buffers[0].slice(..),
                    wgpu::IndexFormat::Uint32);
                render_pass.set_bind_group(0, &self.uniform_bind_groups[0], &[]);
                render_pass.draw_indexed(0..self.indices_lens[0], 0, 0..CHUNKS_COUNT);
            }

            if plot_type == "wireframe_only" || plot_type == "both" {
                render_pass.set_pipeline(&self.pipelines[1]);
                render_pass.set_vertex_buffer(0, self.vertex_buffers[1].slice(..));
                render_pass.set_index_buffer(self.index_buffers[1].slice(..),
```

```
                wgpu::IndexFormat::Uint32);
            render_pass.set_bind_group(0, &self.uniform_bind_groups[1], &[]);
            render_pass.draw_indexed(0..self.indices_lens[1], 0, 0..CHUNKS_COUNT);
        }
    }
    self.fps_counter.print_fps(5);
    self.init.queue.submit(iter::once(encoder.finish()));
    output.present();

    Ok(())
    }
}

fn main() {
    let mut sample_count = 1 as u32;
    let mut width = 200u32;
    let mut height = 200u32;
    let args: Vec<String> = std::env::args().collect();
    if args.len() > 1 {
        sample_count = args[1].parse::<u32>().unwrap();
    }
    if args.len() > 2 {
        width = args[2].parse::<u32>().unwrap();
    }
    if args.len() > 3 {
        height = args[3].parse::<u32>().unwrap();
    }

    env_logger::init();
    let event_loop = EventLoop::new();
    let window = winit::window::WindowBuilder::new().build(&event_loop).unwrap();
    window.set_title(&*format!("ch08_{}", "terrain_water_level"));

    let mut state = pollster::block_on(State::new(&window, sample_count, width, height));

    event_loop.run(move |event, _, control_flow| {
        match event {
            Event::WindowEvent {
                ref event,
                window_id,
            } if window_id == window.id() => {
                if !state.input(event) {
                    match event {
                        WindowEvent::CloseRequested
                        | WindowEvent::KeyboardInput {
                            input:
                                KeyboardInput {
                                    state: ElementState::Pressed,
                                    virtual_keycode: Some(VirtualKeyCode::Escape),
                                    ..
                                },
                            ..
                        } => *control_flow = ControlFlow::Exit,
                        WindowEvent::Resized(physical_size) => {
                            state.resize(*physical_size);
                        }
                        WindowEvent::ScaleFactorChanged { new_inner_size, .. } => {
                            state.resize(**new_inner_size);
                        }
                        _ => {}
```

```
                    }
                }
            }
            Event::RedrawRequested(_) => {
                state.update();

                match state.render() {
                    Ok(_) => {}
                    Err(wgpu::SurfaceError::Lost) => state.resize(state.init.size),
                    Err(wgpu::SurfaceError::OutOfMemory) => *control_flow = ControlFlow::Exit,
                    Err(e) => eprintln!("{:?}", e),
                }
            }
            Event::MainEventsCleared => {
                window.request_redraw();
            }
            _ => {}
        }
    });
}
```

The above code begins by defining three constants:

```
const X_CHUNKS_COUNT:u32 = 4;
const Z_CHUNKS_COUNT:u32 = 4;
const CHUNKS_COUNT:u32 = 16;
```

In this portion, we establish the number of chunks in both the *x* and *z* directions, resulting in a total of 16 terrain chunks. By adjusting the *X_CHUNKS_COUNT* and *Z_CHUNKS_COUNT* parameters, you can effortlessly tailor the terrain size according to the specific requirements of your application.

Inside the *State::new* function, the unlit shader is utilized to generate multiple instances of terrain chunks using terrain chunk data. A notable departure from the previous example is the inclusion of two uniform buffers: one for the model matrix and another for the view-projection matrix. The translation transformation is employed to define the position of each terrain chunk. This is illustrated in the following code segment:

```
let mut model_mat:Vec<[f32; 16]> = vec![];
let chunk_size1 = (terrain.chunk_size - 1) as f32;
for i in 0..X_CHUNKS_COUNT {
    for j in 0..Z_CHUNKS_COUNT {
        let xt = -0.5 * X_CHUNKS_COUNT as f32 * chunk_size1 + i as f32 * chunk_size1;
        let zt = -0.5 * Z_CHUNKS_COUNT as f32 * chunk_size1 + j as f32 * chunk_size1;
        let translation = [xt,10.0, zt];
        let m = wt::create_model_mat(translation, [0.0, 0.0, 0.0], [1.0, 25.0, 1.0]);
        model_mat.push(*(m.as_ref()));
    }
}
let model_storage_buffer = init.device.create_buffer_init(&wgpu::util::BufferInitDescriptor{
    label: Some("Model Matrix Storage Buffer"),
    contents: cast_slice(&model_mat),
    usage: wgpu::BufferUsages::STORAGE | wgpu::BufferUsages::COPY_DST,
});
```

In this snippet, a loop iterates through *X_CHUNKS_COUNT* and *Z_CHUNKS_COUNT* to calculate the translation values for each terrain chunk. The *create_model_mat* function defined in the *wgpu_simplified* module is utilized to generate the model matrix for each chunk, which considers translation, rotation, and scaling factors. These model matrices are stored in the *model_mat* vector. Subsequently, a storage buffer is created for the model matrices using the *create_buffer_init* method. This buffer is intended for storing the model matrices.

Within the *State::update* function, similar to the approach adopted in the previous example, updating both the vertex and index buffers is necessary if any changes are made to the *level_of_detail* parameter.

In the code snippet above, the *State::render* function retains a resemblance to the rendering process employed in the previous example. However, in this example, the code is configured to generate multiple instances of terrain chunks based on the total number of chunks. Specifically, the rendering process is achieved using the following line of code:

```
render_pass.draw_indexed(0..self.indices_lens[0], 0, 0..CHUNKS_COUNT);
```

This code segment efficiently draws indexed vertices to render multiple instances of the terrain chunks.

Additionally, the code permits the user to modify input parameters through keyboard inputs.

Here is a list of controls using keyboard:

- *Space*: Changes plot type among surface, wireframe, and both.
- *LControl*: Changes the *seed* value for the terrain.
- *LAlt*: Changes the *level_of_detail* parameter.
- *Q/A*: Increases/decreases the *scale* parameter.
- *W/S:* Increases/decreases the *octaves* parameter.
- *E/D:* Increases/decreases the *offect_x* parameter.
- *R/F:* Increases/decreases the *offect_z* parameter.
- *T/G:* Increases/decreases the *water_level* parameter.

8.5.3 Run Application

To run this application, add the following code snippet to the *Cargo.toml* file:

```
[[example]]
name = "ch08_terrain_instance"
path = "examples/ch08/ terrain_ instance.rs"
```

Afterward, execute the following *cargo run* commands in the terminal window:

```
cargo run --example ch08_ terrain_ instance 8
```

Fig.8-8 shows the results of this example.

It is evident from Fig.8-8 that each chunk has the identical appearance and acts independently, resulting in a large terrain with obvious seams between terrain chunks. We will resolve this problem in next section.

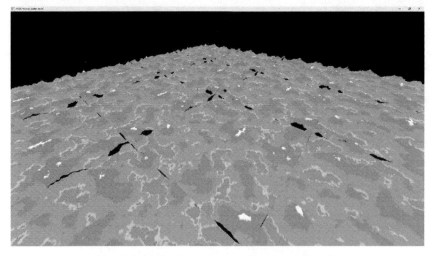

Fig.8-8. Multiple instances of a terrain chunk.

8.6 Multiple Terrain Chunks

The large terrain generated through terrain chunks in the preceding example exhibits discontinuities between the individual chunks. This is attributed to the fact that each chunk generates its distinct set of height map values, thereby leading to non-continuous heights at the borders of neighboring chunks. To address this issue, our foremost objective is to ensure that the terrain chunks possess consistent height maps along their shared borders.

To achieve this goal, we can implement an offset and translation for each chunk. These adjustments should be meticulously calculated, taking into consideration the dimensions of the chunks and the specific positions of each chunk within the overall terrain.

8.6.1 Implementation

In order to achieve a seamless and continuous height map across terrain chunks, we will introduce offset parameters during the creation of these chunks. By subsequently correlating these offsets with the positions of the chunks, we can ensure a cohesive height map experience along the chunk borders.

Begin by navigating to the *terrain_data.rs* file within the *src/* folder and append a new Rust function named *create_terrain_data_multiple_chunks* to the implementation of the *ITerrain* struct. Here is the code for this function:

```
pub fn create_terrain_data_multiple_chunks(&mut self, x_chunks:u32, z_chunks:u32,
translations:&Vec<[f32;2]>) -> (Vec<Vec<Vertex>>, Vec<Vec<Vertex>>, u32) {
    let mut data:Vec<Vec<Vertex>> = vec![];
    let mut data2:Vec<Vec<Vertex>> = vec![];
    let mut vertices_per_row = 0u32;

    let mut k:u32 = 0;
    for _i in 0..x_chunks {
        for _j in 0..z_chunks {
            self.offsets = translations[k as usize];
            let dd = self.create_terrain_data_chunk();
```

```
                    data.push(dd.0);
                    data2.push(dd.1);
                    vertices_per_row = dd.2;
                    k += 1;
                }
            }
        (data, data2, vertices_per_row)
    }
}
```

This function incorporates additional parameters: x_*chunks*, z_*chunks*, and a 2D translation array, as its input arguments. Within the *for* loop, the *offsets* array is explicitly defined using the values from the translation array. This strategic approach guarantees a seamless and uninterrupted noise map across the entire terrain, effectively eliminating any visual seams between adjacent chunks. The function then returns a data array, where each element corresponds to a distinct terrain chunk.

8.6.2 Rust Code

Create a new Rust file named *terrain_multiple_chunks.rs* in the *examples/ch08/* folder and add the following code to it:

```rust
use std:: {iter, mem};
use rand::Rng;
use cgmath::Matrix4;
use wgpu:: {util::DeviceExt, VertexBufferLayout};
use winit::{
    event::*,
    event_loop::{ControlFlow, EventLoop},
    window::Window,
};
use bytemuck::cast_slice;
use wgpu_book_examples:: { wgpu_simplified as ws, transforms as wt, terrain_data };

const X_CHUNKS_COUNT:u32 = 2;
const Z_CHUNKS_COUNT:u32 = 2;

struct State {
    init:  ws::IWgpuInit,
    pipelines: Vec<wgpu::RenderPipeline>,
    vertex_buffers: Vec<wgpu::Buffer>,
    vertex_buffers2: Vec<wgpu::Buffer>,
    index_buffers: Vec<wgpu::Buffer>,
    uniform_bind_groups: Vec<wgpu::BindGroup>,
    uniform_buffers: Vec<wgpu::Buffer>,
    view_mat: Matrix4<f32>,
    project_mat: Matrix4<f32>,
    msaa_texture_view: wgpu::TextureView,
    depth_texture_view: wgpu::TextureView,
    indices_lens: Vec<u32>,
    plot_type: u32,

    terrain: terrain_data::ITerrain,
    update_buffers: bool,
    translations: Vec<[f32; 2]>,
    normalize_mode: u32,
    fps_counter: ws::FpsCounter,
}
```

```rust
impl State {
    async fn new(window:&Window, sample_count:u32, width:u32, height:u32) -> Self {
        let init = ws::IWgpuInit::new(&window, sample_count, None).await;

        let shader = init.device.create_shader_module(wgpu::include_wgsl!("shader_unlit_instance.wgsl"));

        let mut terrain = terrain_data::ITerrain::new();

        // uniform data
        let mut translations:Vec<[f32; 2]> = vec![];
        let mut model_mat:Vec<[f32; 16]> = vec![];
        let chunk_size1 = (terrain.chunk_size - 1) as f32;
        for i in 0..X_CHUNKS_COUNT {
            for j in 0..Z_CHUNKS_COUNT {
                let xt = -0.5 * X_CHUNKS_COUNT as f32 * chunk_size1 + i as f32 * chunk_size1;
                let zt = -0.5 * Z_CHUNKS_COUNT as f32 * chunk_size1 + j as f32 * chunk_size1;
                let translation = [xt, 10.0, zt];
                let m = wt::create_model_mat(translation, [0.0, 0.0, 0.0], [1.0, 25.0, 1.0]);
                model_mat.push(*(m.as_ref()));
                translations.push([xt, zt]);
            }
        }
        let model_storage_buffer = init.device.create_buffer_init(&wgpu::util::BufferInitDescriptor{
            label: Some("Model Matrix Storage Buffer"),
            contents: cast_slice(&model_mat),
            usage: wgpu::BufferUsages::STORAGE | wgpu::BufferUsages::COPY_DST,
        });

        let camera_position = (120.0, 120.0, 150.0).into();
        let look_direction = (0.0,0.0,0.0).into();
        let up_direction = cgmath::Vector3::unit_y();

        let (view_mat, project_mat, vp_mat) =
            wt::create_vp_mat(camera_position, look_direction, up_direction,
            init.config.width as f32 / init.config.height as f32);

        // create vertex uniform buffers
        let vp_uniform_buffer = init.device.create_buffer_init(&wgpu::util::BufferInitDescriptor{
            label: Some("View-Projection Matrix Uniform Buffer"),
            contents: cast_slice(vp_mat.as_ref() as &[f32; 16]),
            usage: wgpu::BufferUsages::UNIFORM | wgpu::BufferUsages::COPY_DST,
        });

        // uniform bind group for vertex shader
        let (vert_bind_group_layout, vert_bind_group) = ws::create_bind_group_storage(
            &init.device,
            vec![wgpu::ShaderStages::VERTEX, wgpu::ShaderStages::VERTEX],
            vec![
                wgpu::BufferBindingType::Uniform,
                wgpu::BufferBindingType::Storage { read_only: true },
            ],
            &[vp_uniform_buffer.as_entire_binding(), model_storage_buffer.as_entire_binding()],
        );

        let (vert_bind_group_layout2, vert_bind_group2) = ws::create_bind_group_storage(
            &init.device,
            vec![wgpu::ShaderStages::VERTEX, wgpu::ShaderStages::VERTEX],
            vec![
                wgpu::BufferBindingType::Uniform,
                wgpu::BufferBindingType::Storage { read_only: true },
```

```
        ],
        &[vp_uniform_buffer.as_entire_binding(), model_storage_buffer.as_entire_binding()],
    );

    let vertex_buffer_layout = VertexBufferLayout {
        array_stride: mem::size_of::<terrain_data::Vertex>() as wgpu::BufferAddress,
        step_mode: wgpu::VertexStepMode::Vertex,
        attributes: &wgpu::vertex_attr_array![0 => Float32x3, 1 => Float32x3], // pos, col
    };

    let pipeline_layout = init.device.create_pipeline_layout(&wgpu::PipelineLayoutDescriptor {
        label: Some("Render Pipeline Layout"),
        bind_group_layouts: &[&vert_bind_group_layout],
        push_constant_ranges: &[],
    });

    let mut ppl = ws::IRenderPipeline {
        shader: Some(&shader),
        pipeline_layout: Some(&pipeline_layout),
        vertex_buffer_layout: &[vertex_buffer_layout],
        ..Default::default()
    };
    let pipeline = ppl.new(&init);

    let vertex_buffer_layout2 = VertexBufferLayout {
        array_stride: mem::size_of::<terrain_data::Vertex>() as wgpu::BufferAddress,
        step_mode: wgpu::VertexStepMode::Vertex,
        attributes: &wgpu::vertex_attr_array![0 => Float32x3, 1 => Float32x3], // pos, col
    };

    let pipeline_layout2 = init.device.create_pipeline_layout(&wgpu::PipelineLayoutDescriptor {
        label: Some("Render Pipeline Layout 2"),
        bind_group_layouts: &[&vert_bind_group_layout2],
        push_constant_ranges: &[],
    });

    let mut ppl2 = ws::IRenderPipeline {
        topology: wgpu::PrimitiveTopology::LineList,
        shader: Some(&shader),
        pipeline_layout: Some(&pipeline_layout2),
        vertex_buffer_layout: &[vertex_buffer_layout2],
        ..Default::default()
    };
    let pipeline2 = ppl2.new(&init);

    let msaa_texture_view = ws::create_msaa_texture_view(&init);
    let depth_texture_view = ws::create_depth_view(&init);

    terrain.scale = 50.0;
    terrain.water_level = 0.3;
    terrain.width = width;
    terrain.height = height;
    let vertex_data = terrain.create_terrain_data_multiple_chunks(X_CHUNKS_COUNT, Z_CHUNKS_COUNT,
        &translations);
    let index_data = terrain.create_indices(vertex_data.2, vertex_data.2);

    let mut vertex_buffers:Vec<wgpu::Buffer> = vec![];
    let mut vertex_buffers2:Vec<wgpu::Buffer> = vec![];
    let mut k:usize = 0;
    for _i in 0..X_CHUNKS_COUNT {
```

```
            for _j in 0..Z_CHUNKS_COUNT {
                let vb = init.device.create_buffer_init(&wgpu::util::BufferInitDescriptor {
                    label: Some("Vertex Buffer"),
                    contents: cast_slice(&vertex_data.0[k]),
                    usage: wgpu::BufferUsages::VERTEX | wgpu::BufferUsages::COPY_DST,
                });
                let vb2 = init.device.create_buffer_init(&wgpu::util::BufferInitDescriptor {
                    label: Some("Vertex Buffer 2"),
                    contents: cast_slice(&vertex_data.1[k]),
                    usage: wgpu::BufferUsages::VERTEX | wgpu::BufferUsages::COPY_DST,
                });
                vertex_buffers.push(vb);
                vertex_buffers2.push(vb2);
                k += 1;
            }
        }

        let index_buffer = init.device.create_buffer_init(&wgpu::util::BufferInitDescriptor{
            label: Some("Index Buffer"),
            contents: bytemuck::cast_slice(&index_data.0),
            usage: wgpu::BufferUsages::INDEX | wgpu::BufferUsages::COPY_DST,
        });

        let index_buffer2 = init.device.create_buffer_init(&wgpu::util::BufferInitDescriptor{
            label: Some("Index Buffer 2"),
            contents: bytemuck::cast_slice(&index_data.1),
            usage: wgpu::BufferUsages::INDEX | wgpu::BufferUsages::COPY_DST,
        });

        Self {
            init,
            pipelines: vec![pipeline, pipeline2],
            vertex_buffers,
            vertex_buffers2,
            index_buffers: vec![index_buffer, index_buffer2],
            uniform_bind_groups: vec![vert_bind_group, vert_bind_group2],
            uniform_buffers: vec![vp_uniform_buffer, model_storage_buffer],
            view_mat,
            project_mat,
            msaa_texture_view,
            depth_texture_view,
            indices_lens: vec![index_data.0.len() as u32, index_data.1.len() as u32],
            plot_type: 0,

            terrain,
            update_buffers: false,
            translations,
            normalize_mode: 0,
            fps_counter: ws::FpsCounter::default(),
        }
    }

    fn resize(&mut self, new_size: winit::dpi::PhysicalSize<u32>) {
        if new_size.width > 0 && new_size.height > 0 {
            self.init.size = new_size;
            self.init.config.width = new_size.width;
            self.init.config.height = new_size.height;
            self.init.surface.configure(&self.init.device, &self.init.config);

            self.project_mat = wt::create_projection_mat(new_size.width as f32 / new_size.height as f32,
```

```
                    true);
            let vp_mat = self.project_mat * self.view_mat;
            self.init.queue.write_buffer(&self.uniform_buffers[0], 0,
                cast_slice(vp_mat.as_ref() as &[f32;16]));

            self.depth_texture_view = ws::create_depth_view(&self.init);
            if self.init.sample_count > 1 {
                self.msaa_texture_view = ws::create_msaa_texture_view(&self.init);
            }
        }
    }

    #[allow(unused_variables)]
    fn input(&mut self, event: &WindowEvent) -> bool {
        match event {
            WindowEvent::KeyboardInput {
                input:
                    KeyboardInput {
                        virtual_keycode: Some(keycode),
                        state: ElementState::Pressed,
                        ..
                    },
                ..
            } => {
                match keycode {
                    VirtualKeyCode::Space => {
                        self.plot_type = (self.plot_type + 1) % 3;
                        true
                    },
                    VirtualKeyCode::LControl => {
                        let mut rng = rand::thread_rng();
                        self.terrain.seed = rng.gen_range(1..65536);
                        self.update_buffers = true;
                        println!("seed = {}", self.terrain.seed);
                        true
                    },
                    VirtualKeyCode::LAlt => {
                        self.terrain.level_of_detail = (self.terrain.level_of_detail + 1) % 7;
                        self.update_buffers = true;
                        println!("LOD = {}", self.terrain.level_of_detail);
                        true
                    },
                    VirtualKeyCode::LShift => {
                        self.normalize_mode = (self.normalize_mode + 1) % 2;
                        self.terrain.normalize_mode = if self.normalize_mode == 0 { "local".to_string() }
                            else { "global".to_string() };
                        self.update_buffers = true;
                        println!("LOD = {}", self.terrain.normalize_mode);
                        true
                    },
                    VirtualKeyCode::Q => {
                        self.terrain.scale += 1.0;
                        self.update_buffers = true;
                        println!("scale = {}", self.terrain.scale);
                        true
                    },
                    VirtualKeyCode::A => {
                        self.terrain.scale -= 1.0;
                        if self.terrain.scale < 1.0 {
                            self.terrain.scale = 1.0;
```

```
                }
                self.update_buffers = true;
                println!("scale = {}", self.terrain.scale);
                true
            },
            VirtualKeyCode::W => {
                self.terrain.octaves += 1;
                self.update_buffers = true;
                println!("octaves = {}", self.terrain.octaves);
                true
            },
            VirtualKeyCode::S => {
                self.terrain.octaves -= 1;
                if self.terrain.octaves < 1 {
                    self.terrain.octaves = 1;
                }
                self.update_buffers = true;
                println!("octaves = {}", self.terrain.octaves);
                true
            },
            VirtualKeyCode::E => {
                self.terrain.offsets[0] += 1.0;
                self.update_buffers = true;
                println!("offset_x = {}", self.terrain.offsets[0]);
                true
            },
            VirtualKeyCode::D => {
                self.terrain.offsets[0] -= 1.0;
                self.update_buffers = true;
                println!("offset_x = {}", self.terrain.offsets[0]);
                true
            },
            VirtualKeyCode::R => {
                self.terrain.offsets[1] += 1.0;
                self.update_buffers = true;
                println!("offset_z = {}", self.terrain.offsets[1]);
                true
            },
            VirtualKeyCode::F => {
                self.terrain.offsets[1] -= 1.0;
                self.update_buffers = true;
                println!("offset_z = {}", self.terrain.offsets[1]);
                true
            },
            VirtualKeyCode::T => {
                self.terrain.water_level += 0.01;
                self.update_buffers = true;
                println!("water_level = {}", self.terrain.water_level);
                true
            },
            VirtualKeyCode::G => {
                self.terrain.water_level -= 0.01;
                self.update_buffers = true;
                println!("water_level = {}", self.terrain.water_level);
                true
            },
            _ => false
        }
    }
    _ => false,
```

```
        }
    }

    fn update(&mut self) {
        // update buffers:
        if self.update_buffers {
            let vertex_data = self.terrain.create_terrain_data_multiple_chunks(X_CHUNKS_COUNT,
                Z_CHUNKS_COUNT, &self.translations);

            let mut k = 0usize;
            for _i in 0..X_CHUNKS_COUNT {
                for _j in 0..Z_CHUNKS_COUNT {
                    self.init.queue.write_buffer(&self.vertex_buffers[k], 0,
                        cast_slice(&vertex_data.0[k]));
                    self.init.queue.write_buffer(&self.vertex_buffers2[k], 0,
                        cast_slice(&vertex_data.1[k]));
                    k += 1;
                }
            }

            let index_data = self.terrain.create_indices(vertex_data.2, vertex_data.2);
            self.init.queue.write_buffer(&self.index_buffers[0], 0, cast_slice(&index_data.0));
            self.init.queue.write_buffer(&self.index_buffers[1], 0, cast_slice(&index_data.1));
            self.indices_lens = vec![index_data.0.len() as u32, index_data.1.len() as u32];
            self.update_buffers = false;
        }
    }

    fn render(&mut self) -> Result<(), wgpu::SurfaceError> {
        //let output = self.init.surface.get_current_frame()?.output;
        let output = self.init.surface.get_current_texture()?;
        let view = output
            .texture
            .create_view(&wgpu::TextureViewDescriptor::default());

        let mut encoder = self
            .init.device
            .create_command_encoder(&wgpu::CommandEncoderDescriptor {
                label: Some("Render Encoder"),
            });

        {
            let color_attach = ws::create_color_attachment(&view);
            let msaa_attach = ws::create_msaa_color_attachment(&view, &self.msaa_texture_view);
            let color_attachment = if self.init.sample_count == 1 { color_attach } else { msaa_attach };
            let depth_attachment = ws::create_depth_stencil_attachment(&self.depth_texture_view);

            let mut render_pass = encoder.begin_render_pass(&wgpu::RenderPassDescriptor {
                label: Some("Render Pass"),
                color_attachments: &[Some(color_attachment)],
                depth_stencil_attachment: Some(depth_attachment),
                occlusion_query_set: None,
                timestamp_writes: None,
            });

            let plot_type = if self.plot_type == 1 { "shape_only" } else if self.plot_type == 2
                {"wireframe_only"} else {"both"};

            if plot_type == "shape_only" || plot_type == "both" {
                render_pass.set_pipeline(&self.pipelines[0]);
```

```
        render_pass.set_bind_group(0, &self.uniform_bind_groups[0], &[]);

        let mut k:u32 = 0;
        for _i in 0..X_CHUNKS_COUNT {
            for _j in 0..Z_CHUNKS_COUNT {
                render_pass.set_vertex_buffer(0, self.vertex_buffers[k as usize].slice(..));
                render_pass.set_index_buffer(self.index_buffers[0].slice(..),
                    wgpu::IndexFormat::Uint32);
                render_pass.draw_indexed(0..self.indices_lens[0], 0, k..k+1);
                k += 1;
            }
        }
    }

    if plot_type == "wireframe_only" || plot_type == "both" {
        render_pass.set_pipeline(&self.pipelines[1]);
        render_pass.set_bind_group(0, &self.uniform_bind_groups[1], &[]);

        let mut k:u32 = 0;
        for _i in 0..X_CHUNKS_COUNT {
            for _j in 0..Z_CHUNKS_COUNT {
                render_pass.set_vertex_buffer(0, self.vertex_buffers2[k as usize].slice(..));
                render_pass.set_index_buffer(self.index_buffers[1].slice(..),
                    wgpu::IndexFormat::Uint32);
                render_pass.draw_indexed(0..self.indices_lens[1], 0, k..k+1);
                k += 1;
            }
        }
    }
}
self.fps_counter.print_fps(5);
self.init.queue.submit(iter::once(encoder.finish()));
output.present();

Ok(())
    }
}

fn main() {
    let mut sample_count = 1 as u32;
    let mut width = 200u32;
    let mut height = 200u32;
    let args: Vec<String> = std::env::args().collect();
    if args.len() > 1 {
        sample_count = args[1].parse::<u32>().unwrap();
    }
    if args.len() > 2 {
        width = args[2].parse::<u32>().unwrap();
    }
    if args.len() > 3 {
        height = args[3].parse::<u32>().unwrap();
    }

    env_logger::init();
    let event_loop = EventLoop::new();
    let window = winit::window::WindowBuilder::new().build(&event_loop).unwrap();
    window.set_title(&*format!("ch08_{}", "terrain_multiple_chunks"));

    let mut state = pollster::block_on(State::new(&window, sample_count, width, height));
```

```
event_loop.run(move |event, _, control_flow| {
    match event {
        Event::WindowEvent {
            ref event,
            window_id,
        } if window_id == window.id() => {
            if !state.input(event) {
                match event {
                    WindowEvent::CloseRequested
                    | WindowEvent::KeyboardInput {
                        input:
                            KeyboardInput {
                                state: ElementState::Pressed,
                                virtual_keycode: Some(VirtualKeyCode::Escape),
                                ..
                            },
                        ..
                    } => *control_flow = ControlFlow::Exit,
                    WindowEvent::Resized(physical_size) => {
                        state.resize(*physical_size);
                    }
                    WindowEvent::ScaleFactorChanged { new_inner_size, .. } => {
                        state.resize(**new_inner_size);
                    }
                    _ => {}
                }
            }
        }
        Event::RedrawRequested(_) => {
            state.update();

            match state.render() {
                Ok(_) => {}
                Err(wgpu::SurfaceError::Lost) => state.resize(state.init.size),
                Err(wgpu::SurfaceError::OutOfMemory) => *control_flow = ControlFlow::Exit,
                Err(e) => eprintln!("{:?}", e),
            }
        }
        Event::MainEventsCleared => {
            window.request_redraw();
        }
        _ => {}
    }
});
}
```

The above code uses the same shader as the one in the previous example, but generates different terrain data using the *create_terrain_data_multiple_chunks* function. It then defines *X_CHUNKS_COUNT* and *Z_CHUNKS_COUNT* parameters used to create a square terrain with 4 chunks.

In the *State::new* function, we first create a 2D translation vector when generating the uniform data, as demonstrated in the following code snippet:

```
let mut translations:Vec<[f32; 2]> = vec![];
let mut model_mat:Vec<[f32; 16]> = vec![];
let chunk_size1 = (terrain.chunk_size - 1) as f32;
for i in 0..X_CHUNKS_COUNT {
    for j in 0..Z_CHUNKS_COUNT {
        let xt = -0.5 * X_CHUNKS_COUNT as f32 * chunk_size1 + i as f32 * chunk_size1;
        let zt = -0.5 * Z_CHUNKS_COUNT as f32 * chunk_size1 + j as f32 * chunk_size1;
```

```
        let translation = [xt, 10.0, zt];
        let m = wt::create_model_mat(translation, [0.0, 0.0, 0.0], [1.0, 25.0, 1.0]);
        model_mat.push(*(m.as_ref()));
        translations.push([xt, zt]);
    }
}
```

Then, we use this translation vector to generate a data array for each chunk by calling the *create_terrain_data_multiple_chunks* function implemented in the previous section. Subsequently, we use the data array to create various vertex buffer arrays, as shown in the following code snippet:

```
let vertex_data = terrain.create_terrain_data_multiple_chunks(X_CHUNKS_COUNT, Z_CHUNKS_COUNT,
    &translations);

let mut vertex_buffers:Vec<wgpu::Buffer> = vec![];
let mut vertex_buffers2:Vec<wgpu::Buffer> = vec![];
let mut k:usize = 0;
for _i in 0..X_CHUNKS_COUNT {
    for _j in 0..Z_CHUNKS_COUNT {
        let vb = init.device.create_buffer_init(&wgpu::util::BufferInitDescriptor {
            label: Some("Vertex Buffer"),
            contents: cast_slice(&vertex_data.0[k]),
            usage: wgpu::BufferUsages::VERTEX | wgpu::BufferUsages::COPY_DST,
        });
        let vb2 = init.device.create_buffer_init(&wgpu::util::BufferInitDescriptor {
            label: Some("Vertex Buffer 2"),
            contents: cast_slice(&vertex_data.1[k]),
            usage: wgpu::BufferUsages::VERTEX | wgpu::BufferUsages::COPY_DST,
        });
        vertex_buffers.push(vb);
        vertex_buffers2.push(vb2);
        k += 1;
    }
}
```

Each element of the data array and various vertex buffer arrays in the above code corresponds to a specific chunk. These arrays are necessary because, to make a continuous large terrain without seams between chunks, each chunk should have different noise map data.

Within the *State::render* function, we need to draw the surface and wireframe of the terrain chunks one by one using for loops because each chunk has different vertex buffers, as illustrated in the following code snippet used to create the surface of the terrain:

```
render_pass.set_pipeline(&self.pipelines[0]);
render_pass.set_bind_group(0, &self.uniform_bind_groups[0], &[]);

let mut k:u32 = 0;
for _i in 0..X_CHUNKS_COUNT {
    for _j in 0..Z_CHUNKS_COUNT {
        render_pass.set_vertex_buffer(0, self.vertex_buffers[k as usize].slice(..));
        render_pass.set_index_buffer(self.index_buffers[0].slice(..),
            wgpu::IndexFormat::Uint32);
        render_pass.draw_indexed(0..self.indices_lens[0], 0, k..k+1);
        k += 1;
    }
}
```

Within the *State::update* function, we update the data array and various vertex buffer arrays using the following code snippet:

```
if self.update_buffers {
    let vertex_data = self.terrain.create_terrain_data_multiple_chunks(X_CHUNKS_COUNT, Z_CHUNKS_COUNT,
        &self.translations);

    let mut k = 0usize;
    for _i in 0..X_CHUNKS_COUNT {
        for _j in 0..Z_CHUNKS_COUNT {
            self.init.queue.write_buffer(&self.vertex_buffers[k], 0, cast_slice(&vertex_data.0[k]));
            self.init.queue.write_buffer(&self.vertex_buffers2[k], 0, cast_slice(&vertex_data.1[k]));
            k += 1;
        }
    }

    let index_data = self.terrain.create_indices(vertex_data.2, vertex_data.2);
    self.init.queue.write_buffer(&self.index_buffers[0], 0, cast_slice(&index_data.0));
    self.init.queue.write_buffer(&self.index_buffers[1], 0, cast_slice(&index_data.1));
    self.indices_lens = vec![index_data.0.len() as u32, index_data.1.len() as u32];
    self.update_buffers = false;
}
```

This code ensures that multiple terrain chunks can be seamlessly connected to form a continuous terrain without any visible seams.

Additionally, the code permits the user to modify input parameters through keyboard inputs.

Here is a list of controls using keyboard:

- *Space*: Changes plot type among surface, wireframe, and both.

- *LControl*: Changes the *seed* value for the terrain.

- *LAlt*: Changes the *level_of_detail* parameter.

- *LShift*: Changes the normalization model: *local* or *global*.

- *Q/A*: Increases/decreases the *scale* parameter.

- *W/S:* Increases/decreases the *octaves* parameter.

- *E/D:* Increases/decreases the *offect_x* parameter.

- *R/F:* Increases/decreases the *offect_z* parameter.

- *T/G:* Increases/decreases the *water_level* parameter.

8.6.3 Run Application

To run this application, add the following code snippet to the *Cargo.toml* file:

```
[[example]]
name = "ch08_terrain_multiple_chunks"
path = "examples/ch08/ terrain_ multiple_chunks.rs"
```

Afterward, execute the following *cargo run* commands in the terminal window:

```
cargo run --example ch08_ terrain_ multiple_chunks 8
```

Fig.8-9 displays the results of this example. It is clear that the terrain looks smooth and continuous across different chunks.

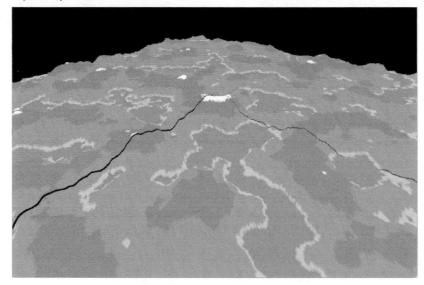

Fig.8-9. A continuous terrain created using multiple chunks.

However, upon close inspection of the terrain, you may notice that the chunks are not lining up perfectly. This is because we are normalizing each chunk locally, and the minimum and maximum noise heights may vary slightly across different chunks. To resolve this issue, we can globally normalize the chunks using the same minimum and maximum heights. This can be achieved by pressing the *LShift* key to change the *normalize_mode* to *global*. By doing so, we can create a seamless terrain using multiple chunks, as depicted in Fig.8-10.

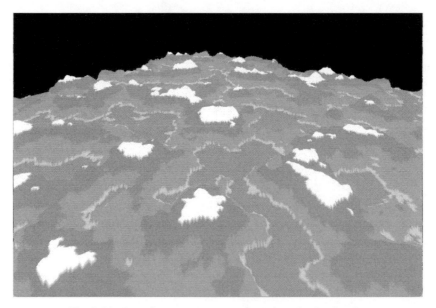

Fig.8-10. A perfect terrain created using multiple chunks.

With the terrain chunks presented in previous sections, it is possible to easily create a seamless, endless procedural terrain dynamically. Additionally, the LOD feature allows for a smoother transition between different levels of detail as the viewer moves closer or further away from the terrain. This means that the terrain can have more detail when viewed up close and less detail when viewed from a distance.

To create an endless terrain, you need to develop a system to dynamically load and unload chunks, ensuring that only the necessary terrain data is loaded into memory. One way to achieve this is to load chunks based on the player's position and unload chunks that are too far away. The detailed implementation of this system is beyond the scope of this book.

8.7 Terrain Animation

Animating the terrain can be a great way to produce special effects and add more visual interest to your scene. For example, you can animate the vertices of the terrain mesh to create a ripping effect, which can be used to simulate water waves. You can also animate the vertices of the terrain mesh to create a swaying effect, which can be used to mimic wind effects.

In this section, I will show you how to simulate an endless terrain by using the terrain scrolling technique. The idea is to animate the entire terrain mesh in one direction and then wrap it around so that it seamlessly connects with the beginning of the mesh.

Create a new Rust file named *terrain_animation.rs* in the *examples/ch08/* folder. This file is similar to the *terrain_water_level.rs* file used earlier to create a terrain with water level. Here, I only list the difference between these two files. To animate the entire terrain using the scrolling technique, we need to move the terrain in one direction by a small amount for each frame within the *State::update* function. Below is the code snippet for doing this:

```
self.terrain.offsets[1] = -20.0*self.animation_speed * dt.as_secs_f32();
let vertex_data = self.terrain.create_terrain_data_with_water_level();
self.init.queue.write_buffer(&self.vertex_buffers[0], 0, cast_slice(&vertex_data.0));
self.init.queue.write_buffer(&self.vertex_buffers[1], 0, cast_slice(&vertex_data.1));
```

The above code snippet sets the *offsets[1]* parameter using a time-dependent value scaled by the animation speed, resulting in movement in the *z* direction. To achieve this, we need to update the terrain data and vertex buffers for every frame, which is a computation-intensity task. For a larger terrain created on the CPU, the framerate is expected to drop.

Fig.8-11 shows the results of this example.

It is clear that for a terrain with a size of 200×200, the framerate drops to 8 FPS. In this case, the animation appears to stutter, resulting in a choppy and less smooth movement of the terrain.

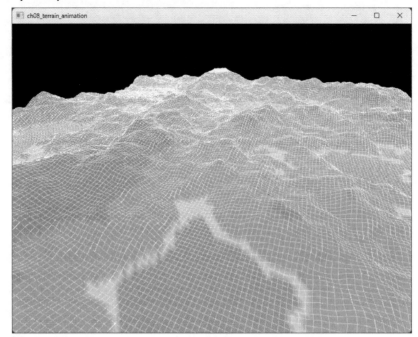

Fig.8-11. Terrain animation.

8.8 Creating Terrain on GPU

In this section, we will use compute shaders to animate the terrain on the GPU. This is because animating a large terrain on the CPU without a significant drop in framerate is almost impossible, as demonstrated in the previous example.

8.8.1 WGSL Code for Noise Model

To create terrains on the GPU using compute shaders, we need to implement a noise model in WGSL shader code. Add a new WGSL shader file named *noise.wgsl* to the *examples/ch08/* folder and include the following code:

```
const MAGIC:f32 = 43758.5453123;

fn random2d(st:vec2<f32>) -> vec2<f32> {
    let x = dot(st, vec2(127.1, 311.7));
    let y = dot(st, vec2(269.5, 183.3));
    let s = vec2(x, y);
    return -1.0 + 2.0 * fract(sin(s) * MAGIC);
}

fn interpolate(t:f32) -> f32 {
    return t * t * t * (10.0 + t * (6.0 * t - 15.0)); // smoothstep
}

fn gradientNoise(p:vec2<f32>) -> vec4<f32> {
    let i = floor(p);
```

```
    let f = fract(p);

    let f11 = dot(random2d(i + vec2(0.0, 0.0)), f - vec2(0.0, 0.0));
    let f12 = dot(random2d(i + vec2(0.0, 1.0)), f - vec2(0.0, 1.0));
    let f21 = dot(random2d(i + vec2(1.0, 0.0)), f - vec2(1.0, 0.0));
    let f22 = dot(random2d(i + vec2(1.0, 1.0)), f - vec2(1.0, 1.0));

    return vec4(f11, f12, f21, f22);
}

fn perlinNoise(p:vec2f) -> f32 {
    let v = gradientNoise(p);

    let f = fract(p);
    let t = interpolate(f.x);
    let u = interpolate(f.y);

    return mix(
        mix(v.x, v.z, t),
        mix(v.y, v.w, t),
        u
    ) * 0.5 + 0.5;
}
```

The *random2d* function in the above code is a 2D random number generator. The function takes a 2D vector as input and returns a 2D random vector. It first calculates two dot products between the input vector and two constant vectors. It then calculates the sine of each dot product and multiplies them with a constant value called MAGIC. Finally, it calculates the fractional part of this result and returns it as a 2D vector. It is worth noting that the MAGIC constant was chosen somewhat arbitrarily, as it provides a good balance between speed and randomness. These two constant vectors are also chosen arbitrarily, but they should be different and not collinear to ensure better distribution of the random values.

The *interpolate* function in the code above applies a *smoothstep* interpolation function to the input value using a third-order polynomial equation. The function returns a value that is a smooth and continuous transition between 0 and 1.

The *gradientNoise* function takes a 2D vector as input and returns a 4D random vector. The function first calculates the floor of the input vector and then calculates the fractional part of it. Next, it calculates four dot products between random 2D vectors and four different offsets from the input vector. Finally, the function returns these four dot products as a 4D vector.

The *perlinNoise* function is used to generate 2D Perlin noise. The function first calculates the gradient noise at the given point using the *gradientNoise* function. The resulting noise value is stored in a 4D vector. Next, the function calculates the fractional part of the input vector. This is used to interpolate the noise value between the neighboring integer coordinates using the *interpolate* function. Finally, the function uses the *mix* function to blend the four noise values calculated by *gradientNoise* using the interpolated values. The resulting value is scaled and shifted to fit in the range of [0, 1] and returned as the final noise value.

To use compute shaders to generate terrains on the GPU, we also need to implement certain utility functions in shader code, as we did earlier in Rust. Add the following two helper functions to the *noise.wgsl* file with the following code:

```
fn lerpColor(colors:array<vec3f,5>, ta1:array<f32,6>, t:f32) -> vec3f {
    var res = vec3(0.0);
    var rgbData = colors;
    var ta = ta1;
```

```
    for(var i = 0u; i < 5u; i = i + 1u){
        if(t >= ta[i] && t < ta[i+1u]){
            res = rgbData[i];
        }
    }

    if(t == ta[5u]){
        res = rgbData[4u];
    }
    return res;
}

fn addTerrainColors(rgbData:array<vec3f,5>, ta:array<f32,6>, tmin:f32, tmax:f32, t:f32,
waterLevel:f32) -> vec3f {
    var tt = t;
    if(t < tmin){tt = tmin;}
    if(t > tmax){tt = tmax;}
    if(tmin == tmax) {return vec3(0.0);}
    tt = (tt-tmin)/(tmax-tmin);

    var t1 = array<f32, 6>(0.0,0.0,0.0,0.0,0.0,0.0);
    let r = (1.0 - waterLevel)/(1.0 - ta[1]);
    var del:f32 = 0.0;
    t1[1] = waterLevel;

    for(var i:u32 = 1u; i < 5u; i = i + 1u) {
        if (i == 1u) {
            del = ta[2u] - ta[1u];
            t1[2] = t1[1] + r * del;
        } else if (i == 2u) {
            del = ta[3u] - ta[2u];
            t1[3] = t1[2] + r * del;
        } else if (i == 3u) {
            del = ta[4u] - ta[3u];
            t1[4] = t1[3] + r * del;
        } else if (i == 4u) {
            del = ta[5u] - ta[4u];
            t1[5] = t1[4] + r * del;
        }
    }

    return lerpColor(rgbData, t1, tt);
}
```

The *lerpColor* and *addTerrainColors* functions in the above code are simply conversions of corresponding counterparts implemented in the *terrain_data.rs* file located in the *src/* folder.

8.8.2 Compute Shader for Terrain data

Create a new WGSL shader file named *terrain_comp.wgsl* in the *examples/ch08/* folder and add the following code to it:

```
struct VertexData{
    position: vec4f,
    color: vec4f,
}

struct VertexDataArray{
```

```
        vertexDataArray: array<VertexData>,
}

struct TerrainParams{
    resolution: f32,
    octaves: f32,
    persistence: f32,
    lacunarity: f32,
    offsetX: f32,
    offsetZ: f32,
    scale: f32,
    waterLevel: f32,
}

@group(0) @binding(0) var<storage, read_write> vda : VertexDataArray;
@group(0) @binding(1) var<storage, read_write> vda2 : VertexDataArray;
@group(0) @binding(2) var<uniform> tps: TerrainParams;

fn terrainFunc(x:f32, z:f32) -> f32 {
    let halfr = 0.5 * tps.resolution;
    var amplitude = 1.0;
    var frequency = 1.0;
    var noiseHeight = 0.0;
    for(var i:u32 = 0u; i < u32(tps.octaves); i = i+1u) {
        let sampleX = (x - halfr + tps.offsetX)/(tps.scale) * frequency;
        let sampleZ = (z - halfr - tps.offsetZ)/(tps.scale) * frequency;
        let y = perlinNoise(vec2(sampleX, sampleZ))*2.0 - 1.0;
        noiseHeight += y * amplitude;
        amplitude *= tps.persistence;
        frequency *= tps.lacunarity;
    }
    return noiseHeight;
}

@compute @workgroup_size(8, 8, 1)
fn cs_main(@builtin(global_invocation_id) id : vec3u){
    var i = id.x;
    var j = id.y;
    var y = terrainFunc(f32(id.x), f32(id.y));
    let waterLevel = 0.1*tps.waterLevel;
    if(y <= waterLevel) { y = waterLevel - 0.000001; }
    let p0 = vec3(f32(id.x), y, f32(id.y));

    // colormap
    let cData = array<vec3<f32>,5>(
        vec3(0.055, 0.529, 0.8),
        vec3(0.761, 0.698, 0.502),
        vec3(0.204, 0.549, 0.192),
        vec3(0.353, 0.302, 0.255),
        vec3(1.0, 0.98, 0.98)
    );
     let cData2 = array<vec3<f32>,5>(
        vec3(1.0),
        vec3(1.0),
        vec3(1.0),
        vec3(1.0),
        vec3(1.0),
    );
    let ta = array<f32, 6>(0.0, 0.3, 0.35, 0.4, 0.7, 1.0);
    let color = addTerrainColors(cData, ta, 0.0, 1.0, p0.y, waterLevel);
```

```
        let color2 = addTerrainColors(cData2, ta, 0.0, 1.0, p0.y, waterLevel);

        var idx = i + j * u32(tps.resolution);
        vda.vertexDataArray[idx].position = vec4(p0, 1.0);
        vda.vertexDataArray[idx].color = vec4(color, 1.0);

        vda2.vertexDataArray[idx].position = vec4(p0, 1.0);
        vda2.vertexDataArray[idx].color = vec4(color2, 1.0);
}
```

The above compute shader is used to generate terrain heightmaps and colors for a given resolution using the *perlinNoise* function implemented in the previous section.

The shader starts by defining two structs: *VertexData* and *TerrainParams*. *VertexData* contains the *position* and *color* of a single vertex, and *TerrainParams* contains the parameters that control the generation of the terrain. The *VertexDataArray* struct defines a dynamic array using the *VertexData* struct, which is used to store the vertex data for the terrain.

The *terrainFunc* function takes the *x* and *z* coordinates as input arguments and generates a noise height map for the terrain at the specified location using Perlin noise. It uses the terrain parameters to control the number of octaves, persistence, lacunarity, scale, and height multiplier of the noise function. This process is very similar to what we did earlier in Rust.

The main function in the code above is *cs_main*, which takes the *global_invocation_id* of the current thread as input. The function first calls *terrainFunc* to generate the noise height of the terrain at the current location. Similar as what we did in Rust, in this example, we also hardcode the water level. Namely, if the height is below the specified water level, it manually sets the height to be the water level. Otherwise, the height is just the noise height value returned by the *perlinNoise* function.

The function then generates the position vector for the current vertex using the height value and the global ID. It uses this position to determine the color of the vertex by invoking the *addTerrainColors* function with the array of RGB colors and an array of terrain altitudes. Finally, the function writes the position and color of the current vertex to the vertex data array at the appropriate index, which will be used to generate the terrain. The two vertex data arrays are used to store the vertex data for the terrain and wireframe.

It is worth noting that in the *cs_main* function, we generate the terrain data in parallel for all vertices at once, and there is no for-loop involved. This is why terrain data generation on the GPU should be much faster than on the CPU, where a double for-loop is necessary to perform computation for each vertex at a time.

In the previous chapter, we implemented a compute shader for indices that is used to generate 3D surfaces. We will reuse this indices shader in this example.

8.8.3 Rust Code

With the noise model and compute shaders presented earlier, we are ready to generate the terrain animation on the GPU. To achieve this, create a new Rust file named *terrain_gpu.rs* in the *examples/ch08/* folder and add the following code to it:

```
use std:: {iter, f32::consts::PI};
use cgmath::Matrix4;
use wgpu:: {util::DeviceExt, VertexBufferLayout};
use winit::{
    event::*,
```

```
        event_loop::{ControlFlow, EventLoop},
        window::Window,
};
use bytemuck::cast_slice;
use wgpu_book_examples:: { wgpu_simplified as ws, transforms as wt };

struct State {
    init:   ws::IWgpuInit,
    pipelines: Vec<wgpu::RenderPipeline>,
    uniform_bind_groups: Vec<wgpu::BindGroup>,
    uniform_buffers: Vec<wgpu::Buffer>,

    cs_pipelines: Vec<wgpu::ComputePipeline>,
    cs_vertex_buffers: Vec<wgpu::Buffer>,
    cs_index_buffers: Vec<wgpu::Buffer>,
    cs_uniform_buffers: Vec<wgpu::Buffer>,
    cs_bind_groups: Vec<wgpu::BindGroup>,

    model_mat: Matrix4<f32>,
    view_mat: Matrix4<f32>,
    project_mat: Matrix4<f32>,
    msaa_texture_view: wgpu::TextureView,
    depth_texture_view: wgpu::TextureView,
    plot_type: u32,

    update_buffers: bool,
    aspect_ratio: f32,
    animation_speed: f32,
    resolution: u32,
    water_level: f32,
    z_offset: f32,
    scale: f32,
    triangles_count: u32,
    lines_count:u32,
    fps_counter: ws::FpsCounter,
}

impl State {
    async fn new(window:&Window, sample_count:u32, resolution:u32) -> Self {
        let init = ws::IWgpuInit::new(&window, sample_count, None).await;

        let resol = ws::round_to_multiple(resolution, 8);
        let vertices_count = resol * resol;
        let triangles_count = 6 * (resol - 1) * (resol - 1);
        let lines_count = 8 * (resol - 1) * (resol - 1);
        println!("resolution = {}", resol);

        let shader = init.device.create_shader_module(wgpu::include_wgsl!("shader_unlit.wgsl"));

        let cs_noise = include_str!("noise.wgsl");
        let cs_terrain = include_str!("terrain_comp.wgsl");
        let cs_combine = [cs_noise, cs_terrain].join("\n");
        let cs_comp = init.device.create_shader_module(wgpu::ShaderModuleDescriptor {
            label: Some("Compute Shader"),
            source: wgpu::ShaderSource::Wgsl(cs_combine.into()),
        });

        let cs_indices =
init.device.create_shader_module(wgpu::include_wgsl!("../ch07/indices_comp.wgsl"));
```

```
    // uniform data
    let model_mat = wt::create_model_mat([-0.65*resol as f32, 5.0, -0.5*resol as f32],
        [0.0, PI/15.0, 0.0], [1.0, 20.0, 1.0]);

    let camera_position = (40.0, 50.0, 60.0).into();
    let look_direction = (0.0,0.0,0.0).into();
    let up_direction = cgmath::Vector3::unit_y();

    let (view_mat, project_mat, vp_mat) =
        wt::create_vp_mat(camera_position, look_direction, up_direction,
        init.config.width as f32 / init.config.height as f32);

    let mvp_mat = vp_mat * model_mat;

    // create vertex uniform buffers
    let vert_uniform_buffer = init.device.create_buffer_init(&wgpu::util::BufferInitDescriptor{
        label: Some("Vertex Uniform Buffer"),
        contents: cast_slice(mvp_mat.as_ref() as &[f32; 16]),
        usage: wgpu::BufferUsages::UNIFORM | wgpu::BufferUsages::COPY_DST,
    });

    // uniform bind group for vertex shader
    let (vert_bind_group_layout, vert_bind_group) = ws::create_bind_group(
        &init.device,
        vec![wgpu::ShaderStages::VERTEX],
        &[vert_uniform_buffer.as_entire_binding()],
    );
    let (vert_bind_group_layout2, vert_bind_group2) = ws::create_bind_group(
        &init.device,
        vec![wgpu::ShaderStages::VERTEX],
        &[vert_uniform_buffer.as_entire_binding()],
    );

    let vertex_buffer_layout = VertexBufferLayout {
        array_stride: 32,
        step_mode: wgpu::VertexStepMode::Vertex,
        attributes: &wgpu::vertex_attr_array![0 => Float32x4, 1 => Float32x4], // pos, col
    };

    let pipeline_layout = init.device.create_pipeline_layout(&wgpu::PipelineLayoutDescriptor {
        label: Some("Render Pipeline Layout"),
        bind_group_layouts: &[&vert_bind_group_layout],
        push_constant_ranges: &[],
    });

    let mut ppl = ws::IRenderPipeline {
        shader: Some(&shader),
        pipeline_layout: Some(&pipeline_layout),
        vertex_buffer_layout: &[vertex_buffer_layout],
        ..Default::default()
    };
    let pipeline = ppl.new(&init);

    let vertex_buffer_layout2 = VertexBufferLayout {
        array_stride: 32,
        step_mode: wgpu::VertexStepMode::Vertex,
        attributes: &wgpu::vertex_attr_array![0 => Float32x4, 1 => Float32x4], // pos, col
    };

    let pipeline_layout2 = init.device.create_pipeline_layout(&wgpu::PipelineLayoutDescriptor {
```

```
        label: Some("Render Pipeline Layout 2"),
        bind_group_layouts: &[&vert_bind_group_layout2],
        push_constant_ranges: &[],
});

let mut ppl2 = ws::IRenderPipeline {
    topology: wgpu::PrimitiveTopology::LineList,
    shader: Some(&shader),
    pipeline_layout: Some(&pipeline_layout2),
    vertex_buffer_layout: &[vertex_buffer_layout2],
    ..Default::default()
};
let pipeline2 = ppl2.new(&init);

let msaa_texture_view = ws::create_msaa_texture_view(&init);
let depth_texture_view = ws::create_depth_view(&init);

// create compute pipeline for indices
let cs_index_buffer = init.device.create_buffer(&wgpu::BufferDescriptor{
    label: Some("Index Buffer"),
    size:  4 * triangles_count as u64,
    usage: wgpu::BufferUsages::INDEX | wgpu::BufferUsages::STORAGE | wgpu::BufferUsages::COPY_DST,
    mapped_at_creation: false,
});

let cs_index_buffer2 = init.device.create_buffer(&wgpu::BufferDescriptor{
    label: Some("Index 2 Buffer"),
    size:  4 * lines_count as u64,
    usage: wgpu::BufferUsages::INDEX | wgpu::BufferUsages::STORAGE | wgpu::BufferUsages::COPY_DST,
    mapped_at_creation: false,
});

let cs_index_uniform_buffer = init.device.create_buffer(&wgpu::BufferDescriptor{
    label: Some("Index Uniform Buffer"),
    size:  4,
    usage: wgpu::BufferUsages::UNIFORM | wgpu::BufferUsages::COPY_DST,
    mapped_at_creation: false,
});
init.queue.write_buffer(&cs_index_uniform_buffer, 0, cast_slice(&[resol]));

let (cs_index_bind_group_layout, cs_index_bind_group) = ws::create_bind_group_storage(
    &init.device,
    vec![
        wgpu::ShaderStages::COMPUTE, wgpu::ShaderStages::COMPUTE,
        wgpu::ShaderStages::COMPUTE,
    ],
    vec![
        wgpu::BufferBindingType::Storage { read_only: false },
        wgpu::BufferBindingType::Storage { read_only: false },
        wgpu::BufferBindingType::Uniform,
    ],
    &[
        cs_index_buffer.as_entire_binding(),
        cs_index_buffer2.as_entire_binding(),
        cs_index_uniform_buffer.as_entire_binding(),
    ],
);

let cs_index_pipeline_layout = init.device.create_pipeline_layout(&wgpu::PipelineLayoutDescriptor{
    label: Some("Compute Index Pipeline Layout"),
```

```
        bind_group_layouts: &[&cs_index_bind_group_layout],
        push_constant_ranges: &[],
    });

    let cs_index_pipeline = init.device.create_compute_pipeline(&wgpu::ComputePipelineDescriptor{
        label: Some("Compute Index Pipeline"),
        layout: Some(&cs_index_pipeline_layout),
        module: &cs_indices,
        entry_point: "cs_main",
    });

    // create compute pipeline for terrain
    let cs_vertex_buffer = init.device.create_buffer(&wgpu::BufferDescriptor{
        label: Some("Vertex Buffer"),
        size:  32 * vertices_count as u64,
        usage: wgpu::BufferUsages::VERTEX | wgpu::BufferUsages::STORAGE |
            wgpu::BufferUsages::COPY_DST,
        mapped_at_creation: false,
    });

    let cs_vertex_buffer2 = init.device.create_buffer(&wgpu::BufferDescriptor{
        label: Some("Vertex Buffer 2"),
        size:  32 * vertices_count as u64,
        usage: wgpu::BufferUsages::VERTEX | wgpu::BufferUsages::STORAGE |
            wgpu::BufferUsages::COPY_DST,
        mapped_at_creation: false,
    });

    let params = [resol as f32, 5.0, 0.5, 2.0, 0.0, 0.0, 50.0, 0.2];
    let cs_vertex_uniform_buffer = init.device.create_buffer_init(&wgpu::util::BufferInitDescriptor{
        label: Some("Vertex Uniform Buffer"),
        contents: bytemuck::cast_slice(&params),
        usage: wgpu::BufferUsages::UNIFORM | wgpu::BufferUsages::COPY_DST,
    });

    let (cs_vertex_bind_group_layout, cs_vertex_bind_group) = ws::create_bind_group_storage(
        &init.device,
        vec![
            wgpu::ShaderStages::COMPUTE, wgpu::ShaderStages::COMPUTE, wgpu::ShaderStages::COMPUTE,
        ],
        vec![
            wgpu::BufferBindingType::Storage { read_only: false },
            wgpu::BufferBindingType::Storage { read_only: false },
            wgpu::BufferBindingType::Uniform,
        ],
        &[
            cs_vertex_buffer.as_entire_binding(),
            cs_vertex_buffer2.as_entire_binding(),
            cs_vertex_uniform_buffer.as_entire_binding(),
        ],
    );

    let cs_pipeline_layout = init.device.create_pipeline_layout(&wgpu::PipelineLayoutDescriptor{
        label: Some("Compute Pipeline Layout"),
        bind_group_layouts: &[&cs_vertex_bind_group_layout],
        push_constant_ranges: &[],
    });

    let cs_pipeline = init.device.create_compute_pipeline(&wgpu::ComputePipelineDescriptor{
        label: Some("Compute Pipeline"),
```

```
            layout: Some(&cs_pipeline_layout),
            module: &cs_comp,
            entry_point: "cs_main",
    });

    Self {
        init,
        pipelines: vec![pipeline, pipeline2],
        uniform_bind_groups: vec![vert_bind_group, vert_bind_group2],
        uniform_buffers: vec![vert_uniform_buffer],

        cs_pipelines: vec![cs_index_pipeline, cs_pipeline],
        cs_vertex_buffers: vec![cs_vertex_buffer, cs_vertex_buffer2],
        cs_index_buffers: vec![cs_index_buffer, cs_index_buffer2],
        cs_uniform_buffers: vec![cs_index_uniform_buffer, cs_vertex_uniform_buffer],
        cs_bind_groups: vec![cs_index_bind_group, cs_vertex_bind_group],

        model_mat,
        view_mat,
        project_mat,
        msaa_texture_view,
        depth_texture_view,
        plot_type: 0,

        //terrain,
        update_buffers: false,
        aspect_ratio: 20.0,
        resolution: resol,
        animation_speed: 1.0,
        water_level: 0.2,
        z_offset: 0.0,
        scale: 50.0,
        triangles_count,
        lines_count,
        fps_counter: ws::FpsCounter::default(),
    }
}

fn resize(&mut self, new_size: winit::dpi::PhysicalSize<u32>) {
    if new_size.width > 0 && new_size.height > 0 {
        self.init.size = new_size;
        self.init.config.width = new_size.width;
        self.init.config.height = new_size.height;
        self.init.surface.configure(&self.init.device, &self.init.config);

        self.project_mat = wt::create_projection_mat(new_size.width as f32 / new_size.height as f32,
            true);
        let mvp_mat = self.project_mat * self.view_mat * self.model_mat;
        self.init.queue.write_buffer(&self.uniform_buffers[0], 0,
            cast_slice(mvp_mat.as_ref() as &[f32;16]));

        self.depth_texture_view = ws::create_depth_view(&self.init);
        if self.init.sample_count > 1 {
            self.msaa_texture_view = ws::create_msaa_texture_view(&self.init);
        }
    }
}

#[allow(unused_variables)]
fn input(&mut self, event: &WindowEvent) -> bool {
```

```rust
match event {
    WindowEvent::KeyboardInput {
        input:
            KeyboardInput {
                virtual_keycode: Some(keycode),
                state: ElementState::Pressed,
                ..
            },
        ..
    } => {
        match keycode {
            VirtualKeyCode::Space => {
                self.plot_type = (self.plot_type + 1) % 3;
                true
            },
            VirtualKeyCode::Q => {
                self.scale += 1.0;
                self.update_buffers = true;
                println!("scale = {}", self.scale);
                true
            },
            VirtualKeyCode::A => {
                self.scale -= 1.0;
                if self.scale < 1.0 {
                    self.scale = 1.0;
                }
                self.update_buffers = true;
                println!("scale = {}", self.scale);
                true
            },
            VirtualKeyCode::W => {
                self.aspect_ratio += 1.0;
                self.update_buffers = true;
                println!("aspect_ratio = {}", self.aspect_ratio);
                true
            },
            VirtualKeyCode::S => {
                self.aspect_ratio -= 1.0;
                self.update_buffers = true;
                println!("aspect_ratio = {}", self.aspect_ratio);
                true
            },
            VirtualKeyCode::E => {
                self.water_level += 0.01;
                self.update_buffers = true;
                println!("water_level = {}", self.water_level);
                true
            },
            VirtualKeyCode::D => {
                self.water_level -= 0.01;
                self.update_buffers = true;
                println!("water_level = {}", self.water_level);
                true
            },
            _ => false
        }
    }
    _ => false,
}
}
```

```
fn update(&mut self, dt: std::time::Duration) {
    // update buffers:
    if self.update_buffers {
        self.model_mat = wt::create_model_mat([-0.65*self.resolution as f32, 5.0,
            -0.5*self.resolution as f32], [0.0, PI/15.0, 0.0], [1.0, self.aspect_ratio, 1.0]);
        let mvp_mat = self.project_mat * self.view_mat * self.model_mat;
        self.init.queue.write_buffer(&self.uniform_buffers[0], 0,
            cast_slice(mvp_mat.as_ref() as &[f32;16]));
        self.update_buffers = false;
    }

    self.z_offset = 20.0*self.animation_speed * dt.as_secs_f32();
    let params = [
        self.resolution as f32,
        5.0, 0.5, 2.0, 0.0,
        self.z_offset,
        self.scale,
        self.water_level,
    ];
    self.init.queue.write_buffer(&self.cs_uniform_buffers[1], 0, cast_slice(&params));
}

fn render(&mut self) -> Result<(), wgpu::SurfaceError> {
    //let output = self.init.surface.get_current_frame()?.output;
    let output = self.init.surface.get_current_texture()?;
    let view = output
        .texture
        .create_view(&wgpu::TextureViewDescriptor::default());

    let mut encoder = self
        .init.device
        .create_command_encoder(&wgpu::CommandEncoderDescriptor {
            label: Some("Render Encoder"),
        });

    // compute pass for indices
    {
        let mut cs_index_pass = encoder.begin_compute_pass(&wgpu::ComputePassDescriptor{
            label: Some("Compute Index Pass"),
            timestamp_writes: None,
        });
        cs_index_pass.set_pipeline(&self.cs_pipelines[0]);
        cs_index_pass.set_bind_group(0, &self.cs_bind_groups[0], &[]);
        cs_index_pass.dispatch_workgroups(self.resolution/8, self.resolution/8, 1);
    }

    // compute pass for vertices
    {
        let mut cs_pass = encoder.begin_compute_pass(&wgpu::ComputePassDescriptor{
            label: Some("Compute Pass"),
            timestamp_writes: None,
        });
        cs_pass.set_pipeline(&self.cs_pipelines[1]);
        cs_pass.set_bind_group(0, &self.cs_bind_groups[1], &[]);
        cs_pass.dispatch_workgroups(self.resolution/8, self.resolution/8, 1);
    }

    // render pass
    {
```

```rust
        let color_attach = ws::create_color_attachment(&view);
        let msaa_attach = ws::create_msaa_color_attachment(&view, &self.msaa_texture_view);
        let color_attachment = if self.init.sample_count == 1 { color_attach } else { msaa_attach };
        let depth_attachment = ws::create_depth_stencil_attachment(&self.depth_texture_view);

        let mut render_pass = encoder.begin_render_pass(&wgpu::RenderPassDescriptor {
            label: Some("Render Pass"),
            color_attachments: &[Some(color_attachment)],
            depth_stencil_attachment: Some(depth_attachment),
            occlusion_query_set: None,
            timestamp_writes: None,
        });

        let plot_type = if self.plot_type == 1 { "shape_only" }
            else if self.plot_type == 2 {"wireframe_only"} else {"both"};

        if plot_type == "shape_only" || plot_type == "both" {
            render_pass.set_pipeline(&self.pipelines[0]);
            render_pass.set_vertex_buffer(0, self.cs_vertex_buffers[0].slice(..));
            render_pass.set_index_buffer(self.cs_index_buffers[0].slice(..),
                wgpu::IndexFormat::Uint32);
            render_pass.set_bind_group(0, &self.uniform_bind_groups[0], &[]);
            render_pass.draw_indexed(0..self.triangles_count, 0, 0..1);
        }

        if plot_type == "wireframe_only" || plot_type == "both" {
            render_pass.set_pipeline(&self.pipelines[1]);
            render_pass.set_vertex_buffer(0, self.cs_vertex_buffers[1].slice(..));
            render_pass.set_index_buffer(self.cs_index_buffers[1].slice(..),
                wgpu::IndexFormat::Uint32);
            render_pass.set_bind_group(0, &self.uniform_bind_groups[1], &[]);
            render_pass.draw_indexed(0..self.lines_count, 0, 0..1);
        }
    }
    self.fps_counter.print_fps(5);
    self.init.queue.submit(iter::once(encoder.finish()));
    output.present();

    Ok(())
    }
}

fn main() {
    let mut sample_count = 1 as u32;
    let mut resolution = 1024u32;
    let args: Vec<String> = std::env::args().collect();
    if args.len() > 1 {
        sample_count = args[1].parse::<u32>().unwrap();
    }
    if args.len() > 2 {
        resolution = args[2].parse::<u32>().unwrap();
    }

    env_logger::init();
    let event_loop = EventLoop::new();
    let window = winit::window::WindowBuilder::new().build(&event_loop).unwrap();
    window.set_title(&*format!("ch08_{}", "terrain_gpu"));

    let mut state = pollster::block_on(State::new(&window, sample_count, resolution));
    let render_start_time = std::time::Instant::now();
```

```
event_loop.run(move |event, _, control_flow| {
    match event {
        Event::WindowEvent {
            ref event,
            window_id,
        } if window_id == window.id() => {
            if !state.input(event) {
                match event {
                    WindowEvent::CloseRequested
                    | WindowEvent::KeyboardInput {
                        input:
                            KeyboardInput {
                                state: ElementState::Pressed,
                                virtual_keycode: Some(VirtualKeyCode::Escape),
                                ..
                            },
                        ..
                    } => *control_flow = ControlFlow::Exit,
                    WindowEvent::Resized(physical_size) => {
                        state.resize(*physical_size);
                    }
                    WindowEvent::ScaleFactorChanged { new_inner_size, .. } => {
                        state.resize(**new_inner_size);
                    }
                    _ => {}
                }
            }
        }
        Event::RedrawRequested(_) => {
            let now = std::time::Instant::now();
            let dt = now - render_start_time;
            state.update(dt);

            match state.render() {
                Ok(_) => {}
                Err(wgpu::SurfaceError::Lost) => state.resize(state.init.size),
                Err(wgpu::SurfaceError::OutOfMemory) => *control_flow = ControlFlow::Exit,
                Err(e) => eprintln!("{:?}", e),
            }
        }
        Event::MainEventsCleared => {
            window.request_redraw();
        }
        _ => {}
    }
});
}
```

In the above code, we first add several new fields to the *State* struct, such as *resolution*, *triangles_count*, and *lines_count*. These fields provide accessible values for different functions without necessitating their explicit input.

within the *State::new* function, we reuse the vertex and fragment shaders created earlier for previous examples, as well as the index shader generated in the preceding chapter. Since both *noise.wgsl* and *terrain_comp.wgsl* are required for generating terrain data, these files are amalgamated to form the compute shader module. The process is demonstrated in the following code:

```
let shader = init.device.create_shader_module(wgpu::include_wgsl!("shader_unlit.wgsl"));
```

```
let cs_noise = include_str!("noise.wgsl");
let cs_terrain = include_str!("terrain_comp.wgsl");
let cs_combine = [cs_noise, cs_terrain].join("\n");
let cs_comp = init.device.create_shader_module(wgpu::ShaderModuleDescriptor {
    label: Some("Compute Shader"),
    source: wgpu::ShaderSource::Wgsl(cs_combine.into()),
});

let cs_indices = init.device.create_shader_module(wgpu::include_wgsl!("../ch07/indices_comp.wgsl"));
```

There is a significant difference compared to previous examples that generate terrains on the CPU: this example does not use data generated from the Rust code to create vertex buffers for positions and colors. Instead, we will use compute shaders to generate these buffers. To achieve this, a slight variation is introduced in the vertex buffer layout: the format *Float32×3* utilized for transmitting position and color data in prior examples is substituted with *Float32×4* in the current instance:

```
let vertex_buffer_layout2 = VertexBufferLayout {
    array_stride: 32,
    step_mode: wgpu::VertexStepMode::Vertex,
    attributes: &wgpu::vertex_attr_array![0 => Float32x4, 1 => Float32x4], // pos, col
};
```

The above code snippet ensures proper buffer alignment when the compute shader is used to generate vertex data.

After creating the render pipelines for rendering the terrain and wireframe, we proceed to define the compute pipeline for handling indices. We first create two index buffers: *cs_index_buffer* and *cs_index_buffer2*, designated for the terrain and wireframe, respectively. Concurrently, a uniform buffer is constructed to pass the *resolution* parameter to the shader. This collection of buffers facilitated the creation of a bind group layout and, subsequently, a bind group, both crucial for the compute pipeline.

The following code segment constructs a compute pipeline customized for terrain data generation. In this context, we introduce two distinct vertex buffers, namely *cs_vertex_buffer* and *cs_vertex_buffer2*, each allocated a size of 32 bytes. This size is derived from two *Float32×4* fields – position and color – with each field spanning a size of 16 bytes.

Subsequently, we proceed to define a uniform buffer for input parameters used in terrain data calculation. By combining these buffers, we lay the groundwork for the formulation of both the bind group layout and the corresponding bind group for the compute pipeline. The code snippet below illustrated this process:

```
let (cs_vertex_bind_group_layout, cs_vertex_bind_group) = ws::create_bind_group_storage(
    &init.device,
    vec![
        wgpu::ShaderStages::COMPUTE, wgpu::ShaderStages::COMPUTE, wgpu::ShaderStages::COMPUTE,
    ],
    vec![
        wgpu::BufferBindingType::Storage { read_only: false },
        wgpu::BufferBindingType::Storage { read_only: false },
        wgpu::BufferBindingType::Uniform,
    ],
    &[
        cs_vertex_buffer.as_entire_binding(),
        cs_vertex_buffer2.as_entire_binding(),
        cs_vertex_uniform_buffer.as_entire_binding(),
    ],
);
```

Here, the collection of three buffers, including two storage buffers and one uniform buffer, aligns seamlessly with the three bindings within the compute shader. Notably, we designate all three buffers for access within the *COMPUTE* shader stage, limiting their accessibility exclusively to the compute shader.

The *State::render* function encompasses three distinctive passes, consisting of two compute passes followed by a render pass.

In the first compute pass, index calculation takes the center stage. Here, the bind group is configured for the pass, and the *dispatch_workgroups* function is invoked. This function orchestrates the launch of a predefined number of workgroups, initiating the execution of the compute shader functions. The *dispatch_workgroups* function requires three inputs: the count of workgroups to dispatch along the x, y, and z dimensions.

A subsequent compute pass is dedicated to terrain data generation. In this case, the bind group configuration remains relevant, as one of the resource attributes depends on the vertex buffer. This setup serves as a precursor to the ensuing render pass.

In the realm of the render pass, we depart from the approach used in previous terrain examples. Here, the vertex buffer and index buffer sourced from the compute pipeline plays a crucial role in defining these buffers within the render pass. This marks a departure from earlier instances where the vertex buffer and index buffer were generated using data originating from Rust code executed on the CPU.

The *State::update* function closely resembles its counterparts in previous terrain examples. However, in this instance, we adopt an innovative approach to animate the vertex data and vertex buffer. Unlike prior scenarios where vertex data and buffers required updates on a per-frame basis, our focus shifts here. Instead, we emphasize updating only the uniform parameters required for vertex data computation within the compute shader. This novel approach is illustrated in the following code excerpt:

```
self.z_offset = 20.0*self.animation_speed * dt.as_secs_f32();
let params = [
    self.resolution as f32,
    5.0, 0.5, 2.0, 0.0,
    self.z_offset,
    self.scale,
    self.water_level,
];
self.init.queue.write_buffer(&self.cs_uniform_buffers[1], 0, cast_slice(&params));
```

Additionally, the code permits the user to modify input parameters through keyboard inputs.

Here is a list of controls using keyboard:

- *Space*: Changes plot type among *surface*, *wireframe*, and *both*.
- *Q/A*: Increases/decreases the *scale* parameter.
- *W/S:* Increases/decreases the *aspect_ratio* parameter.
- *E/D:* Increases/decreases the *water_level* parameter.

8.8.4 Run Application

To run this application, add the following code snippet to the *Cargo.toml* file:

```
[[example]]
name = "ch08_terrain_gpu"
```

path = "examples/ch08/ terrain_gpu.rs"

Afterward, execute the following *cargo run* commands in the terminal window:

cargo run --example ch08_terrain_gpu 8

Fig.8-12 shows the results of this example.

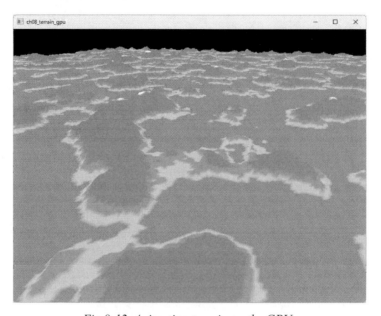

Fig.8-12. Animating terrain on the GPU.

The figure clearly demonstrates that using compute shaders to simulate the terrain provides smooth animation with a framerate of 60 FPS, even at higher resolutions like 1024. In comparison, creating the same animated terrain on the CPU in the previous example, with a resolution of 200, resulted in a framerate of 8 FPS. This highlights the immense computational power of the compute shader in generating terrains.

8.9 Creating Minecraft on GPU

Minecraft terrain is made up of cube-shaped blocks, which can be stacked and arranged in different ways to create structures and landscapes. This unique blocky style is a defining characteristic of Minecraft and has helped to make the game one of the most recognized and beloved titles in the gaming world. In this section, we will reuse the compute shaders from the previous example to create a Minecraft terrain. The compute shader in this example will generate the position and color data used to render the instanced cubes. It is worth noting that since the Minecraft terrain is made up of cubes, we no longer need the indices data to render the surface of the terrain.

8.9.1 Shader Code

Create a new WGSL shader file named *shader_minecraft.wgsl* file in the *examples/ch08/* folder and include the following code:

```
@binding(0) @group(0) var<uniform> mvpMat: mat4x4f;

struct Input {
    @location(0) cubePosition: vec4f,
    @location(1) position: vec4f,
    @location(2) color: vec4f,
}

struct Output {
    @builtin(position) position : vec4f,
    @location(0) vColor: vec4f,
}

// vertex shader
@vertex
fn vs_main(in:Input) -> Output {
    var output: Output;
    var position = in.position + in.cubePosition;
    output.position = mvpMat * position;
    output.vColor = in.color;
    return output;
}

// fragment shader
@fragment
fn fs_main(@location(0) vColor: vec4f) -> @location(0) vec4f {
    return vec4(vColor.rgb, 1.0);
}
```

The vertex shader in the above code takes an input struct *Input* and returns an output struct *Output*. The input struct has three fields: *cubePosition*, *position*, and *color* and the output struct has two fields: *position* and *vColor*.

The vertex shader adds the *cubePosition* and *position* fields from the *Input* struct together and stores the result in the *position* variable. The final vertex position is obtained by multiplying by the *position* variable with the model-view-projection matrix, which is stored in the *mvpMat* uniform variable.

The rest of the code is similar to previous examples.

In the previous example, we implemented a compute shader for generating terrain data. We could reuse the *terrain_comp.wgsl* shader file, but we will use a simplified version of that shader in Minecraft terrain generation instead. This is because the previous shader contains two vertex data arrays, one for the terrain and another for wireframe. Here, we need only one vertex array for the Minecraft terrain. To do this, create a new compute shader file named *minecraft_comp.wgsl* in the *examples/ch08/* folder and include the following code:

```
struct VertexData{
    position: vec4f,
    color: vec4f,
}

struct VertexDataArray{
    vertexDataArray: array<VertexData>,
}

struct TerrainParams{
    resolution: f32,
    octaves: f32,
    persistence: f32,
```

```
        lacunarity: f32,
        offsetX: f32,
        offsetZ: f32,
        scale: f32,
        waterLevel: f32,
        aspect_ratio: f32,
}

@group(0) @binding(0) var<storage, read_write> vda : VertexDataArray;
@group(0) @binding(1) var<uniform> tps: TerrainParams;

fn terrainFunc(x:f32, z:f32) -> f32 {
    let halfr = 0.5 * tps.resolution;
    var amplitude = 1.0;
    var frequency = 1.0;
    var noiseHeight = 0.0;
    for(var i:u32 = 0u; i < u32(tps.octaves); i = i+1u) {
        let sampleX = (x - halfr + tps.offsetX)/(tps.scale) * frequency;
        let sampleZ = (z - halfr - tps.offsetZ)/(tps.scale) * frequency;
        let y = perlinNoise(vec2(sampleX, sampleZ))*2.0 - 1.0;
        noiseHeight += y * amplitude;
        amplitude *= tps.persistence;
        frequency *= tps.lacunarity;
    }
    return noiseHeight;
}

@compute @workgroup_size(8, 8, 1)
fn cs_main(@builtin(global_invocation_id) id : vec3u){
    var i = id.x;
    var j = id.y;
    var y = terrainFunc(f32(id.x), f32(id.y));
    let waterLevel = 0.1*tps.waterLevel;
    if(y <= waterLevel) { y = waterLevel - 0.000001; }
    let p0 = vec3(f32(id.x), y*tps.aspect_ratio, f32(id.y));

    // colormap
    let cData = array<vec3<f32>,5>(
        vec3(0.055, 0.529, 0.8),
        vec3(0.761, 0.698, 0.502),
        vec3(0.204, 0.549, 0.192),
        vec3(0.353, 0.302, 0.255),
        vec3(1.0, 0.98, 0.98)
    );
     let cData2 = array<vec3<f32>,5>(
        vec3(1.0),
        vec3(1.0),
        vec3(1.0),
        vec3(1.0),
        vec3(1.0),
    );
    let ta = array<f32, 6>(0.0, 0.3, 0.35, 0.4, 0.7, 1.0);
    let color = addTerrainColors(cData, ta, 0.0, 1.0*tps.aspect_ratio, p0.y, waterLevel);

    var idx = i + j * u32(tps.resolution);
    vda.vertexDataArray[idx].position = vec4(p0, 1.0);
    vda.vertexDataArray[idx].color = vec4(color, 1.0);
}
```

8. Procedural Terrains |369

This code is a simplified version of the shader implemented in the *terrain_comp.wgsl* file and requires no further explanation.

8.9.2 Rust Code

Create a new Rust file called *minecraft_gpu.rs* in the *examples/ch08/* folder and add the following code to it:

```rust
use std:: {iter, f32::consts::PI};
use cgmath::Matrix4;
use wgpu:: {util::DeviceExt, VertexBufferLayout};
use winit::{
    event::*,
    event_loop::{ControlFlow, EventLoop},
    window::Window,
};
use bytemuck:: {Pod, Zeroable, cast_slice};
use wgpu_book_examples:: { wgpu_simplified as ws, transforms as wt, vertex_data as vd };

#[repr(C)]
#[derive(Copy, Clone, Debug, Pod, Zeroable)]
struct Vertex {
    position: [f32; 4],
}

fn cube_vertices(side: f32) -> (Vec<Vertex>, Vec<u16>) {
    let(pos, _, _, _, ind, _) = vd::create_cube_data(side);
    let mut data:Vec<Vertex> = Vec::with_capacity(pos.len());
    for i in 0..pos.len() {
        data.push(Vertex{position: [pos[i][0], pos[i][1], pos[i][2], 1.0]});
    }
    (data.to_vec(), ind)
}

struct State {
    init:  ws::IWgpuInit,
    pipeline: wgpu::RenderPipeline,
    vertex_buffer: wgpu::Buffer,
    index_buffer: wgpu::Buffer,
    uniform_bind_group: wgpu::BindGroup,
    uniform_buffer: wgpu::Buffer,
    indices_len: u32,

    cs_pipeline: wgpu::ComputePipeline,
    cs_vertex_buffer: wgpu::Buffer,
    cs_uniform_buffer: wgpu::Buffer,
    cs_bind_group: wgpu::BindGroup,

    model_mat: Matrix4<f32>,
    view_mat: Matrix4<f32>,
    project_mat: Matrix4<f32>,
    msaa_texture_view: wgpu::TextureView,
    depth_texture_view: wgpu::TextureView,

    update_buffers: bool,
    data_changed: bool,
    aspect_ratio: f32,
    animation_speed: f32,
```

```
        resolution: u32,
        water_level: f32,
        z_offset: f32,
        scale: f32,
        cube_side: f32,
        fps_counter: ws::FpsCounter,
}

impl State {
    async fn new(window:&Window, sample_count:u32, resolution:u32) -> Self {
        let init = ws::IWgpuInit::new(&window, sample_count, None).await;

        let resol = ws::round_to_multiple(resolution, 8);
        let vertices_count = resol * resol;
        println!("resolution = {}", resol);

        let shader = init.device.create_shader_module(wgpu::include_wgsl!("shader_minecraft.wgsl"));

        let cs_noise = include_str!("noise.wgsl");
        let cs_minecraft = include_str!("minecraft_comp.wgsl");
        let cs_combine = [cs_noise, cs_minecraft].join("\n");
        let cs_comp = init.device.create_shader_module(wgpu::ShaderModuleDescriptor {
            label: Some("Compute Shader"),
            source: wgpu::ShaderSource::Wgsl(cs_combine.into()),
        });

        // uniform data
        let model_mat = wt::create_model_mat([-0.5*resol as f32, -15.0, -0.5*resol as f32],
            [0.0, PI/15.0, 0.0], [1.5, 1.5, 1.5]);

        let camera_position = (40.0, 40.0, 50.0).into();
        let look_direction = (0.0,0.0,0.0).into();
        let up_direction = cgmath::Vector3::unit_y();

        let (view_mat, project_mat, vp_mat) =
            wt::create_vp_mat(camera_position, look_direction, up_direction,
            init.config.width as f32 / init.config.height as f32);

        let mvp_mat = vp_mat * model_mat;

        // create vertex uniform buffers
        let vert_uniform_buffer = init.device.create_buffer_init(&wgpu::util::BufferInitDescriptor{
            label: Some("Vertex Uniform Buffer"),
            contents: cast_slice(mvp_mat.as_ref() as &[f32; 16]),
            usage: wgpu::BufferUsages::UNIFORM | wgpu::BufferUsages::COPY_DST,
        });

        // uniform bind group for vertex shader
        let (vert_bind_group_layout, vert_bind_group) = ws::create_bind_group(
            &init.device,
            vec![wgpu::ShaderStages::VERTEX],
            &[vert_uniform_buffer.as_entire_binding()],
        );

        let vertex_buffer_layout = [
            VertexBufferLayout {
                array_stride: 16,
                step_mode: wgpu::VertexStepMode::Vertex,
                attributes: &wgpu::vertex_attr_array![0 => Float32x4], // cube position
            },
```

```
        VertexBufferLayout {
            array_stride: 32,
            step_mode: wgpu::VertexStepMode::Instance,
            attributes: &wgpu::vertex_attr_array![1=>Float32x4, 2=>Float32x4], // instance pos, col
        }
];

let pipeline_layout = init.device.create_pipeline_layout(&wgpu::PipelineLayoutDescriptor {
    label: Some("Render Pipeline Layout"),
    bind_group_layouts: &[&vert_bind_group_layout],
    push_constant_ranges: &[],
});

let mut ppl = ws::IRenderPipeline {
    shader: Some(&shader),
    pipeline_layout: Some(&pipeline_layout),
    vertex_buffer_layout: &vertex_buffer_layout,
    ..Default::default()
};
let pipeline = ppl.new(&init);

let msaa_texture_view = ws::create_msaa_texture_view(&init);
let depth_texture_view = ws::create_depth_view(&init);

let (cube_vertex_data, cube_index_data) = cube_vertices(2.0);
let cube_vertex_buffer = init.device.create_buffer_init(&wgpu::util::BufferInitDescriptor {
    label: Some("Cube Vertex Buffer"),
    contents: cast_slice(&cube_vertex_data),
    usage: wgpu::BufferUsages::VERTEX | wgpu::BufferUsages::COPY_DST,
});

let cube_index_buffer = init.device.create_buffer_init(&wgpu::util::BufferInitDescriptor{
    label: Some("Cube Index Buffer"),
    contents: cast_slice(&cube_index_data),
    usage: wgpu::BufferUsages::INDEX,
});

// create compute pipeline for terrain
let cs_vertex_buffer = init.device.create_buffer(&wgpu::BufferDescriptor{
    label: Some("Vertex Buffer"),
    size:  64 * vertices_count as u64,
    usage: wgpu::BufferUsages::VERTEX | wgpu::BufferUsages::STORAGE |
        wgpu::BufferUsages::COPY_DST,
    mapped_at_creation: false,
});

let params = [resol as f32, 5.0, 0.5, 2.0, 0.0, 0.0, 50.0, 0.2, 50.0];
let cs_vertex_uniform_buffer = init.device.create_buffer_init(&wgpu::util::BufferInitDescriptor{
    label: Some("Vertex Uniform Buffer"),
    contents: bytemuck::cast_slice(&params),
    usage: wgpu::BufferUsages::UNIFORM | wgpu::BufferUsages::COPY_DST,
});

let (cs_vertex_bind_group_layout, cs_vertex_bind_group) = ws::create_bind_group_storage(
    &init.device,
    vec![
        wgpu::ShaderStages::COMPUTE, wgpu::ShaderStages::COMPUTE,
    ],
    vec![
        wgpu::BufferBindingType::Storage { read_only: false },
```

```
                wgpu::BufferBindingType::Uniform,
            ],
            &[
                cs_vertex_buffer.as_entire_binding(),
                cs_vertex_uniform_buffer.as_entire_binding(),
            ],
        );

        let cs_pipeline_layout = init.device.create_pipeline_layout(&wgpu::PipelineLayoutDescriptor{
            label: Some("Compute Pipeline Layout"),
            bind_group_layouts: &[&cs_vertex_bind_group_layout],
            push_constant_ranges: &[],
        });

        let cs_pipeline = init.device.create_compute_pipeline(&wgpu::ComputePipelineDescriptor{
            label: Some("Compute Pipeline"),
            layout: Some(&cs_pipeline_layout),
            module: &cs_comp,
            entry_point: "cs_main",
        });

        Self {
            init,
            pipeline,
            vertex_buffer: cube_vertex_buffer,
            index_buffer: cube_index_buffer,
            uniform_bind_group: vert_bind_group,
            uniform_buffer: vert_uniform_buffer,
            indices_len: cube_index_data.len() as u32,

            cs_pipeline,
            cs_vertex_buffer,
            cs_uniform_buffer: cs_vertex_uniform_buffer,
            cs_bind_group: cs_vertex_bind_group,

            model_mat,
            view_mat,
            project_mat,
            msaa_texture_view,
            depth_texture_view,

            update_buffers: false,
            data_changed: false,
            aspect_ratio: 50.0,
            resolution: resol,
            animation_speed: 1.0,
            water_level: 0.2,
            z_offset: 0.0,
            scale: 50.0,
            cube_side: 2.0,
            fps_counter: ws::FpsCounter::default(),
        }
    }

    fn resize(&mut self, new_size: winit::dpi::PhysicalSize<u32>) {
        if new_size.width > 0 && new_size.height > 0 {
            self.init.size = new_size;
            self.init.config.width = new_size.width;
            self.init.config.height = new_size.height;
            self.init.surface.configure(&self.init.device, &self.init.config);
```

```
        self.project_mat = wt::create_projection_mat(new_size.width as f32 / new_size.height as f32,
            true);
        let mvp_mat = self.project_mat * self.view_mat * self.model_mat;
        self.init.queue.write_buffer(&self.uniform_buffer, 0,
            cast_slice(mvp_mat.as_ref() as &[f32;16]));

        self.depth_texture_view = ws::create_depth_view(&self.init);
        if self.init.sample_count > 1 {
            self.msaa_texture_view = ws::create_msaa_texture_view(&self.init);
        }
    }
}

#[allow(unused_variables)]
fn input(&mut self, event: &WindowEvent) -> bool {
    match event {
        WindowEvent::KeyboardInput {
            input:
                KeyboardInput {
                    virtual_keycode: Some(keycode),
                    state: ElementState::Pressed,
                    ..
                },
            ..
        } => {
            match keycode {
                VirtualKeyCode::Q => {
                    self.scale += 1.0;
                    self.update_buffers = true;
                    println!("scale = {}", self.scale);
                    true
                },
                VirtualKeyCode::A => {
                    self.scale -= 1.0;
                    if self.scale < 1.0 {
                        self.scale = 1.0;
                    }
                    self.update_buffers = true;
                    println!("scale = {}", self.scale);
                    true
                },
                VirtualKeyCode::W => {
                    self.aspect_ratio += 1.0;
                    self.update_buffers = true;
                    println!("aspect_ratio = {}", self.aspect_ratio);
                    true
                },
                VirtualKeyCode::S => {
                    self.aspect_ratio -= 1.0;
                    self.update_buffers = true;
                    println!("aspect_ratio = {}", self.aspect_ratio);
                    true
                },
                VirtualKeyCode::E => {
                    self.water_level += 0.01;
                    self.update_buffers = true;
                    println!("water_level = {}", self.water_level);
                    true
                },
```

```rust
                VirtualKeyCode::D => {
                    self.water_level -= 0.01;
                    self.update_buffers = true;
                    println!("water_level = {}", self.water_level);
                    true
                },
                VirtualKeyCode::R => {
                    self.cube_side += 0.1;
                    self.data_changed = true;
                    println!("cube_side = {}", self.cube_side);
                    true
                },
                VirtualKeyCode::F => {
                    self.cube_side -= 0.1;
                    if self.cube_side < 0.2 {
                        self.cube_side = 0.2;
                    }
                    self.data_changed = true;
                    println!("cube_side = {}", self.cube_side);
                    true
                },
                _ => false
            }
        }
        _ => false,
    }
}

fn update(&mut self, dt: std::time::Duration) {
    // update buffers:
    if self.update_buffers {
        let mvp_mat = self.project_mat * self.view_mat * self.model_mat;
        self.init.queue.write_buffer(&self.uniform_buffer, 0,
            cast_slice(mvp_mat.as_ref() as &[f32;16]));
        self.update_buffers = false;
    }

    self.z_offset = 20.0*self.animation_speed * dt.as_secs_f32();
    let params = [
        self.resolution as f32,
        5.0, 0.5, 2.0, 0.0,
        self.z_offset,
        self.scale,
        self.water_level,
        self.aspect_ratio,
    ];
    self.init.queue.write_buffer(&self.cs_uniform_buffer, 0, cast_slice(&params));

    if self.data_changed {
        let (cube_vertex_data, _) = cube_vertices(self.cube_side);
        self.init.queue.write_buffer(&self.vertex_buffer, 0, cast_slice(&cube_vertex_data));
    }
}

fn render(&mut self) -> Result<(), wgpu::SurfaceError> {
    //let output = self.init.surface.get_current_frame()?.output;
    let output = self.init.surface.get_current_texture()?;
    let view = output
        .texture
        .create_view(&wgpu::TextureViewDescriptor::default());
```

```
        let mut encoder = self
            .init.device
            .create_command_encoder(&wgpu::CommandEncoderDescriptor {
                label: Some("Render Encoder"),
            });

        // compute pass for vertices
        {
            let mut cs_pass = encoder.begin_compute_pass(&wgpu::ComputePassDescriptor{
                label: Some("Compute Pass"),
                timestamp_writes: None,
            });
            cs_pass.set_pipeline(&self.cs_pipeline);
            cs_pass.set_bind_group(0, &self.cs_bind_group, &[]);
            cs_pass.dispatch_workgroups(self.resolution/8, self.resolution/8, 1);
        }

        // render pass
        {
            let color_attach = ws::create_color_attachment(&view);
            let msaa_attach = ws::create_msaa_color_attachment(&view, &self.msaa_texture_view);
            let color_attachment = if self.init.sample_count == 1 { color_attach } else { msaa_attach };
            let depth_attachment = ws::create_depth_stencil_attachment(&self.depth_texture_view);

            let mut render_pass = encoder.begin_render_pass(&wgpu::RenderPassDescriptor {
                label: Some("Render Pass"),
                color_attachments: &[Some(color_attachment)],
                depth_stencil_attachment: Some(depth_attachment),
                occlusion_query_set: None,
                timestamp_writes: None,
            });

            render_pass.set_pipeline(&self.pipeline);
            render_pass.set_vertex_buffer(0, self.vertex_buffer.slice(..));      // for cube
            render_pass.set_vertex_buffer(1, self.cs_vertex_buffer.slice(..));  // for instance
            render_pass.set_index_buffer(self.index_buffer.slice(..), wgpu::IndexFormat::Uint16);
            render_pass.set_bind_group(0, &self.uniform_bind_group, &[]);
            render_pass.draw_indexed(0..self.indices_len, 0, 0..self.resolution * self.resolution);
        }
        self.fps_counter.print_fps(5);
        self.init.queue.submit(iter::once(encoder.finish()));
        output.present();

        Ok(())
    }
}

fn main() {
    let mut sample_count = 1 as u32;
    let mut resolution = 512u32;
    let args: Vec<String> = std::env::args().collect();
    if args.len() > 1 {
        sample_count = args[1].parse::<u32>().unwrap();
    }
    if args.len() > 2 {
        resolution = args[2].parse::<u32>().unwrap();
    }
```

```rust
    env_logger::init();
    let event_loop = EventLoop::new();
    let window = winit::window::WindowBuilder::new().build(&event_loop).unwrap();
    window.set_title(&*format!("ch08_{}", "terrain_gpu"));

    let mut state = pollster::block_on(State::new(&window, sample_count, resolution));
    let render_start_time = std::time::Instant::now();

    event_loop.run(move |event, _, control_flow| {
        match event {
            Event::WindowEvent {
                ref event,
                window_id,
            } if window_id == window.id() => {
                if !state.input(event) {
                    match event {
                        WindowEvent::CloseRequested
                        | WindowEvent::KeyboardInput {
                            input:
                                KeyboardInput {
                                    state: ElementState::Pressed,
                                    virtual_keycode: Some(VirtualKeyCode::Escape),
                                    ..
                                },
                            ..
                        } => *control_flow = ControlFlow::Exit,
                        WindowEvent::Resized(physical_size) => {
                            state.resize(*physical_size);
                        }
                        WindowEvent::ScaleFactorChanged { new_inner_size, .. } => {
                            state.resize(**new_inner_size);
                        }
                        _ => {}
                    }
                }
            }
            Event::RedrawRequested(_) => {
                let now = std::time::Instant::now();
                let dt = now - render_start_time;
                state.update(dt);

                match state.render() {
                    Ok(_) => {}
                    Err(wgpu::SurfaceError::Lost) => state.resize(state.init.size),
                    Err(wgpu::SurfaceError::OutOfMemory) => *control_flow = ControlFlow::Exit,
                    Err(e) => eprintln!("{:?}", e),
                }
            }
            Event::MainEventsCleared => {
                window.request_redraw();
            }
            _ => {}
        }
    });
}
```

It is worth noting that the above code introduces *vertex_data* module. This is because rendering Minecraft terrain requires the cube data from the *vertex_data.rs* file to be used in the shader code.

In the *State::new* function, we use the following code snippet to define the vertex buffer layout:

```
let vertex_buffer_layout = [
    VertexBufferLayout {
        array_stride: 16,
        step_mode: wgpu::VertexStepMode::Vertex,
        attributes: &wgpu::vertex_attr_array![0 => Float32x4], // cube position
    },
    VertexBufferLayout {
        array_stride: 32,
        step_mode: wgpu::VertexStepMode::Instance,
        attributes: &wgpu::vertex_attr_array![1 => Float32x4, 2 => Float32x4], // instance pos, col
    }
];

let pipeline_layout = init.device.create_pipeline_layout(&wgpu::PipelineLayoutDescriptor {
    label: Some("Render Pipeline Layout"),
    bind_group_layouts: &[&vert_bind_group_layout],
    push_constant_ranges: &[],
});

let mut ppl = ws::IRenderPipeline {
    shader: Some(&shader),
    pipeline_layout: Some(&pipeline_layout),
    vertex_buffer_layout: &vertex_buffer_layout,
    ..Default::default()
};
let pipeline = ppl.new(&init);
```

This is different from the previous example, where the vertex buffer layout contained only one *step_mode*: *Vertex*. In this example, both the *Vertex* and *Instance* step modes are involved. The code first specifies the vertex positions of the cube in the *Vertex* step mode using the cube data generated in Rust. Then, it defines the location and color of each cube instance in the *Instance* step mode using the noise heightmap data generated from the compute shader. Finally, it uses this vertex buffer layout to create the render pipeline.

Additionally, the *State::new* function also defines the vertex and index buffers for the cube using the cube data. This differs from the previous example where all vertex and index data were generated using compute shaders.

Within the *State::new* function, the code for creating compute pipeline is identical to that used in the previous example. However, in the *State::render* function, the code for the compute pass is the same as in the previous example, while the code for the render pass is different. Instead of rendering triangles for the surface of the terrain, this example uses instanced drawing to render multiple instances of the cube, with the number of instances being equal to the number of vertices.

In the *State::input* function, users can modify input parameters using the keyboard controls, such as the cube side and other parameters related to the noise map. To animate the terrain, we set the *z_offset* parameter within the *State::update* function using a time-dependent value scaled by the animation speed, resulting in movement in the *z* direction.

Here is a list of controls using keyboard:

- *Q/A*: Increases/decreases the *scale* parameter.
- *W/S:* Increases/decreases the *aspect_ratio* parameter.
- *E/D:* Increases/decreases the *water_level* parameter.
- *R/F:* Increases/decreases the cube side.

8.9.3 Run Application

To run this application, add the following code snippet to the *Cargo.toml* file:

```
[[example]]
name = "ch08_minecraft_gpu"
path = "examples/ch08/minecraft_gpu.rs"
```

Afterward, execute the following *cargo run* commands in the terminal window:

```
cargo run --example ch08_minecraft_gpu 8
```

Fig.8-13 shows the results of this example.

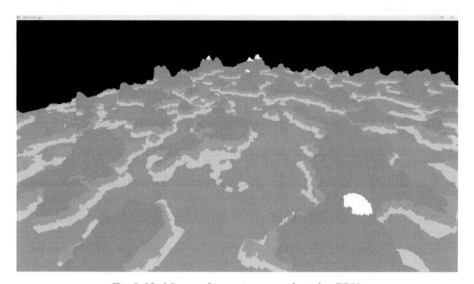

Fig.8-13. Minecraft terrain created on the GPU.

The figure clearly demonstrates that using compute shaders to simulate Minecraft terrain provides smooth animation with a framerate of 60 FPS, even at higher resolutions like 1024. You can also observe the blocky features of Minecraft terrain by reducing the cube side from the default 2 to 0.5 by continuously pressing the *F* key, as shown in Fig.8-14.

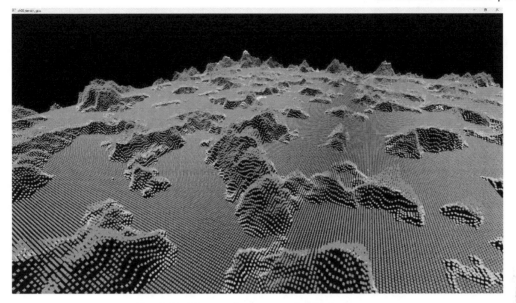

Fig.8-14. Minecraft terrain with blocky feature.

9 Marching Cubes

The marching cubes algorithm is a computer graphics algorithm used to extract a polygonal mesh of an isosurface from a 3D scalar field. The algorithm works by dividing the space into a uniform grid of cubes and then testing the corners of each cube to determine if they are inside or outside of the isosurface. For each cube where some corners are inside and some corners are outside, the surface must pass through that cube, intersecting the edges of the cube in between corners of opposite classification. The algorithm then draws a surface within each cube connecting these intersections.

The marching cubes algorithm is a computationally intensive as it needs to evaluate the scalar field at each point in the 3D grid and determine the topology of the surface that passes through the grid cells. This requires a large number of calculations and comparisons, which can be time-consuming for large grid.

In this chapter, we will apply the marching cubes algorithm to several applications, including implicit 3D surfaces, metaballs, voxel terrains, voxel volcanos, and voxel Minecraft terrains. To improve performance, we will use compute shaders to develop these applications on the GPU. We expect that using the parallel processing power from the GPU can greatly reduce the time required to generate the 3D mesh and optimize memory access patterns, resulting in faster and more efficient rendering of these complex 3D applications.

9.1 Marching Cubes Algorithm

The marching cubes algorithm operates on a 3D grid of scalar values and extracts an isosurface from the grid by dividing it into small cubes called voxels and testing the vertices of each voxel to determine if they lie inside or outside the surface. There are 8 vertices per cube, and each vertex can have a scalar value above or below the threshold that defines the isosurface.

When testing the vertices of each cube, the marching cubes algorithm classifies each cube into one of 256 possible cases based on the arrangement of the vertices that lie inside and outside the isosurface. Each case corresponds to a unique polygonal mesh that connects the edges of the cube that intersect the isosurface.

However, not all 256 cases are required because many of them are symmetrical or equivalent to other cases. For example, a case that is the mirror image of another case can be achieved simply by flipping the isosurface threshold value. Also, some cases can be rotated to produce the same result.

Through analysis and experimentation, it has been found that only 15 cases are necessary to represent all possible arrangements of vertices and edges on the isosurface, as shown in Fig.9-1.

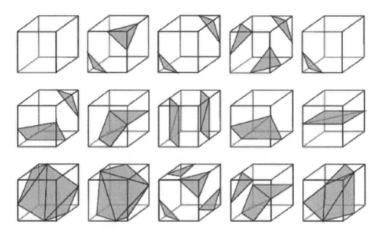

Fig.9-1. Required 15 cases by 3D marching cubes.

These 15 cases are sufficient to generate the full range of shapes and topologies that can arise from the algorithm. By reducing the number of cases required, the algorithm's implementation can be simplified, and its performance can be improved.

The marching cubes algorithm uses two lookup tables: the edge table and triangle table, to determine the triangles that should be drawn for each cube. In this chapter, we will use the tables proposed by W. E. Lorensen and H. R. Cline in 1987.

Create a new Rust file named *marching_cubes_table.rs* in the *examples/ch09/* folder and add the following code to it:

```
pub const EDGE_TABLE: &'static [u32; 256] = &[
    0x000, 0x109, 0x203, 0x30a, 0x406, 0x50f, 0x605, 0x70c,
    0x80c, 0x905, 0xa0f, 0xb06, 0xc0a, 0xd03, 0xe09, 0xf00,
    0x190, 0x099, 0x393, 0x29a, 0x596, 0x49f, 0x795, 0x69c,

    // ... data omitted for brevity

    0x69c, 0x795, 0x49f, 0x596, 0x29a, 0x393, 0x099, 0x190,
    0xf00, 0xe09, 0xd03, 0xc0a, 0xb06, 0xa0f, 0x905, 0x80c,
    0x70c, 0x605, 0x50f, 0x406, 0x30a, 0x203, 0x109, 0x000,
]);

pub const TRI_TABLE: &'static [i32; 4096] = &[
    0, -1, -1, -1, -1, -1, -1, -1, -1, -1, -1, -1, -1, -1, -1, -1,
    3,  0,  8,  3, -1, -1, -1, -1, -1, -1, -1, -1, -1, -1, -1, -1,
    3,  0,  1,  9, -1, -1, -1, -1, -1, -1, -1, -1, -1, -1, -1, -1,

    // ... data omitted for brevity

    3,  0,  9,  1, -1, -1, -1, -1, -1, -1, -1, -1, -1, -1, -1, -1,
    3,  0,  3,  8, -1, -1, -1, -1, -1, -1, -1, -1, -1, -1, -1, -1,
    0, -1, -1, -1, -1, -1, -1, -1, -1, -1, -1, -1, -1, -1, -1, -1,
]);
```

The edge table in the above code is a lookup table consisting of 256 entries, each corresponding to one of the possible arrangements of vertices that lie inside and outside the isosurface in a cube. It is worth noting that the edge table uses hexadecimal numbers because they are more efficient to store than decimal numbers. Hexadecimal numbers are represented by 4 bits, while decimal numbers are represented by 8 bits. This means that hexadecimal numbers can be stored in half the space of decimal numbers.

The tri table is also a lookup table that consists of 256 lines of code. Each line contains a set of 16 values corresponding to one of the possible arrangements of edges that intersect the isosurface in a cube. The first value of each line is the number of valid indices for this entry, and the following 15 values are the triangle indices for this entry, with -1 representing "no index".

Both the edge table and tri table are critical components of the marching cubes algorithm and are widely used in computer graphics, video games, and visualization applications.

9.2 Implicit 3D Surfaces

In previous chapters, we have demonstrated how to render the simple and parametric 3D surfaces in both the CPU and GPU. These surfaces can be explicitly described using a mathematical formula or a set of parametric equations. This means that the surfaces can be defined precisely and accurately using mathematical equations, and they can be easily manipulated and transformed using mathematical operations.

On the other hand, an implicit 3D surface is defined implicitly by a scalar function that describes the value of the function at each point in 3D space. The surface is then represented as a set of points where the scalar function equals a particular threshold value. The implicit surfaces can represent complex and irregular surfaces that may be difficult to define explicitly using a mathematical formula.

Rendering implicit 3D surfaces is more difficult than rendering simple and parametric 3D surfaces. There are several approaches to visualize implicit surfaces, including level sets, isosurfaces, and marching cubes. The level set technique represents implicit 3D surfaces as the zero-level set of a higher-dimensional function. This method can be used to efficiently track the movement of the surface over time, making it a popular choice for simulations and fluid dynamics applications. The isosurfaces method is a technique that starts with a function and then computes the values of the function at a set of points. The points that have the same value are then connected to form an isosurface.

The marching cubes algorithm is a method for approximating implicit 3D surfaces with a set of triangles. The algorithm divides the 3D space into a grid of small cubes, and for each cube, determines whether each vertex is inside or outside the surface using the signed distance function. The algorithm then generates a set of triangles to approximate the surface by selecting a specific configuration of vertices based on their positions relative to the surface. The advantage of the marching cubes algorithm is that it can generate a smooth and continuous surface with a relatively small number of triangles, which makes it a good choice for real-time rendering and interactive applications such as video games and virtual reality.

In this section, we will use the marching cubes algorithm and compute shaders to render various implicit 3D surfaces on the GPU.

9.2.1 Shader Code for Implicit Functions

This subsection implements nine mathematical functions used to create different implicit 3D surfaces, including popular shapes such as the Klein, sphere, blobs, torus, and cube sphere. Create a new WGSL shader file named *implicit_func.wgsl* in the *examples/ch09/* folder and add the following code to it:

```
const pi:f32 = 3.14159265359;

struct DataRange {
    xRange: vec2f,
    yRange: vec2f,
    zRange: vec2f,
    scale: f32,
}

fn sphere(x:f32, y:f32, z:f32, t:f32) -> f32{
    let a = 1.1 + cos(t);
    let v = x*x + y*y + z*z - a;
    return v;
}

fn schwartzSurface(x:f32, y:f32, z:f32, t:f32) -> f32{
    let a = 1.0 + 0.5 * cos(t);
    let v = cos(x*a) + cos(y*a) + cos(z*a);
    return v;
}

fn blobs(x:f32, y:f32, z:f32, t:f32) -> f32{
    let a = 1.01 + cos(2.0*t);
    let v = x*x + y*y + z*z + cos(4.0*x) + cos(4.0*y) + cos(4.0*z) - a;
    return v;
}

fn klein(x:f32, y:f32, z:f32, t:f32) -> f32{
    let a = 1.01 + cos(2.0*t);
    let v = (x*x+y*y+z*z + 2.0*y-a)*((x*x+y*y+z*z - 2.0*y-a)*(x*x+y*y+z*z- 2.0*y-a)
        - 8.0*z*z)+16.0*x*z*(x*x+y*y+z*z - 2.0*y- a);
    return v;
}

fn torus(x:f32, y:f32, z:f32, t:f32) -> f32{
    let a = 1.5*(1.01 + cos(t));
    let b = 0.5*(1.1 + cos(t));
    let v = (sqrt(x*x+y*y)-a)*(sqrt(x*x+y*y)-a) + z*z - b;
    return v;
}

fn gyroid(x:f32, y:f32, z:f32, t:f32) -> f32{
    let a = 1.0 + 0.5 * cos(t);
    let v = cos(x*a) * sin(y*a) + cos(y*a) * sin(z*a) + cos(z*a) * sin(x*a);
    return v;
}

fn orthoCircle(x:f32, y:f32, z:f32, t:f32) -> f32{
    let a = 0.5 * (2.2 + cos(t));
    let v = ((x*x + y*y - a)*(x*x + y*y - a) + z*z)*((y*y + z*z - a)*(y*y + z*z - a) +
            x*x)*((z*z + x*x - a)*(z*z + x*x - a) + y*y) - 0.075*0.075 *(1.0 + 3.0*(x*x + y*y + z*z));
    return v;
}

fn gabrielHorn(x:f32, y:f32, z:f32, t:f32) -> f32{
    let a = 1.0 + cos(t);
    let v = a*y*y + a*z*z - (1.0/x)*(1.0/x);
    return v;
}
```

```
fn spiderCage(x:f32, y:f32, z:f32, t:f32) -> f32 {
    let a = 0.5 * (0.9 + 0.9 * cos(t));
    let x2 = x*x;
    let z2 = z*z;
    let xz2 = x2 + z2;

    let v =  pow(sqrt(pow((x2 - z2), 2.0) / xz2 + 3.0 * pow(y * sin(a), 2.0)) - 3.0, 2.0) +
        6.0 * pow(sqrt(pow(x * z, 2.0) / xz2 + pow(y * cos(a), 2.0)) - 1.5, 2.0) - 0.2;
    return v;
}

fn barthSextic(x:f32, y:f32, z:f32, t:f32) -> f32 {
    let a = 0.5 * (2.2 + 1.036*cos(t));
    let a2 = a*a;
    let x2 = x*x;
    let y2 = y*y;
    let z2 = z*z;
    var v = 3.0 * (a2 * x2 - z2) * (a2 * z2 - y2) * (a2 * y2 - x2)
        - (1.0 + 2.0 * a) * pow(x2 + y2 + z2 - 1.0, 2.0);
    if(x2 + y2 + z2 > 3.1) { v = 0.0; }
    return v - 0.1;
}

fn laplaceGaussian(x:f32, y:f32, z:f32, t:f32) -> f32 {
    let a = 1.4;
    let b = 0.06;
    let c = 1.0/(pi*pow(a, 4.0));
    let temp = (x*x + z*z)/(2.0 * a * a);
    let r = sqrt(x*x + z*z);
    var v:f32;
    if(r > 8.0) {
        v = y + 28.0 * c * ( 1.0 - temp) * exp(-b*temp);
    } else {
        v = y - 4.5*(2.3 + 0.7 * sin(0.0258*(x*x + z*z)));
    }
    return v;
}

fn implicitFunc(x:f32, y:f32, z:f32, t:f32, funcSelection:u32) -> f32{
    var v = 0.0;
    if (funcSelection == 0u) {
        v = sphere(x, y, z, t);
    } else if (funcSelection == 1u) {
        v = schwartzSurface(x, y, z, t);
    } else if (funcSelection == 2u) {
        v = blobs(x, y, z, t);
    } else if (funcSelection == 3u) {
        v = klein(x, y, z, t);
    } else if (funcSelection == 4u) {
        v = torus(x, y, z, t);
    } else if (funcSelection == 5u) {
        v = gyroid(x, y, z, t);
    } else if (funcSelection == 6u) {
        v = orthoCircle(x, y, z, t);
    } else if (funcSelection == 7u) {
        v = spiderCage(x, y, z, t);
    } else if (funcSelection == 8u) {
        v = barthSextic(x, y, z, t);
    }
```

```
        return v;
}

fn getDataRange(funcSelection:u32) -> DataRange{
    var dr:DataRange;
    if (funcSelection == 0u) { // sphere
        dr.xRange = vec2(-2.1, 2.1);
        dr.yRange = vec2(-2.1, 2.1);
        dr.zRange = vec2(-2.1, 2.1);
        dr.scale = 1.4;
    } else if (funcSelection == 1u) { // schwartzSurface
        dr.xRange = vec2(-4.0, 4.0);
        dr.yRange = vec2(-4.0, 4.0);
        dr.zRange = vec2(-4.0, 4.0);
        dr.scale = 0.4;
    } else if (funcSelection == 2u) { // blobs
        dr.xRange = vec2(-2.0, 2.0);
        dr.yRange = vec2(-2.0, 2.0);
        dr.zRange = vec2(-2.0, 2.0);
        dr.scale = 1.1;
    } else if (funcSelection == 3u) { // klein
        dr.xRange = vec2(-3.5, 3.5);
        dr.yRange = vec2(-3.5, 3.5);
        dr.zRange = vec2(-4.5, 4.5);
        dr.scale = 0.5;
    } else if (funcSelection == 4u) { // torus
        dr.xRange = vec2(-4.0, 4.0);
        dr.yRange = vec2(-4.0, 4.0);
        dr.zRange = vec2(-1.2, 1.2);
        dr.scale = 0.6;
    } else if (funcSelection == 5u) { // gyroid
        dr.xRange = vec2(-4.0, 4.0);
        dr.yRange = vec2(-4.0, 4.0);
        dr.zRange = vec2(-4.0, 4.0);
        dr.scale = 0.3;
    } else if (funcSelection == 6u) { // orthoCircle
        dr.xRange = vec2(-1.5, 1.5);
        dr.yRange = vec2(-1.5, 1.5);
        dr.zRange = vec2(-1.5, 1.5);
        dr.scale = 1.7;
    } else if (funcSelection == 7u) { // spiderCage
        dr.xRange = vec2(-5.0, 5.0);
        dr.yRange = vec2(-3.0, 3.0);
        dr.zRange = vec2(-5.0, 5.0);
        dr.scale = 0.5;
    } else if (funcSelection == 8u) { // barthSextic
        dr.xRange = vec2(-2.0, 2.0);
        dr.yRange = vec2(-2.0, 2.0);
        dr.zRange = vec2(-2.0, 2.0);
        dr.scale = 1.7;
    }

    return dr;
}
```

The code above defines nine implicit functions that will be used to create various implicit 3D surfaces. It is worth noting that each function is defined implicitly by a scalar function that describes the value of the function at each point in 3D space. In addition to the x, y, and z coordinates, we also pass an extra argument t to each function, which will be used to animate implicit 3D surfaces. The *setDataRange* function is used to set the data ranges of these functions in 3D space. Meanwhile, the *implicitFunc* function is specifically designed to select one of these nine implicit functions.

9.2.2 Compute Shader for Values

To use marching cubes algorithm to render implicit 3D surfaces on the GPU, we first need to use a compute shader to calculate the scalar values of the implicit functions for given *x*, *y*, and *z* coordinates in 3D space. Create a new WGSL compute shader file named *implicit_value.wgsl* in the *examples/ch09/* folder and include the following code:

```
@group(0) @binding(0) var<storage, read_write> valueBuffer : array<f32>;

struct IntParams {
    resolution: u32,
    funcSelection: u32,
};
@group(0) @binding(1) var<uniform> ips : IntParams;

struct FloatParams {
    animateTime: f32,
}

@group(0) @binding(2) var<uniform> fps : FloatParams;

fn positionAt(index : vec3u) -> vec3f {
    let dr = getDataRange(ips.funcSelection);
    let vmin = vec3(dr.xRange[0], dr.yRange[0], dr.zRange[0]);
    let vmax = vec3(dr.xRange[1], dr.yRange[1], dr.zRange[1]);
    let vstep = (vmax - vmin)/(f32(ips.resolution) - 1.0);
    return vmin + (vstep * vec3<f32>(index.xyz));
}

fn getIdx(id: vec3u) -> u32 {
    return id.x + ips.resolution * ( id.y + id.z * ips.resolution);
}

@compute @workgroup_size(8, 8, 8)
fn cs_main(@builtin(global_invocation_id) id : vec3u) {
    let position = positionAt(id);
    let idx = getIdx(id);
    valueBuffer[idx] = implicitFunc(position.x, position.y, position.z, fps.animateTime,
ips.funcSelection);
}
```

The *valueBuffer* struct contains an array of *f32* values, which is used to store the scalar values of the implicit function. The parameters used to calculate the scalar value are specified using two separate structs: *IntParams* and *FloatParams*. The *IntParams* struct includes parameters of *u32* type, while the *FloatParams* struct consists of parameters of *f32* type, which can help avoid the overhead of data type conversion.

The *positionAt* function in the above code is a helper function that takes an index in 3D space and returns the corresponding position. It first gets the data range for the selected implicit function, which is used to determine the minimum and maximum values for each component. Then it calculates the step size based on the resolution of the implicit surface. Finally, it returns the position corresponding to the given index.

The *getIdx* function takes an index in 3D space and returns the corresponding index in the value buffer. This is a linear index calculated by flattening the 3D index.

The *cs_main* function in the above code calculates the position of the current thread using *positionAt*, gets the corresponding index in the value buffer using *getIdx*, and calculates the implicit function at that position using *implicitFunc*. Finally, it writes the value to the value buffer.

It is worthing noting that the *cs_main* function uses a workgroup size of 8×8×8, meaning that the shader will execute 8×8×8 = 512 threads at once. However, the maximum value of the product of the workgroup size dimensions for a compute stage has a default value of 256. To use a workgroup size of 8×8×8, you must reset the limit for the *maxComputeInvocationsPerWorkgroup* to at least 512 (the maximum possible value is 1024) when creating your GPU *device*.

9.2.3 Compute Shader for Implicit Surfaces

Create a new WGSL compute shader file named *implicit_surface.wgsl* in the *examples/ch09/*folder and add the following code to it:

```
struct Tables {
    edges: array<u32, 256>,
    tris: array<i32, 4096>,
}

@group(0) @binding(0) var<storage, read> tables: Tables;

@group(0) @binding(1) var<storage, read> valueBuffer: array<f32>;

@group(0) @binding(2) var<storage, read_write> positionsOut : array<f32>;

@group(0) @binding(3) var<storage, read_write> normalsOut : array<f32>;

@group(0) @binding(4) var<storage, read_write> colorBuffer: array<f32>;

@group(0) @binding(5) var<storage, read_write> indicesOut: array<u32>;

struct IndirectParams {
    vc: u32,
    vertexCount: atomic<u32>,
    firstVertex: u32,
    indexCount: atomic<u32>,
};
@group(0) @binding(6) var<storage, read_write> indirect: IndirectParams;

@group(0) @binding(7) var<storage> colormap: array<vec4f>;

struct IntParams {
    resolution: u32,
    funcSelection: u32,
    colormapDirection: u32,
    colormapReverse: u32,
};
@group(0) @binding(8) var<uniform> ips: IntParams;

struct FloatParams {
    isolevel: f32,
    scale: f32,
};
```

```
@group(0) @binding(9) var<uniform> fps: FloatParams;

var<private> vmin: vec3f;
var<private> vmax: vec3f;
var<private> vstep: vec3f;
var<private> scale2: f32;

fn getIdx(id: vec3u) -> u32 {
    return id.x + ips.resolution * ( id.y + id.z * ips.resolution);
}

fn valueAt(index: vec3u) -> f32 {
    if (any(index > vec3(ips.resolution, ips.resolution, ips.resolution))) { return 0.0; }
    let idx = getIdx(index);
    return valueBuffer[idx];
}

fn positionAt(index: vec3u) -> vec3f {
    let dr = getDataRange(ips.funcSelection);
    scale2 = dr.scale;
    vmin = vec3(dr.xRange[0], dr.yRange[0], dr.zRange[0]);
    vmax = vec3(dr.xRange[1], dr.yRange[1], dr.zRange[1]);
    vstep = (vmax - vmin)/(f32(ips.resolution) - 1.0);
    return vmin + (vstep * vec3<f32>(index.xyz));
}

fn normalAt(index: vec3u) -> vec3f {
    return vec3<f32>(
      valueAt(index - vec3(1u, 0u, 0u)) - valueAt(index + vec3(1u, 0u, 0u)),
      valueAt(index - vec3(0u, 1u, 0u)) - valueAt(index + vec3(0u, 1u, 0u)),
      valueAt(index - vec3(0u, 0u, 1u)) - valueAt(index + vec3(0u, 0u, 1u))
    );
}

var<private> positions: array<vec3f, 12>;
var<private> normals: array<vec3f, 12>;
var<private> colors: array<vec3f, 12>;
var<private> indices: array<u32, 12>;
var<private> cubeVerts: u32 = 0u;

fn interpX(index: u32, i: vec3u, va: f32, vb: f32) {
    let mu = (fps.isolevel - va) / (vb - va);
    positions[cubeVerts] = positionAt(i) + vec3(vstep.x * mu, 0.0, 0.0);

    let na = normalAt(i);
    let nb = normalAt(i + vec3(1u, 0u, 0u));
    normals[cubeVerts] = mix(na, nb, vec3(mu, mu, mu));

    indices[index] = cubeVerts;
    cubeVerts = cubeVerts + 1u;
}

fn interpY(index: u32, i: vec3u, va: f32, vb: f32) {
    let mu = (fps.isolevel - va) / (vb - va);
    positions[cubeVerts] = positionAt(i) + vec3(0.0, vstep.y * mu, 0.0);

    let na = normalAt(i);
    let nb = normalAt(i + vec3(0u, 1u, 0u));
    normals[cubeVerts] = mix(na, nb, vec3(mu, mu, mu));
```

```
    indices[index] = cubeVerts;
    cubeVerts = cubeVerts + 1u;
}

fn interpZ(index: u32, i: vec3u, va: f32, vb: f32) {
    let mu = (fps.isolevel - va) / (vb - va);
    positions[cubeVerts] = positionAt(i) + vec3(0.0, 0.0, vstep.z * mu);

    let na = normalAt(i);
    let nb = normalAt(i + vec3(0u, 0u, 1u));
    normals[cubeVerts] = mix(na, nb, vec3(mu, mu, mu));

    indices[index] = cubeVerts;
    cubeVerts = cubeVerts + 1u;
}

fn colorLerp(tmin: f32, tmax: f32, t: f32, colormapReverse: u32) -> vec4f{
    var t1 = t;
    if (t1 < tmin) {t1 = tmin;}
    if (t1 > tmax) {t1 = tmax;}
    var tn = (t1-tmin)/(tmax-tmin);

    if(colormapReverse >= 1u) {tn = 1.0 - tn;}

    var idx = u32(floor(10.0*tn));
    var color = vec4(0.0,0.0,0.0, 1.0);

    if(f32(idx) == 10.0*tn) {
        color = colormap[idx];
    } else {
        var tn1 = (tn - 0.1*f32(idx))*10.0;
        var a = colormap[idx];
        var b = colormap[idx+1u];
        color.x = a.x + (b.x - a.x)*tn1;
        color.y = a.y + (b.y - a.y)*tn1;
        color.z = a.z + (b.z - a.z)*tn1;
    }

    return color;
}

@compute @workgroup_size(8, 8, 8)
fn cs_main(@builtin(global_invocation_id) global_id: vec3u) {
    let i0 = global_id;
    let i1 = global_id + vec3(1u, 0u, 0u);
    let i2 = global_id + vec3(1u, 1u, 0u);
    let i3 = global_id + vec3(0u, 1u, 0u);
    let i4 = global_id + vec3(0u, 0u, 1u);
    let i5 = global_id + vec3(1u, 0u, 1u);
    let i6 = global_id + vec3(1u, 1u, 1u);
    let i7 = global_id + vec3(0u, 1u, 1u);

    let v0 = valueAt(i0);
    let v1 = valueAt(i1);
    let v2 = valueAt(i2);
    let v3 = valueAt(i3);
    let v4 = valueAt(i4);
    let v5 = valueAt(i5);
    let v6 = valueAt(i6);
    let v7 = valueAt(i7);
```

```
var cubeIndex = 0u;
if (v0 < fps.isolevel) { cubeIndex = cubeIndex | 1u; }
if (v1 < fps.isolevel) { cubeIndex = cubeIndex | 2u; }
if (v2 < fps.isolevel) { cubeIndex = cubeIndex | 4u; }
if (v3 < fps.isolevel) { cubeIndex = cubeIndex | 8u; }
if (v4 < fps.isolevel) { cubeIndex = cubeIndex | 16u; }
if (v5 < fps.isolevel) { cubeIndex = cubeIndex | 32u; }
if (v6 < fps.isolevel) { cubeIndex = cubeIndex | 64u; }
if (v7 < fps.isolevel) { cubeIndex = cubeIndex | 128u; }

let edges = tables.edges[cubeIndex];
if ((edges & 1u) != 0u) { interpX(0u, i0, v0, v1); }
if ((edges & 2u) != 0u) { interpY(1u, i1, v1, v2); }
if ((edges & 4u) != 0u) { interpX(2u, i3, v3, v2); }
if ((edges & 8u) != 0u) { interpY(3u, i0, v0, v3); }
if ((edges & 16u) != 0u) { interpX(4u, i4, v4, v5); }
if ((edges & 32u) != 0u) { interpY(5u, i5, v5, v6); }
if ((edges & 64u) != 0u) { interpX(6u, i7, v7, v6); }
if ((edges & 128u) != 0u) { interpY(7u, i4, v4, v7); }
if ((edges & 256u) != 0u) { interpZ(8u, i0, v0, v4); }
if ((edges & 512u) != 0u) { interpZ(9u, i1, v1, v5); }
if ((edges & 1024u) != 0u) { interpZ(10u, i2, v2, v6); }
if ((edges & 2048u) != 0u) { interpZ(11u, i3, v3, v7); }

let triTableOffset = (cubeIndex << 4u) + 1u;
let indexCount = u32(tables.tris[triTableOffset - 1u]);
var firstVertex = atomicAdd(&indirect.vertexCount, cubeVerts);
let bufferOffset = getIdx(global_id);
let firstIndex = bufferOffset * 15u;

var rmin = vmin.x;
var rmax = vmax.x;
if(ips.colormapDirection == 1u){
    rmin = vmin.y;
    rmax = vmax.y;
} else if(ips.colormapDirection == 2u){
    rmin = vmin.z;
    rmax = vmax.z;
} else if(ips.colormapDirection == 3u){
    rmin = 0.0;
    rmax = max(max(vmax.x, vmax.y), vmax.z);
}
rmin *= fps.scale * scale2;
rmax *= fps.scale * scale2;

var color:vec4f;
for (var i = 0u; i < cubeVerts; i = i + 1u) {
    positions[i] = fps.scale * scale2 * positions[i];
    positionsOut[firstVertex*4u + i*4u] = positions[i].x;
    positionsOut[firstVertex*4u + i*4u + 1u] = positions[i].y;
    positionsOut[firstVertex*4u + i*4u + 2u] = positions[i].z;
    positionsOut[firstVertex*4u + i*4u + 3u] = 1.0;

    normalsOut[firstVertex*4u + i*4u] = normals[i].x;
    normalsOut[firstVertex*4u + i*4u + 1u] = normals[i].y;
    normalsOut[firstVertex*4u + i*4u + 2u] = normals[i].z;
    normalsOut[firstVertex*4u + i*4u + 3u] = 1.0;

    if(ips.colormapDirection < 3u){
```

```
                color = colorLerp(rmin, rmax, positions[i][ips.colormapDirection], ips.colormapReverse);
        } else {
            let p = positions[i];
            let r = sqrt(p.x * p.x + p.y * p.y + p.z * p.z);
            color = colorLerp(rmin, rmax, r, ips.colormapReverse);
        }
        colorBuffer[firstVertex * 4u + i * 4u] = color.x;
        colorBuffer[firstVertex * 4u + i * 4u + 1u] = color.y;
        colorBuffer[firstVertex * 4u + i * 4u + 2u] = color.z;
        colorBuffer[firstVertex * 4u + i * 4u + 3u] = color.w;
    }

    for (var i = 0u; i < indexCount; i = i + 1u) {
        let index = tables.tris[triTableOffset + i];
        indicesOut[firstIndex + i] = firstVertex + indices[index];
    }

    for (var i = indexCount; i < 15u; i = i + 1u) {
        indicesOut[firstIndex + i] = firstVertex;
    }
}
```

This compute shader is used to implement the main marching cubes algorithm. It starts by introducing the marching cubes tables defined in the *Tables* struct. The *valueBuffer* struct is a storage-read buffer that reads the data computed from the compute shader for values implemented in the *implicit_value.wgsl* file presented the previous section. The other structs, such as position, normal, color, and index, are used for storing various data used to create implicit 3D surfaces.

The *IndirectParams* struct contains several values of *u32* type, as well as two *atomic<u32>* values, used for indirect drawing. The *atomic* variables *vertexCount* and *IndexCount* fields in the struct are used to keep track of the number of vertices and indices that have been generated by the compute shader and are likely being accessed and updated by multiple threads. Using *atomic* variables ensures that these updates are performed atomically, without any race conditions or other synchronization issues that could lead to incorrect results.

As we did in the compute shader for values, this shader code also stores parameters of the u32 and f32 type in two separate structs: *IntParams* and *FloatParams*. The parameters in these two struct will be used to generate implicit 3D surfaces.

The above code continues by defining several helper functions, including getIdx, *valueAt*, *positionAt*, *normalAt*, *interpX*, etc. In particular, the *interp* (X, Y, or Z) function performs a linear interpolation between two values and update the positions, normals, and indices arrays in their respective directions.

The *cs_main* function contains the main code block that implements the marching cubes algorithm. Within the function, it first calculates the indices of eight vertices of a cube using the global ID. It then looks up the scalar values at these vertices using the *valueAt* function, and it computes a bit mask *cubeIndex* based on whether each scalar value stored in the *ValueBuffer.values* array is greater than or less than a given isolevel.

Next, the function looks up a set of edges corresponding to the configuration using an edge table, and for each edge that intersects the isosurface, it calls one of three interpolation functions, *interpX*, *interpY*, and *interpZ*, to compute the position and normal of the intersection point.

Subsequently the function looks up a set of triangle indices corresponding to the cube configuration using another tri table, and computes the number of vertices and the first index of the triangles that will be generated. These values are stored in the atomic field named *vertexCount* in the *IndirectParams* struct for later use in generating the triangles.

The function continues by defining the data range for colormap. It then loops through each vertex and writes the position and normal values to the *positionOutput* and *normalsOut* buffers, respectively. Additionally, the function calculates the colormap for each vertex based on the corresponding data range and the position of the vertex in the direction specified by the colormap direction parameter, and writes the result to the color buffer.

9.2.4 Rust Code

Create a new Rust file named *implicit_surface.rs* in the *examples/ch09/* folder and add the following code to it:

```rust
use std::{iter, collections::HashMap};
use cgmath::{ Matrix, Matrix4, SquareMatrix };
use rand::{Rng, rngs::ThreadRng};
use wgpu:: { VertexBufferLayout, util::DeviceExt };
use winit::{
    event::*,
    event_loop::{ControlFlow, EventLoop},
    window::Window,
};
use bytemuck::cast_slice;
use wgpu_book_examples::{ wgpu_simplified as ws, transforms as wt, colormap };
mod marching_cubes_table;

fn create_color_data(colormap_name: &str) -> Vec<[f32; 4]> {
    let cdata = colormap::colormap_data(colormap_name);
    let mut data:Vec<[f32; 4]> = vec![];
    for i in 0..cdata.len() {
        data.push([cdata[i][0], cdata[i][1], cdata[i][2], 1.0 ]);
    }
    data
}

fn surface_type_map() -> HashMap<u32, String> {
    let mut surface_type = HashMap::new();
    surface_type.insert(0, String::from("Sphere"));
    surface_type.insert(1, String::from("Schwartz Surface"));
    surface_type.insert(2, String::from("Blobs"));
    surface_type.insert(3, String::from("Klein"));
    surface_type.insert(4, String::from("Torus"));
    surface_type.insert(5, String::from("Chmutov"));
    surface_type.insert(6, String::from("Gyroid"));
    surface_type.insert(7, String::from("Cube Sphere"));
    surface_type.insert(8, String::from("Ortho Circle"));
    surface_type.insert(9, String::from("Spider Cage"));
    surface_type.insert(10, String::from("Barth Sextic"));
    surface_type
}

fn get_surface_type(key:u32) -> String {
    let map = surface_type_map();
    map.get(&key).map(|s| s.to_string()).unwrap_or_default()
}

struct State {
```

```
    init:  ws::IWgpuInit,
    pipeline: wgpu::RenderPipeline,
    uniform_bind_groups: Vec<wgpu::BindGroup>,
    uniform_buffers: Vec<wgpu::Buffer>,

    cs_pipelines: Vec<wgpu::ComputePipeline>,
    cs_vertex_buffers: Vec<wgpu::Buffer>,
    cs_index_buffer: wgpu::Buffer,
    cs_uniform_buffers: Vec<wgpu::Buffer>,
    cs_bind_groups: Vec<wgpu::BindGroup>,

    view_mat: Matrix4<f32>,
    project_mat: Matrix4<f32>,
    msaa_texture_view: wgpu::TextureView,
    depth_texture_view: wgpu::TextureView,
    animation_speed: f32,
    rotation_speed: f32,

    resolution: u32,
    index_count: u32,

    surface_type: u32,
    colormap_direction: u32,
    colormap_reverse: u32,
    isolevel: f32,
    scale: f32,

    rng: ThreadRng,
    t0: std::time::Instant,
    random_shape_change: u32,
    fps_counter: ws::FpsCounter,
}

impl State {
    async fn new(window:&Window, sample_count:u32, resolution:u32, colormap_name:&str) -> Self {
        let limits = wgpu::Limits {
            max_storage_buffer_binding_size: 1024*1024*1024, //1024MB, defaulting to 128MB
            max_buffer_size: 1024*1024*1024, // 1024MB, defaulting to 256MB
            max_compute_invocations_per_workgroup: 512, // dafaulting to 256
            ..Default::default()
        };
        let init = ws::IWgpuInit::new(&window, sample_count, Some(limits)).await;

        let resol = ws::round_to_multiple(resolution, 8);
        let marching_cube_cells = (resolution - 1) * (resolution - 1) * (resolution - 1);
        let vertex_count = 3 * 12 * marching_cube_cells;
        let vertex_buffer_size = 4 * vertex_count;
        let index_count = 15 * marching_cube_cells;
        let index_buffer_size = 4 * index_count;
        println!("resolution = {}", resol);

        let vs_shader = init.device.create_shader_module(wgpu::include_wgsl!("../ch05/shader_vert.wgsl"));
        let fs_shader = init.device.create_shader_module(wgpu::include_wgsl!("../ch05/shader_frag.wgsl"));

        let cs_value_file = include_str!("implicit_value.wgsl");
        let cs_func_file = include_str!("implicit_func.wgsl");
        let cs_surface_file = include_str!("implicit_surface.wgsl");

        let cs_value = init.device.create_shader_module(wgpu::ShaderModuleDescriptor {
            label: Some("Compute Shader"),
```

```
        source: wgpu::ShaderSource::Wgsl([cs_func_file, cs_value_file].join("\n").into()),
});

let cs_comp = init.device.create_shader_module(wgpu::ShaderModuleDescriptor {
    label: Some("Compute Shader"),
    source: wgpu::ShaderSource::Wgsl([cs_func_file, cs_surface_file].join("\n").into()),
});

// uniform data
let camera_position = (2.0, 2.0, 3.0).into();
let look_direction = (0.0,0.0,0.0).into();
let up_direction = cgmath::Vector3::unit_y();
let light_direction = [-0.5f32, -0.5, -0.5];

let (view_mat, project_mat, _) =
    wt::create_vp_mat(camera_position, look_direction, up_direction,
    init.config.width as f32 / init.config.height as f32);

// create vertex uniform buffers

// model_mat and vp_mat will be stored in vertex_uniform_buffer inside the update function
let vert_uniform_buffer = init.device.create_buffer(&wgpu::BufferDescriptor{
    label: Some("Vertex Uniform Buffer"),
    size: 192,
    usage: wgpu::BufferUsages::UNIFORM | wgpu::BufferUsages::COPY_DST,
    mapped_at_creation: false,
});

// create light uniform buffer. here we set eye_position = camera_position
let light_uniform_buffer = init.device.create_buffer(&wgpu::BufferDescriptor{
    label: Some("Light Uniform Buffer"),
    size: 48,
    usage: wgpu::BufferUsages::UNIFORM | wgpu::BufferUsages::COPY_DST,
    mapped_at_creation: false,
});

let eye_position:&[f32; 3] = camera_position.as_ref();
init.queue.write_buffer(&light_uniform_buffer, 0, cast_slice(light_direction.as_ref()));
init.queue.write_buffer(&light_uniform_buffer, 16, cast_slice(eye_position));

// set specular light color to white
let specular_color:[f32; 3] = [1.0, 1.0, 1.0];
init.queue.write_buffer(&light_uniform_buffer, 32, cast_slice(specular_color.as_ref()));

// material uniform buffer
let material_uniform_buffer = init.device.create_buffer(&wgpu::BufferDescriptor{
    label: Some("Material Uniform Buffer"),
    size: 16,
    usage: wgpu::BufferUsages::UNIFORM | wgpu::BufferUsages::COPY_DST,
    mapped_at_creation: false,
});

// set default material parameters
let material = [0.1f32, 0.7, 0.4, 30.0];
init.queue.write_buffer(&material_uniform_buffer, 0, cast_slice(material.as_ref()));

// uniform bind group for vertex shader
let (vert_bind_group_layout, vert_bind_group) = ws::create_bind_group(
    &init.device,
    vec![wgpu::ShaderStages::VERTEX],
```

```
                &[vert_uniform_buffer.as_entire_binding()],
        );

        // uniform bind group for fragment shader
        let (frag_bind_group_layout, frag_bind_group) = ws::create_bind_group(
            &init.device,
            vec![wgpu::ShaderStages::FRAGMENT, wgpu::ShaderStages::FRAGMENT],
            &[light_uniform_buffer.as_entire_binding(), material_uniform_buffer.as_entire_binding()],
        );

        let vertex_buffer_layouts = [
            VertexBufferLayout {
                array_stride: 16,
                step_mode: wgpu::VertexStepMode::Vertex,
                attributes: &wgpu::vertex_attr_array![0 => Float32x4], // pos
            },
            VertexBufferLayout {
                array_stride: 16,
                step_mode: wgpu::VertexStepMode::Vertex,
                attributes: &wgpu::vertex_attr_array![1 => Float32x4], // norm
            },
            VertexBufferLayout {
                array_stride: 16,
                step_mode: wgpu::VertexStepMode::Vertex,
                attributes: &wgpu::vertex_attr_array![2 => Float32x4], // col
            },
        ];

        let pipeline_layout = init.device.create_pipeline_layout(&wgpu::PipelineLayoutDescriptor {
            label: Some("Render Pipeline Layout"),
            bind_group_layouts: &[&vert_bind_group_layout, &frag_bind_group_layout],
            push_constant_ranges: &[],
        });

        let mut ppl = ws::IRenderPipeline {
            vs_shader: Some(&vs_shader),
            fs_shader: Some(&fs_shader),
            pipeline_layout: Some(&pipeline_layout),
            vertex_buffer_layout: &vertex_buffer_layouts,
            ..Default::default()
        };
        let pipeline = ppl.new(&init);

        let msaa_texture_view = ws::create_msaa_texture_view(&init);
        let depth_texture_view = ws::create_depth_view(&init);

        // create compute pipeline for value
        let volume_elements = resol * resol * resol;
        let cs_value_buffer = init.device.create_buffer(&wgpu::BufferDescriptor{
            label: Some("Index Buffer"),
            size:  4 * volume_elements as u64,
            usage: wgpu::BufferUsages::STORAGE | wgpu::BufferUsages::COPY_DST,
            mapped_at_creation: false,
        });

        let cs_value_int_buffer = init.device.create_buffer(&wgpu::BufferDescriptor{
            label: Some("Compuet Value Integer Uniform Buffer"),
            size:  16,
            usage: wgpu::BufferUsages::UNIFORM | wgpu::BufferUsages::COPY_DST,
            mapped_at_creation: false,
```

```
});

let cs_value_float_buffer = init.device.create_buffer(&wgpu::BufferDescriptor{
    label: Some("Compuet Value Float Uniform Buffer"),
    size:  16,
    usage: wgpu::BufferUsages::UNIFORM | wgpu::BufferUsages::COPY_DST,
    mapped_at_creation: false,
});

let (cs_value_bind_group_layout, cs_value_bind_group) = ws::create_bind_group_storage(
    &init.device,
    vec![
        wgpu::ShaderStages::COMPUTE, wgpu::ShaderStages::COMPUTE,
        wgpu::ShaderStages::COMPUTE,
    ],
    vec![
        wgpu::BufferBindingType::Storage { read_only: false },
        wgpu::BufferBindingType::Uniform,
        wgpu::BufferBindingType::Uniform,
    ],
    &[
        cs_value_buffer.as_entire_binding(),
        cs_value_int_buffer.as_entire_binding(),
        cs_value_float_buffer.as_entire_binding(),
    ],
);

let cs_value_pipeline_layout = init.device.create_pipeline_layout(&wgpu::PipelineLayoutDescriptor{
    label: Some("Compute Value Pipeline Layout"),
    bind_group_layouts: &[&cs_value_bind_group_layout],
    push_constant_ranges: &[],
});

let cs_value_pipeline = init.device.create_compute_pipeline(&wgpu::ComputePipelineDescriptor{
    label: Some("Compute Value Pipeline"),
    layout: Some(&cs_value_pipeline_layout),
    module: &cs_value,
    entry_point: "cs_main",
});

// create compute pipeline for implicit surface
let cs_table_buffer = init.device.create_buffer(&wgpu::BufferDescriptor{
    label: Some("Compute Table STorage Buffer"),
    size:  (marching_cubes_table::EDGE_TABLE.len() +
        marching_cubes_table::TRI_TABLE.len()) as u64 * 4,
    usage: wgpu::BufferUsages::STORAGE | wgpu::BufferUsages::COPY_DST,
    mapped_at_creation: false,
});
init.queue.write_buffer(&cs_table_buffer, 0, cast_slice(marching_cubes_table::EDGE_TABLE));
init.queue.write_buffer(&cs_table_buffer, marching_cubes_table::EDGE_TABLE.len() as u64 * 4,
    cast_slice(marching_cubes_table::TRI_TABLE));

let cs_position_buffer = init.device.create_buffer(&wgpu::BufferDescriptor{
    label: Some("Compute Position Buffer"),
    size:  vertex_buffer_size as u64,
    usage: wgpu::BufferUsages::VERTEX | wgpu::BufferUsages::STORAGE |
        wgpu::BufferUsages::COPY_DST,
    mapped_at_creation: false,
});
```

```rust
let cs_normal_buffer = init.device.create_buffer(&wgpu::BufferDescriptor{
    label: Some("Compute Normal Buffer"),
    size:  vertex_buffer_size as u64,
    usage: wgpu::BufferUsages::VERTEX | wgpu::BufferUsages::STORAGE |
        wgpu::BufferUsages::COPY_DST,
    mapped_at_creation: false,
});

let cs_color_buffer = init.device.create_buffer(&wgpu::BufferDescriptor{
    label: Some("Compute Color Buffer"),
    size:  vertex_buffer_size as u64,
    usage: wgpu::BufferUsages::VERTEX | wgpu::BufferUsages::STORAGE |
        wgpu::BufferUsages::COPY_DST,
    mapped_at_creation: false,
});

let cs_index_buffer = init.device.create_buffer(&wgpu::BufferDescriptor{
    label: Some("Compute Index Buffer"),
    size:  index_buffer_size as u64,
    usage: wgpu::BufferUsages::INDEX | wgpu::BufferUsages::STORAGE | wgpu::BufferUsages::COPY_DST,
    mapped_at_creation: false,
});

//let indirect_array = [500u32, 0, 0, 0];
let cs_indirect_buffer = init.device.create_buffer(&wgpu::BufferDescriptor{
    label: Some("Compute Indirect Buffer"),
    size:  16,
    usage: wgpu::BufferUsages::INDIRECT | wgpu::BufferUsages::STORAGE |
        wgpu::BufferUsages::COPY_DST,
    mapped_at_creation: false,
});

let cdata = create_color_data(colormap_name);
let cs_colormap_buffer = init.device.create_buffer_init(&wgpu::util::BufferInitDescriptor{
    label: Some("Compute Colormap Uniform Buffer"),
    contents: bytemuck::cast_slice(&cdata),
    usage: wgpu::BufferUsages::STORAGE | wgpu::BufferUsages::COPY_DST,
});

let cs_int_buffer = init.device.create_buffer(&wgpu::BufferDescriptor{
    label: Some("Compute Integer uniform Buffer"),
    size:  16,
    usage: wgpu::BufferUsages::UNIFORM | wgpu::BufferUsages::COPY_DST,
    mapped_at_creation: false,
});

let cs_float_buffer = init.device.create_buffer(&wgpu::BufferDescriptor{
    label: Some("Compute Float uniform Buffer"),
    size:  16,
    usage: wgpu::BufferUsages::UNIFORM | wgpu::BufferUsages::COPY_DST,
    mapped_at_creation: false,
});

let (cs_bind_group_layout, cs_bind_group) = ws::create_bind_group_storage(
    &init.device,
    vec![
        wgpu::ShaderStages::COMPUTE, wgpu::ShaderStages::COMPUTE, wgpu::ShaderStages::COMPUTE,
        wgpu::ShaderStages::COMPUTE, wgpu::ShaderStages::COMPUTE, wgpu::ShaderStages::COMPUTE,
        wgpu::ShaderStages::COMPUTE, wgpu::ShaderStages::COMPUTE, wgpu::ShaderStages::COMPUTE,
        wgpu::ShaderStages::COMPUTE,
```

```rust
        ],
        vec![
            wgpu::BufferBindingType::Storage { read_only: true },      // marching table
            wgpu::BufferBindingType::Storage { read_only: true },      // value buffer
            wgpu::BufferBindingType::Storage { read_only: false },     // position
            wgpu::BufferBindingType::Storage { read_only: false },     // normal
            wgpu::BufferBindingType::Storage { read_only: false },     // color
            wgpu::BufferBindingType::Storage { read_only: false },     // indices
            wgpu::BufferBindingType::Storage { read_only: false },     // indirect params
            wgpu::BufferBindingType::Storage { read_only: true },      // colormap
            wgpu::BufferBindingType::Uniform,                          // int params
            wgpu::BufferBindingType::Uniform,                          // float params
        ],
        &[
            cs_table_buffer.as_entire_binding(),
            cs_value_buffer.as_entire_binding(),
            cs_position_buffer.as_entire_binding(),
            cs_normal_buffer.as_entire_binding(),
            cs_color_buffer.as_entire_binding(),
            cs_index_buffer.as_entire_binding(),
            cs_indirect_buffer.as_entire_binding(),
            cs_colormap_buffer.as_entire_binding(),
            cs_int_buffer.as_entire_binding(),
            cs_float_buffer.as_entire_binding(),
        ],
    );

let cs_pipeline_layout = init.device.create_pipeline_layout(&wgpu::PipelineLayoutDescriptor{
    label: Some("Compute Pipeline Layout"),
    bind_group_layouts: &[&cs_bind_group_layout],
    push_constant_ranges: &[],
});

let cs_pipeline = init.device.create_compute_pipeline(&wgpu::ComputePipelineDescriptor{
    label: Some("Compute Pipeline"),
    layout: Some(&cs_pipeline_layout),
    module: &cs_comp,
    entry_point: "cs_main",
});

Self {
    init,
    pipeline,
    uniform_bind_groups: vec![vert_bind_group, frag_bind_group],
    uniform_buffers: vec![vert_uniform_buffer, light_uniform_buffer, material_uniform_buffer],

    cs_pipelines: vec![cs_value_pipeline, cs_pipeline],
    cs_vertex_buffers: vec![cs_value_buffer, cs_position_buffer, cs_normal_buffer,
        cs_color_buffer],
    cs_index_buffer,
    cs_uniform_buffers: vec![cs_value_int_buffer, cs_value_float_buffer, cs_int_buffer,
        cs_float_buffer, cs_indirect_buffer],
    cs_bind_groups: vec![cs_value_bind_group, cs_bind_group],

    view_mat,
    project_mat,
    msaa_texture_view,
    depth_texture_view,

    animation_speed: 1.0,
```

```
            rotation_speed: 1.0,

            resolution: resol,
            index_count,
            surface_type: 2,
            colormap_direction: 1,
            colormap_reverse: 0,
            isolevel: 0.0,
            scale: 1.0,

            rng: rand::thread_rng(),
            t0:  std::time::Instant::now(),
            random_shape_change: 0,
            fps_counter: ws::FpsCounter::default(),
        }
    }

    fn resize(&mut self, new_size: winit::dpi::PhysicalSize<u32>) {
        if new_size.width > 0 && new_size.height > 0 {
            self.init.size = new_size;
            self.init.config.width = new_size.width;
            self.init.config.height = new_size.height;
            self.init.surface.configure(&self.init.device, &self.init.config);

            self.project_mat = wt::create_projection_mat(new_size.width as f32 / new_size.height as f32,
                true);
            self.depth_texture_view = ws::create_depth_view(&self.init);
            if self.init.sample_count > 1 {
                self.msaa_texture_view = ws::create_msaa_texture_view(&self.init);
            }
        }
    }

    #[allow(unused_variables)]
    fn input(&mut self, event: &WindowEvent) -> bool {
        match event {
            WindowEvent::KeyboardInput {
                input:
                    KeyboardInput {
                        virtual_keycode: Some(keycode),
                        state: ElementState::Pressed,
                        ..
                    },
                ..
            } => {
                match keycode {
                    VirtualKeyCode::Space => {
                        self.surface_type = (self.surface_type + 1) % 9;
                        println!("key = {:?}, surface_type = {:?}", self.surface_type,
                            get_surface_type(self.surface_type));
                        true
                    },
                    VirtualKeyCode::LControl => {
                        self.colormap_direction = (self.colormap_direction + 1) % 4;
                        true
                    },
                    VirtualKeyCode::LShift => {
                        self.random_shape_change = (self.random_shape_change + 1) % 2;
                        true
                    },
```

```
                VirtualKeyCode::LAlt => {
                    self.colormap_reverse = if self.colormap_reverse == 0 { 1 } else { 0 };
                    true
                },
                VirtualKeyCode::Q => {
                    self.animation_speed += 0.1;
                    true
                },
                VirtualKeyCode::A => {
                    self.animation_speed -= 0.1;
                    if self.animation_speed < 0.0 {
                        self.animation_speed = 0.0;
                    }
                    true
                } ,
                VirtualKeyCode::W => {
                    self.rotation_speed += 0.1;
                    true
                },
                VirtualKeyCode::S => {
                    self.rotation_speed -= 0.1;
                    if self.rotation_speed < 0.0 {
                        self.rotation_speed = 0.0;
                    }
                    true
                } ,
                _ => false
            }
        }
        _ => false,
    }
}

fn update(&mut self, dt: std::time::Duration) {
    // update uniform buffer
    let dt1 = self.rotation_speed * dt.as_secs_f32();

    let model_mat = wt::create_model_mat([0.0,0.0,0.0], [dt1.sin(), dt1.cos(), 0.0], [1.0, 1.0, 1.0]);
    let view_project_mat = self.project_mat * self.view_mat;

    let normal_mat = (model_mat.invert().unwrap()).transpose();

    let model_ref:&[f32; 16] = model_mat.as_ref();
    let view_projection_ref:&[f32; 16] = view_project_mat.as_ref();
    let normal_ref:&[f32; 16] = normal_mat.as_ref();

    self.init.queue.write_buffer(&self.uniform_buffers[0], 0, cast_slice(view_projection_ref));
    self.init.queue.write_buffer(&self.uniform_buffers[0], 64, cast_slice(model_ref));
    self.init.queue.write_buffer(&self.uniform_buffers[0], 128, cast_slice(normal_ref));

    let elapsed = self.t0.elapsed();
    if elapsed >= std::time::Duration::from_secs(5) && self.random_shape_change == 0 {
        self.surface_type = self.rng.gen_range(0..=8) as u32;
        self.t0 = std::time::Instant::now();
        println!("key = {:?}, surface_type = {:?}", self.surface_type,
            get_surface_type(self.surface_type));
    }

    // update compute buffers for value
    let value_int_params = [self.resolution, self.surface_type, 0, 0];
```

```
            self.init.queue.write_buffer(&self.cs_uniform_buffers[0], 0, cast_slice(&value_int_params));

        let value_float_params = [self.animation_speed * dt.as_secs_f32(), 0.0, 0.0, 0.0];
        self.init.queue.write_buffer(&self.cs_uniform_buffers[1], 0,
            cast_slice(&value_float_params));

        // update compute buffers for implicit surface
        let int_params = [
            self.resolution,
            self.surface_type,
            self.colormap_direction,
            self.colormap_reverse,
        ];
        self.init.queue.write_buffer(&self.cs_uniform_buffers[2], 0, cast_slice(&int_params));

        let float_params = [self.isolevel, self.scale, 0.0, 0.0];
        self.init.queue.write_buffer(&self.cs_uniform_buffers[3], 0, cast_slice(&float_params));

        let indirect_array = [500u32, 0, 0, 0];
        self.init.queue.write_buffer(&self.cs_uniform_buffers[4], 0, cast_slice(&indirect_array));

    }

    fn render(&mut self) -> Result<(), wgpu::SurfaceError> {
        let output = self.init.surface.get_current_texture()?;
        let view = output
            .texture
            .create_view(&wgpu::TextureViewDescriptor::default());

        let mut encoder = self
            .init.device
            .create_command_encoder(&wgpu::CommandEncoderDescriptor {
                label: Some("Render Encoder"),
            });

        // compute pass for value
        {
            let mut cs_index_pass = encoder.begin_compute_pass(&wgpu::ComputePassDescriptor{
                label: Some("Compute value Pass"),
                timestamp_writes: None,
            });
            cs_index_pass.set_pipeline(&self.cs_pipelines[0]);
            cs_index_pass.set_bind_group(0, &self.cs_bind_groups[0], &[]);
            cs_index_pass.dispatch_workgroups(self.resolution/8, self.resolution/8, self.resolution/8);
        }

        // compute pass for vertices
        {
            let mut cs_pass = encoder.begin_compute_pass(&wgpu::ComputePassDescriptor{
                label: Some("Compute Pass"),
                timestamp_writes: None,
            });
            cs_pass.set_pipeline(&self.cs_pipelines[1]);
            cs_pass.set_bind_group(0, &self.cs_bind_groups[1], &[]);
            cs_pass.dispatch_workgroups(self.resolution/8, self.resolution/8, self.resolution/8);
        }

        // render pass
        {
            let color_attach = ws::create_color_attachment(&view);
```

```
        let msaa_attach = ws::create_msaa_color_attachment(&view, &self.msaa_texture_view);
        let color_attachment = if self.init.sample_count == 1 { color_attach } else { msaa_attach };
        let depth_attachment = ws::create_depth_stencil_attachment(&self.depth_texture_view);

        let mut render_pass = encoder.begin_render_pass(&wgpu::RenderPassDescriptor {
            label: Some("Render Pass"),
            color_attachments: &[Some(color_attachment)],
            depth_stencil_attachment: Some(depth_attachment),
            occlusion_query_set: None,
            timestamp_writes: None,
        });

        render_pass.set_pipeline(&self.pipeline);
        render_pass.set_vertex_buffer(0, self.cs_vertex_buffers[1].slice(..));
        render_pass.set_vertex_buffer(1, self.cs_vertex_buffers[2].slice(..));
        render_pass.set_vertex_buffer(2, self.cs_vertex_buffers[3].slice(..));
        render_pass.set_index_buffer(self.cs_index_buffer.slice(..),
            wgpu::IndexFormat::Uint32);
        render_pass.set_bind_group(0, &self.uniform_bind_groups[0], &[]);
        render_pass.set_bind_group(1, &self.uniform_bind_groups[1], &[]);
        render_pass.draw_indexed(0..self.index_count, 0, 0..1);
    }
    self.fps_counter.print_fps(5);
    self.init.queue.submit(iter::once(encoder.finish()));
    output.present();

    Ok(())
    }
}

fn main() {
    let mut sample_count = 1u32;
    let mut resolution = 192u32;
    let mut colormap_name = "jet";

    let args: Vec<String> = std::env::args().collect();
    if args.len() > 1 {
        sample_count = args[1].parse::<u32>().unwrap();
    }
    if args.len() > 2 {
        resolution = args[2].parse::<u32>().unwrap();
    }
    if args.len() > 3 {
        colormap_name = &args[3];
    }

    env_logger::init();
    let event_loop = EventLoop::new();
    let window = winit::window::WindowBuilder::new().build(&event_loop).unwrap();
    window.set_title(&*format!("ch09_{}", "implict_surface"));

    let mut state = pollster::block_on(State::new(&window, sample_count, resolution, colormap_name));
    let render_start_time = std::time::Instant::now();

    event_loop.run(move |event, _, control_flow| {
        match event {
            Event::WindowEvent {
                ref event,
                window_id,
            } if window_id == window.id() => {
```

```
                    if !state.input(event) {
                        match event {
                            WindowEvent::CloseRequested
                            | WindowEvent::KeyboardInput {
                                input:
                                    KeyboardInput {
                                        state: ElementState::Pressed,
                                        virtual_keycode: Some(VirtualKeyCode::Escape),
                                        ..
                                    },
                                ..
                            } => *control_flow = ControlFlow::Exit,
                            WindowEvent::Resized(physical_size) => {
                                state.resize(*physical_size);
                            }
                            WindowEvent::ScaleFactorChanged { new_inner_size, .. } => {
                                state.resize(**new_inner_size);
                            }
                            _ => {}
                        }
                    }
                }
                Event::RedrawRequested(_) => {
                    let now = std::time::Instant::now();
                    let dt = now - render_start_time;
                    state.update(dt);

                    match state.render() {
                        Ok(_) => {}
                        Err(wgpu::SurfaceError::Lost) => state.resize(state.init.size),
                        Err(wgpu::SurfaceError::OutOfMemory) => *control_flow = ControlFlow::Exit,
                        Err(e) => eprintln!("{:?}", e),
                    }
                }
                Event::MainEventsCleared => {
                    window.request_redraw();
                }
                _ => {}
            }
        });
    }
```

In the above code, we first introduce the marching cubes tables from the *marching_cubes_table.rs* file and add several new fields to the *State* struct, including *resolution*, *marching_cube_cells*, *vertex_count*, *index_count*, *vertex_buffer_size*, and *index_buffer_size*. These fields can be easily accessed by different functions without the need to pass them as input.

Within the *State::new* function, as mentioned earlier, we need to reset certain GPU device limits when creating the device, as illustrated in the following code snippet:

```
let limits = wgpu::Limits {
    max_storage_buffer_binding_size: 1024*1024*1024, //1024MB, defaulting to 128MB
    max_buffer_size: 1024*1024*1024, // 1024MB, defaulting to 256MB
    max_compute_invocations_per_workgroup: 512, // dafaulting to 256
    ..Default::default()
};
let init = ws::IWgpuInit::new(&window, sample_count, Some(limits)).await;
```

The above code snippet resets limits for several properties, including *max_storage_buffer_binding_size*, *max_buffer_size*, and *max_compute_invocation_per_workgroup*. In particular, the last property is changed from the default value of 256 to 512, which is required by the workgroup size of $8 \times 8 \times 8$ used in the current compute shader.

Subsequently, we reuse the vertex and fragment shaders created earlier in Chapter 5, as well as the colormap data implemented in the *colormap.rs* file located in the *src/* folder. Since three shader files, *implicit_func.wgsl*, *implicit_value.wgsl*, and *implicit_surface.wgsl*, are required for generating compute pipelines for the value and vertex data used to create implicit surfaces, these files are amalgamated to form the compute shader module. The process is demonstrated in the following code:

```
let cs_value_file = include_str!("implicit_value.wgsl");
let cs_func_file = include_str!("implicit_func.wgsl");
let cs_surface_file = include_str!("implicit_surface.wgsl");

let cs_value = init.device.create_shader_module(wgpu::ShaderModuleDescriptor {
    label: Some("Compute Shader"),
    source: wgpu::ShaderSource::Wgsl([cs_func_file, cs_value_file].join("\n").into()),
});

let cs_comp = init.device.create_shader_module(wgpu::ShaderModuleDescriptor {
    label: Some("Compute Shader"),
    source: wgpu::ShaderSource::Wgsl([cs_func_file, cs_surface_file].join("\n").into()),
});
```

The rest of the code for the *State::new* function is similar to the one used to create simple 3D surfaces on the GPU in Chapter 7. This example also uses a compute shader to generate the position, normal, and colormap buffers. The key difference is that this example does not create the wireframe for implicit 3D surfaces.

After creating the render pipeline, we proceed to define the compute pipeline for calculating the scalar values of the explicit function. In this context, we introduce a value storage buffer called *cs_value_buffer* to store the scalar value data, along with two uniform buffers, *cs_value_int_buffer* and *cs_value_float_buffer*. These uniform buffers are used to store parameters with the *u32* and *f32* type, respectively, which will be used to generate the scalar values for implicit 3D surfaces.

The following code segment constructs a compute pipeline customized for vertex data generation. Within the segment, we create a table buffer used to pass the edge table and tri table from the Rust code to the compute shader. Next, we create two parameter buffers and an indirect buffer, which will be used to pass various parameters to the compute shader for calculating various vertex data. To store this data, we create various vertex buffers, including position, normal, color, and index buffers, all of which are storage buffers used to store corresponding vertex data in the compute shader.

The *State::render* function in the above code includes two passes: a compute pass and a render pass. The compute pass contains two compute pipelines: one for calculating scalar values and another for calculating vertex data. To achieve this, we set the corresponding bind groups for the compute pass since one of the *resource* attributes of the bind group is specified by either the value buffer or vertex buffers. Then, in the render pass, we use the vertex buffer and index buffer from the compute pipeline to set these buffers for the render pass.

This example animates the implicit 3D surfaces without the need to regenerate the vertex data and vertex buffers for every frame within the *State::update* function. Instead, we only need to update the uniform parameters used to calculate the scalar value data in the compute shader, as shown in the following code snippet:

```
let value_float_params = [self.animation_speed * dt.as_secs_f32(), 0.0, 0.0, 0.0];
self.init.queue.write_buffer(&self.cs_uniform_buffers[1], 0, cast_slice(&value_float_params));
```

Furthermore, a specific condition, denoted by *self.random_shape_change* = 1, triggers a notable behavior. When this condition is met, the subsequent code block engages to update the uniform buffers at 5-second intervals:

```
let elapsed = self.t0.elapsed();
if elapsed >= std::time::Duration::from_secs(5) && self.random_shape_change == 0 {
    self.surface_type = self.rng.gen_range(0..=8) as u32;
    self.t0 = std::time::Instant::now();
    println!("key = {:?}, surface_type = {:?}", self.surface_type,
        get_surface_type(self.surface_type));
}
```

In this code snippet, a new surface type is selected at random, and the chosen surface type will be displayed in the terminal.

Conversely, when *self.random_shape_change* does not equal 1, a scenario attainable through the *LShift* key, you then possess the ability to manually alter the surface type using the *Space* key.

Additionally, the code permits the user to modify input parameters using keyboard inputs.

Here is a list of controls using keyboard:

- *Space*: Changes the surface type when *random_shape_change* != 1.

- *LControl*: Changes the colormap direction.

- *LShift*: Changes the random_shape_change value between 0 and 1.

- *LAlt*: Reverse colormap.

- *Q/A*: Increases/decreases the animation speed.

- *W/S*: Increases/decreases the rotation speed.

9.2.5 Run Application

To run this application, add the following code snippet to the *Cargo.toml* file:

```
[[example]]
name = "ch09_implicit_surface"
path = "examples/ch09/implicit_surface.rs"
```

Afterward, execute the following *cargo run* commands in the terminal window:

```
cargo run --example ch09_implicit_surface 8
```

Fig.9-2 shows the results of this example.

It is evident from the figure that implicit 3D surfaces allow for smoother surfaces with more complex structures compared to polygon-based models. Implicit surfaces are more flexible in that they can be used to represent a wider variety of shapes. They are also more robust since they are less likely to be affected by noise or errors in the data. However, implicit surfaces also have disadvantages. They are more difficult to visualize and manipulate than other types of surfaces and can be more computationally expensive to render.

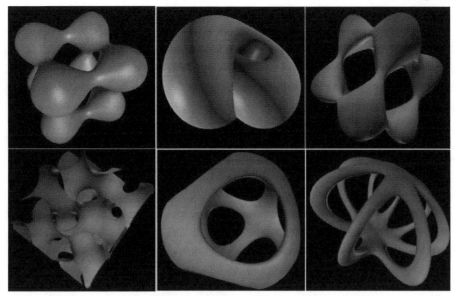

Fig.9-2. Selected implicit 3D surfaces created using marching cubes.

9.3 Metaballs

Metaballs are a type of 3D modeling technique that uses spheres to create a fluid and organic appearance. Each sphere has a radius and a density, and the density of a sphere decreases with distance from the center of the sphere. When two metaballs overlap, the density of the overlapping area increases, resulting in a smooth, continuous surface.

Metaballs are commonly used in computer graphic and visualization applications, including 3D modeling, medical imaging, and fluid dynamics simulation. They can also be used in game design, where they are often used to create visually interesting and dynamic effects, such as explosions, smoke, and other fluid-like phenomena.

In this section, we will use the marching cubes algorithm to simulate metaballs by defining a 3D grid of points or voxels. Each voxel is assigned a value that represents its strength on surrounding space. The algorithm works by iterating over each voxel in the grid and determining its position relative to an isosurface value. Once the inside/outside status of each voxel has been determined, the algorithm constructs a surface mesh that approximates the isosurface. This is done by creating triangles that connect the edges of the voxels that straddle the isosurface.

9.3.1 Compute Shader for Values

To use marching cubes algorithm to render metaballs on the GPU, we first need to use a compute shade to calculate the scalar values of the metaballs. Metaballs are often defined using a mathematical formula that describes how the density of strength of the metaball decreases with distance from its center. The typically used formulas include a Gaussian and inverse distance function. This example will use the following inverse distance formula to simulate metaballs:

$$f(x, y, z) = \frac{strength}{a + x^2 + y^2 + z^2} - b$$

Where the *strength* is a parameter that determines the overall strength of the metaball, *a* is a parameter that determines how quickly the strength of the metaball deceases with distance, and *b* is a parameter that determines the background or ambient level of strength.

Create a new WGSL compute shader file named *metaball_value.wgsl* in the *examples/ch09/* folder and add the following code to it:

```
struct ValueBuffer{
    values: array<f32>,
};
@group(0) @binding(0) var<storage, read_write> valueBuffer : ValueBuffer;

struct IntParams {
    resolution: u32,
    metaballCount: u32,
};
@group(0) @binding(1) var<uniform> ips : IntParams;

struct Metaball {
    position: vec3f,
    radius: f32,
    strength: f32,
    subtract: f32,
};
@group(0) @binding(2) var<storage> metaballs : array<Metaball>;

fn positionAt(index : vec3u) -> vec3f {
    let vmin = vec3(-4.0, -4.0, -4.0);
    let vmax = vec3(4.0, 4.0, 4.0);
    let vstep = (vmax - vmin)/(f32(ips.resolution) - 1.0);
    return vmin + (vstep * vec3<f32>(index.xyz));
}

fn surfaceFunc(position : vec3f) -> f32 {
    var res = 0.0;
    for(var i = 0u; i < ips.metaballCount; i = i + 1u){
        let ball = metaballs[i];
        let dist = distance(position, ball.position);
        let val = ball.strength / (0.000001 + dist * dist) - ball.subtract;
        if(val > 0.0){
            res = res + val;
        }
    }
    return res;
}

fn getIdx(id: vec3u) -> u32 {
    return id.x + ips.resolution * ( id.y + id.z * ips.resolution);
}

@compute @workgroup_size(4, 4, 4)
fn cs_main(@builtin(global_invocation_id) id : vec3u) {
    let position = positionAt(id);
    let idx = getIdx(id);
    valueBuffer.values[idx] = surfaceFunc(position);
}
```

The above code is similar to the *implicit-value.wgsl* file used in the previous example, except that this example uses a different set of parameters. The *IntParams* struct contains a *metaballCount* field that specifies the total number of metaballs used in the simulation, and the *Metalball* struct includes the properties of the metaball, such as position, radius, strength, and subtract (or background strength).

The *positionAt* function in the above code is a helper function that takes an index in 3D space and returns the corresponding position. The function is different from the one used in the previous example, where we used the data range for each implicit function to set the minimum and maximum values for each component, while this example sets these values manually to $[-4, 4]$ for all components. Then it calculates the step size based on the resolution of the metaball surface. Finally, it returns the position corresponding to the given index.

The *surfaceFunc* function implements the mathematical formula we just provided earlier, which describes the strength of metaballs. Note that in our implementation, the parameter *a* in the formula is set to a very small value of 0.000001, and the parameter *b* is set to *ball.subtract*, which can be specified by the user. You can think the *surfaceFunc* function as simply an implicit function that describes metaballs.

The *cs_main* function in the above code calculates the position of the current thread using *positionAt*, gets the corresponding index in the value buffer using *getIdx*, and calculates the metaball function at that position using *surfaceFunc*. Finally, it writes the value to the value buffer.

It is worthing noting that the *cs_main* function uses a smaller workgroup size of 4× 4 × 4, which is different from the previous example where a workgroup size of 8×8×8 was used. This means that the shader will execute 4× 4 × 4 = 64 threads at once, which is smaller than the default value of 256, the maximum value of the product of the workgroup size dimensions for a compute stage. Therefore, we can directly use this default limit for the *maxComputeInvocationsPerWorkgroup* attribute.

Whether to use a larger workgroup size or a smaller one depends on the application requirements and the GPU hardware. Using a smaller workgroup size can result in lower performance, as there is overhead associated with launching new workgroups. This is because a small workgroup size may not fully utilize the hardware resources available on the GPU.

On the other hand, using a large workgroup size can potentially increase performance, as larger workgroups can fully utilize the hardware resources of the GPU. However, using a workgroup size that is too large can also result in decreased performance, as larger workgroups may consume too much shared memory or register space, leading to longer memory access times and register spills.

The optimal workgroup size depends on the specific hardware and workload being executed. It may be necessary to experiment with different workgroup sizes to determine the optimal configuration for a specific compute shader.

9.3.2 Compute Shader for Metaballs

Create a new WGSL compute shader file named *metaball_comp.wgsl* in the *examples/ch09*/folder. The code is essentially similar to that used in the *implicit_surface.wgsl* file in the previous example, so simply copy the code from the *implicit_surface.wgsl* file and paste it into the *metaball_comp.wgsl* file, and then make the following small changes:

First, we need to delete the *funcSelection* field from the *IntParams* struct because this example only has a single function for metaballs and does not need the *funcSelection* field. Another change we need to make is to the *positionAt* function. Instead of using the data range for each implicit function to set the minimum and maximum values for each component, this example sets these values manually to $[-4, 4]$ for all components, as illustrated in the following code snippet:

```
fn positionAt(index : vec3u) -> vec3f {
    vmin = vec3(-4.0, -4.0, -4.0);
    vmax = vec3(4.0, 4.0, 4.0);
    vstep = (vmax - vmin)/(f32(ips.resolution) - 1.0);
    return vmin + (vstep * vec3<f32>(index.xyz));
}
```

The rest of the code is identical to that used in the previous example, so we do not need to make any further changes.

9.3.3 Rust Code

Create a new Rust file named *metaball.rs* in the *examples/ch09/* folder and add the following code to it:

```rust
use std::iter;
use cgmath::{ Matrix, Matrix4, SquareMatrix };
use rand::{Rng, distributions::Uniform};
use wgpu:: { VertexBufferLayout, util::DeviceExt };
use winit::{
    event::*,
    event_loop::{ControlFlow, EventLoop},
    window::Window,
};
use bytemuck::cast_slice;
use wgpu_book_examples::{ wgpu_simplified as ws, transforms as wt, colormap };
mod marching_cubes_table;

fn create_color_data(colormap_name: &str) -> Vec<[f32; 4]> {
    let cdata = colormap::colormap_data(colormap_name);
    let mut data:Vec<[f32; 4]> = vec![];
    for i in 0..cdata.len() {
        data.push([cdata[i][0], cdata[i][1], cdata[i][2], 1.0 ]);
    }
    data
}

#[derive(Clone, Debug)]
struct MetaballPosition {
    x: f32,
    y: f32,
    z: f32,
    vx: f32,
    vy: f32,
    vz: f32,
    speed: f32,
}

struct State {
    init:  ws::IWgpuInit,
    pipeline: wgpu::RenderPipeline,
    uniform_bind_groups: Vec<wgpu::BindGroup>,
    uniform_buffers: Vec<wgpu::Buffer>,

    cs_pipelines: Vec<wgpu::ComputePipeline>,
    cs_vertex_buffers: Vec<wgpu::Buffer>,
    cs_index_buffer: wgpu::Buffer,
```

```
        cs_uniform_buffers: Vec<wgpu::Buffer>,
        cs_bind_groups: Vec<wgpu::BindGroup>,

        view_mat: Matrix4<f32>,
        project_mat: Matrix4<f32>,
        msaa_texture_view: wgpu::TextureView,
        depth_texture_view: wgpu::TextureView,

        resolution: u32,
        index_count: u32,
        metaballs_count: u32,

        colormap_direction: u32,
        colormap_reverse: u32,
        isolevel: f32,
        scale: f32,

        metaball_positions: Vec<MetaballPosition>,
        metaball_array: Vec<f32>,
        strength: f32,
        strength_target: f32,
        subtract: f32,
        subtract_target: f32,
        start: std::time::Instant,
        t0: std::time::Instant,
}

impl State {
    async fn new(window:&Window, sample_count:u32, resolution:u32, colormap_name:&str) -> Self {
        let limits = wgpu::Limits {
            max_storage_buffer_binding_size: 1024*1024*1024, //1024MB, defaulting to 128MB
            max_buffer_size: 1024*1024*1024, // 1024MB, defaulting to 256MB
            ..Default::default()
        };
        let init = ws::IWgpuInit::new(&window, sample_count, Some(limits)).await;

        let resol = ws::round_to_multiple(resolution, 4);
        let metaballs_count = 200;
        let marching_cube_cells = (resolution - 1) * (resolution - 1) * (resolution - 1);
        let vertex_count = 3 * 12 * marching_cube_cells;
        let vertex_buffer_size = 4 * vertex_count;
        let index_count = 15 * marching_cube_cells;
        let index_buffer_size = 4 * index_count;
        println!("resolution = {}", resol);

        let vs_shader = init.device.create_shader_module(wgpu::include_wgsl!("../ch05/shader_vert.wgsl"));
        let fs_shader = init.device.create_shader_module(wgpu::include_wgsl!("../ch05/shader_frag.wgsl"));
        let cs_value = init.device.create_shader_module(wgpu::include_wgsl!("metaball_value.wgsl"));
        let cs_comp = init.device.create_shader_module(wgpu::include_wgsl!("metaball_comp.wgsl"));

        // uniform data
        let model_mat = wt::create_model_mat([0.0,0.0,0.0], [0.0, 0.0, 0.0], [1.0, 1.0, 1.0]);
        let normal_mat = (model_mat.invert().unwrap()).transpose();

        let camera_position = (2.0, 2.0, 3.0).into();
        let look_direction = (0.0,0.0,0.0).into();
        let up_direction = cgmath::Vector3::unit_y();
        let light_direction = [-0.5f32, -0.5, -0.5];

        let (view_mat, project_mat, vp_mat) =
```

```
        wt::create_vp_mat(camera_position, look_direction, up_direction,
        init.config.width as f32 / init.config.height as f32);

// create vertex uniform buffers

// model_mat and vp_mat will be stored in vertex_uniform_buffer inside the update function
let vert_uniform_buffer = init.device.create_buffer(&wgpu::BufferDescriptor{
    label: Some("Vertex Uniform Buffer"),
    size: 192,
    usage: wgpu::BufferUsages::UNIFORM | wgpu::BufferUsages::COPY_DST,
    mapped_at_creation: false,
});
init.queue.write_buffer(&vert_uniform_buffer, 0, cast_slice(vp_mat.as_ref() as &[f32; 16]));
init.queue.write_buffer(&vert_uniform_buffer, 64,
    cast_slice(model_mat.as_ref() as &[f32; 16]));
init.queue.write_buffer(&vert_uniform_buffer, 128, cast_slice(normal_mat.as_ref() as &[f32; 16]));

// create light uniform buffer. here we set eye_position = camera_position
let light_uniform_buffer = init.device.create_buffer(&wgpu::BufferDescriptor{
    label: Some("Light Uniform Buffer"),
    size: 48,
    usage: wgpu::BufferUsages::UNIFORM | wgpu::BufferUsages::COPY_DST,
    mapped_at_creation: false,
});

let eye_position:&[f32; 3] = camera_position.as_ref();
init.queue.write_buffer(&light_uniform_buffer, 0, cast_slice(light_direction.as_ref()));
init.queue.write_buffer(&light_uniform_buffer, 16, cast_slice(eye_position));

// set specular light color to white
let specular_color:[f32; 3] = [1.0, 1.0, 1.0];
init.queue.write_buffer(&light_uniform_buffer, 32, cast_slice(specular_color.as_ref()));

// material uniform buffer
let material_uniform_buffer = init.device.create_buffer(&wgpu::BufferDescriptor{
    label: Some("Material Uniform Buffer"),
    size: 16,
    usage: wgpu::BufferUsages::UNIFORM | wgpu::BufferUsages::COPY_DST,
    mapped_at_creation: false,
});

// set default material parameters
let material = [0.1f32, 0.7, 0.4, 30.0];
init.queue.write_buffer(&material_uniform_buffer, 0, cast_slice(material.as_ref()));

// uniform bind group for vertex shader
let (vert_bind_group_layout, vert_bind_group) = ws::create_bind_group(
    &init.device,
    vec![wgpu::ShaderStages::VERTEX],
    &[vert_uniform_buffer.as_entire_binding()],
);

// uniform bind group for fragment shader
let (frag_bind_group_layout, frag_bind_group) = ws::create_bind_group(
    &init.device,
    vec![wgpu::ShaderStages::FRAGMENT, wgpu::ShaderStages::FRAGMENT],
    &[light_uniform_buffer.as_entire_binding(), material_uniform_buffer.as_entire_binding()],
);

let vertex_buffer_layouts = [
```

```
        VertexBufferLayout {
            array_stride: 16,
            step_mode: wgpu::VertexStepMode::Vertex,
            attributes: &wgpu::vertex_attr_array![0 => Float32x4], // pos
        },
        VertexBufferLayout {
            array_stride: 16,
            step_mode: wgpu::VertexStepMode::Vertex,
            attributes: &wgpu::vertex_attr_array![1 => Float32x4], // norm
        },
        VertexBufferLayout {
            array_stride: 16,
            step_mode: wgpu::VertexStepMode::Vertex,
            attributes: &wgpu::vertex_attr_array![2 => Float32x4], // col
        },
    ];

    let pipeline_layout = init.device.create_pipeline_layout(&wgpu::PipelineLayoutDescriptor {
        label: Some("Render Pipeline Layout"),
        bind_group_layouts: &[&vert_bind_group_layout, &frag_bind_group_layout],
        push_constant_ranges: &[],
    });

    let mut ppl = ws::IRenderPipeline {
        vs_shader: Some(&vs_shader),
        fs_shader: Some(&fs_shader),
        pipeline_layout: Some(&pipeline_layout),
        vertex_buffer_layout: &vertex_buffer_layouts,
        ..Default::default()
    };
    let pipeline = ppl.new(&init);

    let msaa_texture_view = ws::create_msaa_texture_view(&init);
    let depth_texture_view = ws::create_depth_view(&init);

    // create compute pipeline for value
    let volume_elements = resol * resol * resol;
    let cs_value_buffer = init.device.create_buffer(&wgpu::BufferDescriptor{
        label: Some("Index Buffer"),
        size:  4 * volume_elements as u64,
        usage: wgpu::BufferUsages::STORAGE | wgpu::BufferUsages::COPY_DST,
        mapped_at_creation: false,
    });

    let cs_value_int_buffer = init.device.create_buffer(&wgpu::BufferDescriptor{
        label: Some("Compuet Value Integer Uniform Buffer"),
        size:  16,
        usage: wgpu::BufferUsages::UNIFORM | wgpu::BufferUsages::COPY_DST,
        mapped_at_creation: false,
    });

    let single_ball_buffer_size: u32 =
        3 * 4 + // position: vec3<f32>
        1 * 4 + // radius f32
        1 * 4 + // strength: f32
        1 * 4 + // subtract: f32
        2 * 4 + // padding
        0;
    let balls_buffer_size = single_ball_buffer_size * metaballs_count;
    let metaball_array = vec![0f32; (balls_buffer_size/4) as usize];
```

```rust
let cs_value_metaball_buffer = init.device.create_buffer(&wgpu::BufferDescriptor{
    label: Some("Metaball Buffer"),
    size:  balls_buffer_size as u64,
    usage: wgpu::BufferUsages::STORAGE | wgpu::BufferUsages::COPY_DST,
    mapped_at_creation: false,
});

let mut rng = rand::thread_rng();
let range = Uniform::new(0.0, 1.0);
let mut metaball_positions = vec![];

for _ in 0..metaballs_count {
    metaball_positions.push(
    MetaballPosition {
        x: -4.0 * (2.0*rng.sample(range) - 1.0),
        y: -4.0 * (2.0*rng.sample(range) - 1.0),
        z: -4.0 * (2.0*rng.sample(range) - 1.0),
        vx: 1000.0*rng.sample(range),
        vy: 10.0 * (2.0*rng.sample(range) - 1.0),
        vz: 1000.0*rng.sample(range),
        speed: 2.0 * rng.sample(range) + 0.3,
    });
}


let (cs_value_bind_group_layout, cs_value_bind_group) = ws::create_bind_group_storage(
    &init.device,
    vec![
        wgpu::ShaderStages::COMPUTE, wgpu::ShaderStages::COMPUTE,
        wgpu::ShaderStages::COMPUTE,
    ],
    vec![
        wgpu::BufferBindingType::Storage { read_only: false },
        wgpu::BufferBindingType::Uniform,
        wgpu::BufferBindingType::Storage { read_only: true },
    ],
    &[
        cs_value_buffer.as_entire_binding(),
        cs_value_int_buffer.as_entire_binding(),
        cs_value_metaball_buffer.as_entire_binding(),
    ],
);

let cs_value_pipeline_layout = init.device.create_pipeline_layout(&wgpu::PipelineLayoutDescriptor{
    label: Some("Compute Value Pipeline Layout"),
    bind_group_layouts: &[&cs_value_bind_group_layout],
    push_constant_ranges: &[],
});

let cs_value_pipeline = init.device.create_compute_pipeline(&wgpu::ComputePipelineDescriptor{
    label: Some("Compute Value Pipeline"),
    layout: Some(&cs_value_pipeline_layout),
    module: &cs_value,
    entry_point: "cs_main",
});

// create compute pipeline for implicit surface
let cs_table_buffer = init.device.create_buffer(&wgpu::BufferDescriptor{
    label: Some("Compute Table STorage Buffer"),
    size:  (marching_cubes_table::EDGE_TABLE.len() +
```

```
            marching_cubes_table::TRI_TABLE.len()) as u64 * 4,
        usage: wgpu::BufferUsages::STORAGE | wgpu::BufferUsages::COPY_DST,
        mapped_at_creation: false,
    });
    init.queue.write_buffer(&cs_table_buffer, 0, cast_slice(marching_cubes_table::EDGE_TABLE));
    init.queue.write_buffer(&cs_table_buffer, marching_cubes_table::EDGE_TABLE.len() as u64 * 4,
cast_slice(marching_cubes_table::TRI_TABLE));

    let cs_position_buffer = init.device.create_buffer(&wgpu::BufferDescriptor{
        label: Some("Compute Position Buffer"),
        size:  vertex_buffer_size as u64,
        usage: wgpu::BufferUsages::VERTEX | wgpu::BufferUsages::STORAGE |
            wgpu::BufferUsages::COPY_DST,
        mapped_at_creation: false,
    });

    let cs_normal_buffer = init.device.create_buffer(&wgpu::BufferDescriptor{
        label: Some("Compute Normal Buffer"),
        size:  vertex_buffer_size as u64,
        usage: wgpu::BufferUsages::VERTEX | wgpu::BufferUsages::STORAGE |
            wgpu::BufferUsages::COPY_DST,
        mapped_at_creation: false,
    });

    let cs_color_buffer = init.device.create_buffer(&wgpu::BufferDescriptor{
        label: Some("Compute Color Buffer"),
        size:  vertex_buffer_size as u64,
        usage: wgpu::BufferUsages::VERTEX | wgpu::BufferUsages::STORAGE |
            wgpu::BufferUsages::COPY_DST,
        mapped_at_creation: false,
    });

    let cs_index_buffer = init.device.create_buffer(&wgpu::BufferDescriptor{
        label: Some("Compute Index Buffer"),
        size:  index_buffer_size as u64,
        usage: wgpu::BufferUsages::INDEX | wgpu::BufferUsages::STORAGE | wgpu::BufferUsages::COPY_DST,
        mapped_at_creation: false,
    });

    let cs_indirect_buffer = init.device.create_buffer(&wgpu::BufferDescriptor{
        label: Some("Compute Indirect Buffer"),
        size:  16,
        usage: wgpu::BufferUsages::INDIRECT | wgpu::BufferUsages::STORAGE |
            wgpu::BufferUsages::COPY_DST,
        mapped_at_creation: false,
    });

    let cdata = create_color_data(colormap_name);
    let cs_colormap_buffer = init.device.create_buffer_init(&wgpu::util::BufferInitDescriptor{
        label: Some("Compute Colormap Uniform Buffer"),
        contents: bytemuck::cast_slice(&cdata),
        usage: wgpu::BufferUsages::STORAGE | wgpu::BufferUsages::COPY_DST,
    });

    let cs_int_buffer = init.device.create_buffer(&wgpu::BufferDescriptor{
        label: Some("Compute Integer uniform Buffer"),
        size:  16,
        usage: wgpu::BufferUsages::UNIFORM | wgpu::BufferUsages::COPY_DST,
        mapped_at_creation: false,
    });
```

```rust
let cs_float_buffer = init.device.create_buffer(&wgpu::BufferDescriptor{
    label: Some("Compute Float uniform Buffer"),
    size:  16,
    usage: wgpu::BufferUsages::UNIFORM | wgpu::BufferUsages::COPY_DST,
    mapped_at_creation: false,
});

let (cs_bind_group_layout, cs_bind_group) = ws::create_bind_group_storage(
    &init.device,
    vec![
        wgpu::ShaderStages::COMPUTE, wgpu::ShaderStages::COMPUTE, wgpu::ShaderStages::COMPUTE,
        wgpu::ShaderStages::COMPUTE, wgpu::ShaderStages::COMPUTE, wgpu::ShaderStages::COMPUTE,
        wgpu::ShaderStages::COMPUTE, wgpu::ShaderStages::COMPUTE, wgpu::ShaderStages::COMPUTE,
        wgpu::ShaderStages::COMPUTE,
    ],
    vec![
        wgpu::BufferBindingType::Storage { read_only: true },    // marching table
        wgpu::BufferBindingType::Storage { read_only: true },    // value buffer
        wgpu::BufferBindingType::Storage { read_only: false },   // position
        wgpu::BufferBindingType::Storage { read_only: false },   // normal
        wgpu::BufferBindingType::Storage { read_only: false },   // color
        wgpu::BufferBindingType::Storage { read_only: false },   // indices
        wgpu::BufferBindingType::Storage { read_only: false },   // indirect params
        wgpu::BufferBindingType::Storage { read_only: true },    // colormap
        wgpu::BufferBindingType::Uniform,                        // int params
        wgpu::BufferBindingType::Uniform,                        // float params
    ],
    &[
        cs_table_buffer.as_entire_binding(),
        cs_value_buffer.as_entire_binding(),
        cs_position_buffer.as_entire_binding(),
        cs_normal_buffer.as_entire_binding(),
        cs_color_buffer.as_entire_binding(),
        cs_index_buffer.as_entire_binding(),
        cs_indirect_buffer.as_entire_binding(),
        cs_colormap_buffer.as_entire_binding(),
        cs_int_buffer.as_entire_binding(),
        cs_float_buffer.as_entire_binding(),
    ],
);

let cs_pipeline_layout = init.device.create_pipeline_layout(&wgpu::PipelineLayoutDescriptor{
    label: Some("Compute Pipeline Layout"),
    bind_group_layouts: &[&cs_bind_group_layout],
    push_constant_ranges: &[],
});

let cs_pipeline = init.device.create_compute_pipeline(&wgpu::ComputePipelineDescriptor{
    label: Some("Compute Pipeline"),
    layout: Some(&cs_pipeline_layout),
    module: &cs_comp,
    entry_point: "cs_main",
});

Self {
    init,
    pipeline,
    uniform_bind_groups: vec![vert_bind_group, frag_bind_group],
    uniform_buffers: vec![vert_uniform_buffer, light_uniform_buffer, material_uniform_buffer],
```

```
                cs_pipelines: vec![cs_value_pipeline, cs_pipeline],
                cs_vertex_buffers: vec![cs_value_buffer, cs_position_buffer, cs_normal_buffer,
                    cs_color_buffer],
                cs_index_buffer,
                cs_uniform_buffers: vec![cs_value_int_buffer, cs_value_metaball_buffer, cs_int_buffer,
                    cs_float_buffer, cs_indirect_buffer],
                cs_bind_groups: vec![cs_value_bind_group, cs_bind_group],

                view_mat,
                project_mat,
                msaa_texture_view,
                depth_texture_view,

                resolution: resol,
                index_count,
                metaballs_count,

                colormap_direction: 1,
                colormap_reverse: 0,
                isolevel: 20.0,
                scale: 0.5,

                metaball_positions,
                metaball_array,
                strength: 1.0,
                strength_target: 1.0,
                subtract: 1.0,
                subtract_target: 1.0,
                start: std::time::Instant::now(),
                t0: std::time::Instant::now(),
        }
    }

    fn resize(&mut self, new_size: winit::dpi::PhysicalSize<u32>) {
        if new_size.width > 0 && new_size.height > 0 {
            self.init.size = new_size;
            self.init.config.width = new_size.width;
            self.init.config.height = new_size.height;
            self.init.surface.configure(&self.init.device, &self.init.config);

            self.project_mat = wt::create_projection_mat(new_size.width as f32 / new_size.height as f32,
                true);
            let vp_mat = self.project_mat * self.view_mat;
            self.init.queue.write_buffer(&self.uniform_buffers[0], 0,
                cast_slice(vp_mat.as_ref() as &[f32; 16]));

            self.depth_texture_view = ws::create_depth_view(&self.init);
            if self.init.sample_count > 1 {
                self.msaa_texture_view = ws::create_msaa_texture_view(&self.init);
            }
        }
    }
}

#[allow(unused_variables)]
fn input(&mut self, event: &WindowEvent) -> bool {
    match event {
        WindowEvent::KeyboardInput {
            input:
                KeyboardInput {
```

```
                    virtual_keycode: Some(keycode),
                    state: ElementState::Pressed,
                    ..
                },
                ..
        } => {
            match keycode {
                VirtualKeyCode::Space => {
                    self.colormap_direction = (self.colormap_direction + 1) % 4;
                    true
                },
                VirtualKeyCode::LControl => {
                    self.colormap_reverse = if self.colormap_reverse == 0 { 1 } else { 0 };
                    true
                },
                _ => false
            }
        }
        _ => false,
    }
}

fn update(&mut self, _dt: std::time::Duration) {
    // update compute buffers for value
    let value_int_params = [self.resolution, self.metaballs_count, 0, 0];
    self.init.queue.write_buffer(&self.cs_uniform_buffers[0], 0, cast_slice(&value_int_params));

    let time = std::time::Instant::now();
    let dt1 = (time - self.start).as_secs_f32();
    self.start = time;

    self.subtract += (self.subtract_target - self.subtract) * dt1 * 0.2;
    self.strength += (self.strength_target - self.strength) * dt1 * 0.2;

    for i in 0..self.metaballs_count as usize {
        let mbp = &mut self.metaball_positions[i];

        mbp.vx += -mbp.x * mbp.speed * 20.0;
        mbp.vy += -mbp.y * mbp.speed * 20.0;
        mbp.vz += -mbp.z * mbp.speed * 20.0;

        mbp.x += mbp.vx * dt1 * 0.0001;
        mbp.y += mbp.vy * dt1 * 0.0001;
        mbp.z += mbp.vz * dt1 * 0.0001;

        let sz = 3.1f32;
        if mbp.x > sz {
            mbp.x = sz;
            mbp.vx *= -1.0;
        } else if mbp.x < -sz {
            mbp.x = -sz;
            mbp.vx *= -1.0;
        }

        if mbp.y > sz {
            mbp.y = sz;
            mbp.vy *= -1.0;
        } else if mbp.y < -sz {
            mbp.y = -sz;
            mbp.vy *= -1.0;
```

```
        }

        if mbp.z > sz {
            mbp.z = sz;
            mbp.vz *= -1.0;
        } else if mbp.z < -sz {
            mbp.z = -sz;
            mbp.vz *= -1.0;
        }
    }

    for i in 0..self.metaballs_count as usize {
        let mbp = & mut self.metaball_positions[i];
        let offset = i * 8;
        self.metaball_array[offset] = mbp.x;
        self.metaball_array[offset + 1] = mbp.y;
        self.metaball_array[offset + 2] = mbp.z;
        self.metaball_array[offset + 3] = (self.strength/self.subtract).sqrt(); // radius
        self.metaball_array[offset + 4] = self.strength;
        self.metaball_array[offset + 5] = self.subtract;
    }

    self.init.queue.write_buffer(&self.cs_uniform_buffers[1], 0, cast_slice(&self.metaball_array));

    // update compute buffers for implicit surface
    let int_params = [
        self.resolution,
        self.colormap_direction,
        self.colormap_reverse,
    ];
    self.init.queue.write_buffer(&self.cs_uniform_buffers[2], 0, cast_slice(&int_params));

    let float_params = [self.isolevel, self.scale, 0.0, 0.0];
    self.init.queue.write_buffer(&self.cs_uniform_buffers[3], 0, cast_slice(&float_params));

    let indirect_array = [500u32, 0, 0, 0];
    self.init.queue.write_buffer(&self.cs_uniform_buffers[4], 0, cast_slice(&indirect_array));

    // update strength and subtract parameters in every 5 secs
    let elapsed = self.t0.elapsed();
    let mut rng = rand::thread_rng();
    let range = Uniform::new(0.0, 1.0);
    if elapsed >= std::time::Duration::from_secs(5) {
        self.subtract_target = 3.0 * rng.sample(range) + 3.0;
        self.strength_target = 3.0 * rng.sample(range) + 3.0;
    }
}

fn render(&mut self) -> Result<(), wgpu::SurfaceError> {
    let output = self.init.surface.get_current_texture()?;
    let view = output
        .texture
        .create_view(&wgpu::TextureViewDescriptor::default());

    let mut encoder = self
        .init.device
        .create_command_encoder(&wgpu::CommandEncoderDescriptor {
            label: Some("Render Encoder"),
        });
```

```
            // compute pass for value
            {
                let mut cs_index_pass = encoder.begin_compute_pass(&wgpu::ComputePassDescriptor{
                    label: Some("Compute value Pass"),
                    timestamp_writes: None,
                });
                cs_index_pass.set_pipeline(&self.cs_pipelines[0]);
                cs_index_pass.set_bind_group(0, &self.cs_bind_groups[0], &[]);
                cs_index_pass.dispatch_workgroups(self.resolution/4, self.resolution/4, self.resolution/4);
            }

            // compute pass for vertices
            {
                let mut cs_pass = encoder.begin_compute_pass(&wgpu::ComputePassDescriptor{
                    label: Some("Compute Pass"),
                    timestamp_writes: None,
                });
                cs_pass.set_pipeline(&self.cs_pipelines[1]);
                cs_pass.set_bind_group(0, &self.cs_bind_groups[1], &[]);
                cs_pass.dispatch_workgroups(self.resolution/4, self.resolution/4, self.resolution/4);
            }

            // render pass
            {
                let color_attach = ws::create_color_attachment(&view);
                let msaa_attach = ws::create_msaa_color_attachment(&view, &self.msaa_texture_view);
                let color_attachment = if self.init.sample_count == 1 { color_attach } else { msaa_attach };
                let depth_attachment = ws::create_depth_stencil_attachment(&self.depth_texture_view);

                let mut render_pass = encoder.begin_render_pass(&wgpu::RenderPassDescriptor {
                    label: Some("Render Pass"),
                    color_attachments: &[Some(color_attachment)],
                    depth_stencil_attachment: Some(depth_attachment),
                    occlusion_query_set: None,
                    timestamp_writes: None,
                });

                render_pass.set_pipeline(&self.pipeline);
                render_pass.set_vertex_buffer(0, self.cs_vertex_buffers[1].slice(..));
                render_pass.set_vertex_buffer(1, self.cs_vertex_buffers[2].slice(..));
                render_pass.set_vertex_buffer(2, self.cs_vertex_buffers[3].slice(..));
                render_pass.set_index_buffer(self.cs_index_buffer.slice(..),
                    wgpu::IndexFormat::Uint32);
                render_pass.set_bind_group(0, &self.uniform_bind_groups[0], &[]);
                render_pass.set_bind_group(1, &self.uniform_bind_groups[1], &[]);
                render_pass.draw_indexed(0..self.index_count, 0, 0..1);
            }

            self.init.queue.submit(iter::once(encoder.finish()));
            output.present();

            Ok(())
        }
}

fn main() {
    let mut sample_count = 1u32;
    let mut resolution = 64u32;
    let mut colormap_name = "jet";
```

```
let args: Vec<String> = std::env::args().collect();
if args.len() > 1 {
    sample_count = args[1].parse::<u32>().unwrap();
}
if args.len() > 2 {
    resolution = args[2].parse::<u32>().unwrap();
}
if args.len() > 3 {
    colormap_name = &args[3];
}

env_logger::init();
let event_loop = EventLoop::new();
let window = winit::window::WindowBuilder::new().build(&event_loop).unwrap();
window.set_title(&*format!("ch09_{}", "metaball"));

let mut state = pollster::block_on(State::new(&window, sample_count, resolution, colormap_name));
let render_start_time = std::time::Instant::now();

event_loop.run(move |event, _, control_flow| {
    match event {
        Event::WindowEvent {
            ref event,
            window_id,
        } if window_id == window.id() => {
            if !state.input(event) {
                match event {
                    WindowEvent::CloseRequested
                    | WindowEvent::KeyboardInput {
                        input:
                            KeyboardInput {
                                state: ElementState::Pressed,
                                virtual_keycode: Some(VirtualKeyCode::Escape),
                                ..
                            },
                        ..
                    } => *control_flow = ControlFlow::Exit,
                    WindowEvent::Resized(physical_size) => {
                        state.resize(*physical_size);
                    }
                    WindowEvent::ScaleFactorChanged { new_inner_size, .. } => {
                        state.resize(**new_inner_size);
                    }
                    _ => {}
                }
            }
        }
        Event::RedrawRequested(_) => {
            let now = std::time::Instant::now();
            let dt = now - render_start_time;
            state.update(dt);

            match state.render() {
                Ok(_) => {}
                Err(wgpu::SurfaceError::Lost) => state.resize(state.init.size),
                Err(wgpu::SurfaceError::OutOfMemory) => *control_flow = ControlFlow::Exit,
                Err(e) => eprintln!("{:?}", e),
            }
        }
        Event::MainEventsCleared => {
```

```
            window.request_redraw();
        }
        _ => {}
    }
});
}
```

The above code is similar to the one used in previous example. First, we introduce the marching cubes tables from the *marching_cubes_table.rs* file and add several new fields to the *State* struct, including *resolution*, *vertex_count*, and *index_count*. These fields can be easily accessed by different functions without the need to pass them as input. Additionally, we implement a *MetaballPosition* struct that contains positions and velocities of the metaballs.

Within the *State::new* futnction, as we did in the previous example, we reset certain GPU device limits, such as *max_storage_buffer_binding_size* and *max_buffer_size*, when creating the device to accommodate higher-resolution metaballs. However, for *max_compute_invocation_per_workgroup*, we use the default value of 256 since the compute shaders in this example use a smaller workgroup size of $4 \times 4 \times 4$ rather than $8 \times 8 \times 8$ as in the previous example.

Subsequently, we reuse the vertex and fragment shaders created earlier in Chapter 5. Additionally, we introduce two compute shader files generated in the previous sections, namely *metaball-value.wgsl* and *metaball_comp.wgsl*.

The code segment for creating the render pipeline inside the *State::new* function is identical to that used in the previous example. Similarly, the code for creating compute pipelines used to generate the scalar value data and vertex data of the metaballs is also similar to that used in the previous example, but with a different set of parameters specific to metaballs.

The *State::render* function in the above code is also similar to the previous example, but the workgroup size for the metaball compute shader is set to 4 instead of 8.

In the *State::update* function, we animate metaballs using time-dependent parameters, as shown in the following code snippet:

```
self.subtract += (self.subtract_target - self.subtract) * dt1 * 0.2;
self.strength += (self.strength_target - self.strength) * dt1 * 0.2;

for i in 0..self.metaballs_count as usize {
    let mbp = &mut self.metaball_positions[i];

    mbp.vx += -mbp.x * mbp.speed * 20.0;
    mbp.vy += -mbp.y * mbp.speed * 20.0;
    mbp.vz += -mbp.z * mbp.speed * 20.0;

    mbp.x += mbp.vx * dt1 * 0.0001;
    mbp.y += mbp.vy * dt1 * 0.0001;
    mbp.z += mbp.vz * dt1 * 0.0001;

    let sz = 3.1f32;
    if mbp.x > sz {
        mbp.x = sz;
        mbp.vx *= -1.0;
    } else if mbp.x < -sz {
        mbp.x = -sz;
        mbp.vx *= -1.0;
    }

    if mbp.y > sz {
```

```
            mbp.y = sz;
            mbp.vy *= -1.0;
        } else if mbp.y < -sz {
            mbp.y = -sz;
            mbp.vy *= -1.0;
        }

        if mbp.z > sz {
            mbp.z = sz;
            mbp.vz *= -1.0;
        } else if mbp.z < -sz {
            mbp.z = -sz;
            mbp.vz *= -1.0;
        }
    }

    for i in 0..self.metaballs_count as usize {
        let mbp = & mut self.metaball_positions[i];
        let offset = i * 8;
        self.metaball_array[offset] = mbp.x;
        self.metaball_array[offset + 1] = mbp.y;
        self.metaball_array[offset + 2] = mbp.z;
        self.metaball_array[offset + 3] = (self.strength/self.subtract).sqrt(); // radius
        self.metaball_array[offset + 4] = self.strength;
        self.metaball_array[offset + 5] = self.subtract;
    }
```

It is evident from the above code snippet that the strength, subtract, radius, position, and velocity of each metaball are all time-dependent variables.

Additionally, the code permits the user to modify input parameters using keyboard inputs.

Here is a list of controls using keyboard:

- *Space*: Changes the colormap direction.

- *LControl*: Reverse colormap.

9.3.4 Run Application

To run this application, add the following code snippet to the *Cargo.toml* file:

```
[[example]]
name = "ch09_metaball"
path = "examples/ch09/metaball.rs"
```

Afterward, execute the following *cargo run* commands in the terminal window:

```
cargo run --example ch09_metaball 8
```

Fig.9-3 shows the results of this example.

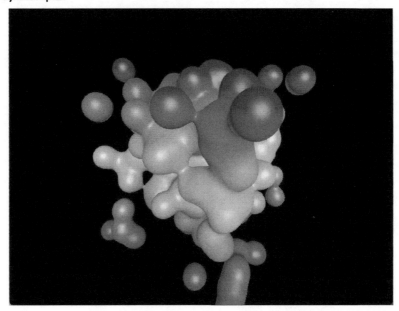

Fig.9-3. Metaballs simulated using marching cubes.

9.4 Voxel Terrains

In the previous chapter, we presented the procedural terrains generated using noise heightmaps, which represent the terrain as a 2D grid of elevation values. Voxel terrain, on the other hand, uses 3D grids of voxels (volumetric pixels) to represent the terrain surface and features. Each voxel contains information about the properties of the terrain at that location, such as its height, texture, color, and other physical attributes.

One of the main advantages of the voxel terrain is its ability to represent complex geometry and features with greater detail and accuracy than conventional terrain. For example, voxel terrain can easily generate overhangs, caves, and tunnels, which are impossible to represent with heightmaps.

Another advantage of voxel terrain is its flexibility and adaptability. Voxel terrain can be modified and manipulated in real-time, allowing for dynamic terrain deformation, destruction, and construction. This can be used for gameplay mechanics such as digging, building, and terraforming.

However, voxel terrain also has some disadvantages compared to conventional terrain. One of the main challenges is performance, as rendering large voxel grids can be computationally expensive. Voxel terrain also requires more memory and storage space than conventional terrain, as each voxel contains more information than a single elevation value. Additionally, creating and modifying voxel terrain can be more difficult than conventional terrain, requiring specialized tools and techniques.

In this section, I will explain how to use the marching cubes algorithm to generate voxel terrain. We start by creating a random scalar field that represents the height of the terrain. Once the scalar field has been created, we divide the terrain into small cubes called voxels and analyze each voxel to determine whether it should be part of the terrain surface or not. Then, we use the marching cubes algorithm to define triangles between adjacent voxels and generate a smooth surface.

9.4.1 Shader Code for 3D Noise

Create a new WGSL shader file named *noise3d.wgsl* in the *examples/ch09/* folder and add the following code to it:

```
fn mod289_3d(x: vec3f) -> vec3f {
    return x - floor(x *(1.0/289.0))*289.0;
}

fn mod289_4d(x: vec4f) -> vec4f {
    return x - floor(x *(1.0/289.0))*289.0;
}

fn permute(x: vec4f) -> vec4f {
    return mod289_4d((x*34.0 + 10.0) *x);
}

fn taylorInvSqrt(x: vec4f) -> vec4f {
    return 1.79284291400159 - x * 0.85373472095314;
}

fn simplex3d(v: vec3f) -> f32 {
    const C = vec2(1.0/6.0, 1.0/3.0) ;
    const D = vec4(0.0, 0.5, 1.0, 2.0);

    // First corner
    var i  = floor(v + dot(v, C.yyy) );
    let x0 =   v - i + dot(i, C.xxx) ;

    // Other corners
    let g = step(x0.yzx, x0.xyz);
    let l = 1.0 - g;
    let i1 = min(g.xyz, l.zxy);
    let i2 = max(g.xyz, l.zxy);

    let x1 = x0 - i1 + C.xxx;
    let x2 = x0 - i2 + C.yyy;
    let x3 = x0 - D.yyy;

    // Permutations
    i = mod289_3d(i);
    let p = permute( permute(permute(i.z + vec4(0.0, i1.z, i2.z, 1.0 ))
            + i.y + vec4(0.0, i1.y, i2.y, 1.0 ))
            + i.x + vec4(0.0, i1.x, i2.x, 1.0 ));

    let n_ = 0.142857142857; // 1.0/7.0
    let ns = n_ * D.wyz - D.xzx;

    let j = p - 49.0 * floor(p * ns.z * ns.z);  //  mod(p,7*7)

    let x_ = floor(j * ns.z);
    let y_ = floor(j - 7.0 * x_ );     // mod(j,N)

    let x = x_ *ns.x + ns.yyyy;
    let y = y_ *ns.x + ns.yyyy;
    let h = 1.0 - abs(x) - abs(y);

    let b0 = vec4( x.xy, y.xy );
    let b1 = vec4( x.zw, y.zw );
```

```
    let s0 = floor(b0)*2.0 + 1.0;
    let s1 = floor(b1)*2.0 + 1.0;
    let sh = -step(h, vec4(0.0));

    let a0 = b0.xzyw + s0.xzyw*sh.xxyy ;
    let a1 = b1.xzyw + s1.xzyw*sh.zzww ;
    var p0 = vec3(a0.xy,h.x);
    var p1 = vec3(a0.zw,h.y);
    var p2 = vec3(a1.xy,h.z);
    var p3 = vec3(a1.zw,h.w);

    // Normalise gradients
    let norm = taylorInvSqrt(vec4(dot(p0,p0), dot(p1,p1), dot(p2, p2), dot(p3,p3)));
    p0 *= norm.x;
    p1 *= norm.y;
    p2 *= norm.z;
    p3 *= norm.w;

    // Mix final noise value
    var m = max(0.5 - vec4(dot(x0,x0), dot(x1,x1), dot(x2,x2), dot(x3,x3)), vec4(0.0));
    m = m * m;
    return 105.0 * dot( m*m, vec4(dot(p0,x0), dot(p1,x1), dot(p2,x2), dot(p3,x3) ));
}

fn rand1d(st: f32, mutator:f32) -> f32 {
    return -1.0 + 2.0 * fract(sin(st + mutator)*143758.5453);
}

fn rand2dTo1d(st: vec2f) -> f32 {
    var v = fract (st * vec2(5.3983, 5.4427));
    v += dot(v.yx, v.xy + vec2(21.5351, 14.3137));
    return fract(v.x * v.y * 95.4337);
}

fn rand2dTo2d(st: vec2f) -> vec2f {
    let rand = vec2(fract(sin(dot(st, vec2(12.9898, 78.233))) * 43758.5453),
                    fract(sin(dot(st, vec2(39.2944, 29.462))) * 23421.631));
    return rand * 2.0 - 1.0;
}


fn rand3d(st:f32) -> vec3f {
    return vec3(
        rand1d(st, 3.9812),
        rand1d(st, 7.1536),
        rand1d(st, 5.7241)
    );
}
```

The 3D simplex noise function in the above code is based on the original WebGL noise library from a GitHub repository found at https://github.com/ashima/webgl-noise. The 3D and 4D *mod289* functions in the code above are used to calculate the modulus of a vector with respect to 289. The reason for using 289 is that it is a prime number that is close to a multiple of 49. The purpose of using a prime number is to prevent any noticeable repetition in the pattern of noise generated by the *simplex3d* function.

The permute function is used to shuffle a 4D vector based on a permutation table, which is generated by using the *mod289_4d* function on a linear combination of the input 4D vector, followed by a multiplication by a constant value of 34 and an addition of 10. The resulting 4D vector is then passed back through the *mod289_4d* function to obtain the final permutation value. The purpose of this shuffling is to ensure that the input coordinates for the noise function are mapped to a unique noise value.

The *taylorInvSqrt* function uses a fast approximation algorithm to calculate the inverse square root of each component of the input vector.

The *simplex3d* function is the main noise function that takes a 3D vector as input and returns a scalar float value. This function generates 3D simplex noise by performing a series of operations on the input vector to calculate the noise value. The reason we use simplex noise rather than Perlin noise is that simplex noise uses a simpler space-filling grid than Perlin noise, which makes it computationally less demanding and visually less directional artifacts.

Additionally, the above code also includes several helper functions, such as *rand2dTo1d*, *rand2dTo2d*, *rand1d*, and *rand3d*, which will be used to generate various random numbers with different dimensions.

9.4.2 Compute Shader for Values

Create a new WGSL compute shader file named *voxel_value.wgsl* in the *examples/ch09/* folder and add the following code to it:

```
struct ValueBuffer{
    values: array<f32>,
}
@group(0) @binding(0) var<storage, read_write> valueBuffer : ValueBuffer;

struct IntParams {
    resolution: u32,
    octaves: u32,
    seed: u32,
}
@group(0) @binding(1) var<uniform> ips : IntParams;

struct FloatParams {
    offset: vec3f,
    terrainSize: f32,
    lacunarity: f32,
    persistence: f32,
    noiseScale: f32,
    noiseHeight: f32,
    heightMultiplier: f32,
    floorOffset: f32,
}
@group(0) @binding(2) var<uniform> fps : FloatParams;

var<private> vmin: vec3f;
var<private> vmax: vec3f;

fn positionAt(index : vec3u) -> vec3f {
    vmin = vec3(-0.5 * fps.terrainSize);
    vmax = vec3(0.5 * fps.terrainSize);
    let vstep = (vmax-vmin)/(f32(ips.resolution) - 1.0);
    return vmin + (vstep * vec3<f32>(index.xyz));
}

fn getIdx(id: vec3u) -> u32 {
    return id.x + ips.resolution * ( id.y + id.z * ips.resolution);
}
```

```
fn noiseFunc(position: vec3f) -> f32 {
    var noise = 0.0;
    var frequency = fps.noiseScale/100.0;
    var amplitude = 1.0;
    var height = 1.0;

    for(var i = 0u; i < ips.octaves; i = i + 1u){
        let r = rand3d(f32(i + ips.seed));
        let offset = 1000.0 * r;
        let n = simplex3d((position  + fps.offset + offset)*frequency );
        var v = 1.0 - abs(n);
        v = v * v;
        v *= height;
        height = max(min(v * fps.heightMultiplier, 1.0), 0.0);
        noise += v * amplitude;
        amplitude *= fps.persistence;
        frequency *= fps.lacunarity;
    }

    let val = -(position.y + fps.floorOffset) + noise * fps.noiseHeight;
    return val;
}

@compute @workgroup_size(8, 8, 8)
fn cs_main(@builtin(global_invocation_id) id : vec3u) {
    var position = positionAt(id);
    var y = (position.y - vmin.y)/(vmax.y - vmin.y);
    if(y <= 0.0) {
        position.y = 0.0;
    }
    let idx = getIdx(id);
    valueBuffer.values[idx] = noiseFunc(position);
}
```

The above code is structurally similar to that used in previous examples, except that this example uses the parameters and a noise function specific for voxel terrain. The *positionAt* function uses the terrain size and resolution to calculate the step size for each index value. The function then calculates the position vector by using the step size.

The *noiseFunc* function in the above code can be used to generate the scalar values, similar to the implicit functions or metaball function used in previous examples. The *noiseFunc* function calculates a noise value at a given position in 3D space using the *simplex3d* function, much like what we did earlier in the previous chapter when creating the noise map for conventional terrains.

The *cs_main* function in the above code calculates the position of the current thread using *positionAt*, gets the corresponding index in the value buffer using *getIdx*, and calculates the noise value at that position using *noiseFunc*. Finally, it writes the value to the value buffer.

9.4.3 Compute Shader for Voxel Terrain

Create a new WGSL compute shader file named *voxel_terrain.wgsl* in the *examples/ch09/*folder and include the following code:

```
struct Tables {
    edges: array<u32, 256>,
    tris: array<i32, 4096>,
```

```
};
@group(0) @binding(0) var<storage> tables : Tables;

struct ValueBuffer{
    values: array<f32>,
};
@group(0) @binding(1) var<storage, read> valueBuffer: ValueBuffer;

struct PositionBuffer {
    values : array<f32>,
};
@group(0) @binding(2) var<storage, read_write> positionsOut : PositionBuffer;

struct NormalBuffer {
    values : array<f32>,
};
@group(0) @binding(3) var<storage, read_write> normalsOut : NormalBuffer;

struct ColorBuffer{
    values: array<f32>,
};
@group(0) @binding(4) var<storage, read_write> colorBuffer: ColorBuffer;

struct IndexBuffer {
    tris : array<u32>,
};
@group(0) @binding(5) var<storage, read_write> indicesOut : IndexBuffer;

struct IndirectParams {
    vc : u32,
    vertexCount : atomic<u32>,
    firstVertex : u32,
    indexCount : atomic<u32>,
};
@group(0) @binding(6) var<storage, read_write> indirect : IndirectParams;

struct IntParams {
    resolution: u32,
};
@group(0) @binding(7) var<uniform> ips : IntParams;

struct FloatParams {
    terrainSize: f32,
    isolevel: f32,
    noiseWeight: f32,
    waterLevel: f32,
};
@group(0) @binding(8) var<uniform> fps : FloatParams;

var<private> vmin: vec3f;
var<private> vmax: vec3f;
var<private> vstep: vec3f;

fn getIdx(id: vec3u) -> u32 {
    return id.x + ips.resolution * ( id.y + id.z * ips.resolution);
}

fn valueAt(index : vec3u) -> f32 {
    if (any(index >= vec3(ips.resolution - 1u, ips.resolution - 1u, ips.resolution - 1u))) { return 0.0; }
    let idx = getIdx(index);
```

```
        return valueBuffer.values[idx];
}

fn positionAt(index : vec3u) -> vec3f {
    vmin = vec3(-0.5 * fps.terrainSize);
    vmax = vec3(0.5 * fps.terrainSize);
    vstep = (vmax-vmin)/(f32(ips.resolution) - 1.0);
    return vmin + (vstep * vec3<f32>(index.xyz));
}

fn normalAt(index : vec3u) -> vec3f {
    return vec3(
      valueAt(index - vec3(1u, 0u, 0u)) - valueAt(index + vec3(1u, 0u, 0u)),
      valueAt(index - vec3(0u, 1u, 0u)) - valueAt(index + vec3(0u, 1u, 0u)),
      valueAt(index - vec3(0u, 0u, 1u)) - valueAt(index + vec3(0u, 0u, 1u))
    );
}

var<private> positions : array<vec3f, 12>;
var<private> normals : array<vec3f, 12>;
var<private> colors : array<vec3f, 12>;
var<private> indices : array<u32, 12>;
var<private> cubeVerts : u32 = 0u;

fn interpX(index : u32, i : vec3u, va : f32, vb : f32) {
    let mu = (fps.isolevel - va) / (vb - va);
    positions[cubeVerts] = positionAt(i) + vec3(vstep.x * mu, 0.0, 0.0);

    let na = normalAt(i);
    let nb = normalAt(i + vec3(1u, 0u, 0u));
    normals[cubeVerts] = mix(na, nb, vec3(mu, mu, mu));

    indices[index] = cubeVerts;
    cubeVerts = cubeVerts + 1u;
}

fn interpY(index : u32, i : vec3u, va : f32, vb : f32) {
    let mu = (fps.isolevel - va) / (vb - va);
    positions[cubeVerts] = positionAt(i) + vec3(0.0, vstep.y * mu, 0.0);

    let na = normalAt(i);
    let nb = normalAt(i + vec3(0u, 1u, 0u));
    normals[cubeVerts] = mix(na, nb, vec3(mu, mu, mu));

    indices[index] = cubeVerts;
    cubeVerts = cubeVerts + 1u;
}

fn interpZ(index : u32, i : vec3u, va : f32, vb : f32) {
    let mu = (fps.isolevel - va) / (vb - va);
    positions[cubeVerts] = positionAt(i) + vec3(0.0, 0.0, vstep.z * mu);

    let na = normalAt(i);
    let nb = normalAt(i + vec3(0u, 0u, 1u));
    normals[cubeVerts] = mix(na, nb, vec3(mu, mu, mu));

    indices[index] = cubeVerts;
    cubeVerts = cubeVerts + 1u;
}
```

```
fn shiftWaterLevel(ta:array<f32, 6>, waterLevel:f32) -> array<f32, 6> {
    var t1 = array<f32, 6>(0.0,0.0,0.0,0.0,0.0,0.0);
    let r = (1.0 - waterLevel)/(1.0 - ta[1]);
    t1[1] = waterLevel;
    var ta1 = ta;
    for(var i:u32 = 1u; i < 5u; i = i + 1u){
        let del = ta1[i + 1u] - ta1[i];
        t1[i+1u] = t1[i] + r*del;
    }
    return t1;
}

fn lerpColor(rgbData:array<vec3f,5>, ta:array<f32,6>, t:f32) -> vec3f {
    let len = 6u;
    var res = vec3(0.0);
    var ta1 = ta;
    var data = rgbData;
    for(var i:u32 = 0u; i < len - 1u; i = i + 1u){
        if(t >= ta1[i] && t < ta1[i + 1u]){
            res = data[i];
        }
    }
    if(t == ta1[len - 1u]){
        res = data[len - 2u];
    }
    return res;
}

fn addTerrainColors(rgbData:array<vec3f,5>, ta:array<f32,6>, tmin:f32, tmax:f32, t:f32, waterLevel:f32) ->
vec3f {
    var tt = t;
    if(t < tmin){tt = tmin;}
    if(t > tmax){tt = tmax;}
    if(tmin == tmax) {return vec3(0.0);}
    tt = (tt-tmin)/(tmax-tmin);

    let t1 = shiftWaterLevel(ta, waterLevel);
    return lerpColor(rgbData, t1, tt);
}

@compute @workgroup_size(8, 8, 8)
fn cs_main(@builtin(global_invocation_id) global_id : vec3u) {
    let i0 = global_id;
    let i1 = global_id + vec3(1u, 0u, 0u);
    let i2 = global_id + vec3(1u, 1u, 0u);
    let i3 = global_id + vec3(0u, 1u, 0u);
    let i4 = global_id + vec3(0u, 0u, 1u);
    let i5 = global_id + vec3(1u, 0u, 1u);
    let i6 = global_id + vec3(1u, 1u, 1u);
    let i7 = global_id + vec3(0u, 1u, 1u);

    let v0 = valueAt(i0);
    let v1 = valueAt(i1);
    let v2 = valueAt(i2);
    let v3 = valueAt(i3);
    let v4 = valueAt(i4);
    let v5 = valueAt(i5);
    let v6 = valueAt(i6);
    let v7 = valueAt(i7);
```

```
var cubeIndex = 0u;
if (v0 < fps.isolevel) { cubeIndex = cubeIndex | 1u; }
if (v1 < fps.isolevel) { cubeIndex = cubeIndex | 2u; }
if (v2 < fps.isolevel) { cubeIndex = cubeIndex | 4u; }
if (v3 < fps.isolevel) { cubeIndex = cubeIndex | 8u; }
if (v4 < fps.isolevel) { cubeIndex = cubeIndex | 16u; }
if (v5 < fps.isolevel) { cubeIndex = cubeIndex | 32u; }
if (v6 < fps.isolevel) { cubeIndex = cubeIndex | 64u; }
if (v7 < fps.isolevel) { cubeIndex = cubeIndex | 128u; }

let edges = tables.edges[cubeIndex];
if ((edges & 1u) != 0u) { interpX(0u, i0, v0, v1); }
if ((edges & 2u) != 0u) { interpY(1u, i1, v1, v2); }
if ((edges & 4u) != 0u) { interpX(2u, i3, v3, v2); }
if ((edges & 8u) != 0u) { interpY(3u, i0, v0, v3); }
if ((edges & 16u) != 0u) { interpX(4u, i4, v4, v5); }
if ((edges & 32u) != 0u) { interpY(5u, i5, v5, v6); }
if ((edges & 64u) != 0u) { interpX(6u, i7, v7, v6); }
if ((edges & 128u) != 0u) { interpY(7u, i4, v4, v7); }
if ((edges & 256u) != 0u) { interpZ(8u, i0, v0, v4); }
if ((edges & 512u) != 0u) { interpZ(9u, i1, v1, v5); }
if ((edges & 1024u) != 0u) { interpZ(10u, i2, v2, v6); }
if ((edges & 2048u) != 0u) { interpZ(11u, i3, v3, v7); }

let triTableOffset = (cubeIndex << 4u) + 1u;
let indexCount = u32(tables.tris[triTableOffset - 1u]);
var firstVertex = atomicAdd(&indirect.vertexCount, cubeVerts);
let bufferOffset = getIdx(global_id);
let firstIndex = bufferOffset * 15u;

var rgbData = array<vec3<f32>,5>(
    vec3(0.055, 0.529, 0.8),
    vec3(0.761, 0.698, 0.502),
    vec3(0.204, 0.549, 0.192),
    vec3(0.353, 0.302, 0.255),
    vec3(1.0, 0.98, 0.98)
);
var ta = array<f32, 6>(0.0, 0.25, 0.27, 0.33, 0.4, 1.0);

for (var i = 0u; i < cubeVerts; i = i + 1u) {
    var y = (positions[i].y - vmin.y)/(vmax.y - vmin.y);
    if(y <= fps.waterLevel) {
        y = fps.waterLevel - 0.0000001;
        positions[i].y = vmin.y + y * (vmax.y - vmin.y);
    }

    positionsOut.values[firstVertex*4u + i*4u] = positions[i].x;
    positionsOut.values[firstVertex*4u + i*4u + 1u] = positions[i].y;
    positionsOut.values[firstVertex*4u + i*4u + 2u] = positions[i].z;
    positionsOut.values[firstVertex*4u + i*4u + 3u] = 1.0;

    normalsOut.values[firstVertex*4u + i*4u] = normals[i].x;
    normalsOut.values[firstVertex*4u + i*4u + 1u] = normals[i].y;
    normalsOut.values[firstVertex*4u + i*4u + 2u] = normals[i].z;
    normalsOut.values[firstVertex*4u + i*4u + 3u] = normals[i].z;

    let color = addTerrainColors(rgbData, ta, vmin.y, vmax.y, positions[i].y, fps.waterLevel);
    colorBuffer.values[firstVertex * 4u + i * 4u] = color.x;
    colorBuffer.values[firstVertex * 4u + i * 4u + 1u] = color.y;
    colorBuffer.values[firstVertex * 4u + i * 4u + 2u] = color.z;
```

```
            colorBuffer.values[firstVertex * 4u + i * 4u + 3u] = 1.0;
    }

    for (var i = 0u; i < indexCount; i = i + 1u) {
      let index = tables.tris[triTableOffset + i];
      indicesOut.tris[firstIndex + i] = firstVertex + indices[index];
    }

    for (var i = indexCount; i < 15u; i = i + 1u) {
      indicesOut.tris[firstIndex + i] = firstVertex;
    }
}
```

The code above is essentially similar to that used in the *implicit_surface.wgsl* file in the previous example, but it uses a different set of parameters specific to the voxel terrains. The other difference is in the *positionAt* function. Instead of using the data range for each implicit function to set the minimum and maximum values for each component, this example sets these values using terrain size, as illustrated in the following code snippet:

```
fn positionAt(index : vec3u) -> vec3f {
    vmin = vec3(-0.5 * fps.terrainSize);
    vmax = vec3(0.5 * fps.terrainSize);
    vstep = (vmax-vmin)/(f32(ips.resolution) - 1.0);
    return vmin + (vstep * vec3<f32>(index.xyz));
}
```

Additionally, this example creates the terrain colormap directly using the *lerpColor*, *shiftWaterLevel*, and *addTerrainColors* function, which is different from previous examples where the colormap data was generated in Rust from the colormap.rs file located in the src folder. Correspondingly, we also need to make changes for the colormap related code within the *cs_main* function, as illustrated in the following code snippet:

```
    let color = addTerrainColors(rgbData, ta, vmin.y, vmax.y, positions[i].y, fps.waterLevel);
```

The rest of the code is identical to that used in the previous example, so we do not need to make any further changes.

9.4.4 Rust Code

Create a new Rust file named *voxel_terrain.rs* in the *examples/ch09/* folder and add the following code to it:

```
use std::{iter, f32::consts::PI};
use cgmath::{ Matrix, Matrix4, SquareMatrix };
use wgpu:: VertexBufferLayout;
use winit::{
    event::*,
    event_loop::{ControlFlow, EventLoop},
    window::Window,
};
use bytemuck::cast_slice;
use wgpu_book_examples::{ wgpu_simplified as ws, transforms as wt };
mod marching_cubes_table;

struct State {
    init:  ws::IWgpuInit,
    pipeline: wgpu::RenderPipeline,
    uniform_bind_groups: Vec<wgpu::BindGroup>,
```

```rust
    uniform_buffers: Vec<wgpu::Buffer>,

    cs_pipelines: Vec<wgpu::ComputePipeline>,
    cs_vertex_buffers: Vec<wgpu::Buffer>,
    cs_index_buffer: wgpu::Buffer,
    cs_uniform_buffers: Vec<wgpu::Buffer>,
    cs_bind_groups: Vec<wgpu::BindGroup>,

    view_mat: Matrix4<f32>,
    project_mat: Matrix4<f32>,
    msaa_texture_view: wgpu::TextureView,
    depth_texture_view: wgpu::TextureView,
    animation_speed: f32,
    animation_direction: u32,

    resolution: u32,
    octaves: u32,
    seed: u32,
    isolevel: f32,
    index_count: u32,
    terrain_size: f32,
    lacunarity: f32,
    persistence: f32,
    noise_scale: f32,
    noise_height: f32,
    water_level: f32,
    height_multiplier: f32,
    floor_offset: f32,
    fps_counter: ws::FpsCounter,
}

impl State {
    async fn new(window:&Window, sample_count:u32, resolution:u32) -> Self {
        let limits = wgpu::Limits {
            max_storage_buffer_binding_size: 1024*1024*1024, //1024MB, defaulting to 128MB
            max_buffer_size: 1024*1024*1024, // 1024MB, defaulting to 256MB
            max_compute_invocations_per_workgroup: 512, // dafaulting to 256
            ..Default::default()
        };
        let init = ws::IWgpuInit::new(&window, sample_count, Some(limits)).await;

        let resol = ws::round_to_multiple(resolution, 8);
        let marching_cube_cells = (resolution - 1) * (resolution - 1) * (resolution - 1);
        let vertex_count = 3 * 12 * marching_cube_cells;
        let vertex_buffer_size = 4 * vertex_count;
        let index_count = 15 * marching_cube_cells;
        let index_buffer_size = 4 * index_count;
        println!("resolution = {}", resol);

        let vs_shader = init.device.create_shader_module(wgpu::include_wgsl!("../ch05/shader_vert.wgsl"));
        let fs_shader = init.device.create_shader_module(wgpu::include_wgsl!("../ch05/shader_frag.wgsl"));

        let cs_value_file = include_str!("voxel_value.wgsl");
        let cs_noise_file = include_str!("noise3d.wgsl");

        let cs_value = init.device.create_shader_module(wgpu::ShaderModuleDescriptor {
            label: Some("Compute Value Shader"),
            source: wgpu::ShaderSource::Wgsl([cs_noise_file, cs_value_file].join("\n").into()),
        });
```

```
let cs_comp = init.device.create_shader_module(wgpu::include_wgsl!("voxel_terrain.wgsl"));

// uniform data
let camera_position = (12.0, 12.0, 12.0).into();
let look_direction = (0.0,0.0,0.0).into();
let up_direction = cgmath::Vector3::unit_y();
let light_direction = [-0.5f32, -0.5, -0.5];

let (view_mat, project_mat, vp_mat) =
    wt::create_vp_mat(camera_position, look_direction, up_direction,
    init.config.width as f32 / init.config.height as f32);

let model_mat = wt::create_model_mat([0.0, 10.0, 0.0], [0.0, 0.1*PI, 0.0], [1.0, 1.0, 1.0]);
let normal_mat = (model_mat.invert().unwrap()).transpose();

// create vertex uniform buffers
let vert_uniform_buffer = init.device.create_buffer(&wgpu::BufferDescriptor{
    label: Some("Vertex Uniform Buffer"),
    size: 192,
    usage: wgpu::BufferUsages::UNIFORM | wgpu::BufferUsages::COPY_DST,
    mapped_at_creation: false,
});
init.queue.write_buffer(&vert_uniform_buffer, 0, cast_slice(vp_mat.as_ref() as &[f32; 16]));
init.queue.write_buffer(&vert_uniform_buffer, 64, cast_slice(model_mat.as_ref() as &[f32; 16]));
init.queue.write_buffer(&vert_uniform_buffer, 128, cast_slice(normal_mat.as_ref() as &[f32; 16]));

// create light uniform buffer. here we set eye_position = camera_position
let light_uniform_buffer = init.device.create_buffer(&wgpu::BufferDescriptor{
    label: Some("Light Uniform Buffer"),
    size: 48,
    usage: wgpu::BufferUsages::UNIFORM | wgpu::BufferUsages::COPY_DST,
    mapped_at_creation: false,
});

let eye_position:&[f32; 3] = camera_position.as_ref();
init.queue.write_buffer(&light_uniform_buffer, 0, cast_slice(light_direction.as_ref()));
init.queue.write_buffer(&light_uniform_buffer, 16, cast_slice(eye_position));

// set specular light color to white
let specular_color:[f32; 3] = [1.0, 1.0, 1.0];
init.queue.write_buffer(&light_uniform_buffer, 32, cast_slice(specular_color.as_ref()));

// material uniform buffer
let material_uniform_buffer = init.device.create_buffer(&wgpu::BufferDescriptor{
    label: Some("Material Uniform Buffer"),
    size: 16,
    usage: wgpu::BufferUsages::UNIFORM | wgpu::BufferUsages::COPY_DST,
    mapped_at_creation: false,
});

// set default material parameters
let material = [0.1f32, 0.7, 0.4, 30.0];
init.queue.write_buffer(&material_uniform_buffer, 0, cast_slice(material.as_ref()));

// uniform bind group for vertex shader
let (vert_bind_group_layout, vert_bind_group) = ws::create_bind_group(
    &init.device,
    vec![wgpu::ShaderStages::VERTEX],
    &[vert_uniform_buffer.as_entire_binding()],
);
```

```rust
    // uniform bind group for fragment shader
    let (frag_bind_group_layout, frag_bind_group) = ws::create_bind_group(
        &init.device,
        vec![wgpu::ShaderStages::FRAGMENT, wgpu::ShaderStages::FRAGMENT],
        &[light_uniform_buffer.as_entire_binding(), material_uniform_buffer.as_entire_binding()],
    );

    let vertex_buffer_layouts = [
        VertexBufferLayout {
            array_stride: 16,
            step_mode: wgpu::VertexStepMode::Vertex,
            attributes: &wgpu::vertex_attr_array![0 => Float32x4], // pos
        },
        VertexBufferLayout {
            array_stride: 16,
            step_mode: wgpu::VertexStepMode::Vertex,
            attributes: &wgpu::vertex_attr_array![1 => Float32x4], // norm
        },
        VertexBufferLayout {
            array_stride: 16,
            step_mode: wgpu::VertexStepMode::Vertex,
            attributes: &wgpu::vertex_attr_array![2 => Float32x4], // col
        },
    ];

    let pipeline_layout = init.device.create_pipeline_layout(&wgpu::PipelineLayoutDescriptor {
        label: Some("Render Pipeline Layout"),
        bind_group_layouts: &[&vert_bind_group_layout, &frag_bind_group_layout],
        push_constant_ranges: &[],
    });

    let mut ppl = ws::IRenderPipeline {
        vs_shader: Some(&vs_shader),
        fs_shader: Some(&fs_shader),
        pipeline_layout: Some(&pipeline_layout),
        vertex_buffer_layout: &vertex_buffer_layouts,
        ..Default::default()
    };
    let pipeline = ppl.new(&init);

    let msaa_texture_view = ws::create_msaa_texture_view(&init);
    let depth_texture_view = ws::create_depth_view(&init);

    // create compute pipeline for value
    let volume_elements = resol * resol * resol;
    let cs_value_buffer = init.device.create_buffer(&wgpu::BufferDescriptor{
        label: Some("Volue Buffer"),
        size:  4 * volume_elements as u64,
        usage: wgpu::BufferUsages::STORAGE | wgpu::BufferUsages::COPY_DST,
        mapped_at_creation: false,
    });

    let cs_value_int_buffer = init.device.create_buffer(&wgpu::BufferDescriptor{
        label: Some("Compute Value Integer Uniform Buffer"),
        size:  16,
        usage: wgpu::BufferUsages::UNIFORM | wgpu::BufferUsages::COPY_DST,
        mapped_at_creation: false,
    });
```

```
let cs_value_float_buffer = init.device.create_buffer(&wgpu::BufferDescriptor{
    label: Some("Compute Value Float Uniform Buffer"),
    size:  48,
    usage: wgpu::BufferUsages::UNIFORM | wgpu::BufferUsages::COPY_DST,
    mapped_at_creation: false,
});

let (cs_value_bind_group_layout, cs_value_bind_group) = ws::create_bind_group_storage(
    &init.device,
    vec![
        wgpu::ShaderStages::COMPUTE, wgpu::ShaderStages::COMPUTE,
        wgpu::ShaderStages::COMPUTE,
    ],
    vec![
        wgpu::BufferBindingType::Storage { read_only: false },
        wgpu::BufferBindingType::Uniform,
        wgpu::BufferBindingType::Uniform,
    ],
    &[
        cs_value_buffer.as_entire_binding(),
        cs_value_int_buffer.as_entire_binding(),
        cs_value_float_buffer.as_entire_binding(),
    ],
);

let cs_value_pipeline_layout = init.device.create_pipeline_layout(&wgpu::PipelineLayoutDescriptor{
    label: Some("Compute Value Pipeline Layout"),
    bind_group_layouts: &[&cs_value_bind_group_layout],
    push_constant_ranges: &[],
});

let cs_value_pipeline = init.device.create_compute_pipeline(&wgpu::ComputePipelineDescriptor{
    label: Some("Compute Value Pipeline"),
    layout: Some(&cs_value_pipeline_layout),
    module: &cs_value,
    entry_point: "cs_main",
});

// create compute pipeline for voxel terrain
let cs_table_buffer = init.device.create_buffer(&wgpu::BufferDescriptor{
    label: Some("Compute Table Storage Buffer"),
    size:  (marching_cubes_table::EDGE_TABLE.len() + marching_cubes_table::TRI_TABLE.len())
        as u64 * 4,
    usage: wgpu::BufferUsages::STORAGE | wgpu::BufferUsages::COPY_DST,
    mapped_at_creation: false,
});
init.queue.write_buffer(&cs_table_buffer, 0, cast_slice(marching_cubes_table::EDGE_TABLE));
init.queue.write_buffer(&cs_table_buffer, marching_cubes_table::EDGE_TABLE.len() as u64 * 4,
    cast_slice(marching_cubes_table::TRI_TABLE));

let cs_position_buffer = init.device.create_buffer(&wgpu::BufferDescriptor{
    label: Some("Compute Position Buffer"),
    size:  vertex_buffer_size as u64,
    usage: wgpu::BufferUsages::VERTEX | wgpu::BufferUsages::STORAGE |
        wgpu::BufferUsages::COPY_DST,
    mapped_at_creation: false,
});

let cs_normal_buffer = init.device.create_buffer(&wgpu::BufferDescriptor{
    label: Some("Compute Normal Buffer"),
```

```
        size:  vertex_buffer_size as u64,
        usage: wgpu::BufferUsages::VERTEX | wgpu::BufferUsages::STORAGE |
            wgpu::BufferUsages::COPY_DST,
        mapped_at_creation: false,
    });

    let cs_color_buffer = init.device.create_buffer(&wgpu::BufferDescriptor{
        label: Some("Compute Color Buffer"),
        size:  vertex_buffer_size as u64,
        usage: wgpu::BufferUsages::VERTEX | wgpu::BufferUsages::STORAGE |
            wgpu::BufferUsages::COPY_DST,
        mapped_at_creation: false,
    });

    let cs_index_buffer = init.device.create_buffer(&wgpu::BufferDescriptor{
        label: Some("Compute Index Buffer"),
        size:  index_buffer_size as u64,
        usage: wgpu::BufferUsages::INDEX | wgpu::BufferUsages::STORAGE | wgpu::BufferUsages::COPY_DST,
        mapped_at_creation: false,
    });

    let cs_indirect_buffer = init.device.create_buffer(&wgpu::BufferDescriptor{
        label: Some("Compute Indirect Buffer"),
        size:  16,
        usage: wgpu::BufferUsages::INDIRECT | wgpu::BufferUsages::STORAGE |
            wgpu::BufferUsages::COPY_DST,
        mapped_at_creation: false,
    });

    let cs_int_buffer = init.device.create_buffer(&wgpu::BufferDescriptor{
        label: Some("Compute Integer Uniform Buffer"),
        size:  16,
        usage: wgpu::BufferUsages::UNIFORM | wgpu::BufferUsages::COPY_DST,
        mapped_at_creation: false,
    });

    let cs_float_buffer = init.device.create_buffer(&wgpu::BufferDescriptor{
        label: Some("Compute Float Uniform Buffer"),
        size:  16,
        usage: wgpu::BufferUsages::UNIFORM | wgpu::BufferUsages::COPY_DST,
        mapped_at_creation: false,
    });

    let (cs_bind_group_layout, cs_bind_group) = ws::create_bind_group_storage(
        &init.device,
        vec![
            wgpu::ShaderStages::COMPUTE, wgpu::ShaderStages::COMPUTE, wgpu::ShaderStages::COMPUTE,
            wgpu::ShaderStages::COMPUTE, wgpu::ShaderStages::COMPUTE, wgpu::ShaderStages::COMPUTE,
            wgpu::ShaderStages::COMPUTE, wgpu::ShaderStages::COMPUTE, wgpu::ShaderStages::COMPUTE,
        ],
        vec![
            wgpu::BufferBindingType::Storage { read_only: true },    // marching table
            wgpu::BufferBindingType::Storage { read_only: true },    // value buffer
            wgpu::BufferBindingType::Storage { read_only: false },   // position
            wgpu::BufferBindingType::Storage { read_only: false },   // normal
            wgpu::BufferBindingType::Storage { read_only: false },   // color
            wgpu::BufferBindingType::Storage { read_only: false },   // indices
            wgpu::BufferBindingType::Storage { read_only: false },   // indirect params
            wgpu::BufferBindingType::Uniform,                        // int params
            wgpu::BufferBindingType::Uniform,                        // float params
```

```
        ],
        &[
            cs_table_buffer.as_entire_binding(),
            cs_value_buffer.as_entire_binding(),
            cs_position_buffer.as_entire_binding(),
            cs_normal_buffer.as_entire_binding(),
            cs_color_buffer.as_entire_binding(),
            cs_index_buffer.as_entire_binding(),
            cs_indirect_buffer.as_entire_binding(),
            cs_int_buffer.as_entire_binding(),
            cs_float_buffer.as_entire_binding(),
        ],
    );

    let cs_pipeline_layout = init.device.create_pipeline_layout(&wgpu::PipelineLayoutDescriptor{
        label: Some("Compute Pipeline Layout"),
        bind_group_layouts: &[&cs_bind_group_layout],
        push_constant_ranges: &[],
    });

    let cs_pipeline = init.device.create_compute_pipeline(&wgpu::ComputePipelineDescriptor{
        label: Some("Compute Pipeline"),
        layout: Some(&cs_pipeline_layout),
        module: &cs_comp,
        entry_point: "cs_main",
    });

    Self {
        init,
        pipeline,
        uniform_bind_groups: vec![vert_bind_group, frag_bind_group],
        uniform_buffers: vec![vert_uniform_buffer, light_uniform_buffer, material_uniform_buffer],

        cs_pipelines: vec![cs_value_pipeline, cs_pipeline],
        cs_vertex_buffers: vec![cs_value_buffer, cs_position_buffer, cs_normal_buffer,
            cs_color_buffer],
        cs_index_buffer,
        cs_uniform_buffers: vec![cs_value_int_buffer, cs_value_float_buffer, cs_int_buffer,
            cs_float_buffer, cs_indirect_buffer],
        cs_bind_groups: vec![cs_value_bind_group, cs_bind_group],

        view_mat,
        project_mat,
        msaa_texture_view,
        depth_texture_view,
        animation_speed: 1.0,
        animation_direction: 2,

        resolution: resol,
        octaves: 10,
        seed: 1232,
        isolevel: 3.0,
        index_count,
        terrain_size: 40.0,
        lacunarity: 2.0,
        persistence: 0.5,
        noise_scale: 4.0,
        noise_height: 7.0,
        water_level: 0.35,
        height_multiplier: 1.5,
```

```
            floor_offset: 9.0,
            fps_counter: ws::FpsCounter::default(),
        }
    }

    fn resize(&mut self, new_size: winit::dpi::PhysicalSize<u32>) {
        if new_size.width > 0 && new_size.height > 0 {
            self.init.size = new_size;
            self.init.config.width = new_size.width;
            self.init.config.height = new_size.height;
            self.init.surface.configure(&self.init.device, &self.init.config);

            self.project_mat = wt::create_projection_mat(new_size.width as f32 / new_size.height as f32,
                true);
            let vp_mat = self.project_mat * self.view_mat;
            self.init.queue.write_buffer(&self.uniform_buffers[0], 0,
                cast_slice(vp_mat.as_ref() as &[f32; 16]));

            self.depth_texture_view = ws::create_depth_view(&self.init);
            if self.init.sample_count > 1 {
                self.msaa_texture_view = ws::create_msaa_texture_view(&self.init);
            }
        }
    }
}

#[allow(unused_variables)]
fn input(&mut self, event: &WindowEvent) -> bool {
    match event {
        WindowEvent::KeyboardInput {
            input:
                KeyboardInput {
                    virtual_keycode: Some(keycode),
                    state: ElementState::Pressed,
                    ..
                },
            ..
        } => {
            match keycode {
                VirtualKeyCode::Space => {
                    self.animation_direction = (self.animation_direction + 1) % 3;
                    true
                },
                VirtualKeyCode::Q => {
                    self.animation_speed += 0.1;
                    true
                },
                VirtualKeyCode::A => {
                    self.animation_speed -= 0.1;
                    if self.animation_speed < 0.0 {
                        self.animation_speed = 0.0;
                    }
                    true
                } ,
                VirtualKeyCode::W => {
                    self.water_level += 0.01;
                    true
                },
                VirtualKeyCode::S => {
                    self.water_level -= 0.01;
                    if self.water_level < 0.0 {
```

```
                                  self.water_level = 0.0;
                              }
                              true
                          } ,
                          _ => false
                      }
                  }
                  _ => false,
              }
          }

    fn update(&mut self, dt: std::time::Duration) {
        // update compute buffers for value
        let value_int_params = [self.resolution, self.octaves, self.seed, 0];
        self.init.queue.write_buffer(&self.cs_uniform_buffers[0], 0, cast_slice(&value_int_params));

        let dt1 = 10.0 * self.animation_speed * dt.as_secs_f32();
        let value_float_params = [
            if self.animation_direction == 0 { -dt1 } else { 0.0 },
            if self.animation_direction == 1 { -dt1 } else { 0.0 },
            if self.animation_direction == 2 { -dt1 } else { 0.0 },
            self.terrain_size,
            self.lacunarity,
            self.persistence,
            self.noise_scale,
            self.noise_height,
            self.height_multiplier,
            self.floor_offset,
            0.0, 0.0 // padding
        ];
        self.init.queue.write_buffer(&self.cs_uniform_buffers[1], 0, cast_slice(&value_float_params));

        // update compute buffers for terrain
        let int_params = [self.resolution, 0, 0, 0];
        self.init.queue.write_buffer(&self.cs_uniform_buffers[2], 0, cast_slice(&int_params));

        let float_params = [self.terrain_size, self.isolevel, self.noise_height, self.water_level];
        self.init.queue.write_buffer(&self.cs_uniform_buffers[3], 0, cast_slice(&float_params));

        let indirect_array = [500u32, 0, 0, 0];
        self.init.queue.write_buffer(&self.cs_uniform_buffers[4], 0, cast_slice(&indirect_array));

    }

    fn render(&mut self) -> Result<(), wgpu::SurfaceError> {
        let output = self.init.surface.get_current_texture()?;
        let view = output
            .texture
            .create_view(&wgpu::TextureViewDescriptor::default());

        let mut encoder = self
            .init.device
            .create_command_encoder(&wgpu::CommandEncoderDescriptor {
                label: Some("Render Encoder"),
            });

        // compute pass for value
        {
            let mut cs_index_pass = encoder.begin_compute_pass(&wgpu::ComputePassDescriptor{
                label: Some("Compute value Pass"),
```

```
                    timestamp_writes: None,
                });
                cs_index_pass.set_pipeline(&self.cs_pipelines[0]);
                cs_index_pass.set_bind_group(0, &self.cs_bind_groups[0], &[]);
                cs_index_pass.dispatch_workgroups(self.resolution/8, self.resolution/8, self.resolution/8);
            }

            // compute pass for vertices
            {
                let mut cs_pass = encoder.begin_compute_pass(&wgpu::ComputePassDescriptor{
                    label: Some("Compute Pass"),
                    timestamp_writes: None,
                });
                cs_pass.set_pipeline(&self.cs_pipelines[1]);
                cs_pass.set_bind_group(0, &self.cs_bind_groups[1], &[]);
                cs_pass.dispatch_workgroups(self.resolution/8, self.resolution/8, self.resolution/8);
            }

            // render pass
            {
                let color_attach = ws::create_color_attachment(&view);
                let msaa_attach = ws::create_msaa_color_attachment(&view, &self.msaa_texture_view);
                let color_attachment = if self.init.sample_count == 1 { color_attach } else { msaa_attach };
                let depth_attachment = ws::create_depth_stencil_attachment(&self.depth_texture_view);

                let mut render_pass = encoder.begin_render_pass(&wgpu::RenderPassDescriptor {
                    label: Some("Render Pass"),
                    color_attachments: &[Some(color_attachment)],
                    depth_stencil_attachment: Some(depth_attachment),
                    occlusion_query_set: None,
                    timestamp_writes: None,
                });

                render_pass.set_pipeline(&self.pipeline);
                render_pass.set_vertex_buffer(0, self.cs_vertex_buffers[1].slice(..));
                render_pass.set_vertex_buffer(1, self.cs_vertex_buffers[2].slice(..));
                render_pass.set_vertex_buffer(2, self.cs_vertex_buffers[3].slice(..));
                render_pass.set_index_buffer(self.cs_index_buffer.slice(..), wgpu::IndexFormat::Uint32);
                render_pass.set_bind_group(0, &self.uniform_bind_groups[0], &[]);
                render_pass.set_bind_group(1, &self.uniform_bind_groups[1], &[]);
                render_pass.draw_indexed(0..self.index_count, 0, 0..1);
            }

            self.fps_counter.print_fps(5);
            self.init.queue.submit(iter::once(encoder.finish()));
            output.present();

            Ok(())
        }
    }
}

fn main() {
    let mut sample_count = 1u32;
    let mut resolution = 192u32;

    let args: Vec<String> = std::env::args().collect();
    if args.len() > 1 {
        sample_count = args[1].parse::<u32>().unwrap();
    }
    if args.len() > 2 {
```

```
            resolution = args[2].parse::<u32>().unwrap();
    }

    env_logger::init();
    let event_loop = EventLoop::new();
    let window = winit::window::WindowBuilder::new().build(&event_loop).unwrap();
    window.set_title(&*format!("ch09_{}", "voxel_terrain"));

    let mut state = pollster::block_on(State::new(&window, sample_count, resolution));
    let render_start_time = std::time::Instant::now();

    event_loop.run(move |event, _, control_flow| {
        match event {
            Event::WindowEvent {
                ref event,
                window_id,
            } if window_id == window.id() => {
                if !state.input(event) {
                    match event {
                        WindowEvent::CloseRequested
                        | WindowEvent::KeyboardInput {
                            input:
                                KeyboardInput {
                                    state: ElementState::Pressed,
                                    virtual_keycode: Some(VirtualKeyCode::Escape),
                                    ..
                                },
                            ..
                        } => *control_flow = ControlFlow::Exit,
                        WindowEvent::Resized(physical_size) => {
                            state.resize(*physical_size);
                        }
                        WindowEvent::ScaleFactorChanged { new_inner_size, .. } => {
                            state.resize(**new_inner_size);
                        }
                        _ => {}
                    }
                }
            }
            Event::RedrawRequested(_) => {
                let now = std::time::Instant::now();
                let dt = now - render_start_time;
                state.update(dt);

                match state.render() {
                    Ok(_) => {}
                    Err(wgpu::SurfaceError::Lost) => state.resize(state.init.size),
                    Err(wgpu::SurfaceError::OutOfMemory) => *control_flow = ControlFlow::Exit,
                    Err(e) => eprintln!("{:?}", e),
                }
            }
            Event::MainEventsCleared => {
                window.request_redraw();
            }
            _ => {}
        }
    });
}
```

The above code is similar to the one used in previous implicit-function example. First, we introduce the marching cubes tables from the *marching_cubes_table.rs* file and add several new fields to the *State* struct, including *resolution*, index_count, *terrain_size*, and other voxel-terrain related parameters. These fields can be easily accessed by different functions without the need to pass them as input.

Within the *State::new* function, as we did in the previous example, we reset certain GPU device limits when creating the device to accommodate higher-resolution voxel terrains. Subsequently, we reuse the vertex and fragment shaders created earlier in Chapter 5. Additionally, we introduce two compute shader files generated in the previous sections, namely *voxel_value.wgsl* and *voxel_terrain.wgsl*.

The code segment for creating the render pipeline inside the *State::new* function is identical to that used in the previous example. Similarly, the code for creating compute pipelines used to generate the scalar value data and vertex data of the voxel terrains is also similar to that used in the previous example, but with a different set of parameters specific to voxel terrains.

The *State::render* function in the above code is also similar to the explicit-function example and the workgroup size for the terrain compute shader is set to 8.

In the *State::update* function, we animate the voxel terrain without the need to regenerate the terrain data and vertex buffers for every frame. Instead, we only need to update the uniform parameters used to calculate the scalar noise value data in the compute shader, as shown in the following code snippet:

```
let dt1 = 10.0 * self.animation_speed * dt.as_secs_f32();
let value_float_params = [
    if self.animation_direction == 0 { -dt1 } else { 0.0 },
    if self.animation_direction == 1 { -dt1 } else { 0.0 },
    if self.animation_direction == 2 { -dt1 } else { 0.0 },
    self.terrain_size,
    self.lacunarity,
    self.persistence,
    self.noise_scale,
    self.noise_height,
    self.height_multiplier,
    self.floor_offset,
    0.0, 0.0 // padding
];
self.init.queue.write_buffer(&self.cs_uniform_buffers[1], 0, cast_slice(&value_float_params));
```

The above code snippet allows the user to select animation direction, with the default being the *z* direction.

Additionally, the code permits the user to modify input parameters using keyboard inputs.

Here is a list of controls using keyboard:

- *Space*: Changes the animation direction.

- *Q/A*: Increases/decreases the animation speed.

- *W/S*: Increases/decreases the water level.

9.4.5 Run Application

To run this application, add the following code snippet to the *Cargo.toml* file:

```
[[example]]
name = "ch09_voxel_terrain"
path = "examples/ch09/voxel_terrain.rs"
```

Afterward, execute the following *cargo run* commands in the terminal window:

```
cargo run --example ch09_voxel_terrain 8
```

Fig.9-4 shows the results of this example.

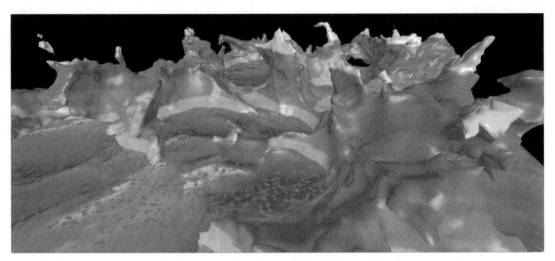

Fig.9-4. Voxel terrain created using marching cubes.

9.5 Voxel Volcanoes

As mentioned earlier, the marching cubes algorithm can be used to simulate a wide range of natural phenomena, including volcanoes. To achieve this, we need to generate a scalar field that represents the density or temperature of the volcano at each voxel in space.

One way to generate this scalar field is to use a combination of simplex (or Perlin) noise and Worley noise functions, which can be used to generate a variety of natural-looking patterns. However, for the sake of simplicity, in this example, we will use two simplex noise functions: one for the volcano located at the center and another for the surrounding terrain.

9.5.1 Compute Shader for Values

Create a new WGSL compute shader file named *volcano_value.wgsl* in the *examples/ch09/* folder and add the following code to it:

```
const pi:f32 = 3.1415926;

struct ValueBuffer{
    values: array<f32>,
}
@group(0) @binding(0) var<storage, read_write> valueBuffer : ValueBuffer;

struct IntParams {
    resolution: u32,
    octaves: u32,
    octaves2: u32,
    seed: u32,
```

```
}
@group(0) @binding(1) var<uniform> ips : IntParams;

struct FloatParams {
    offset: vec3f,
    noiseScale: f32,
    noiseHeight: f32,
    heightMultiplier: f32,
    floorOffset: f32,
    noiseScale2: f32,
    noiseHeight2: f32,
    heightMultiplier2: f32,
    floorOffset2: f32,
}
@group(0) @binding(2) var<uniform> fps : FloatParams;

const terrainSize: f32 = 40.0;
const lacunarity: f32 = 2.0;
const persistence: f32 = 0.5;

var<private> vmin: vec3f;
var<private> vmax: vec3f;

fn positionAt(index : vec3u) -> vec3f {
    vmin = vec3(-0.5 * terrainSize);
    vmax = vec3(0.5 * terrainSize);
    let vstep = (vmax-vmin)/(f32(ips.resolution) - 1.0);
    return vmin + (vstep * vec3<f32>(index.xyz));
}

fn getIdx(id: vec3u) -> u32 {
    return id.x + ips.resolution * ( id.y + id.z * ips.resolution);
}

fn terrainFunc(position: vec3f) -> f32 {
    var noise = 0.0;
    var frequency = fps.noiseScale2/100.0;
    var amplitude = 1.0;
    var height = 1.0;

    for(var i = 0u; i < ips.octaves2; i = i + 1u){
        let rand = rand3d(f32(i + ips.seed));
        let offset = 1000.0 * rand;
        let n = simplex3d((position + offset)*frequency );
        var v = 1.0 - abs(n);
        v = v * v;
        v *= height;
        height = max(min(v * fps.heightMultiplier2, 1.0), 0.0);
        noise += v * amplitude;
        amplitude *= persistence;
        frequency *= lacunarity;
    }
    return -(position.y + fps.floorOffset2) + noise * fps.noiseHeight2;
}

fn volcanoFunc(position: vec3f) -> f32 {
    var noise = 0.0;
    var frequency = fps.noiseScale/100.0;
    var amplitude = 1.0;
    var height = 1.0;
```

```
        let r = sqrt(position.x * position.x + position.z * position.z);
        var offset2 = vec3(0.0);
        if(r < 9.0 + 1.5 * sin(0.05*fps.offset.y)) { offset2 = fps.offset; }
        for(var i = 0u; i < ips.octaves; i = i + 1u){
            let rand = rand3d(f32(i + ips.seed));
            let offset = 1000.0 * rand;
            let n = simplex3d((position  + offset2 + offset)*frequency );
            var v = 1.0 - abs(n);
            v = v * v;
            v *= height;
            height = max(min(v * fps.heightMultiplier, 1.0), 0.0);
            noise += v * amplitude;
            amplitude *= persistence;
            frequency *= lacunarity;
        }
        return -(position.y + fps.floorOffset) + noise * fps.noiseHeight;
}

fn combinedFunc(position: vec3f) -> f32 {
    let terrain = terrainFunc(position);
    let volcano = volcanoFunc(position);
    let r = sqrt(position.x * position.x + position.z * position.z);
    var val: f32;
    if(r < 10.0 + 0.5*sin(0.02*fps.offset.y)) {
        val = volcano;
    } else {
        val = terrain;
    }
    return val;
}

@compute @workgroup_size(8, 8, 8)
fn cs_main(@builtin(global_invocation_id) id : vec3u) {
    var position = positionAt(id);
    var y = (position.y - vmin.y)/(vmax.y - vmin.y);
    if(y <= 0.0) {
        position.y = 0.0;
    }
    let idx = getIdx(id);
    valueBuffer.values[idx] = combinedFunc(position);
}
```

The above code is similar to that used in the previous example, except that we generate the terrain and volcano separately using the simplex noise function with two different sets of parameters. The code for generating the terrain is identical to the previous example. However, the code for generating the volcano contains some changes. In particular, we define a new offset variable called *offset1* in a cylindrical region along the y direction using the following code snippet:

```
let r = sqrt(position.x * position.x + position.z * position.z);
var offset1 = vec3(0.0);
if(r < 9.0 + 1.5 * sin(0.05*fps.offset.y)) { offset1 = fps.offset; }
```

Here, the variable r represents the distance from the center of the terrain to the current point in the x-z plane, and *offset1* is calculated based on the distance r and the uniform parameter *fps.offset* for the volcano. If r is less than a certain threshold, then *offset1* is set to *fps.offset*. Note that since *fps.offset* is a time-dependent uniform parameter used to animate the movement of the volcano, the threshold will vary in the region of [7.5, 10.5] corresponding to $\sin(0.05 * \text{fps.offset.y}) = \pm 1$, resulting in a natural variation of the crater of the volcano.

The *combinedFunc* function combines the terrain and volcano functions to generate a noise heightmap. Within the function, it calls *terrainFunc* and *volcanoFun* to generate two separate heightmaps. Then it calculates r from the center position of the terrain. Next, it sets the noise value to the height of the terrain, for r greater than 10 plus a *sine* wave that varies based on the *fps.offset.y* value. If r is less than the threshold, then it sets the noise value to the height of the volcano instead. In this way, we create a volcano located at the center of the terrain.

9.5.2 Compute Shader for Volcano

Create a new WGSL compute shader file named *volcano_comp.wgsl* in the *examples/ch09/* folder. The code is essentially similar to that used in the previous example, so simply copy the code from the *voxel_terrain.wgsl* file and paste it into the *volcano_comp.wgsl* file, and then make the following small changes:

First, we need to replace the *FloatParams* structs with the following code snippet:

```
struct FloatParams {
    isolevel: f32,
};
```

The *FloatParams* struct in the above code snippet contain only the *isolevel* field, the other fields such as terrain size are specified as constants.

In addition to the *addTerrainColors* function implemented in the previous example, the code above also creates a colormap for the volcano using the following code snippet:

```
fn addVolcanoColors(tmin:f32, tmax:f32, t:f32) -> vec3f {
    let colors = array<vec3f, 11>(
        vec3(1.0, 0.992, 0.98),
        vec3(0.961, 0.863, 0.353),
        vec3(0.906, 0.51, 0.008),
        vec3(0.976, 0.267, 0.008),
        vec3(0.984, 0.584, 0.008),
        vec3(0.612, 0.165, 0.145),
        vec3(0.694, 0.173, 0.024),
        vec3(0.941, 0.341, 0.082),
        vec3(0.588, 0.298, 0.267),
        vec3(0.427, 0.4, 0.408),
        vec3(0.298, 0.255, 0.267),
    );

    var t1 = t;
    if (t1 < tmin) {t1 = tmin;}
    if (t1 > tmax) {t1 = tmax;}
    var tn = (t1-tmin)/(tmax-tmin);

    var idx = u32(floor(10.0*tn));
    var color = vec3(0.0,0.0,0.0);

    if(f32(idx) == 10.0*tn) {
        color = colors[idx];
    } else {
        var tn1 = (tn - 0.1*f32(idx))*10.0;
        var a = colors[idx];
        var b = colors[idx+1u];
        color.x = a.x + (b.x - a.x)*tn1;
        color.y = a.y + (b.y - a.y)*tn1;
```

```
        color.z = a.z + (b.z - a.z)*tn1;
    }
    return color;
}
```

Correspondingly, we also need to make changes for the colormap related code within the *cs_main* function, as illustrated in the following code snippet:

```
let r = sqrt(positions[i].x * positions[i].x + positions[i].z*positions[i].z);
if( r > 10.0){
    color = addTerrainColors(vmin.y, vmax.y, positions[i].y);
} else {
    color = addVolcanoColors(0.0, 10.0, r);
}
```

It is evident from the above code snippet that in the cylindrical region at the center, the colormap for the volcano is used, while the colormap for the terrain is used for the surrounding terrain.

9.5.3 Rust Code

Create a new Rust file named *volcano.rs* in the *examples/ch09/* folder and add the following code to it:

```
use std::iter;
use cgmath::{ Matrix, Matrix4, SquareMatrix };
use wgpu:: VertexBufferLayout;
use winit::{
    event::*,
    event_loop::{ControlFlow, EventLoop},
    window::Window,
};
use bytemuck::cast_slice;
use wgpu_book_examples::{ wgpu_simplified as ws, transforms as wt };
mod marching_cubes_table;

struct State {
    init:  ws::IWgpuInit,
    pipeline: wgpu::RenderPipeline,
    uniform_bind_groups: Vec<wgpu::BindGroup>,
    uniform_buffers: Vec<wgpu::Buffer>,

    cs_pipelines: Vec<wgpu::ComputePipeline>,
    cs_vertex_buffers: Vec<wgpu::Buffer>,
    cs_index_buffer: wgpu::Buffer,
    cs_uniform_buffers: Vec<wgpu::Buffer>,
    cs_bind_groups: Vec<wgpu::BindGroup>,

    view_mat: Matrix4<f32>,
    project_mat: Matrix4<f32>,
    msaa_texture_view: wgpu::TextureView,
    depth_texture_view: wgpu::TextureView,
    rotation_speed: f32,
    animation_speed: f32,

    resolution: u32,
    index_count: u32,
    seed: u32,
    isolevel: f32,

    // for volcano
```

```
        octaves: u32,
        noise_scale: f32,
        noise_height: f32,
        height_multiplier: f32,
        floor_offset: f32,

        // for surrounding terrain
        octaves2: u32,
        noise_scale2: f32,
        noise_height2: f32,
        height_multiplier2: f32,
        floor_offset2: f32,
}

impl State {
    async fn new(window:&Window, sample_count:u32, resolution:u32) -> Self {

        // ...
        // code used to create render pipeline omitted because it is identical to the previous example
        // ...

        // create compute pipeline for value
        let volume_elements = resol * resol * resol;
        let cs_value_buffer = init.device.create_buffer(&wgpu::BufferDescriptor{
            label: Some("Index Buffer"),
            size:  4 * volume_elements as u64,
            usage: wgpu::BufferUsages::STORAGE | wgpu::BufferUsages::COPY_DST,
            mapped_at_creation: false,
        });

        let cs_value_int_buffer = init.device.create_buffer(&wgpu::BufferDescriptor{
            label: Some("Compuet Value Integer Uniform Buffer"),
            size:  16,
            usage: wgpu::BufferUsages::UNIFORM | wgpu::BufferUsages::COPY_DST,
            mapped_at_creation: false,
        });

        let cs_value_float_buffer = init.device.create_buffer(&wgpu::BufferDescriptor{
            label: Some("Compuet Value Float Uniform Buffer"),
            size:  48,
            usage: wgpu::BufferUsages::UNIFORM | wgpu::BufferUsages::COPY_DST,
            mapped_at_creation: false,
        });

        let (cs_value_bind_group_layout, cs_value_bind_group) = ws::create_bind_group_storage(
            &init.device,
            vec![
                wgpu::ShaderStages::COMPUTE, wgpu::ShaderStages::COMPUTE,
                wgpu::ShaderStages::COMPUTE,
            ],
            vec![
                wgpu::BufferBindingType::Storage { read_only: false },
                wgpu::BufferBindingType::Uniform,
                wgpu::BufferBindingType::Uniform,
            ],
            &[
                cs_value_buffer.as_entire_binding(),
                cs_value_int_buffer.as_entire_binding(),
                cs_value_float_buffer.as_entire_binding(),
            ],
```

```
    );

    let cs_value_pipeline_layout = init.device.create_pipeline_layout(&wgpu::PipelineLayoutDescriptor{
        label: Some("Compute Value Pipeline Layout"),
        bind_group_layouts: &[&cs_value_bind_group_layout],
        push_constant_ranges: &[],
    });

    let cs_value_pipeline = init.device.create_compute_pipeline(&wgpu::ComputePipelineDescriptor{
        label: Some("Compute Value Pipeline"),
        layout: Some(&cs_value_pipeline_layout),
        module: &cs_value,
        entry_point: "cs_main",
    });

    // ...
    // code for the compute pipeline used to generate volcano data omitted for brevity
    // ...

    Self {
        init,
        pipeline,
        uniform_bind_groups: vec![vert_bind_group, frag_bind_group],
        uniform_buffers: vec![vert_uniform_buffer, light_uniform_buffer, material_uniform_buffer],

        cs_pipelines: vec![cs_value_pipeline, cs_pipeline],
        cs_vertex_buffers: vec![cs_value_buffer, cs_position_buffer, cs_normal_buffer,
            cs_color_buffer],
        cs_index_buffer,
        cs_uniform_buffers: vec![cs_value_int_buffer, cs_value_float_buffer, cs_int_buffer,
            cs_float_buffer, cs_indirect_buffer],
        cs_bind_groups: vec![cs_value_bind_group, cs_bind_group],

        view_mat,
        project_mat,
        msaa_texture_view,
        depth_texture_view,
        rotation_speed: 1.0,
        animation_speed: 1.0,

        resolution: resol,
        index_count,
        seed: 1232,
        isolevel: 3.0,

        // for volcano
        octaves: 10,
        noise_scale: 10.0,
        noise_height: 9.0,
        height_multiplier: 24.0,
        floor_offset: 10.0,

        // for surrounding terrain
        octaves2: 10,
        noise_scale2: 5.0,
        noise_height2: 5.0,
        height_multiplier2: 3.0,
        floor_offset2: 10.0,
    }
}
```

```rust
    fn resize(&mut self, new_size: winit::dpi::PhysicalSize<u32>) {
        if new_size.width > 0 && new_size.height > 0 {
            self.init.size = new_size;
            self.init.config.width = new_size.width;
            self.init.config.height = new_size.height;
            self.init.surface.configure(&self.init.device, &self.init.config);

            self.project_mat = wt::create_projection_mat(new_size.width as f32 / new_size.height as f32,
                true);
            let vp_mat = self.project_mat * self.view_mat;
            self.init.queue.write_buffer(&self.uniform_buffers[0], 0,
                cast_slice(vp_mat.as_ref() as &[f32; 16]));

            self.depth_texture_view = ws::create_depth_view(&self.init);
            if self.init.sample_count > 1 {
                self.msaa_texture_view = ws::create_msaa_texture_view(&self.init);
            }
        }
    }

    #[allow(unused_variables)]
    fn input(&mut self, event: &WindowEvent) -> bool {
        match event {
            WindowEvent::KeyboardInput {
                input:
                    KeyboardInput {
                        virtual_keycode: Some(keycode),
                        state: ElementState::Pressed,
                        ..
                    },
                ..
            } => {
                match keycode {
                    VirtualKeyCode::Q => {
                        self.animation_speed += 0.1;
                        true
                    },
                    VirtualKeyCode::A => {
                        self.animation_speed -= 0.1;
                        if self.animation_speed < 0.0 {
                            self.animation_speed = 0.0;
                        }
                        true
                    },
                    _ => false
                }
            }
            _ => false,
        }
    }

    fn update(&mut self, dt: std::time::Duration) {
        // update uniform buffers:
        let dt1 = 0.2*self.rotation_speed * dt.as_secs_f32();
        let model_mat = wt::create_model_mat([0.0,5.0,0.0], [0.0, dt1, 0.0], [1.0, 1.0, 1.0]);
        let normal_mat = (model_mat.invert().unwrap()).transpose();
        self.init.queue.write_buffer(&self.uniform_buffers[0], 64,
            cast_slice(model_mat.as_ref() as &[f32;16]));
        self.init.queue.write_buffer(&self.uniform_buffers[0], 128,
```

```
        cast_slice(normal_mat.as_ref() as &[f32;16]));

    // update compute buffers for value
    let value_int_params = [self.resolution, self.octaves, self.octaves2, self.seed];
    self.init.queue.write_buffer(&self.cs_uniform_buffers[0], 0, cast_slice(&value_int_params));

    let dt2 = 10.0*self.animation_speed * dt.as_secs_f32();
    let value_float_params = [
        0.0, -dt2, 0.0,        // offset
        self.noise_scale,
        self.noise_height,
        self.height_multiplier,
        self.floor_offset,
        self.noise_scale2,
        self.noise_height2,
        self.height_multiplier2,
        self.floor_offset2,
    ];
    self.init.queue.write_buffer(&self.cs_uniform_buffers[1], 0, cast_slice(&value_float_params));

    // update compute buffers for terrain
    let int_params = [self.resolution, 0, 0, 0];
    self.init.queue.write_buffer(&self.cs_uniform_buffers[2], 0, cast_slice(&int_params));

    let float_params = [self.isolevel, 0.0, 0.0, 0.0];
    self.init.queue.write_buffer(&self.cs_uniform_buffers[3], 0, cast_slice(&float_params));

    let indirect_array = [500u32, 0, 0, 0];
    self.init.queue.write_buffer(&self.cs_uniform_buffers[4], 0, cast_slice(&indirect_array));

}

fn render(&mut self) -> Result<(), wgpu::SurfaceError> {
    let output = self.init.surface.get_current_texture()?;
    let view = output
        .texture
        .create_view(&wgpu::TextureViewDescriptor::default());

    let mut encoder = self
        .init.device
        .create_command_encoder(&wgpu::CommandEncoderDescriptor {
            label: Some("Render Encoder"),
        });

    // compute pass for value
    {
        let mut cs_index_pass = encoder.begin_compute_pass(&wgpu::ComputePassDescriptor{
            label: Some("Compute value Pass"),
            timestamp_writes: None,
        });
        cs_index_pass.set_pipeline(&self.cs_pipelines[0]);
        cs_index_pass.set_bind_group(0, &self.cs_bind_groups[0], &[]);
        cs_index_pass.dispatch_workgroups(self.resolution/8, self.resolution/8, self.resolution/8);
    }

    // compute pass for vertices
    {
        let mut cs_pass = encoder.begin_compute_pass(&wgpu::ComputePassDescriptor{
            label: Some("Compute Pass"),
            timestamp_writes: None,
```

```
            });
            cs_pass.set_pipeline(&self.cs_pipelines[1]);
            cs_pass.set_bind_group(0, &self.cs_bind_groups[1], &[]);
            cs_pass.dispatch_workgroups(self.resolution/8, self.resolution/8, self.resolution/8);
        }

        // render pass
        {
            let color_attach = ws::create_color_attachment(&view);
            let msaa_attach = ws::create_msaa_color_attachment(&view, &self.msaa_texture_view);
            let color_attachment = if self.init.sample_count == 1 { color_attach } else { msaa_attach };
            let depth_attachment = ws::create_depth_stencil_attachment(&self.depth_texture_view);

            let mut render_pass = encoder.begin_render_pass(&wgpu::RenderPassDescriptor {
                label: Some("Render Pass"),
                color_attachments: &[Some(color_attachment)],
                depth_stencil_attachment: Some(depth_attachment),
                timestamp_writes: None,
                occlusion_query_set: None,
            });

            render_pass.set_pipeline(&self.pipeline);
            render_pass.set_vertex_buffer(0, self.cs_vertex_buffers[1].slice(..));
            render_pass.set_vertex_buffer(1, self.cs_vertex_buffers[2].slice(..));
            render_pass.set_vertex_buffer(2, self.cs_vertex_buffers[3].slice(..));
            render_pass.set_index_buffer(self.cs_index_buffer.slice(..), wgpu::IndexFormat::Uint32);
            render_pass.set_bind_group(0, &self.uniform_bind_groups[0], &[]);
            render_pass.set_bind_group(1, &self.uniform_bind_groups[1], &[]);
            render_pass.draw_indexed(0..self.index_count, 0, 0..1);
        }

        self.init.queue.submit(iter::once(encoder.finish()));
        output.present();

        Ok(())
    }
}

fn main() {
    let mut sample_count = 1u32;
    let mut resolution = 192u32;

    let args: Vec<String> = std::env::args().collect();
    if args.len() > 1 {
        sample_count = args[1].parse::<u32>().unwrap();
    }
    if args.len() > 2 {
        resolution = args[2].parse::<u32>().unwrap();
    }

    env_logger::init();
    let event_loop = EventLoop::new();
    let window = winit::window::WindowBuilder::new().build(&event_loop).unwrap();
    window.set_title(&*format!("ch09_{}", "volcano"));

    let mut state = pollster::block_on(State::new(&window, sample_count, resolution));
    let render_start_time = std::time::Instant::now();

    event_loop.run(move |event, _, control_flow| {
        match event {
```

```
Event::WindowEvent {
    ref event,
    window_id,
} if window_id == window.id() => {
    if !state.input(event) {
        match event {
            WindowEvent::CloseRequested
            | WindowEvent::KeyboardInput {
                input:
                    KeyboardInput {
                        state: ElementState::Pressed,
                        virtual_keycode: Some(VirtualKeyCode::Escape),
                        ..
                    },
                ..
            } => *control_flow = ControlFlow::Exit,
            WindowEvent::Resized(physical_size) => {
                state.resize(*physical_size);
            }
            WindowEvent::ScaleFactorChanged { new_inner_size, .. } => {
                state.resize(**new_inner_size);
            }
            _ => {}
        }
    }
}
Event::RedrawRequested(_) => {
    let now = std::time::Instant::now();
    let dt = now - render_start_time;
    state.update(dt);

    match state.render() {
        Ok(_) => {}
        Err(wgpu::SurfaceError::Lost) => state.resize(state.init.size),
        Err(wgpu::SurfaceError::OutOfMemory) => *control_flow = ControlFlow::Exit,
        Err(e) => eprintln!("{:?}", e),
    }
}
Event::MainEventsCleared => {
    window.request_redraw();
}
_ => {}
}
});
}
```

The above code is similar to the one used in previous example. First, we introduce the marching cubes tables from the *marching_cubes_table.rs* file and add several new fields to the State struct, including *resolution*, *index_count*, and other voxel-volcano related parameters. These fields can be easily accessed by different functions without the need to pass them as input.

Within the *State::new* function, as we did in the previous example, we reset certain GPU device limits when creating the device to accommodate higher-resolution voxel volcanos. Subsequently, we reuse the vertex and fragment shaders created earlier in Chapter 5. Additionally, we introduce two compute shader files generated in the previous sections, namely *volcano_value.wgsl* and *volcano_comp.wgsl*.

The code segment for the render pipeline is identical to that used in the implicit-function example, and its code is not listed here. The code for creating the scalar value and heatmap data of the volcano is also similar to that used in the previous example but with a different set of parameters specific to the volcano.

In the *State::update* function, we animate the volcano without the need to regenerate the terrain data and vertex buffers for every frame. Instead, we only need to update the uniform parameters used to calculate the scalar noise value data in the compute shader, as shown in the following code snippet:

```
let dt2 = 10.0*self.animation_speed * dt.as_secs_f32();
let value_float_params = [
    0.0, -dt2, 0.0,        // offset
    self.noise_scale,
    self.noise_height,
    self.height_multiplier,
    self.floor_offset,
    self.noise_scale2,
    self.noise_height2,
    self.height_multiplier2,
    self.floor_offset2,
];
self.init.queue.write_buffer(&self.cs_uniform_buffers[1], 0, cast_slice(&value_float_params));
```

The above code snippet animates the offset of the volcano along the *y* direction, which mimics the volcano eruption upwards.

Additionally, the code permits the user to modify input parameters using keyboard inputs.

Here is a list of controls using keyboard:

- *Q/A*: Increases/decreases the animation speed.

9.5.4 Run Application

To run this application, add the following code snippet to the *Cargo.toml* file:

```
[[example]]
name = "ch09_volcano"
path = "examples/ch09/volcano.rs"
```

Afterward, execute the following *cargo run* commands in the terminal window:

```
cargo run --example ch09_volcano 8
```

Fig.9-5 shows the results of this example.

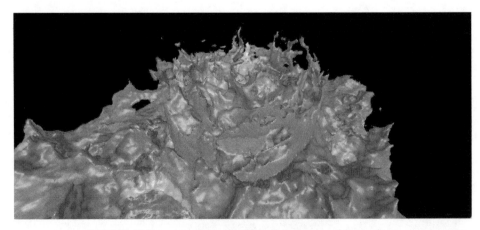

Fig.9-5. Volcano eruption simulated using marching cubes.

9.6 Voxel Minecraft

The voxel Minecraft terrain is a type of terrain generation in Minecraft that uses voxels, or small cubes, to create the landscape. Compared to conventional Minecraft terrain, voxel Minecraft has several advantages. One of the most significant advantages is the ability to create much more detailed and varied landscapes. Voxel Minecraft terrain can create more complex shapes and structures that are difficult or impossible to achieve with conventional terrain generation approaches.

However, voxel terrain also has some disadvantages compared to conventional terrain. One of the disadvantages is performance. Voxel terrain requires more processing power and memory to generate and render than conventional terrain, which can be a significant issue on lower-end hardware.

In this section, we will reuse the compute shaders from the previous voxel-terrain example to create a voxel Minecraft terrain. The compute shader in this example will generate the position and color data used to render the instanced cubes. It is worth noting that since the Minecraft terrain is made up of cubes, we no longer need the indices data to render the surface of the terrain.

9.6.1 Vertex Shader

Create a new WGSL shader file named *minecraft_vert.wgsl* file in the *examples/ch09/* folder and include the following code:

```
// vertex shader
struct Uniforms {
    viewProjectMat: mat4x4f,
    modelMat: mat4x4f,
    normalMat: mat4x4f,
};
@binding(0) @group(0) var<uniform> uniforms: Uniforms;

struct Input {
    @location(0) position: vec4f,
    @location(1) color: vec4f,
    @location(2) boxPosition: vec4f,
    @location(3) boxNormal: vec4f,
}

struct Output {
    @builtin(position) position : vec4f,
    @location(0) vPosition : vec4f,
    @location(1) vNormal : vec4f,
    @location(2) vColor: vec4f,
};

@vertex
fn vs_main(in:Input) -> Output {
    var output: Output;
    let mPosition = uniforms.modelMat * (in.position + in.boxPosition);
    output.vPosition = mPosition;
    output.vNormal =  uniforms.normalMat * in.boxNormal;
    output.position = uniforms.viewProjectMat * mPosition;
    output.vColor = in.color;
    return output;
}
```

This vertex shader takes an input struct *Input* and returns an output struct *Output*. The input struct has four fields: *position*, *color*, *boxPosition*, and *boxNormal*, and the output struct also contains four fields: *position*, *vPosition*, *vNormal*, and *vColor*.

The vertex shader adds the *boxPosition* and *position* fields from the *Input* struct together and stores the result in the *position* variable. The final vertex position is obtained by multiplying by the *position* variable with the model-view-projection matrix, which is stored in the *modelMat* and *viewProjectMat* uniform variables.

9.6.2 Compute Shader for Minecraft

This example can reuse the compute shader for values in the previous voxel-terrain example, but need to implement a compute shader for the Minecraft terrain. To achieve this, create a new WGSL compute shader file named *minecraft_comp.wgsl* in the *examples/ch09/* folder and include the following code:

```
struct Tables {
    edges: array<u32, 256>,
    tris: array<i32, 4096>,
};
@group(0) @binding(0) var<storage> tables : Tables;

struct ValueBuffer{
    values: array<f32>,
};
@group(0) @binding(1) var<storage, read> valueBuffer: ValueBuffer;

struct PositionBuffer {
    values : array<f32>,
};
@group(0) @binding(2) var<storage, read_write> positionsOut : PositionBuffer;

struct ColorBuffer{
    values: array<f32>,
};
@group(0) @binding(3) var<storage, read_write> colorBuffer: ColorBuffer;

struct IndirectParams {
    vc : u32,
    vertexCount : atomic<u32>,
    firstVertex : u32,
};
@group(0) @binding(4) var<storage, read_write> indirect : IndirectParams;

struct IntParams {
    resolution: u32,
};
@group(0) @binding(5) var<uniform> ips : IntParams;

struct FloatParams {
    terrainSize: f32,
    isolevel: f32,
    noiseWeight: f32
};
@group(0) @binding(6) var<uniform> fps : FloatParams;

var<private> vmin: vec3f;
var<private> vmax: vec3f;
```

```
var<private> vstep: vec3f;

fn getIdx(id: vec3u) -> u32 {
    return id.x + ips.resolution * ( id.y + id.z * ips.resolution);
}

fn valueAt(index : vec3u) -> f32 {
    if (any(index > vec3(ips.resolution - 1u, ips.resolution - 1u, ips.resolution - 1u))) { return 0.0; }
    let idx = getIdx(index);
    return valueBuffer.values[idx];
}

fn positionAt(index : vec3u) -> vec3f {
    vmin = vec3(-0.5 * fps.terrainSize);
    vmax = vec3(0.5 * fps.terrainSize);
    vstep = (vmax-vmin)/(f32(ips.resolution) - 1.0);
    return vmin + (vstep * vec3<f32>(index.xyz));
}

var<private> positions : array<vec3f, 12>;
var<private> colors : array<vec3f, 12>;
var<private> cubeVerts : u32 = 0u;

fn interpX(index : u32, i : vec3u, va : f32, vb : f32) {
    let mu = (fps.isolevel - va) / (vb - va);
    positions[cubeVerts] = positionAt(i) + vec3(vstep.x * mu, 0.0, 0.0);
    cubeVerts = cubeVerts + 1u;
}

fn interpY(index : u32, i : vec3u, va : f32, vb : f32) {
    let mu = (fps.isolevel - va) / (vb - va);
    positions[cubeVerts] = positionAt(i) + vec3(0.0, vstep.y * mu, 0.0);
    cubeVerts = cubeVerts + 1u;
}

fn interpZ(index : u32, i : vec3u, va : f32, vb : f32) {
    let mu = (fps.isolevel - va) / (vb - va);
    positions[cubeVerts] = positionAt(i) + vec3(0.0, 0.0, vstep.z * mu);
    cubeVerts = cubeVerts + 1u;
}

fn lerpColor(colors:array<vec3f,5>, ta1:array<f32,6>, t:f32) -> vec3f {
    let len = 6u;
    var res = vec3(0.0);
    var rgb_data = colors;
    var ta = ta1;

    for(var i = 0u; i < len - 1u; i = i + 1u){
        if(t >= ta[i] && t < ta[i + 1u]){
            res = rgb_data[i];
        }
    }
    if(t == ta[len - 1u]){
        res = rgb_data[len - 2u];
    }
    return res;
}

fn addTerrainColors(tmin:f32, tmax:f32, t:f32) -> vec3f {
    let rgb_data = array<vec3f,5>(
```

```
        vec3(0.055, 0.529, 0.8),
        vec3(0.761, 0.698, 0.502),
        vec3(0.204, 0.549, 0.192),
        vec3(0.353, 0.302, 0.255),
        vec3(1.0, 0.98, 0.98)
    );

    let ta = array<f32, 6>(0.0, 0.25, 0.27, 0.33, 0.45, 1.0);
    var tt = t;
    if(t < tmin){tt = tmin;}
    if(t > tmax){tt = tmax;}
    if(tmin == tmax) {return vec3(0.0);}
    tt = (tt - tmin)/(tmax - tmin);

    return lerpColor(rgb_data, ta, tt);
}

@compute @workgroup_size(8, 8, 8)
fn cs_main(@builtin(global_invocation_id) global_id : vec3u) {
    let i0 = global_id;
    let i1 = global_id + vec3(1u, 0u, 0u);
    let i2 = global_id + vec3(1u, 1u, 0u);
    let i3 = global_id + vec3(0u, 1u, 0u);
    let i4 = global_id + vec3(0u, 0u, 1u);
    let i5 = global_id + vec3(1u, 0u, 1u);
    let i6 = global_id + vec3(1u, 1u, 1u);
    let i7 = global_id + vec3(0u, 1u, 1u);

    let v0 = valueAt(i0);
    let v1 = valueAt(i1);
    let v2 = valueAt(i2);
    let v3 = valueAt(i3);
    let v4 = valueAt(i4);
    let v5 = valueAt(i5);
    let v6 = valueAt(i6);
    let v7 = valueAt(i7);

    var cubeIndex = 0u;
    if (v0 < fps.isolevel) { cubeIndex = cubeIndex | 1u; }
    if (v1 < fps.isolevel) { cubeIndex = cubeIndex | 2u; }
    if (v2 < fps.isolevel) { cubeIndex = cubeIndex | 4u; }
    if (v3 < fps.isolevel) { cubeIndex = cubeIndex | 8u; }
    if (v4 < fps.isolevel) { cubeIndex = cubeIndex | 16u; }
    if (v5 < fps.isolevel) { cubeIndex = cubeIndex | 32u; }
    if (v6 < fps.isolevel) { cubeIndex = cubeIndex | 64u; }
    if (v7 < fps.isolevel) { cubeIndex = cubeIndex | 128u; }

    let edges = tables.edges[cubeIndex];
    if ((edges & 1u) != 0u) { interpX(0u, i0, v0, v1); }
    if ((edges & 2u) != 0u) { interpY(1u, i1, v1, v2); }
    if ((edges & 4u) != 0u) { interpX(2u, i3, v3, v2); }
    if ((edges & 8u) != 0u) { interpY(3u, i0, v0, v3); }
    if ((edges & 16u) != 0u) { interpX(4u, i4, v4, v5); }
    if ((edges & 32u) != 0u) { interpY(5u, i5, v5, v6); }
    if ((edges & 64u) != 0u) { interpX(6u, i7, v7, v6); }
    if ((edges & 128u) != 0u) { interpY(7u, i4, v4, v7); }
    if ((edges & 256u) != 0u) { interpZ(8u, i0, v0, v4); }
    if ((edges & 512u) != 0u) { interpZ(9u, i1, v1, v5); }
    if ((edges & 1024u) != 0u) { interpZ(10u, i2, v2, v6); }
    if ((edges & 2048u) != 0u) { interpZ(11u, i3, v3, v7); }
```

```
let triTableOffset = (cubeIndex << 4u) + 1u;
//let indexCount = u32(tables.tris[triTableOffset - 1u]);
var firstVertex = atomicAdd(&indirect.vertexCount, cubeVerts);
let bufferOffset = getIdx(global_id);
//let firstIndex = bufferOffset * 15u;

for (var i = 0u; i < cubeVerts; i = i + 1u) {
    var y = (positions[i].y - vmin.y)/(vmax.y - vmin.y);
    if(y <= 0.25) {
        y = 0.25 - 0.00000001;
        positions[i].y = vmin.y + y * (vmax.y - vmin.y);
    }
    positionsOut.values[firstVertex*4u + i*4u] = positions[i].x;
    positionsOut.values[firstVertex*4u + i*4u + 1u] = positions[i].y;
    positionsOut.values[firstVertex*4u + i*4u + 2u] = positions[i].z;
    positionsOut.values[firstVertex*4u + i*4u + 3u] = 1.0;

    let color = addTerrainColors(vmin.y, vmax.y, positions[i].y);
    colorBuffer.values[firstVertex * 4u + i * 4u] = color.x;
    colorBuffer.values[firstVertex * 4u + i * 4u + 1u] = color.y;
    colorBuffer.values[firstVertex * 4u + i * 4u + 2u] = color.z;
    colorBuffer.values[firstVertex * 4u + i * 4u + 3u] = 1.0;
}
}
```

The code is structurally similar to that used in the previous voxel-terrain example, except that this example does not need to calculate the indices and normal data for the terrain because the Minecraft terrain is made up of cubes, we no longer need the indices and normal data to render the surface of the terrain. Instead, we only need to use the indices and normals data for the cube to render multiple instances of the cube. For this reason, we remove the code related to the calculation of the indices and normal data from the above code.

9.6.3 Rust Code

Create a new Rust file named *minecraft_comp.rs* in the *examples/ch09/* folder and add the following code to it:

```rust
use std::{iter, f32::consts::PI};
use cgmath::{ Matrix, Matrix4, SquareMatrix };
use wgpu::{ VertexBufferLayout, util::DeviceExt};
use winit::{
    event::*,
    event_loop::{ControlFlow, EventLoop},
    window::Window,
};
use bytemuck:: {Pod, Zeroable, cast_slice};
use wgpu_book_examples::{ wgpu_simplified as ws, transforms as wt, vertex_data as vd };
mod marching_cubes_table;

#[repr(C)]
#[derive(Copy, Clone, Debug, Pod, Zeroable)]
struct Vertex {
    position: [f32; 4],
    normal: [f32; 4],
}

fn cube_vertices(side: f32) -> (Vec<Vertex>, Vec<u16>) {
```

```rust
    let(pos, _, norm, _, ind, _) = vd::create_cube_data(side);
    let mut data:Vec<Vertex> = Vec::with_capacity(pos.len());
    for i in 0..pos.len() {
        data.push(Vertex{
            position: [pos[i][0], pos[i][1], pos[i][2], 1.0],
            normal: [norm[i][0], norm[i][1], norm[i][2], 1.0],
        });
    }
    (data.to_vec(), ind)
}

struct State {
    init:  ws::IWgpuInit,
    pipeline: wgpu::RenderPipeline,
    vertex_buffer: wgpu::Buffer,
    index_buffer: wgpu::Buffer,
    uniform_bind_groups: Vec<wgpu::BindGroup>,
    uniform_buffers: Vec<wgpu::Buffer>,
    indices_len: u32,

    cs_pipelines: Vec<wgpu::ComputePipeline>,
    cs_vertex_buffers: Vec<wgpu::Buffer>,
    cs_uniform_buffers: Vec<wgpu::Buffer>,
    cs_bind_groups: Vec<wgpu::BindGroup>,

    view_mat: Matrix4<f32>,
    project_mat: Matrix4<f32>,
    msaa_texture_view: wgpu::TextureView,
    depth_texture_view: wgpu::TextureView,
    animation_speed: f32,
    animation_direction: u32,

    resolution: u32,
    marching_cube_cells: u32,
    octaves: u32,
    seed: u32,
    isolevel: f32,
    terrain_size: f32,
    lacunarity: f32,
    persistence: f32,
    noise_scale: f32,
    noise_height: f32,
    height_multiplier: f32,
    floor_offset: f32,
    cube_side: f32,
    data_changed: bool,
}

impl State {
    async fn new(window:&Window, sample_count:u32, resolution:u32) -> Self {
        let limits = wgpu::Limits {
            max_storage_buffer_binding_size: 1024*1024*1024, //1024MB, defaulting to 128MB
            max_buffer_size: 1024*1024*1024, // 1024MB, defaulting to 256MB
            max_compute_invocations_per_workgroup: 512, // dafaulting to 256
            ..Default::default()
        };
        let init = ws::IWgpuInit::new(&window, sample_count, Some(limits)).await;

        let resol = ws::round_to_multiple(resolution, 8);
        let marching_cube_cells = (resolution - 1) * (resolution - 1) * (resolution - 1);
```

```rust
let vertex_count = 3 * 12 * marching_cube_cells;
let vertex_buffer_size = 4 * vertex_count;
println!("resolution = {}", resol);

let vs_shader = init.device.create_shader_module(wgpu::include_wgsl!("minecraft_vert.wgsl"));
let fs_shader = init.device.create_shader_module(wgpu::include_wgsl!("../ch05/shader_frag.wgsl"));

let cs_value_file = include_str!("voxel_value.wgsl");
let cs_noise_file = include_str!("noise3d.wgsl");
let cs_value = init.device.create_shader_module(wgpu::ShaderModuleDescriptor {
    label: Some("Compute Value Shader"),
    source: wgpu::ShaderSource::Wgsl([cs_noise_file, cs_value_file].join("\n").into()),
});

let cs_comp = init.device.create_shader_module(wgpu::include_wgsl!("minecraft_comp.wgsl"));

// uniform data
let camera_position = (12.0, 12.0, 12.0).into();
let look_direction = (0.0,0.0,0.0).into();
let up_direction = cgmath::Vector3::unit_y();
let light_direction = [-0.5f32, -0.5, -0.5];

let (view_mat, project_mat, vp_mat) =
    wt::create_vp_mat(camera_position, look_direction, up_direction,
    init.config.width as f32 / init.config.height as f32);

let model_mat = wt::create_model_mat([0.0, 5.0, 0.0], [0.0, 0.1*PI, 0.0], [1.7, 1.7, 1.7]);
let normal_mat = (model_mat.invert().unwrap()).transpose();

// create vertex uniform buffers
let vert_uniform_buffer = init.device.create_buffer(&wgpu::BufferDescriptor{
    label: Some("Vertex Uniform Buffer"),
    size: 192,
    usage: wgpu::BufferUsages::UNIFORM | wgpu::BufferUsages::COPY_DST,
    mapped_at_creation: false,
});
init.queue.write_buffer(&vert_uniform_buffer, 0, cast_slice(vp_mat.as_ref() as &[f32; 16]));
init.queue.write_buffer(&vert_uniform_buffer, 64, cast_slice(model_mat.as_ref() as &[f32; 16]));
init.queue.write_buffer(&vert_uniform_buffer, 128, cast_slice(normal_mat.as_ref() as &[f32; 16]));

// create light uniform buffer. here we set eye_position = camera_position
let light_uniform_buffer = init.device.create_buffer(&wgpu::BufferDescriptor{
    label: Some("Light Uniform Buffer"),
    size: 48,
    usage: wgpu::BufferUsages::UNIFORM | wgpu::BufferUsages::COPY_DST,
    mapped_at_creation: false,
});
let eye_position:&[f32; 3] = camera_position.as_ref();
init.queue.write_buffer(&light_uniform_buffer, 0, cast_slice(light_direction.as_ref()));
init.queue.write_buffer(&light_uniform_buffer, 16, cast_slice(eye_position));

// set specular light color to white
let specular_color:[f32; 3] = [1.0, 1.0, 1.0];
init.queue.write_buffer(&light_uniform_buffer, 32, cast_slice(specular_color.as_ref()));

// material uniform buffer
let material_uniform_buffer = init.device.create_buffer(&wgpu::BufferDescriptor{
    label: Some("Material Uniform Buffer"),
    size: 16,
```

```
        usage: wgpu::BufferUsages::UNIFORM | wgpu::BufferUsages::COPY_DST,
        mapped_at_creation: false,
    });

    // set default material parameters
    let material = [0.1f32, 0.7, 0.4, 30.0];
    init.queue.write_buffer(&material_uniform_buffer, 0, cast_slice(material.as_ref()));

    // uniform bind group for vertex shader
    let (vert_bind_group_layout, vert_bind_group) = ws::create_bind_group(
        &init.device,
        vec![wgpu::ShaderStages::VERTEX],
        &[vert_uniform_buffer.as_entire_binding()],
    );

    // uniform bind group for fragment shader
    let (frag_bind_group_layout, frag_bind_group) = ws::create_bind_group(
        &init.device,
        vec![wgpu::ShaderStages::FRAGMENT, wgpu::ShaderStages::FRAGMENT],
        &[light_uniform_buffer.as_entire_binding(), material_uniform_buffer.as_entire_binding()],
    );

    let vertex_buffer_layouts = [
        VertexBufferLayout {
            array_stride: 16,
            step_mode: wgpu::VertexStepMode::Instance,
            attributes: &wgpu::vertex_attr_array![0 => Float32x4], // instance position
        },
        VertexBufferLayout {
            array_stride: 16,
            step_mode: wgpu::VertexStepMode::Instance,
            attributes: &wgpu::vertex_attr_array![1 => Float32x4], // instance color
        },
        VertexBufferLayout {
            array_stride: 32,
            step_mode: wgpu::VertexStepMode::Vertex,
            attributes: &wgpu::vertex_attr_array![2=>Float32x4,3 =>Float32x4], // pos, norm for cube
        },
    ];

    let pipeline_layout = init.device.create_pipeline_layout(&wgpu::PipelineLayoutDescriptor {
        label: Some("Render Pipeline Layout"),
        bind_group_layouts: &[&vert_bind_group_layout, &frag_bind_group_layout],
        push_constant_ranges: &[],
    });

    let mut ppl = ws::IRenderPipeline {
        vs_shader: Some(&vs_shader),
        fs_shader: Some(&fs_shader),
        pipeline_layout: Some(&pipeline_layout),
        vertex_buffer_layout: &vertex_buffer_layouts,
        ..Default::default()
    };
    let pipeline = ppl.new(&init);
    let msaa_texture_view = ws::create_msaa_texture_view(&init);
    let depth_texture_view = ws::create_depth_view(&init);

    // create vertex and index buffers for cube
    let (cube_vertex_data, cube_index_data) = cube_vertices(0.5);
    let cube_vertex_buffer = init.device.create_buffer_init(&wgpu::util::BufferInitDescriptor {
```

```
        label: Some("Cube Vertex Buffer"),
        contents: cast_slice(&cube_vertex_data),
        usage: wgpu::BufferUsages::VERTEX | wgpu::BufferUsages::COPY_DST,
    });

    let cube_index_buffer = init.device.create_buffer_init(&wgpu::util::BufferInitDescriptor{
        label: Some("Cube Index Buffer"),
        contents: cast_slice(&cube_index_data),
        usage: wgpu::BufferUsages::INDEX,
    });

    // create compute pipeline for value
    let volume_elements = resol * resol * resol;
    let cs_value_buffer = init.device.create_buffer(&wgpu::BufferDescriptor{
        label: Some("Compuet Value Buffer"),
        size:  4 * volume_elements as u64,
        usage: wgpu::BufferUsages::STORAGE | wgpu::BufferUsages::COPY_DST,
        mapped_at_creation: false,
    });

    let cs_value_int_buffer = init.device.create_buffer(&wgpu::BufferDescriptor{
        label: Some("Compuet Value Integer Uniform Buffer"),
        size:  16,
        usage: wgpu::BufferUsages::UNIFORM | wgpu::BufferUsages::COPY_DST,
        mapped_at_creation: false,
    });

    let cs_value_float_buffer = init.device.create_buffer(&wgpu::BufferDescriptor{
        label: Some("Compuet Value Float Uniform Buffer"),
        size:  48,
        usage: wgpu::BufferUsages::UNIFORM | wgpu::BufferUsages::COPY_DST,
        mapped_at_creation: false,
    });

    let (cs_value_bind_group_layout, cs_value_bind_group) = ws::create_bind_group_storage(
        &init.device,
        vec![
            wgpu::ShaderStages::COMPUTE, wgpu::ShaderStages::COMPUTE,
            wgpu::ShaderStages::COMPUTE,
        ],
        vec![
            wgpu::BufferBindingType::Storage { read_only: false },
            wgpu::BufferBindingType::Uniform,
            wgpu::BufferBindingType::Uniform,
        ],
        &[
            cs_value_buffer.as_entire_binding(),
            cs_value_int_buffer.as_entire_binding(),
            cs_value_float_buffer.as_entire_binding(),
        ],
    );

    let cs_value_pipeline_layout = init.device.create_pipeline_layout(&wgpu::PipelineLayoutDescriptor{
        label: Some("Compute Value Pipeline Layout"),
        bind_group_layouts: &[&cs_value_bind_group_layout],
        push_constant_ranges: &[],
    });

    let cs_value_pipeline = init.device.create_compute_pipeline(&wgpu::ComputePipelineDescriptor{
        label: Some("Compute Value Pipeline"),
```

```
            layout: Some(&cs_value_pipeline_layout),
            module: &cs_value,
            entry_point: "cs_main",
    });

    // create compute pipeline for implicit surface
    let cs_table_buffer = init.device.create_buffer(&wgpu::BufferDescriptor{
        label: Some("Compute Table STorage Buffer"),
        size:  (marching_cubes_table::EDGE_TABLE.len() + marching_cubes_table::TRI_TABLE.len())
            as u64 * 4,
        usage: wgpu::BufferUsages::STORAGE | wgpu::BufferUsages::COPY_DST,
        mapped_at_creation: false,
    });
    init.queue.write_buffer(&cs_table_buffer, 0, cast_slice(marching_cubes_table::EDGE_TABLE));
    init.queue.write_buffer(&cs_table_buffer, marching_cubes_table::EDGE_TABLE.len() as u64 * 4,
        cast_slice(marching_cubes_table::TRI_TABLE));

    let cs_position_buffer = init.device.create_buffer(&wgpu::BufferDescriptor{
        label: Some("Compute Position Buffer"),
        size:  vertex_buffer_size as u64,
        usage: wgpu::BufferUsages::VERTEX | wgpu::BufferUsages::STORAGE |
            wgpu::BufferUsages::COPY_DST,
        mapped_at_creation: false,
    });

    let cs_color_buffer = init.device.create_buffer(&wgpu::BufferDescriptor{
        label: Some("Compute Color Buffer"),
        size:  vertex_buffer_size as u64,
        usage: wgpu::BufferUsages::VERTEX | wgpu::BufferUsages::STORAGE |
            wgpu::BufferUsages::COPY_DST,
        mapped_at_creation: false,
    });

    let cs_indirect_buffer = init.device.create_buffer(&wgpu::BufferDescriptor{
        label: Some("Compute Indirect Buffer"),
        size:  16,
        usage: wgpu::BufferUsages::INDIRECT | wgpu::BufferUsages::STORAGE |
            wgpu::BufferUsages::COPY_DST,
        mapped_at_creation: false,
    });

    let cs_int_buffer = init.device.create_buffer(&wgpu::BufferDescriptor{
        label: Some("Compute Integer uniform Buffer"),
        size:  16,
        usage: wgpu::BufferUsages::UNIFORM | wgpu::BufferUsages::COPY_DST,
        mapped_at_creation: false,
    });

    let cs_float_buffer = init.device.create_buffer(&wgpu::BufferDescriptor{
        label: Some("Compute Float uniform Buffer"),
        size:  16,
        usage: wgpu::BufferUsages::UNIFORM | wgpu::BufferUsages::COPY_DST,
        mapped_at_creation: false,
    });

    let (cs_bind_group_layout, cs_bind_group) = ws::create_bind_group_storage(
        &init.device,
        vec![
            wgpu::ShaderStages::COMPUTE, wgpu::ShaderStages::COMPUTE, wgpu::ShaderStages::COMPUTE,
            wgpu::ShaderStages::COMPUTE, wgpu::ShaderStages::COMPUTE, wgpu::ShaderStages::COMPUTE,
```

```
            wgpu::ShaderStages::COMPUTE,
        ],
        vec![
            wgpu::BufferBindingType::Storage { read_only: true },    // marching table
            wgpu::BufferBindingType::Storage { read_only: true },    // value buffer
            wgpu::BufferBindingType::Storage { read_only: false },   // position
            wgpu::BufferBindingType::Storage { read_only: false },   // color
            wgpu::BufferBindingType::Storage { read_only: false },   // indirect params
            wgpu::BufferBindingType::Uniform,                        // int params
            wgpu::BufferBindingType::Uniform,                        // float params
        ],
        &[
            cs_table_buffer.as_entire_binding(),
            cs_value_buffer.as_entire_binding(),
            cs_position_buffer.as_entire_binding(),
            cs_color_buffer.as_entire_binding(),
            cs_indirect_buffer.as_entire_binding(),
            cs_int_buffer.as_entire_binding(),
            cs_float_buffer.as_entire_binding(),
        ],
    );

let cs_pipeline_layout = init.device.create_pipeline_layout(&wgpu::PipelineLayoutDescriptor{
    label: Some("Compute Pipeline Layout"),
    bind_group_layouts: &[&cs_bind_group_layout],
    push_constant_ranges: &[],
});

let cs_pipeline = init.device.create_compute_pipeline(&wgpu::ComputePipelineDescriptor{
    label: Some("Compute Pipeline"),
    layout: Some(&cs_pipeline_layout),
    module: &cs_comp,
    entry_point: "cs_main",
});

Self {
    init,
    pipeline,
    vertex_buffer: cube_vertex_buffer,
    index_buffer: cube_index_buffer,
    uniform_bind_groups: vec![vert_bind_group, frag_bind_group],
    uniform_buffers: vec![vert_uniform_buffer, light_uniform_buffer, material_uniform_buffer],
    indices_len: cube_index_data.len() as u32,

    cs_pipelines: vec![cs_value_pipeline, cs_pipeline],
    cs_vertex_buffers: vec![cs_value_buffer, cs_position_buffer, cs_color_buffer],
    cs_uniform_buffers: vec![cs_value_int_buffer, cs_value_float_buffer, cs_int_buffer,
        cs_float_buffer, cs_indirect_buffer],
    cs_bind_groups: vec![cs_value_bind_group, cs_bind_group],

    view_mat,
    project_mat,
    msaa_texture_view,
    depth_texture_view,
    animation_speed: 1.0,
    animation_direction: 2,

    resolution: resol,
    marching_cube_cells,
    octaves: 10,
```

```
                seed: 1232,
                isolevel: 3.0,
                terrain_size: 40.0,
                lacunarity: 2.0,
                persistence: 0.5,
                noise_scale: 5.0,
                noise_height: 7.0,
                height_multiplier: 1.5,
                floor_offset: 10.0,
                cube_side: 0.5,
                data_changed: false,
            }
    }

    fn resize(&mut self, new_size: winit::dpi::PhysicalSize<u32>) {
        if new_size.width > 0 && new_size.height > 0 {
            self.init.size = new_size;
            self.init.config.width = new_size.width;
            self.init.config.height = new_size.height;
            self.init.surface.configure(&self.init.device, &self.init.config);

            self.project_mat = wt::create_projection_mat(new_size.width as f32 / new_size.height as f32,
                true);
            let vp_mat = self.project_mat * self.view_mat;
            self.init.queue.write_buffer(&self.uniform_buffers[0], 0,
                cast_slice(vp_mat.as_ref() as &[f32; 16]));

            self.depth_texture_view = ws::create_depth_view(&self.init);
            if self.init.sample_count > 1 {
                self.msaa_texture_view = ws::create_msaa_texture_view(&self.init);
            }
        }
    }

    #[allow(unused_variables)]
    fn input(&mut self, event: &WindowEvent) -> bool {
        match event {
            WindowEvent::KeyboardInput {
                input:
                    KeyboardInput {
                        virtual_keycode: Some(keycode),
                        state: ElementState::Pressed,
                        ..
                    },
                ..
            } => {
                match keycode {
                    VirtualKeyCode::Space => {
                        self.animation_direction = (self.animation_direction + 1) % 3;

                        true
                    },
                    VirtualKeyCode::Q => {
                        self.cube_side += 0.02;
                        self.data_changed = true;
                        println!("cube size = {}", self.cube_side);
                        true
                    },
                    VirtualKeyCode::A => {
                        self.cube_side -= 0.02;
```

```
                    self.data_changed = true;
                    if self.cube_side < 0.1 {
                        self.cube_side = 0.1;
                    }
                    println!("cube size = {}", self.cube_side);
                    true
                },
                VirtualKeyCode::W => {
                    self.animation_speed += 0.1;
                    true
                },
                VirtualKeyCode::S => {
                    self.animation_speed -= 0.1;
                    if self.animation_speed < 0.0 {
                        self.animation_speed = 0.0;
                    }
                    true
                },
                _ => false
            }
        }
        _ => false,
    }
}

fn update(&mut self, dt: std::time::Duration) {
    // update compute buffers for value
    let value_int_params = [self.resolution, self.octaves, self.seed, 0];
    self.init.queue.write_buffer(&self.cs_uniform_buffers[0], 0, cast_slice(&value_int_params));

    let dt1 = 10.0 * self.animation_speed * dt.as_secs_f32();
    let value_float_params = [
        if self.animation_direction == 0 { -dt1 } else { 0.0 },
        if self.animation_direction == 1 { -dt1 } else { 0.0 },
        if self.animation_direction == 2 { -dt1 } else { 0.0 },
        self.terrain_size,
        self.lacunarity,
        self.persistence,
        self.noise_scale,
        self.noise_height,
        self.height_multiplier,
        self.floor_offset,
    ];
    self.init.queue.write_buffer(&self.cs_uniform_buffers[1], 0, cast_slice(&value_float_params));

    // update compute buffers for terrain
    let int_params = [self.resolution, 0, 0, 0];
    self.init.queue.write_buffer(&self.cs_uniform_buffers[2], 0, cast_slice(&int_params));

    let float_params = [self.terrain_size, self.isolevel, 0.0, 0.0];
    self.init.queue.write_buffer(&self.cs_uniform_buffers[3], 0, cast_slice(&float_params));

    let indirect_array = [500u32, 0, 0, 0];
    self.init.queue.write_buffer(&self.cs_uniform_buffers[4], 0, cast_slice(&indirect_array));

    if self.data_changed {
        let (cube_vertex_data, _) = cube_vertices(self.cube_side);
        self.init.queue.write_buffer(&&self.vertex_buffer, 0, cast_slice(&cube_vertex_data));
        self.data_changed = false;
    }
```

```rust
    }

    fn render(&mut self) -> Result<(), wgpu::SurfaceError> {
        let output = self.init.surface.get_current_texture()?;
        let view = output
            .texture
            .create_view(&wgpu::TextureViewDescriptor::default());

        let mut encoder = self
            .init.device
            .create_command_encoder(&wgpu::CommandEncoderDescriptor {
                label: Some("Render Encoder"),
            });

        // compute pass for value
        {
            let mut cs_index_pass = encoder.begin_compute_pass(&wgpu::ComputePassDescriptor{
                label: Some("Compute value Pass"),
                timestamp_writes: None,
            });
            cs_index_pass.set_pipeline(&self.cs_pipelines[0]);
            cs_index_pass.set_bind_group(0, &self.cs_bind_groups[0], &[]);
            cs_index_pass.dispatch_workgroups(self.resolution/8, self.resolution/8, self.resolution/8);
        }

        // compute pass for vertices
        {
            let mut cs_pass = encoder.begin_compute_pass(&wgpu::ComputePassDescriptor{
                label: Some("Compute Pass"),
                timestamp_writes: None,
            });
            cs_pass.set_pipeline(&self.cs_pipelines[1]);
            cs_pass.set_bind_group(0, &self.cs_bind_groups[1], &[]);
            cs_pass.dispatch_workgroups(self.resolution/8, self.resolution/8, self.resolution/8);
        }

        // render pass
        {
            let color_attach = ws::create_color_attachment(&view);
            let msaa_attach = ws::create_msaa_color_attachment(&view, &self.msaa_texture_view);
            let color_attachment = if self.init.sample_count == 1 { color_attach } else { msaa_attach };
            let depth_attachment = ws::create_depth_stencil_attachment(&self.depth_texture_view);

            let mut render_pass = encoder.begin_render_pass(&wgpu::RenderPassDescriptor {
                label: Some("Render Pass"),
                color_attachments: &[Some(color_attachment)],
                depth_stencil_attachment: Some(depth_attachment),
                timestamp_writes: None,
                occlusion_query_set: None,
            });

            render_pass.set_pipeline(&self.pipeline);
            render_pass.set_vertex_buffer(0, self.cs_vertex_buffers[1].slice(..));
            render_pass.set_vertex_buffer(1, self.cs_vertex_buffers[2].slice(..));
            render_pass.set_vertex_buffer(2, self.vertex_buffer.slice(..));
            render_pass.set_index_buffer(self.index_buffer.slice(..), wgpu::IndexFormat::Uint16);
            render_pass.set_bind_group(0, &self.uniform_bind_groups[0], &[]);
            render_pass.set_bind_group(1, &self.uniform_bind_groups[1], &[]);
            render_pass.draw_indexed(0..self.indices_len, 0, 0..self.marching_cube_cells);
```

```
        }

        self.init.queue.submit(iter::once(encoder.finish()));
        output.present();

        Ok(())
    }
}

fn main() {
    let mut sample_count = 1u32;
    let mut resolution = 64u32;

    let args: Vec<String> = std::env::args().collect();
    if args.len() > 1 {
        sample_count = args[1].parse::<u32>().unwrap();
    }
    if args.len() > 2 {
        resolution = args[2].parse::<u32>().unwrap();
    }

    env_logger::init();
    let event_loop = EventLoop::new();
    let window = winit::window::WindowBuilder::new().build(&event_loop).unwrap();
    window.set_title(&*format!("ch09_{}", "minecraft"));

    let mut state = pollster::block_on(State::new(&window, sample_count, resolution));
    let render_start_time = std::time::Instant::now();

    event_loop.run(move |event, _, control_flow| {
        match event {
            Event::WindowEvent {
                ref event,
                window_id,
            } if window_id == window.id() => {
                if !state.input(event) {
                    match event {
                        WindowEvent::CloseRequested
                        | WindowEvent::KeyboardInput {
                            input:
                                KeyboardInput {
                                    state: ElementState::Pressed,
                                    virtual_keycode: Some(VirtualKeyCode::Escape),
                                    ..
                                },
                            ..
                        } => *control_flow = ControlFlow::Exit,
                        WindowEvent::Resized(physical_size) => {
                            state.resize(*physical_size);
                        }
                        WindowEvent::ScaleFactorChanged { new_inner_size, .. } => {
                            state.resize(**new_inner_size);
                        }
                        _ => {}
                    }
                }
            }
            Event::RedrawRequested(_) => {
                let now = std::time::Instant::now();
                let dt = now - render_start_time;
```

```
            state.update(dt);

            match state.render() {
                Ok(_) => {}
                Err(wgpu::SurfaceError::Lost) => state.resize(state.init.size),
                Err(wgpu::SurfaceError::OutOfMemory) => *control_flow = ControlFlow::Exit,
                Err(e) => eprintln!("{:?}", e),
            }
        }
        Event::MainEventsCleared => {
            window.request_redraw();
        }
        _ => {}
    }
});
}
```

It is worth noting that the above code introduces *vertex_data* module. This is because rendering voxel Minecraft terrains requires the cube data from the *vertex_data.rs* file to be used in the shader code.

The code above is similar to the one used in previous example. First, we introduce the marching cubes tables from the *marching_cubes_table.rs* file and add several new fields to the State struct, including *resolution*, *index_count*, and other parameters related to voxel Minecraft terrains. These fields can be easily accessed by different functions without the need to pass them as input.

In the *State::new* function, we use the following code snippet to define the vertex buffer layout:

```
let vertex_buffer_layouts = [
    VertexBufferLayout {
        array_stride: 16,
        step_mode: wgpu::VertexStepMode::Instance,
        attributes: &wgpu::vertex_attr_array![0 => Float32x4], // instance position
    },
    VertexBufferLayout {
        array_stride: 16,
        step_mode: wgpu::VertexStepMode::Instance,
        attributes: &wgpu::vertex_attr_array![1 => Float32x4], // instance color
    },
    VertexBufferLayout {
        array_stride: 32,
        step_mode: wgpu::VertexStepMode::Vertex,
        attributes: &wgpu::vertex_attr_array![2 => Float32x4, 3 => Float32x4], // pos, norm for cube
    },
];
```

This is different from the previous example, where the vertex buffer layout contained only one step mode: *Vertex*. In this example, both the *Vertex* and *Instance* step modes are involved. The above code snippet first defines the location and color of each cube instance in the "*instance*" step mode using the noise heightmap data generated from the compute shader and then specifies the vertex positions and normals of the cube in the "*vertex*" step mode using the cube data generated in Rust. It then uses this vertex buffer layout to create the render pipeline.

Additionally, the *State::new* function also defines the vertex and index buffers for the cube using the cube data. This differs from the previous voxel-terrain example where all vertex and index data were generated using compute shaders.

The code segment for the compute pipeline used to create a scalar value is identical to the voxel-terrain example because they use the same value compute shader. However, the code block for the compute pipeline used to generate the noise heightmap data for voxel Minecraft terrains is slightly modified compared to the previous example. Specifically, we do not need to create the normal and index buffers, so the corresponding code is removed.

Within the *State::render* function, the code for the compute pass is the same as in the previous example, while the code for the render pass is different. Instead of rendering triangles for the surface of the terrain, this example uses instanced drawing to render multiple instances of the cube, with the number of instances being equal to the number of marching cube cells.

In the *State::update* function, we animate the voxel Minecraft terrain without the need to regenerate the terrain data and vertex buffers for every frame. Instead, we only need to update the uniform parameters used to calculate the scalar noise value data in the compute shader, as shown in the following code snippet:

```
let dt1 = 10.0 * self.animation_speed * dt.as_secs_f32();
let value_float_params = [
    if self.animation_direction == 0 { -dt1 } else { 0.0 },
    if self.animation_direction == 1 { -dt1 } else { 0.0 },
    if self.animation_direction == 2 { -dt1 } else { 0.0 },
    self.terrain_size,
    self.lacunarity,
    self.persistence,
    self.noise_scale,
    self.noise_height,
    self.height_multiplier,
    self.floor_offset,
];
self.init.queue.write_buffer(&self.cs_uniform_buffers[1], 0, cast_slice(&value_float_params));
```

The above code snippet allows the user to select animation direction, with the default being the *z* direction.

Additionally, the code permits the user to modify input parameters using keyboard inputs.

Here is a list of controls using keyboard:

- *Space*: Changes the animation direction.
- *Q/A*: Increases/decreases the cube side.
- *W/S*: Increases/decreases the animation speed.

9.6.4 Run Application

To run this application, add the following code snippet to the *Cargo.toml* file:

```
[[example]]
name = "ch09_minecraft"
path = "examples/ch09/minecraft.rs"
```

Afterward, execute the following *cargo run* commands in the terminal window:

```
cargo run --example ch09_minecraft 8
```

Fig.9-6 shows the results of this example.

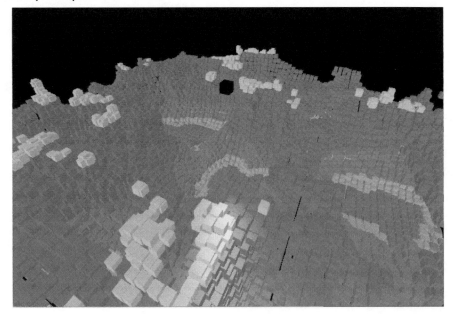

Fig.9-6. Voxel Minecraft terrain generated using marching cubes.

10 Visualizing Complex Functions

Complex numbers, complex functions, and complex analysis are part of an important branch of mathematics. They find wide applications in solving real-world scientific and engineering problems. For any complex function, the values z and their function $f(z)$ from the complex domain may be separated into real and imaginary parts:

$$z = x + iy$$

$$f(z) = f(x + iy) = u(x, y) + iv(x, y)$$

Where x, y, $u(x, y)$, and $v(x, y)$ are all real-valued.

There are several ways to visualize complex functions, including 3D surface plots and domain coloring. Unlike the 3D surface plots for real functions where the y values are color-mapped, the 3D plots for a complex function usually uses colors to represent the angle or argument of the function output. This is because the argument of a complex function represents its direction or orientation in the complex plane, and colors can be used to represent direction in a visually intuitive way. This can provide a useful visual representation of the function's behavior and make it easier to analyze and interpret.

Domain coloring is another visualization method for complex functions that uses color to represent the function's value at each point in the complex plane. In domain coloring, the complex plane is divided into a grid of points, and the color at each point is determined by mapping the complex number at that point to a color in the RGB color space. The hue of the color corresponds to the argument or phase of the complex number, while the saturation and brightness correspond to the magnitude of the complex number.

In this chapter, you will learn how to create 3D surface plots and domain coloring in *wgpu* for various complex functions. We will create 3D surface plots on both the CPU and GPU and compare the performance of these two approaches. While domain coloring is a computation-intensive process because it requires evaluating the function at a large number of points in the complex plane and then mapping each point to a color in the color space, we will use compute shader to accelerate the computation of domain coloring by offloading the computation from the CPU to the GPU. This can greatly improve the performance of the visualization, allowing it to be computed in real-time, even for very large grids in the complex plane.

10.1 Surface Plots on CPU

In this section, I will explain how to create a 3D surface plot for complex functions. A complex function can return several values, including real part (*re*), imaginary part (*im*), magnitude (*abs*), and angle (also called phase or argument). We will plot those values over a complex plan to create a 3D surface plot. Instead of color mapping their values directly, as we did for 3D surfaces for real functions, here we will color the plot using the value of the argument (angle or phase). Thus, the surface plot for the real part, imaginary part, or magnitude of a complex function shows not only the respective values but also corresponding phase information.

10.1.1 Complex Numbers in Rust

Unlike the real functions, there is no built-in functions for complex numbers in Rust. This example will use a crate called *num-complex*, which is a Rust library to work with complex number arithmetic. We need to install this package using the following command:

```
cargo install num-complex
```

This library implements various built-in functions such as arithmetic operations and trigonometric functions. A complex number is an expression of the $a + ib$, where a and b are real numbers and i represents the imaginary number defined as $i = \sqrt{-1}$. The real number a is called the real part of the complex number, and b is the imaginary part.

In the *num-complex* crate, a complex number is created using *Complex* instance. This instance accepts two numbers, representing the real and imaginary parts of the value. Most functions support complex numbers, and complex and real numbers can be used together. The following are some examples using the *num-complex* library:

```
use num-complex::{Complex, ComplexFloat};

const c1 = new Complex::new(2., 3.);        // 2 + 3i
const c2 = new Complex::new(4., 2.);        // 4 - 2i

let re = c1.re;                    // returns real part: number 2
let im = c1.im;                    // returns imaginary part: number 3
let conj = c1.conjugate();         // returns conjugate: 2 - 3i

let add = c1.add(c2);              // 6 + i
let mul = c1.mul(c2);              // 14 + 8i
let div = c1/c2;                   // 0.1 + 0.8i
```

There is an *fdiv* method in the *num-complex* crate, which can also be used for complex division. The *fdiv* method, based on floating-point operations, is more accurate than the above generic division in case where the *denominator.norm_sqrt()* would overflow to infinity or underflow to zero.

```
let div2 = c1.fdiv(c2);
```

Which gives the following result:

```
0.09999999999999998+0.7999999999999999i
```

This result is similar to the generic division but expressed using 64-bit floating-point number.

A classical use case for complex numbers is solving quadratic equations $az^2 + bz + c = 0$, where $z = x + iy$ and a, b, c are real constants, as illustrated in the following code snippet:

```
fn solve_quadratic(a:f64, b:f64, c:f64) -> (Complex<f64>, Complex<f64>) {
    let sqrt = Complex::new(b * b - 4.0 * a * c, 0.0).sqrt();
    let solution1 = (-b + sqrt) / (2.0 * a);
    let solution2 = (-b - sqrt) / (2.0 * a);
    (solution1, solution2)
}

let solution = solve_quadratic(1., 4., 5.); // -2 + i and -2 - i
```

The *num-complex* library also contains properties, functions, and constants that allow you to perform various mathematical operations on complex numbers.

10.1.2 Surface Data

To create a 3D plot for a complex function, we need to generate the vertex data, including position, color, and index data. For the sake of the simplicity, this example will use an unlit shader, meaning that we do not need to generate the normal data. Create a new Rust file named *complex3d_data.rs* in the *src/* folder and add the following code to it:

```
#![allow(dead_code)]
use num_complex::{Complex, ComplexFloat};
use super::colormap;

#[derive(Default)]
pub struct IComplex3DOutput {
    pub positions: Vec<[f32; 3]>,
    pub colors: Vec<[f32; 3]>,
    pub indices: Vec<u32>,
}

pub struct IComplex3D {
    xmin: f32,
    xmax: f32,
    zmin: f32,
    zmax: f32,
    pub func_selection: u32,
    pub x_resolution: u32,
    pub z_resolution: u32,
    pub scale: f32,
    pub aspect_ratio: f32,
    pub colormap_name: String,
    pub t: f32,   // animation time parameter
}

impl Default for IComplex3D {
    fn default() -> Self {
        Self {
            func_selection: 0,
            xmin: -2.0,
            xmax: 2.0,
            zmin: -2.0,
            zmax: 2.0,
            x_resolution: 101,
            z_resolution: 101,
            scale: 1.0,
            aspect_ratio: 1.0,
            colormap_name: "jet".to_string(),
            t: 0.0,
```

```rust
        }
    }
}

impl IComplex3D {
    pub fn new() -> Self {
        Default::default()
    }

    pub fn create_complex_data(&mut self) -> IComplex3DOutput {
        let mut positions:Vec<[f32; 3]> = vec![];
        let mut colors:Vec<[f32; 3]> = vec![];
        let cdr = self.complex_data_range();

        //println!("cmin, cmax = {:?}", cdr.2);

        let cdata = colormap::colormap_data(&self.colormap_name);

        for i in 0..=self.x_resolution as usize{
            for j in 0..=self.z_resolution as usize {
                positions.push(cdr.0[i][j]);
                let color = colormap::color_lerp(cdata, cdr.2[0], cdr.2[1], cdr.1[i][j]);
                colors.push(color);
            }
        }

        // calculate indices
        let mut indices:Vec<u32> = vec![];
        let vertices_per_row = self.z_resolution + 1;
        for i in 0..self.x_resolution {
            for j in 0..self.z_resolution {
                let idx0 = j + i * vertices_per_row;
                let idx1 = j + 1 + i * vertices_per_row;
                let idx2 = j + 1 + (i + 1) * vertices_per_row;
                let idx3 = j + (i + 1) * vertices_per_row;

                let values = vec![idx0, idx1, idx2, idx2, idx3, idx0];
                indices.extend(values);
            }
        }
        IComplex3DOutput { positions, colors, indices }
    }

    fn complex_data_range(&mut self) -> (Vec<Vec<[f32;3]>>, Vec<Vec<f32>>, [f32; 2]) {
        let dx = (self.xmax - self.xmin)/self.x_resolution as f32;
        let dz = (self.zmax - self.zmin)/self.z_resolution as f32;

        let (mut cmin, mut cmax) = (std::f32::MAX, std::f32::MIN);
        let (mut ymin, mut ymax) = (std::f32::MAX, std::f32::MIN);

        let mut pts:Vec<Vec<[f32;3]>> = vec![];
        let mut cps:Vec<Vec<f32>> = vec![];

        for i in 0..=self.x_resolution {
            let x = self.xmin + dx * i as f32;
            let mut pt1:Vec<[f32; 3]> = vec![];
            let mut cp1:Vec<f32> = vec![];
            for j in 0..=self.z_resolution {
                let z = self.zmin + dz * j as f32;
                let pt = self.complex_func(x, z);
```

```
                //let pt = pp.0;
                pt1.push(pt.0);
                cp1.push(pt.1[1]);

                ymin = if pt.0[1] < ymin { pt.0[1] } else { ymin };
                ymax = if pt.0[1] > ymax { pt.0[1] } else { ymax };
                cmin = if pt.1[1] < cmin { pt.1[1] } else { cmin };
                cmax = if pt.1[1] > cmax { pt.1[1] } else { cmax };
            }
        pts.push(pt1);
        cps.push(cp1);
    }

    for i in 0..=self.x_resolution as usize {
        for j in 0..=self.z_resolution as usize {
            pts[i][j] = self.normalize_point(pts[i][j], ymin, ymax);
        }
    }

    (pts, cps, [cmin, cmax])
}

fn normalize_point(&mut self, pt:[f32; 3], ymin:f32, ymax:f32) -> [f32; 3] {
    let mut pt1 = [0f32; 3];
    pt1[0] = self.scale * (-1.0 + 2.0 * (pt[0] - self.xmin) / (self.xmax - self.xmin));
    pt1[1] = self.scale * (-1.0 + 2.0 * (pt[1] - ymin) / (ymax - ymin)) * self.aspect_ratio;
    pt1[2] = self.scale * (-1.0 + 2.0 * (pt[2] - self.zmin) / (self.zmax - self.zmin));
    pt1
}

fn complex_func(&mut self, x:f32, y:f32) -> ([f32; 3], [f32; 3]) {
    let z = Complex::new(x, y);
    let mut fz = z;

    let func_select = self.func_selection;
    let t = self.t;

    if func_select == 0 {
        fz = (z - t)/(z*z + z + t);
        (self.xmin, self.xmax, self.zmin, self.zmax) = (-3.0, 2.0, -2.0, 2.0);
    } else if func_select == 1 {
        let f1 = Complex::new(-z.im - 3.0 * t, z.re);
        let f2 = Complex::new(-z.im + t, z.re);
        fz = (f1.ln()/f2.ln()).sqrt();
        (self.xmin, self.xmax, self.zmin, self.zmax) = (-6.0, 6.0, -6.0, 6.0);
    } else if func_select == 2 {
        fz = t * (t * z).sin();
        (self.xmin, self.xmax, self.zmin, self.zmax) = (-6.0, 6.0, -6.0, 6.0);
    } else if func_select == 3 {
        fz = (0.5 + t) * ((0.5 + t) * z).tan().tan();
        (self.xmin, self.xmax, self.zmin, self.zmax) = (-10.0, 10.0, -1.0, 1.0);
    } else if func_select == 4 {
        fz = t * ((0.5 + t) *z).sin().tan();
        (self.xmin, self.xmax, self.zmin, self.zmax) = (-8.0, 8.0, -2.0, 2.0);
    } else if func_select == 5 {
        let f1 = Complex::new(t + z.re, z.im);
        let f2 = Complex::new(t - z.re, -z.im);
        fz = f1.sqrt() + f2.sqrt();
        (self.xmin, self.xmax, self.zmin, self.zmax) = (-2.0, 2.0, -2.0, 2.0);
    } else if func_select == 6 {
```

```
        fz = ((0.5 + t) * z).exp().tan()/z;
        (self.xmin, self.xmax, self.zmin, self.zmax) = (-1.0, 2.0, -1.0, 1.0);
    } else if func_select == 7 {
        fz = ((0.5 + t) * z).sin().cos().sin()/(z*z - t);
        (self.xmin, self.xmax, self.zmin, self.zmax) = (-2.0, 2.0, -1.0, 1.0);
    } else if func_select == 8 {
        let f1 = 0.5 + t;
        let f2 = 1.0 + ((0.5 + t)*z).powi(5);
        fz = f1/f2;
        (self.xmin, self.xmax, self.zmin, self.zmax) = (-1.0, 1.0, -1.0, 1.0);
    } else if func_select == 9 {
        let f1 = ((0.5 + t) * z).sin();
        let f2 = ((0.5 + t) * z).exp().cos() *(z * z - (0.5 + t)*(0.5 + t));
        fz = f1/f2;
        (self.xmin, self.xmax, self.zmin, self.zmax) = (-4.0, 6.0, -2.0, 2.0);
    } else if func_select == 10 {
        fz = 1.0/(z + t) + 1.0/(z - t);
        (self.xmin, self.xmax, self.zmin, self.zmax) = (-2.0, 2.0, -2.0, 2.0);
    }

    ([x, fz.abs(), y], [x, fz.arg(), y])
    }
}
```

The above code first introduces two structs, *IComplex3DOutput* and *IComplex3D*, which define the output and input fields used to create 3D plots for complex functions. Note that the output struct contains *positions*, *colors*, and *indices*, representing the data used to render the plots. The *normals* are not included because an unlit shader is used to render the plots, which does not require the normal data.

Subsequently, the code uses the *num-complex* crate to add implementations to the *IComplex3D* struct. We first set the default values for the input parameters and then create several functions. The *complex_func* function defines eleven complex functions. Each function can be selected using the *func_selection* field defined in the input struct. In particular, we set the 2D grid range for each complex function, which will be used to generate the vertex and index data. The *complex_func* function returns magnitude and argument with a [*f32, 3*] type.

Both the *normalize_point* and *complex_data_range* are helper functions. The *normalize_point* function maps the region of a surface onto a region of [-1, 1]. This provides a consistent size for different 3D plots in the scene, when using the same camera and transformations. The *scale* and *aspect* parameters in the function allow the user to control the size and aspect ratio of the plot. The *complex_data_range* function calculates the position and colormap, as well as their data ranges for a 3D plot for complex functions. It is worth noting that we use the argument (or angle) of the complex function to calculate the colormap. This way, the plot for the complex function shows not only the respective values but also corresponding phase information.

The main function in the code above is *create_complex_data*, which takes the *IComplex3D* (*self*) as input. The *IComplex3D* struct allows the user to specify the data region and 2D grid points in the complex plane. Within this function, several data arrays are defined to store the *position*, *color*, and *index* data. In the *for*-loop, the *positions* and *colors* arrays are populated with the normalized position data and colormap data returned by the *complex_data_range* function. Additionally, the indices are also calculated within the *create_complex_data* function.

10.1.3 Rust Code

With the background described in the previous sections, we are ready to create 3D surface plots for complex functions. Create a new Rust file called *complex3d_cpu.rs* to the *examples/ch10/* folder and add the following content to it:

```rust
use std:: {iter, mem};
use cgmath::Matrix4;
use wgpu:: {util::DeviceExt, VertexBufferLayout};
use winit::{
    event::*,
    event_loop::{ControlFlow, EventLoop},
    window::Window,
};
use bytemuck:: {Pod, Zeroable, cast_slice};
use wgpu_book_examples:: { wgpu_simplified as ws, transforms as wt, complex3d_data as c3d };

#[repr(C)]
#[derive(Copy, Clone, Debug, Pod, Zeroable)]
pub struct Vertex {
    pub position: [f32; 3],
    pub color: [f32; 3],
}

fn create_vertices(c3d_data: c3d::IComplex3DOutput) -> (Vec<Vertex>, Vec<u32>) {
    let mut data:Vec<Vertex> = vec![];
    for i in 0..c3d_data.positions.len() {
        data.push(Vertex{position: c3d_data.positions[i], color: c3d_data.colors[i]});
    }
    (data.to_vec(), c3d_data.indices)
}

struct State {
    init:  ws::IWgpuInit,
    pipeline: wgpu::RenderPipeline,
    vertex_buffer: wgpu::Buffer,
    index_buffer: wgpu::Buffer,
    uniform_bind_group: wgpu::BindGroup,
    uniform_buffer: wgpu::Buffer,
    view_mat: Matrix4<f32>,
    project_mat: Matrix4<f32>,
    msaa_texture_view: wgpu::TextureView,
    depth_texture_view: wgpu::TextureView,
    indices_len: u32,
    recreate_buffers: bool,
    animation_speed: f32,
    rotation_speed: f32,

    surface: c3d::IComplex3D,
    fps_counter: ws::FpsCounter,
}

impl State {
    async fn new(window:&Window, sample_count:u32, resolution:u32, colormap_name:&str) -> Self {
        let init = ws::IWgpuInit::new(&window, sample_count, None).await;

        let shader = init.device.create_shader_module(wgpu::include_wgsl!("../ch08/shader_unlit.wgsl"));

        // uniform data
```

```
let camera_position = (2.0, 2.0, 2.0).into();
let look_direction = (0.0,0.0,0.0).into();
let up_direction = cgmath::Vector3::unit_y();

let (view_mat, project_mat, _) =
    wt::create_vp_mat(camera_position, look_direction, up_direction,
    init.config.width as f32 / init.config.height as f32);

// create vertex uniform buffers
let vert_uniform_buffer = init.device.create_buffer(&wgpu::BufferDescriptor{
    label: Some("Vertex Uniform Buffer"),
    size: 64,
    usage: wgpu::BufferUsages::UNIFORM | wgpu::BufferUsages::COPY_DST,
    mapped_at_creation: false,
});

// uniform bind group for vertex shader
let (vert_bind_group_layout, vert_bind_group) = ws::create_bind_group(
    &init.device,
    vec![wgpu::ShaderStages::VERTEX],
    &[vert_uniform_buffer.as_entire_binding()],
);

let vertex_buffer_layout = VertexBufferLayout {
    array_stride: mem::size_of::<Vertex>() as wgpu::BufferAddress,
    step_mode: wgpu::VertexStepMode::Vertex,
    attributes: &wgpu::vertex_attr_array![0 => Float32x3, 1 => Float32x3], // pos, col
};

let pipeline_layout = init.device.create_pipeline_layout(&wgpu::PipelineLayoutDescriptor {
    label: Some("Render Pipeline Layout"),
    bind_group_layouts: &[&vert_bind_group_layout],
    push_constant_ranges: &[],
});

let mut ppl = ws::IRenderPipeline {
    shader: Some(&shader),
    pipeline_layout: Some(&pipeline_layout),
    vertex_buffer_layout: &[vertex_buffer_layout],
    ..Default::default()
};
let pipeline = ppl.new(&init);

let msaa_texture_view = ws::create_msaa_texture_view(&init);
let depth_texture_view = ws::create_depth_view(&init);

let mut cc = c3d::IComplex3D::new();
cc.x_resolution = resolution;
cc.z_resolution = resolution;
cc.colormap_name = colormap_name.to_string();
let data = create_vertices(cc.create_complex_data());

let vertex_buffer = init.device.create_buffer_init(&wgpu::util::BufferInitDescriptor {
    label: Some("Vertex Buffer"),
    contents: cast_slice(&data.0),
    usage: wgpu::BufferUsages::VERTEX | wgpu::BufferUsages::COPY_DST,
});

let index_buffer = init.device.create_buffer_init(&wgpu::util::BufferInitDescriptor{
    label: Some("Index Buffer"),
```

```
            contents: bytemuck::cast_slice(&data.1),
            usage: wgpu::BufferUsages::INDEX | wgpu::BufferUsages::COPY_DST,
        });

        Self {
            init,
            pipeline,
            vertex_buffer,
            index_buffer,
            uniform_bind_group: vert_bind_group,
            uniform_buffer: vert_uniform_buffer,
            view_mat,
            project_mat,
            msaa_texture_view,
            depth_texture_view,
            indices_len: data.1.len() as u32,
            recreate_buffers: false,
            animation_speed: 1.0,
            rotation_speed: 1.0,
            surface: cc,
            fps_counter: ws::FpsCounter::default(),
        }
    }

    fn resize(&mut self, new_size: winit::dpi::PhysicalSize<u32>) {
        if new_size.width > 0 && new_size.height > 0 {
            self.init.size = new_size;
            self.init.config.width = new_size.width;
            self.init.config.height = new_size.height;
            self.init.surface.configure(&self.init.device, &self.init.config);

            self.project_mat = wt::create_projection_mat(new_size.width as f32 / new_size.height as f32,
                true);
            self.depth_texture_view = ws::create_depth_view(&self.init);
            if self.init.sample_count > 1 {
                self.msaa_texture_view = ws::create_msaa_texture_view(&self.init);
            }
        }
    }
}

#[allow(unused_variables)]
fn input(&mut self, event: &WindowEvent) -> bool {
    match event {
        WindowEvent::KeyboardInput {
            input:
                KeyboardInput {
                    virtual_keycode: Some(keycode),
                    state: ElementState::Pressed,
                    ..
                },
            ..
        } => {
            match keycode {
                VirtualKeyCode::Space => {
                    self.surface.func_selection = (self.surface.func_selection + 1) % 11;
                    println!("function = {}", self.surface.func_selection);
                    true
                }
                VirtualKeyCode::Q => {
                    self.surface.x_resolution += 1;
```

```rust
                            self.surface.z_resolution += 1;
                            self.recreate_buffers = true;
                            println!("resolution {}", self.surface.x_resolution);
                            true
                        },
                    VirtualKeyCode::A => {
                            self.surface.x_resolution -= 5;
                            if self.surface.x_resolution < 8 {
                                self.surface.x_resolution = 8;
                            }
                            self.surface.z_resolution -= 5;
                            if self.surface.z_resolution < 8 {
                                self.surface.z_resolution = 8;
                            }
                            self.recreate_buffers = true;
                            println!("resolution {}", self.surface.x_resolution);
                            true
                        },
                    VirtualKeyCode::W => {
                            self.animation_speed += 0.1;
                            true
                        },
                    VirtualKeyCode::S => {
                            self.animation_speed -= 0.1;
                            if self.animation_speed < 0.0 {
                                self.animation_speed = 0.0;
                            }
                            true
                        } ,
                    VirtualKeyCode::E => {
                            self.rotation_speed += 0.1;
                            true
                        },
                    VirtualKeyCode::D => {
                            self.rotation_speed -= 0.1;
                            if self.rotation_speed < 0.0 {
                                self.rotation_speed = 0.0;
                            }
                            true
                        } ,
                    _ => false
                }
            }
            _ => false,
        }
    }

    fn update(&mut self, dt: std::time::Duration) {
        // update uniform buffer
        let dt1 = self.rotation_speed * dt.as_secs_f32();

        let model_mat = wt::create_model_mat([0.0,0.5,0.0], [dt1.sin(), dt1.cos(), 0.0], [1.0, 1.0, 1.0]);
        let mvp_mat = self.project_mat * self.view_mat * model_mat;
        self.init.queue.write_buffer(&self.uniform_buffer, 0, cast_slice(mvp_mat.as_ref() as &[f32;16]));

        // recreate vertex and index buffers
        if self.recreate_buffers {
            let data = create_vertices(self.surface.create_complex_data());
            self.indices_len = data.1.len() as u32;
```

```rust
        self.vertex_buffer.destroy();
        self.vertex_buffer = self.init.device.create_buffer_init(&wgpu::util::BufferInitDescriptor {
            label: Some("Vertex Buffer"),
            contents: cast_slice(&data.0),
            usage: wgpu::BufferUsages::VERTEX | wgpu::BufferUsages::COPY_DST,
        });
        self.index_buffer.destroy();
        self.index_buffer = self.init.device.create_buffer_init(&wgpu::util::BufferInitDescriptor {
            label: Some("Index Buffer"),
            contents: cast_slice(&data.1),
            usage: wgpu::BufferUsages::INDEX | wgpu::BufferUsages::COPY_DST,
        });

        self.recreate_buffers = false;
    }

    // update vertex buffer for every frame
    self.surface.t = 0.5 * (1.0 + (self.animation_speed * dt.as_secs_f32()).cos());
    let data = create_vertices(self.surface.create_complex_data());
    self.init.queue.write_buffer(&self.vertex_buffer, 0, cast_slice(&data.0));
}

fn render(&mut self) -> Result<(), wgpu::SurfaceError> {
    let output = self.init.surface.get_current_texture()?;
    let view = output
        .texture
        .create_view(&wgpu::TextureViewDescriptor::default());

    let mut encoder = self
        .init.device
        .create_command_encoder(&wgpu::CommandEncoderDescriptor {
            label: Some("Render Encoder"),
        });

    {
        let color_attach = ws::create_color_attachment(&view);
        let msaa_attach = ws::create_msaa_color_attachment(&view, &self.msaa_texture_view);
        let color_attachment = if self.init.sample_count == 1 { color_attach } else { msaa_attach };
        let depth_attachment = ws::create_depth_stencil_attachment(&self.depth_texture_view);

        let mut render_pass = encoder.begin_render_pass(&wgpu::RenderPassDescriptor {
            label: Some("Render Pass"),
            color_attachments: &[Some(color_attachment)],
            depth_stencil_attachment: Some(depth_attachment),
            timestamp_writes: None,
            occlusion_query_set: None,
        });

        render_pass.set_pipeline(&self.pipeline);
        render_pass.set_vertex_buffer(0, self.vertex_buffer.slice(..));
        render_pass.set_index_buffer(self.index_buffer.slice(..), wgpu::IndexFormat::Uint32);
        render_pass.set_bind_group(0, &self.uniform_bind_group, &[]);
        render_pass.draw_indexed(0..self.indices_len, 0, 0..1);
    }
    self.fps_counter.print_fps(5);
    self.init.queue.submit(iter::once(encoder.finish()));
    output.present();
    Ok(())
}
}
```

```rust
fn main() {
    let mut sample_count = 1 as u32;
    let mut resolution = 256 as u32;
    let mut colormap_name = "jet";

    let args: Vec<String> = std::env::args().collect();
    if args.len() > 1 {
        sample_count = args[1].parse::<u32>().unwrap();
    }
    if args.len() > 2 {
        resolution = args[2].parse::<u32>().unwrap();
    }
    if args.len() > 3 {
        colormap_name = &args[3];
    }

    env_logger::init();
    let event_loop = EventLoop::new();
    let window = winit::window::WindowBuilder::new().build(&event_loop).unwrap();
    window.set_title(&*format!("ch10_{}", "complex3d_cpu"));

    let mut state = pollster::block_on(State::new(&window, sample_count, resolution, colormap_name));
    let render_start_time = std::time::Instant::now();

    event_loop.run(move |event, _, control_flow| {
        match event {
            Event::WindowEvent {
                ref event,
                window_id,
            } if window_id == window.id() => {
                if !state.input(event) {
                    match event {
                        WindowEvent::CloseRequested
                        | WindowEvent::KeyboardInput {
                            input:
                                KeyboardInput {
                                    state: ElementState::Pressed,
                                    virtual_keycode: Some(VirtualKeyCode::Escape),
                                    ..
                                },
                            ..
                        } => *control_flow = ControlFlow::Exit,
                        WindowEvent::Resized(physical_size) => {
                            state.resize(*physical_size);
                        }
                        WindowEvent::ScaleFactorChanged { new_inner_size, .. } => {
                            state.resize(**new_inner_size);
                        }
                        _ => {}
                    }
                }
            }
            Event::RedrawRequested(_) => {
                let now = std::time::Instant::now();
                let dt = now - render_start_time;
                state.update(dt);

                match state.render() {
                    Ok(_) => {}
                    Err(wgpu::SurfaceError::Lost) => state.resize(state.init.size),
```

```
                Err(wgpu::SurfaceError::OutOfMemory) => *control_flow = ControlFlow::Exit,
                Err(e) => eprintln!("{:?}", e),
            }
        }
        Event::MainEventsCleared => {
            window.request_redraw();
        }
        _ => {}
    }
});
}
```

The above code reuses the unlit shader implemented in Chapter 8 for procedural terrains. It also imports the *create_complex_data* function from the *complex3d_data.rs* file created in the previous section, which will be used to generate the vertex and index data for a complex function.

The *State::new* and *State::render* functions are similar to previous examples. Within the *State::new* function, we create vertex, color, and index buffers, as well as a uniform buffer used to pass the model-view-projection matrix to the shader.

In the *State::input* function, we define various input parameters using the keyboard control. This allows the user to manipulate the input parameters via the *keyboard* control, such as the plot type, complex function to be displayed, the colormap of the plot, and the resolution along the *x*- and *z*-axis.

It is worth noting that this example animates the vertex data directly by regenerating it with a time dependent parameter in the *State::update* function. The following code snippet illustrates this process:

```
// recreate vertex and index buffers
if self.recreate_buffers {
    let data = create_vertices(self.surface.create_complex_data());
    self.indices_len = data.1.len() as u32;

    self.vertex_buffer.destroy();
    self.vertex_buffer = self.init.device.create_buffer_init(&wgpu::util::BufferInitDescriptor {
        label: Some("Vertex Buffer"),
        contents: cast_slice(&data.0),
        usage: wgpu::BufferUsages::VERTEX | wgpu::BufferUsages::COPY_DST,
    });
    self.index_buffer.destroy();
    self.index_buffer = self.init.device.create_buffer_init(&wgpu::util::BufferInitDescriptor {
        label: Some("Index Buffer"),
        contents: cast_slice(&data.1),
        usage: wgpu::BufferUsages::INDEX | wgpu::BufferUsages::COPY_DST,
    });

    self.recreate_buffers = false;
}

// update vertex buffer for every frame
self.surface.t = 0.5 * (1.0 + (self.animation_speed * dt.as_secs_f32()).cos());
let data = create_vertices(self.surface.create_complex_data());
self.init.queue.write_buffer(&self.vertex_buffer, 0, cast_slice(&data.0));
```

The above code snippet is executed continuously inside the *State::update* function for every frame. However, this is a computation-intensive process, particularly when the grid points have a high resolution, which is controlled by the *resolution* parameter.

Additionally, the code permits the user to modify input parameters using keyboard inputs.

Here is a list of controls using keyboard:

- *Space*: Select different complex functions to be displayed.
- *Q/A*: Increases/decreases the resolution along both the x- and z-directions.
- *W/S*: Increases/decreases the animation speed.
- *E/D*: Increases/decreases the rotation speed.

10.1.4 Run Application

To run this application, add the following code snippet to the *Cargo.toml* file:

```
[[example]]
name = "ch10_complex3d_cpu"
path = "examples/ch10/complex3d_cpu.rs"
```

Afterward, execute the following *cargo run* commands in the terminal window:

```
cargo run --example ch10_complex3d_cpu 8
```

Fig.10-1 shows the magnitude of several complex functions for different values of the *func_selection* parameter.

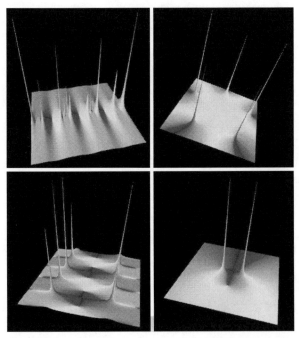

Fig.10-1. 3D plot for complex function created on the CPU.

It is evident from the results displayed in Fig.10-1 that various 3D plots can be created by manipulating the input parameters from the keyboard control. Note that the default values for resolution is set to 256. On my machine with an Nvidia GeForce RTX 3060 GPU, the framerate for creating a 3D plot for a complex function is about 24 FPS. This is a significant drop in the frame rate.

To visualize the poles and zeros of a complex function more clearly, we need to increase the resolution further. Unfortunately, it is impossible to achieve such resolutions with our current implementation. The reason for this is that, in this example, the code used to create the vertex data is written in Rust. This means that vertex data is generated on the CPU, which typically has a limited number of cores and thus limited parallel processing power. Updating the vertex data for every frame with high resolution using the CPU will lead to frame drop, causing the application to become unresponsive and appear to lag or freeze. To overcome this problem, I will show you how to use a compute shader to generate the vertex data directly on the GPU in the following sections. Using the GPU makes it possible to update the vertex data for every frame with high resolution (> 1000) while maintaining a frame rate of 60 FPS.

10.2 Surface Plots on GPU

The previous example demonstrated how to create vertex data, including positions, colors, and indices, for 3D plots of complex functions using the Rust code on the CPU. However, this approach can lead to a drop in framerate when animating the plot at higher resolutions. To address this issue, we can generate the vertex data directly on the GPU using compute shaders. This allows us to take advantage of parallelism by updating the vertex data for multiple vertices at once, rather than one at a time. As a result, we do not need to upload new vertex data for every frame since it is already available on the GPU. By utilizing compute shaders, we can create smooth 3D plot animation for complex functions with resolutions exceeding 1,000 without any loss in frame rate.

10.2.1 Complex Functions in Shader

Unlike real functions, there are no built-in functions for complex numbers in the WGSL shaders. Therefore, we will use *vec2f* data type to represent complex numbers. Create a new WGSL shader file named *complex_func.wgsl* in the *examples/ch10/* folder and include the following code:

```
const pi:f32 = 3.14159265359;
const e:f32 = 2.71828182845;

fn cAdd(a:vec2f, s:f32) -> vec2f{
    return vec2(a.x+s, a.y);
}
fn cMul(a:vec2f, b:vec2f) ->vec2f{
    return vec2(a.x*b.x-a.y*b.y, a.x*b.y + a.y*b.x);
}
fn cDiv(a:vec2f, b:vec2f) ->vec2f{
    let d = dot(b,b);
    return vec2(dot(a,b)/d, (a.y*b.x-a.x*b.y)/d);
}
fn cSqrt(z:vec2f) -> vec2f{
    let m = length(z);
    let s = sqrt(0.5*vec2(m+z.x, m-z.x));
    return s*vec2(1.0, sign(z.y));
}
fn cConj(z:vec2f) -> vec2f{
    return vec2(z.x, -z.y);
}
fn cPow (z:vec2f, n:f32) -> vec2f{
    let r = length(z);
    let a = atan2(z.y, z.x);
    return pow(r, n) * vec2(cos(a*n), sin(a*n));
}
```

```
fn cInv(z:vec2f) -> vec2f{
    return vec2(z.x/dot(z,z), -z.y/dot(z,z));
}
fn cArg(z: vec2f) -> f32{
    var f:f32 = atan2(z.y, z.x);
    if(f<0.0){
        f = f + 6.2831;
    }
    return f/6.2831;
}
fn cLog(z:vec2f) -> vec2f{
    return vec2(log(sqrt(dot(z,z))), atan2(z.y, z.x));
}
fn cSin(z:vec2f) ->vec2f{
    let a = pow(e, z.y);
    let b = pow(e, -z.y);
    return vec2(sin(z.x)*(a+b)*0.5, cos(z.x)*(a-b)*0.5);
}
fn cCos(z:vec2f) ->vec2f{
    let a = pow(e, z.y);
    let b = pow(e, -z.y);
    return vec2(cos(z.x)*(a+b)*0.5, -sin(z.x)*(a-b)*0.5);
}
fn cTan(z:vec2f) ->vec2f{
    let a = pow(e, z.y);
    let b = pow(e, -z.y);
    let cx = cos(z.x);
    let ab = (a - b)*0.5;
    return vec2(sin(z.x)*cx, ab*(a+b)*0.5)/(cx*cx+ab*ab);
}
fn cExp2(z:vec2f) -> vec2f{
    return vec2(z.x*z.x - z.y*z.y, 2.*z.x*z.y);
}

fn cExp(z:vec2f) -> vec2f{
    return vec2(exp(z.x)*cos(z.y), exp(z.x)*sin(z.y));
}

fn cAsinh(z:vec2f) -> vec2f{
    let a = z + cSqrt(cMul(z,z) + vec2<f32>(1.0,0.0));
    return cLog(a);
}
```

The above code defines various mathematical operations and commonly used functions for complex numbers. We can use these operations and functions to create various custom functions. For example, consider the following complex function:

$$f(z) = \frac{z - 1}{z^2 + z + 2}$$

Here, $z = x + iy$ is the complex variable. This function can be expressed in WGSL using the operations and functions defined in the above code, as illustrated in the following code snippet:

```
let fz = cDiv(z - vec2(1.0, 0.0), cMul(z, z) + z + vec2(2.0, 0.0));
```

If your application requires more features, you can easily add your own custom complex operations and functions to the above shader code by following the procedure presented above.

10.2.2 Compute Shader for Surface Data

Create a new compute shader file called *complex3d_comp.wgsl* in the *examples/ch10/* folder and add the following code to it:

```
fn cFunc(z:vec2f, a:f32, selectId:u32) -> vec2f {
    var fz = z;

    if (selectId == 0u) {
        let f1 = z - vec2(a, 0.0);
        let f2 = cMul(z,z) + z + vec2(a, 0.0);
        fz = cDiv(f1, f2);
    } else if (selectId == 1u) {
        fz = cSqrt(cDiv(cLog(vec2(-z.y - 3.0*a, z.x)), cLog(vec2(-z.y + a, z.x))));
    } else if (selectId == 2u){
        fz = a*cSin(a*z);
    } else if(selectId == 3u){
        fz = (a+0.5)*cTan(cTan((a+0.5)*z));
    } else if(selectId == 4u){
        fz = a*cTan(cSin((a+0.5)*z));
    } else if (selectId == 5u){
        fz = cSqrt(vec2(a + z.x, z.y)) + cSqrt(vec2(a - z.x, -z.y));
    } else if (selectId == 6u){
        fz = cDiv(cTan(cExp2((0.5+a)*z)), z);
    } else if (selectId == 7u){
        fz = cDiv(cSin(cCos(cSin((a+0.5)*z))), cMul(z,z) - a);
    } else if (selectId == 8u){
        fz = (a+0.5)*cInv(cAdd(cPow((a+0.5)*z,5.0), 1.0));
    } else if (selectId == 9u){
        fz = cDiv(cSin((a+0.5)*z), cMul(cCos(cExp2((a+0.5)*z)), cMul(z,z)- vec2((a+0.5)*(a+0.5),0.0)));
    } else if (selectId == 10u) {
        fz = cInv(z + vec2(a, 0.0)) + cInv(z - vec2(a, 0.0));
    }

    return fz;
}

struct DataRange {
    xRange: vec2f,
    yRange: vec2f,
    zRange: vec2f,
    cRange: vec2f,
}

fn getDataRange(funcSelection:u32) -> DataRange{
    var dr:DataRange;

    if (funcSelection == 0u) {
        dr.xRange = vec2(-3.0, 2.0);
        dr.zRange = vec2(-2.0, 2.0);
        dr.cRange = vec2(-pi, pi);
        dr.yRange = vec2(0.0, 45.0);
    } else if (funcSelection == 1u) {
        dr.xRange = vec2(-6.0, 6.0);
        dr.zRange = vec2(-6.0, 6.0);
        dr.cRange = vec2(-pi/2.0, pi/2.0);
        dr.yRange = vec2(0.0, 7.0);
    } else if (funcSelection == 2u) {
        dr.xRange = vec2(-6.0, 6.0);
        dr.zRange = vec2(-6.0, 6.0);
```

```
            dr.cRange = vec2(-pi, pi);
            dr.yRange = vec2(0.0, 203.0);
        } else if (funcSelection == 3u) {
            dr.xRange = vec2(-10.0, 10.0);
            dr.zRange = vec2(-1.0, 1.0);
            dr.cRange = vec2(-pi, pi);
            dr.yRange = vec2(0.0, 30.0);
        } else if (funcSelection == 4u) {
            dr.xRange = vec2(-8.0, 8.0);
            dr.zRange = vec2(-2.0, 2.0);
            dr.cRange = vec2(-pi, pi);
            dr.yRange = vec2(0.0, 27.0);
        } else if (funcSelection == 5u) {
            dr.xRange = vec2(-2.0, 2.0);
            dr.zRange = vec2(-2.0, 2.0);
            dr.cRange = vec2(-pi/2.0, pi/2.0);
            dr.yRange = vec2(1.4, 2.9);
        } else if (funcSelection == 6u) {
            dr.xRange = vec2(-1.0, 2.0);
            dr.zRange = vec2(-1.0, 1.0);
            dr.cRange = vec2(-pi, pi);
            dr.yRange = vec2(0.0, 120.0);
        } else if (funcSelection == 7u) {
            dr.xRange = vec2(-2.0, 2.0);
            dr.zRange = vec2(-1.0, 1.0);
            dr.cRange = vec2(-pi, pi);
            dr.yRange = vec2(0.0, 18.5);
        } else if (funcSelection == 8u) {
            dr.xRange = vec2(-1.0, 1.0);
            dr.zRange = vec2(-1.0, 1.0);
            dr.cRange = vec2(-pi, pi);
            dr.yRange = vec2(0.0, 26.0);
        } else if (funcSelection == 9u) {
            dr.xRange = vec2(-4.0, 6.0);
            dr.zRange = vec2(-2.0, 2.0);
            dr.cRange = vec2(-pi, pi);
            dr.yRange = vec2(0.0, 8.0);
        } else if (funcSelection == 10u) {
            dr.xRange = vec2(-2.0, 2.0);
            dr.zRange = vec2(-2.0, 2.0);
            dr.cRange = vec2(-pi, pi);
            dr.yRange = vec2(0.0, 46.0);
        }
        return dr;
}

struct VertexData{
    position: vec4f,
    color: vec4f,
}

struct VertexDataArray{
    vertexDataArray: array<VertexData>,
}

struct ComplexParams {
    resolution: f32,
    funcSelection: f32,
    animationTime: f32,
    scale: f32,
```

```
        aspectRatio: f32,
}

@group(0) @binding(0) var<storage, read_write> vda : VertexDataArray;
@group(0) @binding(1) var<uniform> colormap: array<vec4f, 11>;
@group(0) @binding(2) var<uniform> cp: ComplexParams;

fn colorLerp(tmin:f32, tmax:f32, t:f32) -> vec4f{
    var t1 = t;
    if (t1 < tmin) {t1 = tmin;}
    if (t1 > tmax) {t1 = tmax;}
    var tn = (t1-tmin)/(tmax-tmin);

    var idx = u32(floor(10.0*tn));
    var color = vec4(0.0,0.0,0.0, 1.0);

    if(f32(idx) == 10.0*tn) {
        color = colormap[idx];
    } else {
        var tn1 = (tn - 0.1*f32(idx))*10.0;
        var a = colormap[idx];
        var b = colormap[idx+1u];
        color.x = a.x + (b.x - a.x)*tn1;
        color.y = a.y + (b.y - a.y)*tn1;
        color.z = a.z + (b.z - a.z)*tn1;
    }

    return color;
}

var<private> xmin:f32;
var<private> xmax:f32;
var<private> ymin:f32;
var<private> ymax:f32;
var<private> zmin:f32;
var<private> zmax:f32;
var<private> cmin:f32;
var<private> cmax:f32;
var<private> aspect:f32;

fn getUv(i:u32, j:u32) -> vec2f {
    var dr = getDataRange(u32(cp.funcSelection));
    xmin = dr.xRange[0];
    xmax = dr.xRange[1];
    ymin = dr.yRange[0];
    ymax = dr.yRange[1];
    zmin = dr.zRange[0];
    zmax = dr.zRange[1];
    cmin = dr.cRange[0];
    cmax = dr.cRange[1];

    var dx = (xmax - xmin)/(cp.resolution - 1.0);
    var dz = (zmax - zmin)/(cp.resolution - 1.0);
    var x = xmin + f32(i) * dx;
    var z = zmin + f32(j) * dz;
    return vec2(x, z);
}

fn normalizePoint(pos1: vec3f) -> vec3f {
    var pos = pos1;
```

```
        pos.x = (2.0 * (pos.x - xmin)/(xmax - xmin) - 1.0) * cp.scale;
        pos.y = (2.0 * (pos.y - ymin)/(ymax - ymin) - 1.0) * cp.scale;
        pos.z = (2.0 * (pos.z - zmin)/(zmax - zmin) - 1.0) * cp.scale;
        pos.y = pos.y * cp.aspectRatio;
        return pos;
}

@compute @workgroup_size(8, 8, 1)
fn cs_main(@builtin(global_invocation_id) id : vec3u) {
    let i = id.x;
    let j = id.y;
    let z = getUv(i, j);

    let fz = cFunc(z, cp.animationTime, u32(cp.funcSelection));
    var pt:vec3f = vec3(z.x, length(fz), z.y);

    if(pt.y < ymin) {
        pt.y = ymin;
    }
    if(pt.y > ymax) {
        pt.y = ymax;
    }

    var ps = normalizePoint(pt);
    let color = colorLerp(cmin, cmax, cArg(fz));

    var idx = i + j * u32(cp.resolution);
    vda.vertexDataArray[idx].position = vec4(ps, 1.0);
    vda.vertexDataArray[idx].color = color;
}
```

The *cFunc* function defines eleven complex functions, each of which can be selected using the *selectId* argument. The function returns a complex function with a *vec2f* type. Note that the *cFunc* function is a direct conversion from the Rust code implemented earlier in the *complex3d_data.rs* file.

The *getDataRange* function is used to set the ranges for various data, including the range of the 2D grid in the complex plane represented by the *xRange* and *zRange*, the colormap data range represented by the *cRange*, and *y* value range represented by *yRange*.

The *VertexData* struct in the above code defines the vertex data to be generated for each vertex, including *position* and *color*. The *VertexDataArray* struct defines a dynamic array using the *VertexData* struct, which is used to store the vertex data for a 3D plot of a complex function. Additionally, the *ComplexParams* struct defines various parameters used to generate the vertex data. In addition, we define another uniform buffer named *colormap*, which is used to pass the colormap data, as previously defined in the *colormap.rs* file within the *src/* folder, to the shader components responsible for rendering the surface.

The *getUv* function calculates the *x* and *z* coordinates in a square grid, which will be used to create the 3D plot. Meanwhile, the *normalizePoint* function maps the region of a surface described by different complex functions onto a region of [-1, 1] that is scaled by the aspect ratio in the *y* direction. This provides a consistent size for different 3D plots in the scene when using the same camera and transformations.

The main function in the code above is *cs_main*, which takes the *global_invocation_id* as input. We use this global ID to specify the invocation locations, which is passed to the *getUv* function to calculate the *x* and *z* coordinates. We then use these coordinates to compute the vertex positions for different complex functions. The corresponding vertex data is normalized by invoking the *normalizePoint* function.

Subsequently, we calculate the colormap by calling the *colorLerp* function. Finally, we write the vertex data, such as *position* and *color*, to the *vertexDataArray*, which will be used to generate 3D plots of complex functions.

It is worth noting that in the *cs_main* function, we generate the vertex data in parallel for all vertices at once, and there is no for-loop involved. This is why vertex data generation on the GPU should be much faster than on the CPU, where a double for-loop is necessary to perform computation for each vertex at a time.

10.2.3 Rust Code

Create a new Rust file called *complex3d_gpu.rs* file to the *examples/ch10/* folder and add the following content to it:

```rust
use std::iter;
use cgmath::Matrix4;
use wgpu:: {util::DeviceExt, VertexBufferLayout};
use winit::{
    event::*,
    event_loop::{ControlFlow, EventLoop},
    window::Window,
};
use bytemuck::cast_slice;
use wgpu_book_examples:: { wgpu_simplified as ws, transforms as wt, colormap };

fn create_color_data(colormap_name: &str) -> Vec<[f32; 4]> {
    let cdata = colormap::colormap_data(colormap_name);
    let mut data:Vec<[f32; 4]> = vec![];
    for i in 0..cdata.len() {
        data.push([cdata[i][0], cdata[i][1], cdata[i][2], 1.0 ]);
    }
    data
}

struct State {
    init:  ws::IWgpuInit,
    pipeline: wgpu::RenderPipeline,
    uniform_bind_group: wgpu::BindGroup,
    uniform_buffer: wgpu::Buffer,

    cs_pipelines: Vec<wgpu::ComputePipeline>,
    cs_vertex_buffer: wgpu::Buffer,
    cs_index_buffer: wgpu::Buffer,
    cs_uniform_buffers: Vec<wgpu::Buffer>,
    cs_bind_groups: Vec<wgpu::BindGroup>,

    view_mat: Matrix4<f32>,
    project_mat: Matrix4<f32>,
    msaa_texture_view: wgpu::TextureView,
    depth_texture_view: wgpu::TextureView,
    animation_speed: f32,
    rotation_speed: f32,

    resolution: u32,
    triangles_count: u32,
    surface_type: u32,
    scale: f32,
    aspect_ratio: f32,
```

```
        fps_counter: ws::FpsCounter,
}

impl State {
    async fn new(window:&Window, sample_count:u32, resolution:u32, colormap_name:&str) -> Self {
        let init = ws::IWgpuInit::new(&window, sample_count, None).await;

        let resol = ws::round_to_multiple(resolution, 8);
        let vertices_count = resol * resol;
        let triangles_count = 6 * (resol - 1) * (resol - 1);
        println!("resolution = {}", resol);

        let shader = init.device.create_shader_module(wgpu::include_wgsl!("../ch08/shader_unlit.wgsl"));
        let cs_indices = init.device.create_shader_module(wgpu::include_wgsl!("indices_comp.wgsl"));

        let cs_func_file = include_str!("complex_func.wgsl");
        let cs_comp_file = include_str!("complex3d_comp.wgsl");
        let cs_comp_file = [cs_func_file, cs_comp_file].join("\n");

        let cs_comp = init.device.create_shader_module(wgpu::ShaderModuleDescriptor {
            label: Some("Compute Shader"),
            source: wgpu::ShaderSource::Wgsl(cs_comp_file.into()),
        });

        // uniform data
        let camera_position = (2.0, 2.0, 2.0).into();
        let look_direction = (0.0,0.0,0.0).into();
        let up_direction = cgmath::Vector3::unit_y();

        let (view_mat, project_mat, _) =
            wt::create_vp_mat(camera_position, look_direction, up_direction,
            init.config.width as f32 / init.config.height as f32);

        // create vertex uniform buffers
        let vert_uniform_buffer = init.device.create_buffer(&wgpu::BufferDescriptor{
            label: Some("Vertex Uniform Buffer"),
            size: 64,
            usage: wgpu::BufferUsages::UNIFORM | wgpu::BufferUsages::COPY_DST,
            mapped_at_creation: false,
        });

        // uniform bind group for vertex shader
        let (vert_bind_group_layout, vert_bind_group) = ws::create_bind_group(
            &init.device,
            vec![wgpu::ShaderStages::VERTEX],
            &[vert_uniform_buffer.as_entire_binding()],
        );

        let vertex_buffer_layout = VertexBufferLayout {
            array_stride: 32,
            step_mode: wgpu::VertexStepMode::Vertex,
            attributes: &wgpu::vertex_attr_array![0 => Float32x4, 1 => Float32x4], // pos, col
        };

        let pipeline_layout = init.device.create_pipeline_layout(&wgpu::PipelineLayoutDescriptor {
            label: Some("Render Pipeline Layout"),
            bind_group_layouts: &[&vert_bind_group_layout],
            push_constant_ranges: &[],
        });
```

```
let mut ppl = ws::IRenderPipeline {
    shader: Some(&shader),
    pipeline_layout: Some(&pipeline_layout),
    vertex_buffer_layout: &[vertex_buffer_layout],
    ..Default::default()
};
let pipeline = ppl.new(&init);

let msaa_texture_view = ws::create_msaa_texture_view(&init);
let depth_texture_view = ws::create_depth_view(&init);


// create compute pipeline for indices
let cs_index_buffer = init.device.create_buffer(&wgpu::BufferDescriptor{
    label: Some("Index Buffer"),
    size:  4 * triangles_count as u64,
    usage: wgpu::BufferUsages::INDEX | wgpu::BufferUsages::STORAGE | wgpu::BufferUsages::COPY_DST,
    mapped_at_creation: false,
});

let cs_index_uniform_buffer = init.device.create_buffer(&wgpu::BufferDescriptor{
    label: Some("Index Uniform Buffer"),
    size:  4,
    usage: wgpu::BufferUsages::UNIFORM | wgpu::BufferUsages::COPY_DST,
    mapped_at_creation: false,
});
init.queue.write_buffer(&cs_index_uniform_buffer, 0, cast_slice(&[resol]));

let (cs_index_bind_group_layout, cs_index_bind_group) = ws::create_bind_group_storage(
    &init.device,
    vec![
        wgpu::ShaderStages::COMPUTE, wgpu::ShaderStages::COMPUTE,
    ],
    vec![
        wgpu::BufferBindingType::Storage { read_only: false },
        wgpu::BufferBindingType::Uniform,
    ],
    &[
        cs_index_buffer.as_entire_binding(),
        cs_index_uniform_buffer.as_entire_binding(),
    ],
);

let cs_index_pipeline_layout = init.device.create_pipeline_layout(&wgpu::PipelineLayoutDescriptor{
    label: Some("Compute Index Pipeline Layout"),
    bind_group_layouts: &[&cs_index_bind_group_layout],
    push_constant_ranges: &[],
});

let cs_index_pipeline = init.device.create_compute_pipeline(&wgpu::ComputePipelineDescriptor{
    label: Some("Compute Index Pipeline"),
    layout: Some(&cs_index_pipeline_layout),
    module: &cs_indices,
    entry_point: "cs_main",
});

// create compute pipeline for complex3d surface
let cs_vertex_buffer = init.device.create_buffer(&wgpu::BufferDescriptor{
    label: Some("Vertex Buffer"),
    size:  32 * vertices_count as u64,
```

```
        usage: wgpu::BufferUsages::VERTEX | wgpu::BufferUsages::STORAGE |
            wgpu::BufferUsages::COPY_DST,
        mapped_at_creation: false,
    });

    let cdata = create_color_data(colormap_name);
    let cs_colormap_buffer = init.device.create_buffer_init(&wgpu::util::BufferInitDescriptor{
        label: Some("Colormap Uniform Buffer"),
        contents: bytemuck::cast_slice(&cdata),
        usage: wgpu::BufferUsages::UNIFORM | wgpu::BufferUsages::COPY_DST,
    });

    let cs_vertex_uniform_buffer = init.device.create_buffer(&wgpu::BufferDescriptor{
        label: Some("Vertex Uniform Buffer"),
        size:  32,
        usage: wgpu::BufferUsages::UNIFORM | wgpu::BufferUsages::COPY_DST,
        mapped_at_creation: false,
    });

    let (cs_vertex_bind_group_layout, cs_vertex_bind_group) = ws::create_bind_group_storage(
        &init.device,
        vec![
            wgpu::ShaderStages::COMPUTE, wgpu::ShaderStages::COMPUTE, wgpu::ShaderStages::COMPUTE,
        ],
        vec![
            wgpu::BufferBindingType::Storage { read_only: false },
            wgpu::BufferBindingType::Uniform,
            wgpu::BufferBindingType::Uniform,
        ],
        &[
            cs_vertex_buffer.as_entire_binding(),
            cs_colormap_buffer.as_entire_binding(),
            cs_vertex_uniform_buffer.as_entire_binding(),
        ],
    );

    let cs_pipeline_layout = init.device.create_pipeline_layout(&wgpu::PipelineLayoutDescriptor{
        label: Some("Compute Pipeline Layout"),
        bind_group_layouts: &[&cs_vertex_bind_group_layout],
        push_constant_ranges: &[],
    });

    let cs_pipeline = init.device.create_compute_pipeline(&wgpu::ComputePipelineDescriptor{
        label: Some("Compute Pipeline"),
        layout: Some(&cs_pipeline_layout),
        module: &cs_comp,
        entry_point: "cs_main",
    });

    Self {
        init,
        pipeline,
        uniform_bind_group: vert_bind_group,
        uniform_buffer: vert_uniform_buffer,

        cs_pipelines: vec![cs_index_pipeline, cs_pipeline],
        cs_vertex_buffer,
        cs_index_buffer,
        cs_uniform_buffers: vec![cs_index_uniform_buffer, cs_vertex_uniform_buffer],
        cs_bind_groups: vec![cs_index_bind_group, cs_vertex_bind_group],
```

```rust
                view_mat,
                project_mat,
                msaa_texture_view,
                depth_texture_view,
                animation_speed: 1.0,
                rotation_speed: 1.0,

                resolution: resol,
                triangles_count,
                surface_type: 0,
                scale: 1.5,
                aspect_ratio: 0.8,
                fps_counter: ws::FpsCounter::default(),
        }
    }

    fn resize(&mut self, new_size: winit::dpi::PhysicalSize<u32>) {
        if new_size.width > 0 && new_size.height > 0 {
            self.init.size = new_size;
            self.init.config.width = new_size.width;
            self.init.config.height = new_size.height;
            self.init.surface.configure(&self.init.device, &self.init.config);

            self.project_mat = wt::create_projection_mat(new_size.width as f32 / new_size.height as f32,
                true);
            self.depth_texture_view = ws::create_depth_view(&self.init);
            if self.init.sample_count > 1 {
                self.msaa_texture_view = ws::create_msaa_texture_view(&self.init);
            }
        }
    }
}

#[allow(unused_variables)]
fn input(&mut self, event: &WindowEvent) -> bool {
    match event {
        WindowEvent::KeyboardInput {
            input:
                KeyboardInput {
                    virtual_keycode: Some(keycode),
                    state: ElementState::Pressed,
                    ..
                },
            ..
        } => {
            match keycode {
                VirtualKeyCode::Space => {
                    self.surface_type = (self.surface_type + 1) % 11;
                    println!("function = {}", self.surface_type);
                    true
                }
                VirtualKeyCode::Q => {
                    self.animation_speed += 0.1;
                    true
                },
                VirtualKeyCode::A => {
                    self.animation_speed -= 0.1;
                    if self.animation_speed < 0.0 {
                        self.animation_speed = 0.0;
                    }
```

```
                            true
                        },
                    VirtualKeyCode::W => {
                        self.rotation_speed += 0.1;
                        true
                    },
                    VirtualKeyCode::S => {
                        self.rotation_speed -= 0.1;
                        if self.rotation_speed < 0.0 {
                            self.rotation_speed = 0.0;
                        }
                        true
                    },
                    _ => false
                }
            }
            _ => false,
        }
    }

    fn update(&mut self, dt: std::time::Duration) {
        // update uniform buffer
        let dt1 = self.rotation_speed * dt.as_secs_f32();

        let model_mat = wt::create_model_mat([0.0,0.5,0.0], [dt1.sin(), dt1.cos(), 0.0], [1.0, 1.0, 1.0]);
        let mvp_mat = self.project_mat * self.view_mat * model_mat;
        self.init.queue.write_buffer(&self.uniform_buffer, 0, cast_slice(mvp_mat.as_ref() as &[f32;16]));

        // update uniform buffer for compute pipeline
        let params = [
            self.resolution as f32,
            self.surface_type as f32,
            0.5 * (1.0 + (self.animation_speed*2.0*dt.as_secs_f32()).cos()),
            self.scale,
            self.aspect_ratio,
        ];
        self.init.queue.write_buffer(&self.cs_uniform_buffers[1], 0, cast_slice(&params));
    }

    fn render(&mut self) -> Result<(), wgpu::SurfaceError> {
        let output = self.init.surface.get_current_texture()?;
        let view = output
            .texture
            .create_view(&wgpu::TextureViewDescriptor::default());

        let mut encoder = self
            .init.device
            .create_command_encoder(&wgpu::CommandEncoderDescriptor {
                label: Some("Render Encoder"),
            });
        // compute pass for indices
        {
            let mut cs_index_pass = encoder.begin_compute_pass(&wgpu::ComputePassDescriptor{
                label: Some("Compute Index Pass"),
                timestamp_writes: None,
            });
            cs_index_pass.set_pipeline(&self.cs_pipelines[0]);
            cs_index_pass.set_bind_group(0, &self.cs_bind_groups[0], &[]);
            cs_index_pass.dispatch_workgroups(self.resolution/8, self.resolution/8, 1);
        }
```

```rust
    // compute pass for vertices
    {
        let mut cs_pass = encoder.begin_compute_pass(&wgpu::ComputePassDescriptor{
            label: Some("Compute Pass"),
            timestamp_writes: None,
        });
        cs_pass.set_pipeline(&self.cs_pipelines[1]);
        cs_pass.set_bind_group(0, &self.cs_bind_groups[1], &[]);
        cs_pass.dispatch_workgroups(self.resolution/8, self.resolution/8, 1);
    }

    // render pass
    {
        let color_attach = ws::create_color_attachment(&view);
        let msaa_attach = ws::create_msaa_color_attachment(&view, &self.msaa_texture_view);
        let color_attachment = if self.init.sample_count == 1 { color_attach } else { msaa_attach };
        let depth_attachment = ws::create_depth_stencil_attachment(&self.depth_texture_view);

        let mut render_pass = encoder.begin_render_pass(&wgpu::RenderPassDescriptor {
            label: Some("Render Pass"),
            color_attachments: &[Some(color_attachment)],
            depth_stencil_attachment: Some(depth_attachment),
            timestamp_writes: None,
            occlusion_query_set: None,
        });

        render_pass.set_pipeline(&self.pipeline);
        render_pass.set_vertex_buffer(0, self.cs_vertex_buffer.slice(..));
        render_pass.set_index_buffer(self.cs_index_buffer.slice(..), wgpu::IndexFormat::Uint32);
        render_pass.set_bind_group(0, &self.uniform_bind_group, &[]);
        render_pass.draw_indexed(0..self.triangles_count, 0, 0..1);
    }
    self.fps_counter.print_fps(5);
    self.init.queue.submit(iter::once(encoder.finish()));
    output.present();

    Ok(())
    }
}

fn main() {
    let mut sample_count = 1 as u32;
    let mut resolution = 1024u32;
    let mut colormap_name = "jet";

    let args: Vec<String> = std::env::args().collect();
    if args.len() > 1 {
        sample_count = args[1].parse::<u32>().unwrap();
    }
    if args.len() > 2 {
        resolution = args[2].parse::<u32>().unwrap();
    }
    if args.len() > 3 {
        colormap_name = &args[3];
    }

    env_logger::init();
    let event_loop = EventLoop::new();
    let window = winit::window::WindowBuilder::new().build(&event_loop).unwrap();
    window.set_title(&*format!("ch10_{}", "complex3d_gpu"));
```

```
    let mut state = pollster::block_on(State::new(&window, sample_count, resolution, colormap_name));
    let render_start_time = std::time::Instant::now();

    event_loop.run(move |event, _, control_flow| {
        match event {
            Event::WindowEvent {
                ref event,
                window_id,
            } if window_id == window.id() => {
                if !state.input(event) {
                    match event {
                        WindowEvent::CloseRequested
                        | WindowEvent::KeyboardInput {
                            input:
                                KeyboardInput {
                                    state: ElementState::Pressed,
                                    virtual_keycode: Some(VirtualKeyCode::Escape),
                                    ..
                                },
                            ..
                        } => *control_flow = ControlFlow::Exit,
                        WindowEvent::Resized(physical_size) => {
                            state.resize(*physical_size);
                        }
                        WindowEvent::ScaleFactorChanged { new_inner_size, .. } => {
                            state.resize(**new_inner_size);
                        }
                        _ => {}
                    }
                }
            }
            Event::RedrawRequested(_) => {
                let now = std::time::Instant::now();
                let dt = now - render_start_time;
                state.update(dt);

                match state.render() {
                    Ok(_) => {}
                    Err(wgpu::SurfaceError::Lost) => state.resize(state.init.size),
                    Err(wgpu::SurfaceError::OutOfMemory) => *control_flow = ControlFlow::Exit,
                    Err(e) => eprintln!("{:?}", e),
                }
            }
            Event::MainEventsCleared => {
                window.request_redraw();
            }
            _ => {}
        }
    });
}
```

This example reuses the unlit shader and the indices compute shader created in Chapter 8, as well as the colormap code implemented earlier in the *src/* folder. After the *use* statements, several fields are added to the *State* struct, such as *resolution*, *surface_type*, and *triangles_count*, which can be easily accessed by different functions without passing them as input.

Within the *State::new* function, there is a significant difference compared to the previous example that generates 3D plots of complex functions on the CPU: this example does not use data generated from the

Rust code to create vertex buffers for positions and colors. Instead, we will use compute shaders to generate these buffers.

The code segment for creating compute index pipeline is used to create a compute pipeline for the indices. This segment is the same as that used when creating terrains on the GPU in Chapter 8. The code block for creating compute pipeline is used to generate the vertex data. Within the block, we create a compute pipeline and define a vertex buffer and a parameter buffer. The parameter buffer is a uniform buffer that passes various parameters to the compute shader to calculate the surface data, and the vertex buffer is a storage buffer that is used to store the surface data in the compute shader.

The *State::render* function in the above code includes three passes: two compute passes and a render pass. In the compute passes, we first compute the index data and then the surface data for a complex function by setting the respective bind group to the pass. While in the render pass, we use the vertex buffer and index buffer from the compute pipeline to set these buffers for the render pass. This differs from the previous example, where the vertex buffer and index buffer were created using data from the Rust code.

The rest of the code is similar to that used in the previous example, except that in this example, to animate the plot, we do not need to regenerate the surface data and vertex buffers for every frame within the *State::update* function. Instead, we only need to update the uniform parameters used to calculate the surface data in the compute shader, as shown in the following code snippet:

```
// update uniform buffer for compute pipeline
let params = [
    self.resolution as f32,
    self.surface_type as f32,
    0.5 * (1.0 + (self.animation_speed*2.0*dt.as_secs_f32()).cos()),
    self.scale,
    self.aspect_ratio,
];
self.init.queue.write_buffer(&self.cs_uniform_buffers[1], 0, cast_slice(&params));
```

The above code snippet sets the animation parameter using a time-dependent value scaled by the animation speed.

Additionally, the code permits the user to modify input parameters using keyboard inputs.

Here is a list of controls using keyboard:

- *Space*: Select different surface type to be displayed.

- *Q/A*: Increases/decreases the animation speed.

- *W/S*: Increases/decreases the rotation speed.

10.2.4 Run Application

To run this application, add the following code snippet to the *Cargo.toml* file:

```
[[example]]
name = "ch10_complex3d_gpu"
path = "examples/ch10/complex3d_gpu.rs"
```

Afterward, execute the following *cargo run* commands in the terminal window:

```
cargo run --example ch10_complex3d_gpu 8
```

Fig.10-2 shows the results of this example.

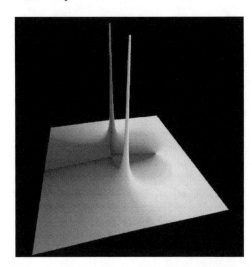

Fig.10-2. 3D plot for a complex function created on the GPU.

The figure demonstrates that using compute shaders to create a 3D plot of a complex function with smooth animation on the GPU results in a framerate of 60 FPS, even for higher resolutions such as 1024. In comparison, creating the same animated plot on the CPU in the previous example with a resolution of 256 only yielded a framerate of 24 FPS. This highlights the enormous computational power of compute shaders in generating 3D plots for complex functions.

10.3 Domain Coloring

As mentioned earlier, domain coloring is a technique for visualizing complex functions by assigning a color to each point of the complex plane. Specifically, in this technique, the complex plane is mapped onto a color wheel, where the hue of the color corresponds to the argument of the complex number, and the saturation and brightness of the color correspond to the magnitude of the complex number.

To implement domain coloring, the complex plane is divided into a grid of points. Then, each point in the grid is evaluated using a complex function, and resulting complex number is mapped onto a color using the hue-saturation-brightness (HSB) color model.

Domain coloring plots can be used to reveal important features of complex functions, such as the location of zeros and poles, the behaviors of the function near singularities or infinity, and the periodicity or symmetry of the function. They can also be used to create visually appealing images of complex functions that can be used for educational or artistic purposes.

Since domain coloring requires evaluating the complex function at a large number of points in the complex plane, which is a computation-intensive process, this section will use compute shaders to perform the computation of domain coloring directly on the GPU.

10.3.1 Color Functions in Shader

While RGB color model is the most common way to mix and create colors in computer graphics, the HSB or HSV (hue, saturation, value) model is considered to be more intuitive and closer to how humans consciously think about color. The RGB model describes colors in terms of red, green, and blue primary colors, while HSV describes colors using their tint (hue), shade (saturation), and brightness (value) .

Domain coloring represents complex functions by assigning a color to each point on the complex plane. The HSV model is usually used to associate hue of the color with the argument or phase, and the saturation and value with the magnitude of the complex function. Then, the HSV model is converted into the RGB model that the fragment shader can use. In this subsection, we will implement several helper functions that can be used to convert the HSV model into the RGB model.

The standard domain coloring technique uses the phase and magnitude of a complex function to determine the hue and the contour lines, respectively. The contours of the magnitude occur around the integer value of $log2(|z|)$. Usually, these contour lines are colored with a light color, while the grid lines of the real and imaginary parts of the complex function are colored with a dark color.

Open the *complex_func.wgsl* file from the *examples/ch10/* folder and add a new shader function named *hsv2Rgb* to the file with the following code:

```
fn hsv2Rgb(z:vec2f) -> vec3f{
    let len = length(z);
    let h = cArg(z);
    var fx = 2.0*(fract(z.x) - 0.5);
    var fy = 2.0*(fract(z.y) - 0.5);
    fx = fx*fx;
    fy = fy*fy;
    var g = 1.0 -(1.0 - fx)*(1.0 - fy);
    g = pow(abs(g), 10.0);
    var c = 2.0*(fract(log2(len)) - 0.5);
    c = 0.7*pow(abs(c), 10.0);
    var v = 1.0 - 0.5*g;
    let f = abs((h*6.0 + vec3(0.0,4.0,2.0))%6.0 - 3.0) - 1.0;
    var rgb = clamp(f, vec3(0.0), vec3(1.0));
    rgb = rgb*rgb*(3.0 - 2.0*rgb);
    rgb = (1.0-c)*v*mix(vec3(1.0), rgb, 1.0);
    return rgb + c*vec3(1.0);
}
```

The above function first calculates the H, S, V values using the magnitude and argument of the complex function and then convert them into RGB color. In this calculation, several built-in WGSL functions are used, including *fract*, *clamp*, and *mix*.

I should point out that various versions of HSV to RGB color conversion have been proposed for domain coloring. The version used in the above code allows you to easily discern the behavior of the complex function.

Fig.10-3 (a) shows a complex function $f(z) = z$ on the complex plane created using the above *hsv2RGB* function. The white circles indicate the magnitude contours and the black gridlines represent the real and imaginary parts. The magnitude contours in white color bunch up, while the black gridlines do not, around $z = 0$, indicating that there is a zero at $z = 0$.

Fig.10-3 (b) shows another complex function $f(z) = 1/z$, where a pole at $z = 0$ is indicated by the way the black gridlines bunch up as white magnitude contours get closer and closer to the pole. From the results displayed in Fig.10-3, you can clearly distinguish the difference between the zeros and poles in the complex plane.

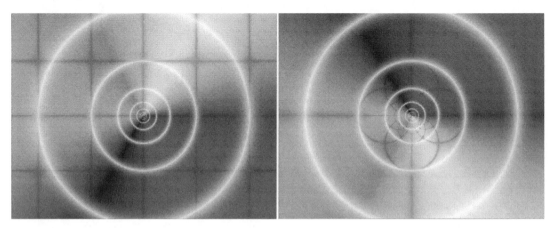

Fig.10-3. (a) f(z)=z (left) and (b) f(z) = 1/z (right) plotted using the hsv2Rgb function.

In Chapter 7, we implemented the colormap functions in Rust in the file named *colormap.rs* file located at *src/* folder. We can also use these colormap functions for domain coloring. To achieve this, add a new WGSL shader function named *colormap2Rgb* to the *complex_func.wgsl* file with the following code:

```
fn colormap2Rgb(z:vec2f, colormap:array<vec4f,11>) -> vec4f {
    var c = colormap;
    let len = length(z);
    var h = atan2(z.y, z.x);
    if(h < 0.0) { h = h + 2.0*pi; }
    if(h >= 2.0*pi) { h = h - 2.0*pi; }
    var s = 0.0;
    var v = vec3f(0.0);

    for(var i:i32 = 0; i < 11; i = i+1){
        if(h >= 0.2*pi*f32(i) && h < 0.2*pi*(f32(i) + 1.0)){
            s = (h - f32(i)*0.2*pi)/(0.2*pi);
            v = s*c[i+1].rgb + (1.0-s)*c[i].rgb;
        }
    }
    let b = fract(log2(len));
    return vec4(v[0]*b, v[1]*b, v[2]*b, 1.0);
}
```

The above function first retrieves the colormap data using the colormap input argument, then uses the complex variable z and the colormap data to create a HSV color model, and finally converts it into the RGB color model. The advantage of using this colormap model is that you can use different colormaps for domain coloring by simply selecting different *colormap* data.

Fig.10-4 shows the complex functions $f(z) = z$ and $f(z) = 1/z$ in the complex plane created using the "*jet*" colormap data. The colormap model allows us to distinguish the difference between the zeros and poles in the complex plane easily.

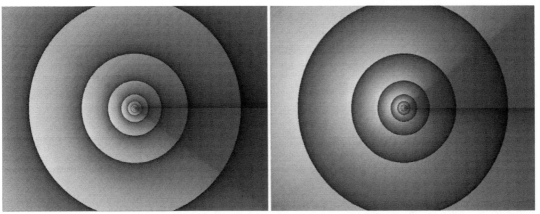

Fig.10-4. (a) f(z)=z (left) and (b) f(z) = 1/z (right) plotted using the colormap2Rgb function.

In the following sections, I will explain how to create domain coloring for complex functions using these implemented color models.

10.3.2 Compute Shader for Domain Coloring

Create a new WGSL compute shader file named *domain_color_comp.wgsl* in the *examples/ch10/* folder and include the following code:

```
fn cFunc(z:vec2f, a:f32, selectId:u32) -> vec2f {
    var fz = z;

    if (selectId == 0u) {
        let f1 = z - vec2(a, 0.0);
        let f2 = cMul(z,z) + z + vec2(a, 0.0);
        fz = cDiv(f1, f2);
    } else if (selectId == 1u) {
        fz = cSqrt(cDiv(cLog(vec2(-z.y - 3.0*a, z.x)), cLog(vec2(-z.y + a, z.x))));
    } else if (selectId == 2u){
        fz = a*cSin(a*z);
    } else if(selectId == 3u){
        fz = (a+0.5)*cTan(cTan((a+0.5)*z));
    } else if(selectId == 4u){
        fz = a*cTan(cSin((a+0.5)*z));
    } else if (selectId == 5u){
        fz = cSqrt(vec2(a + z.x, z.y)) + cSqrt(vec2(a - z.x, -z.y));
    } else if (selectId == 6u){
        fz = cDiv(cTan(cExp2((0.5+a)*z)), z);
    } else if (selectId == 7u){
        fz = cDiv(cSin(cCos(cSin((a+0.5)*z))), cMul(z,z) - a);
    } else if (selectId == 8u){
        fz = (a+0.5)*cInv(cAdd(cPow((a+0.5)*z,5.0), 1.0));
    } else if (selectId == 9u){
        fz = cDiv(cSin((a+0.5)*z), cMul(cCos(cExp2((a+0.5)*z)), cMul(z,z)- vec2((a+0.5)*(a+0.5),0.0)));
    } else if (selectId == 10u) {
        fz = cInv(z + vec2(a, 0.0)) + cInv(z - vec2(a, 0.0));
    } else if(selectId == 11u){
        fz = cInv(z);
    } else if(selectId == 12u){
        fz = z;
```

```
    }
    return fz;
}

struct IntParams {
    funcSelect: u32,
    colorSelect: u32,
}
@group(0) @binding(0) var<uniform> ips: IntParams;

struct FloatParams {
    animateParam: f32,
    width: f32,
    height: f32,
    scale: f32,
}
@group(0) @binding(1) var<uniform> fps: FloatParams;
@group(0) @binding(2) var tex: texture_storage_2d<rgba8unorm, write>;

@compute @workgroup_size(8, 8, 1)
fn cs_main(@builtin(global_invocation_id) id: vec3u) {
    let a = fps.animateParam;
    let w = fps.width;
    let h = fps.height;
    let scale = fps.scale;
    let funcId =  ips.funcSelect;
    let colorId = ips.colorSelect;

    let z = vec2(scale*(f32(id.x) - 0.5*w)/w, -scale*(h/w)*(f32(id.y) - 0.5*h)/h);
    let fz = cFunc(z, a, funcId);

    var color:vec4f;
    if (colorId == 0u) { // default
        color = hsv2Rgb(fz);
    } else { // colormaps
        color = colormap2Rgb(fz, colormap);
    }


    textureStore(tex, vec2(id.xy), color);
}
```

The above code begins with the *cFunc* function, which is the same as the one used in the previous example. It defines thirteen complex functions, each of which can be selected using the *selectId* argument. Then, the code implements a compute shader responsible for generating an image by evaluating a complex function for each pixel in the image and storing the result in a texture.

In the shader, we pass the animation parameter, size of the window, scale, function selection, and colormap selection as uniform variables. Within the *cs_main* function, each point we compute for the complex function corresponds to a pixel, and its computation does not involve any surrounding points. Consequently, we can compute these values by providing the shader with the location of the current pixel in the complex plane. We define the complex variable *z* in the compute shader using the following code snippet:

```
    let z = vec2(scale*(f32(id.x) - 0.5*w)/w, -scale*(h/w)*(f32(id.y) - 0.5*h)/h);
```

Here, *id* corresponds to the built-in global invocation ID of the workgroup, which is available to the compute shader and provides the location of the pixel. Subsequently, we call the *cFunc* function with the *selectId* parameter to retrieve the corresponding complex function, and then create the domain coloring for the complex function by invoking the *hsv2Rgb* or *colormap2Rgb* function. Finally, the data for domain coloring is stored in the texture using the *textureStore* function with the current pixel coordinates and the computed color as parameters.

The fragment shader can access the color data stored in the texture created in the compute shader by sampling the texture using the texture function.

10.3.3 Render Shader

With the data for domain coloring generated using the compute shader, we are ready to render the data in a rendering shader. Create a WGSL shader file named *render_shader.wgsl* in the *examples/ch10/* folder and add the following code to it:

```
@group(0) @binding(0) var texture: texture_2d<f32>;
@group(0) @binding(1) var texSampler: sampler;

struct Output {
    @builtin(position) position: vec4f,
    @location(0) texCoord: vec2f,
}

@vertex
fn vs_main(@builtin(vertex_index) vIndex: u32) -> Output {
    const pos = array(
        vec2( 1.0,  1.0),
        vec2( 1.0, -1.0),
        vec2(-1.0, -1.0),
        vec2( 1.0,  1.0),
        vec2(-1.0, -1.0),
        vec2(-1.0,  1.0),
    );

    var output: Output;
    output.position = vec4(pos[vIndex].x, -pos[vIndex].y, 0.0, 1.0);
    output.texCoord = pos[vIndex] * 0.5 + 0.5;
    return output;
}

@fragment
fn fs_main(in: Output) -> @location(0) vec4f {
    return textureSample(texture, texSampler, in.texCoord);
}
```

This render shader defines a simple vertex and fragment shader that samples a 2D texture and applies it to a quad made up of two triangles.

The vertex shader defines an array of positions for the quad vertices, and returns a struct with a position and texture coordinate for each vertex. The position is set using the vertex index, while the texture coordinates are obtained by manipulating the position data.

The fragment shader takes the output from the vertex shader as input, and samples the texture using *textureSample* function with the texture and sampler variables, and the input texture coordinate. The resulting color is output as a *vec4f* value.

It is worth noting that the 2D texture in this example is generated using a compute shader rather than from an image file.

10.3.4 Rust Code

Create a new Rust file named *domain_color.rs* in the *examples/ch10/* folder and add the following code to it:

```rust
use std::iter;
use wgpu::util::DeviceExt;
use winit::{
    event::*,
    event_loop::{ControlFlow, EventLoop},
    window::Window,
};
use bytemuck::cast_slice;
use wgpu_book_examples:: { wgpu_simplified as ws, colormap, texture_data as td };

fn create_color_data(colormap_name: &str) -> Vec<[f32; 4]> {
    let cdata = colormap::colormap_data(colormap_name);
    let mut data:Vec<[f32; 4]> = vec![];
    for i in 0..cdata.len() {
        data.push([cdata[i][0], cdata[i][1], cdata[i][2], 1.0 ]);
    }
    data
}
struct State {
    init:  ws::IWgpuInit,
    pipeline: wgpu::RenderPipeline,
    uniform_bind_group: wgpu::BindGroup,

    cs_pipeline: wgpu::ComputePipeline,
    cs_uniform_buffers: Vec<wgpu::Buffer>,
    cs_bind_groups: Vec<wgpu::BindGroup>,

    animation_speed: f32,
    function_type: u32,
    colormap_type: u32,
    scale: f32,
    fps_counter: ws::FpsCounter,
}

impl State {
    async fn new(window:&Window, colormap_name:&str) -> Self {
        let init = ws::IWgpuInit::new(&window, 1, None).await;

        let shader = init.device.create_shader_module(wgpu::include_wgsl!("render_shader.wgsl"));

        let cs_func_file = include_str!("complex_func.wgsl");
        let cs_domain_color_file = include_str!("domain_color_comp.wgsl");
        let cs_comp_file = [cs_func_file, cs_domain_color_file].join("\n");

        let cs_comp = init.device.create_shader_module(wgpu::ShaderModuleDescriptor {
            label: Some("Compute Shader"),
            source: wgpu::ShaderSource::Wgsl(cs_comp_file.into()),
        });

        let tex = td::ITexture::create_texture_store_data(&init.device, init.size.width,
            init.size.height).unwrap();
        let (texture_bind_group_layout, texture_bind_group) =
            ws::create_texture_store_bind_group(&init.device, &tex);

        let pipeline_layout = init.device.create_pipeline_layout(&wgpu::PipelineLayoutDescriptor {
```

```rust
        label: Some("Render Pipeline Layout"),
        bind_group_layouts: &[&texture_bind_group_layout],
        push_constant_ranges: &[],
    });

    let mut ppl = ws::IRenderPipeline {
        shader: Some(&shader),
        pipeline_layout: Some(&pipeline_layout),
        vertex_buffer_layout: &[],
        is_depth_stencil: false,
        ..Default::default()
    };
    let pipeline = ppl.new(&init);

    // create compute pipeline for domain coloring
    let cdata = create_color_data(colormap_name);
    let cs_colormap_buffer = init.device.create_buffer_init(&wgpu::util::BufferInitDescriptor{
        label: Some("Colormap Uniform Buffer"),
        contents: bytemuck::cast_slice(&cdata),
        usage: wgpu::BufferUsages::UNIFORM | wgpu::BufferUsages::COPY_DST,
    });

    let cs_int_uniform_buffer = init.device.create_buffer(&wgpu::BufferDescriptor{
        label: Some("Compute Integer Uniform Buffer"),
        size: 16,
        usage: wgpu::BufferUsages::UNIFORM | wgpu::BufferUsages::COPY_DST,
        mapped_at_creation: false,
    });

    let cs_float_uniform_buffer = init.device.create_buffer(&wgpu::BufferDescriptor{
        label: Some("Compute float Uniform Buffer"),
        size: 16,
        usage: wgpu::BufferUsages::UNIFORM | wgpu::BufferUsages::COPY_DST,
        mapped_at_creation: false,
    });

    let (cs_bind_group_layout, cs_bind_group) = ws::create_bind_group_storage(
        &init.device,
        vec![
            wgpu::ShaderStages::COMPUTE, wgpu::ShaderStages::COMPUTE,
            wgpu::ShaderStages::COMPUTE,
        ],
        vec![
            wgpu::BufferBindingType::Uniform,
            wgpu::BufferBindingType::Uniform,
            wgpu::BufferBindingType::Uniform,
        ],
        &[
            cs_colormap_buffer.as_entire_binding(),
            cs_int_uniform_buffer.as_entire_binding(),
            cs_float_uniform_buffer.as_entire_binding(),
        ],
    );

    let (cs_texture_bind_group_layout, cs_texture_bind_group) =
        ws::create_compute_texture_bind_group(&init.device, &tex.view);

    let cs_pipeline_layout = init.device.create_pipeline_layout(&wgpu::PipelineLayoutDescriptor{
        label: Some("Compute Pipeline Layout"),
        bind_group_layouts: &[&cs_bind_group_layout, &cs_texture_bind_group_layout],
```

```rust
            push_constant_ranges: &[],
        });

        let cs_pipeline = init.device.create_compute_pipeline(&wgpu::ComputePipelineDescriptor{
            label: Some("Compute Pipeline"),
            layout: Some(&cs_pipeline_layout),
            module: &cs_comp,
            entry_point: "cs_main",
        });

        Self {
            init,
            pipeline,
            uniform_bind_group: texture_bind_group,

            cs_pipeline,
            cs_uniform_buffers: vec![cs_colormap_buffer, cs_int_uniform_buffer, cs_float_uniform_buffer],
            cs_bind_groups: vec![cs_bind_group, cs_texture_bind_group],

            animation_speed: 1.0,
            function_type: 0,
            colormap_type: 0,
            scale: 5.0,
            fps_counter: ws::FpsCounter::default(),
        }
    }

    fn resize(&mut self, new_size: winit::dpi::PhysicalSize<u32>) {
        if new_size.width > 0 && new_size.height > 0 {
            self.init.size = new_size;
            self.init.config.width = new_size.width;
            self.init.config.height = new_size.height;
            self.init.surface.configure(&self.init.device, &self.init.config);

            // update texture bind groups for both render and compute pipelines when resizing
            let tex = td::ITexture::create_texture_store_data(&self.init.device, self.init.size.width,
                self.init.size.height).unwrap();
            let (_, texture_bind_group) =
                ws::create_texture_store_bind_group(&self.init.device, &tex);
            self.uniform_bind_group = texture_bind_group;

            let (_, cs_texture_bind_group) =
                ws::create_compute_texture_bind_group(&self.init.device, &tex.view);

            self.cs_bind_groups[1] = cs_texture_bind_group;
        }
    }

    #[allow(unused_variables)]
    fn input(&mut self, event: &WindowEvent) -> bool {
        match event {
            WindowEvent::KeyboardInput {
                input:
                    KeyboardInput {
                        virtual_keycode: Some(keycode),
                        state: ElementState::Pressed,
                        ..
                    },
                ..
            } => {
```

```rust
        match keycode {
            VirtualKeyCode::Space => {
                self.function_type = (self.function_type + 1) % 13;
                println!("function = {}", self.function_type);
                true
            }
            VirtualKeyCode::LControl => {
                self.colormap_type = (self.colormap_type + 1) % 2;
                true
            }
            VirtualKeyCode::Q => {
                self.animation_speed += 0.1;
                true
            },
            VirtualKeyCode::A => {
                self.animation_speed -= 0.1;
                if self.animation_speed < 0.0 {
                    self.animation_speed = 0.0;
                }
                true
            } ,
            _ => false
        }
    }
    _ => false,
    }
}

fn update(&mut self, dt: std::time::Duration) {
    // update uniform buffer for compute pipeline
    let int_params = [
        self.function_type,
        self.colormap_type,
    ];
    self.init.queue.write_buffer(&self.cs_uniform_buffers[1], 0, cast_slice(&int_params));

    let dt1 = self.animation_speed * dt.as_secs_f32();
    let float_params = [
        0.5 * (1.0 + dt1.cos()),
        self.init.size.width as f32,
        self.init.size.height as f32,
        self.scale,
    ];
    self.init.queue.write_buffer(&self.cs_uniform_buffers[2], 0, cast_slice(&float_params));
}

fn render(&mut self) -> Result<(), wgpu::SurfaceError> {
    let output = self.init.surface.get_current_texture()?;
    let view = output
        .texture
        .create_view(&wgpu::TextureViewDescriptor::default());

    let mut encoder = self
        .init.device
        .create_command_encoder(&wgpu::CommandEncoderDescriptor {
            label: Some("Render Encoder"),
        });

    // compute pass for vertices
    {
```

```rust
        let mut cs_pass = encoder.begin_compute_pass(&wgpu::ComputePassDescriptor{
            label: Some("Compute Pass"),
            timestamp_writes: None,
        });
        cs_pass.set_pipeline(&self.cs_pipeline);
        cs_pass.set_bind_group(0, &self.cs_bind_groups[0], &[]);
        cs_pass.set_bind_group(1, &self.cs_bind_groups[1], &[]);
        cs_pass.dispatch_workgroups(self.init.size.width/8, self.init.size.height/8, 1);
    }

    // render pass
    {
        let color_attachment = ws::create_color_attachment(&view);
        let mut render_pass = encoder.begin_render_pass(&wgpu::RenderPassDescriptor {
            label: Some("Render Pass"),
            color_attachments: &[Some(color_attachment)],
            depth_stencil_attachment: None,
            timestamp_writes: None,
            occlusion_query_set: None,
        });

        render_pass.set_pipeline(&self.pipeline);
        render_pass.set_bind_group(0, &self.uniform_bind_group, &[]);
        render_pass.draw(0..6, 0..1);
    }
    self.fps_counter.print_fps(5);
    self.init.queue.submit(iter::once(encoder.finish()));
    output.present();

    Ok(())
  }
}

fn main() {
    let mut colormap_name = "jet";
    let args: Vec<String> = std::env::args().collect();
    if args.len() > 1 {
        colormap_name = &args[1];
    }

    env_logger::init();
    let event_loop = EventLoop::new();
    let window = winit::window::WindowBuilder::new().build(&event_loop).unwrap();
    window.set_title(&*format!("ch10_{}", "domain_color"));

    let mut state = pollster::block_on(State::new(&window, colormap_name));
    let render_start_time = std::time::Instant::now();

    event_loop.run(move |event, _, control_flow| {
        match event {
            Event::WindowEvent {
                ref event,
                window_id,
            } if window_id == window.id() => {
                if !state.input(event) {
                    match event {
                        WindowEvent::CloseRequested
                        | WindowEvent::KeyboardInput {
                            input:
                                KeyboardInput {
```

```
                        state: ElementState::Pressed,
                        virtual_keycode: Some(VirtualKeyCode::Escape),
                        ..
                    },
                    ..
                } => *control_flow = ControlFlow::Exit,
                WindowEvent::Resized(physical_size) => {
                    state.resize(*physical_size);
                }
                WindowEvent::ScaleFactorChanged { new_inner_size, .. } => {
                    state.resize(**new_inner_size);
                }
                _ => {}
            }
        }
    }
    Event::RedrawRequested(_) => {
        let now = std::time::Instant::now();
        let dt = now - render_start_time;
        state.update(dt);

        match state.render() {
            Ok(_) => {}
            Err(wgpu::SurfaceError::Lost) => state.resize(state.init.size),
            Err(wgpu::SurfaceError::OutOfMemory) => *control_flow = ControlFlow::Exit,
            Err(e) => eprintln!("{:?}", e),
        }
    }
    Event::MainEventsCleared => {
        window.request_redraw();
    }
    _ => {}
    }
  });
}
```

The above code simple renders a 2D quad shape with a texture map on it, and the texture is generated using a compute shader. In the *State::new* function, we first create shader modules using several WGSL files, including *render_shader.wgsl, complex_func.wgsl,* and *domain_color_comp.wgsl.* We then define a texture and a sampler, which are used to create a uniform bind group for the render pipeline. This texture will be generated using a compute shader. The code segment for creating compute pipeline passes the texture to the compute shader and the compute shader will write the data for domain coloring to the texture.

The *State::render* function contains two passes: one for the compute pass and another for the render pass. In the render pass, we simply draw a quad shape using six vertices (for two triangles). We also animate the plot by passing a time dependent parameter to the compute shader inside the *State::update* function, as shown in the following code snippet:

```
let dt1 = self.animation_speed * dt.as_secs_f32();
let float_params = [
    0.5 * (1.0 + dt1.cos()),
    self.init.size.width as f32,
    self.init.size.height as f32,
    self.scale,
];
self.init.queue.write_buffer(&self.cs_uniform_buffers[2], 0, cast_slice(&float_params));
```

In the *State::input* function, we define several input parameters using the keyboard control, such as selecting function and colormap, allowing the user to manipulate the domain coloring plot.

Here is a list of controls using keyboard:

- *Space*: Select different function type to be displayed.
- *LControl*: Select different colormap.
- *Q/A*: Increases/decreases the animation speed.

10.3.5 Run Application

To run this application, add the following code snippet to the *Cargo.toml* file:

```
[[example]]
name = "ch10_domain_color"
path = "examples/ch10/domain_color.rs"
```

Afterward, execute the following *cargo run* commands in the terminal window:

```
cargo run --example ch10_domain_color
```

Fig.10-5 shows the results of this example for three different complex functions, which are expressed in the following formulas:

$$f_0(z) = \frac{z - 1}{z^2 + z + 1}$$

$$f_1(z) = \tan(\sin z)$$

$$f_2(z) = \frac{\sin[\cos(\sin z)]}{z^2 - 1}$$

Fig.10-5. Domain coloring for three different complex functions.

In the figure, each function has two domain coloring plots: on the top is a plot created using the default *hsv2RGB* function, and on the bottom is a plot created using the *colormap2RGB* function with different colormap names.

10.4 Domain Coloring for Iterated Functions

In mathematics, an iterated function refers to a function that is obtained by repeatedly applying another function to itself. The process of repeatedly applying the same function is called iteration. The iterated functions are frequently used in fractal geometry to generate self-similar and complex patterns by iterating simple mathematical functions. Iterated functions also have applications in computer graphics and image processing, where they can be used to generate patterns and textures or to perform transformations on images.

We will use the notation $f^{(n)}(z)$ to denote the n-th iteration of f, that is

$$f^1(z) = f(z), \ f^{(2)}(z) = f(f(z)), \ f^{(3)}(z) = f\left(f(f(z))\right), \dots$$

This section will use iterated complex functions to generate beautiful domain coloring images, which is similar to the process used to create domain coloring for ordinary complex functions as we did in the previous example.

10.4.1 Compute Shader for iterated functions

Create a new WGSL compute shader file named *iterate_func_comp.wgsl* in the *examples/ch10/* folder and include the following code:

```
// define iterated complex functions
fn cFunc(z:vec2f, a:f32, selectId:u32) -> vec2f {
    var fz = z;

    if (selectId == 0u) {
        fz = cMul(vec2(a, a), cLog(cMul(z,z)));
    } else if (selectId == 1u){
        fz = cDiv(cLog(cMul(z,z)-vec2(0.0, a)), cExp(cMul(z,z))-vec2(a, 0.0));
    } else if (selectId == 2u){
        fz = cDiv(cCos(z), cSin(cMul(z,z) - vec2(0.5*a, 0.0)));
    } else if (selectId == 3u){
        let f1 = cInv(cPow(z, 4.0) + vec2(0.0, 0.1*a));
        fz = cAsinh(cSin(f1));
    } else if (selectId == 4u){
        let f1 = cInv(cPow(z, 6.0) + vec2(0.0, 0.5*a));
        fz = cLog(cSin(f1));
    } else if (selectId == 5u){
        let f1 = cMul(vec2<f32>(0.0,1.0), cCos(z));
        let f2 = cSin(cMul(z,z) - vec2(a, 0.0));
        fz = cDiv(f1, f2);
    } else if (selectId == 6u){
        let f1 = cCos(cMul(vec2<f32>(0.0,1.0), z));
        let f2 = cSin(cMul(z,z) - vec2(a, 0.0));
        fz = cDiv(f1, f2);
    } else if (selectId == 7u){
        let f1 = cTan(z);
        let f2 = cSin(cPow(z,8.0) - vec2(0.5*a, 0.0));
        fz = cDiv(f1, f2);
    } else if (selectId == 8u){
        fz = cInv(z) + cDiv(cMul(z,z), cSin(cPow(z,2.0) - vec2(a, 0.0)));
    } else if (selectId == 9u){
        fz = cConj(z) + cDiv(cMul(z,z), cSin(cPow(z,2.0) - vec2(2.0*a, 0.0)));
    } else if (selectId == 10u){
        fz = cSqrt(cMul(vec2(0.0,1.0), z)) + cDiv(cMul(z,z), cSin(cPow(z,2.0) - vec2(2.0*a, 0.0)));
```

```
    } else {
        fz = cMul(vec2(a), cLog(cMul(z,z)));
    }
    return fz;
}

struct IntParams {
    funcSelect: u32,
    colorSelect: u32,
}
@group(0) @binding(0) var<uniform> ips: IntParams;

struct FloatParams {
    animateParam: f32,
    width: f32,
    height: f32,
    scale: f32,
}
@group(0) @binding(1) var<uniform> fps: FloatParams;
@group(0) @binding(2) var tex: texture_storage_2d<rgba8unorm, write>;

@compute @workgroup_size(8, 8, 1)
fn cs_main(@builtin(global_invocation_id) id: vec3u) {
    let a = fps.animateParam;
    let w = fps.width;
    let h = fps.height;
    let scale = fps.scale;
    var funcId =  ips.funcSelect;
    let colorId = ips.colorSelect;

    var z = vec2(scale*(f32(id.x) - 0.5*w)/w, -scale*(h/w)*(f32(id.y) - 0.5*h)/h);
    let iters:array<u32,11> = array<u32,11>(4,3,4,2,2,5,4,10,6,9,4);
    if(funcId >= 10u) {
        funcId = 0u;
    }

    var i = 0u;
    loop {
        if(i >= iters[funcId]) { break; }
        z = cFunc(z, a, funcId);
        i = i + 1u;
    }

    var color:vec4f;
    if (colorId > 0u && colorId < 22u) { // colormaps
        color = vec4(colormap2Rgb(z, colorId), 1.0);
    } else { // default
        color = vec4(hsv2Rgb(z), 1.0);
    }

    textureStore(tex, vec2<i32>(id.xy), color);
}
```

The above code begins by defining the *cFunc* function that contains eleven complex functions, each of which is selected using the *selectId* parameter. These functions are used as the base function, and the order of iterations will be set inside the *cs_main* function of the compute shader.

The compute shader in the above code is responsible for generating an image by evaluating an iterated complex function for each pixel in the image and storing the result in a texture.

In the shader, we pass the animation parameter, size of the window, scale, function selection, and colormap selection as uniform variables. Within the *cs_main* function, we define an array of *u32* type with each element specifying the iteration order for each function included in the *cFunc* function, as shown in the following code snippet:

```
let iters = array<u32,11>(4,3,4,2,2,5,4,10,6,9,4);
```

Subsequently, we use a loop to iterate the selected complex function. Computing such iterations of functions is a computation-intensive process, but by performing this task inside the compute shader, we free up the CPU and take advantage of the speed at which the GPU can carry out the mathematical operations in parallel. Thus, rather than computing the color one pixel at a time as we would have to do with the CPU-based Rust code, now we can use the multiple GPU cores to compute up to millions of pixel colors concurrently.

The color data for domain coloring is stored in the texture using the *textureStore* function with the current pixel coordinates and the computed color as parameters. The fragment shader can access this color data by sampling the texture using the texture function.

10.4.2 Rust Code

Create a new Rust file named *iterate_func.rs* in the *examples/ch10/* folder and add the following code to it:

```rust
use std::iter;
use wgpu::util::DeviceExt;
use winit::{
    event::*,
    event_loop::{ControlFlow, EventLoop},
    window::Window,
};
use bytemuck::cast_slice;
use wgpu_book_examples:: { wgpu_simplified as ws, colormap, texture_data as td };

fn create_color_data(colormap_name: &str) -> Vec<[f32; 4]> {
    let cdata = colormap::colormap_data(colormap_name);
    let mut data:Vec<[f32; 4]> = vec![];
    for i in 0..cdata.len() {
        data.push([cdata[i][0], cdata[i][1], cdata[i][2], 1.0 ]);
    }
    data
}

struct State {
    init:  ws::IWgpuInit,
    pipeline: wgpu::RenderPipeline,
    uniform_bind_group: wgpu::BindGroup,

    cs_pipeline: wgpu::ComputePipeline,
    cs_uniform_buffers: Vec<wgpu::Buffer>,
    cs_bind_groups: Vec<wgpu::BindGroup>,

    animation_speed: f32,
    function_type: u32,
    colormap_type: u32,
    scale: f32,
    fps_counter: ws::FpsCounter,
}
```

```rust
impl State {
    async fn new(window:&Window, colormap_name:&str) -> Self {
        let init = ws::IWgpuInit::new(&window, 1, None).await;

        let shader = init.device.create_shader_module(wgpu::include_wgsl!("render_shader.wgsl"));

        let cs_func_file = include_str!("complex_func.wgsl");
        let cs_iterate_func_file = include_str!("iterate_func_comp.wgsl");
        let cs_comp_file = [cs_func_file, cs_iterate_func_file].join("\n");

        let cs_comp = init.device.create_shader_module(wgpu::ShaderModuleDescriptor {
            label: Some("Compute Shader"),
            source: wgpu::ShaderSource::Wgsl(cs_comp_file.into()),
        });

        let tex = td::ITexture::create_texture_store_data(&init.device, init.size.width,
            init.size.height).unwrap();
        let (texture_bind_group_layout, texture_bind_group) =
            ws::create_texture_store_bind_group(&init.device, &tex);

        let pipeline_layout = init.device.create_pipeline_layout(&wgpu::PipelineLayoutDescriptor {
            label: Some("Render Pipeline Layout"),
            bind_group_layouts: &[&texture_bind_group_layout],
            push_constant_ranges: &[],
        });

        let mut ppl = ws::IRenderPipeline {
            shader: Some(&shader),
            pipeline_layout: Some(&pipeline_layout),
            vertex_buffer_layout: &[],
            is_depth_stencil: false,
            ..Default::default()
        };
        let pipeline = ppl.new(&init);

        // create compute pipeline for domain coloring
        let cdata = create_color_data(colormap_name);
        let cs_colormap_buffer = init.device.create_buffer_init(&wgpu::util::BufferInitDescriptor{
            label: Some("Colormap Uniform Buffer"),
            contents: bytemuck::cast_slice(&cdata),
            usage: wgpu::BufferUsages::UNIFORM | wgpu::BufferUsages::COPY_DST,
        });

        let cs_int_uniform_buffer = init.device.create_buffer(&wgpu::BufferDescriptor{
            label: Some("Compute Integer Uniform Buffer"),
            size:  16,
            usage: wgpu::BufferUsages::UNIFORM | wgpu::BufferUsages::COPY_DST,
            mapped_at_creation: false,
        });

        let cs_float_uniform_buffer = init.device.create_buffer(&wgpu::BufferDescriptor{
            label: Some("Compute float Uniform Buffer"),
            size:  16,
            usage: wgpu::BufferUsages::UNIFORM | wgpu::BufferUsages::COPY_DST,
            mapped_at_creation: false,
        });

        let (cs_bind_group_layout, cs_bind_group) = ws::create_bind_group_storage(
            &init.device,
```

```
            vec![
                wgpu::ShaderStages::COMPUTE, wgpu::ShaderStages::COMPUTE,
                wgpu::ShaderStages::COMPUTE,
            ],
            vec![
                wgpu::BufferBindingType::Uniform,
                wgpu::BufferBindingType::Uniform,
                wgpu::BufferBindingType::Uniform,
            ],
            &[
                cs_colormap_buffer.as_entire_binding(),
                cs_int_uniform_buffer.as_entire_binding(),
                cs_float_uniform_buffer.as_entire_binding(),
            ],
        );

        let (cs_texture_bind_group_layout, cs_texture_bind_group) =
            ws::create_compute_texture_bind_group(&init.device, &tex.view);

        let cs_pipeline_layout = init.device.create_pipeline_layout(&wgpu::PipelineLayoutDescriptor{
            label: Some("Compute Pipeline Layout"),
            bind_group_layouts: &[&cs_bind_group_layout, &cs_texture_bind_group_layout],
            push_constant_ranges: &[],
        });

        let cs_pipeline = init.device.create_compute_pipeline(&wgpu::ComputePipelineDescriptor{
            label: Some("Compute Pipeline"),
            layout: Some(&cs_pipeline_layout),
            module: &cs_comp,
            entry_point: "cs_main",
        });

        Self {
            init,
            pipeline,
            uniform_bind_group: texture_bind_group,

            cs_pipeline,
            cs_uniform_buffers: vec![cs_colormap_buffer, cs_int_uniform_buffer, cs_float_uniform_buffer],
            cs_bind_groups: vec![cs_bind_group, cs_texture_bind_group],

            animation_speed: 1.0,
            function_type: 0,
            colormap_type: 0,
            scale: 5.0,
            fps_counter: ws::FpsCounter::default(),
        }
    }
}

fn resize(&mut self, new_size: winit::dpi::PhysicalSize<u32>) {
    if new_size.width > 0 && new_size.height > 0 {
        self.init.size = new_size;
        self.init.config.width = new_size.width;
        self.init.config.height = new_size.height;
        self.init.surface.configure(&self.init.device, &self.init.config);

        // update texture bind groups for both render and compute pipelines when resizing
        let tex = td::ITexture::create_texture_store_data(&self.init.device, self.init.size.width,
            self.init.size.height).unwrap();
        let (_, texture_bind_group) =
```

```
                ws::create_texture_store_bind_group(&self.init.device, &tex);
            self.uniform_bind_group = texture_bind_group;

            let (_, cs_texture_bind_group) =
                ws::create_compute_texture_bind_group(&self.init.device, &tex.view);

            self.cs_bind_groups[1] = cs_texture_bind_group;
        }
    }

    #[allow(unused_variables)]
    fn input(&mut self, event: &WindowEvent) -> bool {
        match event {
            WindowEvent::KeyboardInput {
                input:
                    KeyboardInput {
                        virtual_keycode: Some(keycode),
                        state: ElementState::Pressed,
                        ..
                    },
                ..
            } => {
                match keycode {
                    VirtualKeyCode::Space => {
                        self.function_type = (self.function_type + 1) % 11;
                        println!("function = {}", self.function_type);
                        true
                    }
                    VirtualKeyCode::LControl => {
                        self.colormap_type = (self.colormap_type + 1) % 2;
                        true
                    }
                    VirtualKeyCode::Q => {
                        self.animation_speed += 0.1;
                        true
                    },
                    VirtualKeyCode::A => {
                        self.animation_speed -= 0.1;
                        if self.animation_speed < 0.0 {
                            self.animation_speed = 0.0;
                        }
                        true
                    } ,
                    _ => false
                }
            }
            _ => false,
        }
    }

    fn update(&mut self, dt: std::time::Duration) {
        // update uniform buffer for compute pipeline
        let int_params = [
            self.function_type,
            self.colormap_type,
        ];
        self.init.queue.write_buffer(&self.cs_uniform_buffers[1], 0, cast_slice(&int_params));

        let dt1 = self.animation_speed * dt.as_secs_f32();
        let float_params = [
```

```
                    0.5 * (1.0 + dt1.cos()),
                    self.init.size.width as f32,
                    self.init.size.height as f32,
                    self.scale,
                ];
                self.init.queue.write_buffer(&self.cs_uniform_buffers[2], 0, cast_slice(&float_params));
        }

        fn render(&mut self) -> Result<(), wgpu::SurfaceError> {
            let output = self.init.surface.get_current_texture()?;
            let view = output
                .texture
                .create_view(&wgpu::TextureViewDescriptor::default());

            let mut encoder = self
                .init.device
                .create_command_encoder(&wgpu::CommandEncoderDescriptor {
                    label: Some("Render Encoder"),
                });

            // compute pass for vertices
            {
                let mut cs_pass = encoder.begin_compute_pass(&wgpu::ComputePassDescriptor{
                    label: Some("Compute Pass"),
                    timestamp_writes: None,
                });
                cs_pass.set_pipeline(&self.cs_pipeline);
                cs_pass.set_bind_group(0, &self.cs_bind_groups[0], &[]);
                cs_pass.set_bind_group(1, &self.cs_bind_groups[1], &[]);
                cs_pass.dispatch_workgroups(self.init.size.width/8, self.init.size.height/8, 1);
            }

            // render pass
            {
                let color_attachment = ws::create_color_attachment(&view);
                let mut render_pass = encoder.begin_render_pass(&wgpu::RenderPassDescriptor {
                    label: Some("Render Pass"),
                    color_attachments: &[Some(color_attachment)],
                    depth_stencil_attachment: None,
                    timestamp_writes: None,
                    occlusion_query_set: None,
                });

                render_pass.set_pipeline(&self.pipeline);
                render_pass.set_bind_group(0, &self.uniform_bind_group, &[]);
                render_pass.draw(0..6, 0..1);
            }
            self.fps_counter.print_fps(5);
            self.init.queue.submit(iter::once(encoder.finish()));
            output.present();

            Ok(())
        }
    }
}

fn main() {
    let mut colormap_name = "jet";
    let args: Vec<String> = std::env::args().collect();
    if args.len() > 1 {
        colormap_name = &args[1];
```

```
    }

    env_logger::init();
    let event_loop = EventLoop::new();
    let window = winit::window::WindowBuilder::new().build(&event_loop).unwrap();
    window.set_title(&*format!("ch10_{}", "iterate_func"));

    let mut state = pollster::block_on(State::new(&window, colormap_name));
    let render_start_time = std::time::Instant::now();

    event_loop.run(move |event, _, control_flow| {
        match event {
            Event::WindowEvent {
                ref event,
                window_id,
            } if window_id == window.id() => {
                if !state.input(event) {
                    match event {
                        WindowEvent::CloseRequested
                        | WindowEvent::KeyboardInput {
                            input:
                                KeyboardInput {
                                    state: ElementState::Pressed,
                                    virtual_keycode: Some(VirtualKeyCode::Escape),
                                    ..
                                },
                            ..
                        } => *control_flow = ControlFlow::Exit,
                        WindowEvent::Resized(physical_size) => {
                            state.resize(*physical_size);
                        }
                        WindowEvent::ScaleFactorChanged { new_inner_size, .. } => {
                            state.resize(**new_inner_size);
                        }
                        _ => {}
                    }
                }
            }
            Event::RedrawRequested(_) => {
                let now = std::time::Instant::now();
                let dt = now - render_start_time;
                state.update(dt);

                match state.render() {
                    Ok(_) => {}
                    Err(wgpu::SurfaceError::Lost) => state.resize(state.init.size),
                    Err(wgpu::SurfaceError::OutOfMemory) => *control_flow = ControlFlow::Exit,
                    Err(e) => eprintln!("{:?}", e),
                }
            }
            Event::MainEventsCleared => {
                window.request_redraw();
            }
            _ => {}
        }
    });
}
```

The above code is very similar to the one used in the previous example. In particular, the *State::new* and *State::render* functions are identical to the previous example. We also animate the plot by passing a time dependent parameter to the compute shader inside the *State::update* function, as shown in the following code snippet:

```
let dt1 = self.animation_speed * dt.as_secs_f32();
let float_params = [
    0.5 * (1.0 + dt1.cos()),
    self.init.size.width as f32,
    self.init.size.height as f32,
    self.scale,
];
self.init.queue.write_buffer(&self.cs_uniform_buffers[2], 0, cast_slice(&float_params));
```

In the *State::input* function, we define several input parameters in the keyboard control, such as selecting function and colormap, allowing the user to manipulate the domain coloring plot for the iterated complex function.

Here is a list of controls using keyboard:

- *Space*: Select different function type to be displayed.

- *LControl*: Select different colormap.

- *Q/A*: Increases/decreases the animation speed.

10.4.3 Run Application

To run this application, add the following code snippet to the *Cargo.toml* file:

```
[[example]]
name = "ch10_iterate_func"
path = "examples/ch10/iterate_func.rs"
```

Afterward, execute the following *cargo run* commands in the terminal window:

```
cargo run --example ch10_iterate_func
```

Fig.10-6 displays the domain coloring plots of four different complex functions with *selectId* values of 0, 2, 5, and 7, respectively. In the figure, each function has two domain coloring plots. On the top row, the plots for these four functions are created using the default *hsv2RGB* function, while on the bottom row, the plots are create using the *colormap2RGB* function with different colormap names.

Fig.10-6. Domain coloring for iterated complex functions.

The four complex functions are defined using the following formulas:

$$f_0(z) = a(1 + i) \log z^2 \text{ (with } a = 0.5, \text{ iterate to } 4^{th} \text{order)}$$

$$f_1(z) = \frac{\cos z}{\sin(z^2 - a)} \quad \text{(with } a = 1, \text{ iterate to } 4^{th} \text{order)}$$

$$f_2(z) = \frac{i \cos z}{\sin (z^2 - a)} \quad \text{(with } a = 1, \text{ iterate to } 5^{th} \text{order)}$$

$$f_3(z) = \frac{\tan(z)}{\sin (z^8 - a)} \quad \text{(with } a = 1, \text{ iterate to } 10^{th} \text{order)}$$

11 Particle System

Particle simulation is a technique used in computer graphics and game development to model the behavior and movement of a large number of individual particles, such as raindrops, cloud, smoke, sparks, or stars. Each particle is typically represented by a small 2D or 3D object with specific physical properties such as size, mass, velocity, and lifetime.

There are two types of particle simulations: traditional particle simulation and grid-based particle simulation. Traditional particle simulation treats each particle as an individual entity. The particles move freely in space, and their interactions with each other and with the environment are computed based on the laws of physics. The approach is very flexible, and it can be used to simulate a wide variety of particle systems, such as smoke, fire, and fluids. However, it can be computationally expensive, especially for large numbers of particles.

In contrast, grid-based particle simulation divides the simulation space into a grid. The particles are then represented by points in the grid. The forces acting on each particle are calculated by averaging the forces acting on the particles in the surrounding grid cells. This approach is much more computationally efficient, which makes it a good choice for simulating large numbers of particles such as fluid dynamics, cloth simulation, and soft body physics. However, grid-based particle simulation is less flexible than traditional particle simulation in terms of modeling complex interaction and behaviors, as the grid structure can constrain the movement of particles to some extent.

We can perform particle simulation using either the CPU or GPU. CPU-based particle simulations are typically slower than GPU-based particle simulations because to simulate a particle system on the CPU, we need to go through all the particles for every frame, update their parameters according to the rules, and then send the updated positions, velocities, and other information of the particles to the GPU for rendering. This is simple, and it should work. However, if the number of particles in the system is dramatically increased, we not only have to do more work per frame to compute new values of parameters on the CPU, but also have to send a lot more data to the GPU every time we want to render the particles, which is not cheap either.

However, if we run the simulation directly on the GPU, we are then able to harness the parallelism by updating a bunch of particles at a time, instead of one at a time. Thus, we do not need to upload the updated data every frame since it is already available on the GPU. With compute shader and *wgpu*, we can easily run the particle-system simulation on the GPU.

In this chapter, we will look at several examples of particle simulations on the GPU, including two traditional particle systems and five 2D grid-based particle systems. The two-traditional particle systems include the one that mimics the flocking behavior of birds and the other one that simulates gravity on particles, and both systems are modeled using compute shaders and instanced drawing. While the grid-based particle systems can be divided into two categories: the particle systems in one category are simulated using compute shaders and the particle systems in another category are simulated directly in the fragment shader. Theoretically, we can perform same computations on the GPU using either the computer shader or fragment shader, but in certain situations, it is easier to use fragment shader. For example, when we need to manipulate the textures from image files, we can do it easily inside the fragment shader. However, this task is harder to do with computer shader as the compute shader requires textures to be in a specific format and stored in a buffer. This involves several steps, such as creating a texture with the appropriate size, format, and layout, as well as copying the image data into the texture buffer.

11.1 Compute Boids

Compute boids is a technique for simulating the flocking behavior of birds using compute shaders. The basic idea behind compute boids is to use a compute shader to calculate and update the position and velocity of each bird in the flock based on the rules of alignment, separation, and cohesion. These computations are performed on groups of boids in parallel, which allows the simulation to run efficiently even with a large number of boids. The compute-boids example presented in the following subsections is based on the excellent WebGPU sample created by Austin Eng (please see his original sample at https://github.com/webgpu/webgpu-samples/tree/main/src/sample/computeBoids) .

11.1.1 Shader Code

Create a new WGSL shader file named *compute_boids.wgsl* in the *examples/ch11/* folder and add the following code to it:

```
struct Input {
    @location(0) particlePos : vec2f,
    @location(1) particleVel : vec2f,
    @location(2) vertexPos : vec2f,
}

struct Output {
    @builtin(position) vPosition : vec4<f32>,
    @location(0) vColor : vec4<f32>,
}

@vertex
fn vs_main(in: Input) -> Output {
    let angle = -atan2(in.particleVel.x, in.particleVel.y);
    let pos = vec2(
        (in.vertexPos.x * cos(angle)) - (in.vertexPos.y * sin(angle)),
        (in.vertexPos.x * sin(angle)) + (in.vertexPos.y * cos(angle))
    );

    var output: Output;
    output.vPosition = vec4(pos + in.particlePos, 0.0, 1.0);
    output.vColor = vec4(
        1.0 - sin(angle + 1.0) - in.particleVel.y,
        pos.x * 100.0 - in.particleVel.y + 0.1,
        in.particleVel.x + cos(angle + 0.5),
        1.0);
    return output;
}
```

```
@fragment
fn fs_main(in: Output) -> @location(0) vec4<f32> {
    return in.vColor;
}

struct Particle {
  pos : vec2f,
  vel : vec2f,
}
struct SimParams {
  deltaT : f32,
  rule1Distance : f32,
  rule2Distance : f32,
  rule3Distance : f32,
  rule1Scale : f32,
  rule2Scale : f32,
  rule3Scale : f32,
}
struct Particles {
  particles : array<Particle>,
}
@binding(0) @group(0) var<uniform> params : SimParams;
@binding(1) @group(0) var<storage, read> particlesIn : Particles;
@binding(2) @group(0) var<storage, read_write> particlesOut : Particles;

@compute @workgroup_size(64)
fn cs_main(@builtin(global_invocation_id) id : vec3u) {
    var index = id.x;

    var vPos = particlesIn.particles[index].pos;
    var vVel = particlesIn.particles[index].vel;
    var cMass = vec2(0.0);
    var cVel = vec2(0.0);
    var colVel = vec2(0.0);
    var cMassCount = 0u;
    var cVelCount = 0u;
    var pos : vec2f;
    var vel : vec2f;

    for (var i = 0u; i < arrayLength(&particlesIn.particles); i++) {
        if (i == index) {
            continue;
        }

        pos = particlesIn.particles[i].pos.xy;
        vel = particlesIn.particles[i].vel.xy;
        if (distance(pos, vPos) < params.rule1Distance) {
            cMass += pos;
            cMassCount++;
        }
        if (distance(pos, vPos) < params.rule2Distance) {
            colVel -= pos - vPos;
        }
        if (distance(pos, vPos) < params.rule3Distance) {
            cVel += vel;
            cVelCount++;
        }
    }

    if (cMassCount > 0) {
```

```
            cMass = (cMass / vec2(f32(cMassCount))) - vPos;
        }
        if (cVelCount > 0) {
            cVel /= f32(cVelCount);
        }
        vVel += (cMass * params.rule1Scale) + (colVel * params.rule2Scale) + (cVel * params.rule3Scale);

        vVel = normalize(vVel) * clamp(length(vVel), 0.0, 0.1);
        vPos = vPos + (vVel * params.deltaT);

        if (vPos.x < -1.0) {
            vPos.x = 1.0;
        }
        if (vPos.x > 1.0) {
            vPos.x = -1.0;
        }
        if (vPos.y < -1.0) {
            vPos.y = 1.0;
        }
        if (vPos.y > 1.0) {
            vPos.y = -1.0;
        }

        particlesOut.particles[index].pos = vPos;
        particlesOut.particles[index].vel = vVel;
}
```

The above code puts the vertex, fragment, and compute shaders together into a single shader file. The vertex shader takes the position and velocity of the instance particles, as well as the vertex positions of a single bird as input. Within the *vs_main* function, we calculate the angle between the particle's velocity and the *y*-axis, and then use the angle to rotate the vertex position around the particle position. Next, we compute the color using the particle velocity and a combination of sine and cosine functions. The fragment shader simply returns the color processed from the vertex shader.

The compute shader in the code above first defines three structs: *Particle*, *SimParams*, and *Particles*. The *Particle* struct represents a single particle and its position and velocity. *SimParams* stores simulation parameters such as the time step, distances for three different rules that govern the movement of particles, and so on. The *Particles* struct defines an array of particles.

Within the *cs_main* function, we initialize variables to compute the new velocity and position of the particle based on its neighboring particles. We use a loop to iterate over all other particles, calculate their distances to the current particle, and apply the three rules of boids algorithm: cohesion, separation, and alignment. Finally, we compute the new velocity and position of the particle and check to ensure they are within the simulation bounds. The updated particle data is then written to the *particlesOut* buffer at the current index.

11.1.2 Rust Code

Create a new Rust file called *compute_boids.rs* to the *examples/ch11/* folder and enter the following content into it:

```
use std::iter;
use wgpu::{util::DeviceExt, VertexBufferLayout};
use winit::{
    event::*,
    event_loop::{ControlFlow, EventLoop},
```

```
        window::Window,
};
use rand::{
    distributions::{Distribution, Uniform},
    SeedableRng,
};
use wgpu_book_examples::wgpu_simplified as ws;

const NUM_PARTICLES:u32 = 5000;
const PARTICLES_PER_GROUP:u32 = 64;

struct State {
    init:  ws::IWgpuInit,
    pipeline: wgpu::RenderPipeline,
    cs_pipeline: wgpu::ComputePipeline,
    particle_bind_groups: Vec<wgpu::BindGroup>,
    particle_buffers: Vec<wgpu::Buffer>,
    vertices_buffer: wgpu::Buffer,
    work_group_count: u32,
    frame_num: usize,
    fps_counter: ws::FpsCounter,
}

impl State {
    async fn new(window:&Window) -> Self {
        let init = ws::IWgpuInit::new(&window, 1, None).await;

        let shader = init.device.create_shader_module(wgpu::include_wgsl!("compute_boids.wgsl"));

        let pipeline_layout = init.device.create_pipeline_layout(&wgpu::PipelineLayoutDescriptor {
            label: Some("Render Pipeline Layout"),
            bind_group_layouts: &[],
            push_constant_ranges: &[],
        });

        let vertex_buffer_layouts = [
            VertexBufferLayout {
                array_stride: 16,
                step_mode: wgpu::VertexStepMode::Instance,
                attributes: &wgpu::vertex_attr_array![0 => Float32x2, 1 => Float32x2],
            },
            wgpu::VertexBufferLayout {
                array_stride: 8,
                step_mode: wgpu::VertexStepMode::Vertex,
                attributes: &wgpu::vertex_attr_array![2 => Float32x2],
            },
        ];

        let mut ppl = ws::IRenderPipeline {
            shader: Some(&shader),
            pipeline_layout: Some(&pipeline_layout),
            vertex_buffer_layout: &vertex_buffer_layouts,
            is_depth_stencil: false,
            ..Default::default()
        };
        let pipeline = ppl.new(&init);

        let vertex_data = [-0.01f32, -0.02, 0.01, -0.02, 0.00, 0.02];
        let vertices_buffer = init.device.create_buffer_init(&wgpu::util::BufferInitDescriptor {
            label: Some("Vertex Buffer"),
```

```
            contents: bytemuck::bytes_of(&vertex_data),
            usage: wgpu::BufferUsages::VERTEX | wgpu::BufferUsages::COPY_DST,
    });

    // create compute pipeline
    ********************************************************************

    let params = [
        0.04f32, // deltaT
        0.1,     // rule1Distance
        0.025,   // rule2Distance
        0.025,   // rule3Distance
        0.02,    // rule1Scale
        0.05,    // rule2Scale
        0.005,   // rule3Scale
    ];
    let cs_param_buffer = init.device.create_buffer_init(&wgpu::util::BufferInitDescriptor {
        label: Some("Compute Parameter Uniform Buffer"),
        contents: bytemuck::cast_slice(&params),
        usage: wgpu::BufferUsages::UNIFORM | wgpu::BufferUsages::COPY_DST,
    });

    let cs_bind_group_layout = ws::create_bind_group_layout_storage(
        &init.device,
        vec![
            wgpu::ShaderStages::COMPUTE, wgpu::ShaderStages::COMPUTE,
            wgpu::ShaderStages::COMPUTE,
        ],
        vec![
            wgpu::BufferBindingType::Uniform,
            wgpu::BufferBindingType::Storage { read_only: true },
            wgpu::BufferBindingType::Storage { read_only: false },
        ]
    );

    let cs_pipeline_layout = init.device.create_pipeline_layout(&wgpu::PipelineLayoutDescriptor{
        label: Some("Compute Pipeline Layout"),
        bind_group_layouts: &[&cs_bind_group_layout],
        push_constant_ranges: &[],
    });

    let cs_pipeline = init.device.create_compute_pipeline(&wgpu::ComputePipelineDescriptor{
        label: Some("Compute Pipeline"),
        layout: Some(&cs_pipeline_layout),
        module: &shader,
        entry_point: "cs_main",
    });

    let mut initial_particle_data = vec![0.0f32; (4 * NUM_PARTICLES) as usize];
    let mut rng = rand::rngs::StdRng::seed_from_u64(42);
    let unif = Uniform::new_inclusive(-1.0, 1.0);
    for particle_instance_chunk in initial_particle_data.chunks_mut(4) {
        particle_instance_chunk[0] = unif.sample(&mut rng);       // posx
        particle_instance_chunk[1] = unif.sample(&mut rng);       // posy
        particle_instance_chunk[2] = unif.sample(&mut rng) * 0.1; // velx
        particle_instance_chunk[3] = unif.sample(&mut rng) * 0.1; // vely
    }

    let mut particle_buffers = Vec::<wgpu::Buffer>::new();
    let mut particle_bind_groups = Vec::<wgpu::BindGroup>::new();
```

```
        for i in 0..2 {
            particle_buffers.push(
                init.device.create_buffer_init(&wgpu::util::BufferInitDescriptor {
                    label: Some(&format!("Particle Buffer {}", i)),
                    contents: bytemuck::cast_slice(&initial_particle_data),
                    usage: wgpu::BufferUsages::VERTEX | wgpu::BufferUsages::STORAGE
                        | wgpu::BufferUsages::COPY_DST,
                }),
            );
        }

        for i in 0..2 {
            particle_bind_groups.push(init.device.create_bind_group(&wgpu::BindGroupDescriptor {
                layout: &cs_bind_group_layout,
                entries: &[
                    wgpu::BindGroupEntry {
                        binding: 0,
                        resource: cs_param_buffer.as_entire_binding(),
                    },
                    wgpu::BindGroupEntry {
                        binding: 1,
                        resource: particle_buffers[i%2].as_entire_binding(),
                    },
                    wgpu::BindGroupEntry {
                        binding: 2,
                        resource: particle_buffers[(i + 1) % 2].as_entire_binding(),
                    },
                ],
                label: None,
            }));
        }

        let work_group_count = ((NUM_PARTICLES as f32) / (PARTICLES_PER_GROUP as f32)).ceil() as u32;

        Self {
            init,
            pipeline,
            cs_pipeline,
            particle_bind_groups,
            particle_buffers,
            vertices_buffer,
            work_group_count,
            frame_num: 0,
            fps_counter: ws::FpsCounter::default(),
        }
    }
}

fn resize(&mut self, new_size: winit::dpi::PhysicalSize<u32>) {
    if new_size.width > 0 && new_size.height > 0 {
        self.init.size = new_size;
        self.init.config.width = new_size.width;
        self.init.config.height = new_size.height;
        self.init.surface.configure(&self.init.device, &self.init.config);
    }
}

#[allow(unused_variables)]
#[allow(unused_variables)]
fn input(&mut self, event: &WindowEvent) -> bool {
    false
```

```rust
    }

    fn update(&mut self) {
    }

    fn render(&mut self) -> Result<(), wgpu::SurfaceError> {
        let output = self.init.surface.get_current_texture()?;
        let view = output
            .texture
            .create_view(&wgpu::TextureViewDescriptor::default());

        let mut encoder = self
            .init.device
            .create_command_encoder(&wgpu::CommandEncoderDescriptor {
                label: Some("Render Encoder"),
            });

        // compute pass
        {
            let mut cs_pass = encoder.begin_compute_pass(&wgpu::ComputePassDescriptor{
                label: Some("Compute Pass"),
            });
            cs_pass.set_pipeline(&self.cs_pipeline);
            cs_pass.set_bind_group(0, &self.particle_bind_groups[self.frame_num % 2], &[]);
            cs_pass.dispatch_workgroups(self.work_group_count, 1, 1);
        }

        // render pass
        {
            let color_attachment = ws::create_color_attachment(&view);
            let mut render_pass = encoder.begin_render_pass(&wgpu::RenderPassDescriptor {
                label: Some("Render Pass"),
                color_attachments: &[Some(color_attachment)],
                depth_stencil_attachment: None,
            });

            render_pass.set_pipeline(&self.pipeline);
            render_pass.set_vertex_buffer(0, self.particle_buffers[
                (self.frame_num + 1) % 2].slice(..));
            render_pass.set_vertex_buffer(1, self.vertices_buffer.slice(..));
            render_pass.draw(0..3, 0..NUM_PARTICLES);
        }

        // update frame count
        self.frame_num += 1;

        self.init.queue.submit(iter::once(encoder.finish()));
        output.present();
        self.fps_counter.print_fps(5);
        Ok(())
    }
}

fn main() {
    env_logger::init();
    let event_loop = EventLoop::new();
    let window = winit::window::WindowBuilder::new().build(&event_loop).unwrap();
    window.set_title(&*format!("ch11_{}", "compute_boids"));

    let mut state = pollster::block_on(State::new(&window));
```

```
event_loop.run(move |event, _, control_flow| {
    match event {
        Event::WindowEvent {
            ref event,
            window_id,
        } if window_id == window.id() => {
            if !state.input(event) {
                match event {
                    WindowEvent::CloseRequested
                    | WindowEvent::KeyboardInput {
                        input:
                            KeyboardInput {
                                state: ElementState::Pressed,
                                virtual_keycode: Some(VirtualKeyCode::Escape),
                                ..
                            },
                        ..
                    } => *control_flow = ControlFlow::Exit,
                    WindowEvent::Resized(physical_size) => {
                        state.resize(*physical_size);
                    }
                    WindowEvent::ScaleFactorChanged { new_inner_size, .. } => {
                        state.resize(**new_inner_size);
                    }
                    _ => {}
                }
            }
        }
        Event::RedrawRequested(_) => {
            state.update();

            match state.render() {
                Ok(_) => {}
                Err(wgpu::SurfaceError::Lost) => state.resize(state.init.size),
                Err(wgpu::SurfaceError::OutOfMemory) => *control_flow = ControlFlow::Exit,
                Err(e) => eprintln!("{:?}", e),
            }
        }
        Event::MainEventsCleared => {
            window.request_redraw();
        }
        _ => {}
    }
});
}
```

The code above first initializes some global variables, including the number of particles and particles per workgroup, which can be used by different functions without passing them as input.

In the *State::new* function, we define the vertex buffer layout that contains both the "*instance*" and "*vertex*" step modes. In the "*instance*" step mode, we specify the position and velocity of the instanced particles using the data generated from the compute shader, while in the "*vertex*" step mode, we set the vortex position using the data created manually in the following code within the *State::new* function. Next, we use this vertex buffer layout to create the render pipeline. Subsequently, we create the vertex data used to simulate each bird with a small triangle.

In the code segment for creating compute pipeline, we first generate the initial values for simulation parameters that govern the behavior of the boids and use this initial data to create a uniform parameter buffer. These parameters set three rules for controlling the movement of the boids. The first rule is cohesion, which makes each boid try to move towards the average position of its neighbors. The second rule is separation, which makes each boid try to maintain a minimum distance from its neighbors. The third rule is alignment, which makes each boid try to match the velocity of its neighbors.

Subsequently, we initialize the position and velocity of the particles with random values. We then create two sets of particle buffers using the same initial particle data. When we define the bind group for the compute pipeline, we set the *particle_buffers*[i] at binding 1 for reading and set *particle_buffers*[$(i + 1)\%2$] at binding 2 for writing, ensuring that the buffer is used for reading is always different from that used for writing.

In the *State::render* function, we use the following code snippet to set the bind group for compute pass:

```
cs_pass.set_bind_group(0, &self.particle_bind_groups[self.frame_num % 2], &[]);
```

Here, *frame_num* is the increment number, which increases by 1 for each frame. On the other hand, we use the following code snippet to set vertex buffer to the render pass:

```
render_pass.set_vertex_buffer(0, self.particle_buffers[(self.frame_num + 1) % 2].slice(..));
```

This ensures that the reading buffer is always different from the writing buffer.

11.1.3 Run Application

To run this application, add the following code snippet to the *Cargo.toml* file:

```
[[example]]
name = "ch11_compute_boids"
path = "examples/ch11/compute_boids.rs"
```

Afterward, execute the following *cargo run* commands in the terminal window:

```
cargo run --example ch11_compute_boids
```

Fig.11-1 shows the results of this example.

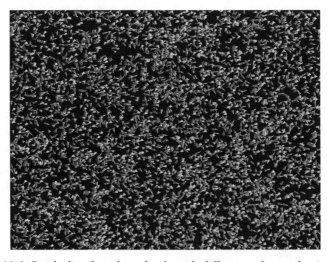

Fig.11-1. Boids distributed randomly with different colors at beginning.

It is evident from the figure that at beginning, the boids are distributed on the scene randomly with different positions, velocities, and colors. However, they will gradually form large clusters with similar velocities and colors. Eventually, they will evolve into several large clusters with same velocity and color. The final color depends on the initial conditions. Fig.11-2 shows the results after several-minute evolution of initial results displayed in Fig.11-1.

Fig.11-2. Boids patterns after several-minute evolution.

11.2 Particles under Gravity

In this section, we will demonstrate how to use a computer shader to simulate the gravity effect on a particle system. The system consists of three mass centers and the particles are attracted towards each mass center with a gravity force. The gravitational force acting on each particle is determined by the combined forces generated by all three mass centers.

In this system, the locations of the three mass centers are moving around with time, so the mass centers can collide. This would result in a change in the gravitational field that affects the motion of the particles and provides rich physics phenomena.

11.2.1 Shader Code

Create a new WGSL shader file called *gravity.wgsl* in the *examples/ch11/* folder and include the following code:

```
// vertex shader
struct VertexUniforms {
    width: f32,
    height: f32,
    particleSize: f32,
}
@binding(0) @group(0) var<uniform> uniforms: VertexUniforms;

struct Input {
    @location(0) vertexPosition: vec2f,
```

```
    @location(1) position: vec2f,
    @location(2) velocity: vec2f,
    @location(3) color: vec4f,
};

struct Output {
    @builtin(position) Position: vec4f,
    @location(0) vColor : vec4f,
};

@vertex
fn vs_main(input: Input) -> Output {
    var output: Output;
    output.vColor = input.color;
    let pos = vec2(
        input.vertexPosition.x * uniforms.particleSize / uniforms.width,
        input.vertexPosition.y * uniforms.particleSize / uniforms.height
    );
    output.Position = vec4(pos + input.position, 0.0, 1.0);
    return output;
}

// fragment shader
@fragment
fn fs_main( @location(0) vColor: vec4f) -> @location(0) vec4f {
    var color = vColor.rgb;
    color = pow(color, vec3(1.0/2.2));
    return vec4(color*vColor.a, vColor.a);
}

// compute shader
struct Particle {
    pos: vec2f,
    vel: vec2f,
};

struct Particles {
    particles: array<Particle>,
}

struct Params {
    mass1Position: vec2f,
    mass2Position: vec2f,
    mass3Position: vec2f,
    mass1Factor: f32,
    mass2Factor: f32,
    mass3Factor: f32,
}

struct AnimateParam {
    time: f32,
    deltaT: f32,
}

@binding(0) @group(0) var<storage, read> particleIn: Particles;
@binding(1) @group(0) var<storage, read_write> particleOut: Particles;
@binding(2) @group(0) var<uniform> ps: Params;
@binding(3) @group(0) var<uniform> ap: AnimateParam;

@compute @workgroup_size(64, 1, 1)
```

```
fn cs_main(@builtin(global_invocation_id) id : vec3u) {
    var index:u32 =  id.x;
    var position = particleIn.particles[index].pos;
    var velocity = particleIn.particles[index].vel;

    var massPositions = array(
        vec2(ps.mass1Position.x * sin(0.05*ap.time), ps.mass1Position.y * sin(0.1*ap.time + 3.0)),
        vec2(ps.mass1Position.x * sin(0.07*ap.time + 1.0), ps.mass1Position.y * sin(0.25*ap.time + 2.0)),
        vec2(ps.mass1Position.x * sin(0.06*ap.time + 2.0), ps.mass1Position.y * sin(0.2*ap.time + 1.0))
    );

    var massFactors = array<f32, 3>(ps.mass1Factor, ps.mass2Factor, ps.mass3Factor);

    var acceleration = vec2(0.0);
    for(var i = 0u; i < 3u; i++) {
        let r = massPositions[i] - position;
        let dist = max(0.1, length(r));
        let dir = normalize(r);
        acceleration += massFactors[i] / (dist * dist) * dir;
    }

    velocity += acceleration * ap.deltaT;
    velocity = 0.995 * velocity;

    position += velocity * ap.deltaT;

    particleOut.particles[index].pos = position;
    particleOut.particles[index].vel = velocity;
}
```

The above code puts the vertex, fragment, and compute shaders together into a single shader file. The vertex shader takes the position, velocity, and color of the instance particles, as well as the vertex positions of a single particle, as input. Within the *vs_main* function, the particle position is calculated by adding its instance position and vertex position together. The vertex buffer provides the color for the particle, which is then passed to the fragment shader for rendering the particle system.

The compute shader first retrieves the initial position and velocity data of the particle from the input buffer. It then defines time-dependent locations for the three mass centers, based on their initial positions specified in the *Params* struct. Next, it calculates the acceleration of the particle due to the gravitational attraction of the three mass centers. The acceleration is then added to the velocity, and the velocity is multiplied by a dampening factor of 0.995. Finally, the updated position and velocity of the particle are written to the output buffer.

It is worth noting that the *max* function is used in order to prevent division by zero when calculating the distance between a particle and a mass center.

11.2.2 Rust Code

Create a new Rust file called *gravity.rs* to the *examples/ch11/* folder and add the following content to it:

```
use std::iter;
use bytemuck::cast_slice;
use wgpu::{util::DeviceExt, VertexBufferLayout};
use winit::{
    event::*,
    event_loop::{ControlFlow, EventLoop},
    window::Window,
```

```
};
use rand::distributions::{Distribution, Uniform};
use wgpu_book_examples::wgpu_simplified as ws;

const NUM_PARTICLES:u32 = 10000;
const PARTICLES_PER_GROUP:u32 = 64;

struct State {
    init:  ws::IWgpuInit,
    pipeline: wgpu::RenderPipeline,
    vertex_buffers: Vec<wgpu::Buffer>,
    uniform_buffer: wgpu::Buffer,
    uniform_bind_group: wgpu::BindGroup,
    particle_size: f32,

    cs_pipeline: wgpu::ComputePipeline,
    particle_bind_groups: Vec<wgpu::BindGroup>,
    particle_buffers: Vec<wgpu::Buffer>,
    cs_uniform_buffers: Vec<wgpu::Buffer>,
    work_group_count: u32,
    frame_num: usize,

    animation_speed: f32,
    delt_t: f32,
    data_changed: bool,
    fps_counter: ws::FpsCounter,
}

impl State {
    async fn new(window:&Window) -> Self {
        let init = ws::IWgpuInit::new(&window, 1, None).await;

        let shader = init.device.create_shader_module(wgpu::include_wgsl!("gravity.wgsl"));

        let uniform_buffer = init.device.create_buffer(&wgpu::BufferDescriptor{
            label: Some("Uniform Buffer"),
            size: 16,
            usage: wgpu::BufferUsages::UNIFORM | wgpu::BufferUsages::COPY_DST,
            mapped_at_creation: false,
        });

        // uniform bind group for vertex shader
        let (uniform_bind_group_layout, uniform_bind_group) = ws::create_bind_group(
            &init.device,
            vec![wgpu::ShaderStages::VERTEX],
            &[uniform_buffer.as_entire_binding()],
        );

        let pipeline_layout = init.device.create_pipeline_layout(&wgpu::PipelineLayoutDescriptor {
            label: Some("Render Pipeline Layout"),
            bind_group_layouts: &[&uniform_bind_group_layout],
            push_constant_ranges: &[],
        });

        let vertex_buffer_layouts = [
            VertexBufferLayout {
                array_stride: 8,
                step_mode: wgpu::VertexStepMode::Vertex,    // vertex position
                attributes: &wgpu::vertex_attr_array![0 => Float32x2],
            },
```

```
            wgpu::VertexBufferLayout {
                array_stride: 16,
                step_mode: wgpu::VertexStepMode::Instance, // instance position, veclocity
                attributes: &wgpu::vertex_attr_array![1 => Float32x2, 2 => Float32x2],
            },
            VertexBufferLayout {
                array_stride: 16,
                step_mode: wgpu::VertexStepMode::Instance, // instance color
                attributes: &wgpu::vertex_attr_array![3 => Float32x4],
            },
        ];

        let mut ppl = ws::IRenderPipeline {
            shader: Some(&shader),
            pipeline_layout: Some(&pipeline_layout),
            vertex_buffer_layout: &vertex_buffer_layouts,
            is_depth_stencil: false,
            ..Default::default()
        };
        let pipeline = ppl.new(&init);

        // create vertex buffer
        let vertex_data = [-1f32, -1., 1., -1., -1., 1., -1., 1., 1., -1., 1., 1.];
        let vertex_buffer = init.device.create_buffer_init(&wgpu::util::BufferInitDescriptor {
            label: Some("Vertex Buffer"),
            contents: bytemuck::bytes_of(&vertex_data),
            usage: wgpu::BufferUsages::VERTEX | wgpu::BufferUsages::COPY_DST,
        });

        let mut rng = rand::thread_rng();
        let unif_mp = Uniform::new_inclusive(-1.0, 1.0);
        let unif_p = Uniform::new_inclusive(0.0, 1.0);
        let mut color_data = [0.0f32; 4 * NUM_PARTICLES as usize];
        for i in (0..color_data.len()).step_by(4) {
            color_data[i + 0] = unif_p.sample(&mut rng);
            color_data[i + 1] = unif_p.sample(&mut rng);
            color_data[i + 2] = unif_p.sample(&mut rng);
            color_data[i + 3] = 0.8;
        }
        let color_buffer = init.device.create_buffer_init(&wgpu::util::BufferInitDescriptor {
            label: Some("Color Buffer"),
            contents: bytemuck::cast_slice(&color_data),
            usage: wgpu::BufferUsages::VERTEX | wgpu::BufferUsages::COPY_DST,
        });

        // create compute pipeline
//**************************************************************************

        // create instance particle buffers
        let mut particle_data = [0.0f32; 4 * NUM_PARTICLES as usize];
        for i in (0..particle_data.len()).step_by(4) {
            particle_data[i + 0] = unif_mp.sample(&mut rng);        // position
            particle_data[i + 1] = unif_mp.sample(&mut rng);
            particle_data[i + 2] = unif_mp.sample(&mut rng) * 0.1;  // velocity
            particle_data[i + 3] = unif_mp.sample(&mut rng) * 0.1;
        }

        let mut particle_buffers:Vec<wgpu::Buffer> = vec![];
        for i in 0..2 {
            particle_buffers.push(init.device.create_buffer_init(&wgpu::util::BufferInitDescriptor{
```

```
            label: Some(&format!("Particle Buffer {}", i)),
            contents: bytemuck::cast_slice(&particle_data),
            usage: wgpu::BufferUsages::VERTEX | wgpu::BufferUsages::STORAGE |
                wgpu::BufferUsages::COPY_DST,
    }));
}

// mass parameters
let params = [
    unif_mp.sample(&mut rng), unif_mp.sample(&mut rng),    // mass 1 position
    unif_mp.sample(&mut rng), unif_mp.sample(&mut rng),    // mass 2 position
    unif_mp.sample(&mut rng), unif_mp.sample(&mut rng),    // mass 3 position
    unif_p.sample(&mut rng) * 2.0,                         // mass 1 factor
    unif_p.sample(&mut rng) * 2.0,                         // mass 2 factor
    unif_p.sample(&mut rng) * 2.0,                         // mass 3 factor
    0.0, 0.0, 0.0
];
let cs_param_buffer = init.device.create_buffer_init(&wgpu::util::BufferInitDescriptor {
    label: Some("Compute Parameter Uniform Buffer"),
    contents: bytemuck::cast_slice(&params),
    usage: wgpu::BufferUsages::UNIFORM | wgpu::BufferUsages::COPY_DST,
});

let animate_data = [0.0f32, 0.003, 0.0, 0.0];
let cs_animate_buffer = init.device.create_buffer_init(&wgpu::util::BufferInitDescriptor {
    label: Some("Compute Animation Parameter Uniform Buffer"),
    contents: bytemuck::cast_slice(&animate_data),
    usage: wgpu::BufferUsages::UNIFORM | wgpu::BufferUsages::COPY_DST,
});

let cs_bind_group_layout = ws::create_bind_group_layout_storage(
    &init.device,
    vec![
        wgpu::ShaderStages::COMPUTE, wgpu::ShaderStages::COMPUTE,
        wgpu::ShaderStages::COMPUTE, wgpu::ShaderStages::COMPUTE,
    ],
    vec![
        wgpu::BufferBindingType::Storage { read_only: true },
        wgpu::BufferBindingType::Storage { read_only: false },
        wgpu::BufferBindingType::Uniform,
        wgpu::BufferBindingType::Uniform,
    ]
);

let cs_pipeline_layout = init.device.create_pipeline_layout(&wgpu::PipelineLayoutDescriptor{
    label: Some("Compute Pipeline Layout"),
    bind_group_layouts: &[&cs_bind_group_layout],
    push_constant_ranges: &[],
});

let cs_pipeline = init.device.create_compute_pipeline(&wgpu::ComputePipelineDescriptor{
    label: Some("Compute Pipeline"),
    layout: Some(&cs_pipeline_layout),
    module: &shader,
    entry_point: "cs_main",
});

let mut particle_bind_groups = Vec::<wgpu::BindGroup>::new();
for i in 0..2 {
    particle_bind_groups.push(init.device.create_bind_group(&wgpu::BindGroupDescriptor {
```

```
                layout: &cs_bind_group_layout,
                entries: &[
                    wgpu::BindGroupEntry {
                        binding: 0,
                        resource: particle_buffers[i%2].as_entire_binding(),
                    },
                    wgpu::BindGroupEntry {
                        binding: 1,
                        resource: particle_buffers[(i + 1) % 2].as_entire_binding(),
                    },
                    wgpu::BindGroupEntry {
                        binding: 2,
                        resource: cs_param_buffer.as_entire_binding(),
                    },
                    wgpu::BindGroupEntry {
                        binding: 3,
                        resource: cs_animate_buffer.as_entire_binding(),
                    },
                ],
                label: None,
            }));
        }

        let work_group_count = ((NUM_PARTICLES as f32) / (PARTICLES_PER_GROUP as f32)).ceil() as u32;

        Self {
            init,
            pipeline,
            vertex_buffers: vec![vertex_buffer, color_buffer],
            uniform_buffer,
            uniform_bind_group,
            particle_size: 5.0,

            cs_pipeline,
            particle_bind_groups,
            particle_buffers,
            cs_uniform_buffers: vec![cs_animate_buffer, cs_param_buffer],
            work_group_count,
            frame_num: 0,
            data_changed: true,
            animation_speed: 1.0,
            delt_t: 0.002,
            fps_counter: ws::FpsCounter::default(),
        }
    }
}

fn resize(&mut self, new_size: winit::dpi::PhysicalSize<u32>) {
    if new_size.width > 0 && new_size.height > 0 {
        self.init.size = new_size;
        self.init.config.width = new_size.width;
        self.init.config.height = new_size.height;
        self.init.surface.configure(&self.init.device, &self.init.config);

        let uniform_data = [
            self.init.size.width as f32,
            self.init.size.height as f32,
            self.particle_size,
            0.0,    // padding
        ];
        self.init.queue.write_buffer(&self.uniform_buffer, 0, cast_slice(&uniform_data));
```

```rust
        }
    }

    #[allow(unused_variables)]
    fn input(&mut self, event: &WindowEvent) -> bool {
        match event {
            WindowEvent::KeyboardInput {
                input:
                    KeyboardInput {
                        virtual_keycode: Some(keycode),
                        state: ElementState::Pressed,
                        ..
                    },
                ..
            } => {
                match keycode {
                    VirtualKeyCode::Q => {
                        self.animation_speed += 0.1;
                        println!("animation speed = {}", self.animation_speed);
                        true
                    },
                    VirtualKeyCode::A => {
                        self.animation_speed -= 0.1;
                        if self.animation_speed < 0.0 {
                            self.animation_speed = 0.0;
                        }
                        println!("animation speed = {}", self.animation_speed);
                        true
                    },
                    VirtualKeyCode::W => {
                        self.particle_size += 0.1;
                        self.data_changed = true;
                        println!("particle size = {}", self.particle_size);
                        true
                    },
                    VirtualKeyCode::S => {
                        self.particle_size -= 0.1;
                        if self.particle_size < 0.1 {
                            self.particle_size = 0.1;
                        }
                        self.data_changed = true;
                        println!("particle size = {}", self.particle_size);
                        true
                    },
                    _ => false
                }
            }
            _ => false,
        }
    }

    fn update(&mut self, dt: std::time::Duration) {
        if self.data_changed {
            // update uniform parameters:
            let uniform_data = [
                self.init.size.width as f32,
                self.init.size.height as f32,
                self.particle_size,
                0.0,    // padding
            ];
```

```rust
        self.init.queue.write_buffer(&self.uniform_buffer, 0, cast_slice(&uniform_data));

        self.data_changed = false;
    }

    let dt1 = self.animation_speed * dt.as_secs_f32();
    let animate_params = [dt1, self.delt_t, 0.0, 0.0];
    self.init.queue.write_buffer(&self.cs_uniform_buffers[0], 0, cast_slice(&animate_params));
}

fn render(&mut self) -> Result<(), wgpu::SurfaceError> {
    let output = self.init.surface.get_current_texture()?;
    let view = output
        .texture
        .create_view(&wgpu::TextureViewDescriptor::default());

    let mut encoder = self
        .init.device
        .create_command_encoder(&wgpu::CommandEncoderDescriptor {
            label: Some("Render Encoder"),
        });

    // compute pass
    {
        let mut cs_pass = encoder.begin_compute_pass(&wgpu::ComputePassDescriptor{
            label: Some("Compute Pass"),
        });
        cs_pass.set_pipeline(&self.cs_pipeline);
        cs_pass.set_bind_group(0, &self.particle_bind_groups[self.frame_num % 2], &[]);
        cs_pass.dispatch_workgroups(self.work_group_count, 1, 1);
    }

    // render pass
    {
        let color_attachment = ws::create_color_attachment(&view);
        let mut render_pass = encoder.begin_render_pass(&wgpu::RenderPassDescriptor {
            label: Some("Render Pass"),
            color_attachments: &[Some(color_attachment)],
            depth_stencil_attachment: None,
        });

        render_pass.set_pipeline(&self.pipeline);
        render_pass.set_bind_group(0, &self.uniform_bind_group, &[]);
        render_pass.set_vertex_buffer(0, self.vertex_buffers[0].slice(..));
        render_pass.set_vertex_buffer(1, self.particle_buffers[
            (self.frame_num + 1) % 2].slice(..));
        render_pass.set_vertex_buffer(2, self.vertex_buffers[1].slice(..));
        render_pass.draw(0..6, 0..NUM_PARTICLES);
    }

    // update frame count
    self.frame_num += 1;

    self.init.queue.submit(iter::once(encoder.finish()));
    output.present();
    self.fps_counter.print_fps(5);

    Ok(())
  }
}
```

```
fn main() {
    env_logger::init();
    let event_loop = EventLoop::new();
    let window = winit::window::WindowBuilder::new().build(&event_loop).unwrap();
    window.set_title(&*format!("ch11_{}", "attractors"));

    let mut state = pollster::block_on(State::new(&window));
    let render_start_time = std::time::Instant::now();

    event_loop.run(move |event, _, control_flow| {
        match event {
            Event::WindowEvent {
                ref event,
                window_id,
            } if window_id == window.id() => {
                if !state.input(event) {
                    match event {
                        WindowEvent::CloseRequested
                        | WindowEvent::KeyboardInput {
                            input:
                                KeyboardInput {
                                    state: ElementState::Pressed,
                                    virtual_keycode: Some(VirtualKeyCode::Escape),
                                    ..
                                },
                            ..
                        } => *control_flow = ControlFlow::Exit,
                        WindowEvent::Resized(physical_size) => {
                            state.resize(*physical_size);
                        }
                        WindowEvent::ScaleFactorChanged { new_inner_size, .. } => {
                            state.resize(**new_inner_size);
                        }
                        _ => {}
                    }
                }
            }
            Event::RedrawRequested(_) => {
                let now = std::time::Instant::now();
                let dt = now - render_start_time;
                state.update(dt);

                match state.render() {
                    Ok(_) => {}
                    Err(wgpu::SurfaceError::Lost) => state.resize(state.init.size),
                    Err(wgpu::SurfaceError::OutOfMemory) => *control_flow = ControlFlow::Exit,
                    Err(e) => eprintln!("{:?}", e),
                }
            }
            Event::MainEventsCleared => {
                window.request_redraw();
            }
            _ => {}
        }
    });
}
```

The code above first initializes some global variables, including the number of particles and particles per workgroup, which can be used by different functions without passing them as input.

In the *State::new* function, we define the vertex buffer layout that contains both the "*vertex*" and "*instance*" step modes. In the "*instance*" step mode, we specify the position, velocity, and color for the instanced particles, with the position and velocity data generated from the compute shader and the color data from the randomly generated data. While in the "*vortex*" step mode, we set the vortex position using the created data. Next, we use this *buffers* attribute to create the render pipeline. Subsequently, we create the vertex data used to simulate each particle with a small quad and define a color buffer using the random data for the instanced particles.

In the segment for creating compute pipeline, we initialize the position and velocity of the particles with random values. We then create two sets of particle buffers using the same initial particle data. When we define the bind group for the compute pipeline, we set the *particle_buffers*[*i*%2] at binding 0 for reading and set *particle_buffers*[(*i* + 1)%2] at binding 1 for writing, ensuring that the buffer is used for reading is always different from that used for writing. Meanwhile, we also generate the initial values for simulation parameters that define the initial positions and mass factors of the three mass centers and use this initial data to create a uniform parameter buffer.

In the *State::render* function, we use the following code snippet to set the bind group for compute pass:

```
cs_pass.set_bind_group(0, &self.particle_bind_groups[self.frame_num % 2], &[]);
```

Here, *frame_num* is the increment number, which increases by 1 for each frame. On the other hand, we use the following code snippet to set vertex buffer to the render pass:

```
render_pass.set_vertex_buffer(1, self.particle_buffers[(self.frame_num + 1) % 2].slice(..));
```

This ensures that the reading buffer is always different from the writing buffer.

Additionally, the code permits the user to modify input parameters using keyboard inputs.

Here is a list of controls using keyboard:

- *Q/A*: Increases/decreases the animation speed.
- *W/S*: Increases/decreases the particle size.

11.2.3 Run Application

To run this application, add the following code snippet to the *Cargo.toml* file:

```
[[example]]
name = "ch11_gravity"
path = "examples/ch11/gravity.rs"
```

Afterward, execute the following *cargo run* commands in the terminal window:

```
cargo run --example ch11_gravity
```

Fig.11-3 shows the results of this example.

Fig.11-3. Particles distributed randomly at beginning.

It is evident from the figure that initially, the particles are distributed randomly. However, after a few minutes, the particles are gradually attracted towards the three mass centers. For the case where the three mass centers have a small animation (or moving) speed, depending on the initial locations and mass factors, the way that the three mass centers attract particles may look very different: one mass center may attract more particles than the others.

Fig.11-4 shows the results after several minutes of evolution. You can clearly see that the particles form three (or less than three) clusters around mass centers.

Fig.11-4. Particles attracted towards mass centers.

The results shown in Fig.11-4 are achieved by setting the animation speed of the mass centers to the default of 1. If we increase the animation speed to, for example, 5, the particles cannot form clusters around the mass centers anymore even after an hour of evolution, as demonstrated in the Fig.11-5.

The reason is that when the mass centers move at a high speed, the particle system is difficult to reach a state of equilibrium. The motion of the mass centers can cause the gravitational forces acting on the particles to be unbalanced, leading to non-uniform motion and complex trajectories for the particles. In particular, when the three mass centers move at a high speed, they have a high probability of colliding with each other, which further disrupts the formation of the particle clusters around the mass centers.

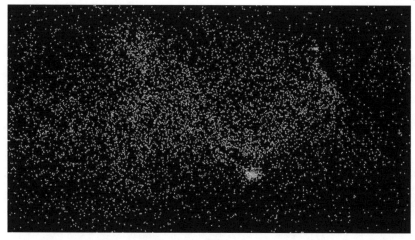

Fig.11-5. Particle clusters cannot be formed when the mass centers move at a high speed.

11.3 Firework Simulation

The two examples presented in the previous sections are traditional particle system simulations, where the particles move freely in space. In the following sections, we will use the grid-based particle simulation to model various phenomena such as the firework, fire, gravity on a 2D grid, electric field distribution, and stars in the universe.

The first example we are going to present in this section is the firework simulation, in which the number of fireworks, number of particles of each firework, and the explosion size of each firework can be specified by the user.

This example is based on a WebGL implementation found at https://www.shadertoy.com/view/Ws3SRS.

11.3.1 Shader Code

This example will reuse the vertex and fragment shader code implemented earlier for domain coloring in the previous chapter. Here, we only need to code a compute shader for firework simulation. To achieve this, we create a new WGSL compute shader file called *firework.wgsl* in the *examples/ch11/* folder and add the following code to it:

```
const pi:f32 = 3.141592653589793;
const speed = 10.0;

struct IntParams {
    width: u32,
    height: u32,
    numFireworks: u32,
    numParticles: u32,
    isGammaCorrection: u32,
}
@group(0) @binding(0) var<uniform> ips: IntParams;

struct FloatParams {
```

```
        time: f32,
        duration: f32,
        radius: f32,
}
@group(0) @binding(1) var<uniform> fps: FloatParams;
@group(0) @binding(2) var outputTex: texture_storage_2d<rgba8unorm, write>;

fn hash31(p:f32) -> vec3f {
        var p3 = fract(vec3(p) * vec3(0.1031, 0.11369, 0.13787));
        p3 += dot(p3, p3.yzx + vec3(19.19));
        return fract(vec3((p3.x + p3.y) * p3.z, (p3.x + p3.z) * p3.y, (p3.y + p3.z) * p3.x));
}

fn fireworks(p: vec2f, aspect:f32) -> vec3f {
        var color = vec3(0.0);
        var origin = vec2(0.0);
        var t = (fps.time + 10.0) % 7200.0;

        for(var i = 0u; i < ips.numFireworks; i = i + 1u) {
                var oh = hash31((f32(i) + 1234.1939) * 641.6974);
                origin = vec2(oh.x, oh.y) * 0.7 - vec2(0.1, 0.3);
                origin.x *= aspect;
                t += (f32(i) + 1.0) * 9.6491 * oh.z;

                for(var j = 0u; j < ips.numParticles; j = j + 1u) {
                        let h = hash31(f32(i)*963.31 + f32(j) + 497.8943);
                        let a = h.x * pi * 2.0;
                        let rs = h.y * fps.radius;
                        if(((t * speed) % fps.duration) > 2.0){
                                var r = ((t * speed) % fps.duration) * rs;
                                var pos = vec2(r * cos(a), r * sin(a));
                                pos.y -= pow(pos.x, 4.0);
                                let spark = 0.0002/pow(length(p - pos - origin), 1.65);
                                let sd = 2.0 * length(origin - pos);
                                let shimmer = max(0.0, sqrt(sd) * (sin((t + h.y * 2.0 * pi) * 20.0)));
                                let threshold = fps.duration * 0.32;
                                let fade = max(0.0, (fps.duration - 5.0) * rs - r);
                                color += mix(spark, shimmer * spark, smoothstep(threshold * rs,
                                        (threshold + 1.0) * rs , r)) * fade * oh;
                        }
                }
        }
        return color;
}

@compute @workgroup_size(8, 8, 1)
fn cs_main(@builtin(global_invocation_id) id: vec3u) {
        var p = vec2<f32>(id.xy) / f32(ips.height) - 0.5;
        p.y *= -1.0;
        let aspect = f32(ips.width) / f32(ips.height);

        var col = fireworks(p, aspect);
        col = max(vec3(0.1), col);
        col += vec3(0.12, 0.06, 0.02) * (1.0 - p.y);
        if(ips.isGammaCorrection == 1) {
                col = pow(col, vec3(1.0/2.2));
        }
        let color = vec4(col, 1.0);
        textureStore(outputTex, vec2<i32>(id.xy), color);
}
```

The above code uses a grid-based particle system to simulate a firework explosion. It begins by defining two parameter structs: *IntParams* and *FloatParams*, which hold integer and floating-point parameters, respectively. It then implements a function *hash31*, which is used to generate a pseudo-random 3D vector with a floating-point input argument.

Subsequently, the code defines a *firework* function, which is used to generate a particle system that simulates a firework explosion. The function uses the *hash31* function to generate random vectors for each particle and calculates the position and color of each particle based on its age and distance from the center of the explosion.

Afterwards, the *cs_main* function generates a 2D grid of particles using the *firework* function and writes the resulting colors to a 2D texture using the *textureStore* function.

11.3.2 Rust Code

Create a new Rust file named *firework.rs* in the *examples/ch11/* folder and include the following code:

```rust
use std::iter;
use winit::{
    event::*,
    event_loop::{ControlFlow, EventLoop},
    window::Window,
};
use bytemuck::cast_slice;
use wgpu_book_examples:: { wgpu_simplified as ws, texture_data as td };

struct State {
    init:  ws::IWgpuInit,
    pipeline: wgpu::RenderPipeline,
    uniform_bind_group: wgpu::BindGroup,

    cs_pipeline: wgpu::ComputePipeline,
    cs_uniform_buffers: Vec<wgpu::Buffer>,
    cs_bind_groups: Vec<wgpu::BindGroup>,

    animation_speed: f32,
    radius: f32,
    fireworks_count: u32,
    particles_count: u32,
    duration: f32,
    fps_counter: ws::FpsCounter,
}

impl State {
    async fn new(window:&Window) -> Self {
        let init = ws::IWgpuInit::new(&window, 1, None).await;

        let shader = init.device.create_shader_module(wgpu::include_wgsl!("../ch10/render_shader.wgsl"));
        let cs_shader = init.device.create_shader_module(wgpu::include_wgsl!("firework.wgsl"));

        let tex = td::ITexture::create_texture_store_data(&init.device, init.size.width,
            init.size.height).unwrap();
        let (texture_bind_group_layout, texture_bind_group) =
            ws::create_texture_store_bind_group(&init.device, &tex);

        let pipeline_layout = init.device.create_pipeline_layout(&wgpu::PipelineLayoutDescriptor {
            label: Some("Render Pipeline Layout"),
```

```
        bind_group_layouts: &[&texture_bind_group_layout],
        push_constant_ranges: &[],
    });

    let mut ppl = ws::IRenderPipeline {
        shader: Some(&shader),
        pipeline_layout: Some(&pipeline_layout),
        vertex_buffer_layout: &[],
        is_depth_stencil: false,
        ..Default::default()
    };
    let pipeline = ppl.new(&init);

    // create compute pipeline for domain coloring
    let cs_int_uniform_buffer = init.device.create_buffer(&wgpu::BufferDescriptor{
        label: Some("Compute Integer Uniform Buffer"),
        size:  16,
        usage: wgpu::BufferUsages::UNIFORM | wgpu::BufferUsages::COPY_DST,
        mapped_at_creation: false,
    });

    let cs_float_uniform_buffer = init.device.create_buffer(&wgpu::BufferDescriptor{
        label: Some("Compute float Uniform Buffer"),
        size:  16,
        usage: wgpu::BufferUsages::UNIFORM | wgpu::BufferUsages::COPY_DST,
        mapped_at_creation: false,
    });

    let (cs_bind_group_layout, cs_bind_group) = ws::create_bind_group_storage(
        &init.device,
        vec![
            wgpu::ShaderStages::COMPUTE, wgpu::ShaderStages::COMPUTE,
        ],
        vec![
            wgpu::BufferBindingType::Uniform,
            wgpu::BufferBindingType::Uniform,
        ],
        &[
            cs_int_uniform_buffer.as_entire_binding(),
            cs_float_uniform_buffer.as_entire_binding(),
        ],
    );

    let (cs_texture_bind_group_layout, cs_texture_bind_group) =
        ws::create_compute_texture_bind_group(&init.device, &tex.view);

    let cs_pipeline_layout = init.device.create_pipeline_layout(&wgpu::PipelineLayoutDescriptor{
        label: Some("Compute Pipeline Layout"),
        bind_group_layouts: &[&cs_bind_group_layout, &cs_texture_bind_group_layout],
        push_constant_ranges: &[],
    });

    let cs_pipeline = init.device.create_compute_pipeline(&wgpu::ComputePipelineDescriptor{
        label: Some("Compute Pipeline"),
        layout: Some(&cs_pipeline_layout),
        module: &cs_shader,
        entry_point: "cs_main",
    });

    Self {
```

```
            init,
            pipeline,
            uniform_bind_group: texture_bind_group,

            cs_pipeline,
            cs_uniform_buffers: vec![cs_int_uniform_buffer, cs_float_uniform_buffer],
            cs_bind_groups: vec![cs_bind_group, cs_texture_bind_group],

            animation_speed: 1.0,
            fireworks_count: 8,
            particles_count: 128,
            radius: 0.06,
            duration: 20.0,
            fps_counter: ws::FpsCounter::default(),
        }
    }

    fn resize(&mut self, new_size: winit::dpi::PhysicalSize<u32>) {
        if new_size.width > 0 && new_size.height > 0 {
            self.init.size = new_size;
            self.init.config.width = new_size.width;
            self.init.config.height = new_size.height;
            self.init.surface.configure(&self.init.device, &self.init.config);

            // update texture bind groups for both render and compute pipelines when resizing
            let tex = td::ITexture::create_texture_store_data(&self.init.device, self.init.size.width,
                self.init.size.height).unwrap();
            let (_, texture_bind_group) =
                ws::create_texture_store_bind_group(&self.init.device, &tex);
            self.uniform_bind_group = texture_bind_group;

            let (_, cs_texture_bind_group) =
                ws::create_compute_texture_bind_group(&self.init.device, &tex.view);

            self.cs_bind_groups[1] = cs_texture_bind_group;
        }
    }

    #[allow(unused_variables)]
    fn input(&mut self, event: &WindowEvent) -> bool {
        match event {
            WindowEvent::KeyboardInput {
                input:
                    KeyboardInput {
                        virtual_keycode: Some(keycode),
                        state: ElementState::Pressed,
                        ..
                    },
                ..
            } => {
                match keycode {
                    VirtualKeyCode::Q => {
                        self.animation_speed += 0.1;
                        true
                    },
                    VirtualKeyCode::A => {
                        self.animation_speed -= 0.1;
                        if self.animation_speed < 0.0 {
                            self.animation_speed = 0.0;
                        }
```

```
                                true
                            } ,
                        VirtualKeyCode::W => {
                            self.radius += 0.001;
                            true
                        },
                        VirtualKeyCode::S => {
                            self.radius -= 0.001;
                            if self.radius < 0.01 {
                                self.radius = 0.01;
                            }
                            true
                        } ,
                        VirtualKeyCode::E => {
                            self.duration += 0.1;
                            true
                        },
                        VirtualKeyCode::D => {
                            self.duration -= 0.1;
                            if self.duration < 5.0 {
                                self.duration = 5.0;
                            }
                            true
                        } ,
                        _ => false
                }
            }
            _ => false,
        }
    }

    fn update(&mut self, dt: std::time::Duration) {
        // update uniform buffer for compute pipeline
        let int_params = [
            self.init.size.width,
            self.init.size.height,
            self.fireworks_count,
            self.particles_count,
        ];
        self.init.queue.write_buffer(&self.cs_uniform_buffers[0], 0, cast_slice(&int_params));

        let dt1 = 0.5 * self.animation_speed * dt.as_secs_f32();
        let float_params = [
            dt1,
            self.duration,
            self.radius,
            0.0,
        ];
        self.init.queue.write_buffer(&self.cs_uniform_buffers[1], 0, cast_slice(&float_params));
    }

    fn render(&mut self) -> Result<(), wgpu::SurfaceError> {
        let output = self.init.surface.get_current_texture()?;
        let view = output
            .texture
            .create_view(&wgpu::TextureViewDescriptor::default());

        let mut encoder = self
            .init.device
            .create_command_encoder(&wgpu::CommandEncoderDescriptor {
```

```
                label: Some("Render Encoder"),
            });

        // compute pass for vertices
        {
            let mut cs_pass = encoder.begin_compute_pass(&wgpu::ComputePassDescriptor{
                label: Some("Compute Pass"),
            });
            cs_pass.set_pipeline(&self.cs_pipeline);
            cs_pass.set_bind_group(0, &self.cs_bind_groups[0], &[]);
            cs_pass.set_bind_group(1, &self.cs_bind_groups[1], &[]);
            cs_pass.dispatch_workgroups(self.init.size.width/8, self.init.size.height/8, 1);
        }

        // render pass
        {
            let color_attachment = ws::create_color_attachment(&view);
            let mut render_pass = encoder.begin_render_pass(&wgpu::RenderPassDescriptor {
                label: Some("Render Pass"),
                color_attachments: &[Some(color_attachment)],
                depth_stencil_attachment: None,
            });

            render_pass.set_pipeline(&self.pipeline);
            render_pass.set_bind_group(0, &self.uniform_bind_group, &[]);
            render_pass.draw(0..6, 0..1);
        }

        self.init.queue.submit(iter::once(encoder.finish()));
        output.present();
        self.fps_counter.print_fps(5);
        Ok(())
    }
}

fn main() {
    env_logger::init();
    let event_loop = EventLoop::new();
    let window = winit::window::WindowBuilder::new().build(&event_loop).unwrap();
    window.set_title(&*format!("ch11_{}", "firework"));

    let mut state = pollster::block_on(State::new(&window));
    let render_start_time = std::time::Instant::now();

    event_loop.run(move |event, _, control_flow| {
        match event {
            Event::WindowEvent {
                ref event,
                window_id,
            } if window_id == window.id() => {
                if !state.input(event) {
                    match event {
                        WindowEvent::CloseRequested
                        | WindowEvent::KeyboardInput {
                            input:
                                KeyboardInput {
                                    state: ElementState::Pressed,
                                    virtual_keycode: Some(VirtualKeyCode::Escape),
                                    ..
                                },
```

```
                                ..
                    } => *control flow = ControlFlow::Exit,
                    WindowEvent::Resized(physical_size) => {
                        state.resize(*physical_size);
                    }
                    WindowEvent::ScaleFactorChanged { new_inner_size, .. } => {
                        state.resize(**new_inner_size);
                    }
                    _ => {}
                }
            }
        }
        Event::RedrawRequested(_) => {
            let now = std::time::Instant::now();
            let dt = now - render_start_time;
            state.update(dt);

            match state.render() {
                Ok(_) => {}
                Err(wgpu::SurfaceError::Lost) => state.resize(state.init.size),
                Err(wgpu::SurfaceError::OutOfMemory) => *control flow = ControlFlow::Exit,
                Err(e) => eprintln!("{:?}", e),
            }
        }
        Event::MainEventsCleared => {
            window.request_redraw();
        }
        _ => {}
    }
});
}
```

The *State::new* and *State::draw* functions in the above code are similar to those used in the previous domain coloring example presented in Chapter 10. Additionally, the code permits the user to modify input parameters using keyboard inputs.

Here is a list of controls using keyboard:

- *Q/A*: Increases/decreases the animation speed.
- *W/S*: Increases/decreases the firework size.
- *E/D*: Increases/decreases the duration of the firework explosion.

11.3.3 Run Application

To run this application, add the following code snippet to the *Cargo.toml* file:

```
[[example]]
name = "ch11_firework"
path = "examples/ch11/firework.rs"
```

Afterward, execute the following *cargo run* commands in the terminal window:

```
cargo run --example ch11_firework
```

Fig.11- 6 shows the results of this example.

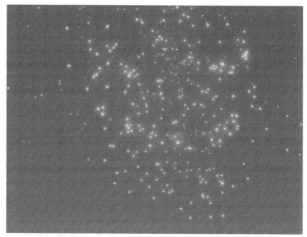

Fig.11-6. Firework simulation using a grid-based particle system.

11.4 Fire Simulation

Fire and smoke simulation is a technique of predicting the behavior of fire and smoke in a given space. In this example, we will use the *simplex3d* noise function, implemented earlier in the *noise3d.wgsl* file located in the *examples/ch09/* folder, to create the fire, smoke, and sparks.

This example is based on a WebGL demo found at https://www.shadertoy.com/view/MlKSWm.

11.4.1 Shader Code

As we did in the previous example, this example will also reuse the vertex and fragment shader code implemented earlier for domain coloring in the previous chapter. Here, we only need to code a compute shader for fire and smoke simulation. To achieve this, we create a new WGSL compute shader file called *fire.wgsl* in the *examples/ch11/* folder and add the following code to it:

```
const pi:f32 = 3.141592653589793;

struct IntParams {
    width: u32,
    height: u32,
    octaves: u32,
}
@group(0) @binding(0) var<uniform> ips: IntParams;

struct FloatParams {
    time: f32,
    fireHeight: f32,
    sparkSize: f32,
}
@group(0) @binding(1) var<uniform> fps: FloatParams;
@group(0) @binding(2) var outputTex: texture_storage_2d<rgba8unorm, write>;

fn noiseStack(p:vec3f, octaves:u32, falloff:f32) -> f32 {
    var noise = simplex3d(vec3(p));
    var off = 1.0;
```

```
        var pos = p;
        for(var i = 1u; i < octaves; i ++) {
            pos *= 2.0;
            off *= falloff;
            noise = (1.0 - off) * noise + off * simplex3d(pos);
        }
        return (1.0 + noise) / 2.0;
}

fn noiseStackUv(p:vec3f, octaves:u32, falloff:f32) -> vec2f {
    let da = noiseStack(p, octaves, falloff);
    let db = noiseStack(p + vec3(3984.293, 423.21, 5235.19), octaves, falloff);
    return vec2(da, db);
}

fn fires(p:vec2f, id:vec2f) -> vec3f {
    var uv = id;
    uv.y *= -1.0;
    var color = vec3(0.0);
    let yclip = p.y / fps.fireHeight;
    let yfalloff = clamp(2.0 - yclip, 0.0, 1.0);
    let yclipped = min(yclip, 1.0);
    let yclippedn = 1.0 - yclipped;
    let xfuel = 1.0 - abs(2.0 * p.x - 1.0);

    let pos = vec3(0.01* uv, 0.0) + vec3(1223.0, 6434.0, 8425.0);
    let flow = vec3(4.1 * (0.5 - p.x) * pow(yclippedn, 4.0), -2.0 * xfuel * pow(yclippedn, 64.0), 0.0);
    let t = fps.time * vec3(0.0, -1.7, 1.1) + flow;

    let displacePos = vec3(1.0, 0.5, 1.0) *2.4 * pos + fps.time * vec3(0.01, -0.7, 1.3);
    let displace3 = vec3(noiseStackUv(displacePos, ips.octaves, 0.5), 0.0);
    let noiseCoord = vec3(2.0, 1.0, 1.0) * pos + t + 0.4 * displace3;
    let noise = noiseStack(noiseCoord, 3u, 0.4);

    // fire
    let flames = pow(yclipped, 0.3 * xfuel) * pow(noise, 0.3 * xfuel);
    let f = yfalloff * pow(1.0 - flames * flames * flames, 8.0);
    let f3 = f * f * f;
    let fire = 1.5 * vec3(f, f3, f3*f3);

    // smoke
    let smokeNoise = 0.5 + simplex3d(0.4 * pos + t * vec3(1.0, 1.0, 0.2)) / 2.0;
    let smoke = vec3(0.3 * pow(xfuel, 3.0) * pow(p.y, 2.0) * (smokeNoise + 0.4 * (1.0 - noise)));

    // sparks
    let sparkGridSize = 30.0;
    var sparkCoord = uv - vec2(0.0, 190.0 * fps.time);
    sparkCoord -= 30.0* noiseStackUv(0.01 * vec3(sparkCoord, 60.0* fps.time), 1, 0.4);
    sparkCoord += 100.0 * flow.xy;
    if (((sparkCoord.y/sparkGridSize) % 2.0) < 1.0) { sparkCoord.x += 0.5 * sparkGridSize; }
    let sparkIndex = vec2(floor(sparkCoord / sparkGridSize));
    let sparkRand = rand2dTo1d(sparkIndex);
    var sparkLife = 1.0 - min(10.0 * (1.0 - min((-sparkIndex.y - (190.0 * fps.time / sparkGridSize)) /
        (24.0 - 20.0 * sparkRand), 1.0)), 1.0);
    let sparkSize = xfuel * xfuel * sparkRand * 0.05 * fps.sparkSize;
    let sparkRadians = 999.0 * sparkRand * 2.0 * pi + 4.0 * fps.time;
    let sparkCircular = vec2(sin(sparkRadians), cos(sparkRadians));
    let sparkOffset = (0.5 - sparkSize) * sparkGridSize * sparkCircular;
    let sparkModulus = ((sparkCoord + sparkOffset) % sparkGridSize) - sparkGridSize * vec2(0.5, -0.5);
    let sparkLength = length(sparkModulus);
```

```
    let sparksGray = max(0.0, 1.0 - sparkLength / (sparkSize * sparkGridSize));
    let sparks = 0.5 * sparkLife * sparksGray * vec3(1.0,0.3,0.0);

    return max(fire, sparks) + smoke;
}

@compute @workgroup_size(8, 8, 1)
fn cs_main(@builtin(global_invocation_id) id: vec3u) {
    var p = vec2f(id.xy) / vec2(f32(ips.width), f32(ips.height)) - vec2(0.0, 1.0);
    p.y *= -1.0;
    let col = fires(p, vec2f(id.xy));

    let color = vec4(col, 1.0);
    textureStore(outputTex, vec2<i32>(id.xy), color);
}
```

The above code uses a grid-based particle system to simulate fire, smoke, and sparks. It begins by defining two parameter structs: *IntParams* and *FloatParams*, which hold integer and floating-point parameters, respectively. It then uses the *simplex3d* noise to implement a function *noiseStack*, which is used to generate a noise value at specified position. The *noiseStack* function takes three input arguments: a 3D vector *p*, an integer *octave*, and a floating-point value *falloff*. The function works by first calculating the noise at the specified position using *simplex3d*, and then calculates the *falloff* factor that determines how much the noise should be attenuated as the distance from the origin increases. The function continues to iterate over the specified number of octaves and add the noise from each octave together. The function finally returns a noise value that is smooth and has a lot of detail. Furthermore, the *noiseStackUv* function generates two noise values using the *noiseStack* function with slightly different input vectors, and returns those two values as a 2D vector.

Inside the *fires* function, we use the *noiseStack* function to simulate fire flames, use the *simplex3d* function to generate smoke, and use *noiseStackUv* function to create sparks. The *flames* variable represents the intensity of the fire, *smokeNoise* represents the smoke at the position of the fire, and the *smoke* variable represents the color of the smoke. We define various variables, including spark coordinates, lifetime, offset, size, and so on to aid the calculation for sparks. The fires function finally returns a color mixed by fire flames, smoke, and sparks.

The *cs_main* function calls the *fires* function to compute the color of the pixel at the current position and the resulting color is stored in the output texture at the corresponding position in the texture using the *textureStore* function.

11.4.2 Rust Code

Create a new Rust file named *fire.rs* in the *examples/ch11/* folder and include the following code:

```
use std::iter;
use winit::{
    event::*,
    event_loop::{ControlFlow, EventLoop},
    window::Window,
};
use bytemuck::cast_slice;
use wgpu_book_examples:: { wgpu_simplified as ws, texture_data as td };

struct State {
    init:  ws::IWgpuInit,
    pipeline: wgpu::RenderPipeline,
    uniform_bind_group: wgpu::BindGroup,
```

```
        cs_pipeline: wgpu::ComputePipeline,
        cs_uniform_buffers: Vec<wgpu::Buffer>,
        cs_bind_groups: Vec<wgpu::BindGroup>,

        animation_speed: f32,
        octaves: u32,
        fire_height: f32,
        spark_size: f32,
        fps_counter: ws::FpsCounter,
}

impl State {
    async fn new(window:&Window) -> Self {
        let init = ws::IWgpuInit::new(&window, 1, None).await;

        let shader = init.device.create_shader_module(wgpu::include_wgsl!("../ch10/render_shader.wgsl"));

        let cs_noise_file = include_str!("../ch09/noise3d.wgsl");
        let cs_fire_file = include_str!("fire.wgsl");
        let cs_comp_file = [cs_noise_file, cs_fire_file].join("\n");

        let cs_shader = init.device.create_shader_module(wgpu::ShaderModuleDescriptor {
            label: Some("Compute Shader"),
            source: wgpu::ShaderSource::Wgsl(cs_comp_file.into()),
        });

        let tex = td::ITexture::create_texture_store_data(&init.device, init.size.width,
            init.size.height).unwrap();
        let (texture_bind_group_layout, texture_bind_group) =
            ws::create_texture_store_bind_group(&init.device, &tex);

        let pipeline_layout = init.device.create_pipeline_layout(&wgpu::PipelineLayoutDescriptor {
            label: Some("Render Pipeline Layout"),
            bind_group_layouts: &[&texture_bind_group_layout],
            push_constant_ranges: &[],
        });

        let mut ppl = ws::IRenderPipeline {
            shader: Some(&shader),
            pipeline_layout: Some(&pipeline_layout),
            vertex_buffer_layout: &[],
            is_depth_stencil: false,
            ..Default::default()
        };
        let pipeline = ppl.new(&init);

        // create compute pipeline for domain coloring
        let cs_int_uniform_buffer = init.device.create_buffer(&wgpu::BufferDescriptor{
            label: Some("Compute Integer Uniform Buffer"),
            size:  16,
            usage: wgpu::BufferUsages::UNIFORM | wgpu::BufferUsages::COPY_DST,
            mapped_at_creation: false,
        });

        let cs_float_uniform_buffer = init.device.create_buffer(&wgpu::BufferDescriptor{
            label: Some("Compute float Uniform Buffer"),
            size:  16,
            usage: wgpu::BufferUsages::UNIFORM | wgpu::BufferUsages::COPY_DST,
            mapped_at_creation: false,
```

```
        });

        let (cs_bind_group_layout, cs_bind_group) = ws::create_bind_group_storage(
            &init.device,
            vec![
                wgpu::ShaderStages::COMPUTE, wgpu::ShaderStages::COMPUTE,
            ],
            vec![
                wgpu::BufferBindingType::Uniform,
                wgpu::BufferBindingType::Uniform,
            ],
            &[
                cs_int_uniform_buffer.as_entire_binding(),
                cs_float_uniform_buffer.as_entire_binding(),
            ],
        );

        let (cs_texture_bind_group_layout, cs_texture_bind_group) =
            ws::create_compute_texture_bind_group(&init.device, &tex.view);

        let cs_pipeline_layout = init.device.create_pipeline_layout(&wgpu::PipelineLayoutDescriptor{
            label: Some("Compute Pipeline Layout"),
            bind_group_layouts: &[&cs_bind_group_layout, &cs_texture_bind_group_layout],
            push_constant_ranges: &[],
        });

        let cs_pipeline = init.device.create_compute_pipeline(&wgpu::ComputePipelineDescriptor{
            label: Some("Compute Pipeline"),
            layout: Some(&cs_pipeline_layout),
            module: &cs_shader,
            entry_point: "cs_main",
        });

        Self {
            init,
            pipeline,
            uniform_bind_group: texture_bind_group,

            cs_pipeline,
            cs_uniform_buffers: vec![cs_int_uniform_buffer, cs_float_uniform_buffer],
            cs_bind_groups: vec![cs_bind_group, cs_texture_bind_group],

            animation_speed: 1.0,
            octaves: 2,
            fire_height: 0.4,
            spark_size: 1.4,
            fps_counter: ws::FpsCounter::default(),
        }
    }

    fn resize(&mut self, new_size: winit::dpi::PhysicalSize<u32>) {
        if new_size.width > 0 && new_size.height > 0 {
            self.init.size = new_size;
            self.init.config.width = new_size.width;
            self.init.config.height = new_size.height;
            self.init.surface.configure(&self.init.device, &self.init.config);

            // update texture bind groups for both render and compute pipelines when resizing
            let tex = td::ITexture::create_texture_store_data(&self.init.device, self.init.size.width,
                self.init.size.height).unwrap();
```

```
        let (_, texture_bind_group) =
            ws::create_texture_store_bind_group(&self.init.device, &tex);
        self.uniform_bind_group = texture_bind_group;

        let (_, cs_texture_bind_group) =
            ws::create_compute_texture_bind_group(&self.init.device, &tex.view);

        self.cs_bind_groups[1] = cs_texture_bind_group;
    }
}

#[allow(unused_variables)]
fn input(&mut self, event: &WindowEvent) -> bool {
    match event {
        WindowEvent::KeyboardInput {
            input:
                KeyboardInput {
                    virtual_keycode: Some(keycode),
                    state: ElementState::Pressed,
                    ..
                },
            ..
        } => {
            match keycode {
                VirtualKeyCode::Space => {
                    self.octaves = (self.octaves + 1) % 6;
                    println!("octaves = {}", (self.octaves + 1));
                    true
                },
                VirtualKeyCode::Q => {
                    self.animation_speed += 0.1;
                    true
                },
                VirtualKeyCode::A => {
                    self.animation_speed -= 0.1;
                    if self.animation_speed < 0.0 {
                        self.animation_speed = 0.0;
                    }
                    true
                },
                VirtualKeyCode::W => {
                    self.fire_height += 0.01;
                    true
                },
                VirtualKeyCode::S => {
                    self.fire_height -= 0.01;
                    if self.fire_height < 0.1 {
                        self.fire_height = 0.1;
                    }
                    true
                },
                VirtualKeyCode::E => {
                    self.spark_size += 0.01;
                    true
                },
                VirtualKeyCode::D => {
                    self.spark_size -= 0.01;
                    if self.spark_size < 0.1 {
                        self.spark_size = 0.1;
                    }
                }
```

```
                        true
                  },
                  _ => false
              }
          }
          _ => false,
      }
}

fn update(&mut self, dt: std::time::Duration) {
    // update uniform buffer for compute pipeline
    let int_params = [
        self.init.size.width,
        self.init.size.height,
        self.octaves + 1,
        0,
    ];
    self.init.queue.write_buffer(&self.cs_uniform_buffers[0], 0, cast_slice(&int_params));

    let dt1 = 0.5 * self.animation_speed * dt.as_secs_f32();
    let float_params = [
        dt1,
        self.fire_height,
        self.spark_size,
        0.0,
    ];
    self.init.queue.write_buffer(&self.cs_uniform_buffers[1], 0, cast_slice(&float_params));
}

fn render(&mut self) -> Result<(), wgpu::SurfaceError> {
    let output = self.init.surface.get_current_texture()?;
    let view = output
        .texture
        .create_view(&wgpu::TextureViewDescriptor::default());

    let mut encoder = self
        .init.device
        .create_command_encoder(&wgpu::CommandEncoderDescriptor {
            label: Some("Render Encoder"),
        });

    // compute pass for vertices
    {
        let mut cs_pass = encoder.begin_compute_pass(&wgpu::ComputePassDescriptor{
            label: Some("Compute Pass"),
        });
        cs_pass.set_pipeline(&self.cs_pipeline);
        cs_pass.set_bind_group(0, &self.cs_bind_groups[0], &[]);
        cs_pass.set_bind_group(1, &self.cs_bind_groups[1], &[]);
        cs_pass.dispatch_workgroups(self.init.size.width/8, self.init.size.height/8, 1);
    }

    // render pass
    {
        let color_attachment = ws::create_color_attachment(&view);
        let mut render_pass = encoder.begin_render_pass(&wgpu::RenderPassDescriptor {
            label: Some("Render Pass"),
            color_attachments: &[Some(color_attachment)],
            depth_stencil_attachment: None,
        });
```

```
            render_pass.set_pipeline(&self.pipeline);
            render_pass.set_bind_group(0, &self.uniform_bind_group, &[]);
            render_pass.draw(0..6, 0..1);
        }

        self.init.queue.submit(iter::once(encoder.finish()));
        output.present();
        self.fps_counter.print_fps(5);
        Ok(())
    }
}

fn main() {
    env_logger::init();
    let event_loop = EventLoop::new();
    let window = winit::window::WindowBuilder::new().build(&event_loop).unwrap();
    window.set_title(&*format!("ch11_{}", "firework"));

    let mut state = pollster::block_on(State::new(&window));
    let render_start_time = std::time::Instant::now();

    event_loop.run(move |event, _, control_flow| {
        match event {
            Event::WindowEvent {
                ref event,
                window_id,
            } if window_id == window.id() => {
                if !state.input(event) {
                    match event {
                        WindowEvent::CloseRequested
                        | WindowEvent::KeyboardInput {
                            input:
                                KeyboardInput {
                                    state: ElementState::Pressed,
                                    virtual_keycode: Some(VirtualKeyCode::Escape),
                                    ..
                                },
                            ..
                        } => *control_flow = ControlFlow::Exit,
                        WindowEvent::Resized(physical_size) => {
                            state.resize(*physical_size);
                        }
                        WindowEvent::ScaleFactorChanged { new_inner_size, .. } => {
                            state.resize(**new_inner_size);
                        }
                        _ => {}
                    }
                }
            }
            Event::RedrawRequested(_) => {
                let now = std::time::Instant::now();
                let dt = now - render_start_time;
                state.update(dt);

                match state.render() {
                    Ok(_) => {}
                    Err(wgpu::SurfaceError::Lost) => state.resize(state.init.size),
                    Err(wgpu::SurfaceError::OutOfMemory) => *control_flow = ControlFlow::Exit,
                    Err(e) => eprintln!("{:?}", e),
```

```
            }
        }
        Event::MainEventsCleared => {
            window.request_redraw();
        }
        _ => {}
    }
});
}
```

In the above code, the *State::new* and *State::render* functions are similar to those used in the previous example, with the exception that the shader module for the compute pipeline combines the noise shader code from Chapter 9 with the fire shader. This combination is necessary because the fire shader uses the *simplex3D* and *rand2dTo1d* functions that were implemented in the noise shader.

Additionally, the code permits the user to modify input parameters using keyboard inputs.

Here is a list of controls using keyboard:

- *Space*: Changes the *octaves* level.
- *Q/A*: Increases/decreases the animation speed.
- *W/S*: Increases/decreases the fire height.
- *E/D*: Increases/decreases the spark size.

11.4.3 Run Application

To run this application, add the following code snippet to the *Cargo.toml* file:

```
[[example]]
name = "ch11_fire"
path = "examples/ch11/fire.rs"
```

Afterward, execute the following *cargo run* commands in the terminal window:

```
cargo run --example ch11_fire
```

Fig.11-7 shows the result of this example.

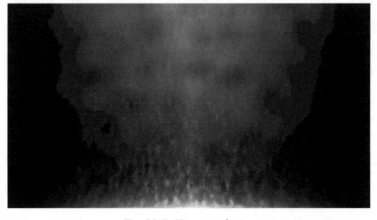

Fig.11-7. Fire simulation.

11.5 Gravity on a 2D Grid

The particle examples presented so far always use compute shaders to simulate different particle systems in order to perform complex computations on the GPU. While compute shaders are generally better suited for performing general-purpose calculations on the GPU, there are some situations where performing computations directly inside the fragment shader can be more efficient, especially when manipulating image textures.

One reason is that the fragment shader runs in parallel for each pixel on the screen, which can make it more efficient for image processing tasks that require manipulating each pixel independently, such as color correction or image filtering. Additionally, the fragment shader has access to texture samplers, which allow it to sample and write to textures directly, without the need for a separate compute pipeline.

Another reason is that using the fragment shader can be more convenient when integrating with other rendering operations, such as rendering a scene and applying post-processing effects. By using the same pipeline for both rendering and computation, it can simplify the overall pipeline and reduce the amount of data transfers between CPU and GPU.

However, it is important to note that for more complex computation tasks, such as physics simulations or large-scale data processing, compute shaders are still the preferred approach due to their flexibility and parallelism. Ultimately, the choice between using the fragment shader or compute shader for computation depends on the specific requirements of the task at hand.

In this section, we will use the fragment shader to simulate the gravity on a 2D grid-based particle system. The system consists of four mass centers and the particles are attracted towards each mass center with a gravity force. The gravitational force acting on each particle is determined by the combined forces generated by all three mass centers.

In this system, the locations of the four mass centers are moving around with time, so the mass centers can collide. This would result in a change in the gravitational field that affects the motion of the particles and provides rich physics phenomena. To render this particle system, we apply an image texture by using either a UV coordinate vector or a velocity vector as its texture coordinates. The final code is a mixture of the image texture and the velocity.

11.5.1 Shader Code

Create a new WGSL shader file named *gravity_grid.wgsl* in the *examples/ch11/* folder and add the following code to it:

```
@vertex
fn vs_main(@builtin(vertex_index) vIndex: u32) -> @builtin(position) vec4f {
    const pos = array(
        vec2( 1.0,  1.0),
        vec2( 1.0, -1.0),
        vec2(-1.0, -1.0),
        vec2( 1.0,  1.0),
        vec2(-1.0, -1.0),
        vec2(-1.0,  1.0),
    );
    return vec4(pos[vIndex], 0.0, 1.0);
}

struct Params {
    time: f32,
```

```
        timeSteps: f32,
        deltaT: f32,
        width: f32,
        height: f32,
        scale: f32,
        colorIntensity: f32,
        isGammaCorrection: f32,
        isUv: f32,
        isAttraction: f32,
}
@group(0) @binding(0) var<uniform> ps: Params;
@group(1) @binding(0) var texture: texture_2d<f32>;
@group(1) @binding(1) var texSampler: sampler;

@fragment
fn fs_main(@builtin(position) coord: vec4f) -> @location(0) vec4f {
        let t = ps.time;
        let dt = ps.deltaT;
        let w = ps.width;
        let h = ps.height;
        let scale = ps.scale;
        let ts = u32(ps.timeSteps);
        let ci = ps.colorIntensity;
        let gamma = u32(ps.isGammaCorrection);
        let isUv = u32(ps.isUv);
        let isAttraction = u32(ps.isAttraction);

        var uv = vec2(scale*(f32(coord.x) - 0.5*w)/w, -scale*(h/w)*(f32(coord.y) - 0.5*h)/h);
        var v = 0.1 * uv;

        // define mass centers
        let massPositions = array(
            0.1*vec2(sin(0.05*t + 0.0), 0.5*sin(0.10*t + 3.0)),
            0.3*vec2(sin(0.07*t + 1.0), 0.5*sin(0.25*t + 2.0)),
            0.5*vec2(sin(0.06*t + 2.0), 0.5*sin(0.20*t + 1.0)),
            0.7*vec2(sin(0.04*t + 3.0), 0.5*sin(0.15*t + 0.0))
        );

        for(var i = 0u; i < ts; i++) {
            uv += v;
            var acceleration = vec2(0.0);
            for(var j = 0u; j < 4; j++) {
                let r = uv - massPositions[j];
                let dist = 0.15 + length(r);
                var dir = normalize(r);
                if(isAttraction < 1) {
                    dir = -dir;
                }
                acceleration += 1.0/(dist * dist) * dir;
            }
            v += dt*acceleration;
            v *= 0.995;
        }

        var texCoord = uv;
        if(isUv < 1){
            texCoord = v;
        }

        let tex = textureSample(texture, texSampler, texCoord);
```

```
    var color = vec3(tex.r*v[0]*ci, tex.g*v[1]*ci, tex.b*length(v)*ci);
    if(gamma > 0) {
        color = pow(color, vec3(1.0/2.2));
    }
    return vec4(color, 1.0);
}
```

The vertex shader in the above code simply defines a 2D quad shape with six vertices on which the particle system will be rendered by the fragment shader. The fragment shader begins by defining a *Params* struct that allows the user to manipulate the particle system by modifying the fields of the struct. Meanwhile, we also pass the image texture and sampler to the shader, which will be used to set the output color.

The fragment shader first defines time-dependent locations for the four mass centers and then calculates the acceleration of the particle due to the gravitational forces of the four mass centers. In this example, the gravitational force from the mass center acting on a particle can be either attractive or repulsive, controlled by the *isAttraction* parameter. The acceleration is then added to the velocity, and the velocity is multiplied by a dampening factor of 0.995 for the stability and realism of the simulation. Next, the shader calls the *textureSample* function to get the texture color by sampling the image texture using either the UV coordinates or velocity as its texture coordinates, controlled by the *isUv* parameter. By directly manipulating the texture coordinates, the particle system will show much richer features. The final color is obtained by mixing the velocity components with the texture color.

It is worth noting that all computations for the particle systems under gravity are performed in the fragment shader rather than compute shaders. This is because this example uses an image texture to color the particle system, and the fragment shader has access to texture samplers, which allow it to sample and write to textures directly, without the need for a separate compute pipeline.

11.5.2 Rust Code

Create a new Rust file named *gravity_grid.rs* in the *examples/ch11/* folder and add the following code to it:

```
use std::{iter, collections::HashMap};
use winit::{
    event::*,
    event_loop::{ControlFlow, EventLoop},
    window::Window,
};
use bytemuck::cast_slice;
use wgpu_book_examples::wgpu_simplified as ws;

fn image_file_map(n:u32) -> Option<String> {
    let mut d: HashMap<u32, String> = HashMap::new();
    d.insert(0, String::from("assets/universe.png"));
    d.insert(1, String::from("assets/cloth2.png"));
    d.insert(2, String::from("assets/grass.png"));
    d.insert(3, String::from("assets/wood.png"));
    d.get(&n).cloned()
}
const ADDRESS_MODE:wgpu::AddressMode = wgpu::AddressMode::ClampToEdge;

struct State {
    init:  ws::IWgpuInit,
    pipeline: wgpu::RenderPipeline,
    uniform_bind_groups: Vec<wgpu::BindGroup>,
```

```
    uniform_buffer: wgpu::Buffer,

    animation_speed: f32,
    image_selection: u32,
    force_type: u32,
    texture_coord_type: u32,
    gamma_correction: u32,
    time_steps: u32,
    delta_t: f32,
    scale: f32,
    color_intensity: f32,
    fps_counter: ws::FpsCounter,
}

impl State {
    async fn new(window:&Window) -> Self {
        let init = ws::IWgpuInit::new(&window, 1, None).await;

        let shader = init.device.create_shader_module(wgpu::include_wgsl!("gravity_grid.wgsl"));

        let param_uniform_buffer = init.device.create_buffer(&wgpu::BufferDescriptor{
            label: Some("Parameter Uniform Buffer"),
            size: 48,
            usage: wgpu::BufferUsages::UNIFORM | wgpu::BufferUsages::COPY_DST,
            mapped_at_creation: false,
        });

        let (uniform_bind_group_layout, uniform_bind_group) = ws::create_bind_group(
            &init.device,
            vec![wgpu::ShaderStages::FRAGMENT],
            &[param_uniform_buffer.as_entire_binding()]
        );

        // create image texture and image texture bind group
        let img_file = image_file_map(0).unwrap();
        let(texture_bind_group_layout, texture_bind_group) =
            ws::create_texture_bind_group(&init.device, &init.queue, vec![&img_file], ADDRESS_MODE,
                ADDRESS_MODE);

        let pipeline_layout = init.device.create_pipeline_layout(&wgpu::PipelineLayoutDescriptor {
            label: Some("Render Pipeline Layout"),
            bind_group_layouts: &[&uniform_bind_group_layout, &texture_bind_group_layout],
            push_constant_ranges: &[],
        });

        let mut ppl = ws::IRenderPipeline {
            shader: Some(&shader),
            pipeline_layout: Some(&pipeline_layout),
            vertex_buffer_layout: &[],
            is_depth_stencil: false,
            ..Default::default()
        };
        let pipeline = ppl.new(&init);

        Self {
            init,
            pipeline,
            uniform_bind_groups: vec![uniform_bind_group, texture_bind_group],
            uniform_buffer: param_uniform_buffer,
```

```
            animation_speed: 1.0,
            image_selection: 0,
            force_type: 1,
            texture_coord_type: 0,
            gamma_correction: 1,
            time_steps: 20,
            delta_t: 0.001,
            scale: 1.0,
            color_intensity: 50.0,
            fps_counter: ws::FpsCounter::default(),
        }
    }

    fn resize(&mut self, new_size: winit::dpi::PhysicalSize<u32>) {
        if new_size.width > 0 && new_size.height > 0 {
            self.init.size = new_size;
            self.init.config.width = new_size.width;
            self.init.config.height = new_size.height;
            self.init.surface.configure(&self.init.device, &self.init.config);
        }
    }

    #[allow(unused_variables)]
    fn input(&mut self, event: &WindowEvent) -> bool {
        match event {
            WindowEvent::KeyboardInput {
                input:
                    KeyboardInput {
                        virtual_keycode: Some(keycode),
                        state: ElementState::Pressed,
                        ..
                    },
                ..
            } => {
                match keycode {
                    VirtualKeyCode::Space => {
                        self.image_selection = (self.image_selection + 1) % 4;
                        let img_file = image_file_map(self.image_selection).unwrap();
                        println!("image file = {:?}", img_file);
                        let(_, texture_bind_group) =
                            ws::create_texture_bind_group(&self.init.device, &self.init.queue,
                                vec![&img_file], ADDRESS_MODE, ADDRESS_MODE);
                        self.uniform_bind_groups[1] = texture_bind_group;
                        true
                    },
                    VirtualKeyCode::LControl => {
                        self.force_type = (self.force_type + 1) % 2;
                        if self.force_type == 0 {
                            self.color_intensity = 100.0;
                        } else {
                            self.color_intensity = 50.0;
                        }
                        true
                    },
                    VirtualKeyCode::LShift => {
                        self.texture_coord_type = (self.texture_coord_type + 1) % 2;
                        true
                    },
                    VirtualKeyCode::LAlt => {
                        self.gamma_correction = (self.gamma_correction + 1) % 2;
```

```
                        true
                    },
                    VirtualKeyCode::Q => {
                        self.time_steps += 1;
                        true
                    },
                    VirtualKeyCode::A => {
                        self.time_steps -= 1;
                        if self.time_steps < 1 {
                            self.time_steps = 1;
                        }
                        true
                    } ,
                    VirtualKeyCode::W => {
                        self.animation_speed += 0.1;
                        true
                    },
                    VirtualKeyCode::S => {
                        self.animation_speed -= 0.1;
                        if self.animation_speed < 0.0 {
                            self.animation_speed = 0.0;
                        }
                        true
                    } ,
                    _ => false
                }
            }
            _ => false,
        }
    }

    fn update(&mut self, dt: std::time::Duration) {
        // update uniform buffer for compute pipeline
        let dt1 = 5.0 * self.animation_speed * dt.as_secs_f32();
        let params = [
            dt1,
            self.time_steps as f32,
            self.delta_t,
            self.init.size.width as f32,
            self.init.size.height as f32,
            self.scale,
            self.color_intensity,
            self.gamma_correction as f32,
            self.texture_coord_type as f32,
            self.force_type as f32,
        ];
        self.init.queue.write_buffer(&self.uniform_buffer, 0, cast_slice(&params));
    }

    fn render(&mut self) -> Result<(), wgpu::SurfaceError> {
        let output = self.init.surface.get_current_texture()?;
        let view = output
            .texture
            .create_view(&wgpu::TextureViewDescriptor::default());

        let mut encoder = self
            .init.device
            .create_command_encoder(&wgpu::CommandEncoderDescriptor {
                label: Some("Render Encoder"),
            });
```

```
        // render pass
        {
            let color_attachment = ws::create_color_attachment(&view);
            let mut render_pass = encoder.begin_render_pass(&wgpu::RenderPassDescriptor {
                label: Some("Render Pass"),
                color_attachments: &[Some(color_attachment)],
                depth_stencil_attachment: None,
            });

            render_pass.set_pipeline(&self.pipeline);
            render_pass.set_bind_group(0, &self.uniform_bind_groups[0], &[]);
            render_pass.set_bind_group(1, &self.uniform_bind_groups[1], &[]);
            render_pass.draw(0..6, 0..1);
        }

        self.init.queue.submit(iter::once(encoder.finish()));
        output.present();
        self.fps_counter.print_fps(5);
        Ok(())
    }
}

fn main() {
    env_logger::init();
    let event_loop = EventLoop::new();
    let window = winit::window::WindowBuilder::new().build(&event_loop).unwrap();
    window.set_title(&*format!("ch11_{}", "gravity_grid"));

    let mut state = pollster::block_on(State::new(&window));
    let render_start_time = std::time::Instant::now();

    event_loop.run(move |event, _, control_flow| {
        match event {
            Event::WindowEvent {
                ref event,
                window_id,
            } if window_id == window.id() => {
                if !state.input(event) {
                    match event {
                        WindowEvent::CloseRequested
                        | WindowEvent::KeyboardInput {
                            input:
                                KeyboardInput {
                                    state: ElementState::Pressed,
                                    virtual_keycode: Some(VirtualKeyCode::Escape),
                                    ..
                                },
                            ..
                        } => *control_flow = ControlFlow::Exit,
                        WindowEvent::Resized(physical_size) => {
                            state.resize(*physical_size);
                        }
                        WindowEvent::ScaleFactorChanged { new_inner_size, .. } => {
                            state.resize(**new_inner_size);
                        }
                        _ => {}
                    }
                }
            }
```

```
Event::RedrawRequested(_) => {
    let now = std::time::Instant::now();
    let dt = now - render_start_time;
    state.update(dt);

    match state.render() {
        Ok(_) => {}
        Err(wgpu::SurfaceError::Lost) => state.resize(state.init.size),
        Err(wgpu::SurfaceError::OutOfMemory) => *control_flow = ControlFlow::Exit,
        Err(e) => eprintln!("{:?}", e),
    }
}
Event::MainEventsCleared => {
    window.request_redraw();
}
_ => {}
}
});
}
```

Unlike previous examples in this chapter, the above code does not contain the compute pipeline. In the *State::new* function, we create a parameter uniform buffer, which will be passed to the fragment shader for simulating the particle system under gravity. Additionally, we create a texture bind group that contains the texture and sampler generated from an image file.

Within the *State::render* function, we define only the render pass because this example does not use a compute pass.

Additionally, the code permits the user to modify input parameters using keyboard inputs.

Here is a list of controls using keyboard:

- *Space*: Changes the image file.
- *LControl*: Changes the force type: attractive or repulsive.
- *LShift*: Changes texture coordinate type: UV or velocity.
- *LAlt*: Controls gamma correction or not for the color.
- *Q/A*: Increases/decreases the time steps.
- *W/S*: Increases/decreases the animation speed.

11.5.3 Run Application

To run this application, add the following code snippet to the *Cargo.toml* file:

```
[[example]]
name = "ch11_gravity_grid"
path = "examples/ch11/gravity_grid.rs"
```

Afterward, execute the following *cargo run* commands in the terminal window:

```
cargo run --example ch11_gravity_grid
```

Fig.11-8 shows the results of this example.

Fig.11-8. The particle system with different textures under attractive gravity.

In the figure, the left column shows four different image textures, and the rest of the columns displays the results under the attractive gravity mapped with these four textures. Specifically, the middle column displays the results using the UV coordinates as the texture coordinates, while the right column displays the results using the velocity as the texture coordinates.

We can also obtain the results under repulsive gravity by pressing the LControl key. Fig.11-9 shows some results under repulsive gravity.

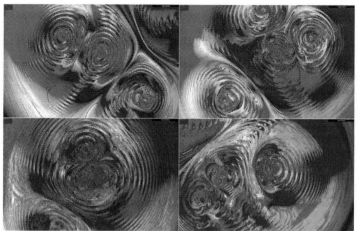

Fig.11-9. Selected results under repulsive gravity.

11.6 Electric Field

Electric field distribution from point charges represents the spatial distribution of electric fields around point charges. We can visualize the distribution using field lines, which are a graphical representation of the direction and strength of the electric field at a point. The density of the field lines is proportional to the strength of the electric fields.

In this section, we will use the same approach as the one used in the previous example to simulate the electric field distribution from point charges in the fragment shader.

11.6.1 Shader Code

Create a new WGSL shader file named *electric_field.wgsl* in the *examples/ch11/* folder and add the following code to it:

```
@vertex
fn vs_main(@builtin(vertex_index) vIndex: u32) -> @builtin(position) vec4f {
    const pos = array(
        vec2( 1.0,  1.0),
        vec2( 1.0, -1.0),
        vec2(-1.0, -1.0),
        vec2( 1.0,  1.0),
        vec2(-1.0, -1.0),
        vec2(-1.0,  1.0),
    );
    return vec4(pos[vIndex], 0.0, 1.0);
}

struct Params {
    time: f32,
    width: f32,
    height: f32,
    scale: f32,
    isGammaCorrection: f32,
    numCharges: f32,
```

```
        sameCharges: f32,
}
@group(0) @binding(0) var<uniform> ps: Params;

@fragment
fn fs_main(@builtin(position) coord: vec4f) -> @location(0) vec4f {
    let t = ps.time;
    let w = ps.width;
    let h = ps.height;
    let scale = ps.scale;
    let gamma = u32(ps.isGammaCorrection);
    let num = u32(ps.numCharges);
    let sameCharges = u32(ps.sameCharges);

    var uv = vec2(scale*(f32(coord.x) - 0.5*w)/w, -scale*(h/w)*(f32(coord.y) - 0.5*h)/h);

    let ps = array(
        0.1*vec2(sin(0.05*t + 0.0), 0.5*sin(0.10*t + 3.0)),
        0.3*vec2(sin(0.07*t + 1.0), 0.5*sin(0.25*t + 2.0)),
        0.5*vec2(sin(0.06*t + 2.0), 0.5*sin(0.20*t + 1.0)),
        0.7*vec2(sin(0.04*t + 3.0), 0.5*sin(0.15*t + 0.0))
    );

    // electric field
    var ef = vec2(0.0);

    for(var i = 0u; i < num; i++) {
        let r = uv - ps[i];
        let dist = length(r);
        var dir = normalize(r);
        if(sameCharges < 1){
            if((i + 1) % 2u == 0) {
                dir = -dir;
            }
        }
        ef += dir * 0.01/(0.01 + dist * dist);
    }

    var color = mix(vec3(ef.x, ef.y, length(ef)), vec3(1.0, 1.0, 0.0), sin(4.0 * t + 75.0 * length(ef)));

    if(gamma > 0) {
        color = pow(color, vec3(1.0/2.2));
    }
    return vec4(color, 1.0);
}
```

The vertex shader in the above code is identical to the previous example. The fragment shader begins by defining a *Params* struct that allows the user to manipulate the electric field distribution by modifying the fields of the struct.

The *fs_main* function first defines time-dependent locations for the four point charges and then calculates the electric field distribution of the four charges. In the calculation, the *sameCharges* parameter indicates whether the same types of charges or different types of charges are used by setting its value to 1 or 0 respectively. When the parameter is set to zero, i.e., different types of charges are used, we assign a positive charge at locations 1 and 3 and a negative charge at locations of 2 and 4. Finally, we use the resulting electric field to generate the color.

11.6.2 Rust Code

Create a new Rust file named *electric_field.rs* in the *examples/ch11/* folder and add the following code to it:

```rust
use std::iter;
use winit::{
    event::*,
    event_loop::{ControlFlow, EventLoop},
    window::Window,
};
use bytemuck::cast_slice;
use wgpu_book_examples::wgpu_simplified as ws;

struct State {
    init:  ws::IWgpuInit,
    pipeline: wgpu::RenderPipeline,
    uniform_bind_group: wgpu::BindGroup,
    uniform_buffer: wgpu::Buffer,

    animation_speed: f32,
    charges_count: u32,
    charge_type: u32,
    gamma_correction: u32,
    scale: f32,
    fps_counter: ws::FpsCounter,
}

impl State {
    async fn new(window:&Window) -> Self {
        let init = ws::IWgpuInit::new(&window, 1, None).await;

        let shader = init.device.create_shader_module(wgpu::include_wgsl!("electric_field.wgsl"));

        let param_uniform_buffer = init.device.create_buffer(&wgpu::BufferDescriptor{
            label: Some("Parameter Uniform Buffer"),
            size: 32,
            usage: wgpu::BufferUsages::UNIFORM | wgpu::BufferUsages::COPY_DST,
            mapped_at_creation: false,
        });

        let (uniform_bind_group_layout, uniform_bind_group) = ws::create_bind_group(
            &init.device,
            vec![wgpu::ShaderStages::FRAGMENT],
            &[param_uniform_buffer.as_entire_binding()]
        );

        let pipeline_layout = init.device.create_pipeline_layout(&wgpu::PipelineLayoutDescriptor {
            label: Some("Render Pipeline Layout"),
            bind_group_layouts: &[&uniform_bind_group_layout],
            push_constant_ranges: &[],
        });

        let mut ppl = ws::IRenderPipeline {
            shader: Some(&shader),
            pipeline_layout: Some(&pipeline_layout),
            vertex_buffer_layout: &[],
            is_depth_stencil: false,
            ..Default::default()
        };
```

```rust
    let pipeline = ppl.new(&init);

    Self {
        init,
        pipeline,
        uniform_bind_group,
        uniform_buffer: param_uniform_buffer,

        animation_speed: 1.0,
        charges_count: 4,
        charge_type: 0,
        gamma_correction: 1,
        scale: 1.5,
        fps_counter: ws::FpsCounter::default(),
    }
}

fn resize(&mut self, new_size: winit::dpi::PhysicalSize<u32>) {
    if new_size.width > 0 && new_size.height > 0 {
        self.init.size = new_size;
        self.init.config.width = new_size.width;
        self.init.config.height = new_size.height;
        self.init.surface.configure(&self.init.device, &self.init.config);
    }
}

#[allow(unused_variables)]
fn input(&mut self, event: &WindowEvent) -> bool {
    match event {
        WindowEvent::KeyboardInput {
            input:
                KeyboardInput {
                    virtual_keycode: Some(keycode),
                    state: ElementState::Pressed,
                    ..
                },
            ..
        } => {
            match keycode {
                VirtualKeyCode::Space => {
                    self.charges_count = (self.charges_count + 1) % 4;
                    true
                },
                VirtualKeyCode::LControl => {
                    self.charge_type = (self.charge_type + 1) % 2;
                    true
                },
                VirtualKeyCode::LAlt => {
                    self.gamma_correction = (self.gamma_correction + 1) % 2;
                    true
                },
                VirtualKeyCode::Q => {
                    self.scale += 0.1;
                    true
                },
                VirtualKeyCode::A => {
                    self.scale -= 0.1;
                    if self.scale < 0.2 {
                        self.scale = 0.2;
                    }
```

```
                    true
                },
                VirtualKeyCode::W => {
                    self.animation_speed += 0.1;
                    true
                },
                VirtualKeyCode::S => {
                    self.animation_speed -= 0.1;
                    if self.animation_speed < 0.0 {
                        self.animation_speed = 0.0;
                    }
                    true
                },
                _ => false
            }
        }
        _ => false,
    }
}

fn update(&mut self, dt: std::time::Duration) {
    // update uniform buffer for compute pipeline
    let dt1 = self.animation_speed * dt.as_secs_f32();
    let params = [
        dt1,
        self.init.size.width as f32,
        self.init.size.height as f32,
        self.scale,
        self.gamma_correction as f32,
        (self.charges_count + 1) as f32,
        self.charge_type as f32,
    ];
    self.init.queue.write_buffer(&self.uniform_buffer, 0, cast_slice(&params));
}

fn render(&mut self) -> Result<(), wgpu::SurfaceError> {
    let output = self.init.surface.get_current_texture()?;
    let view = output
        .texture
        .create_view(&wgpu::TextureViewDescriptor::default());

    let mut encoder = self
        .init.device
        .create_command_encoder(&wgpu::CommandEncoderDescriptor {
            label: Some("Render Encoder"),
        });

    // render pass
    {
        let color_attachment = ws::create_color_attachment(&view);
        let mut render_pass = encoder.begin_render_pass(&wgpu::RenderPassDescriptor {
            label: Some("Render Pass"),
            color_attachments: &[Some(color_attachment)],
            depth_stencil_attachment: None,
        });

        render_pass.set_pipeline(&self.pipeline);
        render_pass.set_bind_group(0, &self.uniform_bind_group, &[]);
        render_pass.draw(0..6, 0..1);
    }
```

```rust
            self.init.queue.submit(iter::once(encoder.finish()));
            output.present();
            self.fps_counter.print_fps(5);
            Ok(())
        }
    }

fn main() {
    env_logger::init();
    let event_loop = EventLoop::new();
    let window = winit::window::WindowBuilder::new().build(&event_loop).unwrap();
    window.set_title(&*format!("ch11_{}", "electric_field"));

    let mut state = pollster::block_on(State::new(&window));
    let render_start_time = std::time::Instant::now();

    event_loop.run(move |event, _, control_flow| {
        match event {
            Event::WindowEvent {
                ref event,
                window_id,
            } if window_id == window.id() => {
                if !state.input(event) {
                    match event {
                        WindowEvent::CloseRequested
                        | WindowEvent::KeyboardInput {
                            input:
                                KeyboardInput {
                                    state: ElementState::Pressed,
                                    virtual_keycode: Some(VirtualKeyCode::Escape),
                                    ..
                                },
                            ..
                        } => *control_flow = ControlFlow::Exit,
                        WindowEvent::Resized(physical_size) => {
                            state.resize(*physical_size);
                        }
                        WindowEvent::ScaleFactorChanged { new_inner_size, .. } => {
                            state.resize(**new_inner_size);
                        }
                        _ => {}
                    }
                }
            }
            Event::RedrawRequested(_) => {
                let now = std::time::Instant::now();
                let dt = now - render_start_time;
                state.update(dt);

                match state.render() {
                    Ok(_) => {}
                    Err(wgpu::SurfaceError::Lost) => state.resize(state.init.size),
                    Err(wgpu::SurfaceError::OutOfMemory) => *control_flow = ControlFlow::Exit,
                    Err(e) => eprintln!("{:?}", e),
                }
            }
            Event::MainEventsCleared => {
                window.request_redraw();
            }
```

```
        _ => {}
      }
   });
}
```

The above code does not contain the compute pipeline, which is similar to the previous example. In the *State::new* function, we create a parameter buffer, which will be passed to the fragment shader for simulating the electric field distribution of point charges.

The *State::render* function defines only the render pass because this example does not use a compute pass, which is also similar to the previous example.

Additionally, the code permits the user to modify input parameters using keyboard inputs. Particularly, we can display the electric field distribution for a system with one, two, three, or four point charges by modifying the charge count parameter.

Here is a list of controls using keyboard:

- *Space*: Changes the charge count.
- *LControl*: Changes the charge type: attractive or repulsive.
- *LAlt*: Controls gamma correction or not for the color.
- *Q/A*: Increases/decreases the scale.
- *W/S*: Increases/decreases the animation speed.

11.6.3 Run Application

To run this application, add the following code snippet to the *Cargo.toml* file:

```
[[example]]
name = "ch11_electric_field"
path = "examples/ch11/electric_field.rs"
```

Afterward, execute the following *cargo run* commands in the terminal window:

```
cargo run --example ch11_electric_field
```

Fig.11-10 displays the electric field distribution for a single point charge.

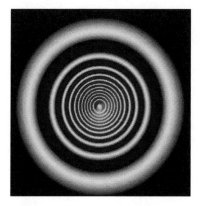

Fig.11-10. Electric field distribution of a single point charge.

Fig.11-11 presents the results for a system with two, three, and four point charges. The top row shows the electric field distribution for charges of the same types located at the point charges, while the bottom row shows the results for charges of different types located at the point charges. The density of the field lines provides insight into the strength of the electric field around the point charges.

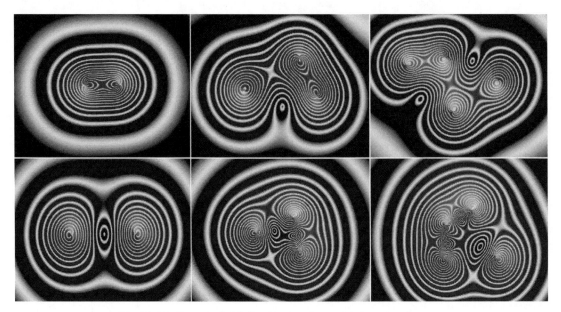

Fig.11-11. Electric field distribution for multiple point charges.

11.7 Universe and Stars

In this section, we will be using a grid-based particle system to simulate stars in the universe. For each unit cell on the grid, we assign a particle (or star) inside the cell and then draw a line from each particle to the adjacent cells, resulting in a mesmerizing effect. The particle inside each cell is placed randomly using the *rand2dTo2d* function that was implemented earlier in Chapter 9.

This example is based on a YouTube video found at https://www.youtube.com/watch?v=3CycKKJiwis.

11.7.1 Shader Code

Create a new WGSL shader file named *universe.wgsl* in the *examples/ch11/* folder and add the following code to it:

```
@vertex
fn vs_main(@builtin(vertex_index) vIndex: u32) -> @builtin(position) vec4f  {
    const pos = array(
        vec2( 1.0,  1.0),
        vec2( 1.0, -1.0),
        vec2(-1.0, -1.0),
        vec2( 1.0,  1.0),
        vec2(-1.0, -1.0),
        vec2(-1.0,  1.0),
    );
```

```
        return vec4(pos[vIndex], 0.0, 1.0);
}

struct Params {
    time: f32,
    numLayers: f32,
    width: f32,
    height: f32,
    scale: f32,
    isGammaCorrection: f32,
}
@group(0) @binding(0) var<uniform> ps: Params;
@group(0) @binding(1)  var<uniform> rotMat: mat2x2f;

fn distanceToLine(p:vec2f, a:vec2f, b:vec2f) -> f32 {
    let pa = p - a;
    let ba = b - a;
    let t = clamp(dot(pa, ba)/dot(ba, ba), 0.0, 1.0);
    return length(pa - ba * t);
}

fn getLine(p:vec2f, a:vec2f, b:vec2f) -> f32 {
    let d = distanceToLine(p, a, b);
    var m = smoothstep(0.03, 0.01, d);
    let d2 = length(a-b);
    m *= smoothstep(1.2, 0.8, d2) + smoothstep(0.05, 0.03, abs(d2 - 0.75));
    return m;
}

fn getPosition(id:vec2f, offset:vec2f) -> vec2f {
    let n = rand2dTo2d(id + offset) * ps.time;
    return offset + sin(n)*0.4;
}

fn layer(uv: vec2f) -> f32 {
    let gv = fract(uv) - 0.5;
    let id = floor(uv);
    var m = 0.0;

    var pp:array<vec2f, 9>;
    var i = 0;
    for( var x = 0; x < 3; x++) {
        for( var y = 0; y < 3; y++) {
            pp[i] = getPosition(id, vec2(f32(x-1), f32(y-1)));
            i++;
        }
    }

    for(var i = 0; i<9; i++){
        m += getLine(gv, pp[4], pp[i]);
        let s = (pp[i] - gv)*20.0;
        let sparkle = 1.0/dot(s, s);
        m += sparkle * (0.5 + 0.5*sin(10.0*ps.time + fract(pp[i].x)*10.0));
    }
    m += getLine(gv, pp[1], pp[3]);
    m += getLine(gv, pp[1], pp[5]);
    m += getLine(gv, pp[7], pp[3]);
    m += getLine(gv, pp[7], pp[5]);
    return m;
}
```

```
@fragment
fn fs_main(@builtin(position) coord: vec4f) -> @location(0) vec4f {
    let t = ps.time;
    let w = ps.width;
    let h = ps.height;
    let scale = ps.scale;
    let gamma = u32(ps.isGammaCorrection);
    let num = u32(ps.numLayers);

    let uv0 = vec2(scale*(f32(coord.x) - 0.5*w)/w, -scale*(h/w)*(f32(coord.y) - 0.5*h)/h);
    var uv = uv0;
    uv *= rotMat;

    var m = 0.0;
    for (var i = 0u; i < num; i++) {
        let depth = fract(f32(i)/f32(num) + 0.1 * t);
        let size = mix(10.0, 0.5, depth);
        let fade = smoothstep(0.0, 0.5, depth) * smoothstep(1.0, 0.8, depth);
        m += layer(uv * size + f32(i)/f32(num)*20.0)*fade;
    }

    let baseColor = sin(2.0 * t * vec3(0.345, 0.656, 0.878)) * 0.4 + 0.6;
    var color = (m - 0.5*uv0.y) * baseColor;

    if(gamma == 1){
        color = pow(color, vec3(1.0/2.2));
    }
    return vec4(color, 1.0);
}
```

The vertex shader in the above code is identical to that used in the previous example. The fragment shader begins by defining a *Params* struct that allows the user to manipulate the particle system by modifying the fields of the struct. The fragment shader then defines several helper functions, including *distanceToLine*, *getLine*, *getPosition*, and *layer*.

The *distanceToLine* function calculates distance between a point and a line segment and then clamps it between 0 and 1 to ensure that the projection is within the line segment. The *getLine* function uses the *distanceToLine* function to calculate the distance between a point and a line segment. It then applies some smoothing using the *smoothstep* function based on the distance and length of the line segment to produce a value between 0 and 1.

The *getPosition* function applies some random noise using the *rand2dTo2d* function and a time variable. The function returns a 2D position vector. The *layer* function takes the 2D texture coordinates, *uv*, as input and returns a floating-point value. Within the function, it first calculates the fractional (*gv*) and integer (*id*) parts of *uv*. It then calculates the position array with nine points surrounding the current coordinates using the *getPosition* function. For each of these points in the array, it calculates the distance between the point and the line segment defined by its adjacent points using the *getLine* function, and adds some sparkle using the sine function and the position of the point. Finally, it calculates the distance between *gv* and some additional line segments using the *getLine* function and returns the sum of all these values.

Subsequently, the *fs_main* function first calculates the UV coordinates and rotates the UV coordinates with a rotation matrix. It then calculates the pattern by iterating over the number of layers and summing the values returned by the layer function. The depth, size, and fade of each layer are determined based on the layer index and the current time. The final color is calculated by multiplying the pattern value by a base color that varies sinusoidally with time.

11.7.2 Rust Code

Create a new Rust file named *universe.rs* in the *examples/ch11/* folder and include the following code:

```rust
use std::iter;
use winit::{
    event::*,
    event_loop::{ControlFlow, EventLoop},
    window::Window,
};
use bytemuck::cast_slice;
use wgpu_book_examples::wgpu_simplified as ws;

struct State {
    init:  ws::IWgpuInit,
    pipeline: wgpu::RenderPipeline,
    uniform_bind_group: wgpu::BindGroup,
    uniform_buffers: Vec<wgpu::Buffer>,

    animation_speed: f32,
    layers_count: u32,
    gamma_correction: u32,
    scale: f32,
    fps_counter: ws::FpsCounter,
}

impl State {
    async fn new(window:&Window) -> Self {
        let init = ws::IWgpuInit::new(&window, 1, None).await;

        let noise_file = include_str!("../ch09/noise3d.wgsl");
        let universe_file = include_str!("universe.wgsl");
        let shader_file = [noise_file, universe_file].join("\n");

        let shader = init.device.create_shader_module(wgpu::ShaderModuleDescriptor {
            label: Some("Shader"),
            source: wgpu::ShaderSource::Wgsl(shader_file.into()),
        });

        let param_uniform_buffer = init.device.create_buffer(&wgpu::BufferDescriptor{
            label: Some("Parameter Uniform Buffer"),
            size: 32,
            usage: wgpu::BufferUsages::UNIFORM | wgpu::BufferUsages::COPY_DST,
            mapped_at_creation: false,
        });

        let rotation_uniform_buffer = init.device.create_buffer(&wgpu::BufferDescriptor{
            label: Some("rotation Uniform Buffer"),
            size: 16,
            usage: wgpu::BufferUsages::UNIFORM | wgpu::BufferUsages::COPY_DST,
            mapped_at_creation: false,
        });

        let (uniform_bind_group_layout, uniform_bind_group) = ws::create_bind_group(
            &init.device,
            vec![wgpu::ShaderStages::FRAGMENT, wgpu::ShaderStages::FRAGMENT],
```

```rust
        &[
            param_uniform_buffer.as_entire_binding(),
            rotation_uniform_buffer.as_entire_binding(),
        ],
    );

    let pipeline_layout = init.device.create_pipeline_layout(&wgpu::PipelineLayoutDescriptor {
        label: Some("Render Pipeline Layout"),
        bind_group_layouts: &[&uniform_bind_group_layout],
        push_constant_ranges: &[],
    });

    let mut ppl = ws::IRenderPipeline {
        shader: Some(&shader),
        pipeline_layout: Some(&pipeline_layout),
        vertex_buffer_layout: &[],
        is_depth_stencil: false,
        ..Default::default()
    };
    let pipeline = ppl.new(&init);

    Self {
        init,
        pipeline,
        uniform_bind_group,
        uniform_buffers: vec![param_uniform_buffer, rotation_uniform_buffer],

        animation_speed: 1.0,
        layers_count: 4,
        gamma_correction: 0,
        scale: 5.0,
        fps_counter: ws::FpsCounter::default(),
    }
}

fn resize(&mut self, new_size: winit::dpi::PhysicalSize<u32>) {
    if new_size.width > 0 && new_size.height > 0 {
        self.init.size = new_size;
        self.init.config.width = new_size.width;
        self.init.config.height = new_size.height;
        self.init.surface.configure(&self.init.device, &self.init.config);
    }
}

#[allow(unused_variables)]
fn input(&mut self, event: &WindowEvent) -> bool {
    match event {
        WindowEvent::KeyboardInput {
            input:
                KeyboardInput {
                    virtual_keycode: Some(keycode),
                    state: ElementState::Pressed,
                    ..
                },
            ..
        } => {
            match keycode {
                VirtualKeyCode::Space => {
                    self.gamma_correction = (self.gamma_correction + 1) % 2;
                    true
```

```
            },
            VirtualKeyCode::Q => {
                self.layers_count += 1;
                println!("layoers count = {}" , self.layers_count);
                true
            },
            VirtualKeyCode::A => {
                self.layers_count -= 1;
                if self.layers_count < 1 {
                    self.layers_count = 1;
                }
                println!("layoers count = {}" , self.layers_count);
                true
            } ,
            VirtualKeyCode::W => {
                self.scale += 0.1;
                true
            },
            VirtualKeyCode::S => {
                self.scale -= 0.1;
                if self.scale < 0.2 {
                    self.scale = 0.2;
                }
                true
            } ,
            VirtualKeyCode::E => {
                self.animation_speed += 0.1;
                true
            },
            VirtualKeyCode::D => {
                self.animation_speed -= 0.1;
                if self.animation_speed < 0.0 {
                    self.animation_speed = 0.0;
                }
                true
            } ,
            _ => false
        }
    }
    _ => false,
    }
}

fn update(&mut self, dt: std::time::Duration) {
    // update uniform buffer for compute pipeline
    let dt1 = self.animation_speed * dt.as_secs_f32();
    let params = [
        dt1,
        self.layers_count as f32,
        self.init.size.width as f32,
        self.init.size.height as f32,
        self.scale,
        self.gamma_correction as f32,
    ];
    self.init.queue.write_buffer(&self.uniform_buffers[0], 0, cast_slice(&params));

    let angle = -0.1 * dt1;
    let rot_mat = [angle.cos(), -angle.sin(), angle.sin(), angle.cos()];
    self.init.queue.write_buffer(&self.uniform_buffers[1], 0, cast_slice(&rot_mat));
}
```

```rust
    fn render(&mut self) -> Result<(), wgpu::SurfaceError> {
        let output = self.init.surface.get_current_texture()?;
        let view = output
            .texture
            .create_view(&wgpu::TextureViewDescriptor::default());

        let mut encoder = self
            .init.device
            .create_command_encoder(&wgpu::CommandEncoderDescriptor {
                label: Some("Render Encoder"),
            });

        // render pass
        {
            let color_attachment = ws::create_color_attachment(&view);
            let mut render_pass = encoder.begin_render_pass(&wgpu::RenderPassDescriptor {
                label: Some("Render Pass"),
                color_attachments: &[Some(color_attachment)],
                depth_stencil_attachment: None,
            });

            render_pass.set_pipeline(&self.pipeline);
            render_pass.set_bind_group(0, &self.uniform_bind_group, &[]);
            render_pass.draw(0..6, 0..1);
        }

        self.init.queue.submit(iter::once(encoder.finish()));
        output.present();
        self.fps_counter.print_fps(5);
        Ok(())
    }
}

fn main() {
    env_logger::init();
    let event_loop = EventLoop::new();
    let window = winit::window::WindowBuilder::new().build(&event_loop).unwrap();
    window.set_title(&*format!("ch11_{}", "electric_field"));

    let mut state = pollster::block_on(State::new(&window));
    let render_start_time = std::time::Instant::now();

    event_loop.run(move |event, _, control_flow| {
        match event {
            Event::WindowEvent {
                ref event,
                window_id,
            } if window_id == window.id() => {
                if !state.input(event) {
                    match event {
                        WindowEvent::CloseRequested
                        | WindowEvent::KeyboardInput {
                            input:
                                KeyboardInput {
                                    state: ElementState::Pressed,
                                    virtual_keycode: Some(VirtualKeyCode::Escape),
                                    ..
                                },
                            ..
```

```
            } => *control_flow = ControlFlow::Exit,
            WindowEvent::Resized(physical_size) => {
                state.resize(*physical_size);
            }
            WindowEvent::ScaleFactorChanged { new_inner_size, .. } => {
                state.resize(**new_inner_size);
            }
            _ => {}
        }
    }
}
Event::RedrawRequested(_) => {
    let now = std::time::Instant::now();
    let dt = now - render_start_time;
    state.update(dt);

    match state.render() {
        Ok(_) => {}
        Err(wgpu::SurfaceError::Lost) => state.resize(state.init.size),
        Err(wgpu::SurfaceError::OutOfMemory) => *control_flow = ControlFlow::Exit,
        Err(e) => eprintln!("{:?}", e),
    }
}
Event::MainEventsCleared => {
    window.request_redraw();
}
_ => {}
        }
    });
}
```

The above code does not contain the compute pipeline, which is similar to the previous example. In the *State::new* function, we create a parameter buffer, which will be passed to the fragment shader for simulating the particle system.

The *State::render* function defines only the render pass because this example does not use a compute pass, which is also similar to the previous example.

Additionally, the code permits the user to modify input parameters using keyboard inputs.

Here is a list of controls using keyboard:

- *Space*: Controls gamma correction or not for the color.
- *Q/A*: Increases/decreases the layer count.
- *W/S*: Increases/decreases the scale.
- *E/D*: Increases/decreases the animation speed.

11.7.3 Run Application

To run this application, add the following code snippet to the *Cargo.toml* file:

```
[[example]]
name = "ch11_universe"
path = "examples/ch11/universe.rs"
```

Afterward, execute the following *cargo run* commands in the terminal window:

```
cargo run --example ch11_universe
```

Fig.11-12 shows the results of this example.

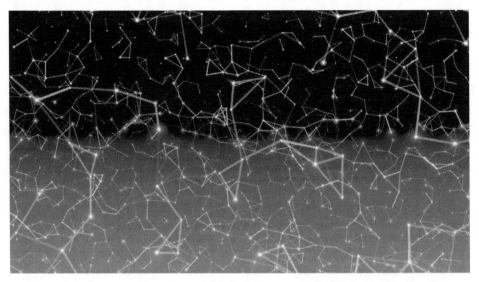

Fig.11-12. Stars in the universe simulated using a grid-based particle system.

12 Text Rendering

The *wgpu* API does not have a built-in function for rendering text, which is more complicated than other types of graphics due to its unique characteristics. Text consists of individual characters that need to be positioned correctly and spaced out evenly, and it requires specific font, size, color, and style, which can be loaded and rendered as textures. Text can also be interacted with in various ways, requiring additional calculations.

Several methods exist for rendering text in computer graphics, each with its own advantages and disadvantages. One approach is to create a texture with the desired text and map it onto 3D objects using texture mapping techniques. Another approach is bitmap-font technique, which rasterizes all unique characters into a single texture atlas, allowing for the creation of any given text string at runtime. However, this method can result in pixelated text when scaled or rendered at large size and is not ideal for dynamic text.

A third approach is font glyph geometry, which involves generating triangles for each character in a font and using that geometry to render the text. This method provides complete control over the appearance and layout of the text, allowing for custom fonts and styles and supporting dynamic or changing text content. However, it can be computationally expensive, especially when rendering large amounts of text.

In this chapter, we will demonstrate how to render text in *wgpu* using various techniques, including bitmap fonts and font glyph geometry.

12.1 Bitmap Fonts

Bitmap fonts are a type of font that uses a texture atlas to render text in computer graphics. Each character in the font is represented as a small image within the texture atlas, and these images are arranged in a grid pattern. When rendering text, the application uses the texture atlas to look up the appropriate image for each character in the text string and then renders the characters using these images as textures.

In this example, we will render text in *wgpu* using a bitmap fonts atlas file named *font.png*, which is included in the *assets/fonts/* folder. Fig.12-1 shows the atlas image.

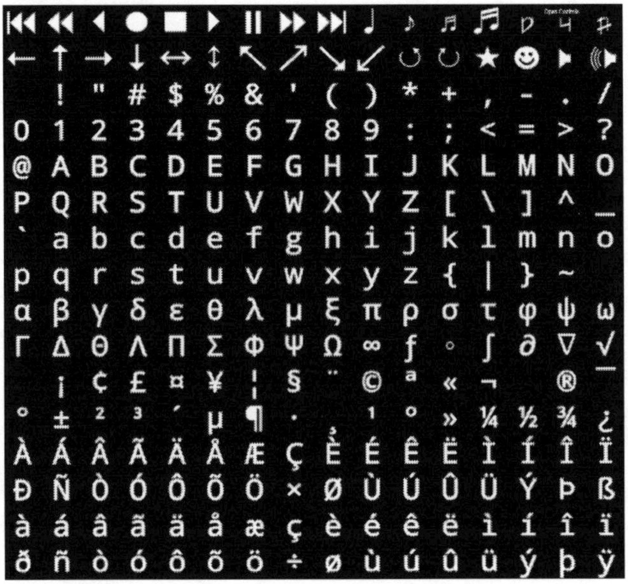

Fig.12-1. Bitmap font atlas.

It is evident from the figure that the atlas can be divided into a 16×16 grid. If we use i and j to represent the row and column index respectively, we can use a single index to specify any character in the grid using the following formula:

$$\text{index} = i * 16 + j$$

Here, i and j take values from 0 to 15. For example, the letter A is located second column ($j = 1$) and fifth row ($i = 4$), so we can use index = 65 to uniquely identify the letter A. This approach can be used to identify any character in the grid.

12.1.1 Shader Code

Create a WGSL shader file named *bitmap-fonts.wgsl* in the *examples/ch12/* folder and add the following code to it:

```
@vertex
fn vs_main(@builtin(vertex_index) vIndex: u32) -> @builtin(position) vec4f {
    var pos = array(
        vec2( 1.0,  1.0),
        vec2( 1.0, -1.0),
        vec2(-1.0, -1.0),
        vec2( 1.0,  1.0),
        vec2(-1.0, -1.0),
        vec2(-1.0,  1.0),
    );
    return vec4(pos[vIndex], 0.0, 1.0);
}

struct Params {
    originalFont: f32,
    width: f32,
    height: f32,
```

```
        time: f32,
}

@group(0) @binding(0) var<uniform> ps: Params;
@group(1) @binding(0) var texture: texture_2d<f32>;
@group(1) @binding(1) var texSampler: sampler;

fn getTitle(i:i32) -> i32 {
    var codes = array<i32, 18> (
        87, 101, 98, 71, 80, 85, 32, 98, 121, 32, 69, 120, 97, 109, 112, 108, 101, 115
    );
    return codes[i];
}

fn getText(i:i32) -> i32 {
    var codes = array<i32, 62> (
        76, 101, 97, 114, 110, 32, 97, 110, 100, 32, 69, 120, 112, 108, 111, 114, 101, 32,
        78, 101, 120, 116, 45, 71, 101, 110, 101, 114, 97, 116, 105, 111, 110, 32,
        87, 101, 98, 32, 71, 114, 97, 112, 104, 105, 99, 115, 32, 97, 110, 100, 32,
        67, 111, 109, 112, 117, 116, 101, 32, 65, 80, 73
    );
    return codes[i];
}

fn getChar(p:vec2f, i:i32) -> f32 {
    var pos = vec2(f32(i % 16), floor(f32(i/16)));
    pos += clamp(p, vec2(0.0), vec2(1.0));
    return textureSample(texture, texSampler, pos/16.0).x;
}

fn getIndex(x:i32, n:i32) -> i32 {
    return i32(f32(n)*(f32(x)/f32(n)) - floor(f32(x)/f32(n)));
}

@fragment
fn fs_main(@builtin(position) coord: vec4f) -> @location(0) vec4f {
    let w = ps.width;
    let h = ps.height;
    let orig = u32(ps.originalFont);
    let t = i32(ps.time);

    var uv = coord.xy/ vec2(w, h);
    var color = vec3(1.0);
    var col = 0.0;

    if(orig == 1u) {
        let tex = textureSample(texture, texSampler, uv);
        color = vec3(tex.x);
    } else {
        var p = uv - 0.5;
        p.x *= w/h;
        var p1 = 8.5*(p + vec2(0.55, 0.4));

        // book title
        for(var i = 0; i < 18; i++) {
            col = getChar(p1, getTitle(i));
            if(i < 6){
                color -= vec3(0.0, col, col);
            } else if (i >= 7 && i < 9) {
                color -= vec3(0.0, col, 0.0);
```

```
        } else {
            color -= vec3(col, 0.0, col);
        }
        p1.x -= 0.5;
    }

    // book subtitle
    p1 = 16.0 * (p + vec2(0.52, 0.18));
    for(var i = 0; i < 34; i++) {
        col = getChar(p1, getText(i));
        color -= 0.5 * col;
        p1.x -= 0.5;
    }

    p1 = 16.0 * (p + vec2(0.45, 0.1));
    for(var i = 34; i < 62; i++) {
        col = getChar(p1, getText(i));
        color -= col;
        p1.x -= 0.5;
    }

    // draw letter
    p1 = 5.0 * (p + vec2(0.1, -0.1));
    let idx = getIndex(t, 255*2);
    col = getChar(p1, idx);
    var colors = array<vec3f, 6>(
        vec3(0.0, col, col),
        vec3(col, 0.0, col),
        vec3(col, col, 0.0),
        vec3(col, 0.0, 0.0),
        vec3(0.0, col, 0.0),
        vec3(0.0, 0.0, col),
    );
    color -= colors[t % 6];
}

return vec4(color, 1.0);
}
```

The vertex shader in the above code simply creates a quad shape with six vertices. In the fragment shader, we pass the font image atlas texture and sampler to the shader, which will be used to render text.

The *getTitle* function selects the characters using an index array for the title "*WebGPU by Examples*", in which the index of 32 represents the empty spacing. While the *getText* function returns an index array used to generate text for "*Learn and Explore Next-Generation Web Graphics and Compute API*".

The *getChar* function takes in a 2D position p and an index i as input and return the x component of the texture color, which is a floating-point value representing the brightness of the color. The function first calculates the grid position of the character in the font atlas based on the given index i. Next, it adjusts the grid position based on the pixel offset represented by the input position p. Subsequently, it samples the font atlas texture using the *textureSample* function at a normalized texture coordinate of the specified character.

The *getIndex* function is used to select any character from the font atlas grid. For a 16×16 grid, $n = 2 * 255$ and x can be any integer. This function ensures that for any x, it can always select a unique character from the grid.

The *fs_main* function first defines the UV coordinates using the built-in position and the initial color. It then uses the *originalFont* uniform parameter to determine whether we want to display the original font atlas or the book's title and subtitle. In the *else* block, the function computes the position of the current pixel in the font atlas. The variable *p* is the position of the pixel relative to the center of the viewport, and *p1* is the position of the pixel in the font atlas. The constant vector (0.55, 0.4) shifts the position to the top-left corner of the atlas, and the scaling factor 8.5 adjusts the size of the atlas to match the viewport.

Next, we use a for-loop to draw the book title using characters from the font atlas. The *getChar* function is called with the position *p1* and an index returned by the *getTitle* function to get the color of a character. The loop also applies some color adjustments based on the position of the character in the title. We then do the same thing for the book's subtitle. Finally, we draw the character at the center of the texture coordinates. The different characters with different colors will be displayed depending on the current time.

12.1.2 Rust Code

Create a new Rust file named *bitmp_fonts.rs* in the *examples/ch12/* folder and include the following code:

```rust
use std::iter;
use winit::{
    event::*,
    event_loop::{ControlFlow, EventLoop},
    window::Window,
};
use bytemuck::cast_slice;
use wgpu_book_examples::wgpu_simplified as ws;

const ADDRESS_MODE:wgpu::AddressMode = wgpu::AddressMode::ClampToEdge;

struct State {
    init:  ws::IWgpuInit,
    pipeline: wgpu::RenderPipeline,
    uniform_bind_groups: Vec<wgpu::BindGroup>,
    uniform_buffer: wgpu::Buffer,
    msaa_texture_view: wgpu::TextureView,
    animation_speed: f32,
    show_original_font: u32,
    fps_counter: ws::FpsCounter,
}

impl State {
    async fn new(window:&Window, sample_count:u32) -> Self {
        let init = ws::IWgpuInit::new(&window, sample_count, None).await;

        let shader = init.device.create_shader_module(wgpu::include_wgsl!("bitmap_fonts.wgsl"));

        let param_uniform_buffer = init.device.create_buffer(&wgpu::BufferDescriptor{
            label: Some("Parameter Uniform Buffer"),
            size: 16,
            usage: wgpu::BufferUsages::UNIFORM | wgpu::BufferUsages::COPY_DST,
            mapped_at_creation: false,
        });

        let (uniform_bind_group_layout, uniform_bind_group) = ws::create_bind_group(
            &init.device,
```

```
            vec![wgpu::ShaderStages::FRAGMENT],
            &[param_uniform_buffer.as_entire_binding()]
    );

    // create image texture and image texture bind group
    let img_file = "assets/fonts/font.png";
    let(texture_bind_group_layout, texture_bind_group) =
        ws::create_texture_bind_group(&init.device, &init.queue, vec![img_file], ADDRESS_MODE,
            ADDRESS_MODE);

    let pipeline_layout = init.device.create_pipeline_layout(&wgpu::PipelineLayoutDescriptor {
        label: Some("Render Pipeline Layout"),
        bind_group_layouts: &[&uniform_bind_group_layout, &texture_bind_group_layout],
        push_constant_ranges: &[],
    });

    let mut ppl = ws::IRenderPipeline {
        shader: Some(&shader),
        pipeline_layout: Some(&pipeline_layout),
        vertex_buffer_layout: &[],
        is_depth_stencil: false,
        ..Default::default()
    };
    let pipeline = ppl.new(&init);

    let msaa_texture_view = ws::create_msaa_texture_view(&init);

    Self {
        init,
        pipeline,
        uniform_bind_groups: vec![uniform_bind_group, texture_bind_group],
        uniform_buffer: param_uniform_buffer,
        msaa_texture_view,
        animation_speed: 1.0,
        show_original_font: 0,
        fps_counter: ws::FpsCounter::default(),
    }
}

fn resize(&mut self, new_size: winit::dpi::PhysicalSize<u32>) {
    if new_size.width > 0 && new_size.height > 0 {
        self.init.size = new_size;
        self.init.config.width = new_size.width;
        self.init.config.height = new_size.height;
        self.init.surface.configure(&self.init.device, &self.init.config);

        if self.init.sample_count > 1 {
            self.msaa_texture_view = ws::create_msaa_texture_view(&self.init);
        }
    }
}

#[allow(unused_variables)]
fn input(&mut self, event: &WindowEvent) -> bool {
    match event {
        WindowEvent::KeyboardInput {
            input:
                KeyboardInput {
                    virtual_keycode: Some(keycode),
                    state: ElementState::Pressed,
```

```
                    ..
                },
            ..
        } => {
            match keycode {
                VirtualKeyCode::Space => {
                    self.show_original_font = (self.show_original_font + 1) % 2;
                    true
                },
                _ => false
            }
        }
        _ => false,
    }
}

fn update(&mut self, dt: std::time::Duration) {
    // update uniform buffer for compute pipeline
    let dt1 = 2.0 * self.animation_speed * dt.as_secs_f32();
    let params = [
        self.show_original_font as f32,
        self.init.size.width as f32,
        self.init.size.height as f32,
        dt1
    ];
    self.init.queue.write_buffer(&self.uniform_buffer, 0, cast_slice(&params));
}

fn render(&mut self) -> Result<(), wgpu::SurfaceError> {
    let output = self.init.surface.get_current_texture()?;
    let view = output
        .texture
        .create_view(&wgpu::TextureViewDescriptor::default());

    let mut encoder = self
        .init.device
        .create_command_encoder(&wgpu::CommandEncoderDescriptor {
            label: Some("Render Encoder"),
        });

    // render pass
    {
        let color_attach = ws::create_color_attachment(&view);
        let msaa_attach = ws::create_msaa_color_attachment(&view, &self.msaa_texture_view);
        let color_attachment = if self.init.sample_count == 1 { color_attach } else
            { msaa_attach };
        let mut render_pass = encoder.begin_render_pass(&wgpu::RenderPassDescriptor {
            label: Some("Render Pass"),
            color_attachments: &[Some(color_attachment)],
            depth_stencil_attachment: None,
        });

        render_pass.set_pipeline(&self.pipeline);
        render_pass.set_bind_group(0, &self.uniform_bind_groups[0], &[]);
        render_pass.set_bind_group(1, &self.uniform_bind_groups[1], &[]);
        render_pass.draw(0..6, 0..1);
    }

    self.init.queue.submit(iter::once(encoder.finish()));
    output.present();
```

```
        self.fps_counter.print_fps(5);
        Ok(())
    }
}

fn main() {
    let mut sample_count = 1 as u32;
    let args: Vec<String> = std::env::args().collect();
    if args.len() > 1 {
        sample_count = args[1].parse::<u32>().unwrap();
    }

    env_logger::init();
    let event_loop = EventLoop::new();
    let window = winit::window::WindowBuilder::new().build(&event_loop).unwrap();
    window.set_title(&*format!("ch11_{}", "gravity_grid"));

    let mut state = pollster::block_on(State::new(&window, sample_count));
    let render_start_time = std::time::Instant::now();

    event_loop.run(move |event, _, control_flow| {
        match event {
            Event::WindowEvent {
                ref event,
                window_id,
            } if window_id == window.id() => {
                if !state.input(event) {
                    match event {
                        WindowEvent::CloseRequested
                        | WindowEvent::KeyboardInput {
                            input:
                                KeyboardInput {
                                    state: ElementState::Pressed,
                                    virtual_keycode: Some(VirtualKeyCode::Escape),
                                    ..
                                },
                            ..
                        } => *control_flow = ControlFlow::Exit,
                        WindowEvent::Resized(physical_size) => {
                            state.resize(*physical_size);
                        }
                        WindowEvent::ScaleFactorChanged { new_inner_size, .. } => {
                            state.resize(**new_inner_size);
                        }
                        _ => {}
                    }
                }
            }
            Event::RedrawRequested(_) => {
                let now = std::time::Instant::now();
                let dt = now - render_start_time;
                state.update(dt);

                match state.render() {
                    Ok(_) => {}
                    Err(wgpu::SurfaceError::Lost) => state.resize(state.init.size),
                    Err(wgpu::SurfaceError::OutOfMemory) => *control_flow = ControlFlow::Exit,
                    Err(e) => eprintln!("{:?}", e),
                }
            }
```

```
            Event::MainEventsCleared => {
                window.request_redraw();
            }
            _ => {}
        }
    });
}
```

The *State::new* function in the above code first defines the shader module from the *bitmap-fonts.wgsl* file implemented earlier in the previous section. It then creates a parameter buffer, texture, and sampler using the font atlas file named *font.png* located at *assets/fonts/* folder. Subsequently, it generates a uniform bind group using the parameter buffer, texture, and sampler.

The *State:render* function in the code above simply draws a 2D quad shape. Additionally, the code permits the user to select whether the original font atlas or custom text should be displayed using the *Space* key.

12.1.3 Run Application

To run this application, add the following code snippet to the *Cargo.toml* file:

```
[[example]]
name = "ch12_bitmap_fonts"
path = "examples/ch12/bitmap_fonts.rs"
```

Afterward, execute the following *cargo run* commands in the terminal window:

```
cargo run --example ch12_bitmap_fonts 8
```

Fig.12-2 shows the results of this examples. If you press the *Space* key, the original font atlas will be displayed, as shown in Fig.12-1.

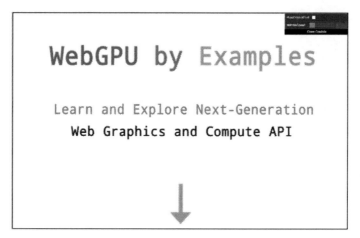

Fig.12-2. Book title and subtitle created using a font atlas.

It is evident from the figure that we only use a single texture for all of the text and only need to render as little as one unit cell in the font atlas grid per glyph. Additionally, the font size and font color can be set as needed. However, to use a different font style, you need to have a different font atlas.

12.2 Glyph Geometry

Because the bitmap-font approach presented in the previous sections rasterizes the text into a texture, they suffer from the same problem as regular images. When you zoom in or scale the text, you start seeing a pixelated and blurry mess. To avoid this issue, we can use the glyph geometry to render text. This approach involves creating a mesh representation of the text using the geometry data of individual characters in a font. One way to achieve this is by using the *meshtext* crate. To use this library, install it using the following command:

```
Cargo intsall meshtext
```

The *meshtext* package is a Rust font triangulation tool for 3D scenes. It can generate indexed or non-indexed meshes, which can be used to create flat 2D text (in 3D space) or 3D text.

The following examples will use the meshtext tool to create 2D and 3D glyph geometry for each character in a text string and render the text string in wgpu. To achieve this, I have included three font files in the TrueType font (TTF) format: *fira-mono-regular.ttf*, *regular-webfont.ttf*, and *changa-regular.ttf*, located in the *assets/fonts/* folder.

12.2.1 Font Data

In this section, we will use the *meshtext* crate to generate the vertex (or mesh) data for 2D and 3D text. Create a new Rust file called *font_data.rs* to the *examples/ch12/* folder and include the following code:

```rust
#![allow(dead_code)]
use std::{collections::HashMap, fs};
use meshtext::{IndexedMeshText, MeshText, MeshGenerator, TextSection};
use cgmath::{Vector3, InnerSpace};
use bytemuck:: {Pod, Zeroable};

pub fn font_file_map(font_selection:u32) -> Option<String> {
    let mut d: HashMap<u32, String> = HashMap::new();
    d.insert(0, String::from("assets/fonts/fira-mono-regular.ttf"));
    d.insert(1, String::from("assets/fonts/regular-webfont.ttf"));
    d.insert(2, String::from("assets/fonts/changa-regular.ttf"));
    d.get(&font_selection).cloned()
}

pub fn get_text_vertices_2d(font_selection: u32, text: &str, pos:[f32; 2], scale:f32, aspect:f32) ->
(Vec<u8>, Vec<u8>, u32) {
    let mut scale1 = 0.22 * scale;
    let font_data = fs::read(font_file_map(font_selection).unwrap()).unwrap();
    if font_selection == 1 {
        scale1 *= 1.5;
    } else if font_selection == 2 {
        scale1 *= 2.0;
    }
    let font_data_static = Box::leak(font_data.into_boxed_slice());

    let mut generator = MeshGenerator::new(font_data_static);
    let transform = [scale1, 0.0, 0.0, 0.0, scale1*aspect, 0.0, pos[0], pos[1], 1.0];
    let data:IndexedMeshText = generator.generate_section_2d(text,
        Some(&transform)).expect("failed to generate glyph.");

    let mut vertex_data:Vec<u8> = Vec::new();
    for vert in data.vertices.iter() {
```

```
        vertex_data.extend_from_slice(vert.to_le_bytes().as_slice());
    }

    let mut index_data:Vec<u8> = Vec::new();
    for ind in data.indices.iter() {
        index_data.extend_from_slice(ind.to_le_bytes().as_slice());
    }

    (vertex_data, index_data, data.indices.len() as u32)
}

pub fn get_text_vertices(font_selection: u32, text: &str) -> Vec<[f32; 3]> {
    let mut scale = 1.0;
    let font_data = fs::read(font_file_map(font_selection).unwrap()).unwrap();
    if font_selection == 1 {
        scale *= 1.5;
    } else if font_selection == 2 {
        scale *= 2.0;
    }
    let font_data_static = Box::leak(font_data.into_boxed_slice());

    let mut generator = MeshGenerator::new(font_data_static);
    let transform = [scale, 0.0, 0.0, 0.0, 0.0, scale, 0.0, 0.0, 0.0, 0.0, 0.1*scale,
        0.0, 0.0, 0.0, 0.0, 1.0];
    let data:MeshText = generator.generate_section(text, false,
        Some(&transform)).expect("failed to generate glyph.");
    let vertices = data.vertices;
    let positions: Vec<[f32; 3]> = vertices.chunks(3).map(|c| [c[0] - 0.5*data.bbox.size().x,
        c[1] , c[2]]).collect();

    positions
}

#[repr(C)]
#[derive(Copy, Clone, Debug, Pod, Zeroable)]
pub struct Vertex {
    pub position: [f32; 3],
    pub normal: [f32; 3],
}

impl Vertex {
    pub fn new(position:[f32; 3], normal:[f32; 3]) -> Self {
        Self { position, normal }
    }
}

pub fn create_text_vertices(font_selection: u32, text: &str) -> Vec<Vertex> {
    let pos = get_text_vertices(font_selection, text);
    let mut vertices:Vec<Vertex> = vec![];

    for chunk in pos.chunks_exact(3) {
        let p1 = Vector3::from(chunk[0]);
        let p2 = Vector3::from(chunk[1]);
        let p3 = Vector3::from(chunk[2]);
        let normal = (p2 - p1).cross(p3 - p1).normalize();

        vertices.push(Vertex::new(p1.into(), normal.into()));
        vertices.push(Vertex::new(p2.into(), normal.into()));
        vertices.push(Vertex::new(p3.into(), normal.into()));
    }
```

```
    vertices
}
```

The code above first introduces several structs and traits from the *meshtext* crate. The *font_file_map* function takes a *font_select* as input and returns a string representing the path to a font file. The function uses a HashMap to map different *font_selection* values to corresponding file paths and returns the path associated with the provided *font_selection*.

The *get_text_vertices_2d* function in the above code is responsible for generating vertices (or meshes) and indices for rendering 2D text. It takes several input parameters, including font selection, text, position, scale, and aspect ratio. Inside this function, we calculate a modified scaling factor based on the provided *scale* parameter and *font_selection*, and use a *MeshGenerator* to generate text mesh data. Subsequently, we convert the mesh data into bytes and store it in *vertex_data* and *index_data* vectors. The function finally returns a tuple containing the vertex data, index data, and the length of the index data vector.

The *get_text_vertices* function is used to generate vertices for rendering 3D text. It takes two input arguments, *font_selection* and *text*. As we did earlier in the *get_text_vertices_2d* function, we make scaling adjustment based on *font_selection*. The main difference between these two functions lies in the method of text generation and the dimensionality of the resulting vertices. Specifically, the 2D function uses the *generator.generate_section_2d* method to generate the text vertices, while the 3D function uses the *generator.generate_section* to generate the text vertices.

The remaining code is used to generate vertex data for rendering 3D text with a lighting effect. To achieve this, we begin by defining a *Vertex* struct that contains two fields, *position* and *normal*. The *create_text_vertices* function first retrieves the positions of text vertices by calling the *get_text_vertices* function that we implemented earlier. Next, the function iterates over the *position* variable in chunks of three, calculating the normal vector for each triangle formed by the three consecutive positions. Finally, the function returns the *vertices* vector, which now contains the necessary data for rendering the provided text in 3D space, including normals for shading.

12.2.2 2D Glyph Text

With the background presented in the previous sections, we can now generate 2D glyph text. To do this, we first need to create a simple shader. Add a new WGSL file named *glyph_2d.wgsl* to the *examples/ch12/* folder with the following code:

```
@vertex
fn vs_main(@location(0) position: vec2f) -> @builtin(position) vec4f {
    return vec4(position.x - 1.0, position.y, 0.0, 1.0);
}

@group(0) @binding(0) var<uniform> color : vec4f;

@fragment
fn fs_main() -> @location(0) vec4f {
    return color;
}
```

The code above defines a simple vertex shader that shifts the vertex position to the left along the *X*-axis and a fragment shader that uses a uniform color variable to determine the color of each fragment.

Next, create a new Rust file named *glyph_2d.rs* to the *examples/ch12/* folder and add the following code to it:

```rust
use std::iter;
use wgpu::util::DeviceExt;
use winit::{
    event::*,
    event_loop::{ControlFlow, EventLoop},
    window::Window,
};
use bytemuck::cast_slice;
use wgpu_book_examples::wgpu_simplified as ws;
mod font_data;

struct State {
    init:  ws::IWgpuInit,
    pipeline: wgpu::RenderPipeline,
    vertex_buffer: wgpu::Buffer,
    index_buffer: wgpu::Buffer,
    uniform_bind_group: wgpu::BindGroup,
    uniform_buffer: wgpu::Buffer,
    msaa_texture_view: wgpu::TextureView,

    color_selection: u32,
    font_selection: u32,
    text_position: [f32; 2],
    scale: f32,
    index_count: u32,
    data_changed: bool,
    text: String,
    fps_counter: ws::FpsCounter,
}

impl State {
    async fn new(window:&Window, sample_count:u32, text:&str) -> Self {
        let init = ws::IWgpuInit::new(&window, sample_count, None).await;

        let shader = init.device.create_shader_module(wgpu::include_wgsl!("glyph_2d.wgsl"));

        let color_uniform_buffer = init.device.create_buffer(&wgpu::BufferDescriptor{
            label: Some("Color Uniform Buffer"),
            size: 16,
            usage: wgpu::BufferUsages::UNIFORM | wgpu::BufferUsages::COPY_DST,
            mapped_at_creation: false,
        });
        init.queue.write_buffer(&color_uniform_buffer, 0, cast_slice(&[1.0f32, 0.0, 0.0, 1.0]));

        let (uniform_bind_group_layout, uniform_bind_group) = ws::create_bind_group(
            &init.device,
            vec![wgpu::ShaderStages::FRAGMENT],
            &[color_uniform_buffer.as_entire_binding()]
        );

        let pipeline_layout = init.device.create_pipeline_layout(&wgpu::PipelineLayoutDescriptor {
            label: Some("Render Pipeline Layout"),
            bind_group_layouts: &[&uniform_bind_group_layout],
            push_constant_ranges: &[],
        });

        let vertex_buffer_layout = wgpu::VertexBufferLayout {
            array_stride: 8,
            step_mode: wgpu::VertexStepMode::Vertex,
            attributes: &wgpu::vertex_attr_array![0 => Float32x2],
```

```
        };

    let mut ppl = ws::IRenderPipeline {
        shader: Some(&shader),
        pipeline_layout: Some(&pipeline_layout),
        vertex_buffer_layout: &[vertex_buffer_layout],
        is_depth_stencil: false,
        ..Default::default()
    };
    let pipeline = ppl.new(&init);

    let msaa_texture_view = ws::create_msaa_texture_view(&init);

    let (vertex_data, index_data, index_count) =
        font_data::get_text_vertices_2d(0, text, [0f32, 0.0], 1.0,
            (init.size.width/init.size.height) as f32);

    let vertex_buffer = init.device.create_buffer_init(&wgpu::util::BufferInitDescriptor {
        label: Some("Vertex Buffer"),
        contents: vertex_data.as_slice(),
        usage: wgpu::BufferUsages::VERTEX | wgpu::BufferUsages::COPY_DST,
    });

    let index_buffer = init.device.create_buffer_init(&wgpu::util::BufferInitDescriptor {
        label: Some("Index Buffer"),
        contents: index_data.as_slice(),
        usage: wgpu::BufferUsages::INDEX | wgpu::BufferUsages::COPY_DST,
    });

    Self {
        init,
        pipeline,
        vertex_buffer,
        index_buffer,
        uniform_bind_group,
        uniform_buffer: color_uniform_buffer,
        msaa_texture_view,
        index_count,
        color_selection: 0,
        font_selection: 0,
        text_position: [0.0f32, 0.0],
        scale: 1.0,
        data_changed: false,
        text: text.to_string(),
        fps_counter: ws::FpsCounter::default(),
    }
}

fn resize(&mut self, new_size: winit::dpi::PhysicalSize<u32>) {
    if new_size.width > 0 && new_size.height > 0 {
        self.init.size = new_size;
        self.init.config.width = new_size.width;
        self.init.config.height = new_size.height;
        self.init.surface.configure(&self.init.device, &self.init.config);

        if self.init.sample_count > 1 {
            self.msaa_texture_view = ws::create_msaa_texture_view(&self.init);
        }
        self.data_changed = true;
    }
```

```
}

#[allow(unused_variables)]
fn input(&mut self, event: &WindowEvent) -> bool {
    match event {
        WindowEvent::KeyboardInput {
            input:
                KeyboardInput {
                    virtual_keycode: Some(keycode),
                    state: ElementState::Pressed,
                    ..
                },
            ..
        } => {
            match keycode {
                VirtualKeyCode::Space => {
                    self.font_selection = (self.font_selection + 1) % 3;
                    println!("font file = {:?}", font_data::font_file_map(self.font_selection));
                    self.data_changed = true;
                    true
                },
                VirtualKeyCode::LControl => {
                    self.color_selection = (self.color_selection + 1) % 4;
                    self.data_changed = true;
                    true
                },
                VirtualKeyCode::Q => {
                    self.scale += 0.1;
                    self.data_changed = true;
                    true
                },
                VirtualKeyCode::A => {
                    self.scale -= 0.1;
                    if self.scale < 0.1 {
                        self.scale = 0.1;
                    }
                    self.data_changed = true;
                    true
                },
                VirtualKeyCode::W => {
                    self.text_position[0] += 0.1;
                    self.data_changed = true;
                    true
                },
                VirtualKeyCode::S => {
                    self.text_position[0] -= 0.1;
                    self.data_changed = true;
                    true
                },
                VirtualKeyCode::E => {
                    self.text_position[1] += 0.1;
                    self.data_changed = true;
                    true
                },
                VirtualKeyCode::D => {
                    self.text_position[1] -= 0.1;
                    self.data_changed = true;
                    true
                },
                _ => false
```

```
                }
            }
            _ => false,
        }
    }

    fn update(&mut self, _dt: std::time::Duration) {
        // update buffers
        if self.data_changed {
            let mut color = [1.0f32, 0.0, 0.0, 1.0];
            if self.color_selection == 1 {
                color = [0.0f32, 1.0, 0.0, 1.0];
            } else if self.color_selection == 2 {
                color = [0.0f32, 0.0, 1.0, 1.0];
            } else if self.color_selection == 3 {
                color = [1.0f32, 1.0, 1.0, 1.0];
            }
            self.init.queue.write_buffer(&self.uniform_buffer, 0, cast_slice(&color));

            let (vertex_data, index_data, index_count) =
                font_data::get_text_vertices_2d(self.font_selection, &self.text, self.text_position,
                    self.scale, (self.init.size.width/self.init.size.height) as f32);
            self.vertex_buffer.destroy();
            self.index_buffer.destroy();
            self.vertex_buffer = self.init.device.create_buffer_init(&wgpu::util::BufferInitDescriptor {
                label: Some("Vertex Buffer"),
                contents: vertex_data.as_slice(),
                usage: wgpu::BufferUsages::VERTEX | wgpu::BufferUsages::COPY_DST,
            });
            self.index_buffer = self.init.device.create_buffer_init(&wgpu::util::BufferInitDescriptor {
                label: Some("Index Buffer"),
                contents: index_data.as_slice(),
                usage: wgpu::BufferUsages::INDEX | wgpu::BufferUsages::COPY_DST,
            });
            self.index_count = index_count;

            self.data_changed = false;
        }
    }

    fn render(&mut self) -> Result<(), wgpu::SurfaceError> {
        let output = self.init.surface.get_current_texture()?;
        let view = output
            .texture
            .create_view(&wgpu::TextureViewDescriptor::default());

        let mut encoder = self
            .init.device
            .create_command_encoder(&wgpu::CommandEncoderDescriptor {
                label: Some("Render Encoder"),
            });

        // render pass
        {
            let color_attach = ws::create_color_attachment(&view);
            let msaa_attach = ws::create_msaa_color_attachment(&view, &self.msaa_texture_view);
            let color_attachment = if self.init.sample_count == 1 { color_attach } else
                { msaa_attach };
            let mut render_pass = encoder.begin_render_pass(&wgpu::RenderPassDescriptor {
                label: Some("Render Pass"),
```

```
                color_attachments: &[Some(color_attachment)],
                depth_stencil_attachment: None,
            });

            render_pass.set_pipeline(&self.pipeline);
            render_pass.set_vertex_buffer(0, self.vertex_buffer.slice(..));
            render_pass.set_index_buffer(self.index_buffer.slice(..), wgpu::IndexFormat::Uint32);
            render_pass.set_bind_group(0, &self.uniform_bind_group, &[]);
            render_pass.draw_indexed(0..self.index_count, 0, 0..1);
        }

        self.init.queue.submit(iter::once(encoder.finish()));
        output.present();
        self.fps_counter.print_fps(5);
        Ok(())
    }
}

fn main() {
    let mut sample_count = 1 as u32;
    let mut text = "Hello, Rust wgpu!";

    let args: Vec<String> = std::env::args().collect();
    if args.len() > 1 {
        sample_count = args[1].parse::<u32>().unwrap();
    }
    if args.len() > 2 {
        text = &args[2];
    }

    env_logger::init();
    let event_loop = EventLoop::new();
    let window = winit::window::WindowBuilder::new().build(&event_loop).unwrap();
    window.set_title(&*format!("ch11_{}", "glyph_2d"));

    let mut state = pollster::block_on(State::new(&window, sample_count, text));
    let render_start_time = std::time::Instant::now();

    event_loop.run(move |event, _, control_flow| {
        match event {
            Event::WindowEvent {
                ref event,
                window_id,
            } if window_id == window.id() => {
                if !state.input(event) {
                    match event {
                        WindowEvent::CloseRequested
                        | WindowEvent::KeyboardInput {
                            input:
                                KeyboardInput {
                                    state: ElementState::Pressed,
                                    virtual_keycode: Some(VirtualKeyCode::Escape),
                                    ..
                                },
                            ..
                        } => *control_flow = ControlFlow::Exit,
                        WindowEvent::Resized(physical_size) => {
                            state.resize(*physical_size);
                        }
                        WindowEvent::ScaleFactorChanged { new_inner_size, .. } => {
```

```
                    state.resize(**new_inner_size);
                }
                _ => {}
            }
        }
    }
    Event::RedrawRequested(_) => {
        let now = std::time::Instant::now();
        let dt = now - render_start_time;
        state.update(dt);

        match state.render() {
            Ok(_) => {}
            Err(wgpu::SurfaceError::Lost) => state.resize(state.init.size),
            Err(wgpu::SurfaceError::OutOfMemory) => *control_flow = ControlFlow::Exit,
            Err(e) => eprintln!("{:?}", e),
        }
    }
    Event::MainEventsCleared => {
        window.request_redraw();
    }
    _ => {}
    }
});
}
```

The above code first introduces the *font_data* module using the statement:

```
mod font_data;
```

It then adds several new fields to the *State* struct, including color selection, font selection, scaling factor, and text position.

Inside the *State::new* function, we create a color uniform buffer and corresponding bind group. Subsequently, we generate the vertex and index data for rendering 2D text by calling the *get_text_vertices_2d* method implemented earlier in the *font_data* file. This data is then used to create vertex and index buffers.

Within the *State::update* function, we regenerate the vertex data and corresponding buffers for rendering the text when the *data_changed* parameter is true.

Additionally, the code permits the user to modify input parameters using keyboard inputs.

Here is a list of controls using keyboard:

- *Space*: Changes font files.
- *LControl*: Changes text color.
- *Q/A*: Increases/decreases the font size.
- *W/S*: Moves text in the positive/negative x direction.
- *E/D*: Moves text in the positive/negative y direction.

To run this application, add the following code snippet to the *Cargo.toml* file:

```
[[example]]
name = "ch12_glyph_2d"
path = "examples/ch12/glyph_2d.rs"
```

Afterward, execute the following *cargo run* commands in the terminal window:

```
cargo run --example ch12_glyph_2d 8
```

Fig.12-3 shows the result of this example.

Fig.12-3. 2D glyph text.

12.2.3 3D Glyph Text

This example will reuse the vertex and fragment shader files named *shader_vert.wgsl* and *blinn_phong_frag.wgsl* implemented earlier in Chapter 3 for create simple 3D shapes such as cube and sphere.

Now, create a new Rust file named *glyph_3d.rs* in the *examples/ch12/* folder and include the following code:

```rust
use std::{iter, mem};
use cgmath::{Matrix, Matrix4, SquareMatrix};
use wgpu:: {util::DeviceExt, VertexBufferLayout};
use winit::{
    event::*,
    event_loop::{ControlFlow, EventLoop},
    window::{Window, WindowBuilder},
};
use bytemuck::cast_slice;
use wgpu_book_examples:: { wgpu_simplified as ws, transforms as wt };
mod font_data;

struct State {
    init: ws::IWgpuInit,
    pipeline: wgpu::RenderPipeline,
    vertex_buffer: wgpu::Buffer,
    uniform_bind_groups: Vec<wgpu::BindGroup>,
    uniform_buffers: Vec<wgpu::Buffer>,
    view_mat: Matrix4<f32>,
    project_mat: Matrix4<f32>,
    msaa_texture_view: wgpu::TextureView,
    depth_texture_view: wgpu::TextureView,
    vertex_count: u32,
    animation_speed: f32,
    text: String,

    font_selection: u32,
    color_selection: u32,
    data_changed: bool,
    scale: f32,
    fps_counter: ws::FpsCounter,
}

impl State {
    async fn new(window: &Window, sample_count: u32, topology:wgpu::PrimitiveTopology, text: &str) -> Self
    {
```

```
let init = ws::IWgpuInit::new(&window, sample_count, None).await;

let vs_shader = init.device.create_shader_module(wgpu::include_wgsl!("../ch03/shader_vert.wgsl"));
let fs_shader = init.device.create_shader_module(
    wgpu::include_wgsl!("../ch03/blinn_phong_frag.wgsl"));

// uniform data
let camera_position = (2.0, 2.0, 4.0).into();
let look_direction = (0.0,0.0,0.0).into();
let up_direction = cgmath::Vector3::unit_y();

let (view_mat, project_mat, _) =
    wt::create_vp_mat(camera_position, look_direction, up_direction,
    init.config.width as f32 / init.config.height as f32);

// model_mat and vp_mat will be stored in vertex_uniform_buffer inside the update function
let vert_uniform_buffer = init.device.create_buffer(&wgpu::BufferDescriptor{
    label: Some("Vertex Uniform Buffer"),
    size: 192,
    usage: wgpu::BufferUsages::UNIFORM | wgpu::BufferUsages::COPY_DST,
    mapped_at_creation: false,
});

// create light uniform buffer. here we set eye_position = camera_position and
// light_position = eye_position
let light_uniform_buffer = init.device.create_buffer(&wgpu::BufferDescriptor{
    label: Some("Light Uniform Buffer"),
    size: 64,
    usage: wgpu::BufferUsages::UNIFORM | wgpu::BufferUsages::COPY_DST,
    mapped_at_creation: false,
});

let light_position:&[f32; 3] = camera_position.as_ref();
let eye_position:&[f32; 3] = camera_position.as_ref();
init.queue.write_buffer(&light_uniform_buffer, 0, cast_slice(light_position));
init.queue.write_buffer(&light_uniform_buffer, 16, cast_slice(eye_position));

// set specular light color to white
let specular_color:[f32; 3] = [1.0, 1.0, 1.0];
init.queue.write_buffer(&light_uniform_buffer, 48, cast_slice(specular_color.as_ref()));

// set default object color to red:
let object_color:[f32; 3] = [1.0, 0.0, 0.0];
init.queue.write_buffer(&light_uniform_buffer, 32, cast_slice(object_color.as_ref()));

// material uniform buffer
let material_uniform_buffer = init.device.create_buffer(&wgpu::BufferDescriptor{
    label: Some("Material Uniform Buffer"),
    size: 16,
    usage: wgpu::BufferUsages::UNIFORM | wgpu::BufferUsages::COPY_DST,
    mapped_at_creation: false,
});

// set default material parameters
let material = [0.2 as f32, 0.8, 0.4, 30.0];
init.queue.write_buffer(&material_uniform_buffer, 0, cast_slice(material.as_ref()));

// uniform bind group for vertex shader
let (vert_bind_group_layout, vert_bind_group) = ws::create_bind_group(
    &init.device,
```

```
        vec![wgpu::ShaderStages::VERTEX],
        &[vert_uniform_buffer.as_entire_binding()],
    );

    // uniform bind group for fragment shader
    let (frag_bind_group_layout, frag_bind_group) = ws::create_bind_group(
        &init.device,
        vec![wgpu::ShaderStages::FRAGMENT, wgpu::ShaderStages::FRAGMENT],
        &[light_uniform_buffer.as_entire_binding(), material_uniform_buffer.as_entire_binding()],
    );

    let vertex_buffer_layout = VertexBufferLayout {
        array_stride: mem::size_of::<font_data::Vertex>() as wgpu::BufferAddress,
        step_mode: wgpu::VertexStepMode::Vertex,
        attributes: &wgpu::vertex_attr_array![0 => Float32x3, 1 => Float32x3],
    };

    let pipeline_layout = init.device.create_pipeline_layout(&wgpu::PipelineLayoutDescriptor {
        label: Some("Render Pipeline Layout"),
        bind_group_layouts: &[&vert_bind_group_layout, &frag_bind_group_layout],
        push_constant_ranges: &[],
    });

    let mut ppl = ws::IRenderPipeline {
        topology,
        vs_shader: Some(&vs_shader),
        fs_shader: Some(&fs_shader),
        pipeline_layout: Some(&pipeline_layout),
        vertex_buffer_layout: &[vertex_buffer_layout],
        ..Default::default()
    };
    let pipeline = ppl.new(&init);

    let msaa_texture_view = ws::create_msaa_texture_view(&init);
    let depth_texture_view = ws::create_depth_view(&init);

    let vertex_data = font_data::create_text_vertices(0, text);
    let vertex_buffer = init.device.create_buffer_init(&wgpu::util::BufferInitDescriptor {
        label: Some("Vertex Buffer"),
        contents: cast_slice(&vertex_data),
        usage: wgpu::BufferUsages::VERTEX | wgpu::BufferUsages::COPY_DST,
    });

    Self {
        init,
        pipeline,
        vertex_buffer,
        uniform_bind_groups: vec![vert_bind_group, frag_bind_group],
        uniform_buffers: vec![vert_uniform_buffer, light_uniform_buffer, material_uniform_buffer],
        view_mat,
        project_mat,
        msaa_texture_view,
        depth_texture_view,
        animation_speed: 1.0,
        vertex_count: vertex_data.len() as u32,

        text: text.to_string(),
        font_selection: 0,
        color_selection: 0,
        data_changed: false,
```

```
            scale: 1.0,
            fps_counter: ws::FpsCounter::default(),
        }
    }

    pub fn resize(&mut self, new_size: winit::dpi::PhysicalSize<u32>) {
        if new_size.width > 0 && new_size.height > 0 {
            self.init.size = new_size;
            self.init.config.width = new_size.width;
            self.init.config.height = new_size.height;
            self.init.surface.configure(&self.init.device, &self.init.config);

            self.project_mat = wt::create_projection_mat(new_size.width as f32 / new_size.height as f32,
                true);
            self.depth_texture_view = ws::create_depth_view(&self.init);
            if self.init.sample_count > 1 {
                self.msaa_texture_view = ws::create_msaa_texture_view(&self.init);
            }
            self.data_changed = true;
        }
    }

    #[allow(unused_variables)]
    fn input(&mut self, event: &WindowEvent) -> bool {
        match event {
            WindowEvent::KeyboardInput {
                input:
                    KeyboardInput {
                        virtual_keycode: Some(keycode),
                        state: ElementState::Pressed,
                        ..
                    },
                ..
            } => {
                match keycode {
                    VirtualKeyCode::Space => {
                        self.font_selection = (self.font_selection + 1) % 3;

                        println!("font file = {:?}", font_data::font_file_map(self.font_selection));
                        self.data_changed = true;
                        true
                    },
                    VirtualKeyCode::LControl => {
                        self.color_selection = (self.color_selection + 1) % 4;
                        self.data_changed = true;
                        true
                    },
                    VirtualKeyCode::Q => {
                        self.scale += 0.1;
                        self.data_changed = true;
                        true
                    },
                    VirtualKeyCode::A => {
                        self.scale -= 0.1;
                        if self.scale < 0.1 {
                            self.scale = 0.1;
                        }
                        self.data_changed = true;
                        true
                    },
```

```
                    VirtualKeyCode::W => {
                        self.animation_speed += 0.1;
                        true
                    },
                    VirtualKeyCode::S => {
                        self.animation_speed -= 0.1;
                        if self.animation_speed < 0.0 {
                            self.animation_speed = 0.0;
                        }
                        true
                    },
                    _ => false
                }
            }
            _ => false,
        }
    }

    fn update(&mut self, dt: std::time::Duration) {
        // update uniform buffer
        let dt = self.animation_speed * dt.as_secs_f32();
        let model_mat = wt::create_model_mat([0.0, 0.0, 0.0],
            [0.0, dt, 0.0], [self.scale, self.scale, self.scale]);
        let vp_mat = self.project_mat * self.view_mat;

        let normal_mat = (model_mat.invert().unwrap()).transpose();
        let model_ref:&[f32; 16] = model_mat.as_ref();
        let vp_ref:&[f32; 16] = vp_mat.as_ref();
        let normal_ref:&[f32; 16] = normal_mat.as_ref();

        self.init.queue.write_buffer(&self.uniform_buffers[0], 0, cast_slice(vp_ref));
        self.init.queue.write_buffer(&self.uniform_buffers[0], 64, cast_slice(model_ref));
        self.init.queue.write_buffer(&self.uniform_buffers[0], 128, cast_slice(normal_ref));

        if self.data_changed {
            let mut color = [1.0f32, 0.0, 0.0];
            if self.color_selection == 1 {
                color = [0.0f32, 1.0, 0.0];
            } else if self.color_selection == 2 {
                color = [0.0f32, 0.0, 1.0];
            } else if self.color_selection == 3 {
                color = [1.0f32, 1.0, 1.0];
            }
            self.init.queue.write_buffer(&self.uniform_buffers[1], 32, cast_slice(&color));

            let vertex_data = font_data::create_text_vertices(self.font_selection, &self.text);
            self.vertex_buffer.destroy();
            self.vertex_buffer = self.init.device.create_buffer_init(&wgpu::util::BufferInitDescriptor {
                label: Some("Vertex Buffer"),
                contents: cast_slice(&vertex_data),
                usage: wgpu::BufferUsages::VERTEX | wgpu::BufferUsages::COPY_DST,
            });
            self.vertex_count = vertex_data.len() as u32;

            self.data_changed = false;
        }
    }

    fn render(&mut self) -> Result<(), wgpu::SurfaceError> {
        let output = self.init.surface.get_current_texture()?;
```

```
        let view = output
            .texture
            .create_view(&wgpu::TextureViewDescriptor::default());

        let mut encoder = self
            .init.device
            .create_command_encoder(&wgpu::CommandEncoderDescriptor {
                label: Some("Render Encoder"),
            });

        {
            let color_attach = ws::create_color_attachment(&view);
            let msaa_attach = ws::create_msaa_color_attachment(&view, &self.msaa_texture_view);
            let color_attachment = if self.init.sample_count == 1 { color_attach } else { msaa_attach };
            let depth_attachment = ws::create_depth_stencil_attachment(&self.depth_texture_view);

            let mut render_pass = encoder.begin_render_pass(&wgpu::RenderPassDescriptor {
                label: Some("Render Pass"),
                color_attachments: &[Some(color_attachment)],
                depth_stencil_attachment: Some(depth_attachment),
            });

            render_pass.set_pipeline(&self.pipeline);
            render_pass.set_vertex_buffer(0, self.vertex_buffer.slice(..));
            render_pass.set_bind_group(0, &self.uniform_bind_groups[0], &[]);
            render_pass.set_bind_group(1, &self.uniform_bind_groups[1], &[]);
            render_pass.draw(0..self.vertex_count, 0..1);
        }

        self.init.queue.submit(iter::once(encoder.finish()));
        output.present();
        self.fps_counter.print_fps(5);
        Ok(())
    }
}

fn main() {
    let mut sample_count = 1 as u32;
    let mut topology1 = wgpu::PrimitiveTopology::TriangleList;
    let mut text = "Hello, wgpu!";
    let args: Vec<String> = std::env::args().collect();
    if args.len() > 1 {
        sample_count = args[1].parse::<u32>().unwrap();
    }
    if args.len() > 2 {
        if args[2].contains("line") {
            topology1 = wgpu::PrimitiveTopology::LineList;
        } else {
            topology1 = wgpu::PrimitiveTopology::TriangleList;
        }
    }
    if args.len() > 3 {
        text = &args[3];
    }

    env_logger::init();
    let event_loop = EventLoop::new();
    let window = WindowBuilder::new().build(&event_loop).unwrap();
    window.set_title(&*format!("{}", "ch12_glyph_3d"));
    let mut state = pollster::block_on(State::new(&window, sample_count, topology1, text));
```

```
    let render_start_time = std::time::Instant::now();
    event_loop.run(move |event, _, control_flow| {
        match event {
            Event::WindowEvent {
                ref event,
                window_id,
            } if window_id == window.id() => {
                if !state.input(event) {
                    match event {
                        WindowEvent::CloseRequested
                        | WindowEvent::KeyboardInput {
                            input:
                                KeyboardInput {
                                    state: ElementState::Pressed,
                                    virtual_keycode: Some(VirtualKeyCode::Escape),
                                    ..
                                },
                            ..
                        } => *control_flow = ControlFlow::Exit,
                        WindowEvent::Resized(physical_size) => {
                            state.resize(*physical_size);
                        }
                        WindowEvent::ScaleFactorChanged { new_inner_size, .. } => {
                            state.resize(**new_inner_size);
                        }
                        _ => {}
                    }
                }
            }
            Event::RedrawRequested(_) => {
                let now = std::time::Instant::now();
                let dt = now - render_start_time;
                state.update(dt);

                match state.render() {
                    Ok(_) => {}
                    Err(wgpu::SurfaceError::Lost) => state.resize(state.init.size),
                    Err(wgpu::SurfaceError::OutOfMemory) => *control_flow = ControlFlow::Exit,
                    Err(e) => eprintln!("{:?}", e),
                }
            }
            Event::MainEventsCleared => {
                window.request_redraw();
            }
            _ => {}
        }
    });
}
```

The code above is similar to the code used for creating a 3D cube with Blinn-Phong lighting, as presented earlier in Chapter 3. It begins by introducing the *font_data* module using the statement:

```
mod font_data;
```

It then adds several new fields to the *State* struct, including color selection, font selection, and font size (scaling).

The *State::new* function is nearly identical to the one used for creating simple 3D shapes with a lighting effect, with one exception: in this example, it generates vertex data for rendering 3D text by calling the *create_text_vertices* method implemented earlier in the *font_data.rs* file and uses this vertex data to create a vertex buffer.

Within the *State::update* function, we regenerate the vertex data and corresponding buffers for rendering the text when the *data_changed* parameter is true.

Additionally, the code permits the user to modify input parameters using keyboard inputs.

Here is a list of controls using keyboard:

- *Space*: Changes font files.
- *LControl*: Changes text color.
- *Q/A*: Increases/decreases the font size.
- *W/S*: Increases/decreases the animation speed.

To run this application, add the following code snippet to the *Cargo.toml* file:

```
[[example]]
name = "ch12_glyph_3d"
path = "examples/ch12/glyph_3d.rs"
```

Afterward, execute the following *cargo run* commands in the terminal window:

```
cargo run --example ch12_glyph_3d 8
```

Fig.12-4 shows the results of this example.

Fig.12-4. 3D Text with different fonts and colors created using the glyph geometry.

Rendering text using glyph geometry has several advantages. One of the advantages is that it allows for high-quality, scalable text rendering. Since the text is represented as a series of shapes, it can be scaled up or down without losing quality. Additionally, since the shapes are created using vector graphics, they can be rendered at any resolution, resulting in crisp and clear text.

Another advantage is that it allows for more creative control over the appearance of the text. By manipulating the shapes that make up the glyphs, we can create unique and stylized text effects that would be difficult or impossible to achieve with traditional font rendering techniques.

However, there are also some disadvantages to rendering text using glyph geometry. One of the main disadvantages is that it can be more computationally intensive than texture-based font rendering. Since the text is represented as a series of shapes, rather than pre-rendered pixels, the computer must perform additional calculations to render the text on screen.

Another disadvantage is that it can be more difficult to edit or manipulate the text once it has been rendered as glyph geometry. Since the text is no longer represented as a series of characters, but rather as a series of shapes, making changes to the text can be more time-consuming and labor-intensive.

Index

Made in United States
Troutdale, OR
01/14/2024

16936866R00354